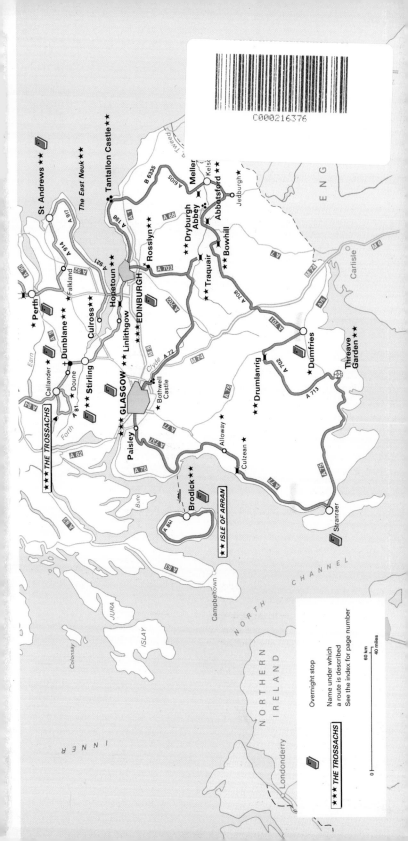

C000216376

St Andrews ★★

The East Neuk ★★

Tantallon Castle ★★

B 6355

A 5019

Meller

Kelso

A 198

A 1

A 68

Dryburgh Abbey ★★

Abbotsford

Jedburgh ★

ENG

A 917

A 914

Perth ★★

A 9

A 823

A 91

A 921

A 26

Falkland

Culross ★

Hopetoun ★

Rosslyn ★

Traquair

Bowhill ★★

A 703

A 708

A 702

Dumfries ★

A 7

Carlisle

M 6

A 7

Dunblane ★★

EDINBURGH

Linlithgow ★★

A 702/1

M 8

Clyde

A 72

M 74

Threave Garden ★★

A 713

Callander

Earn

THE TROSSACHS
★★★

Stirling ★

Doune

GLASGOW

Bothwell Castle

A 81

Forth

A 82

Paisley

A 737

A 77

A 76

Drumlanrig ★

A 75

A 74

A 713

Bute

A 78

Alloway ★

Culzean ★

Stranraer

JURA

Brodick ★★

ISLE OF ARRAN
★★

A 841

Campbeltown

NORTH   CHANNEL

Colonsay

ISLAY

INNER

NORTHERN
IRELAND

Londonderry

Dunblane ★★

★★★ *THE TROSSACHS*

Overnight stop

Name under which
a route is described

See the index for page number

0   60 km
         40 miles

SCOTLAND

Scottish Viewpoint

Editorial Director   Cynthia Clayton Ochterbeck

THE GREEN GUIDE SCOTLAND

Editor   Jonathan P. Gilbert
Contributing Writers   Paul Murphy
Production Manager   Natasha G. George
Cartography   Alain Baldet, Peter Wrenn
Photo Editors   Cecile Koroleff, Yoshimi Kanazawa
Proofreaders   Alison Coupe, Rachel Mills
Layout & Design   John Higginbottom
Cover Design   Ute Weber, Laurent Muller

Contact Us: The Green Guide
                                Michelin Maps and Guides
                                One Parkway South
                                Greenville, SC 29615
                                USA
                                www.michelintravel.com
                                michelin.guides@us.michelin.com

                                Michelin Maps and Guides
                                Hannay House
                                39 Clarendon Road
                                Watford, Herts WD17 1JA
                                UK
                                ☏ (01923) 205 240
                                www.ViaMichelin.com
                                travelpubsales@uk.michelin.com

Special Sales: For information regarding bulk sales,
                                customized editions and premium sales,
                                please contact our Customer Service
                                Departments:
                                USA   1-800-432-6277
                                UK   (01923) 205 240
                                Canada 1-800-361-8236

Note to the Reader
While every effort is made to ensure that all information printed in this guide is
correct and up-to-date, Michelin Apa Publications Ltd. accepts no liability for
any direct, indirect or consequential losses howsoever caused so far as such
can be excluded by law.

One Team…
A Commitment to Quality

There's just one reason our team is dedicated to producing quality travel publications—you, our reader.

Throughout our guides we offer **practical information**, **touring tips** and **suggestions** for finding the best places for a break.

Michelin driving tours help you hit the highlights and quickly absorb the best of the region. Our descriptive **walking tours** make you your own guide, armed with directions, maps and expert information.

We scout out the attractions, classify them with **star ratings**, and describe in detail what you will find when you visit them.

Michelin maps featured throughout the guide offer vibrant, detailed and easy-to-follow outlines of everything from close-up museum plans to international maps.

Places to stay and eat are always a big part of travel, so we research **hotels and restaurants** that we think convey the essence of the destination and arrange them by geographic area and price. We walk you through the best shopping districts and point you towards the host of entertainment and recreation possibilities available.

We **test**, **retest**, **check and recheck** to make sure that our guidebooks are truly just that: a personalized guide to help you make the most of your visit. And if you still want a speaking guide, we list local tour guides who will lead you on all the boat, bus, guided, historical, culinary, and other tours you shouldn't miss.

In short, we remove the guesswork involved with travel. After all, we want you to enjoy exploring with Michelin as much as we do.

The Michelin Green Guide Team

PLANNING YOUR TRIP

INTRODUCTION TO SCOTLAND

P. Tomkins/VisitScotland/Scottish Viewpoint

CONTENTS

DISCOVERING SCOTLAND

HOW TO USE THIS GUIDE

PLANNING YOUR TRIP

The blue-tabbed PLANNING YOUR TRIP section at the front of the guide gives you **ideas for your trip** and **practical information** to help you organise it. You'll find tours, a host of breaks in the great outdoors, a calendar of events, information on shopping, sightseeing, kids' activities and more.

INTRODUCTION

The orange-tabbed INTRODUCTION section explores **Nature** from the Highlands to the Lowlands. The **History** section spans from the Neolithic and Skara Brae to the Scottish Parliament. The **Art and Culture** section covers architecture, art, literature, traditions and folklore,

Sidebars

Throughout the guide you will find peach-colored text boxes (like this one), with lively anecdotes, detailed history and background information.

while the **Country Today** delves into modern Scotland.

DISCOVERING

The green-tabbed DISCOVERING section features Scotland's Principal Sights, arranged alphabetically and by region, featuring the most interesting local **Sights**, **Walking Tours**, nearby **Excursions**, and detailed **Driving Tours**.

🛈 Contact information, ⊚ admission charges, 🕒 hours of operation, and a host of other **visitor information** is given wherever possible. Admission prices shown are normally for a single adult.

STAR RATINGS★★★

Michelin has given star ratings for more than 100 years. If you're pressed for time, we recommend you visit the ★★★, or ★★ sights first:

★★★   Highly recommended
★★   Recommended
★   Interesting

Address Books - Where to Stay, Eat and more...

WHERE TO STAY

We've made a selection of hotels and arranged them within the cities by price category to fit all budgets (👌 *see the Legend on the cover flap for an explanation of the price categories*). For the most part, we've selected accommodations based on their unique regional quality, their regional feel, as it were. So, unless the individual hotel embodies local ambience, it's rare that we include chain properties, which typically have their own imprint.
👌 *See the back of the guide for an index to the accommodations featured throughout the guide.*

WHERE TO EAT

We thought you'd like to know the popular eating spots in Scotland. So, we selected restaurants that capture the regional experience—those that have a unique regional flavor (👌 *see the Legend on the cover flap for an explanation of the price categories*). We're not rating the quality of the food per se; as we did with the hotels, we selected restaurants for many towns and villages, categorized by price to appeal to all wallets.
👌 *See the back of the guide for an index to the restaurants featured throughout the guide.*

MAPS

- 🌀 Regional **Driving Tours** map.
- 🌀 Scotland map with the **Principal Sights** highlighted.
- 🌀 Places to Stay map.
- 🌀 Maps for major **cities** and **villages**.
- 🌀 **Local tour** maps.

All maps in this guide are oriented north, unless otherwise indicated by a directional arrow. The term "Local Map" refers to a map within the chapter or Tourism Region. A complete list of the maps

🌀 A Bit of Advice 🌀

Green advice boxes found in this guide contain practical tips and handy information relevant to the sight in the Discovering section.

found in the guide appears at the back of this book, as well as a comprehensive index and list of restaurants and accommodations.

🌀 *See the map Legend at the back of the guide for an explanation of map symbols.*

ORIENT PANELS

Vital statistics are given for each principal sight in the DISCOVERING section:

- ☒ **Information**: Tourist Office/Sight contact details.
- ▶ **Orient Yourself:** Geographic location of the sight with reference to surrounding boroughs, towns, and roads.
- ☐ **Parking:** Where to park.
- 🌀 **Don't Miss:** Unmissable things to do.
- ◔ **Organizing Your Time:** Tips on organizing your stay; what to see first, how long to spend, crowd avoidance, market days and more.
- 🄺 **Especially for Kids:** Sights of particular interest to children.
- ◔ **Also See:** Nearby PRINCIPAL SIGHTS featured elsewhere in the guide.

SYMBOLS

🄂	**Spa Facilities**	🗺	**Tours**
🄺	**Interesting for Children**	☐	**On-site Parking**
◔	**Also See**	▶	**Directions**
☒	**Tourist Information**	✖	**On-site eating Facilities**
◔	**Hours of Operation**	☌	**Swimming Pool**
◔	**Periods of Closure**	⚠	**Camping Facilities**
⊶	**Closed to the Public**	☯	**Beaches**
∞	**Entry Fees**	☕	**Breakfast Included**
⇾	**Credit Cards not Accepted**	🌀	**A Bit of Advice**
♿	**Wheelchair Accessible**	🌀	**Warning**

Contact - Addresses, phone numbers, opening hours and prices published in this guide are accurate at the time of press. We welcome corrections and suggestions that may assist us in preparing the next edition. Please send your comments to:

UK
Michelin Maps and Guides
Hannay House
39 Clarendon Road
Watford, Herts WD17 1JA
travelpubsales@uk.michelin.com
www.michelin.co.uk

USA
Michelin Maps and Guides
Editorial Department
P.O. Box 19001
Greenville, SC 29602-9001
michelin.guides@us.michelin.com
www.michelintravel.com

The Highland dancing competition at
the Cowal Games, Dunoon, Argyll
P. Tomkins/VisitScotland/Scottishviewpoint

MICHELIN DRIVING TOURS

Regional Drives

⚹ *Use the Driving Tours Map on the cover flap to plan a sightseeing trip to:*

- **Southern Scotland & Arran**
  (550 miles - 9 days)
- **Eastern Scotland**
  (800 miles - 12 days)
- **Western Highlands and Islands**
  (800 miles - 8 days)

Local Drives

⚹ *Use the A–Z Discovering section to explore Scotland's hidden routes in:*

- **ALFORD**
- **ISLE OF ARRAN**
- **AVIEMORE**
- **AYR**
- **BANFF**
- **BRECHIN**
- **CASTLE DOUGLAS**
- **CRIEFF**
- **DEESIDE**

- **EYEMOUTH**
- **FORT WILLIAM**
- **GREAT GLEN**
- **HADDINGTON**
- **KELSO**
- **KIRCUDBRIGHT**
- **KYLE OF LOCHALSH**
- **MELROSE**
- **NORTH BERWICK**
- **OBAN**
- **ORKNEY ISLANDS (mainland)**
- **ST ANDREWS**
- **SHETLAND ISLANDS**
- **THURSO**
- **TROSSACHS**
- **LOCH TAY**
- **STANRAER**
- **STIRLING**
- **ISLE OF SKYE**
- **TWEED VALLEY**
- **ULLAPOOL**
- **WESTER ROSS**
- **WHITHORN**
- **WICK**

WHEN AND WHERE TO GO

When to Go

The best time of year to visit Scotland, and especially the islands, is in the late **spring** and early summer when the natural beauty of the country is at its peak; the sunniest months are May and June. It is also the ideal time to enjoy all sorts of outdoor leisure activities. The roads are not too busy and the midges (small, biting insects) are not yet active.

The remaining months also have their special appeal. July and August are warm but can be wet. It is essential to pack **insect repellent** for trips into the countryside in midge season (usually Jun–Aug). Many events and festivals are held all over the country during these two months. Edinburgh and Glasgow are particularly lively centres for a short break or longer

holidays, especially during the festivals. Be sure to take in the museums and art galleries and enjoy the relaxed atmosphere. In **summer**, the longest days may be enjoyed in the Shetland and Orkney Islands. September and October are also very pleasant months, but the temperature is cooler and the evenings are shorter. The west coast – warmed by the Gulf Stream – enjoys a mild but wet climate while the east coast is cool and dry.

In **winter**, the Grampians and Highlands offer cross-country skiing while Aviemore in the Cairngorms is the main winter sports resort. Winter is also a good time to visit Glasgow and Edinburgh when rates may be negotiable and the world-class galleries and museums, not to mention restaurants, bars and nightlife are not dependent on weather.

Where to Go

Scotland is a relatively small country and it's quite possible to stay in either Edinburgh or Glasgow and make trips as far afield as the Highlands. However, there's a lot to see and do in most of the regions, so the best strategy is to concentrate on two or three adjacent regions.

BORDERS

The main gateway to Scotland from the south, the Borders is a region of rolling hills and moorland punctuated by picturesque villages, as well as the castles, abbeys, stately homes and museums that illustrate the exciting and bloody history of the area. **Sir Walter Scott**'s novels made it famous historically, today the **River Tweed** attracts visitors to some of the best fishing in Scotland. *See ABBOTS-FORD, BOWHILL, DRYBURGH ABBEY, FLOORS CASTLE, KELSO, MELLERSTAIN, TRAQUAIR HOUSE, TWEED VALLEY...*

GREAT CITIES AND BEYOND

No visitor to Scotland should miss **Edinburgh** (*see EDINBURGH*); it is one of Europe's most beautiful and beguiling cities. The crag-top castle is the stuff of fairy tales and the Old Town below is a veritable film set of dark narrow alleys and covered passageways. By contrast, the New Town is an elegant Georgian masterpiece. The **Edinburgh Festival** in August is one of the world's great celebrations of the arts in the very broadest sense and appeals to just about everyone. For many years the ugly sister to beautiful Edinburgh, **Glasgow** (*see GLASGOW*) has re-invented itself, shaken off its sooty coating and is now also a must see. The city is an architectural treat, most famous for its Art Nouveau designer **Charles Rennie Mackintosh**. Its shopping opportunities are second only to London and its range of stylish bars, boutique hotels and vibrant nightlife equals, if not outclasses Edinburgh. Like Edinburgh, the city's arts scene is world-class.

Both cities are within easy reach of bucolic countryside. The **Lothians**, steeped in history and filled with castles, great houses and battle sites, is Edinburgh's southern "backyard" (*see ROSSLYN CHAPEL, TANTALLON CASTLE, LENNOXLOVE, LINLITHGOW...*). A short drive cross the Firth of Forth to the north is the ancient kingdom of **Fife**, home to Dunfermline, St Andrews and a whole raft of charming fishing villages (*see DUNFERMLINE, CULROSS, FALKLAND, EAST NEUK...*). To the south west of Glasgow, **Dumfries and Galloway** is a quite unspoilt area where you can escape the bustle of the city (*see DUMFRIES, CAERLAV-EROCK CASTLE, WHITHORN...*).

Due west, **Ayrshire and Arran** are a mecca for all golfers with over forty quality courses, including three Open Championship courses. Ancient castles, country parks and gardens, bustling market towns, spectacular granite mountains, ancient stone circles and the waters of the Firth of Clyde act as a magnet for walkers, cyclists, fishermen and sailing enthusiasts alike. Ayrshire is the birthplace of world-renowned poet **Robert Burns**, and there are plentiful reminders of the man and his world to explore here. The **Isle of Arran**, 'Scotland in miniature' is a fascinating island. *See ISLE OF ARRAN, AYR, CULZEAN CASTLE...*

ARGYLL AND THE ISLES

Just northwest of Glasgow this area takes in Scottish folklore icons such as Loch Lomond and William Wallace in the historic city of **Stirling** (*see STIRLING*) with its magnificent castle. You can also tread in the footsteps of Robert the Bruce, Mary Queen of Scots and Rob Roy.

At the heart of this region the mention of "The Trossachs" (*see TROSSACHS*) may not conjure up the same images as "The Highlands", but the scenery here is quintessential Scotland. These are lands where you can glimpse an eagle, an osprey, a wildcat, a fine antlered stag – and while making the short crossing to the **Inner Hebridean** islands (*see ISLE OF MULL*), whales and dolphins. Moreover, it is all within reach of Edinburgh and Glasgow.

CENTRAL SCOTLAND

Situated in the very heart of Scotland, **Perthshire** enjoys a majestic landscape of mountain, water, farmlands and particularly forest. Perthshire is the adventure capital of Scotland offering a wide range of outdoor pursuits on land, water and in the air: world-class fishing, walking from waymarked forest trails to lofty treks in the mountains, cycling routes both on- and off-road and excellent golf courses. (♿see PITLOCHRY, SCONE PALACE, PERTH, DUNKELD...). Bordering Perthshire to the east is the ancient land of **Angus**, once Scotland's ancient and historic heartland with unspoiled highland glens, rugged coastlines and miles of sandy beaches. Its main city, **Dundee**, is a blossoming cultural centre with some fine visitor attractions. ♿See DUNDEE, ARBROATH, GLAMIS, EDZELL CASTLE...

ABERDEEN AND GRAMPIANS

This Eastern Highlands region is blessed with outstanding scenery. With its signature granite buildings, **Aberdeen** (♿see ABERDEEN)– Scotland's third-largest city – has a distinctive skyline and an atmospheric Old Town. First-class restaurants, vibrant nightlife and a thriving cultural calendar make it an excellent base.
The **Grampian Mountains** dominate the skyline in the central highlands, while miles of unspoilt and often dramatic coastline frame the area in the east. Castles and whisky are local specialities and you can sample the 'water of life' while visiting the many distilleries on the world's only Malt Whisky trail in the famous **Speyside** region. ♿See AVIEMORE, CAIRNGORMS, DEESIDE, DUFFTOWN, PITMEDDEN.

HIGHLANDS

The Central, Western and Northern Highlands cover a vast tract of the country, much of the northern part being sparsely inhabited. This is classic Scotland with majestic scenery, awesome wild places, towering mountains, ancient pine forests and broad expanses of dark and shimmering lochs. The most famous stretch of water is **Loch Ness** (♿see LOCH NESS) with **Inverness** (♿see INVERNESS) as the burgeoning centre for the region. The West Highlands include **Fort William** (♿see FORT WILLIAM) and the romantic **isle of Skye** (♿see SKYE). Towards the northern tip of mainland Britain the bleak grandeur of **Caithness** and **Sutherland** make up one of Europe's last great wild places. Wildlife flourishes here and you can expect to see dolphins, whales, eagles, deer, otters and much more besides. ♿See INVEREWE, WESTER ROSS.

WESTERN ISLES

The **Outer Hebrides**, or Western Isles, stretch for 130 mi/208km along the northwest coast. Here on the edge of Europe is a striking mix of landscapes from windswept golden sands to harsh, heather-backed mountains and peat bogs. An elemental beauty pervades the 200-plus islands that make up the archipelago, only a handful of which are actually inhabited. **Lewis** and **Harris** are the best known names. The Hebrides remain the heartland of Scottish Gaelic culture. ♿See W. ISLES.

ORKNEYS AND SHETLANDS

Just off the northern tip of Scotland 70 or so scattered islands make up the **Orkneys** archipelago, famous for its prehistoric sites. Modern day Orkney is also a hive of creativity, with several internationally renowned jewellery manufacturers and professional craftspeople at work here. The **Shetland Isles** are an entrancing blend of Scotland and Norway, much influenced by the Vikings. Neolithic sites date back over 2,000 years. The scenery is surprisingly varied for such a small area and is often truly spectacular. So too are the sunsets and the Northern Lights, and in summer it never really gets dark. ♿See ORKNEY, SHETLAND.

KNOW BEFORE YOU GO

Useful Websites

www.visitscotland.com
The Official Scottish Tourist Board website. Accommodation, holidays, what to see and do, links to all geographical areas. Large subsections on sports, culture, eating and many other topics.

www.rampantscotland.com
This site claims over 13,000 Scottish-related links and over 3,700 webpage features on Scotland and the Scots, all regularly updated. Good for practical planning as well as browsing for fun.

www.scotland-info.co.uk
The 80,000 word Internet Guide to Scotland is a personal labour of love by a Scottish author, largely based on her personal travels. A very professional site with excellent suggestions on accommodation and much more.

www.undiscoveredscotland.co.uk
Deceptively named in some ways – this site trawls mainstream Scotland's many attractions, hotels and restaurants, but also unearths lots of facts on places that rarely get a mention (often deservedly) on other sites.

http://adventure.visitscotland.com
An offshoot of the official visitor guide, this is mostly (but not exclusively) for adrenaline junkies, covering every sinew-stretching sport that you can do in Scotland. If it's just a wee game of golf or curling you're after, stick to the mainstream sites.

www.aboutscotland.com
Clickable maps, good pictures, personally tested accommodation and lively articles about visiting Scotland.

www.edinburgh.org
Sooner or later everyone visits Edinburgh, and with good reason. You may as well know before you go, so click onto the official site of Scotland's favourite city.

www.seeglasgow.com
Though not quite so well known, nor visited, as Edinburgh, Scotland's second city (don't call it that while you're there!) definitely deserves a visit, too.

Tourist Offices

BRITISH TOURIST OFFICES ABROAD

The **British Tourist Authority** (**BTA**) provides assistance in planning a trip to Scotland and an excellent range of brochures and maps.

Postal addresses given below are for walk-in offices only. There are BTA offices in many other parts of the world including Belgium, Brazil, Denmark, Hong Kong, Italy, Norway, Netherlands, Spain, Sweden and Switzerland.

Australia
Level 2 15 Blue Street
North Sydney, NSW 2060,
☎9021 4400 or 1300 85 85 89.
www.visitbritain.com.au

Canada
☎1 888 VISIT UK or 1 905 405 1720.
www.visitbritain.com/ca

France
www.visitbritain.fr

New Zealand
☎0800 700 741 or 64 (0)9 309 1899.
www.visitbritain.co.nz

USA - New York
551 5th Avenue,
Suite 701, NY 10176
☎1 800 462 2748.
www.visitbritain.com/usa

USA - Los Angeles
☎1 310 470 2782.
www.visitbritain.com/usa

SCOTTISH TOURIST INFORMATION

Edinburgh and Scotland Information Centre
3 Princes St, Edinburgh. ☎08452 255 121. www.visitscotland.com.

Tourist Information Centres
Visit Scotland has a large network of local tourist boards and over 140 tourist information centres. The addresses and telephone numbers of the main TICs to be found in large towns and tourist resorts are listed in the *Discovering Scotland* section. The centres can supply town plans, timetables and information on local accommodation, entertainment facilities, sports and sightseeing.

Britain Visitor Centre is located at 1 Lower Regent Street, London SW1Y 4NS (personal callers only).

International Visitors

CONSULATES

Australia
21–23 Hill Street, Edinburgh EH2 3JP. ☎0131 226 8161.

Canada
Festival Square, 50 Lothian Road, Edinburgh EH3 9WJ. ☎0131 473 6320.

France
11 Randolph Crescent, Edinburgh EH3 7TT. ☎0131 225 7954.

Germany
16 Eglinton Crescent, Edinburgh EH12 5DJ. ☎0131 337 2323.

Japan
2 Melville Crescent, Edinburgh EH3 7HW. ☎0131 225 4777.

USA
3 Regent Terrace, Edinburgh EH7 5BW. ☎0131 556 8315.

DOCUMENTS

It is essential for EU nationals to hold a **passport** or national identity card in order to enter the UK. Non-EU nationals must be in possession of a valid national passport. Loss or theft should be reported to the appropriate embassy or consulate and to the local police.
A **visa** to visit the United Kingdom is not required by nationals of the member states of the European Union and of the Commonwealth (including Australia, Canada, New Zealand and South Africa) and the USA. Nationals of other countries should check with the British Embassy and apply for a visa, if necessary, in good time.
For general travel advice, US nationals should visit http://travel.state.gov/travel.

CUSTOMS

Tax-free allowances for various commodities are governed by EU legislation. Details of these allowances and restrictions are available at most ports of entry to Great Britain.
British customs regulations and "duty free" allowances are posted online at www.hmrc.gov.uk (then click on Travel information).
US Citizens should visit the US Customs and Borders Protection website, www.cbp.gov.

HEALTH

Visitors to Britain are entitled to treatment at the Accident and Emergency Departments of National Health Service hospitals. For an overnight or longer hospital stay, payment will most likely be required.
Visitors from EU countries should apply to their own National Social Security Offices for a **European Health Insurance Card** which entitles them to medical treatment under an EU Reciprocal Medical Treatment

arrangement. Nationals of non-EU countries should take out comprehensive insurance. American Express offers Global Assist for any medical, legal or personal emergency. From outside the US ☎(call collect) 715 3437977. www.americanexpress.com.

Accessibility

Some of the sights described in this guide are accessible to disabled people. The **red-cover Michelin Guide Great Britain & Ireland** indicates hotels with facilities suitable for disabled people.
Capability Scotland is Scotland's largest disability organisation, contact: Advice Service Capability Scotland (ASCS) 11 Ellersly Road, Edinburgh EH12 6HY, ☎0131 313 5510, www.capability-scotland.org.uk.
Holiday Care is a national charity and the UK's central source of holiday and travel information and support for disabled people and their carers, contact:

Medical Insurance

It is important to take out medical insurance prior to departure as treatment in Great Britain may be extremely expensive.

Holiday Care, 7th Floor, Sunley House, 4 Bedford Park, Croydon, Surrey CR0 2AP, ☎0845 124 9971.
The Royal Association for Disability and Rehabilitation (RADAR) publishes an annual guide with details on holiday facilities for disabled travellers: ☎0207 250 3222, www.radar.org.uk.

Facilities for Disabled Travellers
The symbol ♿ indicates access for wheelchairs. However, because the range/scope/quality of facilities (also for impaired mobility, sight and hearing) is open to interpretation by site managers, readers are advised to telephone in advance to specify their requirements and to check precisely what is available on site.

GETTING THERE AND GETTING AROUND

By Plane

As airport security and baggage regulations change frequently, it is always advisable to check the rules before you fly. Visit www.dft.gov.uk/transportforyou/airtravel/airportsecurity for more information regarding UK airports. US travellers should visit www.tsa.gov/travelers/airtravel. International airlines operate flights to Edinburgh, Glasgow, Prestwick and Aberdeen. There are also low-cost flights from Europe and several parts of the UK to Inverness, Dundee and eight small airports in the Highlands and Islands (see www.hial.co.uk). All airports are linked by bus to the neighbouring towns. Fly-Drive schemes are operated by most airlines.

The most romantic and spectacular air service is provided by Loch Lomond seaplanes who fly straight off the water by Glasgow Science Centre to Loch Lomond, Oban, Tobermory and other destinations (see www.lochlomondseaplanes.com for details.)

By Ship

Details of passenger ferry and car ferry services to Scotland from Ireland can be obtained from travel agencies or from the carrier:
- **Stena Line**, (Belfast to Stranraer). ☎08705 70 70 70. www.stenaline.co.uk.
- **P&O Irish Sea Ferries**, (Larne to Troon, Larne to Cairnryan). ☎0871

66 44 999 (book online only).
www.poirishsea.com

Ferry operators to the islands:

- **Caledonian MacBrayne Ltd**:
  ☎08000 66 5000.
  www.calmac.co.uk.
- **P&O Scottish Ferries**: Orkney
  and Shetland Services.
  Online bookings only,
  www.poscottishferries.com.
- **John O'Groats**: John O' Groats
  to Burwick (Orkney).
  ☎0195 561 1353.
  www.jogferry.co.uk.
- **Orkney Ferries**: ☎0185 687 2044.
  www.orkneyferries.co.uk.
- **Pentland Ferries**: Caithness to St.
  Margarets Hope, Orkney.
  ☎0185 683 1226.
  www.pentlandferries.co.uk.

By Train

- **FirstScotRail:** ☎08457 55 00 33.
  www.firstgroup.com/scotrail. If
  you are travelling from London
  the *Caledonian Sleeper* departs
  from Euston around midnight and
  arrives in Edinburgh or Glasgow
  around 7.15am.
- **Virgin West Coast, Virgin Cross
  Country**: ☎08457 222 333.
  www.virgintrains.co.uk.
- **National Express East Coast**:
  ☎Online bookings only, www.
  nationalexpresseastcoast.com

Discounts – Britrail and **Eurail**
passes are available to visitors from
North America and certain Asia-Pacific
countries including Australia.
For details visit www.raileurope.com
and www.railpass.com.
For all rail service **timetable
enquiries**: ☎08457 48 49 50.
www.nationalrail.co.uk.

By Coach

National Express (☎08717 81 81 81;
www.nationalexpress.com/coach) and
Scottish Citylink (☎08705 50 50 50;
www.citylink.co.uk) operate a regular

coach service throughout Scotland
and between the major Scottish and
English cities and towns. **Megabus**
(online booking only, www.megabus.
com) is a budget service operating
between London (and other English
cities) to Edinburgh and Glasgow and
onwards to Perth, Dundee, Aberdeen
and Inverness.
Remote areas are served by
Royal Mail Postbuses. Visit
www.postbus.royalmail.com
for routes and timetables.

By Car

DOCUMENTS

Nationals of EU countries require a
valid **national driving licence**. US
nationals require a driving licence
valid for 12 months; a permit is available from the National Auto Club
(☎650-294-7000; www.nationalauto-
club.com) or from a local branch of
the American Automobile Association.
Other nationals require an international driving licence.
It is also necessary to have the **reg-
istration papers** (log book) and a
nationality plate within the vehicle.

INSURANCE

Insurance coverage is compulsory in
the United Kingdom. Although an
International Insurance Certificate
(Green Card) is not a legal require-
ment, it is the most effective proof
of insurance and is internationally
recognised by the police and other
authorities.
Certain UK motoring organisations
(⌖*see opposite page, top left*) run
accident insurance and breakdown
service schemes covering holiday periods. Special policies are provided by
Europ-Assistance (☎0870 737 5720.
www.europ-assistance.co.uk). Drivers
in the US should visit the American
Automobile Association website
www.aaapublicaffairs.com and
click on Around the World/
International Clubs.

MOTORING ORGANISATIONS

The major motoring organisations in Great Britain are the Automobile Association (AA) and the Royal Automobile Club (RAC). Each provides services in varying degrees for non-resident members of affiliated clubs.

Automobile Association ☏0800 085 2721 (breakdown cover sales); www.theaa.com.

Royal Automobile Club breakdown cover sales ☏08000 966 999 or 0800 82 82 82 (at the scene); www.rac.co.uk.

HIGHWAY CODE

The **minimum driving age** is 17 years old. Traffic drives **on the left** and overtakes on the right. Headlights must be used at night even in built-up areas and at other times when visibility is poor. There are severe penalties for driving after drinking more than the legal limit of alcohol. In the case of a **breakdown** hazard warning lights are obligatory and a red warning triangle is advisable. On single track roads drivers should take extra care and use the passing places to allow traffic to flow.

Seat belts
In Britain the compulsory wearing of **seat belts** includes rear seat passengers when rear belts are fitted and all children under 14.

Speed limits
Maximum speeds are:
- 70mph/112kph: motorways or dual carriageways
- 60mph/96kph: other roads (unless specified otherwise)
- 30mph/48kph: in towns and cities.

Parking Regulations
Off-street parking is indicated by blue signs with white lettering (Parking or P); payment is made on leaving or in advance for a certain period. There are also parking meters, disc systems and pay to park zones; in the last case tickets must be obtained from ticket machines (small change necessary)

and displayed inside the windscreen. Illegal parking is liable to fines and also in certain cases to the vehicle being clamped or towed away.
- Double red line/wide red line = no stopping at any time (freeway)
- Double yellow line = no parking at any time
- Single yellow line = no parking for set periods as indicated on panel
- Dotted yellow line = parking limited to certain times only.
- No stopping or parking on white zigzag lines before and after a zebra crossing at any time. Remember to give way to pedestrians on zebra crossings and when traffic lights flash amber.

PETROL/GAS

Dual-pumps are the rule with **unleaded pumps** being identified by green pump handles.

ROUTE PLANNING

Michelin Map 501 (scale 1: 400,000) and the **Michelin** Road Atlas of Great Britain and Ireland (scale 1: 300,000) show the motorways (M), major roads (A) and many of the minor roads (B) in Scotland and give highly detailed road information.

RENTAL CARS

There are car rental agencies at airports, railway stations and in all large towns throughout Scotland. European cars usually have manual transmission but automatic cars are available on demand. An **international driving licence** is required for non-EU nationals. Most companies will not rent to drivers aged under 21 or 25.

- Avis: ☏online booking only, www.avis.co.uk.
- Budget: ☏0844 581 9998, www.budget.co.uk.
- Europcar: ☏0870 607 5000, www.europcar.co.uk
- Hertz: ☏see website for local offices, www.hertz.co.uk.

WHERE TO STAY AND EAT

 Refer to the Address Books in the Discovering section for local restaurant and accommodations listings. For coin ranges and for a description of the symbols used in the Address Books, see the Legend on the cover flap. The red-cover **Michelin Guide Great Britain and Ireland** is an annual publication that presents a selection of accommodation and restaurants. The range is wide, from modest guesthouses to luxurious grand hotels, from centrally situated lodging to secluded retreats.

Where to Stay

BOOKING A ROOM

The Scottish Regional Tourist Boards and the Tourist Information Centres operate an accommodation booking service for a small booking fee. Beware that room prices, even for a double room, are usually quoted per person.

BED AND BREAKFAST

Many private individuals take in a limited number of guests. Prices include bed and hot breakfast. Some also offer an evening meal.

UNIVERSITY ACCOMMODATION

During student vacations many universities and colleges offer low-cost accommodation in residence halls and dormitories in Dumfries, Dunfermline, Edinburgh, Glasgow and Stirling. Contact **Venuemasters** ☏0114 249 3090. www.venuemasters.co.uk.

YOUTH HOSTELS

There are many hostels in Scotland. Package holidays that comprise youth

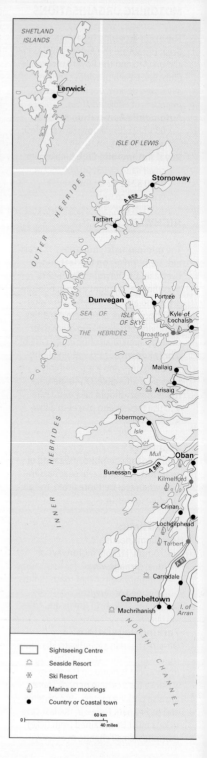

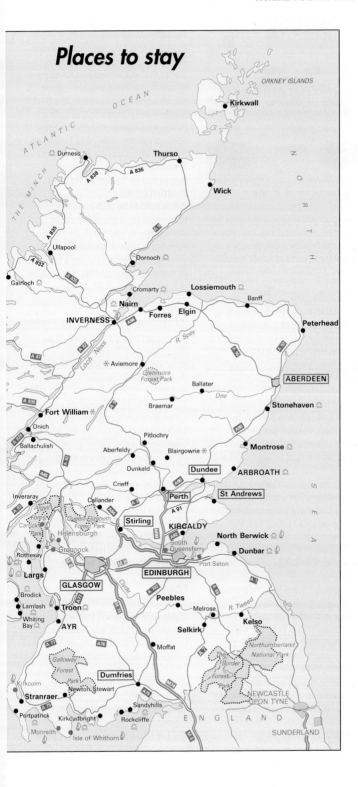

Places to stay

Seafood restaurant, Ile of Skye

F. Sichet/ MICHELIN

hostel vouchers, rail and bus pass or hostel vouchers, return rail fare and cycle hire are available by application to:

- **Scottish Youth Hostels Association**, 7 Glebe Crescent, Stirling FK8 2JA. ☏0870 155 3255. www.syha.org.uk.
- **Scottish Independent Hostels**, SIH, PO Box 7024 Fort William, PH33 6YX (or online). www.hostel-scotland.co.uk.

CAMPING

Scotland has many officially graded caravan and camping parks with modern facilities and a variety of additional sports facilities. For official sites recommended by Visit Scotland, see http://families.visitscotland.com/accommodation. Another useful organistaion is The Camping and Caravanning Club (visit www.campingand caravanningclub.co.uk.)

Where to Eat

Dining out in the UK has undergone a revolution in the last couple of decades and while changes may have taken longer to get to the farthest outposts, eating out in Edinburgh, Glasgow and many other major Scottish towns can be a very rewarding experience. Thanks to its colonial past and its cosmopolitan present, the UK offers authentic tastes from all over the world. In particular Scotland's "Auld Alliance", (with France) has

translated into a significant number of **French restaurants**. In recent years, as Indian and Asian restaurants have burgeoned, Glasgow has become one of Britain's best places for **curry**. Whereas Modern European cuisine is highly popular in London, the best Scottish restaurants, particularly in Edinburgh, feature top quality Scottish ingredients married to European, Asian or even Pacific influences and flavours that produce a splendid hybrid cuisine known as **Modern Scottish** cooking.

Prices tend to be high compared to many other parts of the world, particularly in Edinburgh and Glasgow. Eating out in the big cities at lunchtime, however, can be a bargain as many restaurants offer competitive pricing aimed at office workers.

VENUES

Restaurant hours are often flexible in the major cities but less so elsewhere. Most rural restaurants serve lunch only between noon and 2 or 2.30pm and dinner from about 7pm to 10pm. The rise of bistros, brasseries and continental style cafes has brought all-day, pan-European eating and snacking to many places but these establishments are rare outside major cities. Though many Scottish pubs serve food, what's on offer tends to be palatable rather than memorable. There are a growing number of "gastropubs", however, where the food is given top priority. For guaranteed good food in a pub pick up a copy of **Michelin Eating Out in Pubs**.

FOOD

Scotland is renowned for the quality of its beef and its fish. Aberdeen Angus and Galloway beef are always reliable. Scottish seafood is equally famous; fish lovers can enjoy salmon or trout, either fresh from the stream or via the smoke house.

For more information on traditional Scottish cooking and produce, see THE REGION TODAY in the INTRODUCTION.

WHAT TO SEE AND DO

Outdoor Fun

Information on all the activities listed below is available from Visit Scotland either online (www.visitscotland.com) or in brochure form from tourist information centres.

CYCLING

From dedicated mountain biking centres – Scotland is one of the best places in Europe for this sport – and forest trails, to quiet countryside lanes and miles upon miles of the National Cycle Network, Scotland is an excellent destination for cyclists.

Airlines, ferry companies and the rail network will transport accompanied bicycles. Tourist Information Centres will give advice on shops hiring out cycles in Scotland and provide leaflets on local cycling routes (150 are available on the website alone).

For more details go to the official Visit Scotland cycling website: http://cycling.visitscotland.com.

FISHING

Scotland is a world-class fishing destination. Salmon, sea trout and brown trout abound in the many lochs and rivers. Coarse fishing may be enjoyed in the southern part of the country. The waters around the coast provide ample opportunities for sea anglers to test their skills. The main centres include Eyemouth, Arbroath, Stonehaven, Kippford, Ullapool and the Shetland Islands, where there is a ready supply of boats for hire. Sea angling festivals are regular features in some resorts.

For more information on the seasons, fisheries, price of licences and permits, boat and tackle hire and accommodation, go to the official Visit Scotland fishing website, http://fish.visitscotland.com where you can also download or request by post the brochure *Fish in Scotland*.

Fishing permits are available from local tackle shops, hotels, grocers and post offices.

GOLF

The traditional home of golf, Scotland has over 550 public and private courses in addition to the world famous venues at St Andrews, Turnberry, Carnoustie, Muirfield and Dornoch. Most courses are open to the public on payment of a green fee, and golfers are admitted without introduction or the need to belong to a club. For more detailed information on golf courses, see the **Michelin** map 501, the red-cover **Michelin Guide Great Britain & Ireland** and go to the Visit Scotland website, http://golf.visitscotland.com.

HIKING

Walking Scotland is available as a brochure or to download from the Visit Scotland website http://walking.visitscotland. It gives details on short walk, family walks and, at the other extreme, in-depth information sheets

P.TOMKINS/VisitScotland/SCOTTISH VIEWPOINT

Fly fishing on the River Teith, Callander

Walkers looking over to Loch Duich and the Five Sisters of Kintail from Mam Ratagan (Ratagain), Highland

for individual long-distance walks. There are also leaflets, guides and maps detailing Scotland's three **long-distance footpaths,** the Speyside Way, the South Upland Way and the West Highland Way.

Each route has a ranger service to help and advise ramblers. Official guides and route maps are published by HMSO and a free information and accommodation leaflet is available from Scottish Natural Heritage. Another good contact the **Ramblers' Association (Scotland)**, ☎0157 786 1222; www.ramblers.org.uk/scotland.

West Highland Way

This route runs 95mi/150km from Milngavie on the outskirts of Glasgow, north to Fort William. It follows the eastern shore of Loch Lomond, crosses the remote Rannoch Moor and the mountains of Lochaber, passing Ben Nevis on the way.

Speyside Way

The route passes through varied countryside as it follows the river from the coast to the Cairngorms. Of the 60mi/96km from Tugnet on Spey Bay to Glenmore Lodge, east of Aviemore, only the northern section to Ballindalloch (30mi/48km) has been completed. In addition there is a spur from Craigellachie to Dufftown (3mi/5km) and a more arduous one (17mi/27km)

from Ballindalloch to Tomintoul in the foothills of the Grampian Mountains.

South Upland Way

This coast to coast footpath (212mi/341km) links Portpatrick in the west to Cockburnspath in the east. Some of the longer stretches are arduous, covering remote hill country. There is also a section on Munros, the colloquial term for Scottish mountains above 3,000ft (914.4m. There are 284 Munros and climbing them all – 'Munro-bagging' – is a popular pursuit amongst the climbing and hillwalking fraternity.

HORSE RIDING

A wide choice of centres throughout Scotland welcomes the beginner or the experienced rider for single day or longer holiday spells. Trekking and trail riding are good ways to discover the countryside.

For more information visit the website of The Trekking and Riding Society of Scotland, www.ridinginscotland.com for details of trail riding, residential centres, horse riding holidays, etc.

HUNTING

In Scotland you can hunt for Roe Buck, Red Stag, Sika, Red Hind, pheasant, partridge, duck, pigeon and, most famously, grouse. The season for the latter starts on the Glorious Twelfth (12 August) until 10 December. Other birds and animals may also only be hunted seasonally. Perthshire is famous for grouse shooting, otherwise hunting takes places nationally. Countrysports is Scotland's longest established private agency. Initial contact only via website: www.countrysports.co.uk.

MOUNTAINEERING

Scotland provides ideal country for hill walking, mountaineering, orienteering and rock climbing. Many Scottish peaks lie within easy reach of a public road, while some areas in the Cairngorms, Skye and Knoydart are very remote.

The relatively low altitude of most peaks – only four are over 4,000ft/1,200m – is deceptive as rapid weather changes make them hazardous. All climbers should be aware of the potential dangers and equip themselves properly. Climbers are also advised to inform the police or another responsible person of their plans before venturing on hazardous climbs. Winter may present an entirely different environment from spring and summer.

Some of the principal climbing centres include Arran, Skye, Ben Nevis, Glencoe and the Cairngorms. There are more remote ranges and peaks in the western and northern Highlands. The more popular centres, especially Bens Nevis and Lomond, have well marked footpaths.

The indoor **Edinburgh International Climbing Arena** at Ratho (☎0131 333 6333; www.eica-ratho.com) offers experienced climbers the opportunity to brush up on their skills or alternatively it can give complete beginners a taste of the sport. With climbing walls from 39ft/12m to 115ft/35m high, and routes from simple to complex, there is something for all levels and abilities. Keen climbers might like to visit the website of the **Mountaineering Council of Scotland**; ☎www.mcofs.org.uk.

Guided walking holidays and mountain courses in the Highlands are run by **Mountain innovations** ☎01479 831 331. www.scotmountain.co.uk.

NATURE RESERVES AND NATIONAL FOREST PARKS

Scotland has numerous **nature reserves**, **country parks** and **forest parks** managed for public use and recreation.

Nature conservation is the main aim of these reserves and most employ a warden. In general visitors are welcome, with amenities that include visitor interpretation centres, nature trails and observation hides. The reserves provide the visitor with a good chance to see wildlife, though there are restrictions in some cases. In addition to bird sanctuaries on the cliffs and offshore islands (such as Bass Rock, Isle of May, Ailsa Craig, St Kilda), the Forestry Commission – Scotland's largest landowner – has created forest parks in areas of scenic attraction. These include Glenmore Park, Queen Elizabeth Park, Argyll Forest Park, Galloway Forest Park and Border Forest Park.

Timber growing is the main activity in these parks but recreation is also encouraged. In addition to designated forest drives and marked trails there are picnic sites, camping and caravan sites and visitor centres.

For additional information apply to:
- **The Forestry Commission**, 231 Costorphine Road, Edinburgh EH12 7AT. ☎0845 367 3787. www.forestry.gov.uk/scotland.
- **Scottish Wildlife Trust**, Cramond House, Kirk Cramond, Cramond Glebe Road, Edinburgh EH4 6NS. ☎0131 312 7765. www.swt.org.uk.
- **Scottish Natural Heritage**, 2 Great Glen House, Leachkin Road, Inverness IV3 8NW. ☎01463 725000. www.snh.org.uk.
- **Royal Society for the Protection of Birds Scotland** ☎www.rspb.org.uk.

SAILING AND WATERSPORTS

Unsurprisingly, in a land where sea and freshwater lochs abound, there is no lack of sailing or watersports. The western seaboard with its many isles and sheltered waters is a safe playground. Many sailing centres hold local regattas; some of the main centres are Largs, Tobermory, Lamlash Bay, Oban (Kimelford), Crammond Port, Aberdour, Helensburgh, Crinan and Tarbert.

Inland, sailing and watersports facilities are good on Loch Earn, Loch Lomond and Loch Morlich.

Yachts can be hired on the western seaboard and the Caledonian Canal. There are sailing marinas all round the coast of Scotland and on the inland lochs. All yacht clubs and sailing schools are linked to the Royal Yachting Association Scotland, Caledonia House, South Gyle, Edinburgh EH12 9DQ; ☎0131 317 7388; www.ryascotland.org.uk.

SKIING

The main centres are:

Glenshee: 26 Wellmeadow, Blairgowrie. ☎08450 50 50 52. www.ski-glenshee.co.uk.

The Lecht Ski Centre: The Mews, Mar Road, Braemar. ☎013397 41600. www.lecht.co.uk.

Glencoe Mountain Resort: ☎0871 871 9929. www.glencoemountain.com.

The Nevis Range: Cameron Centre, Cameron Square, Fort William. ☎01397 703781. www.nevisrange.co.uk.

Aviemore: Grampian Road, Aviemore. ☎01479 810363. www.cairngormmountain.org.

There are dry ski slopes all over the country; the longest in Britain is at the Midlothian Snowsports Centre (☎0131 445 4433; www.midlothian. gov.uk), south of Edinburgh.

Ski Scotland is the official ski site of VisitScotland; www. ski.visitscotland. com. From here UK and Ireland visitors can obtain the latest VisitScotland 'Scottish Adventure Guide' featuring full information about Scottish ski centres and winter sports.

ADVENTURE SPORTS

With its extraordinary range of adventure sports and activities Scotland has a justifiable claim to be Europe's Adventure Sports Capital.

On the **water**: adventure-tubing, bodyboarding, canyoning, diving (sub aqua), kayak-surfing, kitesurfing, open canoeing, powerboating, river-bugging (riding a single person inflatable craft), sea-kayaking, surfing, wakeboarding, whitewater kayaking, whitewater rafting, windsurfing.

On **land**: caving and potholing, land yachting, mountain biking, mountainboarding, scrambling, weaseling (wriggling through an underground labyrinth of tunnels).

Adrenaline sports: kart racing, off-road driving, paintball, quad biking, skateboarding, sphereing (hurtling down the mountainside on the inside of a large transparent inflatable ball).

On **ice**: ice climbing, ski mountaineering, snowboarding, sled dog racing, telemark skiing.

In the **air**: gliding, hang-gliding, Hot Air Ballooning, microlighting, paragliding, power kiting, sky diving

You can find more details of all these on www.adventure.visitscotland.com, the official adventure sport website.

WILDLIFE WATCHING

Scotland is home to a diverse range of species, from the bottlenose dolphins of the Moray Firth to the capercaillie of the Central Highlands and the thousands of seals and puffins inhabiting the coastline. For an excellent overview visit the official Wildlife Scotland website at http://wildlife.visitscotland.com. For reputable wildlife tour operators ask at tourist information centres.

Spas

Scotland has a growing number of spas with many country house hotels and 4- and 5-star hotels in the cities now adding the latest luxury facilities. Recommended are:

The Cowshed,
The Scotsman Hotel, Edinburgh.
www.thescotsmanhotel.co.uk.

One Spa, The Sheraton, Edinburgh.
www.one-spa.com.

The Spa at The Westin Turnberry Resort, Ayrshire.
www.turnberry.co.uk.

Stobo Castle, Stobo, Peebleshire.
www.stobocastle.co.uk.

Dunblane Hydro Hotel, Dunblane.
www.dunblanehydrohotel.com.

Activities for Children Kids

In this guide, sights of particular interest to children are indicated with a Kids symbol. All attractions/tours offer discounted admission/tour fees for children and most have family tickets. Scotland isn't the easiest place in the world to bring children, with a culture that has in the past not really catered for them and weather that often doesn't encourage them to play outside for long. The weather hasn't changed much but things have improved immeasurably in recent years in other aspects, with, for example, museums and other interpretive attractions becoming far more hands-on. New cutting-edge attractions, such as Edinburgh's Our

Dynamic Earth and Glasgow Science Centre, have been designed especially for the family. The big cities all cater well for family visitors and Edinburgh in particular is a wonderful place for children at festival time.

Calendar of Events

Listed below are a few of the more popular events among Scotland's many colourful customs and traditions. For more details on these and other events visit www.visitscotland.com, or ask at a local Tourist Information Centres.
For a selection of Highland Games and Common Ridings, see INTRODUCTION: Traditional Scotland.

JANUARY

Throughout Scotland — Burns Night: Burns Suppers to celebrate the birthday of the national poet with haggis as the main dish
Lerwick, Shetland — Last Tuesday. Up-Helly-Ha: torchlit procession followed by burning of Viking warship, singing and all night dancing. www.visitshetland.com/major-events/up-helly-aa.
Glasgow — Celtic Connections: large festival of Celtic-inspired music throughout the city. www.glasgowwestend.co.uk.

FEBRUARY

Jedburgh, Scottish Borders — Ba' Game (mob or village football)
Inverness, Highland — mid-February to early March. Inverness Music Festival: Classical music. www.invernessmusicfestival.org.

MARCH

Lanark, South Lanarkshire — 1 March. Whuppity Scourie: banishing winter.
Glenshee — early March — Snow Fun Week: www.ski-glenshee.co.uk.

Edinburgh — mid-March.
Edinburgh Book Fair.
www.edinburghbookfair.co.uk.

MARCH–APRIL

Edinburgh — Ceilidh Culture.
Music dance and story-telling:
www.ceilidhculture.co.uk.
Kirkcaldy, Fife — 1 week around
Easter. Links Market: Europe's
longest (1mi/1.6km) street funfair.
www.linksmarket.org.uk.

MARCH–OCTOBER

Pitlochry, Perthshire and Kinross
— Pitlochry Festival Theatre
Season. www.pitlochry.org.uk.

APRIL

Ayr, South Ayrshire —
Scottish Grand National.
www.ayr-racecourse.co.uk.
Mull, Argyll and Bute — late April.
Mull Traditional Music Festival.

APRIL–MAY

Lerwick, Shetland — early April.
Shetland Folk Festival.
www.shetlandfolkfestival.com.

MAY

Ayr, Alloway, Ayrshire —
mid–late May. Burns and A' That:
a celebration of the life of Robert
Burns with contemporary artists
and performers. http://burns.
visitscotland.com/festival.

MAY

Blair Castle, Perthshire and Kinross
— Late May.
Atholl Highlanders' Parade.
www.blair-castle.co.uk/events.

JUNE

Lanark, South Lanarkshire —
6–12 June. Lanark Lanimer Festival. www.lanarklanimers.co.uk.

Kirkwall and Stromness, Orkney
— Late June.
St Magnus Festival. Arts festival.
www.stmagnusfestival.com.
Ingliston, near Edinburgh —
Late June. Royal Highland Agricul-
tural Show. www.rhass.org.uk.
Glasgow — Late June.
Glasgow International
Jazz Festival. www.jazzfest.co.uk.

JULY–AUGUST

Aberdeen — Late July–early August.
International Youth Festival of
Music and the Arts. www.aiyf.org.
Variable venue — World Pipe Band
Championship. www.rspba.org.
South Queensferry, West Lothian
— August. Burry Man Festival:
Burry man clad in sticky burrs
tours the town collecting for char-
ity, on the last day of fair week.
www.ferryfair.co.uk.
Edinburgh — August. Edinburgh
International Festival, Military
Tattoo and Edinburgh Fringe,
Jazz Festival.
www.edinburgh-festivals.com.

AUGUST–SEPTEMBER

Largs, North Ayrshire —
Largs Viking Festival.
www.largsvikingfestival.com
Inverness, Highland — early
September. Northern Meeting
Piping Competition.
www.northern-meeting.org

SEPTEMBER

Highlands (various venues) —
Blas Festival. The Highlands premier Gaelic and traditional music
festival. www.blas-festival.com.

OCTOBER

Variable venue (2009, Oban) —
The Royal National Mod.
Scotland's premier Gaelic festival.
www.the-mod.co.uk.
Blair Castle, Perthshire and Kinross
— Late October. Glenfiddich

World Piping Championship.
www.blairatholl.org.uk.

NOVEMBER

Edinburgh — Late November onwards. Edinburgh's Christmas. www.edinburghschristmas.com.
Glasgow — Late November onwards. Winterfest Glasgow. www.winterfestglasgow.com.

DECEMBER

Kirkwall, Orkney — Christmas and New Year's Day. Ba' Games. Street/ Mob Football. www.bagame.com.
Stonehaven, Aberdeenshire — 31 Dec, midnight. Swinging Fireball Ceremony. www.stonehavenfireballs.co.uk.
Hogmanay — 31 Dec. New Year's Eve Celebrations. Nationwide but particularly vibrant in Edinburgh and Glasgow.

Shopping

Glasgow and Edinburgh are wonderful places for shoppers whether in search of cheap touristy tartan souvenirs or the very latest in household and clothing fashions. There is much less choice in the provinces but here, too, the quality of merchandise has improved immeasurably over the last decade or so. For more details on shopping in Scotland visit http://liveit.visit scotland.com.

BUYING

Crafts

Many craft studios (pottery, ceramics, weaving, lacemaking, knitting, basketmaking, metalwork, woodcraft, jewellery) are open to visitors in summer. There are demonstrations of obsolete crafts in some Folk Museums and Folk Villages and at festivals.

Textiles

Everywhere there is a wide choice of woollen articles, in particular cashmere, Shetland and lambswool,

as well as tweed and tartan garments. Jewellery in Celtic designs, Caithness glass and Edinburgh crystal make ideal gifts.

Whisky

Scotch whisky, especially single malt, is recommended. The most popular food products are smoked salmon, marmalade, Dundee cake and shortbread. ¢ *See INTRODUCTION, Food and Drink for more information on whisky production in Scotland.*

OPENING HOURS

Shops in the major cities are open Mondays to Saturdays, 9am–5.30/6pm. There is late-night shopping (7–8pm) in most large cities on Thursdays. Smaller individual shops may open later, close during the lunch hour or stay open until late at night. Many towns are closed all day or have an early closing day (ECD), when shops are closed during the afternoon (Mondays, Wednesdays or Thursdays). Shops are often open on Sundays, especially in large towns during the summer.

Sightseeing

HERITAGE

National Trust for Scotland (NTS)

Head Office, 28 Charlotte Square, Edinburgh EH2 4ET. ☎0131 243 9300. www.nts.org.uk.
The Trust owns and conserves places of historic interest or natural beauty, including coast and countryside properties. Discovery Tickets (valid for 7 or 14 days) giving access to all NTS properties are available from staffed properties, the head office and major TICs.
Some properties host special events such as festivals, exhibitions and concerts; enquire in advance for details. There are reciprocal arrangements between the NTS and similar overseas national trusts (for example the Royal Oak Foundation in the US, etc.).

P. Tomkins/VisitScotland/Scottish Viewpoint

Strathisla Distillery, Grampian

Historic Scotland (HS)

Head Office, Longmore House, Salisbury Place, Edinburgh EH9 1SH. ☎0131 668 8600. www.historic-scotland.gov.uk.
HS restores, conserves and maintains over 300 properties representing Scotland's varied architectural heritage. Explorer Passes (valid 3, 7 and 10 days) are available for individuals and families. These are available from all HS properties, TICs, and online at www.historic-scotland.gov.uk/explorer. HS has reciprocal arrangements with English Heritage and Cadw (Welsh Historic Monuments).

Great British Heritage Pass

This useful pass (15-day or one-month available) gives access to over 580 stately homes, castles and gardens throughout Britain, and is available to non-UK residents via some BTA

offices (☎*see Tourist Offices*) or online at www.britishheritagepass.com.

Scotland's Gardens

42a Castle Street, Edinburgh EH2 3BN. ☎0131 226 3714. www.gardensof scotland.org. These are private gardens that open to the public for a limited period in aid of charity. The handbook, **Gardens of Scotland**, is available direct (£5.50 plus £1.00 post and packaging), or from major retail outlets.

TRACING ANCESTORS

There are organisations in Edinburgh and clan centres that can assist people of Scottish descent who wish to trace their ancestors. For information on clan gatherings, enquire at tourist information centres.

- **Scotland's People** is the government source of genealogical data; www.scotlandspeople.gov.uk. Linked to this is Ancestral Scotland, an initiative by Visit Scotland; www.ancestralscotland.com.
- **National Archives of Scotland**, HM General Register House, 2 Princes Street, Edinburgh EH1 3YY. ☎0131 535 1314. www.nas.gov.uk.
- **The National Library of Scotland**, George IV Bridge, Edinburgh EH1 1EW. ☎0131 623 3700. www.nls.uk/family-history.
- **General Register Office**, New Register House, 3 West Register Street, Edinburgh EH1 3YY; ☎0131 334 0380. www.gro-scotland.gov.uk.

TARTANS

Information on Scottish tartans is available from:

- James Pringle Weavers, Leith Mills, Leith, Edinburgh. ☎0131 553 5161.
- The Tartan Weaving Mills Exhibition, 555 Castlehill, Edinburgh. ☎0131 226 1555. www.geoffreykilts.co.uk/tartan-weavingmill.htm

World Heritage Sites

Over 500 sites of "outstanding universal value" are on the UNESCO World Heritage List. Sites may be exceptional natural locales, monuments with unique historical, artistic or scientific features; groups of buildings, or sites which are the combined works of man and nature of exceptional beauty. Scotland boasts four such sites: St Kilda; the Old Town and New Town of Edinburgh; Neolithic Orkney; New Lanark.

GAELIC EVENTS

An Comunn Gaidhealach, 109 Church Street, Inverness IVI IEJ. ☎01463 231 226. www.ancomunn.co.uk.

WHISKY TOURS

The Scotch Whisky Association, 20 Atholl Crescent, Edinburgh EH3 8HF. www.scotch-whisky.org.uk. *For more information, see Shopping, and INTRODUCTION, Food and Drink.*

SCENIC ROUTES

Tourist information centres have leaflets on scenic routes. The road signs have white lettering on a brown background with a blue thistle symbol.

Books

The History of Scotland – P and F Somerset Fry, Routledge and Kegan Paul 1982
The Story of Scotland – Nigel Tranter, Lochar Publishing Ltd 1991
Scotland, A New History – Michael Lynch, Pimlico 1992
Anatomy of Scotland – Eds. Magnus Linklater and Robin Denniston, Chambers 1992
The Manufacture of Scottish History – Eds. Ian Donnachie and Christopher Whatley, Polygon 1992
A Concise History of Scotland – Fitzroy Maclean, Thames & Hudson
Highlanders, A History of the Highland Clans – Fitzroy Maclean, Adelphi
The Battle for Scotland – Andrew Marr, Penguin 1992
Robert the Bruce – Ronald McNair Scott, Edinburgh 1989
Bonnie Prince Charlie – Fitzroy MacLean, Canongate Publishing, Edinburgh 1989
Mary Queen of Scots – Antonia Fraser, Mandarin Paperbacks 1969
The Royal House of Scotland – Eric Linklater, Macmillan & Co Ltd 1970
Poetical Works of Robert Burns edited by W & R Chambers Ltd 1990
Whisky Galore – Compton Mackenzie, Penguin Books 1957

A Traveller's History of Scotland – Andrew Fischer, The Windrush Press 1990

Films

Macbeth (1948)
Orson Welles directs and plays the tragic king; restructured, but the dialogue is Shakespeare's.
Whisky Galore (1949)
A comedy classic of Scottish islanders trying to plunder whisky from a stranded ship.
Brigadoon (1954)
Two Americans on a hunting trip in Scotland discover a village set two hundred years in the past.
The Prime of Miss Jean Brodie (1969)
Oscar-winning Maggie Smith as a liberated young schoolteacher at an Edinburgh girls' school.
Gregory's Girl (1981)
Romantic comedy of teens in love at a Scottish school in the 1970s.
*Local Hero (*1983)
An American oil company sends their representative to buy up an entire village where they want to build a refinery
Highlander (1986)
An immortal Scottish swordsman pits himself against an equally immortal barbarian.
Hamlet (1990)
Franco Zeffirelli's Oscar-winning adaptation starring Mel Gibson.
Rob Roy (1995)
Liam Neeson plays Rob in a violent tale of treachery and revenge.
Braveheart (1995)
Mel Gibson plays William Wallace in an iconic role fighting English oppression.
Loch Ness (1995).
Heartwarming monster drama starring Ted Danson.
Trainspotting (1996).
Violent portrayal of Edinburgh drugs culture in the 1990s.
Stone of Destiny (2009)
How a group of Scottish students stole the coronation stone from Westminster Abbey in the 1950s.

BASIC INFORMATION

Business Hours

Standard business and office hours are 9am to 5pm Monday to Friday. Museums and visitor attractions in the cities generally open year-round daily around 10am (noon on Sunday) to 5.30pm or 6pm. In winter opening times may be reduced. In the provinces and more remote areas attractions may close for the winter, hours will be shorter and they may be closed on quieter days.

Pubs generally open Mondays to Saturdays 11am–11pm, and Sundays, 12.30pm–2.30pm and 6.30pm–11pm, though in the bigger cities and towns they may stay open much later. Young people under 18 years of age are subject to various restrictions.

Electricity

240 volts AC (50 HZ) is the usual voltage; 3-pin flat wall sockets are standard. An adaptor or multiple point plug is required for non-British appliances.

Emergencies

Dial 999 (free) for nationwide emergency assistance; ask for **Fire**; **Police**; **Ambulance**; **Coastguard**, etc.

Mail/Post

Post Offices are generally open Mondays to Fridays, 9.30am to 5.30pm and Saturday mornings, 9.30am to 12.30pm.

Somewhat confusingly, Royal Mail pricing is now based on the *size* of a letter as well as the more traditional weight.

Postcard/standard small letter rate: UK 24p, Europe 48p, rest of the world 54p. You will need to visit a Post Office if you are sending anything else. Stamps are also available from newsa-gents and tobacconists and even some supermarkets. Poste Restante items are held for 14 days; proof of identity is required. Airmail delivery usually takes 3 to 4 days in Europe and 4 to 7 days elsewhere in the world.

Money

BANKS

Banks are generally open from Mondays to Fridays, 9.30am to 3.30pm; some banks offer a limited service on Saturday mornings; all banks are closed on Sundays and bank holidays. Most banks have cash dispensers (ATMs) that accept international credit cards; most do not charge a fee for cash withdrawals (be sure to look for a notice to that effect). Exchange facilities outside these hours are available at airports, currency exchange companies, travel agencies and hotels. Some form of identification is necessary when cashing travellers cheques or Eurocheques in banks. Commission charges vary; hotels usually charge more than banks.

CREDIT CARDS

The main credit cards (American Express; Access/Eurocard/Mastercard; Diners Club; Visa/Barclaycard) are widely accepted in shops, hotels, restaurants and petrol stations. Most banks have cash dispensers which accept international credit cards. In case of loss or theft, phone:

CURRENCY

The official currency in Great Britain is the **pound sterling**. The decimal system (100 pence = £1) is used throughout Great Britain; Scotland has different notes including £1 and £100 notes, which are legal tender outside Scotland, though you may well have difficulty getting English shopkeepers to accept them; the Channel Islands and Isle of Man have different notes and coins, which are not valid elsewhere. The common currency – in descending order of value – is £50, £20, £10 and £5 (notes); £2, £1 (gold coins), 50p, 20p, 10p, 5p (silver coins) and 2p and 1p (copper coins). The Euro may be accepted in some stores in London; check in advance.

Dialling codes	
00 61:	Australia
00 1:	Canada
00 353:	Republic of Ireland
00 64:	New Zealand
00 44:	United Kingdom (including Northern Ireland)
00 1:	United States of America

Public Holidays

The following are days when museums and other monuments may be closed or vary their admission hours:
- 1, 2 January
- Good Friday
- Monday nearest 1 May
- Last Monday in May
- First Monday in August
- 30 November (St Andrew's Day)
- 25 December
- 26 December

There are school holidays at Christmas spring and summer, and half-term breaks in February and October.

Reduced Rates

Discounts are generally available for senior citizens (over 65), students and youths (usually under 15/16) on visitor attractions and tours, public transport and other leisure activities such as movies. Proof of age may be required.

Smoking

In the UK it is illegal to smoke in enclosed public spaces and some outdoor spaces, such as train platforms.

Taxes

In Great Britain a **Value Added Tax** (VAT) of 17.5 % is added to almost all retail goods. Non-Europeans may reclaim this tax at the Customs office of the airport of their departure; each shop sets its own minimum purchase. See www.globalrefund.com.

Communications

TELEPHONES

Pre-paid phonecards for national and international calls from public phones are available from Post Offices and some shops (such as newsagents and tobacconists). Some public phones also accept credit cards.

Since deregulation a number of telephone operators have set up in competition with the previous state-run British Telecommunications (BT). Rates vary enormously between operators. For calls made through BT daytime rates are Mon–Fri, 6am–6pm; evening, Mon–Fri, before 6am and after 6pm; weekend midnight Friday to midnight Sunday.

℘ 100: Operator
℘ 118 500: BT Directory Enquiries-within the UK and International Operator/Enquiries.

International Calls
To make an international call dial 00 followed by the country code, then the area code (without the initial 0) then the subscriber's number. Below are some of the more popular visitors home country codes The codes for direct dialling to other countries are printed in telephone directories.

Time

In winter standard time throughout Scotland is Greenwich Mean Time (GMT). In summer (mid-March to October) clocks are advanced by 1hr to give British Summer Time (BST) which is the same as Central European Time.

Dunnottar Castle, South of
Stonehaven, Aberdeenshire
P. Tomkins/VisitScotland/Scottish Viewpoint

NATURE

Scotland is renowned for its unspoiled natural state and the attractions of the great outdoors; from a majestic stag in Monarch of the Glen pose, or endearing shaggy Highland Cattle, to the humble thistle and purple heather, all are powerful icons of a land which has remained close to its roots.

Topography

A FEW FACTS

The mainland of Scotland and the numerous fringing islands cover an area of 30,414sq mi/78,936km². The coastline is deeply penetrated by the Atlantic on the west and by the North Sea on the east; most places are within 60mi/96km of the sea. There are 787 islands (under one quarter are inhabited) and 6,214mi/10,000km of coastline. The resident population is slightly less than 5,100,000, giving an average density of 167 per square mile (270/km²). 98% of Scotland is classified as countryside. Although Scotland is generally recognised as a mountainous country, the infinite variety of landscapes is one of its major tourist assets. The country is traditionally divided into three areas, the Southern Uplands, Central Lowlands or Midland Valley and the Highlands.

SOUTHERN UPLANDS

Here the hills are lower and more rounded than their northern counterparts. In the southwest the smoothly rounded forms of the Galloway hills are dominated by the more rugged granitic masses of the Merrick (2,764ft/843m), Criffel (1,886ft/569m) and Cairnsmore of Fleet (2,331ft/711m). Both the **Clyde** and **Tweed** have their sources in the vicinity of the lead-bearing Lowther Hills. The Nith, Annan and Esk drain southwards to the Solway Firth. Hill country continues eastward with the **Moorfoot** and **Lammermuir Hills** which demarcate the **Southern Upland Fault**.

CENTRAL LOWLANDS

The **Highland Boundary Fault** extending from Stonehaven to Helensburgh and the Southern Upland Fault delimit this low-lying rift valley which has little land below 400ft/122m and is not without its own hill masses – **Campsie Fells**, **Kilpatrick Hills**, **Ochils** and **Sidlaws.**

The Lothian plains fringing the Firth of Forth and stretching to the sea at Dunbar are interrupted on the southern outskirts of Edinburgh by the Pentland Hills. Lowland continues along the carselands of the Forth up through Strathearn to the Tay and the rich Carse of Gowrie, overlooked by the **Sidlaw Hills**. To the north the fertile sweep of **Strathmore** passes northeastwards, to become, beyond Brechin, the more restricted **Howe of the Mearns.** Dumbarton, Stirling and Edinburgh Castle rocks, North Berwick and the Bass Rock are associated with volcanic activity.

HIGHLANDS

Though altitudes are low by Alpine standards, much of this area lies above 2,000ft/610m. The **Great Glen Fault**, stretching from Loch Linnhe to the Moray Firth, acts as a divide between the Grampian Mountains and the North West Highlands. The **Cairngorms** are an extensive tract of land above 3,500ft/1,067m punctuated by peaks rising to over 4,000ft/1,219m (**Cairn Gorm** 4,084ft/1,245m; **Ben Macdui** 4,296ft/1,309m and **Braeriach** 4,248ft/1,295m). West of the Spey are the Monadhliath Mountains, a rolling upland of peat and moorland.

Some of the highest peaks (**Ben Nevis** 4,406ft/1,344m, **Ben Lawers** 3,984ft/1,214m), finest saltwater (**Lochs Fyne** and **Long**) and freshwater lochs (**Lochs Lomond, Katrine, Awe** and **Tay**) and greatest rivers (Spey, Tay, Dee and Don) can be found here. The Buchan and Moray Firth (Laigh of Moray) lowlands fringe the mountains to the east and north.

The Highlands to the north and west of the Great Glen are a wilder and more remote area where isolated peaks rise above a plateau surface with an average height of 2,000ft/610m. Outstanding examples are the spectacular Torridon peaks of **Suilven** (2,399ft/731m), **Canisp** (2,779ft/846m) and **Quinag** (2,653ft/808m), and in Sutherland **Bens Hope** (3,042ft/927m) and **Loyal** (2,504ft/764m). The indented western coastline where sea lochs separate peninsulas, is fringed offshore by the **Inner** and **Outer Hebrides**.

COASTLINE

Scotland's long coastline is deeply indented and largely rocky, although the east coast is generally smoother and straighter. The coastline is one of impressive cliff faces with offshore arches and stacks as at Hoy in Orkney, Cape Wrath and St Abb's Head, or great stretches of dune-backed sandy beaches, the asset of such east coast resorts as Montrose, Aberdeen, Fraserburgh and Nairn.

ISLANDS

Mainland Scotland is fringed by approximately 787 islands with the Hebrides strung out along the western seaboard, as the largest group (500). The Inner Hebrides include such evocative isles as Skye, Mull, Iona, Jura and Islay. The Minch separates the mainland from the Outer Hebrides, an archipelago stretching 140mi/225km from the Butt of Lewis to Barra Head. The principal islands in the Firth of Clyde are Arran, Bute and the Cumbraes. Beyond the Pentland Firth in the north are two important clusters of isles and islets, the Orkney Islands comprising 90 in all and farther north the Shetland Islands, a group of about 100. Fair Isle, St Kilda and Rockall are isolated outliers of this island fringe. Many are now uninhabited but it was on these distant isles that the Norse and Gaelic cultures resisted the longest. Today each one has a jealously guarded character of its own.

THE MUNROS

A large percentage of Scotland lies above 800ft/244m and hills and mountains are an ever-present aspect of the landscape. In 1891 **Sir Hugh Munro** drew up tables of all the Scottish peaks over 3,000ft/910m. With perfected surveying techniques the total includes some 280. To some climbers Munro-bagging, chalking off every single one, is a lifetime task.

CONSERVATION POLICY

The task of reconciling the increasing demand for public access and recreation with the conservation of the countryside and in particular the areas of outstanding scenic value is met in Scotland by the cooperation of numerous bodies. Agreements ensure the conservation of Scotland's scenic heritage with its wildlife. The National Trust for Scotland owns and administers some of Scotland's most important mountain areas – Balmacara-Kintail, Glencoe and Torridon – where ranger-naturalists meet the need for public access to the countryside.

In an attempt to reverse the destruction of native forests, Scottish Natural Heritage has launched schemes to regenerate woodland areas. Hawthorn, rowan and alder are planted to replace non-native tree species such as sycamore, larch and beech.

Gardens

Somewhat surprisingly given Scotland's northern latitude, gardens are an important part of the country's natural heritage, both historically and horticulturally.

GULF STREAM GARDENS

For the foreign visitor these gardens are perhaps the most unexpected. In secluded spots all along Scotland's Atlantic seaboard gardens with a profusion of tropical and sub-tropical plants flourish. The outstanding example is Osgood Mackenzie's woodland garden at Inverewe, in its perfect Highland setting. Moving southwards others include Crarae Woodland Garden, the Younger Botanic Gardens, Benmore and the Logan Botanic Gardens, to name a few of those open all year round.

GARDENS WITH A DIFFERENCE

The formal gardens at Pitmedden, Edzell and Drummond Castle reflect the spread of Renaissance ideas from the continent and from France in particular. Gardens came to be mere adornment for ancestral homes as at Brodick, Falkland and Kellie. The intimate enclosures at the garden at Crathes Castle are distinguished by colour, season and plant species.

Wildlife

Scotland is endowed with a rich natural heritage of wildlife, vegetation and land. Humans have been largely responsible for destroying certain habitats (deforestation and in particular the loss of the native pinewoods) and the extinction of the fauna. The first to suffer were the larger animals – reindeer, elk, brown bear and wild boar – which are extinct in Scotland in the wild. However recent cooperation between government and specialised organisations is responsible for the successful conservation of many habitats and wildlife. **Scottish Natural Heritage** is responsible for establishing reserves to safeguard certain wildlife communities and the **Scottish Wildlife Trust** was founded in 1964 to combat the increasing dangers to Scotland's wildlife

BIRDS OF PREY

The most majestic, if elusive, Scottish raptor is the golden eagle, found on Skye, the Outer

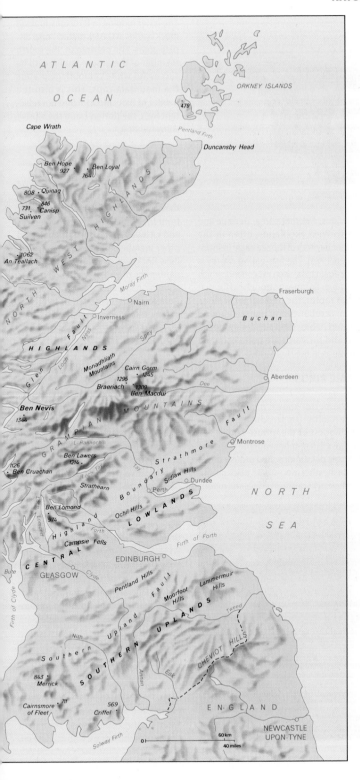

ATLANTIC

OCEAN

ORKNEY ISLANDS

•479

Pentland Firth

Cape Wrath

Duncansby Head

Ben Hope •
927   • Ben Loyal
        764

808 • Quinag
    • 846
731 • Canisp
Suilven

• 1062
An Teallach

N O R T H

W E S T   H I G H L A N D S

Moray Firth

• Nairn   Fraserburgh

Inverness   B u c h a n

H I G H L A N D S

Spey

Glen   Fault

Ness

Loch

Monadhliath
Mountains   Cairn Gorm
            •1245
        1295 •
    Braeriach •1309
        Ben Macdui   Dee   Aberdeen

Ben Nevis
•1344   G R A M P I A N   M O U N T A I N S   Fault

L. Rannoch   Strathmore

Ben Lawers   Boundary
1126   1214 •
• Ben Cruachan   Tay   Sidlaw Hills
            Perth • Dundee   Montrose
    Strathearn

Highland   Ochl Hills   L O W L A N D S   N O R T H

Ben Lomond
•974   Forth

L. Lomond   Campsie Fells   Firth of Forth   S E A

C E N T R A L   EDINBURGH

Bute   GLASGOW   Clyde   Pentland Hills   Fault

Firth of Clyde   Upland   Moorfoot   Lammermuir
                Hills   Hills

S o u t h e r n   S O U T H E R N   U P L A N D S   Tweed

Nith   CHEVIOT HILLS

• 843   Esk
Merrick

Cairnsmore •711   569 •
of Fleet   Criffel   E N G L A N D

Annan   NEWCASTLE
                UPON-TYNE

Solway Firth   0   60km
            40 miles

Golden Eagle

Hebrides, Aviemore area, Deeside and North West Highlands, often in the former territory of the sea eagle (reintroduced 1985). The fish-eating osprey is once again to be seen in Scotland, which is a major European stronghold for that other raptor, the hen harrier with its aerial acrobatics and unusual ground nesting habits. Both the peregrine falcon and buzzards are quite common sightings in the Highlands.

GAME BIRDS

Of the better known game birds the capercaillie (reintroduced c 1770), the biggest of the grouse family, has increased in number with the spread of forestry plantations. Red grouse thrive on the heather moors, with black grouse or blackcocks on forest edges and moors.

Puffin

The latter indulge in ferocious-looking mock battles at the lek or traditional display areas. The ptarmigan, the fourth member of the grouse family, with its successful white camouflage prefers the mountain tops. This is also the habitat of that colourful bird but reluctant flyer, the dotterel, and the elusive snow bunting.

SEA BIRDS

The offshore islands (Bass Rock, Ailsa Craig, St Kilda) and cliffs of Scotland are the haunts of a wide variety of sea birds from the comical puffin, to guillemots and kittiwakes, razorbills, fulmars and other members of the gull family. The Bass Rock, which is one of the easier gannetries to visit, gave the gannet its scientific name *Sula bassana*. Excursions from Anstruther take visitors to the Isle of May, thronged with sea birds.

MAMMALS

The early mammal population counted elks, northern lynx, brown bear, beaver, reindeer, wild boar, ponies, white cattle with black points (still found in some parks today) and the wolf (& *see Box on following page*). With re-afforestation Scotland has become the last British stronghold of otters, wildcats, and the secretive pine marten. The fox is a newcomer to the northeastern coastal lowlands and badgers have re-colonised most of the mainland. Some of these animals can now be seen in the Highland Wildlife Park near Kincraig in Speyside or Edinburgh Zoo. Rare breeds such as the Soay sheep from the St Kilda group of islands are part of the Highland Wildlife Park at Kincraig while famously photogenic shaggy Highland cattle pasture the parklands of Scotland's castles.

SHARKS AND WHALES

The **Basking Shark**, most frequently spotted in summer, is the second largest animal in the world, measuring 36ft/11 m long and weighing up to 7 tonnes/ 7,000 kg. It is usually seen swimming slowly near the surface with its huge fin,

The Big Bad Wolf...

Once common in Scotland, wolves were hunted to extinction by the late 18C, but now naturalists are calling for their reintroduction. The argument is that deer are close to reaching the maximum capacity that the local ecosystem (trees and plants in particular) can support. Culls by man would not be economically effective, so instead wolves would cull the deer. The negative side is that wolves may also cull farmers' livestock, most notably sheep. However wolves do not typically slaughter whole flocks, but just take individuals when they are hungry. Farmers are cautious but are not completely averse to the idea provided they are adequately reimbursed for any lost stock. While the public are generally positive to the idea of wolf reintroduction, people living in rural areas are more sensitive. The debate rumbles on.

up to 6ft/2m high, breaking the water along with the tip of the tail fin and the tip of its nose. As it swims it opens its mouth, which can be over 1m wide, gulping hundreds of litres of seawater, equivalent to around a swimming pool-full an hour, which flows out through its gills trapping plankton.

Orcas, among the fastest sea creatures and the top predators in the ocean, are seen in Scottish waters year-round. Males can grow between 21ft/7m and 23ft/8m and weigh over 5 tonnes/5,000kg. The dorsal surface is mostly black, the underside is white, with a white eyespot behind each eye. The huge dorsal fin can measure 1.8m (6ft) high. Orcas are highly social and live in groups called pods. **Minke whales** are even bigger, up to 31ft/10 m long and up to 10 tonnes/10,000kg.

DOLPHINS

Bottlenose dolphins may be seen all around the coast of Scotland in spring and summer – the Moray Firth colony is the most renowned. Their single nostril (blowhole) allows the dolphin to take in air when it comes to the surface. The distinctive bulging forehead contains an organ called a melon, which holds a mass of fat and oily tissue. This allows dolphins to echo-locate food and to communicate with each other in schools.

The **harbour porpoise** is the most common cetacean in Scottish waters. It may be found year-round in any shallow seas and particularly around the Hebrides

and Northern Isles. The animals tend to gather together in pods of 2 to 5.

SEALS

Seals may be seen year-round. **Common seals** are often found around shallow inland waters, hauled up on sandbanks and around estuaries, but they will use rocky outcrops on the west coast. This species is roughly 5ft/1.5m to 6ft/2m long with the male (bull) weighing up to 550lb/250kg and the female (cow) around half that size. They fish over wide area, feeding on anything from shrimps to whole herring, and breed between June and July.

The **grey seal** is slightly bigger and widespread on Scotland's rocky west coast. They feed on all types of fish, plus crabs, squid and sandeels, and breed in the autumn. The Scottish population is estimated at up to 120,000, 40% of the world total.

Otter on the shore of Isle of Mull

P. Tomkins/VisitScotland/Scottish Viewpoint

HISTORY

PREHISTORIC PERIOD: EARLY MIGRATIONS

4000-2500 BC — Neolithic settlers arrive by the Atlantic route

2000-1000 BC — Bronze Age agriculturalists arrive from the continent

800 BC-AD 400 — Iron Age peoples from central Europe

THE ROMANS 1C AD – 4C AD

The Roman conquest of **Caledonia** was never fully accomplished although there were two main periods of occupation. The initial one (c 80-c 100), which started with Julius Agricola's push northwards, is notable for the victory at **Mons Graupius** (©see INVERURIE). The second period followed the death in 138 of the Emperor Hadrian (builder of the wall in the 120s). His successor Antoninus Pius advanced the frontier to its earlier limits but by the mid 160s the **Antonine Wall** was definitively abandoned.

55, 54 BC — Caesar invades Britain; conquest begins AD 43

AD 71-84 — Romans push north into **Caledonia**; Agricola establishes a line of forts between the Clyde and Forth

84 — **Mons Graupius**: Agricola defeats the Caledonian tribes

142 – c 145 — Building of turf rampart, the **Antonine Wall** (39mi/63km long)

End 4C — Roman power wanes

DARK AGES 4C - 11C

The Barbarian invasions of Britain forced the Britons to take refuge in the barren mountains and moorlands of Cornwall, Wales, and even beyond Hadrian's Wall in southwest Scotland. It was at Whithorn, in the native kingdom of **Strathclyde** with its main fortress at Dumbarton (©see GLASGOW: Excursions), that the Romano-Briton St Ninian established the first Christian community in the late 4C. Over the next centuries, Christianity gained a firm foothold.

The early Scottish nation owed much to its western territories. The royal line descended from the Dalriadic royal house with the accession of Kenneth MacAlpine as king of Alba. Scottish kings had their ancient burial place, **Reilig Odhrian**, on Iona and the nation took its name from the western kingdom of the Scots.

In the 8C and 9C the first Norse raiders arrived by sea. These were followed by peaceful settlers in search of new lands who occupied the western isles. Gradually the isles became independent territories over which the Dalriadic kings had no power. The kingdoms of the Picts and Scots merged, under the Scot Kenneth MacAlpine, to form **Alba**, the territory north of the Forth and Clyde which later became known as **Scotia**, while the western fringes remained under Norse sway. Territorial conflicts with the English and the Norsemen marked the next two centuries.

397 — **St Ninian** establishes a Christian mission at **Whithorn**

563 — **St Columba** and his companions land on **Iona**. The Celtic Church evolves in isolation until the **Synod of Whitby** (663/4) when certain Celtic usages were abandoned to conform with the practices of Rome

8C — Beginning of Norse raids. The Western Isles remain under Norse domination until 1266, the Orkney and Shetland Islands until 1468-69

843 — **Kenneth MacAlpine** obtains the Pictish throne unifying the Picts and the Scots

MEDIEVAL SCOTLAND

Under the influence of Queen Margaret, a pious English princess, and during the reigns of her sons, in particular Edgar, Alexander I and David I, the Celtic kingdom took on a feudal character as towns grew and royal charters were granted. Monastic life flourished as religious communities from France set up sister houses throughout Scotland.

In 1098, King **Edgar**, the son of Malcolm III (Canmore), ceded to **Magnus Barefoot**, King of Norway (1093-1103), "all the islands around which a boat could sail". Magnus included Kintyre having had his galley dragged across the isthmus. On the death of Magnus the native ruler of Argyll, **Somerled** (d 1164), seized power and assumed the kingship of the Isles and briefly of Man, under the tutelage of Norway. Somerled died in 1164 fighting the Scots. Alexander II (1214-49) set out on a campaign to curb Norse rule but he died on Kerrera. It was his son **Alexander III** (1249-86) who, following the **Battle of Largs** (see LARGS) against King Haakon IV, negotiated the Treaty of Perth in 1266 returning the Western Isles to Scotland.

Relations with England remained tense. In the 12C, after his defeat and capture at Alnwick, **William I the Lion** paid homage to Richard I the Lionheart. Northumbria remained a contentious issue until 1236 when Alexander II renounced his claim. The country enjoyed a degree of stability during the reign of Alexander III before plunging into centuries of conflict over rival claims to the throne and attempts to gain its independence.

1034 — **Strathclyde** becomes part of the Scottish Kingdom

1058-93 — **Malcolm III**; his second queen, **Margaret**, introduces the Catholic Church

1124-53 — **David I**, last of the Margaretsons, reorganises the church, settles monastic orders and creates royal burghs, all of which increase the monarchy's prestige

1249-86 — **Alexander III**, the last Canmore king; brief period of peace and prosperity

1263 — **Battle of Largs**

1290 — **Margaret**, the Maid of Norway, dies

WARS OF INDEPENDENCE

On the death in 1290 of the Maid of Norway, the direct heir to the throne,

Edward I was instrumental in choosing from among the various **Competitors** the ultimate successor. In 1292 John Balliol became king and the vassal of Edward. Following Balliol's 1295 treaty with the French, Edward set out for the north on the first of several pacification campaigns. Strongholds fell one by one and thus started a long period of intermittent warfare.

The years of struggle for independence from English overlordship helped to forge a national identity. Heroes were born. The unknown knight **William Wallace** (1270-1305) rallied the resistance in the early stages achieving victory at Stirling Bridge (1277). He assumed the Guardianship in the name of Balliol. Wallace was captured in 1305 and taken to London where he was executed.

The next to rally the opposition was **Robert the Bruce** (1274-1329), grandson of one of the original Competitors and therefore with a legitimate claim to the throne. Following the killing of **John Comyn**, who was the son of another Competitor and the representative of the Balliol line, Bruce had himself crowned at Scone (1306).

Slowly Bruce forced the submission of the varying fiefs and even achieved the allegiance of Angus Og, natural son of the 4th Lord of the Isles. The victory at **Bannockburn** (1314) was crucial in achieving independence but formal recognition only came eight years after the **Declaration of Arbroath** (1320) with the **Treaty of Northampton**.

1296 — Edward I's choice, **John Balliol**, abdicates during the first of the Hammer of the Scots' punitive conquering campaigns in Scotland 1296, 1298, 1303 and 1307

1297 — Wallace wins the **Battle of Stirling Bridge**; Falkirk, the following year, is a defeat

1306-29 — Robert the Bruce kills the Comyn, is crowned at Scone, then starts the long campaign to free Scotland

1314 — Battle of **Bannockburn**

1320 — **Declaration of Arbroath**; the Treaty of Northampton (1328) recognises Scotland's Independence

AKG-IMAGES/ Erich Lessing Bibliotheque Nationale, Paris

Portrait of Marie Stuart
by Jean Clouet, 1559

THE STEWARTS (LATER STUARTS)

Following independence, royal authority was undermined by feuds and intrigue as bloody power struggles broke out among the clan chiefs; but the monarchy prevailed. The powerful Albany and Douglas clans were subdued in the 15C. The Scots supported France in its rivalry with England and alliances were forged.

1406-37 — **James I**; James takes the reins of power in 1424 after 18 years in English captivity

1410 — Teaching begins at St Andrews University, officially founded 1412; confirmation by Papal Bull 1413

1437-60 — Accession of **James II** following the assassination of his father at Perth

1440 — **Black Dinner** at Edinburgh Castle

1451 — Founding of Glasgow University

1455 — Fall of the Black Douglases

1460-88 — Accession of **James III** following the death of James II at the siege of Rox-burgh Castle

1468-9 — Orkney and Shetland pass to Scotland as the dowry of Margaret of Denmark

1488-1513 — Accession of **James IV** following his father's death after Sauchieburn

1493 — Forfeiture of the Lordship of the Isles

1495 — Founding of Aberdeen's first University (King's College); Marischal founded 1593

1513-42 — Death of **James IV** at the **Battle of Flodden**; Accession of **James V**

In the 16C, to punish the Scots for refusing an alliance between the young Mary and Henry VIII's son, English troops, led by the Marquess of Hertford, invaded repeatedly and inflicted a harsh treatment on the country. The growing French influence at court was resented by the nobility and the Reformation gained ground. The regent Mary of Guise was deposed by Protestant leaders fired by John Knox's sermons; monastic houses were destroyed and Catholicism was banned. During her short tragic reign (1561-67) when conspiracies and violence were rife, the young queen advocated religious tolerance but murderous intrigues (see EDINBURGH, *Palace of Holyroodhouse*), probably with Mary's tacit approval, caused great scandal. Rebellion broke out after her marriage to Bothwell who was suspected of involvement in the murder of Darnley. Her flight to England, after her abdication in favour of her infant son and her escape from captivity, ended in imprisonment and execution by Elizabeth I to thwart the formation of factions around a rival claimant to the English throne.

1542-67 — **Mary**, Queen of Scots

1544-47 — **Rough Wooing** or Hertford's invasions

1548 — The five-year-old Mary is sent to France for safety and affianced to the French Dauphin

1559 — Riot at Perth; the Lords of the Congregation set out from Perth on their campaign

1560 — **Reformation**; death of Mary's French husband, François II

1561 — Mary returns to Scotland as an 18-year-old widow; 4 years later she marries her cousin, Henry Stewart, Lord Darnley

1567 — Murder of Darnley; Bothwell becomes Mary's third husband; she abdicates, and flees to England after the Battle of Langside (1568); executed after 19 years in captivity (1587)

THE STUARTS AND
THE COMMONWEALTH

In the largely Protestant Scotland of the 17C James VI attempted to achieve a situation similar to that in England by re-establishing Episcopacy. This implied royal control of the church through the bishops appointed by the Crown. His son Charles I aroused strong Presbyterian opposition with the forced introduction of the *Scottish Prayer Book*. By February of 1638 the **National Covenant** or Solemn Agreement was drawn up, which pledged the signatories to defend the Crown and true religion.

In 1643 the **Solemn League and Covenant** united the Covenanters and English parliamentary cause against Charles I. Many like the Marquess of Montrose were torn between their loyalty to the King and Covenant. In 1644 Montrose pledged to win back Scotland for the King. At the end of a year of campaigning with a largely Highland army he was master of Scotland. Defeat came at the **Battle of Philiphaugh** (1645) and Montrose was forced into exile. In England the struggle led to the execution of Charles I (1649).

The Covenanters were quick to offer Charles II the throne on his acceptance of the Covenant. Montrose was captured and executed. Cromwell marched north defeating the Covenanters' army at **Dunbar** (1650) and Scotland became an occupied country (1651-60) and part of the Commonwealth.

On the **Restoration** of Charles II, made possible by Monck's march on the capital, the king rejected his promise and restored Episcopacy (1661). The 1st Duke of Lauderdale ruled Scotland and the Covenanters suffered severe persecution. The years around 1685 were known as the Killing Times with Lord Advocate, Sir George ("Bluidy") Mackenzie responsible for much of the persecution.

The death of Charles II and the prospect of a new line of openly Catholic monarchs, with the accession of his brother James VII, inspired the ill-fated **Monmouth Rebellion** led by Charles II's natural son. The two landings, one in western Scotland under the 9th Earl of

Articles of Union between England and Scotland from the House of Lords record office, 1707

Argyll and the second in western England under Monmouth, both failed.

The Protestant Mary and William were invited to rule (1689). Viscount Dundee rallied the Jacobites or those faithful to King James VII who had already fled the country.

The initial victory at Killiecrankie 1689 cost the life of the Jacobite leader and the Highland army was later crushed at Dunkeld. The 1690 Act established for good the Presbyterian Church of Scotland.

The Act of Union guaranteed the maintenance of the Scottish legal system and church.

1567-1625 — **James VI** of Scotland reigns as **James I** of England
1582 — Raid of Ruthven
1600 — Gowrie Conspiracy

James I

1603 — **Union of the Crowns** with the accession of James VI to the throne of England

1625-49 — **Charles I**; Scottish coronation ceremony in Edinburgh (1633)

1638 — **National Covenant**; Glasgow General Assembly abolishes Episcopacy

1643 — The **Solemn League and Covenant**

1645 — Montrose loses the Battle of Philiphaugh

1650 — Execution of Montrose following that of Charles I the previous year

1651 — Cromwellian occupation, the **Commonwealth**

1660 — General Monck and his regiment set out from Coldstream on 1 January 1660 on the long march south to London which leads to the Restoration

1660-85 — **Charles II**

1661 — Restoration of Episcopacy

1685-8 — Accession of **James VII (James II of England)**: Monmouth Rebellion 1685

1688 — James VII flees the country in late December

1689 — William and Mary are offered the crown; **Battle of Killiecrankie**

1692 — Massacre of **Glencoe**

1702-14 — **Queen Anne**

1707 — **Union of the Parliaments**

HOUSE OF HANOVER

The Jacobite uprisings of 1715 and 1745 aiming to restore the Stuarts to their throne reflected in some measure the discontent of post-Union (1707) Scotland. The rising ended at the indecisive Battle of **Sheriffmuir**. James VIII or the **Old Pretender** (1688-1766) not only arrived too late but also lacked the power to inspire his followers. His departure by boat from Montrose was furtive and final. Following this, General George Wade set out to pacify the Highlands with a programme of road and bridge building to facilitate military access.

A generation later, the 1745 rising was led by **Charles Edward Stuart** or **Bonnie Prince Charlie** (1720-88) born 5 years after the first rising. After

The Auld Alliance

The longstanding friendship between Scotland and France is known as the Auld Alliance. Its 700th anniversary was celebrated in 1995.

In the 12C David I (1124-54) developed close ties with Normandy: many Normans settled in Scotland and the king himself owned land in the Cotentin. At his behest monastic houses were set up by French religious orders: Selkirk, Kelso, Arbroath. He also founded great Cistercian abbeys at Melrose, Dundrennan and Kinloss.

In 1295 Robert the Bruce signed the first treaty between Scotland and France as part of his fight to gain independence from England.

In the 15C Scottish troops fought alongside the French army at the Battle of Vieux Baugé (1421) to drive the English from Angers.

During the 16C France's reputation as a seat of learning attracted many Scots. In 1512 James IV signed a second treaty with France. James V married two French princesses successively. His second wife, Mary of Guise, gave birth to a daughter, Mary. In 1548 at the tender age of five Mary Stuart was sent to France where she lived at St-Germain-en-Laye until she reached 16. In 1558 she married the dauphin François II and became Queen of France. A year after her husband's death (1560) she returned to Scotland at the age of 18 to live out her tragic destiny.

During the 17C the Royal Scots Regiment was part of Louis XIII's royal guard; three centuries later they fought at the Battle of the Marne (1914). From 1688 to 1692 numerous supporters of James II (James VII of Scotland) went into exile in France. Further emigration occurred until the first half of the 18C especially after the Jacobite risings of 1715 and 1745.

Crofting

Crofts are small agricultural holdings worked by tenant farmers. Crofting is a unique form of land tenure which became popular, especially on remote islands, in the 19C after the Highland Clearances. The Crofters Act of 1886 gave tenants security of tenure and other valuable rights. The 1976 Act allowed crofters to buy the land but they also lost many rights including grazing their herds on common land. The solution was to form a trust to buy the crofts and to rent the crofts back from the trust. Crofting is a hard life but holdings are in great demand as more and more people dream of escaping from large cities and living off the land.

landing near Arisaig, the 24-year-old Prince raised his standard at Glenfinnan and with an essentially Highland army won an initial victory at Prestonpans where he routed the government troops under Sir John Cope. At Derby his military advisers counselled retreat which ended in the defeat of **Culloden** (1746). For 5 months the Prince wandered the Highlands and Hebrides as a hunted fugitive with a bounty of £30,000 on his head. Shortly after this, **Flora Macdonald** assisted him in escaping from the Outer Hebrides. The Prince embarked for lifelong exile.

The aftermath rather than the failure of the '45 was tragic for the Highlands: Highlanders were disarmed, their national dress proscribed and chieftains deprived of their rights of heritable justice. Economic and social change was accelerated.

Eviction and loss of the traditional way of life ensued; this period became known as the **Highland Clearances**. Mass emigration followed for the many who faced abject poverty. A small number became crofters with no security of tenure. This uncertainty was later alleviated by the **Crofters Act**. The clearances were complete by 1860.

George IV's visit organised by **Sir Walter Scott** in 1822 made Highland dress and other accoutrements (bagpipes, arms) acceptable again. By making Balmoral Castle a favoured residence, Queen Victoria and Prince Albert later gave the royal seal of approval to the Highlands.

1714-27 — Accession of **George I**
1715 — **Jacobite Rising, Battle of Sheriffmuir**
1719 — Jacobite Rising in Glen Shiel
1727-60 — **George II**

1745 — Jacobite Rising; The Year of the Prince opens with the raising of the standard at Glenfinnan
1746 — **Battle of Culloden**
1747-82 — **Proscription Act**
1760-1820 — **George III**
1790 — Opening of Forth-Clyde Canal
1803-22 — Building of the Caledonian Canal
1822 — George IV State Visit
1843 — The Disruption: Founding of the Free Church
1871-78 — Tay Railway Bridge; disaster the following year
1883-90 — Forth Railway Bridge
1886 — **Crofters Act**
1906-13 — Home Rule Bills
1928 — National Party of Scotland formed; SNP founded in 1934
1951 — Stolen **Stone of Destiny** found in Arbroath
1964 — Opening of the Forth Road Bridge; Tay Bridge opens two years later
1964-1970s — Discovery and development of major oil and natural gas fields in the North Sea with the subsequent growth of the North Sea oil industry
1974-5 — Reorganisation of local government; the old counties and burghs replaced by nine regions and island areas
1979 — Referendum on proposed Assembly failed to produce the necessary 40%
1990 — Glasgow nominated Cultural Capital of Europe
1995 — 700th anniversary of the **Auld Alliance** between Scotland and France. Further reorganisation of local government – election of 29

unitary councils and three islands councils

1996 — After 700 years the **Stone of Destiny** is returned to Scotland

Scottish Parliament

Since the decline of Scottish industry in the 1930s relations between Scotland and the central government have proved uneasy although the Scots had their own legal and education systems. Economic decline and discontent about the lack of adequate benefits from North Sea Oil fostered nationalist feelings. The remoteness of central government, the imposition of the poll-tax and local government reorganisation were all contentious issues. As direct election of representatives to the European Parliament had given Scotland renewed confidence in its ability to control its own affairs, the 1997 referendum was a resounding vote for devolution. Scotland greeted the opening of the Scottish Parliament with pride some 290 years after the last parliament was dissolved.

The new body has 120 members; the Executive consists of a First Minister and a team of ministers and law officers. The Parliament has responsibility over wide areas of Scottish affairs and has tax-raising powers. Among areas which remain under Westminster control are the constitution, foreign policy, defence and national security, border controls and economic policy.

In 2005 the Scottish Parliament moved to the foot of the Royal Mile to take up their new permanent residence in Britain's most controversial post-Millennium building. Designed by the Spanish architect, Enric Miralles (1955-2000), it arrived four years late and, most scandalously, ten times over budget, costing over £430 million. Miralles did not live to see its completion and tragedy also struck the Parliament in 2000, when its recently elected first ever First Minister, Donald Dewar, died of a heart attack in office. His successor, Henry McLeish, lasted just over a year before resigning over financial irregularities. He was succeeded by Jack McConnell who was in turn been succeeded by the current First Minister., Alex Salmond in 2007.

Famous Scottish names

Mungo Park (1771-1806), explored West Africa; **David Livingstone** (1813-73), the first man to cross Africa from east to west; **Sir John Ross** (1777-1856), Arctic explorer; **John McDouall Stuart** (1815-66), explored the Australian desert; **Alexander Mackenzie** (1764-1820), the first man to cross the North American continent by land (1783).

James McGill (1774-1813), founded McGill University; **John Paul Jones** (1747-1792), admiral in the American Navy; **John Muir** (1838-1914), founded the American National Parks; **Andrew Carnegie** (1835-1919), philanthropist and steel magnate; **John Hunter** (1728-1793) and **William Hunter** (1718-1783), leaders in anatomy and obstetrics;

Sir Joseph Lister (1827-1912), pioneer of antiseptics; **William Thomson, Lord Kelvin** (1824-1907), formulated the second law of thermodynamics; **James Hutton** (1726-97), wrote A Theory of the Earth which formed the basis of modern geology; **Thomas Telford** (1757-1834) and **John Rennie** (1761-1821), built bridges, roads, canals, docks and harbours. **Robert Napier** (1791-1876), built the first Cunard steamships and the first ironclad battleships.

Great inventions and scientific discoveries: **John Napier of Merchiston** (1560-1617) – logarithms; **Sir James Simpson** (1811-70) Chloroform as an anaesthetic; **James Watt** (1736-1819) – the steam engine; **John MacAdam** (1756-1836) – the road surface which bears his name; **Alexander Graham Bell** (1847-1922) – the telephone; John Logie Baird (1888-1946) – television; **Sir Robert Watson-Watt** (1892-1973) – radar; **Alexander Fleming** (1881-1955) – penicillin. Scientists at the **Roslin Research Institute** made history with the cloning of Dolly the Sheep in 1996.

Scottish Parliament

©Andrew Cowan/SPCB

1997 — Second referendum approves the motion for a devolved tax-raising Assembly.

1999 — Opening of **Scottish Parliament** in a temporary home in the Church of Scotland Assembly Hall

2005 — **Scottish Parliament** transferred to Holyrood

2008 — Pro-independence Scottish Nationalist Party elected to the Scottish Government, with Alex Salmond as First Minister.

ART AND CULTURE

Shaped by Celtic beginnings, the early influence of invading Norsemen and the recurrent colonisation—peaceful or otherwise—by the English, the nation's culture has developed into a fascinating hybrid that is impossible to pin down. Rugged and romantic, traditional and modern, it is always evolving, yet remains true to its roots.

Monuments And Sculpture

In prehistoric times seafaring invasions left a rich legacy of monuments and ancient sites.

NEOLITHIC AGE (4400 BC-2000 BC)

Skara Brae is the best example of a Neolithic settlement where the local stone slabs have been used in every conceivable way. The settlers practised collective burials in chambered tombs, which took the form of either a galleried grave or passage grave. Orkney is rich in examples as at Unstan and Maes Howe. Other sites on the mainland include the Clava Cairns near Inverness, the Grey Cairns of Camster near Wick and Cairn Holy I and II in the southwest.

BRONZE AGE (2000 BC-1000 BC)

The Beaker people were continental agriculturalists who buried their dead in individual cists or graves. They erected the round cairns, stone circles and alignments as at Callanish, Ring of Brodgar, Hill o'Many Stanes and Cairnpapple.

Snake and Z-rod   Crescent and V-rod   Double disc and Z-Rod

E. Sevo/ MICHELIN

IRON AGE (800 BC-AD 400)

This period left the largest group of monuments. These include the hill forts and settlements (Traprain, Eildon Hill North, White Caterthun and Dunadd), crannogs or lake dwellings, earth houses or souterrains (Rennibister, Tealing) and wheelhouses (Jarlshof). This period is also marked by the **brochs**. These hollow round towers of drystone masonry are unique to Scotland. The outstanding broch, Mousa in the Shetland Islands, dates from 1C-2C AD.

ROMAN SCOTLAND

The Romans left a considerable heritage. Along the route of penetration (Dere Street) were marching camps for Julius Agricola's army, intent on the subjugation of the native tribes. A chain of forts across the Forth-Clyde isthmus was built prior to his retirement to Rome.
In the 2C Antoninus Pius built the turf **Antonine Wall** with walkway and ditch, along the Forth-Clyde line. Forts were placed at intervals laong the wall. Both were abandoned by the 160s.

EARLY RELIGIOUS SYMBOLS

The **Latinus Stone** AD 450 (see WHITHORN) and a group of three other 5C-6C tombstones at Kirkmadrine (see STRANRAER: Excursions) are a few of the rare examples of this period when the Britons established the first Christian communities in the southwest.

ANGLO-SAXON INFLUENCE

The monumental **Anglian crosses** with their sculptured figures and patterns of vine scroll are the rich artistic heritage of the Northumbrian Kingdom. The 7C

Ruthwell Cross (see DUMFRIES, Excursions) is an outstanding example.

THE CELTIC TRADITION

The characteristic monument of the Scots was the **free-standing cross** with ring of glory, spiral patterns and high bosses. St Martin's and St John's Crosses (8C) on Iona are among the better examples. The Scots brought with them their Celtic ornamental tradition which they applied to stonecarving, metalwork and manuscript illumination. The tradition was continued to some extent in the art of the Picts and the influence is also clearly seen in the works of the 14C-16C school of West Highland Sculpture (see ARCHITECTURE).

PICTISH ART

In the Pictish Kingdom of the east and north, a flowering of this native culture produced the **Pictish Symbol Stones.** These incised and carved boulders and stones portray animal symbols (boar, fish, goose, snake and bull as at Burghead), or purely abstract symbols (mirror and comb, double disc and Z-rod, crescent and V-rod, snake and Z-rod). This art died out once the Scots had become rulers of Pictland c AD 843. **Sueno's Stone** near Forres remains a unique monument closely covered with sculpture of intertwined foliage and beasts and the serried ranks of troops on the shaft.

Architecture

ECCLESIASTICAL

Celtic foundations

Mainland Scotland retains two of the earliest buildings erected by the Celtic clergy, the round towers of Brechin and Abernethy. Dating from the late 10C to early 11C these refuges or belfries are outliers of an Irish tradition. Although tangible remains are few, the Christian faith was an important unifying factor in Dark Age Scotland.

Anglo-Norman period
Scotland of the mid 11C with its Celtic and Norse influences was soon to undergo a new and gradual Anglo-Norman colonisation. It was the west and north, the strongholds of the old cultures, that resisted the new imprint. The 11C and 12C were a time of church reorganisation and all building efforts were concentrated on ecclesiastical works. **Queen Margaret** and her sons were the principal promoters. David I's church at Dunfermline has in the nave (12C) one of the most outstanding examples of Norman art. The parish churches of **Leuchars** and **Dalmeny** are equally well-preserved examples of this period.

Gothic Tradition
Early monastic foundations included Arbroath, Dryburgh, Dundrennan, Holyrood and Jedburgh. Outstanding 13C Gothic buildings include Elgin, Dunblane and Glasgow cathedrals where the lancet window, pointed arch and vaulting are triumphant. War and strife brought building to a standstill and wreaked much havoc on existing buildings. Melrose Abbey, rebuilt in the 14C, is in the pure Gothic tradition. Prosperity returned to the burghs in the 15C and the great burghal churches were an expression of renewed wealth and civic pride (Holy Rude, Stirling; St John's, Perth; St Nicholas, Aberdeen and St Mary's, Haddington). The period also saw the flourishing of collegiate churches built by the baronial class (Dunglass, Seton, Tullibardine, Crichton and Dalkeith). The style was truly Scottish, with a martial influence where buttresses were stepped, towers crenellated, and roofs stone-slabbed. Some of the loveliest churches date from this last Gothic phase, such as Tullibardine and Kirk o'Steil.

The Late Gothic King's College Chapel in Old Aberdeen still has a splendid crown spire (*see ABERDEEN*) as does St Giles', in Edinburgh.

SECULAR

Castles
The earliest predecessors of the Scottish castle were the enigmatic stone-built brochs of the 1C AD. An outstanding example is at Mousa in Shetland.
The feudalisation of Scotland was marked by the introduction of the Norman motte and bailey castles. Several imposing earthen mounds or mottes remain at Duffus, Inverurie and Invernochty. The earliest stone-built castles had a stone curtain wall, as a replacement for the wooden palisade, as seen at Rothesay, Sween and Dunstaffnage.

Medieval period
During the Wars of Independence **Edward I** altered a few strongholds including Kildrummy, giving it a Harlech type gatehouse. From then on the gatehouse replaced the keep as the place of strength.
In 14C Scotland weak kings and a disunited kingdom encouraged turbulent and ambitious feudal lords to build fortresses. Early examples include Drum, Threave, Castle Campbell and Craigmil-

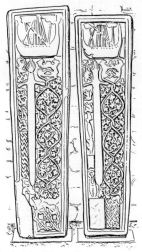

Tomb slabs, Kilmory Knap

After photo E. Sevo/ MICHELIN

51

Plasterwork ceilings

In England the Elizabethan period introduced plasterwork ceilings with their ornate strapwork. In Scotland the early 17C saw the introduction of ornate plaster ceilings as at Craigievar (1625), Glamis (1621), Muchalls (1624), and The Binns (1630). The ceilings were often accompanied by magnificent heraldic achievements (Craigievar and Muchalls) or elaborate fireplaces (Glamis). This art evolved and was adapted by Sir William Bruce for the Classical interiors of Holyroodhouse and Thirlestane. The series at the latter include the magnificent Lauderdale eagles. All this is only a step away from the delicately detailed neo-Classical designs of Robert Adam (Mellerstain, Culzean and Hopetoun House).

lar. The tradition continued with Cardoness and Newark.

The impact of the European Renaissance was limited to the royal works at Stirling, Falkland and Linlithgow.

Post Reformation innovation

The tower house reached its apotheosis in the late 16C and early 17C in the Grampian area, where a local school of architecture flourished. These **baronial** masterpieces—Craigievar, Crathes, Fyvie and Castle Fraser—all show a skilful handling of traditional features and a concentration on the skyline.

The 17C saw the infiltration of foreign influences as at Crichton with its Italianate façade, Edzell with its pleasance, at Huntly Castle, the Earl's Palace in Kirk-

wall and the inner courtyard façade of Caerlaverock.

The Restoration brought a new series of royal works, designed by the Architect Royal **Sir William Bruce** (c 1630-1710). Bruce excelled in the Classical style which he used for the courtyard at Holyroodhouse Palace (1671), Hopetoun House and his own home, Kinross House. Bruce enlarged and remodelled the main front of the Duke of Lauderdale's principal Scottish seat, Thirlestane Castle. Bruce's successor as surveyor to the king in Scotland in 1683 was **James Smith** (c 1644-1731). Smith refitted the Chapel Royal and converted the old palace at Hamilton and the castle at Dalkeith.

Georgian elegance

Apart from Smith the main exponent of this style in the early 18C was **William Adam** (d 1748), father of a family of famous architects. "Old Stone and Lime" dominated the period between the two Jacobite Risings. His better known works are Hopetoun House, the House of Dun, Haddo House and Duff House. Of the sons **Robert Adam** (1728-92) was the most famous and creator of the Adam style. With his brothers, he finished Hopetoun after the death of his father. Following four years of travel in Europe in the entourage of Charles Hope and a period when he worked on a series of London mansions (Osterley, Syon and Kenwood), Adam returned to Scotland. From this period we have Mellerstain, a house of homely proportions with all the refinement of his neo-Classical interiors. Altogether more grandiose are Culzean, Seton and Airthrey castles.

The Glasgow School of Art

The Mackintosh Library,
The Glasgow School of Art

19C

The Romantic movement was accompanied by a revival of medieval styles, as at Scone Palace, Abbotsford and Dalmeny House. David Bryce and Gillespie Graham both revived the baronial style in the Victorian period, notably at Blair and Brodick castles respectively. Balmoral Castle is the best-known example of the Scottish neo-baronial style. These imitations lacked the vigour and sculptural qualities of their 17C predecessors.

Mercat Cross, Aberdeen

20C and beyond

At the close of the 19th century, **Charles Rennie Mackintosh** (1868-1928) revived the Scottish vernacular tradition in his design for the Glasgow School of Art. Mackintosh followed this early design in the Art Nouveau style with Hill House in Helensburgh, a work which even today, more than 100 years later, still seems modern. The Glasgow Herald building has been successfully converted into The Lighthouse, a Centre for Architecture and Design.

Another exponent of the distinctly Scottish style was **Sir Robert Lorimer** with his many restorations (Earlshall and Dunrobin castles) and creations (Thistle Chapel in St Giles', and the National War Memorial in Edinburgh Castle).

Contemporary landmark buildings have won acclaim for imaginative design: the Museum of Scotland, Dynamic Earth, International Conference Centre in Edinburgh, the Armadillo Conference Centre in Glasgow, and the Contemporary Arts Centre in Dundee. In 1999 Glasgow was celebrated as the UK City of Architecture and Design.

The first great Scottish building of the 21C is the Parliament Building at Holyrood. Designed by Spanish architect Enric Miralles (1955-2000) it is also destined to be one of the most controversial for many years to come for being massively over-budget.

Burghs

While several towns (Haddington, Elgin and Old Edinburgh) retain their medieval layouts, relatively few medieval buildings exist, in part due to their timber construction. As a rule the main street linked the castle and church and was the site of the market and tolbooth. Pends and wynds led off to closes with burgess plots extending back to the town wall pierced by gates or ports. The burghs tended to lavish funds on such symbols of civic authority and pride as the tolbooth and mercat cross, with the result that the townscapes of today are still enhanced by some fine examples.

Market crosses

Known in Scotland as **mercat crosses**, these provided the focal point of the burgh, where goods for sale were presented, proclamations made and public punishment executed. Of the larger platform type an outstanding example is at Aberdeen, where a series of royal portrait medallions adorn the platform. Others are topped by the royal unicorn (Edinburgh, Cockburnspath). There is a rare pre-Reformation cross at Banff.

Tolbooth

Originally for collecting taxes, the booths gradually came to embody civic authority and house the council chamber, court and prison. Today they represent one of the most attractive elements of Scottish townscapes. Kelso and Haddington have handsomely elegant buildings reflecting periods of agricultural prosperity. Tolbooths incorporated a tower (Glasgow, Aberdeen and Stirling) which was often adjoined by a later range of buildings. Fine examples exist at Linlithgow, Crail, Culross, Dumfries and Old Aberdeen, Kirkcudbright, North Berwick, and the Canongate, Edinburgh. The most renowned of all was Edinburgh's now vanished Heart of Midlothian, as popularised by Scott's novel.

Lectern dovecot, Tealing

Cylindrical Dovecot, Boath

Tron

Now a rare feature, the public weigh-beam was once a common sight. Both Culross and the village of Stenton still have examples.

Dovecots

Dovecots (doocots in Scotland) are a familiar and attractive sight in rural Scotland and are found in their greatest number in the rich farming areas of the Lothians, Fife, Angus and Moray where grain growing predominated.

Design

Most are stone-built. They vary in type from the fairly common beehive as at Phantassie, Craigmillar, Dirleton and Aberdour castles to the more typically Scottish lectern of Tantallon Castle and Tealing. Others were cylindrical (Lady Kitty's Garden, Haddington). The majority were freestanding, although nesting boxes were incorporated into towers of certain castles (Hailes, Rothesay and Huntingtower) or even a church belfry (Aberlady, Stenton and Torphichen). 18C and 19C versions were built as part of farm buildings.

Beehive dovecot, Phantassie

ARCHITECTURAL GLOSSARY

Aisle – ⓘ *see Introduction: Ecclesiastical Architecture*

Barmkin – outer enclosing wall

Box pew – enclosed pew

Broch – ⓘ *see SHETLAND ISLANDS: Mousa Broch*

Cap-house – small chamber at the head of turnpike stairs serving as guardroom

Close – courtyard or passage leading to other buildings

Crow steps – stepped gable ends

Donjon – castle's main tower or keep

Doocot – dovecot

Forestair – external stair

Gait or Gate – street leading to...

Garth – cloisters or garden

Harling – wall plastered with roughcast. Often painted or with colour incorporated

Laird's loft – ⓘ *see Introduction: Ecclesiastical Architecture*

Laird's lug – listening post or spy hole

Land – tenement

Marriage lintel – dated lintel inscribed with couple's initials

Pend – covered passageway

Port – town gateway

Skewputt – gable's corner stone

Tolbooth – ⓘ *see Introduction: Secular Architecture—Burghs*

Tron – weigh-beam

Turnpike – spiral stair

Tower house – fortified house

Wynd – subsidiary street

Yett – wrought-iron gate usually at the main doorway

"Storm Cloud", W. McTaggart

Painting

Scottish painting is closely linked with the English artistic tradition as many artists worked in London. Some were also great travellers and were influenced by the evolution of artistic movements in Europe. Many artists, however, remained relatively unknown outside Scotland.

PORTRAITURE

In the 17C the Aberdonian George **Jamesone** (1588-1644) was the leading portraitist. His sensitive works are reminiscent of Van Dyck.

The 18C is marked by the portraitist **Allan Ramsay** (1713-84), responsible for the founding of Edinburgh's first important art academy and painter to George III. His delicate portraits of women are notable. **Henry Raeburn** (1756-1823), George IV's Limner for Scotland, also has a well deserved reputation as a portrait painter *(The Reverend Robert Walker skating, Sir Walter Scott, Mrs Lumsden, Mrs Liddell)*. These two artists painted the gentry and leading personalities of the period and are well represented in the major art galleries and country houses.

NATURAL AND HISTORICAL THEMES

Alexander Nasmyth (1785-1859), Ramsay's assistant, became a successful landscape artist *(Robert Burns, The Windings of the Forth, Distant Views of Stirling)*. The idealised treatment of nature is illustrated in *The Falls of Clyde* by the neo-Classical master Jacob More. Gavin **Hamilton** (1723-98) painted vast historical compositions (illustrations of Homer's *Illiad, The Abdication of Mary, Queen of Scots*) and became very successful in Rome. In the 19C Walter Scott's novels brought about renewed interest in Scottish landscape: *Glencoe, Loch Katrine, Inverlochy Castle* by Horatio **McCullough** (1805-67) who is famous for his Highland scenes. David **Wilkie**'s (1785-1841) artistry is evident in his realistic popular scenes *(Pitlessie Fair, Distraining for Rent)* and portraits *(George IV)* which show Raeburn's influence. *The Gentle Shepherd* illustrates Ramsay's pastoral poem.

The Faed brothers (late 19C – early 20C), who were members of an artists' colony in Galloway, specialised in detailed genre scenes. The romantic landscapes and religious works of William **Dyce**

The Bridgeman Art Library/ "Storm Cloud" W. McTaggart Private Collection

(1806-64) heralded the Pre-Raphael-ites who influenced Noel Paton (1821-1901). Nature is depicted in great detail in the latter's fairy scenes *(Oberon and Titania)* and other paintings full of symbolism. The portraitist John "Spanish" Phillip (1817-67) is better known for his exotic paintings.

In the Victorian era Highland scenery gained great popularity through the English artist Edwin **Landseer** (1802-73), the official Animal Painter for Scotland, who is famous for his romantic depiction of Scotland (stags at bay and other Highland scenes). Another Englishman John Everett **Millais** (1829-96), whose wife came from Perthshire and who spent many years near Perth, painted romantic landscapes *(Chill October)*.

INNOVATION

The founding of the Scottish Academy in 1836 brought about a flowering of native talent. In reaction against Victorian conventions, William **McTaggart** (1835-1910) developed a highly individual style – bold brushwork, light effects, rich colours – evident in his dramatic seascapes *(The Storm, Dawn at Sea, The Fishers' Landing)* and landscapes *(Corn in the Ear, Spring, Rosslyn Castle: Autumn)*.

In the second half of the 19C artistic activity in Glasgow was given a boost by rich art collectors and dealers. The works of the **Glasgow School** (James Guthrie, E A Walton, George Henry, E A Hornel, Joseph Crawhall, John Lavery among others under the leadership of W Y MacGregor) reveal the influence of Impressionism and other European movements (The Hague School). Their interest in Realism is expressed in an original decorative style: *A Galloway Landscape* (Henry), *Gathering Primroses* (Hornel), *The Gypsy Fires* (Guthrie), *Carse of Lecropt* (MacGregor), *The Tennis Party* (Lavery). Artists' colonies flourished at Brig o'Turk, Kirkcudbright, Cockburnspath and Cambuskenneth. *Tollcross 10* and *Girls at Play* are good examples of J Q Pringle's original style.

The **Scottish Colourists** (J D Fergusson, F Caddell, S J Peploe, L Hunter) were the next important group to emerge from Glasgow in the early 20C. Their canvases are striking with the strong lines and vibrant colours reminiscent of Post Impressionism and Fauvism: *Bathers, Le Voile Persan, Les Eus* (Fergusson), *The Red Chair* (Caddell), *The Brown Crock, Iona, Tulips and Cup* (Peploe). Joan **Eardley** (1921-63) is an important artist who drew inspiration from slum life *(Street Kids)* and dramatic weather at sea *(Salmon Nets and the Sea, A Stormy Sea)*.

The Glasgow School of Art nurtured many outstanding artists: R Colquhoun (1914-62) – *The Dubliners, Figures in a Farmyard* showing the influence of Cubism – and R MacBryde (1913-66) – *The Backgammon Player, Fish on a Pedestal Table* (original combination of unusual objects). Anne **Redpath** (1895-1965), well known for her still-life paintings, flower pieces, landscapes and church interiors *(Pinks, Red Slippers)*, and William Gillies (1893-1973), who painted gentle landscapes *(Temple Village)* and still-life compositions, were both associated with the Edinburgh School of Art. The work of Ian Hamilton **Finlay** (b 1925) combines classical allusions and form. Russell Flint's (1880-1969) watercolours celebrate the pleasures of life.

MODERN TRENDS

Another important group of artists was open to international influences. William Gear (b 1915) and Stephen Gilbert joined the COBRA movement. Alan Davie (b 1920) became an exponent of Abstract Expressionism *(Jingling Space)* while William Turnbull's (b 1922) interest in modernist abstraction is expressed in geometrical or painterly compositions. **Eduardo Paolozzi** (b 1924) creates collages in the Pop Art idiom using discarded artefacts of the consumer society and showing the influence of Dadaism and Surrealism. *Celebration of Earth, Air, Fire and Water* by William Johnstone is a good example of landscape abstraction. John Bellany (b 1942) tackles the inhumanity of people and the mysteries of existence and human relations. He shows victims of horror in domestic interiors invaded by a nightmarish atmosphere *(Woman with*

Skate). The triptych *"Journey to the End of Night"* is a visionary creation.

The **New Image** group from Glasgow is blazing a trail on the contemporary scene. The influence of Fernand Léger and the Mexican muralists is evident in the graphic emphasis of the human figure and the raw vigour of the large compositions by Ken **Currie** (b 1960) – *The Glasgow Triptych* mural. Social realism is also tackled with poetic vision by Peter Howson (b 1958). The works of Adrian Wiszniewski (b 1958) show great imaginative fantasy while Stephen Campbell (b 1953) poses conundrums in natural philosophy. Stephen **Conroy** (b 1964) who seems to distance himself from human life is famous for his strangely typecast characters (clubmen, actors, singers, businessmen) depicted with great flair and craftsmanship.

Other artists making a name for themselves on the contemporary scene include Jock McFayden (b 1950) and the "Wilde Malerei" group (Fiona Carlisle, June Redfern, Joyce Cairns) who paint in lively, vivid colours.

Robert Louis Stevenson by Count Girolamo Nerli

The Bridgeman Art Library/ Scottish National Portrait Gallery, Edinburgh

Thomas the Rhymer, the 13C Scottish seer and poet, was famous for his verse prophecies. The wizard Michael Scott (1117-1232) won fame as a scholar and linguist at the court of Emperor Frederick II. **John Duns Scotus** (1266-1308), a Franciscan scholar, was a leading philosopher who dominated the European scene.

Literature

EARLY TRADITION

Gaelic folklore celebrates the legendary 3C bard **Ossian** who was thought to be the author of *"The Ossianic Fragments"*; the poems were a literary fraud perpetrated by James Macpherson in the 18C which won great acclaim.

St Columba arrived in Iona in AD 563 and there is a tradition that the community's scribes and illuminators worked on the *Book of Kells*. The 9th abbot St Adamnan (c 624-704) wrote *The Life of St Columba*. The *Book of Deer* (now at Cambridge University) is a 9C Latin manuscript annotated in Scottish Gaelic in the 11C or 12C (the earliest known example).

In medieval times learning was associated with the monastic houses (Jedburgh, Dryburgh, Melrose, Arbroath, Dunfermline) but their treasures were lost following raids by the English and the religious conflicts in the 16C.

EVOLUTION

Printing was introduced in 1507 and the earliest printed works included those of Bishop Gavin Douglas (1474-1522) who translated Virgil's **Aeneid** into Scots, and of the court poet William Dunbar (1460-1520). Both belonged to a group of poets known as the Makars which also included Robert Henryson (1430-1506).

In the 16C Andrew Melville (1554-1622), a celebrated theologian, scholar and linguist, had a close association with the universities of Glasgow and St Andrews. The humanist George Buchanan (1506-82) was the tutor of Mary, Queen of Scots and of James VI. The 16C was an era of religious ferment dominated by the reformer **John Knox** (1512-72) who held famous debates with Mary, Queen of Scots and whose fiery sermons led to unfortunate excesses.

B. Perousse/ MICHELIN

Pipers at Callander Highland games

NATIONAL PRIDE

The Age of Enlightenment witnessed a flowering of talented men in all fields of endeavour who frequented clubs and learned societies. Leading figures included the prolific and influential poet and writer **Sir Walter Scott** (1771-1832), the revered bard **Robert Burns** (1759-96) who epitomised the national spirit, the poet Allan Ramsay (1686-1758) who fostered the use of the Scottish language in literary works *(The Gentle Shepherd)*, the writer James Boswell (1740-95), Dr Johnson's close friend and biographer, the novelist Tobias Smollett (1721-71), the philosophers David Hume (1716-86), Dugald Stewart (1753-1828) and Adam Smith (1723-90). James Hogg (1770-1835), the "Ettrick Shepherd", was known for his pastoral poetry. The first edition of the *Encyclopaedia Britannica* was published between 1768-71 in Edinburgh. Literary magazines *(Edinburgh Review, Blackwood's Magazine)* disseminated the new ideas and theories of the period.

In the 19C the essayist and historian **Thomas Carlyle** (1795-1881) was widely acclaimed and his seminal works *(The French Revolution, Oliver Cromwell)* wielded enormous influence. **James Barrie**'s (1860-1937) original works show great wit and imagination *(Peter Pan, The Admirable Crichton)*. Robert Louis Stevenson (1850-94) wrote thrilling tales of adventure *(Treasure Island, Master of Bal-*

lantrae). The gripping stories *(The Thirty-Nine Steps, Prester John, Greenmantle)* told by John Buchan (1875-1940) were much admired. Another famous figure was the poet Charles Murray (1864-1941) who penned his verses in the Doric (rustic Scotch dialect).

CONTEMPORARY SCENE

The **Scottish Literary Renaissance** of the early 20C attempted to foster a national language and included the poet Hugh MacDiarmid (1892-1978), the poet and journalist Lewis Spence (1874-1955), Helen Cruickshank (1896-1973), the novelists Lewis Grassic Gibbon (1901-35), Compton Mackenzie (1883-1972) and Neil Gunn (1891-1973) and the poet and literary critic E Muir (1887-1959). William McGonagall (1830-1902) took up the role of itinerant bard although he wrote indifferent verse. John Joy Bell (1871-1961) wrote fiction, comic novels, travel books and recollections *(I remember)*. George Blake (1893-1961) is known for his naturalistic treatment of life in Glasgow and Clydeside *(The Shipbuilders)*. The novelist and playwright Eric Linklater (1899-1974) *(The Man of Ness, The Dark of Summer, A Year of Space)* was born in Orkney. George Mackay Brown (1921-97) drew his inspiration from the Norse tradition and wrote in a limpid style *(Winter Tales, Beside the Ocean of Time)*. Famous names on the modern scene include Muriel Spark (b 1918) with her witty satirical novels *(The Prime of Miss Jean Brodie, Girls of Slender Means)*, Alan Massie, William Boyd, James Kelman *(How Late it was, How Late, The Bus-conductor Hines)*. Alasdair Gray, A L Kennedy and D Maclean are also notable figures.

The Edinburgh International Festival which was launched in 1947 draws new and established theatrical talent from all over the world and the city has acquired a well deserved reputation as a cultural centre. Glasgow's Mayfest founded in 1983 also attracts much international interest; in 1990 the city was nominated Cultural Capital of Europe.

Music

ORIGINS

Scottish **folk music** has its roots in the Gaelic (Celtic) tradition while the islands have a Nordic heritage. The *òran mor* (great song) comprises the Heroic Lays, the Ossianic Ballads and songs linked with pipe music (laments and pibroch songs). There were also songs which set the rhythm for certain tasks such as linen making, cloth fulling, reaping, spinning, churning, as well as lullabies, fairy songs, love songs and mourning songs *(coronach)*. *Puirt-a-Beul* (mouth music) was a popular form of vocal dance music, often with humorous lyrics.

Communities scattered in remote areas of the Highlands held gatherings *(ceilidhs),* when songs, music, dance and poetry were performed for entertainment. Itinerant musicians were always welcome. The Skene manuscript (c 1615) is the earliest example of Lowland music and there are collections of Lowland ballads (narrative songs).

Bothy ballads are associated with farming life and many have been collected in Aberdeenshire and neighbouring counties.

TRADITIONAL INSTRUMENTS

The most ancient musical instrument is the **harp** *(clarsach)* as evidenced from stone carvings dating from the 9C. Queen Mary's Harp and the Lamont Harp

in the Royal Museum of Scotland are the earliest surviving examples from the 15C-16C although no ancient harp music has survived in its original form.

The modern revival of the harp dates from 1892 when the first Mod was held by The Highland Society (An Comunn Gaidhealach) which aims to stimulate interest in Gaelic culture. In 1931 the Comunn na Clàrsach (Clarsach Society) was founded.

The fiddle, lute and flute were also popular instruments. There are many references to fiddlers from the 13C; music collections have been recorded from the 15C onwards with manuscripts and printed music collections from the late 17C.

BAGPIPES

These are now generally acknowledged as the national musical instrument, but are of uncertain origin. Already in use in 14C Scotland they developed from the original one drone instrument to the modern example with three drones, chanter (for the melody) and blow stick (mouthpiece).

Bagpipe music is unquestionably a Scottish art, be it the *ceol mor* (big or great music) or *ceol beag* (small or light music). The latter, more recent and common, covers the lighter music for marching and dancing (strathspeys and reels). The older or classical music of the bagpipes is known as pibroch *(piobairochd)*.

RELIGIOUS INFLUENCE

The monastic and church music schools maintained a high musical standard but the religious conflicts exacted a heavy toll as the music collections were dispersed. The earliest document is a manuscript compiled at St Andrews c 1250. The flowering of **sacred music** which occurred from the reign of James IV (1488-1513) to the Reformation is marked by three notable 16C composers: Patrick Hamilton, Robert Johnson and David Peebles. The Protestant tradition favoured simple metrical psalm settings but an important and independent development was the Gaelic "long psalms" which are still sung today.

The "Mike Vass Band" leads one of the McEwan's sessions held during the Edinburgh Festival in the Royal Mile Tavern

NEW TRENDS

In the 18C folk songs arranged for stringed instruments and keyboard were very popular. The Edinburgh Musical Society concerts were founded in 1720. There was an influx of Italian composers and Scottish composers went to study abroad: Sir John Clerk (1676-1755), who studied with Corelli, composed solo cantatas and Thomas Alexander Erskine (1732-81) wrote symphonies and chamber music. Also of note were chamber music by William McGibbon (c 1690-1756) and violin sonatas by David Foulis (1710-73). Sir Walter Scott's poems (The Lady of the Lake) and novels (Ivanhoe, The Bride of Lammermoor) were a source of inspiration for many composers (Schubert, Donizetti, Auber).

REVIVAL

Robert Burns was active in collecting and rewriting Scottish songs which were published in The Scots Musical Museum (1787-1803) and Select Scottish Airs (1793-1818). Many of Burns' own poems were also set to music.

Scottish musical inspiration was at its lowest ebb in the 19C but a rebirth became evident in the late 19C with the formation of choral and orchestral societies, the changing attitudes of the church and the celebration of Scotland by native composers (Sir Alex Campbell Mackenzie, Hamish MacCunn, William Wallace).

At the turn of the century, the philanthropist Andrew Carnegie donated organs to remote parishes to promote new interest in church music. 20C composers who adopted Scottish idioms include Eric Chisholm (1904-65), Ian Whyte (1902-69), Cedric Thorpe Davie (b 1913) and Lyell Creswell (b 1944). Celtic culture inspired two outstanding composers: Ronald Stevenson (b 1928) who wrote songs, piano works and concertos and Francis George Scott (1880-1958), who, together with his disciple Hugh MacDiarmid (1892-1978), promoted the **Scottish Renaissance**, a musical and literary movement in the 1920s.

Many Scottish artists have won great respect on the international scene : the pianist Frederic Lamond (1868-1948), the singers Mary Garden (1874-1967) and Joseph Hislop (1884-1977), and the choral conductor Hugh S Robertson (1874-1952). In the 20 C operas by the Scottish composers Robin Orr, Iain Hamilton, Thomas Wilson and Thea Musgrave have been well received.

Scotland's natural attractions have drawn several composers. The scenery of the Hebrides inspired Felix Mendelssohn to write the Overture to the Hebrides. Since 1970 Sir Peter Maxwell Davies, the avant-garde English composer, has written all his music on Hoy in the Orkney Islands and in 1977 inaugurated the **St Magnus Arts Festival** held every summer in Kirkwall and Stromness.

The **Edinburgh International Festival** and **Glasgow Mayfest** offer a wide range of classical music and the **Jazz Festivals** are very popular events. The reputation of the Scottish National Orchestra is second to none. It commissions new music from aspiring Scottish composers who contribute to the dynamism of the musical world in Scotland.

THE COUNTRY TODAY

As Scotland enters the 21st century it is shaking off the old tourist stereotype of shortbread in tartan tins, bagpipers and haggis. Instead it is incorporating such icons into contemporary life, often with humour and verve. On the streets of Edinburgh, Glasgow and other major towns, there is a buzz and confidence equal to any modern European city, albeit with a definite Scottish twist.

Economy

The economy of Scotland has always been closely linked with the rest of the United Kingdom and in recent times also to the European Union. At the time of the Industrial revolution Scotland was one of the powerhouses of Europe, famous for **shipbuilding**, as well as its thriving **coal mining**, **steel** and other manufacturing industries. As these traditional industries went into decline or moved to other parts of the world Scotland has become a **technology** and **service** based economy – it is estimated that around 80 per cent of all Scotland's employees now work in services and this sector has enjoyed significant rates of growth over the last decade.

The "**Silicon Glen**" corridor between Glasgow and Edinburgh is home to many companies specialising in information systems, electronics, instrumentation, defence and semi-conductors, while Edinburgh is one of the largest **banking** and **financial services** centres in Europe.

Despite the passing of its halcyon Clyde shipbuilding days, Glasgow still builds ships, is Scotland's leading seaport and is the fourth largest manufacturing centre in the UK. The city also boasts the UK's largest commercial and retail district after London's West End.

In the late 1970s the discovery and exploitation of **North Sea oil** and natural gas in fields around the Shetland Isles proved a massive boon to Scotland in general and to the Highlands and Islands, particularly Aberdeen. Today, even though the best years of oil have passed, this sector continues to underpin a local economy which has barely survived – particularly in the islands – on traditional fishing and agricultural activities. The services sector has also spread far north however with Shetlanders and Orcadians involved in software and microprocessors.

Other important Scottish traditional sectors are textiles, whisky and shortbread, not only important as highly visible flagships to the tourist sector but also exported all over the world. Tourism is an important and growing area but highly susceptible to external influences as demonstrated in the 2001 and 2005 terror attacks in London.

Government

In 1997 Scotland re-opened the Scottish Parliament, almost 300 years after the last parliament was dissolved.

The Parliament has responsibility over wide areas of Scottish affairs and has tax-raising powers, though in theory at least the UK Parliament at Westminter) retains powers to amend or even abolish the Scottish Parliament.

Among areas which remain under Westminster control are the constitution, foreign policy, defence and national security, border controls and economic policy, including Scottish taxes, though the Scottish Parliament has limited power to vary local income tax, known as the Tartan Tax.

The head of state in Scotland is still the British monarch.

The new Scottish Parliamentary body has 120 members. Tthe Executive comprises a First Minister and a team of ministers and law officers.

The Parliament is a single house legislature made up of 129 Members, 73 of whom represent individual constituencies and are elected on a first-past-the-post voting system.

Population

Scotland's population based on the results of the 2001 Census was 5,062,000. Recent estimates suggest that a truer figure is around 5,117,000.

Glasgow is the largest city with a population of approximately 619,000 while the capital, Edinburgh, has around 448,000 with Aberdeen next at just under 219,000.

Scotland's population reached its peak in the mid 1970s, and has slowly declined since then. However the trend of people leaving the country, usually for better paid jobs in England, has been arrested with significant movements of population to Scotland from the rest of the United Kingdom. Also, since 2004 and the expansion of the EU—offering economic migration without frontiers in much of Europe—incomers from countres such as as Poland, Latvia, Lithuania and the Czech Republic, have joined the local population.

Traditions and Customs

CLANS

Clann in Gaelic means children or family. All members of a clan owed loyalty to the head of the family or the chief. In return for their allegiance, he acted as leader, protector and dispenser of justice. Castle pit prisons, gallows hills and beheading pits are all common features in clan territories. The ties of kinship created a powerful social unit

Tartan

which flourished north of the Highland Line where Scottish monarchs found it hard to assert their authority. There the Lord of the Isles ruled as an independent monarch. As late as 1411, with the Battle of Harlaw, the monarchy was threatened by combined clan action. Clan ties ran deep and rivalries and feuds, often for land or cattle, were common. Scott popularised the Campbell–MacGregor feud in *Rob Roy*. The late 17C was marked by the Massacre of Glen Coe. The mainly Catholic clans pinned their hopes on the "King over the water" and the Jacobite risings were based on clan support. Sweeping changes followed the Battle of Culloden (1746) with the passing of the Act of Proscription (1747-82). The wearing of tartan in any form and carrying of arms were banned and heritable jurisdictions abolished. This was the destruction of the clan system and the death knell came with the clearances of the early 19C.

The battles and feuds, loyalty and traditions live on in legends and literature. Today Clan Societies and Associations are active organisations, both in Scotland and abroad. Some of them finance museums (Macpherson at Newtonmore, Donnachaid north of Blair Atholl), others undertake the restoration of clan seats (Menzies Castle) or building of clan centres (Clan Donald Centre, Armadale Skye).

TARTANS

The colourful clothing material, tartan, now so symbolic of Scotland, has ancient origins while clan tartans are an invention of the early 19C. In the Highlands a coarse woollen cloth (*tartaine* in French) was dyed using vegetable plant sources (bracken for yellow; blaeberries for blue, whin bark or broom for green). Originally patterns or setts corresponded to the district in which a particular weaver, with his distinctive pattern, operated. In early portraits it is common to see a variety of patterns being worn at one time. Some of the best examples are Francis Cote's splendidly defiant *Pryse Campbell, 18th Thane of Cawdor* (see CAWDOR CASTLE), *The MacDonald Boys* (c 1750), Raeburn's series of Highland chiefs including *Macnab* and J Michael Wright's 17C *Highland Chieftain* at Holyroodhouse Palace.

The repeal of the Proscription Act (1782) led to the commercialisation of tartans and standardisation on a clan basis and a more rigid observation of clan or family tartans. The first tartan pattern books appeared at this time. George IV's 1822 visit, when the monarch wore a kilt, initiated the tartan boom of the 19C, a vogue continued by Queen Victoria and Albert with their interest in all things Highland.

Colours

Any given **sett** or pattern may be woven in modern, ancient or reproduction colours. With the introduction of aniline dyes in the 19C the colours became bright and harsh and were termed **"modern"**. After the First World War an attempt was made, again using chemical dyes, to achieve the softer shades of the natural dyes. These were defined as **"ancient"** and created a certain amount of confusion on the tartan scene as some tartans, like the Old Stewart or Old Munro, already had "old" as part of their title. More recent developments include the invention of **"reproduction"** and **"muted"** colours.

The introduction in the 19C of synthetic dyes gave vivid colours and the kilt began to lose its camouflage quality on the hills. **Hunting tartans** were created where the bright red backgrounds were replaced by green, blue or brown. The **dress tartan** was another innovation of the period. The clan tartan was given a white ground and used for men's evening dress.

A tartan exists for every occasion be it everyday, hunting or evening wear. The most common form is the kilt which constitutes the principal item of Highland dress. By the 16C a belted plaid *(feileadh mor)* was in use for everyday wear. The little kilt *(feileadh beag)* developed from this and was popular in the 18C. A proper kilt may use as much as 8yd/7m of tartan. Both the Scottish Tartans Museum in Stirling run by the Scottish Tartans Society and the Scottish Experience, Royal Mile, Edinburgh have costume

Harris tweed

displays. The former has registered as many as 1,600 tartans or setts.

TRACING YOUR ANCESTORS

Before applying for professional help eliminate any home sources of information that you may have to hand. Check out old letters, diaries, albums and newspaper cuttings and books with inscriptions, including the family Bible or school prizes. Ensure that research has not already been done on the family with a visit to the **National Library of Scotland** in Edinburgh.

Birth, marriage and death certificates from 1855 onwards, Census Returns from 1801 and Parish Registers pre-1855 may be consulted in the **General Register Office**. The **National Archives of Scotland** holds property records (Sasines and Deeds Registers) and will furnish names of researchers experienced in using such documents. For those with titled or eminent ancestors, *Burke's* and *Debrett's Peerages,* the *Dictionary of National Biography* and *Who's Who* are useful sources. The names of professional genealogists can be obtained from the Scots Ancestry Research Society which also furnishes the addresses of Clan Associations.

B. Perousse/ MICHELIN

Tossing the caber

GAELIC

Spoken Gaelic

Although on the decline there were 65,978 speakers in 1991, representing 1.2% of the resident population. The majority of Gaelic speakers are bilingual. As a living language Gaelic continues to flourish in the Northwest Highlands, the Hebrides where 76% of the population are Gaelic speakers and Skye (58%). Outside these regions Glasgow has a pocket of Gaelic speakers.

One of the oldest European languages and a Celtic one, Scottish Gaelic is akin to the Irish version. The Gaeldom culture has given much that is distinctive to Scotland (tartans, kilt, bagpipes, music). An Comunn Gaidhealach (f 1891) with its headquarters in Inverness promotes the use of Gaelic, its literature and music and organises an annual festival, the **Mod**, of Gaelic song and poetry (♨ *see Calendar of Events).*

SCOTTISH CRAFTS

Craftsmen offer a wide variety of quality objects, which make perfect souvenirs of a visit to Scotland. Of the many traditional Scottish crafts, the best-known is the **knitwear** of Fair Isle and Shetland. These include the natural colours of Shetland sweaters, the extremely fine lace shawls and the complicated multicoloured patterned Fair Isle jerseys. **Harris tweed**, woven exclusively on handlooms in the Outer Hebrides is a quality product well meriting its high reputation. **Tartans** are nearly all

machine woven but **kiltmaking** has remained a handicraft.

Both **glassmaking** and **engraving** are thriving crafts today. The best-known products, other than cut crystal, are the engraving and handblown paperweights, in particular the delightful **millefiori**. Jewellery making includes the setting of semi-precious stones such as the Cairngorm or Tay pearls. Both serpentine and granite are employed for various ornaments and objects (paperweights, penholders) and granite is used for the polished curling stones.

The straw-backed and hooded **Orkney chairs,** white fleecy **sheepskin rugs** and **leather** and hornwork articles (cutlery handles and buttons) are also popular.

Both individual craftsmen and larger firms usually welcome visitors to their workshops and showrooms. For further information apply to the local tourist information centres.

HIGHLAND GAMES AND GATHERINGS

Visitors are well advised to attend one of these colourful occasions where dancing, piping and sporting events are all part of the programme. As early as the 11C contests in the arts of war were organised to permit clan chiefs to choose their footrunners and bodyguards from the winners.

Following the repeal of the Proscription Act, Highland Societies were formed to ensure the survival of traditional dances and music. Today these events are popular with locals and visitors alike. Of particular interest and charm are those of the Grampian and Highland areas.

Traditional events include dancing, piping, athletics and the never failing attraction of massed pipe bands. The heavy events include putting the shot, throwing the hammer and tossing the caber as straight as possible and not as far as possible.

The map below shows a selection of Highland Games, Gatherings and Common Ridings. The background colour indicates the month, and for certain games the principal attraction is also given.

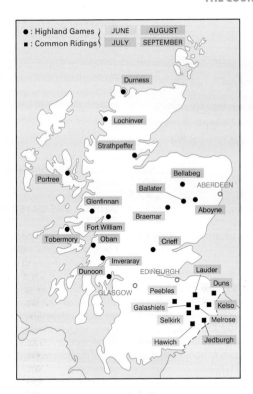

● : Highland Games ⎱ JUNE   AUGUST
■ : Common Ridings ⎰ JULY   SEPTEMBER

Durness
Lochinver
Strathpeffer
Bellabeg
Portree
Ballater   ABERDEEN
Glenfinnan   Aboyne
Braemar
Fort William
Tobermory   Oban   Crieff
Inveraray
Dunoon   EDINBURGH   Lauder
        Duns
GLASGOW   Peebles
    Galashiels   Kelso
    Selkirk   Melrose
    Hawick   Jedburgh

Food and Drink

SCOTTISH FARE

Scottish cooking is characterised by the excellence and quality of the natural products from river, moor, sea and farm.

Soups

These number **Cock-a-Leekie** using fowl, cut leeks and prunes; **Scots** or **Barley Broth**, a vegetable and barley soup; **Game Soup; Partan Bree** a crab soup and **Cullen Skink** made with smoked haddock.

Fish

Of the many varieties of fish, pride of place goes to the **salmon**, be it farmed or wild, from the famous fisheries of the Tay, Spey or Tweed. Served fresh or smoked, it is a luxury dish. **Trout** and **salmon-trout** with their delicately pink flesh are equally appreciated. Breakfast menus often feature the **Arbroath Smokie** – a small salted and smoked haddock; the **Finnan Haddie**, a salted haddock dried on the beach prior to smoking over a peat fire; and the **kipper** a split, salted and smoked herring.

Game

The hills and moors provide a variety of game. The best-known are the superb **red grouse** and **venison**. The raw material is either farmed or wild.

Meat

With such first class beef cattle as the angus from Aberdeen and Galloway in addition to home-bred sheep, it is hardly surprising that the quality of Scotch **beef**

Taste of Scotland

The Taste of Scotland is a website (www.taste-of-scotland.com) devoted to selected restaurants, tearooms and other eating placed which offer 'a true 'taste of scotland' via their menus.It also includes Scottish food producers and Scottish farmers markets.

Haggis, Neeps and Tatties

and **mutton** is unsurpassed. **Haggis** is the national dish.

Desserts

Succulent **soft fruits** (strawberries, raspberries and black currants) ripened slowly make an excellent sweet. Other creamsweets like **Cranachan** often incorporate one of the soft fruits. **Atholl Brose** is a mixture of honey, oatmeal, malt whisky and cream.

Cheeses

Although not of international repute, Scotland is home to several very high quality home-made cheeses. Both the **Dunlop** cheese from Orkney, Arran and Islay and the **Scottish Cheddar** are hard cheeses. **Caboc** is a rich double cream cheese rolled in oatmeal while **Crowdie** is similar to a cottage cheese.

All over the world the **Burns Supper** starts with the recitation of a humorous ode To a Haggis.

Fair fa' your honest sonsie face,
Great chieftain o' the puddin'-race!
Aboon them a' ye tak your place
Painch, tripe or thain:
Weel are ye wordy o' a grace
Aslang's my arm...

...Ye Pow'rs, wha mak mankind your care,
And dish them out their bill o' fare,
Auld Scotland wants nae skinking ware
That jaups in luggies;
But, if ye wish her gratefu' prayer,
Gie her a Haggis!

Breakfast and tea-time

These two famously British meals provide the chance to taste porridge, a smokie or kipper, a rasher or two of Ayrshire bacon with eggs, oatcakes, an Aberdeen buttery or a softie. Tea-time includes shortbread and Dundee cake.

Preserves

Heather honey or Scottish-made jam and marmalade are not only perfect at breakfast time but make ideal presents.

WHISKY, THE WATER OF LIFE

Scotland's national drink, whisky – in Gaelic, *uisge beatha* (pronounced oosh-ga beh-huh), meaning water of life, is thought to have begun centuries ago as a way of using up rain-soaked barley after a wet harvest. Whatever its origins, the highly competitive whisky industry is nowadays Scotland's biggest export earner (over £900 million a year) and one of the government's main sources of revenue.

It is often asked, what makes a good whisky. The answer is that the quality and subtle differences in character depend essentially on a combination of certain factors, of which the key ones are: the barley (not always home grown); the water, filtered through peat or over granite; the equipment, such as the shape of the still, and of course the experience and skill of the stillmen.

To learn more about whisky in Scotland visit the official website www.scotland-whisky.com. this gives details of places to visit, whisky festivals, tours, tastiing guides and links to a whole host of other whisky-related websites

A troubled past

Undoubtedly among the earliest distillers of whisky, the Scots have played a major part in the perfection of this art. In the 15C monks were distilling a spirit and soon after it became an everyday domestic occupation. The Union of 1707 brought exorbitant taxation, including the 1713 malt tax. Distilling went underground and smuggling became a way of life. From the illicit stills on the hillsides, the spirit was transported along a smugglers' trail from Speyside to Perth over 140mi/225km of hill country. Excisemen became the scourge of the Highlands. A succession of new laws in the early 19C did nothing to halt illicit distilling until the 1824 Act. The latter sanctioned distillation on payment of a licence fee and duty per gallon produced. Many famous distilleries were founded after this date. Whisky production developed rapidly in the 1880s as the replacement spirit for gin and brandy. Blending produced a more palatable drink which rapidly achieved universal success. Although blended whiskies still dominate the market, the subtler and finer qualities of a single malt are gaining recognition.

Malt whisky

The original spirit was a malt or straight unblended product of a single malt whisky.

There are around 116 single malts, classified into Highland, Lowland or Islay.

The subtle flavours of pure malt whisky distilled according to age-old methods are greatly prized by connoisseurs throughout the world. The distilleries on Speyside (Cardhu, Glenfarclas, Strathisla, Glen Grant, Glenfiddich, Tamnavulin, The Glenlivet and Dallas Dhu) enjoy a prestigious reputation and many welcome visitors to see the process and sample a wee dram.

Islay in the Hebrides produces distinctive smoky, peaty malts such as Laphroaig, Bowmore, Bunnahabhain.

There are also many lesser-known malt whisky distilleries close to Edinburgh and Glasgow and all over the Highland region which welcome visitors. The Scotch Whisky Heritage Centre in Edinburgh (see EDINBURGH) also provides a comprehensive introduction to the celebrated drink.

Blended whisky

Grain whisky is made from a malted barley and other cereals. The blends are a mixture of a lighter grain with a malt. Blended varieties are subdivided into two categories: de luxe and standard.

Whisky making

Scotch whisky is made from only three ingredients: malted barley, water and yeast. The processes have been refined down through the centuries but apart from the scale and complexity of the hardware, in essence they have remained the same for much of this time.

Malting

Best quality barley is first steeped in water and then spread out on malting floors to germinate. It is turned regularly to prevent the build up of heat. Traditionally, this was done by tossing the barley into the air with wooden shovels in a malt barn adjacent to the kiln.

During this process enzymes are activated which convert the starch into sugar when mashing takes place. After 6 to 7 days of germination the barley, , goes to the kiln for drying. This halts the germination. Peat may be added to the fire to impart flavour from the smoke.

Mashing

The dried malt is ground into a coarse flour or grist, which is mixed with hot water in the mash tun.

The quality of the pure Scottish water is important. The mash is stirred, helping to convert the starches to sugar. After mashing, the sweet sugary liquid is known as wort.

Fermentation

The wort is cooled and pumped into washbacks, where yeast is added and fermentation begins. After about 2 days the fermentation dies down and the wash contains 6-8% alcohol by volume.

Pot Stills

In some mysterious way the shape of the pot still affects the character of the individual malt whisky, and each distillery keeps its stills exactly the same over the years.

The still is heated to just below the boiling point of water and the alcohol and other compounds vaporize and pass over the neck of the still into either a condenser or a worm – a large copper coil immersed in cold running water where the vapour is condensed into a liquid.

www.scotlandwhisy.com

Whisky Barrels

Distillation

The wash is distilled twice – first in the wash still, to separate the alcohol from the water, yeast and residue

The distillate from the wash still, then goes to the spirit still for the second distillation. The more volatile compounds which distil off first, are channelled off to be redistilled. Only the pure heart of the run, which is about 68% alcohol by volume is collected in the spirit receiver.

Spirit Safe

All the distillates pass through the spirit safe – whose locks were traditionally controlled by the Customs & Excise. The stillman uses all his years of experience to test and judge the various distillates without being able to come into physical contact with the spirit.

The newly distilled, colourless, fiery spirit , reduced to maturing strength, 63% alcohol by volume, is filled into oak casks which may have previously contained Scotch whisky, bourbon or sherry, and the maturation process begins.

Maturation

By law all Scotch whisky must be matured for at least 3 years, but most single malts lie in the wood for 8, 10, 12, 15 years or longer. Customs & Excise allow for a maximum of 2% of the whisky to evaporate from the cask each year – the Angels' Share. Unlike wine, whisky does not mature further once it is in the bottle.

Grain whisky and blending

Scotch grain whisky is usually made from 10-20% malted barley and then other unmalted cereals such as maize or wheat. The starch in the non-malted cereals is released by pre-cooking and converted into fermentable sugars. The mashing and fermentation processes are similar to those used for malt whisky.

While the distinctive single malts produced by individual distilleries are becoming increasingly popular, blending creates over 90% of the Scotch whisky enjoyed throughout the world. By nosing samples in tulip-shaped glasses the blender selects from a wide palate – from the numerous Highland and Speyside malts to the strongly flavoured and peaty Island malts, and the softer and lighter Lowland malts. These malts are combined with grain whiskies – usually 60-80% grain whiskies to 20-40% malt whiskies, and are then left to 'marry' in casks before being bottled as one of the world-renowned blended whiskies.

A blend of a range of malt whiskies, with no grain whisky included, is known as a vatted malt.

Little Red Riding Hood

ut Little Red Riding Hood had her regional map with her, and so she did not fall into the trap. She did not take the path through the wood and she did not meet the big bad wolf. Instead, she chose the picturesque touring route straight to Grandmother's house, and arrived safely with her cake and her little pot of butter.

The End

With Michelin maps, go your own way.

MICHELIN
A better way forward

Tobermory Harbour & Town, Isle of Mull
Edmund Nagele/Pictures Colour Library

ABBOTSFORD★★
SCOTTISH BORDERS
&LOCAL MAP SEE THE TWEED VALLEY

Abbotsford, a fantasy in stone, is typical of **Sir Walter Scott** (1771–1832), the man who did so much to romanticise and popularise all things Scottish. Here you can see souvenirs of the man, his friends and contemporaries, his literary works and his cherished collection of **"curiosities of small intrinsic value"**.

- **Information:** Abbey House, Abbey Street, Melrose. ☎0870 60804046. www.scot-borders.co.uk.
- **Orient Yourself:** Abbotsford is 2mi/3km from Melrose. Take the A 68, A 6091 Melrose bypass, heading north towards Galashiels. Turn left at the second roundabout onto the B 6360. Car parking can be found on the left opposite Abbotsford.
- **Organizing Your Time:** Allow around 90min to see the house and grounds.
- **Also See:** BOWHILL, DRYBURGH ABBEY, JEDBURGH, KELSO, MELLERSTAIN, TRAQUAIR.

A Bit of History

The Wizard of the North
Walter Scott was born on 15 August 1771 and he was the youngest of 13 children of an Edinburgh solicitor. His earliest contacts with the region began at **Sandyknowe**, his grandfather's farm (&see KELSO: Excursions). At the age of eight he attended Edinburgh High School and then the university where he qualified as an advocate. In 1799 he became sheriff-depute of Selkirkshire. To be nearer his work he acquired a property at **Ashiestiel** in 1804 and then in 1812, the small farmhouse of Cartley Hall, which he renamed Abbotsford, on the banks of the Tweed. He extended the building but later demolished the farmhouse replacing it with the present exuberant structure which reflects his romantic spirit.

Scott's narrative poems, *The Lay of the Last Minstrel*, *Marmion* and *The Lady of the Lake* were written before he came to Abbotsford, as were his Scottish novels: *Waverley* (1814), *Guy Mannering* (1815), *The Antiquary* and *Old Mortality* (1816), *Rob Roy* (1818), *The Heart of Midlothian* (1818), *The Bride of Lammermoor*, *Ivanhoe* (1820), *A Legend of Montrose* (1819) and *Redgauntlet* (1824). The literary reputation of Scott is largely based on these novels, where he shows a genius for

character and a masterful handling of Scots dialogue.

Conundrum Castle
On 7 January 1828 Scott recorded in his journal, "It is a kind of Conundrum Castle to be sure and I have great pleasure in it for while it pleases a fantastic person in the stile and manner of its architecture and decoration it has all the comforts of a commodious habitation." Scott lavished much thought and effort on the building of his beloved Abbotsford, bristling with turrets and gables in the baronial style, which was to house his collection of "gabions", a word he invented to cover "curiosities of small intrinsic value". They often related some part of Scotland's chequered history.

Visit

&Open mid-Mar–Oct, daily 9.30am–5pm; Sun in Mar, Apr, May, Oct 2pm–5pm. £6.20; gardens only, £3. ☎01896 752 043. www.scottsabbotsford.co.uk.

Study
The small book-lined room is almost entirely occupied by the massive writing desk and is adjoined by a "speak-a-bit" turret room.

House of Sir Walter Scott

Library

The moulded ceiling is a copy of **Rosslyn Chapel** (&see *ROSSLYN CHAPEL*). The Chantrey bust of Scott is dated 1820, the year **George IV** knighted the author. The showcase in the bow window contains many of the treasured "gabions" including Rob Roy's purse and Burns' tumbler. The painting on the easel records the one and only meeting between Burns and the 15-year-old Scott. On the shleves are over 9,000 rare volumes.

Drawing-Room

The paintings include portraits of Scott's mother and father and, over the fireplace, **Henry Raeburn**'s *Portrait of Sir Walter* with his dog, Camp, at his feet. In one of the wall alcoves (to the right of the fireplace) is the silver urn which Byron gave to Scott. It also figures in the Sciennes House painting.

Armoury

This was a smoking corridor in Scott's time; the items on display include a Highland broadsword with basket hilt by Andrea Farara, Rob Roy souvenirs, including his gun, a Landseer painting of *Ginger* (the companion portrait of his master is in the National Portrait Gallery in Edinburgh) and a still-life of the Regalia of Scotland, a reminder that Scott was instrumental in their rediscovery. The miniatures include one of **Bonnie Prince Charlie** and **John Graham of Claverhouse**.

Dining-Room

It was here, where he could command a view of the Tweed to the last, that Scott died on 21 September 1832. His death was undoubtedly precipitated by the burden of overwork in his last years. Following a financial crisis in 1826, Scott produced a phenomenal three novels a year in an age when there were no mechanical aids.

Entrance Hall

Panelling from **Dunfermline Abbey**'s church is surmounted by arms of the Border families, while the fireplace and statues are copied from details in Melrose Abbey. Other souvenirs include people and events prominent in Scottish history.

South Court

Note the door from the Heart of Midlothian, Edinburgh's Old Tolbooth.

Chapel

Along with the neighbouring wing, it is a 19C addition. Ghirlandaio's *Madonna and Child* dominates the fireplace.

Grounds

There is a Walled Garden, a Woodland Walk and the chance to stroll down to the famous River Tweed.

ABERDEEN★★
CITY OF ABERDEEN
POPULATION 202,370

The "Granite City" lies between the Don and the Dee, backed by a rich agricultural hinterland and facing the North Sea oilfields which has given her a new role, that of Offshore Capital of Europe.

- ▯ **Information:** 23 Union Street ☏0124 288 828. www.agtb.org.
- ▶ **Orient Yourself:** Most of the major attractions are clustered in Old Aberdeen and the city centre.
- ⟲ **Don't Miss:** The heraldic ceiling in St Machar's Cathedral, Aberdeen Art Gallery, Grampian Castles.
- ◷ **Organizing Your Time:** Allow about 1 hour to stroll around Old Aberdeen. Allow another 2 hours to see the sights of the city centre.
- **Kids** **Especially for Kids:** The maze at Hazelhead.
- ♿ **Also See:** Follow the signed routes of the Victorian Heritage Trail, Scotland's Castle Trail, the Coastal Trail, and the Malt Whisky Trail which includes famous distilleries and coopers (barrel makers).

A Bit of History

Twin burghs – The present city developed from two separate fishing villages on the Dee and Don. By the 12C Old Aberdeen was the seat of an episcopal see. The cathedral city acquired burgh status in the 12C, and in the late 15C Bishop Elphinstone founded a university. The second distinct burgh grew up around the king's castle (13C) to become an active trading centre based on coastal and Baltic trade. While the Reformation brought ruin to Old Aberdeen, the city centre continued to prosper, acquired its own university (1593) and by the late 17C had started to break out of its medieval bounds.

The Granite City – Following Edinburgh and Perth, Aberdeen implemented its own plan for expansion with the laying out of Union and King streets (1801). Local architect **Archibald Simpson** (1790–1847) was responsible for giving the city much of its present character by his masterly use of Aberdeen granite as a building material. He gave his buildings a simplicity and dignity fully in keeping with the nature of the stone. The streets were lined with dignified public buildings (Medical Hall, 29 King Street: 1818–20, Assembly Rooms now the Music Hall, Union Street: 1822) and

there were imaginative private ventures, such as the Athenaeum and a successful design for the Clydesdale Bank at the Union and King Street corner site. Until the middle of the 20C, Aberdeen continued to be built in granite, giving its townscape a rare homogeneity, though few of its later suburbs can match the harmony of Simpson's essay in town planning centred on Bon Accord Square, Terrace and Crescent to the southwest of the city centre.

Maritime Past – The tradition of shipbuilding has always been strong in Aberdeen as the yards produced vessels for whaling and line fishing. Then came that age of international fame, the **clipper ship era** when the city's boatyards specialised in fast sailing ships. With the legendary and graceful tea clippers, *Stornoway, Chrysolite* and *Thermopylae*, Britain gained supremacy in the China tea trade. Wooden clippers gave way to composite and finally iron built vessels in the 1870s. Sail yielded to steam. Throughout, the local shipbuilding industry remained to the fore and continues today as an important aspect of the city's economy, although now geared to the oil industry.

The earliest fisheries included whaling (1752–1860s) and line fishing. Aberdeen became a fishing port with the herring

Address Book

For coin ranges, see the Legend on the cover flap.

WHERE TO STAY

Penny Meadow – *189 Gt. Western Rd. ☎01224 588037. frances@penny meadow.freeserve.co.uk.* Attractive welcoming period house built of local granite, with light and airy bedrooms and some thoughtful touches.

Express by Holiday Inn – *Chapel Street. ☎01224 623 500, www. hieaberdeen.co.uk.* Well equipped, in the heart of the city, with functional contemporary bedrooms.

Atholl – *54 King's Gate. ☎01224 323 505. www.atholl-aberdeen.co.uk.* This Baronial-style hotel is set in the leafy suburbs. Rooms are light and airy with Tartan decor. Its popular restaurant servies fresh local produce , the lounge bar has a wide selection of malt whiskies, ales and wines.

The Mariner – *349 Great Western Road. ☎01224 588 901. www. the marinerhotel.co.uk.* A nautical theme welcomes visitors to this elegant hotel set in a residential district 5 min dfrom the city centre. Bedrooms are spacious and colourful with extensive facilities. Good restaurant.

Simpson's Hotel – *59 Queen's Road. ☎01224 327 777. www.simpsonshotel.co.uk.* This vibrantly decorated boutique hotel is very stylish. Bedrooms have CD players. Superb bar-brasserie (*see Where to Eat, opposite*).

Skene House, Holburn – *6 Union Grove. ☎01224 580 000. www. skene-house.co.uk.* Based on the American concept of an all-suite hotel, this row of five typical local granite town houses have been converted into well-appointed serviced apartments, with kitchens, ideal for longer stays.

WHERE TO EAT

Black Olive Brasserie – *32–34 Queen's Road. ☎01224 208 877. www. olive-tree.co.uk. Closed Sun.* Smart modern brasserie serving all day from breakfast to Mediterranean inspired evening meals in a very attractive conservatory with tinted glass.

Rendezvous at Nargile – *106–108 Forest Avenue. ☎01224 323 700. www.rendezvousatnargile.co.uk.* Part of an acclaimed small chain, this stylish modern restaurant serves authentic Turkish cuisine, from snacks to full meals, with flair.

Lairhillock Inn – *Netherley. ☎01569 730 001. www.lairhillock.co.uk.* Former coaching inn a 15-min drive from the city centre with a cosy bar, conservatory with open fires, and serving rustic dishes showcasing local produce such as langoustines and venison.

Restaurant and Brasserie at Simpson's Hotel – *59 Queen's Road. ☎01224 327 799. www.simpsonshotel. co.uk.* A colonnade of arches, a fountain, palms and exotic flowers plus a split-level conservatory, make an extraordinary Alhambra-meets Roman Baths setting for modern international cuisine.

Silver Darling – *Pocra Quay, North Pier. ☎01224 576 229. www.silverdarlingrestaurant.co.uk.* Diners enjoy panoramic views of the harbour from this attractive old Customs House while savouring imaginatively prepared seafood.

---

boom (1875–96) and by 1900 had converted to trawling; it remains Scotland's premier white fishing port. The decline in trawling has in some way been counteracted by the increase in oil activities and today Aberdeen is one of Scotland's more vibrant cities, with a wide choice of good eating, drinking and cultural opportunities of all kinds.

Old Aberdeen★★ *3hr*

Old Aberdeen became a burgh of barony in 1489 under the patronage of the bishops and retained its separate burghal identity until 1891.
Today, the quarter stretching from King's College Chapel to St Machar's Cathedral, is part of a conservation area where the

old burgh's essential character has been well retained. The medieval streets – College Bounds (6), High Street, Don Street and the Chanonry – are now bordered by a variety of single and double storey cottages, and some more substantial detached mansions; a happy mix.

From King's College Chapel to the Brig o'Balgownie

King's College Old Town House and Chapel★

Open year-round Mon–Sat, 9am–5pm. Closed two weeks over Christmas and New Year. ☎*01224 237 650. www.abdn.ac.uk/oldtownhouse.*

The Old Town House, built in 1788, was the hub of the Burgh and the focal point for a busy trading community. Recently restored it is now the focal point of Old Aberdeen and is the visitor gateway to both the University and its charming medieval campus

Of the university founded in 1495 by **Bishop Elphinstone** (1431–1514), the beautiful chapel, in its campus setting, is the only original building. The chapel in the Flamboyant Gothic style (1500–05) is famous for its attractive Renaissance **crown spire**★★★ of great delicacy. It was restored in the 17C following storm damage. The bronze **monument** in front of the chapel is a 19C tribute to the founder. The tinctured arms on the buttresses of the west front are those of the sovereign James IV, his Queen Margaret Tudor, the founder Bishop Elphinstone, and a royal bastard, Archibald of St Andrews.

Inside is an extremely rare ensemble of **medieval fittings**★★★: rood screen, canopied stalls, pulpit and desk all richly and vigorously carved. The plain Tournoi marble tomb is that of the founder's and the plaque commemorates the first principal of the college, Hector Boece (c. 1465–1536).

The square Cromwell Tower in the northeast corner of the quadrangle was designed in 1658 to serve originally as student lodgings.

Old Town House

Now a branch library, this attractive 18C Georgian town house stands astride the High Street. The Old Aberdeen coat of arms above the door belonged to an earlier building.

The Chanonry

The layout of this once walled precinct is still apparent. Within this area were grouped dependent residences, from the Bishop's Palace to the manses of the secular canons and dwellings of the choir chaplains.

On the left are the university's **Cruickshank Botanic Gardens**.

St Machar's Cathedral★★

Open daily, summer 9am–5pm, winter 10am–4pm. ☎*01224 485 988, www.stmachar.com.*

The twin spires of St Machar's have long been one of Old Aberdeen's most famous landmarks. Its highly individual style – so very Scottish – reflects the nature of the granite building material. The present edifice, which dates from the 14C and 15C, overlooks the haughlands of the Don. According to legend, the original Celtic (c. 580) settlement was established by St Machar slightly to the west so as to overlook the "crook" of the Don and comply with instructions from **St Columba**. When the bishopric was transferred from **Mortlach**, now **Dufftown**, to St Machar's in 1131, a programme of rebuilding was undertaken. The present building is the nave as finally completed in the 15C.

Exterior

The **west front**★★★, the cathedral's most distinctive feature, is immediately impressive for the austerity and strength of its unusual design, where the role of the doorway is reduced to a minimum. Buttressed and crenellated towers, topped by tapering sandstone spires, flank the majestic seven-light window. The whole is devoid of decorative details.

Move round past the south porch (*entrance*) to the east end. The church was truncated at the transept crossing when the choir was demolished at the Reformation and further shortened in

1688 when the central tower and spire collapsed, destroying the transepts. Here are to be found the **tombs** of two of the bishop builders: in the north transept that of Bishop Henry Leighton (1422–40) – his effigy is inside the cathedral – and in the south, now glazed over, that of Bishop Gavin Dunbar (1518–32).

Interior

Take binoculars to examine the heraldic ceiling. Enter by the south porch.

A majestically simple but effective interior is the setting for this 16C **heraldic ceiling**★★★ attributed to the enterprising Bishop Gavin Dunbar. The flat, coffered oak ceiling is decorated with 48 brightly tinctured coats of arms arranged in three rows of 16 each running from east to west. Ingeniously designed, this unique ceiling presents a vision of the European scene around 1520 and a strong assertion of Scottish nationalism. The central axis representing the Holy Church, until then the traditional unifying force in Europe, is headed by the arms of Pope Leo X followed by other ecclesiastical arms. The absence of York and Trondheim is significant. On the right are the King of Scots (closed crown) and his nobles while on the left, headed by the Holy Roman Emperor, are the other Kings of Christendom. The King of England comes fourth after his fellow monarchs of France, Scotland's traditional ally, and Spain!

The stained glass is all 19C and 20C: the west window with cusped round arches and the Bishops Window (third from east end in the south aisle) 1913, an early example of Douglas Strachan's work showing the three great builder bishops, are noteworthy.

Brig O'Balgownie★

Approach via Don Street.

This early 14C bridge, one of Aberdeen's most important medieval buildings, is set astride the Don. The single span bridge with its pointed Gothic arch has cobbled approaches and a defensive kink at the south end.

Farther downstream is the **Bridge of Don**, by Aberdeen's first city architect, John Smith, with modifications by Thomas Telford (1827–30). The cost of building was financed by its illustrious neighbour's 17C maintenance fund.

the development of the North Sea oil industry brought conversion to the building of oil supply and fishery protection vessels.

City Centre

Maritime Museum★

Provost Ross's House, Shiprow. ♿🕐*Open year-round Mon–Sat, 10am–5pm, Sun noon–3pm.* 🕐 *Closed 25–26, 31 Dec, 1–2 Jan.* ☎*01224 337 700. www.aagm. co.uk.*

The museum is housed in two 16C town houses (alongside the National Trust of Scotland Visitor Centre) bordering Shiprow, one of the medieval thoroughfares winding up from the harbour. Provost Ross's House was owned by a succession of wealthy merchants, provosts and landed gentry. The museum has recently been enlarged and redeveloped with the introduction of interactive displays (touch screen, computerised visual databases, hands-on exhibits) complementing the ship models, paintings and artefacts tracing the story of the fishing, shipping and oil industries.

Castlegate

The gait or way to the castle on Castle Hill (marked by two high-rise blocks behind the Salvation Army Citadel) was the medieval market place. Near the paved area known as the "plain-stones" stands the Mannie Fountain (1706), a reminder of Aberdeen's first piped water supply.

Marischal Street, leading to the harbour, was laid out in 1767-68 on the site of the former tenement of the Earls Marischal. The new street was given a uniform design of three storeys and an attic. In the middle of the Castlegate is the splendid **mercat cross**★★ dating from 1686 (♿*see Introduction: Secular Architecture*). The unicorn surmounts the cross which rises from the roof of an arcaded structure. The decoration includes a frieze of oval panels containing 10 portraits of the royal **Stuarts** from James I to James VII and the series is

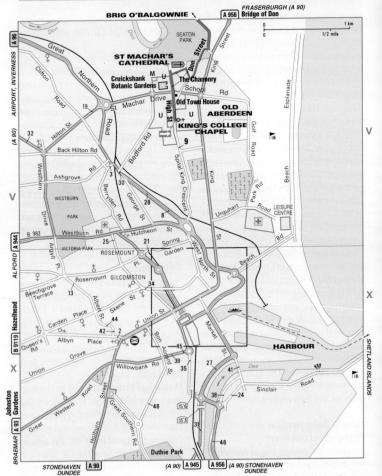

completed by the royal and Aberdeen coats of arms.

Northwards along King Street the integrated design of the various buildings was the result of collaboration between **John Smith** and **Archibald Simpson**. On the north side of Castle Street, the

19C **Town House** dominates all. Rising from behind this relatively recent façade is the tower of the 17C **Tolbooth**. Inside there is Aberdeen's **Museum of Civic History** (⏱ open year-round Tue–Sat 10am–4pm, Sun 12.30pm–3.30pm; ⏱Closed 25–26, 31 Dec, 1–2 Jan;☎01224

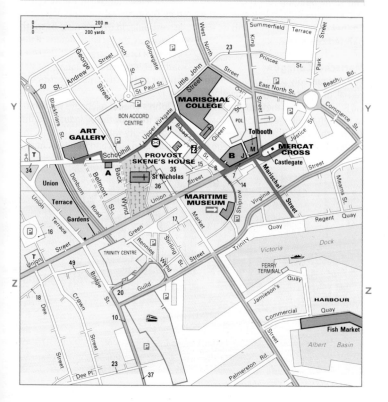

621 167; www.aberdeencity.gov.uk), with a fine model of the city as it was in 1661. Spiral stairs and cramped passageways lead to chambers and cells with lifelike figures evoking the tollbooth's ancient use as a prison. The tower is best viewed from the opposite side of Castle Street.

Provost Skene's House★

Open Mon–Sat 10am–5pm, Sun 1pm–4pm. Closed 25–26, 31 Dec, 1–2 Jan. 01224 641 086. www.aagm.co.uk.

This 17C town house is named after a wealthy merchant and one time provost of the town, **Sir George Skene** (1619–1707). His portrait by Medina hangs in the 17C bedroom. Although title deeds go as far back as 1545, the house acquired its present form under the ownership of Skene.

Following restoration in the 1950s, a series of tastefully furnished period rooms were created. Original features include plasterwork ceilings (Cromwellian, Restoration and 17C bedroom), panelling (1732, Regency) and stone flagging (Georgian Dining Room). Outstanding, however, is the **Chapel** or Painted Gallery with its 16C **painted ceiling**★★.

Marischal College★

The undoubtedly striking, but controversial, granite façade (1905) overlooking Broad Street was the latest extension to Marischal College. In 1593 George Keith, 5th Earl Marischal (*see DUNNOTTAR CASTLE*) founded a college in the buildings of Greyfriars Monastery, appropriated following the Reformation. Marischal was to be the counterpart of King's – older by a century – and for over two and a half centuries the two universities coexisted, a situation unique in Britain.

At the far end of the quadrangle and reached by a splendid stairway, are the halls of the **Marischal Museum** (*open year-round Mon–Fri 10am–5pm, Sun 2pm–5pm; 01224 274 301; www.abdn.ac.uk/marischal_museum*). The displays relating to the history and prehistory of Northeast Scotland are complemented by the University's fine ethnographical collections, recently arranged and reinterpreted.

St Nicholas Kirk

Enter from Correction Wynd and the south transept. Open May–Sept, Mon–Fri noon–4pm, Sat 1–3pm; Sun 9.30am–1pm. 01224 643 494. www.kirk-of-st-nicholas.org.uk.

The once vast medieval burgh church was divided into two at the Reformation. The medieval transepts now serve as vestibule. In Drum's Aisle or south transept are the reclining figures of the Irvines of Drum Castle (*see DEESIDE*) and a tablet to Edward Raban, master printer to the city and universities in the 17C.

St John's Chapel celebrates the contribution made by the oil industry to the life of the city with striking contemporary stained glass and furniture. At the

Detail of the Heraldic Coat of Arms, Marischal College

P. Tomkins/ Scottish Viewpoint/ Visit Scotland

far end in Collison's Aisle is the effigy of Provost Davidson who fell at Harlaw (ℹ️*see INVERURIE: Excursions*).

West Church

The church was rebuilt c. 1752 by the Aberdonian architect, **James Gibbs** (1682–1754), the designer of St Martin-in-the-Fields, London. commission. The interior has dark oak pews and galleries with a splendid canopied "Council Loft".

East Church

🔒*Closed following an archaeological dig; see website for re-opening details. There is a viewing window.*
Originally designed by Archibald Simpson (1835–37), the church was restored by William Smith after fire damage in 1875. Steps lead to the restored 15C **St Mary's Chapel**. The transepts are also 15C. The central roof boss depicts the legend of St Nicholas.The Gothic spire (1876) has a carillon of 48 bells and is occasionally used for concerts.

James Dun's House

This late-18C house takes its name from its builder James Dun (1708–89). He was the rector of the Old Grammar School which stood nearby and was attended by Byron.

Art Gallery★★

♿🕐*Open year-round daily 10am–5pm (Sun from 2pm).* 🕐*Closed 25–26 & 31 Dec, 1–2 Jan.* 🍴.☎*01224 523 700. www.aagm. co.uk.*
The permanent collection, in pleasant well-lit surroundings, has a strong emphasis on contemporary art, work by the Impressionists and the Scottish Colourists.
The sculpture court and adjoining rooms contain the larger works of sculpture, while additional pieces are also on display throughout the first floor rooms. Foreign sculptors (Degas, Rodin and Zadkine) and British artists (Hepworth, Moore and Butler) are represented by a variety of techniques and materials.

▶ *At the top of the stairs turn left to visit the rooms in numerical order, 1 to 6.*

City Art Gallery sculptures

The painting section on the first floor has a well represented **Scottish collection. William McTaggart** (1835–1910) provided a turning point on the 19C Scottish scene, when he broke with the grandeur of the Romantics and commercial sentimentalism of the *genre* artists in his search for realism. Inspired by nature, his works are notable for their clarity and vitality culminating in his own personal "impressionist" style (*A Ground Swell*-1). Other works in Room 1 include those of the versatile William Dyce (1806–64), another Aberdonian with an international outlook. Dyce's *Ferryman* and Titian's *First Essay in Colour* are first and foremost figure compositions with the landscape playing a secondary role. They also show his care for detail and naturalism in outdoor scenes, as does *A Scene in Arran* where the figures are reduced to a minor role while the treatment of landscape anticipates the Pre-Raphaelites.

The **MacDonald Collection**★★ of British artists' portraits in Room 2 numbers 92, many of which are self-portraits. This unique series is a highly revealing survey of the art world in the 19C. It includes the patron himself, Alexander MacDonald.

Room 3 presents some of the earliest Scottish portraitists, including a self-portrait by Aberdeen's own **George Jamesone** (1588–1644), *Mrs Janet Shairp* by Allan Ramsay (1713–84) who excelled in his delicate treatment of women, and works by Raeburn (1756–1823), portraitist to George IV.

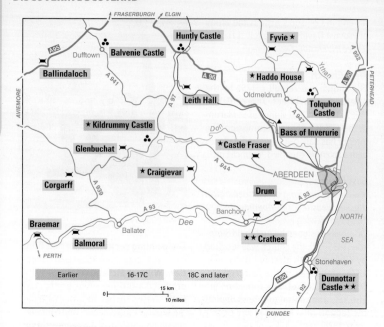

A selection of works by the French Impressionists is displayed among the 19C foreign works in Room 4, while an array of mostly British prints and water-colours are hung in the dim light of Room 5. The 20C British paintings hung in Room 6 and on the balcony include works by Paul Nash, Stanley Spencer, Ben Nicholson, Peploe, William McTaggart, and Joan Eardley.

Additional Sights

Parks and Gardens

Known as The Flower of Scotland, the city has been many times winner of the Britain in Bloom competition, and Aberdeen's parks and gardens are justly worthy of a mention. Take the time to visit at least one, be it **Union Terrace Gardens** (off Union Street) with their celebrated floral displays including Aberdeen's coat of arms, the unrivalled Winter Gardens in **Duthie Park**, the Rose Garden, the delightful **Johnston Gardens** and the university's **Cruickshank Botanic Gardens**. At **Hazlehead Park** (Kids ⏱open 8am–1hr before dusk; ⬥£1.40; ☎01224 814773; www.aberdeencity.gov.uk) you can explore the oldest **Maze** in Scotland. A pets'

corner, crazy golf and putting green are attached.

Excursions

Deeside★★ – 𝒸See DEESIDE.

Grampian Castles★★

The map (𝒸see above) shows those castles described elsewhere in the guide. All are easily reached from Aberdeen. In addition to these there are other castles which are open to the public by appointment only. Enquire locally for further details.

Aberdeen's hinterland is rich in castles with examples from all periods.

These range from the earliest Norman motte and bailey to the formidable strongholds (Kildrummy) which were the centres of government in the troubled Middle Ages. The golden age of castle building (16C–17C) is well represented. In this far from rich area, stability engendered prosperity and encouraged lairds to build castles worthy of their newly acquired status or wealth. A flourishing native school produced the baronial style. Master masons skilfully worked the local stone creating a native tradition unparalleled elsewhere.

ABERDOUR ★
FIFE
POPULATION 1,460

Aberdour, a small resort on the Fife shore of the Forth estuary, is famous for its castle and silver sands, which make it a popular destination for day trips from Edinburgh or as a base from which to explore the Forth Valley.

- **Information:** 1 High Street, Dunfermline. ☎01383 720999. www.standrews.co.uk.
- ▶ **Orient Yourself:** Aberdour is 7.5 mi/12km east of the Forth Bridges on the A921.
- 🕐 **Organizing Your Time:** Allow a full day in summer.
- **Also See:** SOUTH QUEENSFERRY (FORTH BRIDGES), DUNFERMLINE.

Aberdour Castle 30min

(HS). Open Apr–Sept, daily 9.30am–5.30pm; Oct–Mar, Sat–Wed 9.30am–4.30pm. £4. (summer and winter weekends). ☎01383 860 519. www.historic-scotland.gov.uk.

Seat of the Earls of Morton

Initially granted by **Robert the Bruce** to his nephew, Thomas Randolph, Earl of Moray c. 1325, it passed to William Douglas in 1342 who also acquired the lands of Dalkeith (see DALKEITH). The latter became the principal seat of this branch of the Douglas family. James, 4th Lord Dalkeith was created Earl of Morton prior to his marriage with James I's daughter, Joanna.

Regent Morton, James Douglas, 4th Earl of Morton (1516–81), inherited Aberdour in 1548. This Scottish lord, who played an active part in the overthrow of Mary, Queen of Scots, is remembered for his iron rule as Regent (1572–78) during James VI's minority when he achieved peace in a time of religious strife. Forced to resign the regency in 1578 he was tried, convicted and beheaded in 1581 for complicity in the murder of Darnley 14 years earlier.

William, 6th Earl (d. 1648) and Lord Treasurer of Scotland, was obliged to sell the lands of Dalkeith in 1642 and in consequence Aberdour became the principal Morton family seat. Extensions and improvements followed. By 1725 the castle was abandoned in favour of nearby Aberdour House.

Buildings

Today the castle consists of the original 14C west **tower**, which was rebuilt in its upper part in the 15C. A rectangular extension was added in the 16C to the southeast. This is distinguished by Renaissance decoration on the windows overlooking the courtyard. The internal layout was innovative in that a corridor served the rooms on both levels. The L-shaped extension to the east was built for William, 6th Earl and contained a picture gallery on the first floor. In accordance with the fashion of the time this was in all probability panelled with a painted timber ceiling.

Gardens

To the east is the **walled garden** which was once a typical 17C formal garden. It became a bowling green and its lawn is now fringed with herbaceous borders. The pediment over the kirk lane entrance displays the monogram of the 6th Earl and his wife and the date 1632.

The sloping ground to the south of the castle was once laid out as formal terraces, with a dovecot and orchard beyond. The late-16C terrace gardens have been reinstated. It is interesting to note that two of the family's near relations in the late-16C/early-17C included the owners of other famous gardens, namely Edzell (see EDZELL CASTLE) and Glamis (see GLAMIS CASTLE).

Silver Sands

The large sandy beach is a popular recreation spot for watersports and walks.

ABERFELDY★
PERTHSHIRE AND KINROSS
POPULATION 1,477

The small Perthshire town of Aberfeldy, pleasantly set in Strath Tay, was immortalised by Burns, who advised: *"Come let us spend the lichtsome days, In the birks of Aberfeldy"* and the deep pools and majestic waterfalls of the **Birks** (birches), just outside the town, remain one of its most popular attractions.

- **Information:** The Square. ☎0188 782 0276. www.perthshire.co.uk.
- ▶ **Orient Yourself:** Aberfeldy is 10 mi/16km off the main A9 road heading north from Perth. Take the A827 west at Ballinluig
- **Don't Miss:** The Water Mill, Dewar's World of Whisky distillery tour.
- **Also See:** BLAIR CASTLE, PITLOCHRY, LOCH TAY.

Sights

The Water Mill
🕐*Open year-round daily, 10am–5pm (Sun noon–5pm).* 🕐*Closed 25–26 Dec, 1 Jan.* ☎01887 822 896. www.aberfeldywatermill.com.
in the centre of the town the Watermill brings together the largest bookshop in the rural Highlands, a contemporary art gallery, music and coffee shop set in an impressive former early-19C watermill. Water from the Birks is led through a 1,500ft/500m tunnel to power the big overshot water-wheel of the restored mill. Inside, atmospheric rumblings and creakings accompany the grinding of oats.

General Wade's Bridge
This elegant five-arched bridge was built by Wade to carry his military road north from Crieff to Dalwhinnie.

Black Watch Monument
The kilted figure, dressed in a uniform of the time, commemorates the formation of the Black Watch Regiment in 1739 and marks the site of the first parade.

Dewar's World of Whisky
🕐 *Open Apr–Oct, Mon–Sat 10am–6pm, Sun noon–4pm. Nov–Mar Mon–Sat 10am–4pm. Last admission 1 hr before closing. Note during Oct–Nov maintenance work may mean there is no distillery tour.* £5 standard tour and Brand Centre. ☎01887 822 010. www.dewars wow.com.

Just on the edge of town is distilled one of Scotland's most famous drinks brands. The tour does a good job of explaining the process and the Brand Centre tells you the history of Dewar's. And of course there is a tasting session, which may be upgraded to include sampling superior whiskies.

Excursions

Castle Menzies
1.5mi/2.5km to the west. Leave by B 846 crossing General Wade's Bridge. Take the second entrance. 🕐*Open 1 Apr (or Easter) to mid-Oct, daily, 10.30am–5pm (from 2pm Sun). £4.50. ☎01887 820 982. www.menzies.org/castle.*
This 16C Z-plan castle, which has been repeatedly besieged, was the chief seat of the Menzies (pronounced "Mingus") until some 80 years ago when the main line died out. There are two fine plaster-work ceilings.

St Mary's Church
2mi/3km northeast of Aberfeldy, sign-posted off the A 827. Take the farm road up to Pitcairn Farm. Electric time switch; handboards available. Call the tourist office for opening times.
The 16C church, a low unassuming whitewashed edifice, stands behind the farm buildings. Inside is an extraordinary 17C **painted ceiling**★. The elaborate design includes heraldic devices of local Stewarts and colourful Biblical scenes.

ALFORD ★
ABERDEENSHIRE
POPULATION 861

This market town is set in the **Howe of Alford**, a rich arable basin encircled by hills, notably the Correen Hills to the northwest and Bennachie to the northeast.

- **Information:** Railway Museum, Station Yard. ☎019755 62052.
- **Orient Yourself:** Alford lies 28 mi/45km west of Aberdeen on the A944.
- **Don't Miss:** the March of the Men of Lonarch, on Games Day (August) in Bellabeg in Upper Donside.
- **Also See:** ABERDEEN, CRATHES, DEESIDE, INVERURIE.

Sights

Grampian Transport Museum
Beside the main car park. ○*Open late-Mar–Oct, 10am–5pm (Oct 4pm).* ✆£5.50. ♿☎*01975 562 292. www.gtm.org.uk.*
The main collection evokes the transport (cars, cycles and carriages) history of the North East amid a variety of side exhibits. Look out for the "sociable safety cycle", which was anything but safe, and The Craigievar Express, a local postman's 19C steam tricycle. There is a fine collection of Scottish-built cars.

Alford Valley Railway Museum
○*Open Jun Mon–Fri 10.30am–2.30pm, Sat–Sun 1–4.30pm; Jul–Aug daily 1–4.30pm. May and Sept, Sat–Sun 1–4.30pm.* ✆£2.50. *Trains run Easter/Apr–Sept every half-hour, see website for schedule.* ☎*019755 62292 (museum).* ♿☎*07879 293934 (trains). www.alfordvalley railway.org.uk.*
The station houses a small museum describing the arrival of the railway. The Alford Valley Railway operates diesel locomotives along a 2 mi/3km stretch of track to Haughton Country Park.

Excursion

Craigievar Castle★
5mi/8km south. ○*closed during 2008 for conservation work. Grounds open daily.*
This attractive 17C tower house is a fine example of baronial architecture.

Driving Tour

Upper Donside
28mi/45km from Alford to Corgarff.
This tour follows the Don Valley through the changing scenery of its upper reaches.

- *Leave Alford by the A 944 which follows the river closely to break through the hill rim. Turn left to take the A 97, Tomintoul road.*

In the grounds of Kildrummy Castle Hotel an attractive **alpine garden** has been laid out in a former quarry.

Kildrummy Castle★ –
○*See KILDRUMMY CASTLE.*

Five miles further on is Glenbuchat Castle, in a strategic site commanding both the Don and Water of Buchat Valleys.

Highland Gathering

On Games Day in August the tiny village of Bellabeg in Upper Donside is the scene of a 160-year-old tradition, the **March of the Men of Lonach**. The Men of Lonach, traditionally Forbeses and Wallaces, resplendently attired in full Highland dress with pikes aloft, march proudly through the strath to the scene of the Gathering in the park at Bellabeg. Traditional games, pipe music and dance create a lively atmosphere.

ARBROATH ★
ANGUS
POPULATION 23,934

Known as the "auld red town" because of the distinctive stonework of its close-packed fishing quarter, Arbroath is famous for the lovely ruins of its Abbey Church and for its cured herrings. Expansive shoreline parklands and promenades recall the town's mid-century aspirations as a seaside resort.

- **Information:** Market Place. ☎01241 872 609.
- **Orient Yourself:** Arbroath is 17.5mi/28km north east of Dundee on the A92.
- **Don't Miss:** Sampling Arbroath "smokies", tasty hot-cured herrings which can be eaten hot or cold, best from M&M Spink's at 10 Marketgate; a clifftop walk.
- **Especially for Kids:** The town's long sandy beaches.
- **Also See:** DUNDEE, GLAMIS, MONTROSE.

Abbey ★

(*HS*). ○*Open year-round daily, 9.30am–5.30pm (4.30pm Oct–Mar).* ☞*£4.50.* ☎*01 241 878 756, www.historic-scotland.gov.uk.*
William the Lion (1143-1214) founded a priory here in 1178 in memory of his childhood friend Thomas à Becket, murdered in Canterbury Cathedral eight years previously. By 1233 the building was finished and in 1285 the establishment was accorded abbey status and

was colonised by Tironensian monks from Kelso (☞*see KELSO*).
The abbey's most historic moment was the drawing up and signing of the **Declaration of Arbroath** on 6 April 1320 during the Wars of Independence.
A wealthy and influential establishment the abbey flourished untilthe early 17C. Thereafter neglect led to decay and today it is a romantic ruin.
A visitor centre provides an insight into the abbey's history and an exhibition on the Declaration is within the Abbey.

ISLE OF ARRAN ★★
NORTH AYRSHIRE
POPULATION 4,726

Arran, the largest of the Clyde islands, with an area of 165sq mi/427 sq km, measures 20mi/32km long and 10mi/16km wide. "Scotland in miniature", the island is cut in two by the Highland Boundary Fault. The mountainous northern part, with Goat Fell (2,866ft/874m) the highest peak, has deep valleys and moorland while the southern half has more typically Lowland scenery. Around the coast, sheltered sandy bays, rugged cliffs and small creeks alternate. Protected by the arm of the Kintyre Peninsula, the island has a particularly mild climate.

- **Information:** The Pier, Brodick. ☎0845 225 512. www.ayrshire-arran.com.
- **Orient Yourself:** Ardrossan ferry to Brodick ☎01294 463470. www.calmac.co.uk.
- **Drivers :** Make sure the petrol tank is full before setting out on an island tour as there are few filling stations.
- **Don't Miss:** Brodick Castle rhododendron garden in bloom (late spring).
- **Organizing Your Time:** Allow at least one full day to look around (☞*see suggested Driving Tour*) and spend a night at Brodick.
- **Especially for Kids:** Sandy beaches.
- **Also See:** AYR, GLASGOW

S. Richard/ Britainonview.com

Isle of Arran

A Bit of History

Prehistory – The heritage of prehistoric times is particularly rich with the island set on the main migration route up the western seaboard. The long cairn collective tombs of the Neolithic agriculturalists, standing stone circles of the Bronze Age (Machrie Moor) and forts of the Iron Age are all to be found on Arran.

Arran today – The economy is essentially based on agriculture with large sheep runs on the moorland areas and arable farming or dairying restricted to the improved areas of valleys and coastal fringes. Forestry is on the increase on the east coast but the main industry is undoubtedly tourism, exploiting the isle's natural assets: its scenic beauty and its changelessness. Facilities for the visitor include golf, cycle and boat hiring, pony trekking, rock climbing, hill and ridge walking, fishing, sea angling, yachting, water skiing and fine sandy beaches with safe bathing.

Brodick Castle★★ 45min

(NTS). &.(ᐧ)Castle: open Easter–Oct, daily 11am–4pm (Oct 3pm). (ᐧ)Country Park open: year-round, daily 9.30am–sunset ☜£10 (includes garden). ⓟ£2. ☕. ☎0844 4932152, www.nts.org.uk.

As you approach the isle by steamer one of the first things you can pick out against the towering backdrop of Goat Fell is the red sandstone mass of Brodick Castle, overlooking the bay. In a grand yet homely setting are displayed fine silver, porcelain and painting collections, the heirlooms of Hamilton generations. Added to this are the splendours and beauty of an outstanding rhododendron garden.

Castle

A stronghold from earliest times, the castle soon became royal and from 1503 Hamilton property, when the 2nd Lord Hamilton inherited the earldom of Arran. Following the 2nd Duke's death at Worcester (1652), Cromwellian troops occupied the castle and extended it westwards. In 1844, a further extension, complete with a four-storey tower, all in the baronial style, was made by the ageing Gillespie Graham (1776–1855).

Interior

In the Hall and first floor staircase landing we meet many of those responsible for the Brodick seen today. Busts portray William the IIth Duke and Princess Marie of Baden who decided to make Brodick their home and for whom Gillespie designed the 19C extensions and decorations, and their son the 12th Duke, gambler, racing man and collector of the many sporting

Address Book

&For coin ranges, see the Legend on the cover flap.

WHERE TO STAY

⊜⊜**Dunvegan House** – *Shore Road, Brodick.* ☎*01770 302 811. www.dunveganhouse.co.uk. 9 rooms.* This attractive guesthouse is located on the seafront with fine views over the bay. Guests can enjoy the lawned garden and comfortable lounge.

⊜⊜**Lilybank** – *Shore Road, Lamlash.* ☎*01770 600 230. www.lilybank-arran.co.uk. 7 rooms.* This whitewashed cottage on the bayfront looks onto Holy Island. Rooms are modern but cosy.

⊜⊜–⊜⊜⊜**Royal Arran** – *Shore Road, Whiting Bay.* ☎*01770 700 286. www.royalarran.co.uk.* This traditional Victorian sandstone building has been tastefully refurbished. Each bedroom has its own distinctive character. A comfortable lounge with open fire and an elegant dining room offer stunning views of Whiting Bay and Holy Isle.

⊜⊜⊜⊜**Kilmichael Country House** – *Glen Cloy, near Brodick.* ☎*01770 302 219. www.kilmichael.com. 5 rooms, 2 suites.* The oldest dwelling on Arran, this elegant Mansion House offers luxury with character. Set in delightful tranquil countryside, all rooms are individually styled with antique funishings; there is an award-winning restaurant (⊜⊜⊜) and self-catering cottages.

items. Portraits on the landing show the 10th Duke and his Duchess, Susan Beckford, who assembled many of the exquisite treasures now on display. The first and more intimate suite of rooms was that of the Duchess of Montrose, heiress of the 12th Duke, who made it her life's work to preserve the house and its collections which are now in the care of the National Trust for Scotland. The dressing room provides the setting for the fan collection, two lovely 18C marquetry pieces, one Dutch and one English (Boudoir), and Gainsborough landscape sketches (Boudoir).

The Boudoir Landing introduces the Beckford link, with William Beckford portrayed on his deathbed (Willes Maddox) and a Turner watercolour of his home Fonthill Abbey. David Teniers' *The Temptations of St Anthony*, to the left of the cabinet, well rewards a careful study. The cabinet itself is a treasure trove of exquisite art objects: ivories, porcelain, glass.

In the **Drawing-Room** the richness of the gilded heraldic ceiling matches that of the contents. Notable paintings include two small Watteaus, a Clouet portrait and the late Duchess of Montrose by de Laszlo. A pair of goose tureens, masterpieces of late-18C Chinese art (Chien Lung), graces the 18C Italian commodes between the windows. On display in the two following rooms, part of the Cromwellian extension, are many sporting pictures and items from Brodick's magnificent silver collection.

Gardens

The slope down to Brodick Bay is the setting for another of Brodick's gems, justly of international repute, the two beautiful gardens. Firstly comes the colour and formality of the 1710 walled garden, then beyond, the 65-acre **woodland garden**, a creation of the late Duchess and her son-in-law, and now considered one of the finest **rhododendron** gardens of its kind (*main display April to mid-June*).

The gardens form part of Brodick Country Park which provides many facilitie including waymarked trails, guided hill walks and an adventure playground. On a sunny day the Park is ideal for a picnic.

Driving Tour of the Isle

56mi/90km – allow half a day.

The visit can be done in either direction or in two trips by taking the String Road between Brodick and Blackwater-

foot to cut across the waist of the island (10mi/16km).

This mainly coastal route gives a good view of the island and its diversity of scenery, from the moors, glens and mountains of the north to the more pastoral landscapes and rocky cliff coastline of the south.

Brodick

Population 884. With its sandy beach and many hotels and boarding houses, this is the isle's largest resort and the port of call for the ferry.

Rosaburn Heritage Museum

1mi/1.5km out of Brodick on the Lochranza road. ○*Open mid-March/Easter–late Oct, daily 10.30am–4.30pm.* ⊜*£3; garden and cafe only, 50p.* ▭. ☎*01770 302 636. www. arranmuseum.co.uk.*

Visit the blacksmith's shop, milk house, and cottage furnished in late-19C and early-20C styles, alongside an exhibition area with displays of local social history, geology and archeology.

Paths lead to the castle (*1mi/1.5km*) and Goat Fell (*3mi/5km*).

▸ *Take the Lochranza road (right).*

Brodick Castle★★

Entrance for visitors with cars. Walkers should take the path indicated above. ⟳*See main entry above for description of the castle.*

Corrie

Population 188. This former fishing hamlet consisting of a line of whitewashed cottages makes a convenient starting point for ridge walkers and mountaineers.

Sannox Bay

Another sheltered sandy stretch.

The road moves inland, up Glen Sannox climbing to higher, bleaker moorland scenery in the shadow of the surrounding peaks and crests. Once over the watershed, the road drops steeply towards Lochranza.

Lochranza

Population 283. Once an active herring-fishing village and port of call for the Clyde steamers, this rather scattered community has several holiday homes. The island was once famous for its whisky, and in 1995 the **Arran Distillery** (○*Visitor Centre: open mid-Mar–Oct, 10am (Sun 11am)–6pm; Nov–Feb 10am–4pm Mon, Wed, Fri, Sat.* ☞*Tours: mid-Mar–Oct, daily 10.30am–4.30pm (Sun from 11.30am).* ⊜*£4.* ✕☎*01770 830264. www.arranwhisky.com*), became the first (legal!) whisky producers to open on the island in over 150 years. The tour finishes with the usual, complimentary "wee dram".

The roofless ruin of 16C **Lochranza Castle** (*HS;* ○*open at all reasonable times*) stands on a spit jutting out into Loch Ranza. In summer a ferry operates between Lochranza and Claonaig on the Kintyre Peninsula.

Once round the point the view extends over Kilbrannan Sound to the Kintyre coast. The road becomes more twisting but remains close to the shore. Beyond is the shingle beach of Catacol Bay. Farming country appears again in the vicinity of Dougarie.

Machrie Moor Stone Circles

1.5mi/2.4km inland off the road.

These five ruined stone circles in an impressive setting date from the Bronze Age. Their exact purpose remains unsure; sepulchral or ritualistic? Four of the five had associated short cist burials and in two cases accompanying food vessels, which have been attributed to the period 1650–1500 BC (Stonehenge c. 2800–1550 BC).

Kilmory

The creamery produces Arran Dunlop cheese. Just offshore lies Pladda with its lighthouse.

Whiting Bay

Population 352. This is another popular resort, with views to **Holy Isle,** before the road rounds to **Lamlash Bay** affording a classic view of Brodick Castle on the north shore of Brodick Bay dominated by Goat Fell.

AVIEMORE★
HIGHLAND
POPULATION 1,510

Set in the Spey valley on the western fringes of the Cairngorms (☝ see The CAIRN-GORMS), Aviemore is Scotland's premier all-year sports resort. The building of the Aviemore Centre in the mid 1960s transformed this small village, which had grown up around the railway station, into a bustling centre offering day and night entertainment and indoor and outdoor sports and pastimes. Attractions include indoor swimming pools, ice rink, watersports centre and a dry ski slope.

- **Information:** Grampian Road. ☎01479 810 636. www.cairngorms.co.uk. www.visitaviemore.com.
- ▸ **Orient Yourself:** Take bus number 31 to the mountain railway at Cairn Gorm.
- **Don't Miss:** the spectacular view (on a clear day) from the top of Cairn Gorm and a meal in their award-winning restaurant at 1079m; the Highland Wildlife Park.
- **Organizing Your Time:** Depending on how sporty you are (and, in winter, the weather conditions), you could spend several days here.
- **Especially for Kids:** Strathspey Steam Railway. Landmark Forest Theme Park. Highland Wildlife Park.
- **Also See:** LOCH NESS.

Excursion

1 Strathspey Railway [Kids]

&.⏰Steam trains operate from the main station in Aviemore (15 min single journey to Boat of Garten, 40 min to Broomhill. Time-table Jun–Sept, daily 10am–4.40pm; Apr, May and Oct, Wed, Thu, Sat, Sun; also at Christmas and New Year. See website for full schedule. ☜Return ticket (US: round trip) £10.50. Refreshments on board. ☎01479 810 725. www.strathspeyrailway.co.uk.

The sounds and smells on this 5mi/8km journey between Aviemore and Boat of Garten are evocative reminders of times not so distant.

Driving Tours

2 Southeast and North
42mi/67km.

▸ Leave Aviemore by B 970.

Panorama from Cairn Gorm★★★
– ☝See The CAIRNGORMS.

▸ Return to Coylumbridge and take B 970 to the right.

Osprey Centre (Loch Garten)

Off B 970. Access to the Royal Society for the Protection of Birds' hide within the sanctuary area is by a clearly marked path only 5min walk. The hide is equipped with binoculars and telescopes. ⏰Open Apr–Aug, 10am–6pm. Last entrance 5pm. ☜£3. ☎01479 831476. www.rspb.org.uk/reserves/guide/l.

After an absence of 40 years, the osprey returned to breed in Britain choosing a nest site by Loch Garten, within the ancient Abernethy pine forest. Operation Osprey was started to give total protection during the breeding season, and the area round the tree-top eyrie was declared a bird sanctuary. In 1975 the nesting area, and surrounding woodland, loch and moor, was declared a nature reserve with open access to visitors, and includes a Visitor Centre.

▸ Return to Boat of Garten and continue to the A 95, then branch off on the B 9153 towards Carrbridge.

Landmark Forest Theme Park [Kids]

⏰Open year-round daily 10am–6pm; (7pm mid-Jul–mid-Aug; 5pm Nov–Mar & Sept–Oct). ⏰Closed 25 Dec, 1 Jan. ☜£10.05 (adult), £7.85 child. (Nov–Easter

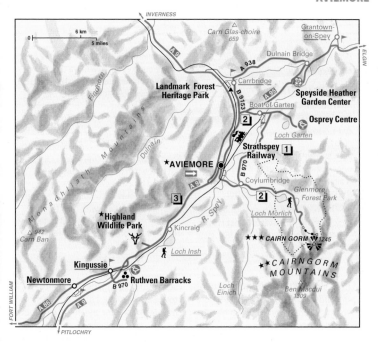

adult £3.20, child £2.35. ✖ ☲. ☏ 01479
841 613, 0800 731 3446 (freephone information line), www.landmark-centre.
co.uk.
A combination of forestry heritage
park meets modern theme park with
a tree-top trail, huge slides, a water-
coaster adventure playground and
various white-knuckle experiences
are themed to fit in with the beautiful
surroundings.

▷ Continue on the A 938 east to
Dulnain Bridge and the local road to
Skye of Curr.

Speyside Heather
Garden Centre

♿ ◷ Open year-round Mon–Sat 9am–
5.30pm, Sun 10am–5pm. ◷ Closed 25
Dec, 1 Jan ◉ Small charge for some
exhibitions. ✖. ☏ 01479 851 359. www.
heathercentre.com.
A colourful display of over 300 varieties
of heather in a beautiful setting near the
River Spey. An exhibition in the visitor
centre presents the historical and modern uses of heather: thatching, basket-
ware, wool dyeing. An art gallery and
antique shop completes the visit.

③ South 16mi/26km

▷ Leave Aviemore to the south to take
A 9 to beyond Kincraig.

Highland Wildlife Park★ ⟨Kids⟩

♿ ◷ Open daily (weather permitting in
winter) Apr–Oct 10am–5pm, Nov–Mar
10am–4pm. Last entry 1 hr before closing.
◷ Closed 25 Dec. ◉ £10 (child £7.50).
☲. ☏ 01540 651 270. www.highland
wildlifepark.org.
An initial drive-through area includes
herds of free ranging European bison,
red deer, wild horses, Soay sheep from
St Kilda, ibex (wild goat) and shaggy
Highland cattle. In the walk-about section are wild cats, badgers, polecats,
pine martens, beavers, golden eagles,
wolves, grouse and capercaillie.

▷ Take the A 9 and branch off to
Newtonmore via Kingussie.

Highland Folk Museum,
Newtownmore

♿ ◷ Open Easter–Aug, daily 10.30am–
5.30pm; Sept–Oct, daily 11am–4.30pm.
☲. ☏ 01540 661 631. www.highland
folk.com.

Address Book

For coin ranges, see the Legend on the cover flap.

WHERE TO STAY

Ardlogie Guest House. *Dalfaber Road.* ☎*01479 810 747. www.ardlogie. co.uk. 5 rooms.* This cosy guest house enjoys a quiet location with attractive light and airy bedrooms, two of which offer wonderful mountain views. There is a terrace with seating over-looking the garden and a petanque/boules pitch. Excellent value.

The Old Minister's Guest House – *Rothiemurchus.* ☎*01479 812 181. www.*
theoldministershouse.co.uk. *4 rooms.* Set on the outskirts of Aviemore this 100-year old former church minister's house enjoys fine views and has been beautifully restored with charming and bright modern-traditional guestrooms.

Corrour House – *Inverdruie.* ☎*01479 810 220. www.corrourhouse hotel.co.uk. 8 rooms.* One mile (1.6km) out of town in a bucolic setting surrounded by 4 acres of gardens and woodlands, this Victorian dower house is immaculately kept with furniture and fittings contemporary to its age. The dining room enjoys views to the Cairngorms.

Within sight of the Cairngorm Mountains, this 1 mi(1.6km)-long 80 acre (32ha) site is devoted to living history. In addition to re-located and re-created buildings and architectural features, there are working demonstrations and actors interpreting the past. It includes a township from the 1700s, an 1800s farm (reinterpreted for the 1930s) a school house, church, clockmaker's shop, tailors shop, joinery, the estate sawmill and more. A vintage bus covers the site.

AYR★
SOUTH AYRSHIRE
POPULATION 48,493

Ayr, the leading holiday resort on the Firth of Clyde coast, makes a good centre for exploring Burns country. This lively resort has a vast expanse of sandy beach backed by an esplanade, several delightful parks, traditional amusements and Scotland's premier racecourse. The latter is the venue for the Scottish Grand National (see Calendar of Events) and the Ayr Gold Cup.

- **Information:** 22 Sandgate. ☎0845 2255 121. www.ayrshire-arran.com.
- **Orient Yourself:** The town centre is a short walk from the seaside though you will need a car to visit the outlying historical attractions.
- **Don't Miss:** Alloway for its Robert Burns connection.
- **Organizing Your Time:** Allow one to two days unless you are a "Burnsophile" or a keen golfer – in which case you will want to stay longer.
- **Also See:** CULZEAN CASTLE, ISLE OF ARRAN.

A Bit of History

The town grew up around its medieval castle to become the principal centre of Carrrick, later an earldom. The original castle seems to have been obliterated by a huge new citadel built by Cromwell of which a few fragments of wall remain.

By the 16C and 17C the town was the busiest port on the west coast, just ahead of Glasgow for size.

Trade was essentially with France until the late 17C when the West Indian and North American markets opened up. The railway age brought new life to Ayr, with the holidaymakers and commuting businessmen. At the beginning of the 19C Ayr expanded in a planned way southwards from its medieval core, and the orderly rectangular street pattern and many substantial terraced houses remain from this time. There are few traces left of an older Ayr.

Today this market town with its excellent shopping centre, has a thriving tourist trade dependent on the proximity of the international airport at Prestwick, the reputation of nearby golfing centres (Turnberry, Troon) and its role as hub of Burns country.

Sights

Auld Brig

This 13C bridge, immortalised by Burns, is said to have been financed by two sisters who lost their fiancés, drowned while trying to ford the river. The narrow cobbled bridge remains firm while its rival collapsed in the storm of 1870.

Tam O'Shanter Inn

230 High Street.
A tavern in Burns' time, this is now an inn. It was from here that Tam set out on his famous ride one stormy night (◉see *Tam O'Shanter Experience, below*).

Burns Country Driving Tour

▶ *60mi. Allow at least one day. Leave Ayr south on B 7024 for 3mi/5km.*

Alloway★

Alloway is famed worldwide as the birthplace of Scotland's bard, **Robert Burns** (1759–96).

Burns Cottage and Museum★

&.◉*Open Apr–Sept, daily 10am–5.30pm; Oct–Mar, 10am–5pm.* ◉*Closed Dec 25–6, Jan 1–2.* ◎*£4 (includes Tam O'Shanter Experience).* ☎. ☎ *01292 443 700. www.burnsheritage park.com.*

This roadside cottage built by William Burns is where his eldest son Robert was born on 25 January 1759. The but, ben and byre evoke the spartan living conditions of the 18C. The museum has

a most extensive collection of Burns' manuscripts, letters, documents and other relics.

▶ *Continue along the main road.*

Tam O'Shanter Experience

◉*Times and contact details as Burns Cottage.* ◎*£2.* &.✕.

This visitor centre makes a good starting point for any excursion into Burns country. A short audio-visual presentation shows the poet in the context of his life, work and travels in Ayrshire and beyond. A longer spectacle, the Tam O'Shanter Experience itself, is an almost too vivid evocation of Tam's nightmare ride.

Robert Burns, Scottish National Portrait Gallery, Edinburgh

The Bridgeman Art Library/ Scottish National Portrait Gallery, Edinburgh

A footpath leads from the visitor centre to highly manicured gardens overlooking the 13C **Brig o'Doon**, to which Tam was chased by the "hellish legion" and where his poor Meg lost her tail. A tiny pavilion contains jolly 19C statues of Tam, Souter Johnnie and Nanse and here too is the imposing Neoclassical **Burns Monument** (○ *open Apr–Sept, daily 10am–5pm; Oct–Mar 10am–4pm*) and attached gardens.

Beyond, on the far side of the main road, stands **Alloway Kirk**, where William Burns is buried and where the hapless Tam, emboldened by "bold John Barleycorn", saw an "unco Sight! Warlocks and witches in a dance".

Kirkoswald

10.4mi detour south of Alloway by A 77 (return to Alloway afterwards).
Population 320. This village boasts the thatched and limewashed **Souter Johnnie's Cottage** (*NTS;* ⏱ ○ *open daily Good Fri–Sept, Fri–Tue 11.30am–5pm;* ⊛*£5;* ☎*0844 493214;, www.nts.org.uk*), home of the cobbler (souter), that "ancient, trusty, drouthy, cronie" of Tam O'Shanter, the central figure in Burns' poem of the same name. Burns had met the real life figures (a cobbler, John Davidson and farmer, Douglas Graham), of this rollicking narrative, during his 1775 summer stay at Kirkoswald when he came to study under the local dominie (schoolmaster-minister) Hugh Roger. In addition to the two rooms and cobbler's workshop is the original set of life-size figures by James Thom in the garden. that depict Souter Johnnie, Tam, the innkeeper and his wife.

Douglas Graham (Tam) and his wife are buried in the local churchyard.

▶ *From Alloway take Doonholm Rd, turn left onto A77, then right onto A713.*

Doon Valley

The Doon Valley southeast of Ayr has a number of evocative reminders of Ayrshire's industrial past.

Scottish Industrial Railway Centre

Dunaskin, 3.2mi southeast of Alloway on the A 713. ○ *Open first and last Sun May, last Sun Jun, all Sun in Jul–Aug, first and last Sun Sept, 11am–4.30pm.* ⊛*£2.50.* ☎*01292 269 260. www.arpg.org.uk.*
Steam locomotives hauled colliery trains in the Doon Valley into the 1970s, long after their demise elsewhere, and surviving engines are put through their paces here on summer Sundays.

▶ *Continue on A 713 to Dalmellington; left on B 741 for New Cumnock; then left on A 76; continue to Mauchline.*

Mauchline

Population 3,776. Following the death of Burns' father, the family moved to Mossgiel Farm. Mauchline was where Burns met and eventually married a local girl, Jean Armour, by whom he had nine children. On returning from his triumphant visit to Edinburgh in 1788, Burns leased an upper room in a Castle Street house, now the **Burns House Museum** (⏱○ *open Tue–Sat 10am–4pm;* ☎*01290 550 045; www.burnsscotland.com/tours/mauchline*), for Jean and his children. Wed later in the year, they all moved to Ellisland Farm (🕯 *see DUMFRIES: Excursions*). In addition to the Jean Armour Room upstairs, the museum has books, letters, documents and several personal items (including a watch and walking stick). Downstairs, a folk section includes 19C Mauchline ware and Cumnock pottery. The house next door (*now the curator's,* ⚬ *closed to the public*) was the home of Dr Mackenzie, who gave Burns a letter of introduction to Henry Mackenzie, editor of *The Lounger*, based in Edinburgh.

In the churchyard are buried four of Burns' children. On the far side of the churchyard is **Poosie Nansie's/Nanse Tinnock's Inn**, still a pub today, which figured large in his poetry of the period (*The Mauchline Lady, Mary Morrison, The Holy Fair, Holy Willie's Prayer, Address to the Deil*).

▶ *Leave Mauchline on B 743 west towards Ayr, then turn right onto B 730 for Tarbolton.*

Tarbolton

Population 2,010. During the period when Burns' father farmed nearby Lochlea Farm (1777–84), Tarbolton was a muslin and silk weavers' village. Here Robert and some friends started a debating society in 1780. The building today is known as the **Bachelors Club**. (*NTS, ⏰open Good Fri–Sept, Fri–Tue 1pm–5pm; ☎£5; ☎0844 4932146; www.nts.org.uk*). Downstairs, an early 19C kitchen adjoins the byre, while above is the hall where the debating club met. Burns' relics include his Masonic belongings.

▶ *Continue North on B 730. Return to Ayr on A 719 and A 77.*

Excursions

Prestwick
4mi/6.5km north of Ayr.
The town is known for its international airport and its top-class golf course. It was on the Prestwick course in 1860 that the very first golf open was played for a Challenge Belt. The following year the competition was declared "open to all the world" and was won by Tom Morris.

Irvine
12mi/20km N. of Ayr by A 77; then A 78.
Former royal burgh and one-time port for Glasgow, Irvine was designated as a New Town in 1996. The old town centre with its skyline of church towers is no longer connected to the railway station by a stone bridge but by a huge shopping mall.

Harbourside
Close to where the River Garnock and River Irvine merge, the quayside is approached through an innovative and picturesque housing scheme, a good neighbour to the old buildings lining the waterfront. The still-evolving **Scottish Maritime Museum**★ (⏰*open Apr–Oct, daily, 10am–5pm; ☎£3; ☐; ☎01294 278 283; www.scottishmaritimemuseum.org*) captures Scotland's maritime history in a lively manner.

BANFF★
ABERDEENSHIRE
POPULATION 3,843

Set at the mouth of the River Deveron, Banff is a distinguished small coastal town with a wealth of 18C buildings. This rich heritage dates from the time when Banff was a winter seat for wealthy local landowners. A royal burgh as early as the 12C, the town had at one time both a castle and a monastery.

- 🗐 **Information:** Collie Lodge. ☎01261 812 419.
- ▶ **Orient Yourself:** Banff lies 45mi/72km north of Aberdeen and 25mi/40km west of Fraserburgh (Scotland's north easternmost town) on the B9031.
- ☺ **Don't Miss:** Duff House for its interiors and paintings from the National Gallery of Scotland.
- ⏰ **Organizing Your Time:** Allow a long day, to include excursions.
- ☾ **Also See:** ELGIN, FRASERBURGH, FYVIE CASTLE, HADDO HOUSE.

Duff House★★ *1hr*

♿⏰*Open Apr–Oct, daily 11am–5pm; Nov–Mar, Thu–Sun 11am–4pm. ☎£5.50. ☐. ☎01261 818 181. www.duffhouse. org.uk.*
The most sophisticated country house in the northeast of Scotland, this splendid Baroque mansion was designed around 1735 by William Adam for William Duff MP, later Lord Braco and Earl of Fife. Architect and patron fell out; a prolonged lawsuit was settled only shortly before Adam's death in 1748 and an embittered Braco never took up residence. Sold by the Fifes in the early 20C, during WWII, Duff House accommodated Norwegian and Polish troops and German POWs. Resplendently restored, it now houses paintings from the Scot-

tish National Gallery, which, together with a rich array of loan furnishings and fittings, has recreated something of the atmosphere it enjoyed in its heyday.

Exterior

With its four corner towers Duff House rises dramatically from level parkland in the valley of the River Deveron just inland from its mouth between Banff and Macduff. The mansion consists of a great central block rising over a basement and entered by a double curving staircase above which Corinthian pilasters support a richly decorated pediment. Adam's proposed flanking pavilions and colonnades were never built, but the house is held in place visually by mature trees. Upstream the river emerges from a gorge whose woodlands conceal an ice house and a mausoleum ornamented with an effigy taken from St Mary's Church at Banff.

Interior

The centre of the building is occupied by the vast and sumptuous spaces of the **Vestibule** on the first floor and the **Great Drawing-Room** on the second, contrasting with the more intimate rooms to either side which served as boudoirs, bedrooms, libraries and closets. The Vestibule is dominated by William Etty's grandiose painting entitled *The Combat, Woman pleading for the Vanquished – an ideal groupe,* while the Drawing-Room is hung with a superb set of Gobelins **tapestries** as well as with a trio of *Pastorales* by Boucher. Other fine paintings in first floor rooms include an early portrait by Ramsay of *Elizabeth, Mrs Daniel Cunyngham* (Dining-Room), fragments of a large picture by Cuyp and a magnificent **El Greco** of *St Jerome in Penitence* (in Countess Agnes' Boudoir). The Great Staircase is densely hung with portraits and other pictures, but the most remarkable object here is a porphyry lion's paw and marble wine cooler mounted on a dense black block of polished Parrot coal. On the second floor, the North Drawing-Room has a number of Raeburn portraits, while the pier-glass over the mantelpiece is the sole surviving item of the house's original fittings. Another room has displays on the history of the house, while the Libraries are hung with portraits of kings of Scotland, exiled monarchs and Pretenders.

Upper and Lower Towns

Low Street

Of particular interest are the 18C Carmelite House, the only reminder of the former monastery, and the **town house** with its unusual steeple. On the plainstones in front of the house is the rare pre-Reformation **mercat cross**★.

High Shore

Numbers 1 to 5 on the left are an attractive group of 18C buildings. The doorway of no 3, with its straight-headed pediment and grotesque, contrasts with the more vernacular inn with its pend.

Boyndie Street

On the north are two examples of 18C town houses. The first Boyndie House has a date stone and curvilinear gable.

High Street

On the west side is another series, nos 47 to 41, of two-storeyed 18C buildings with, farther along on the other side, Abercrombie Tower House, an attractive rubblework mid-18C town house. At the south end are more 18C houses, nos 5 to 1 with the Old Banff Academy beyond. **Banff Museum** (🕐 *open Jun–Sept, Mon–Sat 2pm–4.30pm;* ☏ *01261 815704*) concerns itself with local matters.

Driving Tour

Fishing Villages

15mi/24km drive through farming country to former fishing villages.

▶ *Leave by the Fraserburgh road A 98; once over the Deveron, turn left to Macduff.*

Macduff

Population 3,894. Facing Banff across the river Deveron, Macduff – formerly called

Doune – was renamed in the 18C by the 1st Earl of Fife when he built the harbour. Today the town still boasts an active fishing fleet, fish market and boat building yards, owing in large part to its deep water harbour and the silting up of the Banff one. Another attraction is the open-air swimming pool at Tarlair, amid the rocks.

Gardenstown
Population 823. A winding narrow road leads down to this village which is terraced on the cliffs of the south side of Gamrie Bay. The small harbour is still the base for lobster boats.

Crovie
Population 95. On the east of Gamrie Bay, the cottages of this tiny picturesque village stand, gables on to the sea, only a path's width from the shore.
Troup Head (*no access*), with its 300ft/100m cliffs, is a prominent rocky headland. Just to the east is **Castle Point**, an exhilaratingly exposed headland, fortified and refortified since about 700BC, most recently in the 18C, when **Fort Fiddes**, was added. There are magnificent **views**★★ of Pennan, of the cliffs and headlands of this splendid coastline, and of Hell's Lum, a cleft in the cliffs leading to a sea tunnel.

Pennan
Population 92. Hairpin bends and steep gradients lead down to this attractive village of white-painted cottages with their gable ends on to the rocky shore. Pennan figures as "Ferness" in Bill Forsyth's film *Local Hero* (see Box).
For a longer excursion, from Pennan continue along the picturesque road B 9031 which runs inland before rejoining the coast at Rosehearty to Fraserburgh (see FRASERBURGH).

BANFF

Back Path	2	Gallowhill St	9
Bellevue Rd	3	Reid St	10
Boyndie St	5	Strait Path	12
Boyndie St West	6	Water Path	13
Carmelite St	7		

Abercrombie Tower House	A	No 1-5 High Street	D
Boyndie House	B	No 41-47 High Street	E
		Town House	H

Pilgrims for the 'Local Hero'

Thousands of film fans have made the "pilgrimage" to **Pennan** to have their photographs taken next to the red telephone box which feature in the film, Local Hero (1983). In fact it was a movie prop, set up because the actual phone box was not in the best position for filming. The hotel in the film was also faked, with interiors from elsewhere used. But don't let any of that put you off visiting or bringing your camera; the phone box and the hotel exterior still look very much the part!

BIGGAR ★
SOUTH LANARKSHIRE
POPULATION 1,931

This small but attractive market centre with its pleasantly wide main street serves an area of marvellously varied scenery of hills, moors, glens and farmland.

- **Information:** 155 High Street. ☎01899 221 066.
- **Orient Yourself:** Biggar is 30mi/50km south of Edinburgh on the A702.
- **Don't Miss:** Gladstone Court Museum, a reconstructed slice of Victorian life.
- **Organizing Your Time:** Allow a full day to see Biggar and Broughton.
- **Especially for Kids:** Biggar Puppet Theatre.
- **Also See:** NEW LANARK.

Sights

Gladstone Court Museum ★
North Back Road. Open Easter weekend & May–Sept, Mon–Sat 11am–4.30pm. Sun 2pm–4.30pm. £2. ☎01899 221 050. www.biggarmuseumtrust.co.uk.
This unusual museum, laid out as a shop-lined street, presents an authentic record of life a century ago. The original and entertaining presentation of various commercial premises passes from schoolroom to bank, ironmonger's to bootmaker's, photographer's studio and chemist's shop.

Greenhill Covenanting Museum ★
Open Easter weekend & May–Sept, Mon–Sat 11am–4.30pm. Sun 2pm–4.30pm. £1. ☎ 01899 221 050. www.biggarmuseumtrust.co.uk.
The displays and relics in this relocated 17C farmhouse, evoke the dark **Covenanting Times** (17C), a period of religious persecution and many deaths. The southwest with its strong Covenanting faction is rich in memories of "outed" ministers, illegal open-air conventicles, martyrs and skirmishes.

Biggar Puppet Theatre
Phone for access. Open most of year, see Web site for performance times. ☎01899 220 631. Booking essential. www.purvespuppets.com.
The old coach house of a Victorian mansion has magically metamorphosed into an enchanting puppet theatre with Punch and Judy caryatids and a star-spangled ceiling. There are shows designed to appeal to all ages, while the history of puppetry is told in the little **Puppet Museum**.

Biggar Gasworks Museum
HS. Open Jun–Sept, daily 2pm–5pm. £1. ☎ 01899 221050. www.biggarmuseumtrust.co.uk.
This unusual industrial heritage site is typical of many small town coal-gas works, common before the advent of natural gas. Today it is the only one surviving in Scotland. The oldest part of the works dates from 1839; it ceased supplying gas in 1973.

Excursion

Broughton
Population 220. 7mi/11km from Biggar by the B 7016.
Broughton is a tidy and colourful village with well tended gardens, the **Beechgrove Garden** (open all reasonable hours, "honesty box") being an outstanding example. The **John Buchan Centre**, (open Easter weekend & May–Sept, daily 2pm–5pm; £1; 01899 221050; www.biggarmuseumtrust.co.uk) in the old church, is a tribute to the author and statesman, John Buchan (1875–1940), who as lst Baron Tweedsmuir was Governor-General of Canada between 1935 and 1940, but is most famous for writing *The 39 Steps*.

(HOUSE OF) THE BINNS
WEST LOTHIAN

This 17C hilltop house with fine views to the Forth is as colourful for its architecture as for the history of its most famous owner, Tam Dalyell (pronounced Dee-yell).

- **Information:** High Street, Linlithgow. ☎01506 77 5000. www.edinburgh.org.
- ▶ **Orient Yourself:** 15mi/24km west of Edinburgh.

A Bit of History

The Jamesone portrait in the Business Room shows Thomas Dalyell, an Edinburgh butter merchant, who made his fortune in London with James VI and who on his return to Scotland in 1612 purchased this property. In 1630 he enlarged and redecorated the house. His son **Thomas Dalyell** (1615–1685), better known as **General Tam**, is the colourful family personality who dominates the house's history. A military man and staunch Royalist, on the execution of Charles I (1649) he swore never to cut his hair or beard until the monarchy was restored. Following capture at the Battle of Worcester (1651) and imprisonment in the Tower of London, Tam eventually made his way to Russia where he served the Czar in a military capacity. He gained a fearsome reputation, became known as the "Muscovy Brute", was accused of roasting his enemies in the Bake House oven at the Binns, and introducing the thumbscrews into Scotland. With Charles II's Restoration in 1660, Tam returned to command the king's forces in Scotland and proved to be an unrelenting opponent of the Covenanters, defeating their forces at Rullion Green.

Tam was also responsible for the forming of **The Royal Scots Greys**, holding the first muster at The Binns in 1681. Eventual amalgamation with the 3rd Carabiniers created the new cavalry, the Royal Scots Dragoon Guards.

The current (11th) baronet, also Tam Dalyell (b. 1932–) is a Scottish politician and was an outspoken Labour member of the House of Commons 1962–2005. He was often his own party's fiercest critic, particularly when it came to foreign conflicts and in 1978–1979 famously voted against his own government over 100 times.

Visit *1hr*

(NTS). ♿🕐Open Jun–Sept, Sat–Wed 2pm–5pm. Parkland open daily. ⊜£8. ☎0844 4932127. www.nts.org.uk

Despite successive alterations and additions, the present house retains much that dates from the 1630 reconstruction. Of particular interest are the **plasterwork ceilings**★ dated 1630 in the Drawing Room or High Hall and the King's Room. They are among the earliest examples of this kind of work in Scotland. Amid the many mementoes of General Tam, his Russian boots and sword, huge comb and 1611 "Great She Bible", there are other family and regimental souvenirs. In the Dining Room hang Allan Ramsay's well known portrait of *Christian Shairp* and a portrait of General Tam after the Restoration.

Excursion

Abercorn Parish Church
3mi/5km east of The Binns.

The old village church (refitted 1579, restored 1838) has a particularly fine example of a laird's loft. The **Hopetoun Loft**★★ is unusual in that when Sir William Bruce fitted it out in 1707–8 he included a suite of rooms comprising a retiring room with a burial vault underneath. The panelled loft, not unlike a theatre box, is decorated with Alexander Eizat's carvings and Richard Wiatt's highly colourful Hope coat of arms.

BLAIR CASTLE★★
PERTHSHIRE AND KINROSS

The white form of Blair Castle bristling with turrets, crow-stepped gables, chimneys and crenellated parapets, stands against forested slopes in a site of great strategic importance commanding a route into the Central Highlands. The castle, the family and the nation's history are closely interwoven.

▶ **Orient Yourself:** The castle is on the outskirts of Blair Atholl village 8mi/13km northwest of Pitlochry on the A9 and B8079.
◉ **Organizing Your Time:** Allow 1hr 30min.
▥ **Especially for Kids:** the formidable display of weaponry in the Entrance Hall.
◔ **Also See:** PITLOCHRY.

A Bit of History

Kingdom, earldom, dukedom – The original ancient province or kingdom of Atholl had its main stronghold at Logierait. Cumming's Tower was built on the present site in 1269 and it became the seat of the Atholl earldom, eventually dukedom, held successively by the Stewart and Murray families. The castle has been considerably altered over the years. The Murrays were given the castle in 1629. It was in the lifetime of the royalist 1st Earl that Montrose raised the king's standard at Blair (1644). This act of rebellion was paid for by a Cromwellian occupation in 1652. In the early 18C further troubles ensued as the Hanoverian 1st Duke, John Murray, had several Jacobite sons. Four members of the family raised

regiments of Athollmen in the '15 rising. In 1745 it was one of the former, **Lord George Murray** (1694–1760), an able military tactician, who became Bonnie Prince Charlie's lieutenant general and subsequently laid siege to his own home (1746). Following the '45 rising (1745), the 2nd Duke made many improvements on the estate, including the larch plantings – and transformed the castle into a Georgian mansion house. In the 19C Sir David Bryce added features in the baronial style to the castle.

Visit

♿◉*Castle: open late-Mar–late-Oct , 9.30am–4.30pm (last admission); early Nov–late Mar, Tue & Sat 9.30am–12.30pm*

Blair Castle

D. Barnes/ Scottish Viewpoint

The Atholl Highlanders

The Duke retains the only private army in the British Isles, known as the Atholl Highlanders. The 80-strong army, composed mainly of estate workers, still fulfils certain ceremonial duties. It is the sole survivor of the clan system of pre-army days, when the king relied on each chief to bring out his clan forces in order to raise an army. The annual parade is on the last Sunday in May.

(last admission). ⏱*Closed two weeks of Christmas and New Year.* 🎫*House and grounds £7.20 (£6.50, winter); grounds only, £2.30 (free, winter).* ✕. ☎*01796 481 207. www.blair-castle.co.uk.*
There are 30 rooms to see. Outstanding are the 18C interiors (enhanced by furniture of the same period), the Clayton plasterwork, family portraits, arms and porcelain collections.

Stewart Room (1)
Stewart relics, 16C and 17C furniture and portraits depicting *Mary, Queen of Scots*, her son *James VI* and her parents, *James V and Mary of Guise.*

Earl John's Room (2)
Note in particular one of four original copies of the National Covenant (1638); the 17C bed and lovely walnut chairs; and portraits.

Picture Staircase (4)
The 2nd Duke employed Thomas Clayton for over nine years on the interior decoration, during his alterations on the castle. The stucco ceiling is an example of his work. Between panels and frames of stucco decoration hang the portraits of the 2nd Duke's grandparents, *John, the 2nd Earl* as Julius Caesar (Jacob de Wet) and *Lady Amelia Stanley* (Lely).

Small Drawing-Room (5)
An elegant Georgian room with an unusual set of mahogany chairs (1756).

Tea Room (6)
Fine frieze, fireplace and overmantel and Gerard Honthorst portraits of *Elizabeth, the Winter Queen* and her son *Prince Rupert* (copies). The 18C china cabinets are Chippendale and Sheraton.

Dining-Room (7)
Pale green walls and elaborate white stucco work set off Thomas Bardwell's ceiling medallions of the *Four Seasons* and the landscapes of Atholl estate.

Blue Bedroom (9)
There is a delightful portrait of the 7th Duke's wife, the Victorian beauty *Louisa Moncrieffe,* who had six children, none of whom had an heir!

Fourth Duke's Corridor (11)
Here is the work by David Allan, painted shortly after the 1782 act ending the proscription on Highland dress, showing the *4th Duke*, resplendently attired, with his family.

Study (12)
Some of the books in the library belonged to Lord George Murray during his exile in Holland.

Derby Dressing Room (13)
The unusual wood is broom and the cabinet is by Sandeman of Perth.

Drawing-Room (16)
The crimson damask wall hangings of this sumptuous apartment, set off the all-white coved and compartmented Clayton ceiling. Above the fireplace, the Johann Zoffany conversation piece of the *3rd Duke and family* is flanked by portraits of the *4th Duke* (Hoppner). The settees and chairs are Chipchase (1783) and the pier-glasses are by George Cole.

Tullibardine Room (17)
This contains the famous portrait of *Lord George Murray* in Highland dress and other Jacobite mementoes.

Tapestry Room (18)
Set on the top floor of Cumming's Tower, this chamber is hung with Brussels tap-

The Men of Lonach

Terrace Room (25)

Exhibits include the famous 18C Doune (Highland) pistols (&see DOUNE) by gunsmiths T Cadell and Alexander Campbell. Made entirely of metal, richly engraved, they have the very characteristic ram's horn butts and fluted breech end.

Ballroom (29)

A 19C addition, the walls are decorated with arms, antlers and portraits. On display is Henry Raeburn's painting of *Neil Gow*, the legendary fiddler to the dukes.

China Room (30)

Rich collection of English, continental and oriental fine china.

Grounds

The walk via Diana's Grove and over the Banvie Burn, passing towering larches planted in the 18C, leads to the ruins of St Bride's.

The **Blair Castle Trekking Centre** set in the grounds of the Castle adjacent to the Deer Park has been operating since the 1950s and is open to all levels of rider.

estries entitled *Atalanta and Meleager*. The magnificent state bed (1700) with Spitalfields silk hangings originally came from Holyroodhouse.

BOTHWELL CASTLE ★
SOUTH LANARKSHIRE

The ruins of this outstanding fortress – once Scotland's largest and finest 13C castle – remain impressive in their commanding site high above the Clyde Valley.

- **Information:** Horsemarket, Ladyacre Road, Lanark. ☎01555 661661. www.visitscotland.com.
- **Orient Yourself:** The castle is in the village of Uddingston off the B707, 8 mi/13km south east of Glasgow.
- **Also See:** NEW LANARK.

A Bit of History

A much disputed stronghold – Built in the late 13C, the castle figured largely in the Wars of Independence. It fell into English hands in 1301 and on being retaken in 1314 after Bannockburn, it suffered its first dismantling. The castle was repaired during a second period of English occupation when Edward III made it his headquarters in 1336. By 1367 the Scots were again in command and Bothwell was again dismantled. The

castle lay in ruin until it passed by marriage to **Archibald the Grim**, the 3rd Earl of Douglas, in 1362 and he made this his chief residence. The late 14C and early 15C saw further additions.

Visit

Castle ruins

⊙*Open Apr–Sept, daily 9.30am–5.30pm; Oct–Mar, Sat–Wed 9.30am–4.30pm.*

☏£3.50. ☎01698 816894. www.historic-scotland.gov.uk.

Your first impression of this red sandstone ruin, all towers and curtain walls, will be one of sheer size, yet only part of the original 13C plan was executed.

Take the stairs in the northeast tower to reach the courtyard enclosure. At the far end, the oldest and most impressive part, the 13C circular **keep** or donjon, designed to serve as the last bastion of defence, shows "masterly design and stonework". The keep itself is protected by a moat on the courtyard side, with the drawbridge giving access to the doorway, sheltering behind a beak construction. Walled up following partial dismantling, three storeys and a fighting level rise above the basement. The tower communicates with the 13C prison tower and postern in the south curtain wall. In the southeast corner, the early-15C chapel, marked at first-floor level by two pointed windows, communicates with the other great four storey tower, also 15C. Beyond, against the east curtain wall is the **great hall** with its succession of elegant windows.

Walk around the outside to appreciate the setting, the site, the dimensions and the fine masonry of the 13C parts.

Bothwell

Population 4,840. The town grew up in the shadow of its great castle at an important bridging point on the Clyde. Bothwell developed rapidly in the 19C when it was favoured by wealthy Glasgow merchants. The choir of the parish church belongs to the collegiate church founded in 1398. A good example of the Decorated Gothic style, it has a unique stone slab roof. The 3rd Earl is said to be buried here, in front of the communion table.

A memorial beside Bothwell Bridge (north bank) commemorates the battle of 1679 when the Covenanters suffered their worst defeat. 400 were killed and 1,200 taken prisoner. Most were imprisoned for several months in inhumane conditions in Greyfriars Churchyard, Edinburgh, where many died from exposure and starvation.

Excursions

David Livingstone Centre, Blantyre

1mi/2km from Main Street via Blantyre Mill Road and a footbridge over the Clyde. ♿ ⏱*Open late Mar–Dec 24, 10am–5pm, Sun 12.30pm–5pm (last admission 1hr before closing).* ☏ *£5.* ⛾.🅿.☎01698 823 140, www.nts.org.uk.

The late-18C mill tenement, Shuttle Row, now a **David Livingstone Museum**★, vividly presents the missionary-cum-explorer, his life, work and achievements. David Livingstone (1813–73) was born in one of these single-room family homes which in their time were considered to be model accommodation. Like his father he worked in the local cotton mill, as a piecer then spinner. The young David attended evening classes locally and then medical classes at Anderson's Institution, Glasgow.

A man of strong religious beliefs, he set out as a medical missionary but soon embarked on the travels which were to make his name as an explorer. Pilkington Jackson's wood carving, *The Last Journey,* is a moving tribute to both Livingstone and his faithful African followers.

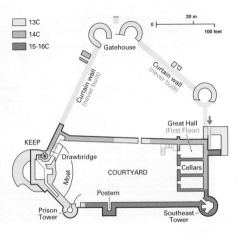

□ 13C
□ 14C
■ 15-16C

Gatehouse

Curtain wall (never built)

Curtain wall (never built)

Great Hall (First Floor)

KEEP

Drawbridge

Moat

COURTYARD

Cellars

Postern

Prison Tower

Southeast Tower

BOWHILL ★★
SCOTTISH BORDERS

On high ground between the Yarrow and Ettrick Waters, **Bowhill**, with its many treasures, is the Border home of the Scotts of Buccleuch.

- **Information:** Selkirk Glass Visitor Centre, Selkirk. ☎0870 6080404 . www.visitscotland.com
- ▶ **Orient Yourself:** The house is in the Ettrick Forest just outside Selkirk, approached by the A7, A707 and A708 (signposted). 3mi/5km west of Selkirk.

A Bit of History

The Scotts of Buccleuch

The estate was formerly part of the ancient Ettrick Forest which Robert the Bruce granted to the Douglas family in 1322. It then reverted to the Crown in 1450 for about 100 years before finally becoming the property of the Scott family. Walter Scott, the **Bold Buccleuch** of the Border raids, was knighted by Queen Elizabeth who is said to have declared: "With ten thousand such men our brethren in Scotland might shake the firmest throne in Europe". His granddaughter **Anne** married **James, Duke of Monmouth**, the eldest natural son of King Charles II and Lucy Walter. Anne retired to live in Dalkeith Palace (◐*see DALKEITH*) on the execution of her husband following his unsuccessful rebellion against James VII.

Henry, 3rd Duke, married Lady Elizabeth Montagu, heiress to Boughton, thus uniting the Scott and Montagu families and it was later in 1810, on Old Q's death, that Henry inherited the estates and titles of the Douglases of Drumlanrig (◐*see DRUMLANRIG CASTLE*) giving the present name, Montagu Douglas Scott.

Visit *1hr*

♿︎🐾*Visit house by guided tour only (1hr), Jul daily 1pm–4.30pm. Country Park: open Easter holidays; May–Jun weekends and bank hols; Jun, Sat–Thu; Jul–Aug daily; 10am–5pm.* 🍴*House and park £7; park only, £3.* ☕. ☎*01750 222 04. www.discovertheborders.co.uk/ places/85.html.*

P. Tomkins/ Scottish Viewpoint/ Visit Scotland

The luxurious furnishings in one of the rooms in Bowhill House

Entrance Hall

Added during 19C alterations, the hall is hung with portraits of four Huntsmen of the Buccleuch Hounds, whose service totals 160 years.

Gallery Hall

This rises through two storeys; the upper walls are hung with four 17C Mortlake tapestries, while an impressive array of family portraits overlooks the BQ monogrammed English carpet in the Savonnerie manner, and fine French furniture, including Aubusson-covered canapé and chairs. Most of the portraits are by the Van Dyck school although *Lady Anne Scott* is by Peter Lely. The children are William II Prince of Orange and Henrietta Mary Stuart, sister of Charles II.

Scott Room

This houses a collection of portraits and mementoes of Sir Walter Scott. They include Henry Raeburn's (1808) *Sir Walter Scott and Camp* with Hermitage Castle in the background, and David Wilkie's *King George IV* in Highland dress; the king's state visit to Scotland in 1822 was stage-managed by Scott and started the vogue for Highland dress. Scott mementoes include the manuscript of *The Lay of the Last Minstrel*, which was dedicated to Harriet, the 4th Duke's wife. Other items recall the poet James Hogg, "the Ettrick Shepherd", a friend of both Scott and the Duke.

Monmouth Room

This room was built as the chapel but now contains a variety of Monmouth relics including his Dutch cradle, saddlery as Master of the Horse, execution shirt and coral teething ring. The young Monmouth is portrayed with the last-mentioned, in a painting by Mytens. The wall opposite the doorway is hung with Lely's majestic portrait of *Monmouth* wearing the robes of a Knight of the Garter, and Kneller's fine family group.

Italian Room

Originally the billiard room, it was renamed after the Italian masterpieces, including scenes of his native Venice by Francesco Guardi. There are two delightful 18C Dutch marquetry tables. The clock (c. 1780) plays Scottish tunes.

Dining-Room

The highlight of this handsome room, in both proportion and detail, is the collection of paintings, in particular the family portraits. On either side of the fireplace are two enchanting portraits by Reynolds of "**Winter**", Lady Caroline Scott, and her brother Charles, Earl of Dalkeith, "**The Pink Boy**". Also included in the array are the children's parents: the *3rd Duke of Buccleuch* by Gainsborough, his wife, *Elizabeth Montagu* by Reynolds, and her mother, *Mary Duchess of Montagu* again by Gainsborough.

Drawing Room

Resplendently rich under an attractively patterned ceiling and cornice highlighted with gold are the red carpet, red silk brocade wall hangings (now faded to pink) and Aubusson-covered chairs and settees by the greatest French craftsmen. The paintings include landscapes by Vernet (18C) and Ruysdael (17C). There are fine pieces of French **furniture**: a table with Sèvres plaques, side tables with red tortoiseshell and brass inlay, parquetry and ormolu commodes. Between the two Boulle glazed cabinets with Sèvres and Meissen porcelain, is Reynolds' appealing portrait of *Elizabeth*, the Montagu heiress with her daughter Lady Mary Scott, and various family pets. Between the Claude landscapes is an early Kneller portrait. The highlight is the only **Leonardo da Vinci** in a private collection, *The Madonna with the Yarn-Winder*.

Library

The centrepiece is the white marble **fireplace** emblazoned with an A, for Duchess Anne, originally from Dalkeith Palace, with her portrait by William Wissing.

Primrose Room

An impressive **collection of miniatures** includes works by such masters as Samuel Cooper, John Hoskins, Laurence and Nicholas Hilliard and Peter and Isaac Oliver.

BRECHIN
ANGUS
POPULATION 7,674

On the banks of the River South Esk, this small cathedral city developed around its original Celtic monastery at a convenient fording point. The city is known for its Round Tower and cathedral.

- **Information:** Brechin Castle Centre, Haughmuir ☎01356 626813. www.brechincastlecentre.co.uk.
- ▶ **Orient Yourself:** Brechin is 26.5mi/43km Northeast of Dundee on the A935.
- **Don't Miss:** the Round Tower and Aberlemno Stones respectively.
- **Especially for Kids**: Brechin Castle Centre Country Park & Pictavia.
- **Also See:** EDZELL CASTLE, MONTROSE.

Sights

Round Tower★
View the tower from the churchyard.
This Round Tower is one of only two of the Irish type in Scotland and dates from c 1000. The 106-ft/34-m structure (the spire is 14C) was originally free standing and may well have served as a belfry, look-out and place of refuge. The narrow **doorway** 6ft/2m above the ground is noteworthy for its carvings..

Cathedral
🕐*Open year-round daily 9am–5pm.* ☎01356 629360. www.brechincathedral. org.uk.
Although the present church had its beginnings in the 13C it has been much altered since. The west doorway is, however, a good example of 13C work. The square tower alongside is 13C-15C. Inside, there are two early **sculptured stones** (St Mary Stone – north wall of chancel arch, and Aldbar Stone – west end of south aisle), both good examples of Pictish art. The hogback tomb is probably 11C. The stained glass is by such 20C masters as Douglas Strachan (War Memorial Window), Herbert Hendrie, Gordon Webster and William Wilson.

Brechin Castle Centre Country Park & Pictavia   Kids
♿🕐*Country Park: open Easter to mid-Oct, Mon–Sat 9am–6pm, Sun 10am–6pm. Mid-Oct to Easter Mon–Fri 9am–5pm, Sat 9am–6pm, Sun 10am–6pm. In summer Pictavia opens 30min later/closes 30min earlier than above times; winter open weekends only: Sat 9am–5pm, Sun 10am–5pm.* ☜*Country Park £3 (adult, Pictavia £3.25 (adult); child £1.50/£2.25.* ✕. ☎01356 626813 (Country Park) or ☎01356 626 241 (Pictavia). www.brechincastle centre.co.uk. www.pictavia.org.uk.*
Inside the visitor centre Pictavia is a lively exhibition which tells the story of Scotland's ancient Pictish tribes, the warrior people who roamed this region nearly two thousand years ago.
The centre is also gateway to a 65-acre country park, including a lake, children's play areas, a miniature railway, nature trails, wetland area and model farm with tame and friendly animals, plus display of vintage farm implements.

Excursions

Aberlemno Stones★
6mi/10km to the southwest. Leave Brechin by the Forfar road (A 935) and once past the castle gates turn sharp left to take the B 9134. The stones are boarded up in winter.
The gently climbing road offers splendid views northwards over Strathmore and the winding South Esk, away to the ramparts of the Highland rim.
The village of Aberlemno has four **Pictish sculptured stones**★ (🕐*see Introduction: Arts and Culture*) dating from the 7C–9C AD. Of the roadside stones, the one nearest to the village hall bears a cross with flanking angels and on the reverse, a hunting scene with Pictish

symbols. Other examples of these enigmatic symbols are discernible on the roadside face of the eastern stone. A road to the left leads to the churchyard with its **stone**★, another outstanding example of this Dark Age art form. On one side a cross with intricate interlacing is flanked by intertwined beasts while on the second, a battle scene evolves.

Driving Tour

Cairn o'Mount Road ★

31mi/50km from Brechin to Banchory. Allow 1hr for the drive, excluding visits.

This scenic route follows one of the most popular passages over the hills to Deeside. Livestock drovers, whisky smugglers, Royalty and their armies have all marched this way. Macbeth fled north to his final defeat and Edward I negotiated it twice.

▶ *Leave Brechin by the B 9667 to join the A 94, (Aberdeen road) then turn left almost immediately to Edzell.*

Edzell Castle – ⓒ*See EDZELL CASTLE.*

▶ *Follow the Fettercairn road (B 966) out of Edzell, and once across the River North Esk turn left.*

Glen Esk ★

Go up the valley to reach the **Glenesk Museum** at The Retreat (♿ⓒ*open Jul–Oct, daily noon–6pm; late-Mar–Jun, Sat–Sun. ⬩£2. ⬩. ☎01356 648 070. www.angusglens.co.uk*). This folk museum gives a fascinating account of the close-knit life in the glen and is locally famous for its tearoom. The road continues up to just before the ruin of Invermark Castle, a Lindsay stronghold.

▶ *Continue along the foothills to Fettercairn.*

Fettercairn

Population 312. This red-sandstone village with picturesque square has a certain charm; its imposing arch commemorates Queen Victoria's 1861 visit.

▶ *Take the Cairn o'Mount road and continue round the foothills.*

Shortly after passing the Fasque Estate (closed to the public), away to the right, a green mound is all that remains of Kincardine Castle, once a royal residence. The foothills were part of the King's Deer Park.

The road then follows a glen up to the Clatterin Brig. Keep left to climb rapidly through moorland to the **Cairn o'Mount** (1,488ft/454m). From near the top there is a splendid **view**★★.

The road then descends to Deeside through hills, and forested countryside with several narrow bridges, over the Water of Dye with some steep gradients to negotiate.

▶ *Cross the Water of Feugh at the village of Strachan (pronounced Struan); then right to follow B 974 to Banchory.*

Bridge of Feugh – ⓒ*See DEESIDE.*

▶ *Cross the Dee to reach Banchory.*

White Caterthun

5mi/8km northwest. Leave Brechin to the north towards Menmuir.

Two Iron Age hill forts stand either side of the road. The **White Caterthun** (*400yd/about 400m by a grassy track to the left*) is the nearer and better. Two massive ruined stone walls enclose a 2-acre site on the hill top.

After photo E. Sevo/ MICHELIN

Pictish Symbol Stone, Aberlemno

Caerlaverock Castle

CAERLAVEROCK CASTLE ★
DUMFRIES AND GALLOWAY
9MI/14KM SOUTHEAST OF DUMFRIES

The substantial handsome ruins of Caerlaverock (Lark's nest in Gaelic) is girt by a moat and earthen ramparts and stands in a green and pleasant setting on the north shore of the Solway Firth. Still formidable from the outside this medieval fortress has an inner façade of great refinement and charm and is an early example of the Scottish Renaissance style.

- **Information:** 64 Whitesands, Dumfries. ☎01387 245555. www.visitdumfriesandgalloway.co.uk.
- **Especially for Kids:** Adventure playground.
- **Also See:** DUMFRIES, SWEETHEART ABBEY.

Castle

♿ 🕐 *Open Apr–Sept, daily 9.30am–5.30pm. Oct–Mar, daily 9.30am–4.30pm.* 🎫£5. ☕ *(summer daily, winter Fri–Sun).* ☎*01387 770244. www.historic-scotland.gov.uk.*

The present castle on the site was built in the late 13C (1290–1300). The defences were soon put to the test by Edward I's famous siege of 1300. By then it was the principal seat of the Maxwells, and alterations were made in the following centuries, the most important being the Renaissance façade of 1634, the work of the Philosopher Ist Earl of Nithsdale. Following a Protestant attack during the Covenanting Wars, the castle

was abandoned for Terregles and then Traquair (♿*see TRAQUAIR HOUSE*) and subsequently fell into disrepair.

Triangular in shape, the great keep **gatehouse** stands impressively at the apex with tall curtain walls receding to towers at the farther extremities, all with 15C machicolations. Inside the courtyard, the splendid **Renaissance façade**★★ of the Nithsdale Building (1634) shows both a symmetry of design and refinement of execution. The main elements, triangular or semicircular window and door pediments, are enriched with heraldic or mythological carvings.

An exhibition area features siege warfare, recalling the castle's violent past.

THE CAIRNGORMS★★
HIGHLAND AND MORAY
🌢LOCAL MAP SEE AVIEMORE

This granitic mountain range between the Spey Valley and Braemar is an area of wild and dramatic scenery. It lies mainly above 3,000ft/1,000m and the highest point is Ben Macdui (4,296ft/1,309m) although three other peaks top the 4,000ft/1,200m mark, including Cairn Gorm (4,084ft/1,245m). The summits have been planed down by glacial erosion to form flat plateaux while glaciers have gouged the trough of Loch Avon and the River Dee. The mountain mass is split in a north-south direction by the great cleft of the Lairig Ghru, continued by the Dee Valley. Braeriach is the main feature to the west of this divide with Ben Macdui, Scotland's second highest peak to the east.

- **Information:** National Park Authority, Grantown-on Spey. ☎01479 873 535. www.cairngorms.co.uk. www.visitcairngorms.com.
- ▶ **Orient Yourself:** Aviemore (🌢see AVIEMORE) is the base for sports enthusiasts and for most outdoor activities. The Mountain Railway means anyone can approach the summit of this impressive massif.
- 👁 **Don't Miss:** the spectacular view (on a clear day) from the top of Cairn Gorm.
- 👁 **Walkers and climbers:** It is essential to obey the mountain code and always leave a note of route and expected time of return with someone responsible. Proper clothing and mountain equipment are vital.
- 🕐 **Organizing Your Time:** Depending on how sporty you are (and, in winter, the weather conditions), you could easily spend several days here.
- Kids **Especially for Kids:** the Cairngorm Reindeer Centre.

Flora and Fauna

The severe climate of these high-altitude plateaux and summits, so often windswept, allows only an Arctic-Alpine flora to flourish. Lichen, heather and moss serve as background to the brilliant splashes of colour provided by the starry saxifrage and moss campion. These windswept tracts are the domain of such elusive creatures as the snow bunting, dotterel and ptarmigan. The objectives of the **Cairngorms National Nature Reserve**, designated in 1954, are to protect the scientific, scenic and wilderness values of its 64,000 acres.

A female reindeer, Rangifer tarandus, and her calf on Glen More, part of the Cairngorms National Park in the Highlands of Scotland

The **Cairngorm Reindeer Centre** (Kids) is located close to the Forestry Commission's visitor centre in the Glenmore Forest Park. The centre has an exhibition and paddocks with a small number of deer (*Easter to early Jan*), but most visitors make the short journey out into the wild to where a guide takes them to the only reindeer herd in Britain which ranges freely in the open. The deer are very friendly and can be stroked and hand-fed. &⊙*Exhibition and paddocks: open early Feb–early Jan (weather permitting);* ←*guided tour available daily 11am, also 2.30pm, May–Sept and 3.30pm, Mon–Fri, Jul–Aug;* ⊙ *Paddock only, £2.50 adult, £1.50 child; Tour (includes exhibition and paddocks) £8 adult, £6 child;* ⊙*wear warm and waterproof clothing and sturdy footwear;* ☎*01479 861 228; www.reindeer-company.demon.co.uk.*

Mountaineering and walking

No roads suitable for motor vehicles traverse these wild and awesome mountains and their very remoteness makes them all the more attractive to the mountaineer or hillwalker. To the inexperienced and ill-equipped, however, they are treacherous owing to rapid weather changes bringing conditions which are sometimes Arctic in severity. If you are planning your own itinerary, get a copy of the Scottish Mountaineering Club's *Climber's Guide to the Cairngorms*. &*See PLANNING YOUR TRIP.*

Skiing

The northern and western slopes of Cairn Gorm (&*see opposite*) provide Scotland's top ski area. The ski slopes are within easy reach of all Spey Valley towns and villages. The main access road passes Loch Morlich before dividing to serve the two distinct skiing corries, Coire Cas and Coire na Ciste. Chair-lifts and ski tows transport the skiers to the various ski runs ranging from easy to difficult. There is also skiing off the Lecht Road on the eastern side of the Cairngorms.

Panorama from Cairn Gorm★★★

For the non-hillwalker or skier, the funicular **Cairngorm Mountain Railway** (&⊙*operates early Dec–early or mid-Nov, daily 10am–5.30pm (last train departs around 4pm–4.30pm, times vary by season; trains run every 15–20 min:* ⊙*Funicular and exhibition £8.75;* ✗; ☎*01479 861 261; www.cairngorm mountain.org.uk)* is an ideal way of discovering the area's austere beauty.

The railway transports visitors to two levels. The first is Base Station, with a Mountain Garden. The Ptarmigan Top Station, nestled just below the summit of Cairn Gorm includes a shop, a bar, the excellent Ptarmigan restaurant and a mountain exhibition. Allow 2 hours for your full visit including transport.

The already excellent view from the car park unfolds further as the train climbs. At the terminal, at 3,600ft/1,100m, there is an extensive **view**★★★ westwards of the Spey Valley. A path leads up another 500ft/150m to the summit of **Cairn Gorm** (4,084ft/1,245m) which affords a wonderful **panorama**★★★ in all directions well beyond the Cairngorm mountains.

The Big Grey Man

The slopes and corries of **Ben Macdui** are a wild primeval place and legends of a strange presence had long been known when, in 1899, Professor Normal Collie, an acclaimed climber, confirmed he, too, had felt the presence of the Big Grey Man. "I was returning from the summit in a mist when I began to think I heard something else than merely the noise of my own footsteps. Every few steps I took I heard a crunch, as if someone was walking after me but taking steps three or four times the length of my own. As I walked on and the eerie crunch, crunch sounded behind me I was seized with terror and took to my heels. Whatever you make of it I do not know, but there is something very queer about the top of Ben MacDhui and will not go back there again by myself I know."

CALLANDER ★
STIRLING
POPULATION 2,286

Known to millions of older television viewers as the Tannochbrae of *Dr Finlay's Casebook*, Callander is a busy summer resort on the banks of the River Teith. Astride one of the principal routes into the Highlands, the town was built on Drummond lands confiscated after the 18C Jacobite risings. Its popularity has grown ever since, owing in large part to its proximity to the Trossachs.

- **Information:** Ancaster Square. ☎08707 200 628. www.incallander.co.uk.
- **Don't Miss:** Venturing out into the Trossachs countryside.
- **Organizing Your Time:** Callander is an excellent base for exploring the Trossachs which can easily occupy 2–3 days.
- **Especially for Kids:** Hamilton Toy Collection.
- **Also See:** THE TROSSACHS, DOUNE, DUNBLANE.

Sights

Hamilton Toy Collection   Kids
11 Main Street. ♿ ⏲*Open Easter–Oct, Mon–Sat 10am–4.30pm, Sun noon–4.30pm.* ☞*£2; child £0.50p.* ☎*01877 330004. www.thehamiltontoycollection. co.uk.*

This charming small museum-cum-shop takes parents (and grandparents) back to their childhood days, while children are fascinated to see the things that were fashionable then.

Excursions

The Trossachs ★★★
⚲*See The TROSSACHS.*

Rob Roy Country
Leave Callander by A 84 following the above itinerary. Turn left at Kingshouse. Inverlochlarig is 11.5mi/18km from the main road. The road is single track with passing places.

The valley, the home ground of Rob Roy, provides a pleasant change from the bustle of the main road. The scenery is wilder but less dramatic.

Balquhidder
The railed enclosure in the churchyard marks the last resting place of Rob Roy MacGregor (⚲*see Box*), his wife Helen, and two of their sons.

Loch Voil
This peaceful stretch of water is overlooked to the north by the rounded outlines of the Braes of Balquhidder and Ben More (3,852ft/1,174m) with lower forest-clad slopes to the south.

Inverlochlarig
At the road end, one mile above the head of Loch Doine, is the site of Rob Roy's house, where he died. Rob moved here from Glen Gyle, the latter being too near for comfort to the recently established garrison at Inversnaid. This is the departure point for several hill walks with paths leading north to Glen Dochart, Ben More and west to Glen Falloch.

Rob Roy

Often referred to as Scotland's Robin Hood, Rob Roy MacGregor (1671–1734), – unlike his English counterpart – was a real person, born at Glengyle, at the head of Loch Katrine. A respected cattleman, he fell foul of the law through no fault of his own and his land and house were seized by the Crown. First Daniel Defoe, in *Highland Rogue* (1723), then Sir Walter Scott's famous *Rob Roy* (1818) embellished his exploits and gave birth to a legend, revived most recently in the eponymous 1995 movie starring Liam Neeson. A short film on Rob Roy is shown in the visitor centre (☞*£1.50; £1 off peak*).

CASTLE DOUGLAS
DUMFRIES AND GALLOWAY
POPULATION 3,546

Spaciously laid out to the north of Carlingwark Loch, this inland market town with its important auction mart serves the local farming industry. The settlement assumed its present name and gridiron street plan in the late 18C. It was named after a local merchant, Sir William Douglas (1745–1809) who, with the fortune he had made in the West Indies, bought local estates and established a cotton industry in the town.

🛈 **Information:** Markethill Car Park. ☎01556 502 611.
www.visitdumfriesandgalloway.co.uk.

▶ **Orient Yourself:** 18mi/29km Southwest of Dumfries on the A75.

⏱ **Also See:** DUMFRIES.

Carlingwark Loch

Beside the town, this lovely lake, dotted with islands, is a perfect place for a picnic or birdwatching. In summer there are boats for hire and you can even learn to sail (enquire at the tourist office).

Threave Garden and Castle Driving Tour

2mi/about 3km.

▶ *Leave Castle Douglas to the southwest by B 736.*

Threave Garden★★
(NTS). ♿⏱*Walled garden and glasshouses: open year-round daily 9:30am–5pm (Fri 4.30pm). Visitor Centre: open Easter–Oct, daily 9.30am–5.30pm; Feb–Easter & Nov–Dec 23, daily 10am–4pm. House: open Easter–Oct, Wed–Fri & Sun, 11am–3.30pm.* ☜*£10, garden only, £6.* ✗.
☎*01556 502 575. www.nts.org.uk.*
The estate comprises four farms, 120 acres of woodland, a mansion and 65 acres belonging to the house. Opened in 1960, the Threave School of Gardening welcomes eight students annually for a two-year course on all aspects of theoretical and practical gardening. The Victorian mansion serves as a school and the 65-acre garden has evolved from the students' work.

Beautifully kept, the garden, with its rich variety of flowers, plants, shrubs and trees, is a sheer delight with something for everyone. The main sections are roses (*June and July*), peat, rock, heather gardens, herbaceous borders, walled garden, glasshouses, patio, arboretum and woodland walk which boasts a mass of daffodils in April.

▶ *Back on the main road and 0.5mi/1km further on, a farm road to the right leads to the car park.*

Threave Castle★
10min walk from car park; ring the bell for ferry. (HS). ⏱*Open Apr–Sept, daily 9.30am–4.30pm (last outward sailing); Oct, Sat–Wed 9.30am–3.30pm (last outward sailing).* ☜*£4 (inc ferry).* ☎*07711 223101. www.historic-scotland.gov.uk.*
Ruined but still impressively grim on its island site in the Dee, Threave Castle is a symbol of the turbulence and insecurity which reigned in medieval Scotland. This tower house was the stronghold of that most powerful and noble house, the **Black Douglases**. Rising four storeys above its cellars, it was built in the late 14C by **Archibald the Grim**, 3rd Earl of Douglas (1330–1400). As part of a campaign against the Douglas ascendancy, James II besieged the castle in 1455. Additional defences – the outer wall and towers – were built following Flodden in 1513. The castle was dismantled in 1640 when it fell into the hands of the Covenanters.

CASTLE FRASER★
ABERDEENSHIRE
&LOCAL MAP SEE ABERDEEN – GRAMPIAN CASTLES

Castle Fraser, the grandest of Midmar Castles, is a typical product of that period of castle building (1560–1636) when native genius reached its apogee.

- **Information:** 23 Union Street, Aberdeen. ☎0124 288 828. www.agtb.org.
- **Orient Yourself:** 19mi/30km north west of Aberdeen on the A96 and B994.
- **Organizing Your Time:** Allow a couple of hours to visit the castle and to take a waymarked walk in the grounds
- **Especially for Kids:** Children's woodland play area with wigwam, bamboo snake walk and giant xylophone.
- **Also See:** ABERDEEN, ALFORD, DRUM CASTLE

Visit 45min

(NTS). Open Jul–Aug, daily 11am–5pm; Easter–Jun & Sept , Wed–Sun (from noon, Sept); bank holiday weekends, also open Mon. Last admission 45min before closing) £8. ☎ 01330 833 463. www.nts.org.uk.

Exterior★★
The glory of Castle Fraser, reminiscent of a French Chateau, lies in its elevations. Here, bare lower walls contrast with the flourish of decorative detail at roof level while harling sets off the sculptured granite work. As you approach from the car park, the layout of this largest and most elaborate of Scottish castles built on the Z plan design, becomes apparent. The **central block**, distinguished by a magnificent heraldic achievement, is adjoined by towers, one round and one square (Michael Tower) at diagonally opposite corners. The two-storey service wings, flanking the courtyard, serve to emphasise the height of the main buildings.

Above the stepped and highly decorative corbelling, a variety of traditional features – turrets, conical roofs, crow-stepped gables, chimney stacks, decorative dormers and gargoyles – is deployed to achieve a harmonious composition. The lantern and balustrade are essentially Renaissance features but the decorative effect as a whole is Scotland's unique contribution to Renaissance architecture.

- Pass round to the main entrance on the south side.

Interior
The visit is arranged to include those rooms which have been restored. Of particular note are the **Great Hall** and the suite of rooms in the Round Tower reserved for the laird's family. The rooftop balustraded area (101 steps) affords an excellent **view** of the surrounding farmland and of the walled garden, and in the distance the **Bennachie hills** (&see Box, below).

Mons Graupius
Rising to a height of 1,733ft (528m), **Bennachie** is the best known and most climbed hill range in northeast Scotland. Although there are no fewer than nine peaks, Mither Tap is the most prominent with the remnants of both a prehistoric and a pictish fort. It is though that Bennachie is the site of the Battle of Mons Graupius, fought in 84 AD when the Romans defeated the Picts. To explore this theme further visit the **Archaeolink Prehistory Park**, (open Easter–Oct, 11am–5pm; £5.50; ☎01464 851500; www.archaeolink.co.uk) which traces 10,000 years of local history from the Mesolithic age to a Roman Marching Camp, with indoor and outdoor exhibitions, hands-on activities, workshops and guided tours.

CAWDOR CASTLE ★
HIGHLAND

Cawdor is the title that Shakespeare's witches promised to Macbeth and the castle is reputed to be the place where Duncan was murdered. The Thanes of Cawdor built the castle, and lived in it from the late 14C.

- **Information:** Castle Wynd/Bridge Street, Inverness. ☎01463 234 353. www.visithighlands.com.
- **Orient Yourself:** 14mi/22km east of Inverness.
- **Also See:** INVERNESS.

A Bit of History

The Scottish Play

William Shakespeare wrote *The Tragedie of Macbeth* in 1606. Its narrative of witches, prophesy, treason, execution and murder were topics that fascinated King James VI of Scotland. This opportunity was not lost on the Bard, who put the finishing touches to his script in time for a special royal performance at Hampton Court that summer to entertain the King. The history books tell us tha Macbeth did indeed slay King Duncan, but as Cawdor Castle was not built until the late 14C, and Macbeth was born c 1005 then it is impossible for Duncan to have lost any blood or Lady Macbeth much sleep in this particular castle!

Visit

Open daily May–mid-Oct, 10am–5.30pm (last admission 5pm). £7.90. ☎01667 404 615. www.cawdorcastle.com.

Exterior

The approach to the castle from the drawbridge side gives a view of the central tower which is the 14C keep with the 17C wings to the right. Later additions and transformations created the fairytale like castle of today.

Interior

In the Drawing Room, the original great hall, Francis Cote's **portrait of Pryse Campbell**, 18th Thane of Cawdor, shows him resplendently attired in an assortment of tartans. This ardent Jacobite defied all by having himself portrayed thus in 1762, during the period of Proscription of Highland dress. The painting also helps to prove that the idea of one clan, one sett (pattern) was in reality a concept of the 19C. Emma Hamilton, a friend of John 1st Lord Cawdor and his wife, is portrayed by Romney.

The **Tapestry Bedroom** is so named after the set of 17C Flemish tapestries depicting events from the life of Noah. The imposing 17C Venetian four-poster retains its original velvet hangings. The Yellow Room is a good example of Jacobean design. The centre window of the Tower Sitting Room was the original, and only, entrance to the castle in the 14C, served by removable wooden steps. The fine set of 17C Bruges tapestries is after designs by Rubens on the theme of the house's thorn tree legend. The **Thorn Tree Room** is a vaulted chamber, where the remains of a holly tree have been carbon dated back to 1372. By legend it is the original marker for the site of the castle and is also an ancient pagan symbol to ward off evil.

Antwerp tapestries grace the front stairs while the Dining-Room has English panels (c. 1690) showing scenes from Cervantes' *Don Quixote* and a most unusual carved stone fireplace.

The walled **garden, flower garden and wild gardens** are well worth a visit as is the **Big Wood** which is particularly lovely in spring. Red deer occasionally enter the wood.

CRATHES CASTLE★★
ABERDEENSHIRE
♿ LOCAL MAP SEE ABERDEEN – GRAMPIAN CASTLES

The 16C tower house of Crathes Castle is an impressive example of the traditional architectural style enhanced by a series of delightful gardens. The interiors include some outstanding painted ceilings and some particularly fine early vernacular furniture. The castle is the ideal place to see the home and lifestyle of a 16C–17C Scottish laird.

- **Information:** Bridge Street, Banchory. ☎01330 822000.
- ▸ **Orient Yourself:** Crathes Castle lies 16mi/26km south west of Aberdeen on the A 93.
- **Parking:** Pay and display £2.
- **Organizing Your Time:** Allow 1 hour for the castle, at least 30 minutes for the gardens. Try to visit the gardens in June to see the famous June Border.
- **Especially for Kids:** Play area.
- **Also See:** ABERDEEN, DEESIDE, DRUM CASTLE.

Castle★★

(NTS). ♿Garden and park year-round daily 9am–dusk. Castle: open Easter–Sept, 10.30am–5.30pm; Oct, 10.30am–4.30pm; Nov–March: Wed–Sun 10.30am–3.45pm. Last admission 45min before closing. ♿Castle: closed Christmas and New Year holidays. ☎£10 castle and gardens, £8 garden only. ✕. ☕. ☎0844 4932 166. www.nts.org.uk.

Exterior
The roof line is enhanced by a variety and quality of decorative detail – spot the many gargoyles – making it one of the best examples of the local baronial style. Also note the series of coats of arms.

Interior
The tour starts with three vaulted kitchen chambers where family documents are on display and passes by the prison hole and the **yett**, now remounted outside. The construction is typically Scottish with an ingenious system of interwoven bars reversed in diagonally opposite corners giving great strength to the yett.

Upstairs, the barrel-vaulted **High Hall** has armorial paintings on the window embrasures and three unusual stone pendants. Above the fireplace is the family's most prized heirloom, the deli-cate **Horn of Leys**, the original token to tenure (1322) given by Robert the Bruce. The motif is found throughout the castle. The family **portraits** by George Jamesone (1588–1644) include the most well-known family member, Bishop Burnett, author of A History of My Own Times and adviser to William of Orange. Note on the great marriage chest the portraits of Alexander, 12th laird, and his wife.

In the **Laird's Bedroom** is the outstanding oak bed (1594), resplendent with the carved heads of Alexander and Katherine, their heraldic devices and colourful crewel work. The highlight of the **Room of the Nine Nobles** is the lovely **painted ceiling** (1602). As was usual, the composition was drawn in black and then colourfully filled in. This bright and lively form of decoration was common on the east coast, no doubt influenced by trading contacts with Scandinavia where similar techniques flourished. Plasterwork ceilings superseded this form of decoration. The Crathes examples are some of the best in existence (restored). The figures of the Nine Nobles (Hector, Alexander the Great, Julius Caesar, Joshua, David, Judas Maccabeus, King Arthur, Charlemagne and Godfrey de Bouillon) are portrayed on the ceiling boards with Biblical quotations on the sides of the beams. In view of the foreignness of their costumes it is

National Trust for Scotland

Painted ceiling (detail), Green Lady's Room

supposed that they were copied from a continental source, as were the garden sculptures at Edzell (*see EDZELL CAS-TLE*). Beside the 1641 inlaid bed with its colourful crewel work hangings are two lovely carved chairs dated 1597 with the initials of Alexander and Katherine.

The **Green Lady's Room**, which is said to be a haunted chamber, has another ornate ceiling where the figures (ceiling boards) and decorative patterns (underside of beams) bear no relation to the maxims and Biblical quotations (sides of beams). Stairs again lead upwards.

The **Long Gallery**, running the entire width of the house, is unique for its oak-panelled roof decorated with armorials and the horn motif. Documents illustrate the 600 years of family history. The gardens may be admired from this good vantage point.

Proceed to the **Muses Room** which boasts another vividly painted ceiling showing the nine muses and Seven Virtues. The tapestry is a William Morris commission (1881). Look for the mouse trademark on the stool by Robert Thompson (1876–1955).

Gardens★★★

Full of variety and beauty, the gardens at Crathes were the lifetime achievement of the late Sir James and Lady Burnett. The whole is composed of a series of distinct and separate gardens where the visitor is lured on by yet another secluded enclosure beyond. The shape, colour, design and fragrance defy description but here the expert gardener and amateur alike will be enthralled by the display. The yew hedges dating from 1702 separate the **Pool Garden** (yellows, reds and purples) from the formal **Fountain** (blues) and **Rose Gardens**. In the lower area a double herbaceous border separates the Camel and Trough Gardens with, beyond, the White and June borders and a Golden Garden as a memorial to Lady Burnett.

Woodland walks offer the chance to discover the natural life of the Crathes estate. Well signposted, they start from the shop and vary in length fom 1mi to 5mi (1.6km to 8km).

The Royal Deeside Railway

Inugurated in 1845 the Royal Deeside Railway was one of the region's most scenic railway lines and for many years was used by members of the Royal Family en-route to Balmoral Castle. It became uneconomical however and closed in 1966 and its tracks were taken up. Recently a group of enthusiasts have relaid part of the line and a service now runs a short way towards Banchory. Next door to the castle a visitor centre (*open Easter–Oct, Sat–Sun*; www.deeside-railway.co.uk), housed in two railway carriages shows the railway in historical times as well as detailing the plans and progress made by the present-day volunteers.

CRIEFF ★
PERTHSHIRE AND KINROSS
POPULATION 6,800

The pleasant spa resort of Crieff is well situated on a hillside overlooking the fertile sweep of Strathearn. On the Highland rim, with fine scenery all around, it makes an ideal touring centre.

- **Information:** Town Hall. ☎01764 652 578.
- ▶ **Orient Yourself:** Crieff lies 18mi/28.5km west of Perth on the A85.
- **Don't Miss:** The Crieff Highland Gathering; Drummond Castle Gardens; Tullibardine Chapel.
- ◷ **Organizing Your Time:** Allow 2–3 hours in Crieff, longer for excursions.
- **Also See:** PERTH.

A Bit of History

At a convergence point of routes from the north, Crieff was (prior to 1770), a centre of the cattle trade and one of the great cattle trysts. The town's 7C cross dates from the period when the town was known as Drummond. Burnt down by the Jacobites after the 1715 rising, it was rebuilt by the Crown Commissioners and by the end of the 18C it was a minor resort. The railway arrived in 1856 and by the late 19C Crieff Hydro was flourishing. The face of Crieff today testifies to its Victorian popularity as a spa.

The **Crieff Highland Gathering** (*see Introduction: Calendar of Events*) with the official Scottish Heavyweight Championship is always a popular event.

Sights

Crieff Visitor Centre

Muthill Road. ♿ ◷Open year-round 9am–5pm; factory and pottery Mon–Fri only.✕. ☎01764 654 014.

In addition to offering an introduction to the area the Visitor Centre is also the home of Caithness Glass (*www.caithnessglass.co.uk*) who produce beautiful handmade paperweights, crystal and arty studio pieces. A visitor's gallery lets you see the whole production process. On a smaller scale is Crieff Pottery where again you can watch a master craftsman at work.

Across the road is the factory shop of another glass-maker, Stuart Crystal.

Glenturret Distillery (Famous Grouse Experience)

0.25mi/400m outside Crieff on the Comrie road, A 85. ♿ Visit by guided tour only, Jan–Feb, 10am–4.30pm (first tour 10.30am, last tour 3pm). Mar–Dec, 9am–6pm (first tour 9.30am, last tour 4.30pm. ◷Closed Dec 25–26 & 1 Jan. Finest Tour (warehouse, inc 1 dram). Distillery Tour (inc 1 dram). Experience Tour £7.75 (inc 2 drams); Malt Tasting Tour £10.95 (inc 5 drams). No tours Jan except Finest Tour. ✕. ☎01764 656 565. www.famousgrouse.co.uk.

On the banks of the Turret, the Glenturret distillery, established in 1775 (making it the oldest in Scotland), still employs traditional methods, and is the most visited distillery in Scotland. A wide choice of tours, quite literally, caters for all tastes.

Excursions

Drummond Castle Gardens ★

2mi/3km south of Crieff. ◷Open Easter weekend & May–Oct, 1pm–6pm (last admission 5pm). £4. ☎01764 681 257. www.drummondcastlegardens.co.uk.

The Drummond family seat, consisting of a 1491 tower and later buildings, is set high on a rocky eminence. Laid out below in a series of terraces, the **formal gardens** are in the form of St Andrew's Cross. Against the background of lawns and gravel areas, boxwood hedging and the many shaped and pruned trees and bushes present a medley of greens and shapes and detailed patterns.

Strathearn Driving Tour★

15mi/24km round tour. Take the Dunblane road out of Crieff, on the A 822.

Drummond Castle Gardens★ –
See previous page.

Muthill

Population 595. This Strathearn village, destroyed in 1715 after the Battle of Sheriffmuir, is dominated by its 70ft/21m high 12C **tower**, one of a group in the area. The saddlebacked and crowstepped tower is now embedded in the west end of the ruined 15C church.

▶ *Continuing on the main A 822 road, cross the Machany Water, before branching left to take the A 823. Signposts indicate Tullibardine Chapel to the left.*

Tullibardine Chapel★
(HS) ◷*Open summer only.*
www.historic-scotland.gov.uk.
This attractive red sandstone church stands on its own in the middle of rich agricultural land, sheltered by a couple of gnarled and windswept trees. It was founded in 1446, enlarged c. 1500 and it has survived unaltered ever since.

▶ *Return to the A 823, at the road junction turn left to take the A 824 in the direction of Auchterarder.*

Nearby, standing in spacious grounds, is the famous **Gleneagles Hotel**, a name synonymous with gracious living and championship golf.

▶ *Return to Crieff.*

CROMARTY★
HIGHLAND
POPULATION 865

Dramatically sited on the northern tip of the Black Isle – which is actually a peninsular – where the narrow mouth of the Cromarty Firth is guarded by the twin heights known as the Sutors, the tiny port of Cromarty has been described as "the jewel in the crown of Scottish (18C–19C) vernacular architecture".

- **Information:** Castle Wynd/Bridge Street, Inverness. ☎01463 234 353. www.visithighlands.com.
- ▶ **Orient Yourself:** Cromarty lies 23mi/37km north of Inverness on the A832.
- ◷ **Organizing Your Time:** Allow at least a day; try to stay overnight to appreciate the peace of Cromarty.
- **Also See:** INVERNESS.

A Bit of History

Cromarty was a 13C Royal Burgh, but owes much of its present appearance and allure to its development in the late 18C by Sir George Ross, who encouraged a high standard of building and rebuilding, improved the harbour, and established industries, including a ropeworks (now housing) and a brewery (now a university study centre). Once used by royal pilgrims to the shrine at Tain, the ferry across the deep water of the Firth still operates, but since the building of the railway and the improvement of roads, Cromarty no longer lies on the main route north; little more than a village, it seems content with its tranquillity and its present status as a popular holiday backwater. Once a haven for the Royal Navy, Cromarty Firth has become a base for the rigs used in the offshore oil industry.

Sights

Hugh Miller Museum & Birthplace Cottage

🕐 (NTS). Easter–Oct, daily 1pm–5pm (Oct Sun–Wed). £5. 🅿. ☎01381 600 245. www.nts.org.uk.

Cromarty's most famous son, **Hugh Miller** (1802–56) was a mason turned writer and geologist. His birthplace, a thatched cottage with crow-step gables, is now a museum, with a collection of geological specimens (including some outstanding fossils) and personal souvenirs.

Cromarty Courthouse

🕐 Open Easter weekends and Apr–Oct 10am–5pm, rest of the year by appointment. £3.50. ☎013 81 600 418. www.cromarty-courthouse.org.uk.

Built by Sir George Ross in 1773, the courthouse is a splendid five-bay structure dominated by an octagonal clock tower. The interior gives a good account of local history, while courtroom scenes are brought to life by talking figures.

Groam House Museum

Rosemarkle. 🕐Open May–Sept Mon–Sat 10am–5pm, Sun 2pm–4.30pm. Oct–Apr Sat & Sun 2pm–4pm. ☎01381 620961. www.groamhouse.org.uk.

The Black Isle has a concentration of prehistoric and Pictish sites and Groam house displays 15 intricately carved Pictish standing stones including the famous Rosemarkie Cross Slab.

The exhibition is focussed on 15 intricately carved Pictish stones. All the stones originated in Rosemarkie, some dating back to the 8C, when it was an important centre of early Christianity.

Ecoventures

🕐Trips depart Cromarty Harbour up to three times daily, weather permitting. Call for sailing times. £20. ☎01381 600 323 www.ecoventures.co.uk.

High speed RIBs (rigid inflatable boats) scoot out to visit the most northerly colony of Bottlenose Dolphins in the world, one of only two resident populations (around 130 in total) in the UK.

CULROSS★★

FIFE

POPULATION 460

Culross (pronounced Cu' ross) is an attractive small Scottish burgh of the 16C and 17C on the north shore of the Firth of Forth. A programme of restoration has ensured the preservation of its essential charm, a wealth of Scottish vernacular architecture.

- **Information:** 1 High Street, Dunfermline. ☎01383 720 999. www.visitfife.com.
- **Orient Yourself:** Culross is located 15mi/24km W of Edinburgh city centre off the A985.
- **Don't Miss:** The atmospheric Palace, which is, in fact, not at all palatial!
- **Organizing Your Time:** Allow 2–3 hours to see everything
- **Also See:** DUNFERMLINE.

A Bit of History

16C–17C industrial royal burgh – Legend has it that this was the landing place and subsequent birthplace of St Kentigern (Mungo of Glasgow) following his mother's flight from Traprain in Lothian. The 13C saw the founding of a Cistercian house high on the hill, beside the then main road. In the 16C coal mining, salt panning and trade with the Low Countries were the principal activities. The port of Sandhaven was a flourishing one and the ensuing prosperity was followed by royal burgh status in 1588, accorded by James VI.

The golden age continued until the end of the 17C, the decline setting in with the

Culross Village

VisitScotland Fife

growth of transatlantic trade and developing industrial centres in the west and central belt. The village was forgotten for almost 200 years. Its renaissance was triggered off by the purchase of The Palace in 1932 by the National Trust for Scotland only shortly after its own foundation in 1931. An extensive restoration programme has since followed, and in 1981 to mark The Trust's Golden Jubilee, Culross was twinned with Veere in the Netherlands, re-creating a link of the past. The village as it stands gives a glimpse of an east coast burgh of the 16C and 17C.

Vernacular architecture – The visitor may enjoy the details and richness of Scottish domestic architecture with a walk through Culross: white or pale colour-washed harling or rubble stonework, dressed stone window and door trims, red pantiles with the occasional glass one, half or pedimented dormer windows, gable ends, crow stepping, skewputts, decorative finials, inscribed or dated lintels and forestairs.

The Palace★★ 45min

⏱Palace, Study, Town House open Good Fri–May & Sept–Oct, Thu–Mon noon–5pm (Oct 4pm). Jun–Aug daily noon–5pm. Garden all year, daily 10am–6pm or sunset if earlier. ✋Visit the Study and Town House by guided tour only (1hr). First tour 1pm, last tour 4pm (Oct, last tour 3pm). £8. 🍽 P . ☎0844 4932189. www. nts.org.uk.

Built between 1597 and 1611 by George Bruce, the Palace is a monument to both a period and a man. James VI's reign (1578–1625) was a time of economic change when merchants such as Bruce, Danzig Willie Forbes and Provost Skene of Aberdeen acquired wealth from trade, which financed the construction of substantial dwellings (The Palace, Craigievar Castle and Provost Skene's House). The man, **Sir George Bruce** (d. 1625), was an enterprising merchant, a burgessman at the height of the burgh's prosperity, with interests in the local coal mines, salt panning and foreign trade.

Despite the fact that many of the materials (pantiles, Baltic pine, Dutch floor tiles and glass) were obtained by Baltic barter, the buildings are a superb example of 16C and 17C domestic architecture. The interior provides an insight into the domestic surroundings of a prosperous merchant of the period. Rooms are small with Memel pine panelling for warmth and have interesting examples of the decorative painting typical of the late 16C and early 17C. Surprisingly, 21 fires burned coal rather than logs as elsewhere, but this was perhaps only natural for a coalmine owner.

West wing

To the left of the main courtyard is the earliest building with George Bruce's initials and the date 1597 on one of the dormer pediments. The initial lodging was later extended to the north and to the south with the creation of the Long Gallery. On the ground floor the Nomad's Room for passing travellers has a **painted ceiling** (1620, *not restored*) with beyond, one of the rooms of the domestic quarters paved with perforated Dutch tiles. In the northern extension alongside the inner court are the kitchen and bakery with the wine cellar across the passage.

Outside stairs give access to the first floor where the **Long Gallery** (*explanatory noticeboards*) is now subdivided. The term "palace" (it was neither royal nor episcopal) may come from the word *palatium*, meaning long hall, which was a typical feature of Elizabethan or Jacobean houses in the south. The Lady's Drawing Room at the south end is panelled with Baltic pine while the Sun Room beyond derives its name from the tempera paintings. Commanding a view of the port, the Business Room where Bruce received his captains has half shuttered and half glazed windows – a window-tax dodge. In the adjoining fireproof Strong Room, glazed Dutch tiles pave the floor and wall safes and iron doors ensure security.

On the second floor in the West Bedroom, the insertion of the occasional glass pantile is again a window-tax dodge. The second panelled room has the **Allegory ceiling**, a fine example of decorative painting, on the pine barrel vaulting.

North wing

A separate building, this extension dates from 1611 and the initials SGB commemorate Sir George's knighthood. The three storey building has a stables, byre and hay loft on the ground floor with additional apartments above. The rooms are panelled and both ceiling and wall paintings, although faint, can be deciphered: in one

first floor room the painting depicts the Judgement Steps of King Solomon while in the other rooms there are more 400-year-old paintings, depicting heraldic devices, fruit and geometrical patterns.

Village★★★ *1hr (excl. visits)*

Moving away from The Palace along the Sandhaven, note, on the left, the sundial at first floor level on the gable end, with the **tron** (⏱*see Introduction: Arts and Culture*) in front, then look up the close to see the Tron Shop with its forestair.

Town House

⏱*See The Palace (above).*

The Sandhaven is dominated by the stone and slate Town House which contrasts with the white harling and red pantiles all around. Built in 1625, with the tower dating from 1783, the edifice has a strong Flemish influence. The exhibition and audio-visual presentation are a must before visiting the burgh of Culross. The former council chambers on the first floor have typical 16C interiors.

The Back Causeway is a cobbled way with a central line of paving stones slightly higher than the rest. Known as

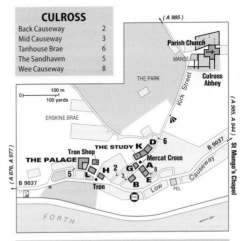

CULROSS	
Back Causeway	2
Mid Causeway	3
Tanhouse Brae	6
The Sandhaven	5
Wee Causeway	8

Ark	A	Oldest House	G
Bishop Leighton's House	B	Sea Captain's House	K
Butcher's House	D	Sundial	L
Nunnery	E	Town House	H

the "crown o'the causie", it was reserved for notables. Note the corbelled tower of the Study.

The Study★

🕐 See The Palace (preceding page).
This delightful example of Scottish burgh architecture dates from 1610. The main room has a restored original painted ceiling and original 1633 panelling. The marriage cupboard is Norwegian and the imposing portrait is of the town's merchant hero, George Bruce. Opposite is the **oldest house** in Culross with, in front of its gable end, a replica of the 1588 **mercat cross.** On the left on Tanhouse Brae, a former **Sea Captain's House** has a window lintel with a Greek inscription.

The wall plaque on the **Butcher's House** displays the tools of the occupant's trade. The road climbs up to the present parish church and remains of the abbey; through the gaps in the wall you can admire the **view** across the Forth and

glimpse of Abbey House (*private*). Built in 1608, for Sir George Bruce's brother, it was one of Scotland's earliest Classical mansions.

Culross Abbey

(*HS*). ☎01383 880 359.
Little remains of the abbey founded in 1217 by Malcolm, Earl of Fife.

Parish Church

🕐 Open daily 10am–dusk.
This occupies the monks' choir of the former Cistercian abbey. In the Bruce vault off the north transept stands Sir George Bruce's **funeral monument** – with alabaster effigies of Sir George, his wife and eight children – a type unusual in Scotland. The churchyard has some interesting tombstones.

Go downhill again to the square, noting the 17C **Nunnery** in Wee Causeway marked by its forestair and statue, and pass the **Ark**, a former seamen's hostel, then **Bishop Leighton's House**.

CULZEAN CASTLE★
SOUTH AYRSHIRE

Culzean (pronounced Cullane) Castle, in its dramatic clifftop **setting**★★★, provides another testimony to "the taste and skill of Mr Adam".

- 🛈 **Information:** 22 Sandgate, Ayr. ☎0845 2255 121. www.ayrshire-arran.com.
- ▶ **Orient Yourself:** 12mi/19km southwest of Ayr.
- 🖾 **Don't Miss:** The Oval Staircase.
- 🕐 **Organizing Your Time:** Allow around three hours including the Country Park. There is a range of daily activities on offer via the Ranger Service , see the website for details. The walled garden is a picture in July and August.
- 📷 **Especially for Kids:** An adventure playground and access to the beach via the Country Park.
- 👣 **Also See:** AYR, ISLE OF ARRAN.

A Bit of History

Always a Kennedy property, Culzean took precedence over Dunure, the traditional family seat when Sir Thomas, the 9th Earl of Cassillis, inherited in 1744. His brother, David, the 10th Earl (d. 1792 commissioned **Robert Adam** (1728–92) to transform the old castle. The work was executed in three stages. Initially there was the conversion of the

tower house, then the creation of a magnificent suite of rooms on the seaward side with the construction of the oval staircase as the final project. Of Adam's castle houses of the 1780s this is perhaps the most spectacular. Adam was a confirmed classicist, but the exteriors have, nevertheless, medieval touches in the mock battlements and arrow slits. The seaward front with the great drum tower is by far the most imposing. Addi-

Culzean Castle

E. Morris/ MICHELIN

tions were made in the 19C and since 1945 the National Trust for Scotland has undertaken an extensive restoration programme.

Castle

(NTS). *Castle and walled garden: open Easter–Oct, 10.30am–5pm (last admission 4pm). Visitor Centre also open: Oct–Easter Thu–Sun 11am–4pm. Country Park: open year-round daily 9.30am–sunset. £12 (park only, £8). 0844 493 2149. www.culzeanexperience.org. www.nts.org.uk.*
For an overview, begin your tour in the **Visitor Centre**, housed in converted buildings which were part of Robert Adam's Home Farm. It features an exhibition, an audio-visual presentation on the history of the castle (available on request, 17min), the Park Ranger Sevice, plus shops and a restaurant.

The Adam interiors characterise "The Age of Elegance". Delicately patterned ceilings – concentric or compartmented – with Antonio Zucchi paintings as focal points, are echoed in equally detailed friezes, chimney-pieces and furniture.

The centrepiece of the house and an Adam masterpiece is the **Oval Staircase**★★ as it rises soberly elegant through three tiers of columns. An impression of movement is created by the interplay of curving lines, the spiralling serried ranks of delicate ironwork balusters and the upward soaring of the superimposed orders. Outstanding on the first floor is **The Saloon**, the epitome of disciplined 18C elegance, which contrasts so strikingly with the wildness of the seascape framed by the windows. Adam-designed furnishings include the carpet (a copy of the original said to have been made locally), mirrors, wall sconces and a pair of semicircular side-tables curved to fit.

In the **Armoury** is one of the most important collections of flintlock pistols (18C–19C) in the world. Also of interest are items that belonged to General (later President) **Eisenhower** who was invited by the 5th Marquess and the Kennedy family to accept the tenancy of a specially created guest flat on the top floor of the Castle for his lifetime, as a gesture of Scottish thanks for America's support during World War II.

Culzean Country Park

In 1970 this 565-acre estate was designated Scotland's first country park. A series of walks have been designed so that visitors can discover the seashore, the walled garden with its herbaceous border, the Swan Lake, the 19C Camellia House, Orangery and terrace garden.

DALMENY ★
CITY OF EDINBURGH
POPULATION 319

This charming village, set around several large greens, is graced not only by its 12C parish church, one of the finest examples of Norman architecture in Scotland, but by Dalmeny House with its internationally renowned collections of porcelain and paintings.

- **Information:** 3 Princes Street, Edinburgh. ☎0845 225 5121. www.edinburgh.org.
- **Orient Yourself:** Dalmeny is 11 mi/18 km west of Edinburgh city centre, signposted (South Queensferry) off the A 90 Forth Bridge Road.
- **Organizing Your Time:** If you want to see Dalmeny House plan your visit around their (restricted) opening times.
- **Also See:** SOUTH QUEENSFERRY (FORTH BRIDGES), HOPETOUN HOUSE.

St Cuthbert's Church ★

Open Apr–Sept, Sun 2pm–4.30pm. Rest of the year, key available from the post office or 5 Main Street (in front of the church). ☎0131 331 1479 or 018452 255 121.

The church is set near the pilgrim route to Dunfermline which has another Norman church and there is evidence to believe that the same masons worked at both places. The simple plan is clearly discernible from outside: a stout western tower, a 20C Lorimer addition, abuts the long nave which in turn is prolonged by the shorter chancel and semicircular apse. Above the string course, round-headed and narrow windows are framed by chevron recessed orders but the jewel of the exterior is the superb **Norman south doorway ★★**, originally the main entrance. Tall, narrow and round-headed without its carved tympanum, the recessed orders are intricately carved showing fabulous animals from the Bestiary, figures and heads. Above is a panel of interlaced arches.

Interior

Seen from the west end, the two decreasing arches focus attention on the high altar. The handsome arches of the chancel and apse have orders of chevron mouldings, while the ribs of the chancel and apse vaulting spring from a series of **carved corbels** in the form of monstrous heads. The Rosebery Aisle built in 1671 was remodelled in the 19C. The family arms are carved on the panel.

Dalmeny House ★
2mi/3.2km east of the village.

Closed during 2008 for refurbishment, due to reopen in 2009. ☎0131 331 1888. www.dalmeny.co.uk.

Sir Archibald Primrose (1616–79) purchased the estate in 1662. His son was created the 1st Earl of **Rosebery** in 1703 and the then family seat was Barnbougle Castle on the Forth shore. **Archibald, 4th Earl** of Rosebery (1783–1868), commissioned William Wilkins to build the Gothic Revival house we see today, still the family seat, presently home to the 7th Earl.

Carved Corbel

After photo E. Sevo/ MICHELIN

Interior

The family portraits in the hall include the *4th Earl of Rosebery*, the builder of the house, by Raeburn and *The PM* by Millais. The set of five Madrid tapestries are after designs by Goya. The library has a painting by Stubbs and lotus-leaf furniture custom made by Wilkins. The Grecian interior of the Drawing Room is the setting for the Rothschild collection of 18C French **furniture and tapestries**. The carpet is Savonnerie while some pieces of furniture have the interlaced I's or dauphin stamp on them. In the corridor are 16C and 17C pieces of Scottish furniture.

The Napoleon Room was the work of the 5th Earl, a great historical collector who wrote Napoleon's biography. One of David's coronation sketches is here. In the Dining Room there are Reynolds and Gainsborough portraits of such personalities as *Dr Johnson*, *Edward Gibbon*, *William Pitt the Younger* and *Henry Dundas, the first Viscount Melville*.

The Old Private Apartments, a suite of five rooms, include the 6th Earl's Sitting Room with the famous rose and primrose racing colours amidst other racing mementoes. The Boudoir contains more of the Mentmore collection of furniture. Also on display is the **porcelain** collection, rich in Sèvres and Vincennes pieces.

DEESIDE ★★
ABERDEENSHIRE

The Dee, a splendid salmon river, flows from its source 4,000ft/1,219m up on the Cairngorm plateau at the Wells of Dee through the Lairig Ghru and then due east to the sea at Aberdeen. Scenically attractive with its many fine castles and its royal associations which have earned it the title of "Royal Deeside", this beautiful valley is a tourist honeypot and very busy in summer.

- **Information:** Bridge Street, Banchory. ☎01330 822 000. Old Royal Station, Ballater ☎01339 755306. The Mews, Braemar. ☎013397 41600. www.visitaberdeen-grampian.com.
- ▶ **Orient Yourself:** Travelling by car is the best way to see Deeside though there is no circular route; you have to backtrack from Braemar. Stagecoach Bluebird Bus 201 from Aberdeen services the A 93, calling at many of the main towns and attractions featured below.
- **Don't Miss:** The scenic stretch between Braemar and Ballater; Crathes Castle; if dates allow, Highland Games and/or a Braemar Highland Gathering.
- **Organizing Your Time:** Allow at least a day, two would be much better! Beware of crowds in the summer holidays.
- **Especially for Kids:** Highland Games or a Braemar Highland Gathering.
- **Also See:** ABERDEEN, CRATHES CASTLE.

Driving Tour

From Aberdeen to Linn O'Dee 64mi/102km

Aberdeen★★ – *see ABERDEEN*.

- ▶ *Leave Aberdeen by the A 93.*

Drum Castle

Easter–Jun & Sept–Oct, Sat–Mon & Wed–Thu 12.30pm–5pm. Jul–Aug daily 11am–5pm. Also open on Fri during bank hol weekends. Last admission 45mins before closing.
Rose Garden Easter–Oct, daily 10am–6pm;. Grounds year-round daily dawn–dusk. £8 (Gardens and park only, £2.50). £2. ☎01330 811 204.

Address Book

🪙 *For coin ranges, see the Legend on the cover flap.*

WHERE TO STAY

🛏️🛏️ **Callater Lodge Guest House** – 9 Glenshee Road, Braemar. ☎01339 741 275. www.hotel-braemar.co.uk. This Victorian villa stands in spacious attractive grounds. It features a library with inglenook and large bedrooms, some with valley views. Good value.

WHERE TO EAT

🍽️🍽️ **Larhillock Inn** – *Netherley* (🪙 *see ABERDEEN*).

🍽️🍽️🍽️🍽️ **The Milton** – *Milton of Crathes, North Deeside Road, Crathes.* ☎01330 844 566, www.themilton.co.uk. Set in a stone barn in a Craft Village next to Crathes Castle this smart, highly acclaimed modern restaurant serves a range of eclectic contemporary dishes.

Robert the Bruce granted the lands to his armour bearer William de Irwin but the castle remained in the same family until 1976 when it was donated to the National Trust for Scotland. The massive rectangular **tower**, dating from the 13C, has as its main defensive features its sheer height and massiveness. The walls taper from 12ft/3.7m at the base to 6ft/1.8m near the parapet and are rounded at the corners. External stairs lead up to the first floor entrance and the interior which was divided by timber roofs into three vaulted chambers. Ninety steps in all, including a ladder, lead to the battlements. In addition to the tower there is the Jacobean wing with attractively furnished rooms and a 17C family chapel in the grounds.

The property is famous for its tradition of beautiful and varied gardens and its **garden of historic roses** is a special feature which alone attracts many visitors.

▶ *A 957 to the left, otherwise known as the Slug Road, leads to Stonehaven (14mi/22km).*

Crathes Castle★★
🪙*see CRATHES CASTLE.*

Banchory
Population 6,270. Banchory, Deeside's largest community, is mainly residential.

The South Deeside Road branches off to the left forking from the Cairn o'Mount road (B 974) to Fettercairn. At the **Bridge of Feugh**, the Water of Feugh negotiates a narrow gorge giving spectacular falls and the chance for salmon to display their leaping abilities.

▶ *Proceed along A 93 which follows the course of the Dee.*

Aboyne
Population 1,477. This popular summer centre is set around a large green, the venue for the **Highland Games**. Part of the traditional pageantry is the ceremonial entry of the Cock o'the North, Chief of clan Gordon attended by his chieftains. The **Burn o'Vat** (*2mi/3.2km from the main road*) is a popular picnic site. The more enclosed valley marks the beginning of the upper reaches and the change to Highland scenery begins with the Cambus o'May defile. Ahead is the rounded form of Craigendarroch, pinpointing the site of Ballater.

Ballater
Population 1,500. This dignified little town developed as a watering place in the 18C and became the railway terminal in 1863. The line closed in 1966. The **Old Royal Station** with its unique Royal Waiting Room has been restored and contains displays on its 100-year history of Royal use. The Royal Saloon railway carriage, as used by Queen Victoria to journey between Ballater and Windsor in the late 19C, is also here and open to visitors. Ballater is a lively resort in

P. Tomkins/ Scottish Viewpoint/ Visit Scotland

Balmoral Castle

summer, famous for its **Highland Games** and its unique hill race up to Craig Coillich.

Crathie Church

🕐*May–Sept 9.30am–5pm. Apr & Oct 9.30am–12.30pm, 1.30pm–5pm. Service Sun 11.30am.*

The church, which is attended by the Royal Family, is the fifth on the site. The foundation stone for the church was laid in September 1893 by Queen Victoria. In the churchyard is a memorial to John Brown, the Queen's manservant, made famous in the 1997 film, *Mrs Brown*.

Balmoral Castle

Car park to the left of the main road.
♿🕐*Open Apr–Jul 10am–5pm. Winter: visit by guided tour only, first three Sats in Nov & Dec, 11am–2pm on the hour. £7 summer. £8 Winter tours. 🍴. ☎01339 742 534. www.balmoralcastle.com.*

Purchased by Queen Victoria in 1848, the Balmoral Estate is the Scottish home of the British Royal Family. Visitors are allowed into the formal and vegetable gardens, and there are exhibitions in the Carriage Room and the Ballroom, which is the largest room in the Castle. All other rooms within the Castle are private.

Royal Lochnagar Distillery

🕐*Visitor Centre Apr–Oct Mon–Sat 10am –4pm or 5pm, Sun noon–4pm or 5pm. Nov–Mar Mon–Fri 10am–4pm*
👣*Distillery, visit by guided tour only Jan–Mar & Nov–Dec, Mon–Fri 11am, 12.30pm, 2pm, 3pm. Apr–Oct daily at 30 minute intervals, with the last tour leaving 1hr before closing. £5. ☎01339 742 700. www.discovering-distilleries. com/royal-lochnagar*

Next to Balmoral Castle the Lochnagar Distillery has been on this site since 1841. Only three days after Victoria had moved

---

Victoria at Balmoral

In her journals Queen Victoria described Balmoral as "my dear paradise in the Highlands". When the queen – at the time, ruler of the largest Empire the world had ever seen – first arrived she was greeted by a crowd of locals estimated to be 80,000 strong. Not everyone was enthusiastic – the local press complained that the area was to be "desolated by cockneys" but over the years most locals have become fiercely protective of the royal connection, as embodied in the 1997 movie *Mrs Brown* (👣*see CRATHIE CHURCH*). Many of the queen's visitors from London were unimpressed by the rustic nature of the Royal retreat and some foreign dignitaries were particularly scathing. Tsar Nicholas II complained "the weather is awful, rain and wind every day" and a Prussian count thought it "astonishing that the Royal Power of England should reside amid this lonesome, desolate mountain scenery".

into Balmoral the Distillery invited her to visit. To their delight and surprise, the next day she did, and the distillery received a Royal Warrant of Appointment as supplier to the Queen.

The road now follows the alignment of the Old Military Road. Cross the Dee at the Invercauld Bridge which replaces Telford's bridge downstream.

Braemar Castle

☞ *Closed for refurbishment, telephone or see website for 2007/2008 opening details.* ☎ *01339 741 219, 01339 741 695.*

This L-plan tower house, set back from the roadside, was built in 1628 by the Earl of Mar as a hunting seat. Burned by Farquharson of Inverey, ancestor of the present owners, the castle was rebuilt and strengthened with a star-shaped curtain wall and crenellations to serve as a military post for Hanoverian troops after the '45 rising.

Braemar

Population 400. This scattered village is a busy summer resort in fine mountain scenery. The two original villages grew up at a strategic convergent point of the routes from the south via the Cairnwell Pass, from Atholl by Glen Tilt (of marble fame) and from Speyside via Glen Feshie. Each year on the first Saturday in September the **Braemar Highland Gathering** (⟨ *see Calendar of Events*) is a highly popular event attended by members of the Royal Family.

▷ *Take the secondary road out following the south bank of the Dee as it winds in its flood plain.*

Linn o'Dee★

This famous beauty spot is where the placid river suddenly tumbles through a narrow channel to drop into rocky pools. Salmon may be seen leaping here.

DIRLETON★

EAST LOTHIAN

POPULATION 740

A village full of charm, where highly individual 17C and 18C cottages and houses enhanced by well tended gardens, stand round two greens. The church (built 1612), has at its gate the session house and school house, adjoined by the schoolroom. The pride of the village is its romantic ruined castle, which dates back to the 13C, and predated the establishment of the village and church.

- ▤ **Information:** Quality Street, North Berwick. ☎01620 892 197. www.visiteastlothian.org.
- ▷ **Orient Yourself:** Dirleton lies 2.75mi/4.5km west of North Berwick on the A 198 and B 1346.
- ⟨ **Also See:** NORTH BERWICK.

Dirleton Castle★

🕐 *Open year-round daily 9.30am–5.30pm; (Oct–Mar 4.30pm). Last admission 30min before closing).* 🕐 *Closed 25, 26 Dec, 1, 2 Jan.* ▤ *£4.50* ☎ *01620 850330, www.historic-scotland.gov.uk.*

In the mainstream of Scottish history the stronghold was owned at different times by the de Vaux family, the Halyburtons and the Ruthvens. In 1650 it was besieged and destroyed by Commonwealth soldiers.

Rising up out of a rocky mound, the castle is adjoined by attractive **gardens**. The **13C part**, to the left of the entrance, includes three towers, surrounding a lesser courtyard. The two storey round tower contains two apartments, the lower one with window slits and the upper one – or Lord's Chamber – with windows and stone benches, a great hooded fireplace and antechamber.

Next to the castle ruins is a lovely **garden** featuring the world's longest herbaceous border.

DOLLAR
STIRLING
POPULATION 2,480

The fame of this small residential town, at the southern edge of the Ochil Hills in Clackmannanshire, lies in its Academy (school) and nearby Castle Campbell. The unusual town name probably derives from "doilleir", a Gaelic word meaning dark and gloomy – Castle Campbell was originally known as Castle Gloom.

- **Information:** 41 Dumbarton Road. Stirling. ☎08707 200 620.
- **Orient Yourself:** 13mi/21km east of Stirling on the B 8052, A 9 and A 91.
- **Also See:** STIRLING.

Castle Campbell★

1.25mi/2km from the main street up Dollar Glen. The road up is narrow and winding with a limited number of parking places (🅿), thereafter it is a 5min walk to the castle. ◷*Open Apr–Sept daily 9.30am–5.30pm. Oct–Mar, Sat–Wed 9.30am–4.30pm. Last admission 30min before closing.* ◷*Closed 1–2 Jan; 25–26 Dec.* ☞*£4.50.* ☕ *(summer only).* ☎*01259 742 408, www.historic-scotland.gov.uk.*

Castle Campbell has a dramatic **site★★★**, on a promontory, with burn-filled clefts on either side, dominating Dollar Glen and Dollar with the Ochil Hills as a backdrop; the lands and property passed by marriage to the Campbell family. The builder of the tower house was **Colin Campbell, 1st Earl of Argyll** (d 1493) and Lord High Chancellor to James IV. The castle was adopted as the Campbell lowland seat conveniently close to the various royal residences. Alterations and extensions in the 16C and 17C included the creation of an enclosed courtyard and additional domestic ranges and gardens. The Campbell family was staunchly Presbyterian and legend has it that John Knox visited the castle and preached here in 1556. The personal animosity between Archibald, 8th Earl of Argyll (1607–61), and the Marquess of Montrose, no doubt made the estate a target for ravaging raids during Montrose's campaign of 1645 but it is doubtful if the castle was attacked. Damage more probably came nine years later during General Monck's campaign and by the late 19C the castle was in a considerable state of disrepair.

Castle buildings

The main part is the late-15C four-storey **tower house** which rises to an overhanging parapet. Prior to the construction of the turnpike stair, access was by a stair in the thickness of the wall or by an outside stair or ladder to first floor level. The vaulted great hall with its massive fireplace has a vaulted cellar below and two chambers above. The topmost room is noteworthy for its ribbed barrel vault and two unusual grotesque masks. The parapet walk (*84 steps from the courtyard*) provides an excellent **view★** away over Dollar to the Forth Valley and Pentlands in the distance.

The School Built on Slavery

Dollar Academy is the oldest co-educational school in Britain and is claimed to be the oldest co-educational boarding school in the world. In terms of academic results it is frequently the best performing school in Scotland. It was founded in 1818 at the bequest of John McNabb, a former slave trader who bequeathed his fortune to provide 'a charity or school for the poor of the parish of Dollar wheir I was born.'

DORNOCH ★
HIGHLAND
POPULATION 1,006

Away from the bustle of the main A 9 road north, Dornoch has a quiet charm. This former royal burgh with its beaches and famous championship golf course of Royal Dornoch is a popular family resort.

- **Information:** The Coffee Shop, The Square. ☎01845 2255 121. www.visithighlands.com.
- ▶ **Orient Yourself:** Dornoch is 43mi/70km north of Inverness on the A 82, the A 9 and the A 949.
- **Also See:** CROMARTY.

Dornoch Cathedral

🕐*Open all reasonable times.* ☎*www. dornoch-cathedral.com.*
In the early 13C the then bishop of Caithness, **Gilbert de Moravia** (1222–45), made Dornoch his episcopal seat and set about building a cathedral. The site had been occupied by a Celtic community since the 6C. The cathedral has, however, been much altered since the 13C. From the outside, the rather squat church is dominated by its square tower and broach spire. The interior, although of modest proportions, has a fine sense of dignity enhanced by the original 13C stonework.

DOUNE ★
STIRLING
POPULATION 1,055

Strategically set on one of the main routes into the Central Highlands, this neat little burgh, famed in the past for its pistol making and cattle and sheep fairs, is now known for its impressive castle ruins.

- **Information:** Stirling Road, Dunblane. ☎08707 200 613. www.visitscottishheartlands.com.
- ▶ **Orient Yourself:** 8mi/13km northwest of Stirling on the A 84.
- **Also See:** CALLANDER, DUNBLANE, STIRLING.

Doune Castle ★

Access by car from the A 820. (HS) 🕐*Open Apr–Sept, daily 9.30am–5.30pm. Oct–Mar, Sat–Wed 9.30am–4.30pm. Last entry 30min before closing.* 🕐*Closed 1–2 Jan; 25–26 Dec.* ☎£4. ☎01786 841742, www.historic-scotland.gov.uk.
This formidable castle overlooks the Ardoch Burn and River Teith. It was built in the late 14C by the Regents, Robert Duke of Albany and his son Murdoch. On the latter's execution it passed to the Crown and was used as a dower house by successive Queens before becoming the property of the Stewarts.
The key to the defence of this 14C fortified castle is the keep-gatehouse. The castle was unusual for its period in that consideration was also given to the provision of practical living quarters.
The **keep-gatehouse** (95ft/30m high) rises through four storeys and is flanked to the right by the range of buildings containing the halls. The well-defended portal gives onto a vaulted passage flanked by prison, guardroom and cellars. The latter and the well chamber

Doune or Highland Pistols

In the 17C and 18C the village was renowned for the manufacture of fine pistols. The trade originated in the mid-17C and catered mainly for the Highland cattle drovers. Of a high quality and entirely of metal, Doune pistols are recognisable by their shape and decoration: a ram's horn butt, fluted breech, flared muzzles and rich embellishment; but they lacked a safety catch. They were manufactured in pairs for left or right hand use. The 1747 **Proscription Act** prohibiting the wearing of Highland dress and the carrying of arms, destroyed the traditional market. By the early-19C revival of Highland dress, mass production had taken over.

have hatches allowing victuals to be hoisted upstairs in the eventuality of a siege. Curtain walls with wall walks enclose the **courtyard** on three sides; the keep-gatehouse, adjoining range and second tower form the fourth.

A well defended outside staircase – compare to the second one – climbs to the first floor lord's hall. The portcullis was operated from a window embrasure here.

Steps beside the double fireplace lead down to the lord's private chamber with escape hatch, and up to the solar and other apartments of the keep-gatehouse, a truly self-contained and secure unit. From the courtyard, take the second outside staircase up to the retainers' hall where the soldiers were garrisoned. From here access is gained to the impressive **kitchen** area in the second tower, which contained the royal apartments or guest rooms on the upper floors.

Argaty Red Kites

4km northeast Doune. ◑*Hide: open all day. Ranger visit to hide and feeding time daily last Sat Oct to late Feb 1.30pm, rest of year 2.30pm.* ◉*£4.* ☎*01786 841373 www.argatyredkites.co.uk.*

Aound 130 years ago the Red Kite became extinct in Scotland. It was re-introduced in 1996, and numbers are now growing again. To enable the general public to see this magnificent bird at close quarters the Argaty viewing centre places a small amount of food daily near the hide (though it should be emphasised that the birds are still wild and do not rely on it for survival) and rangers talk about the Red Kites in situ.

D. Barnes/ Scottish Viewpoint

Doune Castle

DRUMLANRIG CASTLE ★★
DUMFRIES AND GALLOWAY

With its theatrical skyline Drumlanrig Castle makes an arresting picture in a splendid setting. The interiors are graced by a superb collection of priceless family treasures.

- **Information:** ☎ 01848 331 555. www.drumlanrig.co.uk.
- ▶ **Orient Yourself:** 18mi/29km northwest of Dumfries on the A 76 and A 702.
- ◷ **Organizing Your Time:** Allow 1hr.
- **Especially for Kids:** Good adventure playground for young and older kids; spotting wildlife on camera at the Visitor Centre. Hire a bike and cycle the estate.
- ⚲ **Also See:** DUMFRIES.

A Bit of History

A Douglas seat

As early as the 14C this was the site of a Douglas stronghold and son succeeded father until the late 18C. **William, 3rd Earl and 1st Duke of Queensberry** (1637–97), a man of high position under the Stuarts and of an artistic nature, built in 1679–91 a mansion worthy of his status. However it is said that he was so appalled by the total cost of the project that he spent only one night in his new palace before returning to the ancestral seat at Sanquhar. His son **James, 2nd Duke of Queensberry** (1672–1711) is known for his part in negotiating the Treaty of Union (1707). Since both his grandsons predeceased the 2nd Duke, the title passed to William (known as Old Q) in 1778 and he bled his Scottish estates dry with his profligate life in London. Through Jane Douglas, the 2nd Duke's sister and an heiress in her own right, her grandson Henry Scott, 3rd Duke of Buccleuch, inherited the estate in 1810.

Visit

⚲◷ *Castle: open Good Friday–Aug daily. 11am–5pm (last tour 4pm). Country Park Stableyard Studios (Visitor Centre) and gardens open: Good Friday–Sept daily 10am–5pm. £7.* ⛾.

The newly refurbished Visitor Centre in the Stableyard provides visitors with an insight into how a large Country Estate is managed and the wildlife it supports.

Live cameras are trained on the nests of resident red squirrels and barn owls. There is also an underground tunnel and a nocturnal chamber.

Castle

The square towers quartering the structure, built around a courtyard are typical of the native tradition. The main façade, with its terraces, horseshoe staircase and dramatic turreted skyline, is a departure from such. The whole is rich in sculptural detail. The inner courtyard has turret staircases at each corner.

Inside is a superb collection of paintings, including Old Masters and family portraits, a varied selection of clocks and fine French furniture (mainly 17C and 18C) from the workshops of master cabinet makers. The Winged Heart motif on plasterwork ceilings, ironwork, wall hangings, wood carvings... is a reminder that Drumlanrig is a Douglas seat.

Ground floor

In the **Hall** are paintings by Kneller and Thomas Hudson (1701–79) including *Charles, 3rd Duke and His Grace's Family Group*. The family group by Seago in the **Inner Hall** shows the present duke as a youth. There are interesting watercolours of Drumlanrig in the **Passage**. The splendid oak staircase with its barley sugar banisters rises in three flights from the **Staircase Hall** where the highlights are a series of Old Masters, in particular Rembrandt's *Old Woman Reading* (1655). Here Rembrandt has created an atmosphere and attitude of calm introspection. Compare this with the infinitely

P. Tomkins/ Scottish viewpoint/ Visit Scotland

Drumlanrig Castle

more detailed portraits (16C) by Holbein (*Sir Nicolas Carew*) and Joost Van Cleef (*François I, Eleanor of Austria*).

In the splendid oak-panelled **Dining Room**, carved panels attributed to Grinling Gibbons alternate with 17C silver sconces and family portraits. *William, 1st Duke*, the builder of the castle in peer's robes (Kneller), is next to *William, 4th Duke of Queensberry* (Old Q) as an 18-year-old (Ramsay) and his heir *Henry, 5th Duke* (1746–1812). There are two of Monmouth (Kneller and Huysmans), one in a medallion with his mother Lucy Walter. It is interesting to compare the Kneller and Reynolds portraits (between the windows) of the two heiresses responsible for uniting the Montagu, Douglas and Scott families, namely *Lady Jane Douglas* and *Lady Elizabeth Montagu*.

First floor

Both **Bonnie Prince Charlie's Bedroom** and the **Anteroom** are hung with 17C Brussels tapestries and graced by fine pieces of furniture.

In the **Drawing Room**, amidst a selection of very fine pieces of French furniture, are two outstanding **cabinets**★ commissioned in 1675 for Versailles. Louis XIV gifted these to Charles II, his cousin. The portraits include a series of full lengths: *King James VI* and his Queen, *Anne of Denmark* (Jamesone; the stance is similar to both the de Critz and Adam Colone portraits) with their grandson, *Charles II*, between them, and *Francis 2nd Duke of Buccleuch* by Ramsay. The Porcelain Collection includes the delightful Meissen Monkey Band. The fine pier glasses are 17C.

From the **staircase gallery**, the superb 1680 **silver chandelier** is seen to its best advantage. On the panelled walls are magnificent Chippendale sconces and full length portraits: *William and Mary, Queen Anne* and her consort *Prince George*, all contemporaries of the Union Duke who, as High Commissioner, presented Queen Anne with the Treaty of the Union (1707). In recognition he was given an English dukedom. Fine Dutch and Flemish paintings (Teniers, Breughel, Cuyp) hang in the **Boudoir**. In the **Principal Bedroom** are canvases by two 18C artists, Gainsborough and Hudson, of *Mary Duchess of Montagu* and *Kitty Duchess of Queensberry*.

Stableyard Studios

Smart food and craft shops, a cycle hire shop – the estate is perfect for exploring by bike – and a Cycle Museum are housed here.

DRYBURGH ABBEY★★
SCOTTISH BORDERS
LOCAL MAP SEE THE TWEED VALLEY

Majestic and evocative, the extensive ruins of Dryburgh Abbey stand in a splendid, secluded **setting**★★★ on a sheltered meander of the Tweed. The mellow red tones of the Dryburgh stone amid the green swards of well tended grass and majestic old trees, make this one of the most attractive of the Border abbeys.

- **Information:** ☎01835 822381. www.historic-scotland.gov.uk.
- ▶ **Orient Yourself:** 7mi/11km southeast of Melrose on the A 72 and A 7.
- ◔ **Also See:** ABBOTSFORD, MELLERSTAIN, JEDBURGH.

A Bit of History

Dryburgh Abbey was the first Scottish home of the Order of Premonstratensians. Building began in 1150 and the abbey led a peaceful and prosperous existence with the monks tending the lands. The Wars of Independence and subsequent Border troubles resulted in destruction and fire damage on at least three occasions 1322, 1385 and 1544; the latter also included the razing of the town of Dryburgh. The religious life of the abbey ended at the beginning of the 17C. It was then inhabited by the commendators (their descendants), which explains why the conventual buildings have been so well preserved.

Visit 45min

♿🕐Open daily Apr–Sept, 9.30am–5.30pm (Oct–Mar 4.30pm). Last admission 30min before closing. 🕐Closed 25, 26 Dec, 1, 2 Jan. 🎫 £4.50.

Dryburgh Abbey

Abbey Church

Little remains of the mainly 12C and 13C church, dedicated to St Mary. The west front, robbed of its facing, is pierced by a 15C round-arched and recessed doorway, devoid of capitals, and adorned by square, conventionalised leaf motifs.

Transepts

The transepts are late-12C and early-13C in the First Pointed style, best seen in the north transept and its eastern chapels. The main arcade with pointed arches is surmounted by a compressed middle section with cusped circular lights opening onto the interior while the clerestory arcade, taller again, is one storey of triple lancets. The north transept and eastern chapel with moulded, ribbed vaulting and carved bosses are the resting places of Field Marshal Earl Haig (**1**) and Sir Walter Scott (**2**).

The south transept has the remains of a night stair leading to the first floor canons' dormitory and a door to the library and vestry. The great window in the upper part of the transept gable is partly blocked where the roof of the dormitory abutted.

Conventual buildings

These are among the best preserved of their kind in Scotland, and are laid out on the middle and lower levels, around the cloister, with two storeys on the east.

Cloister

The east range is the best preserved.

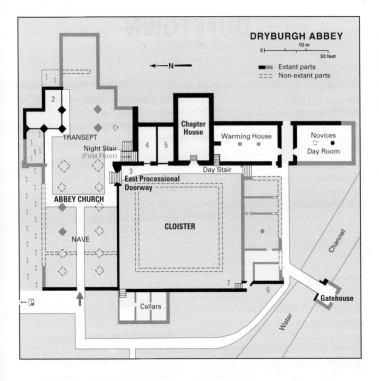

DRYBURGH ABBEY

0 ├────────┤ 10 m
├────────────┤ 50 feet

■■ Extant parts
--- Non-extant parts

← N →

2

TRANSEPT

Night Stair
(First Floor)

4   5

Chapter
House

3

East Processional
Doorway

Day Stair

Warming House

Novices
Day Room

ABBEY CHURCH

NAVE

CLOISTER

Channel

7   6

Cellars

Gatehouse

Water

← P

East Processional Doorway

This is an attractive example of late 12C work, still round-headed with dissimilar capitals and dog-tooth ornament.

On the left, the aumbry (**3**) or book alcove is complete with shelf grooves. The first door leads to the library and vestry (**4**), a barrel-vaulted chamber later adopted as a family vault by the Earls of Buchan, while the parlour beyond is the Erskine vault (**5**).

Chapter-house

The doorway with its flanking openings makes an attractive unit. Stairs lead down to the barrel-vaulted chamber, with its stone bench and attractive interlaced arcading on the east wall.

Next comes the day stair which gave access to the dormitory and treasury. Ahead, the doorway leads down steps to the lowest level where a door on the left opens onto the warming house (calefactory) with two central pillars. The original fireplace was in the east wall as in the novices' day room across the passage.

Dormitory

Access was by the night stair from the south transept.

Extending the full length of the eastern range, it was altered following fire damage and in the 16C when dwelling rooms were made.

Frater and subcroft

Lying on the south side of the cloister are two barrel-vaulted chambers which were surmounted by the refectory. The most outstanding feature is the **wheel window** (**6**) in the west gable.

The west wall of the cloister has a lavatory (**7**), a recess for hand washing before meals.

Gatehouse

To the south of the frater on the far side of the water channel is this 15C gatehouse which was at one time connected to the main building by a covered bridge.

DUFFTOWN
MORAY
POPULATION 1,636

The old local rhyme, "Rome was built on seven hills, Dufftown stands on seven stills", is still valid today as Dufftown is capital of the malt whisky industry. This trim little town was laid out in 1817 by James Duff, 4th Earl of Fife, initially to give employment after the Napoleonic Wars. Glenlivet, the first of Dufftown's numerous distilleries, was established in 1823.

- **Information:** Clock Tower. ☎01340 820 501. www.dufftown.co.uk.
- **Orient Yourself:** Dufftown is 17mi/28km south of Elgin on the A 941.
- **Don't Miss:** If you see only one distillery make it Glenfiddich.
- **Organizing Your Time:** There are the two whisky festivals, one in early May and the other in September. The Highland Games take place on the last weekend in July. You will need a car to explore the many distilleries.
- **Also See:** ELGIN.

Visit

Glenfiddich Distillery★

0.5mi/800m north of the town centre on the east side of the A 941. ♿☕🚃*Visit by guided tour only: Easter–Oct Mon–Sat. 9.30am–4.30pm, Sun noon–4.30pm; Oct–Easter, Mon–Fri 9.30am–4.30pm. Connoisseur tour: includes warehouse and tutored nosing and tasting session.* ☕*£20 (standard tour free).* ⏱*Closed 2 weeks at Christmas.* ☎ *01340 820 373. http://uk.glenfiddich.com/distillery*

Set in the heart of the Highlands, Glenfiddich (meaning "Valley of the Deer" in Gaelic) is a place of great beauty, as well the brand name of the world's best-selling single-malt whisky. The film and tour provide an excellent introduction to the history of this family firm founded in 1886 and the art of malt whisky distilling (☕*see Introduction: Food and drink*) through all the stages from malting to bottling.

Balvenie Castle

Behind Glenfiddich Distillery. (HS). ⏱*Open Apr–Sept, daily 9.30am–5.30pm. Oct–Mar Sat–Wed 9.30am–4.30pm. Last admission 30mins before closing.* ☕ *£3.50.* ☎*01340 820121, www.historic-scotland.gov.uk.*

Set on a strategic route from Donside to Moray, this now ruined courtyard castle was successively the seat of Comyns, Douglases and Stewarts. The initial structure with its massive curtain wall and moat dated from the period of Comyn ownership in the late 13C and early 14C. In the mid 16C the 4th Earl of Atholl, a Stewart, built a Renaissance dwelling. The latter, along the entrance front, is clearly distinguished by richer architectural ornament: carved armorial panels, mouldings and corbellings.

Excursion

Speyside Cooperage

About 4mi/6km northwest to Craigellachie on the far bank of the Spey by A 941. ♿⏱*Open Mon–Fri 9am–4pm.* ⏱*Closed*

P. Tomkins/ Scottish Viewpoint/ Visit Scotland

The still room of the Glenfiddich Distillery

Whisky Trail

This signposted tour (*about 70mi/113km*) takes in eight malt whisky distilleries. For more details enquire at Tourist Information Centres or visit www.maltwhiskytrail.com. The following are suggested highlights:

The Glenlivet Distillery *southwest off B 9136* (⌚🕐*Open Apr–Oct, 9.30am–4pm, Sun noon–4pm.* ☎*01340 821 720, www.chivas.com*), is the first licensed distillery in the Highlands (1824). The original maltings are the setting for the visitor centre.

Glenfarclas Distillery *Marypark, west off A 95,* ⌚🕐*Open Jul–Sept, Mon–Sat 10am–5pm. rest of year Mon–Fri 10am–5pm (Oct–March 4pm). Last admission 1hr 30mins before closing.* ☎*£3.50.* ☎*01807 500 245, www.glenfarclas.co.uk.*

Cardhu Distillery *west B 9102,* 🕐*Open Jul–Sept, 10am–5pm, Sun noon–4pm; Oct–Easter 11am–3pm, guided tour. 11am, 1pm, 2pm; Easter–Jun, Mon–Fri 10am–5pm (last admission 1hr before closing).* ☎*£4.* ☎*01340 872 555. www.maltwhiskytrail.com.*

2 weeks in Dec. ☎*£3.20.* ☕*.* ☎*01340 871 108, www.speysidecooperage.com.* This modern cooperage has a viewing gallery which allows visitors to enjoy the sights, smells and sounds of coopers making and repairing some of the 100,000 barrels which the workshop turns out annually for the maturing of the area's whiskies. In addition there is an intriguing exhibition which recalls the antiquity of the cooper's craft.

DUMFRIES ★
DUMFRIES AND GALLOWAY
POPULATION 31,307

Known as the "Queen of the South" – the name was given by a local poet in 1857 and has been adopted by the town's premier football team – the attractive and bustling town of Dumfries has long been the southwest's most important town. Farming remains the principal industry with diversification provided by the administrative services of the regional headquarters and some manufacturing. The town is also a busy tourist centre. Dumfries has important historical associations with the national bard, **Robert Burns** and the national warrior hero, **Robert the Bruce**, as it was here that he slew Scotland's co-guardian, thus opening the second stage of the Wars of Independence.

- 🛈 **Information:** 64, Whitesands. ☎01387 253 862. www.visitdumfriesandgalloway.co.uk.
- ▶ **Orient Yourself:** Dumfries is around 25mi/40km northwest of the border with England on the A 75.
- ⊘ **Don't Miss:** Sweetheart Abbey.
- 🕐 **Organizing Your Time:** Allow a good half-day to see the town, at least a full day for excursions. The town has a fairly complex one-way system and it is advisable to visit on foot. Dumfries makes a good base for excursions.
- 👣 **Also See:** THREAVE GARDEN.

Sights

Burns Mausoleum
To the right, behind the prominent red sandstone church, rebuilt in 1745, is the mausoleum where Burns, his wife Jean Armour and several of their children are buried. A plan (to the right of the church) indicates where some of Burns' associates and friends are laid to rest.

P. Tomkins/VisitScotland/Scottish Viewpoint

Dumfries

Burns House

🕐*Open Apr–Sept, Mon–Sat 10am–5pm; Sun 2pm–5pm. Oct–March, Tue–Sat 10am–1pm, 2pm–5pm.* ☎*01387 255 297. www.dumgal.gov.uk/museums.*

Burns spent the last three years of his life in this house, which now serves as a museum. The ground floor room has examples of the poet's correspondence. The small upstairs room with writing desk and chair retains the window pane engraved with the bard's name.

Midsteeple★

This imposing building makes a striking focal point for the High Street. The rather angular outline is relieved by the detailed delicacy of the matching pierced balustrades and wrought ironwork of the forestairs' railings. The resemblance with Stirling's Tolbooth (📖*see STIRLING*) is not unexpected since the mason, Tobias Bauchop, had

worked under Sir William Bruce on the Stirling project prior to erecting the Midsteeple in 1707 to serve as a prison and courthouse. The royal coat of arms emblazons the front; there are also a standard measurement of the Ell and a plan of the town in Burns' day.

Burns Statue

At the north end of the High Street, the 1882 statue commemorates Dumfries' most famous citizen.

A wall plaque on the west of the statue marks the site of Grey-friars Monastery where Robert the Bruce killed the Red Comyn in 1306.

Devorgilla Bridge

This narrow six-arch bridge with pointed cutwaters built in the 15C replaced the original wooden structure built by Devorgilla (📖*see Sweetheart Abbey, following page*).

Address Book

💰*For coin ranges, see the Legend on the cover flap.*

WHERE TO STAY

🛏 **Hazeldean House** – *4 Moffat Road.* ☎*01387 266 178, www.hazeldeanhouse. com.* This 19C villa is full of character. There is a conservatory breakfast room and spacious bedrooms.

🛏 **Redbank House** – *New Abbey Road.* ☎*01387 247 034, redbankhouse@talk21. com.* Just outside town, this spacious Victorian villa is set in formal mature gardens. Bedrooms are homely with floral furnishings.

🛏 **Rivendell** – *105 Edinburgh Road.* ☎*01387 252 251. www.rivendellbnb. co.uk.* Very attractive Charles Rennie Mackintosh-style villa with parquet floors, distinctive woodwork and brass fittings. The comfortable bedrooms have views over the large garden.

WHERE TO EAT

🍽🍽 **The Linen Room** – *53 St Michael Street.* ☎*01387 255 689, www.linenroom. com.* This dynamic modern fine-dining restaurant uses only top quality local produce to create original dishes; tasting menus are their forte.

DUMFRIES

		High St	B		Pleasance Ave	AB	29
		Hoods Loaning	B	17	St Andrew St	B	31
Annan Rd	B	2	Howgate St	A	18	St Mary's St	B	32
Assembly St	B	3	Irving St	B	20	St Michael's Bridge Rd	B	34
Castle St	AB	5	Leafield Rd	B	21	Station Rd	B	35
Church Crescent	B	6	Loreburn Centre	B		Suspension Brae	B	36
Craigs Rd	B	7	Market Square	A	22	Terregles St	A	38
David St	A	9	Mill Rd	A	24	Troqueer Rd	B	39
Dockhead	B	10	Nith Bank	B	25	Well St	A	41
Galloway St	A	13	Nith Pl.	B	27			
Great King St	B	14	Nith St	B	28			

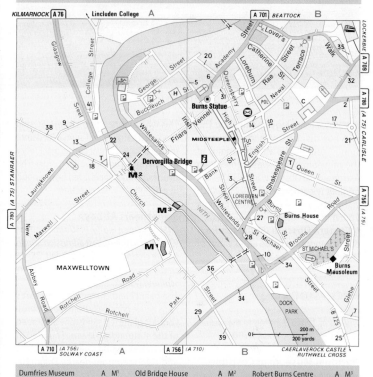

Dumfries Museum	A	M¹	Old Bridge House	A	M²	Robert Burns Centre	A	M³

Old Bridge House

🕐 *Open Apr–Sept Mon–Sat 10am–5pm; Sun 2pm–5pm.* ☎ *01387 256 904, www.dumgal.gov.uk/museums.*
Built in 1660 into the sandstone of the bridge, Dumfries' oldest house is now a museum of everyday life in the town. The family kitchen, nursery and bedroom of a Victorian home have been re-created, as well an early dentist's surgery.

Robert Burns Centre

♿ 🕐 *Open Apr–Sept, Mon–Sat 10am–8pm; Sun 2pm–5pm. Oct–Mar, Tue–Sat 10am–1pm, 2pm–5pm.* 👓*Free (audio-visual theatre £1.80).* ☎ *01387 264 808, www.dumgal.gov.uk/museums.*

The centre, which is housed in a restored 18C water mill, traces the bard's links with the town. The exhibition is illuminated by several original manuscripts and belongings of the poet. There is a fascinating scale model of Dumfries in the 1790s and an atmospheric audio-visual presentation.

Dumfries Museum

♿ 🕐 *Open Apr–Sept, 10am–5pm; Sun 2pm–5pm. Oct–Mar, Tue–Sat 10am–1pm; Sun 2pm–5pm.* 👓*Free. (Camera Obscura £2).* 🅿 ☎*01387 253 374. www.dumgal.gov.uk/museums.*
A converted 18C windmill and later extensions house local collections of

P. Tomkins/VisitScotland/Scottish Viewpoint

The ruins of Sweetheart Abbey (dating from the 13C)

geology, archeology and history. The mill has displays of early Christian stones, country life and the origins of the museum which was formerly an Astronomical Observatory in 1836. The original telescope (8in/200cm), which still exists, was used to observe Halley's Comet in July 1836.

A **Camera Obscura** on the top floor of the windmill affords good views of Dumfries in clear weather.

Excursions

7mi/11km. Leave Dumfries to the south-west by New Abbey Road, A 710.

National Museum of Costume

Shambellie House, signposted just before New Abbey village. ⏲*Open Apr–Oct, 10am–5pm.* ₤3. ⌣. ☎*01387 850 375, www.nms.ac.uk.*

Set in luxuriantly wooded grounds, the house (mid 19C) was designed in the Scottish baronial style by David Bryce. In 1977 Charles Stewart donated both his house and rich **costume collection**★ (late 18C–early 20C) to the former Royal Scottish Museum.

New Abbey Corn Mill

At the entrance to the village of New Abbey (HS). ⏲*Open daily 9.30am–1pm & 2–5.30pm (Oct–Mar 4.30pm. Last admission 30 min before closing.* ⏲*Closed 1–2 Jan; 25–26 Dec.* ₤4. ☎*01387 850260. www.historic-scotland.gov.uk.*

This whitewashed two-storey 18C mill produced oatmeal and animal feed until the Second World War and its machinery remains intact and in working order. The overshot waterwheel is fed from a pond in a delightful village setting.

Sweetheart Abbey★

(HS). ⏲*Open daily 9.30am–5.30pm (Oct–Mar 4.30pm). Last admission 30min before closing.* ⏲*Closed 1–2 Jan, 25–26 Dec.* ₤3. ☎*01387 850397. www.historic-scotland.gov.uk.*

The beauty and charm of Sweetheart's ruins derive principally from the colourful contrast of the red sandstone and green of the surrounding lawns. Founded in 1273 by **Devorgilla**, wife of John Balliol, and colonised from nearby Dundrennan, Sweetheart was the last Cistercian foundation in Scotland. Walter Scott's novel *The Abbot* features Gilbert Brown, the last and most famous of Sweetheart's incumbents.

The whole is enclosed by a rare precinct wall which was originally interrupted by two gateways.

With the claustral buildings gone, the chief interest of the ruins is the completeness of its **church**. Corbels on the west front indicate the former presence of an entrance porch, above which there is a reconstructed and now partially infilled west window. Inside, directly above the great striding arches of the six-bay nave, is an interesting clerestory. Triple openings on the inside are paralleled outside by semicircular arches filled with five graded lancets. The stout tower above the crossing is adorned with rows of masks and heads supporting the battlements. The foundress Dervorgilla was laid to rest in the presbytery, along with the casket containing the embalmed heart of her husband – thus explaining the unusual name.

Ruthwell Cross
16mi/25km. Leave Dumfries to the south-east by the B 725.
Inside Ruthwell Church this 7C cross is an outstanding example of early Christian art, the vivid and realistic sculpture tell the story of the Life and Passion of Christ. The artistic skill and craftsmanship of the 7C sculptor is most evident in the vine tracery intertwined with birds and other creatures. The margins are inscribed with Runic characters. The many vicissitudes of the Cross included its demolition on the orders of the General Assembly in 1642 and removal to the churchyard in 1780. In 1823 the Rev Dr Henry Duncan rebuilt the cross in the grounds of the manse prior to its final installation and restoration in the church in 1887.

Ellisland Farm
6mi/10km. Leave Dumfries by A 76. ◷*Open Apr–Sept, Mon–Fri 10am–1pm & 2pm–5pm, Sun 2–5pm. Oct–Mar, Tue–Sat 10am–4pm.* ⬚ *£2.50.* ☎*01387 740 426. www.ellislandfarm.co.uk.*
Burns leased this farm in June 1788. He introduced new farming methods but the soil was poor and his first crops failed. He accepted an appointment in the Excise in the district and in 1791, on being offered promotion, he gave up farming and moved to Dumfries as a full-time exciseman. His first house was in the Wee Vennel, now Bank Street. It was at Ellisland, on the banks of the Nith, that Burns wrote what many consider to be his greatest work *Tam O'Shanter*. One room of the farmhouse, which is still lived in, has a display of Burns relics with documents concerning family, patrons and friends. In the granary there is a video presentation of Burns' life.

DUNBAR
EAST LOTHIAN
POPULATION 5,795

This east coast holiday resort and day excursion centre takes its name from the once powerful stronghold, around which the town grew up.

- ℹ **Information:** 143 High Street. ☎01368 863 353. www.visiteastlothian.org.
- ▶ **Orient Yourself:** Dunbar is 12.5mi/20km southeast of North Berwick on the B 1346, A 198 and A 1087.
- 🧒 **Especially for Kids:** The beach at Bellhaven Park.
- ⌚ **Also See:** HADDINGTON, TANTALLON CASTLE.

A Bit of History

Battles of Dunbar
Set on the main east coast road and in the path of invading armies, Dunbar has been the site of two important battles, both Scottish defeats. In the opening stages of the Wars of Independence, Edward I, on his first Scottish campaign, sacked Berwick and then inflicted a defeat on the Scots army near Spott (1296). The 1650 battle was part of Cromwell's campaign to subdue Scotland. The Covenanting General David Leslie, with a numerically superior army, abandoned a strong position on Doon Hill to fall prey to General Monck.

Sights

Dunbar Town House Museum
High Street. ◷ *Apr–Oct 12.30pm–4.30pm. Nov–Mar Sat–Sun 2–4.30pm.* ☎*01368863734. www.eastlothian.gov. uk/museums/dth.*

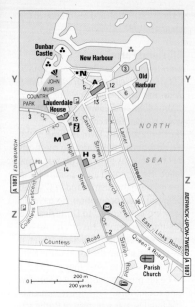

DUNBAR			
		Square	Y 6
		Silver St	Z 9
Abbey Rd	Z 2	Victoria Pl.	Y 12
Bayswell Rd	Y 3	Victoria St	Y 13
Castle Gate	Y 5	West Port	Z 14
Custom House		Woodbush	Z 16

Basil Spence Housing Complex		YA
John Muir's Birthplace	Y	M
Tolbooth	Z	H
Yellow Craig	Y	N

Dunbar Town House was built around the end of the 16C. It is now home to an archaeology and local history centre, as well as temporary exhibitions about Dunbar and district.

Tolbooth★

This attractive 17C tolbooth with its steepled octagonal tower and crow-

The making of John Muir

"When I was a boy in Scotland I was fond of everything that was wild... I loved to wander in the fields to hear the birds sing, and along the shore to gaze and wonder at the shells and the seaweeds, eels and crabs in the pools when the tide was low; and best of all to watch the waves in awful storms thundering on the black headlands and craggy ruins of old Dunbar Castle." John Muir

stepped gable is built of red rubblework sandstone.

John Muir's Birthplace★

Open Apr–Oct, Mon–Sat 10am–5pm; Sun 1pm–5pm. Nov–Mar, Wed–Sat 10am–5pm; Sun 1pm–5pm. ☎01368 865 899. www.jmbt.org.uk.

The home for 11 years of **John Muir** (1838–1914), the pioneer geologist, explorer, naturalist and conservationist *par excellence*, who was responsible for the creation of America's National Park system. The flat where he lived with his six brothers and sisters before emigrating to the States, is appropriately furnished while the rest of the house is devoted to the man and his work

The birthplace is set within the **John Muir Country Park.** There is a cliff top walk which passes the harbour and ruined castle (see Harbour, below).
Belhaven Bay is a glorious, sandy beach fringed by low, sheltering sand dunes, rich salt marsh and colourful grasslands. From here there are splendid views across the Forth Estuary.

Dunbar Castle

The ruins, jagged and red, of what was once, strategically, one of the most important castles in the Middle Ages, rises above the waters of the harbour. The castle was much fought over but it was the stout defence in 1339 by Black Agnes, Countess of March and Dunbar, against English troops led by Salisbury that stands out most clearly in its history. The orders to demolish came from the Scots Parliament in the same year that Mary, Queen of Scots, visited it with Lord Darnley (1567).

Harbour

The **New** or **Victoria Harbour** was opened in 1842 to accommodate the growing number of trading and fishing vessels. The arrival of the railway four years later, however, brought about a decline in the port's activities. The pantiled, dormer-windowed house Yellow Craig, on the right, makes an attractive point of comparison for the Basil Spence housing complex between the harbours. The **Old Harbour** with its cobbled quays and rubble walls was built by Cromwell in 1650.

DUNBLANE ★
STIRLING
POPULATION 6,783

This mainly residential town, on the Allan Water, is famous historically for its lovely 13C Gothic cathedral in its close setting. Unfortunately the town gained unwanted national and worldwide fame In 1996 when a crazed gunmen entered a school, killing 16 children and their teacher. It was Britain's worst gun tragedy and precipitated drastic new gun ownership laws in the United Kingdom. A modern memorial in the cathedral commemorates the victims.

- **Information:** Stirling Road. ☎01786 824 428.
- ▶ **Orient Yourself:** Dunblane is 6mi/10km north of Stirling on the B 8052, the A 84, the M 9, and B 8033.
- ⏱ **Organizing Your Time:** Allow 2hrs for the town centre and the cathedral.
- **Also See:** STIRLING.

Dunblane Cathedral ★★

⏱ *Open Apr–Sep, Mon–Sat 9.30am–12.30pm, 1.30pm–6pm, Sun 2pm–6pm. (Oct–Mar 4pm).* ☎01786 825388, www. dunblanecathedral.org.uk.

Although Dunblane was already an ecclesiastical centre in Celtic times, it was David I who created the bishopric c.1150. The cathedral led a peaceful existence and numbered among its bishops, Clement (1233–58), the builder of the cathedral, and that rare ecclesiastic **Robert Leighton** (1611–84), an enlightened conciliator during the religious strife of the 17C. Leighton sorely regretted leaving Dunblane when translated to Glasgow c.1671. Despite 15C alterations, neglect following the Reformation, but no pillaging, and finally several 19C and 20C restorations, the cathedral is a fine example of 13C Gothic architecture. Adjoining the nave on the south side to the left of the entrance is a 12C **tower** which belonged to the early Celtic building. The upper storeys and parapet are later additions. Continue round to the west end overlooking the Allan Water where the masterful design of the **west front**★★ combines a deeply recessed doorway with a tall triplet of lancets and Ruskin's small vesica (oval window) above, all framed by two buttresses.

Interior

The building (210ft/54m long) passes from nave to choir uninterrupted by transepts or crossing. The initial impressions are of simplicity, height and soaring lines (mostly achieved by the predominance of the pointed arch). Built after the Lady Chapel, the pointed arcades of the eight-bay nave descend onto clustered columns and are surmounted by a double clerestory where window tracery is repeated inside the gallery. This device is copied at the west end, where the great window shows the Tree of Jesse (1906). Below are two sets of the canopied 15C **Chisholm stalls** deeply and vigorously carved with a wealth of detail. The misericords are of great interest. Like the nave, the wooden barrel-vaulted roof with tinctured armorials has also been restored (19C). Around the pulpit are carved figures of St Blane, who gave his name to the town, King David I, Bishops Clement and Leighton, and John Knox, while those on the screen depict Biblical personages.

The glory of the building is the **choir** with its great height emphasised by soaring lancets in the south and east sides. Level with the high altar are the early-15C **Ochiltree stalls**, showing a similar verve of execution. The present stalls and organ case were designed by Robert Lorimer during his 1914 restoration of the choir. Three stone slabs in the floor mark the burial places of the Drummond sisters, allegedly poisoned

Ruskin's Praise

The great Victorian art critic John Ruskin said of Dunblane Cathedral "I know not anything so perfect in its simplicity and so beautiful, in all the Gothic with which I am acquainted".

in 1501 to prevent Margaret, the eldest, from becoming James IV's Queen in preference to Henry VIII's sister, Margaret Tudor. The effigy in the north wall tomb recess is said to be that of Clement, the builder bishop. The oldest part, the **Lady Chapel** opening off the north side of the choir, has ribbed vaulting with carved bosses. The memorial windows, panelling and flooring are all 20C.

Precincts

The Dean's House (1624) contains the **Dunblane Museum** (♿🕐*open early*

May–early Oct, Mon–Sat 10.30am–4.30pm. ☎01786 823 440, www.dunblane museum.org.uk). The house has had several incarnations including a butcher's shop and a chemical laboratory. Now it is devoted to both town and cathedral. Of particular interest is the collection of Communion Tokens, the predecessors of today's cards. Within the manse grounds is a 1687 building, the home of Bishop Leighton's personal library, which is the oldest private library in Scotland. **Leighton Library** (🕐*open year-round Wed–Fri 10am–12.30pm & 2–4.30pm)* houses 4500 books in 90 languages printed between 1500 and 1840. Here visitors can browse through some of the country's rarest books, including a first edition of Sir Walter Scott's *Lady of the Lake*.

From the northeast corner there is a lovely view along the north side of the cathedral.

DUNDEE ★
CITY OF DUNDEE
POPULATION 172,294

Dundee enjoys a near perfect situation on the northern shore of the Tay with the Sidlaw Hills as a backdrop. Prosperity accrued from the three j's: jute, jam and journalism in the Victorian era. Traditional industries have given way to modern, high technology industries and the city centre reflects this with a blend of fine Victorian buildings and modern shopping facilities. The Dundee Contemporay Arts (DCA) centre complements its thriving cultural scene. As Scotland's fourth city, it is a busy seaport, educational centre and capital of Tayside Region.

- **Information:** 21 Castle Street. ☎01382 527 527. www.angusanddundee.co.uk.
- ▶ **Orient Yourself:** 22mi/36km northeast of Perth via the A 85 and A 90.
- **Don't Miss:** Discovery Point , the Frigate Unicorn, McManus Galleries, Verdant Works.
- 🕐 **Organizing Your Time:** Allow one to two days; Discovery Point and the Verdant Works alone can take half a day each. All the main sights can be covered on foot though you will probably need a bus or taxi to avoid getting too tired.
- **Kids Especially for Kids:** Sensation, RSS Discovery, the Frigate Unicorn.
- 👣 **Also See:** ARBROATH, MONTROSE.

A Bit of History

Dundee was home to **James Chalmers** (1823–53), who is now generally acknowledged as the inventor of the adhesive postage stamp. Others with a claim to fame include Desperate Dan,

Denis the Menace, Korky the Kat and Our Wullie, comic characters from the Thomson publishing empire.

Premier whaling port – Dundee took over as Britain's chief whaling port in the 1860s with a new generation of steamers for the whale and seal fishery in the far north. The fleet spent eight months away from March to October. Crews were local but there was a tradition of hiring seamen from Lerwick or Stromness as oarsmen for the whaleboats. The oil found a ready market in the burgeoning jute mills where it was used to soften the raw jute fibres. Whaling continued until the First World War. The museum in **Broughty Castle** (*just outside the city centre.* Oopen year-round Mon–Sat (Oct closed Mon) 10am–4pm, Sun 12.30–4pm; ☎01382 436916; www.dundeecity.gov.uk/broughtycastle) has a section on whaling featuring ships' models, whaling gear, paintings and prints.

Sights

Discovery Point★   Kids
Discovery Quay. &Oopen daily, Mon–Sat, 10am–6pm; Sun 11am–6pm. Nov–Mar closes 5pm. Last admission 1hr prior to closing. OClosed 25–26 Dec, 1–2 Jan. £6.95 (child, £4.25); combined ticket with the Verdant Works £11.25 (child £7). ☎01382 309060. www.rrsdiscovery.com.
Dundee is immensely proud of RRS (Royal Research Ship) *Discovery*, Captain Scott's famous Antarctic exploration vessel, built here in 1901 and commanded by him on the 1901–04 Antarctic Expedition. *Discovery* returned to the Tay in 1986, and now, in dry dock, forms the centrepiece of an ambitious celebration of her historic voyage.

A tour begins in the purpose-built visitor centre on the quayside, where no effort has been spared in preparing comprehensive displays to evoke the excitements of construction, the launch, the voyage, and the two winters spent in Antarctica, justifiably described as an "epic of human endurance". The high point is a spectacular audio-visual presentation, "Locked in the Ice".

Discovery continued her career as a research vessel, and is presented as she was fitted out for a collaborative British/Australian/New Zealand expedition to the Antarctic in 1929.

During the guided tour, note the teak main deck with skylights (icebergs precluded portholes), the now empty engine rooms, laboratories, radio and chart rooms, storerooms, cold store, the mess deck for the 26 crew members and the teak-panelled officers' wardroom and adjoining cabins. The harsh environment of Antarctica is presented in the Polarama Gallery with hands-on exhibits.

The Frigate Unicorn★   Kids
Victoria Dock. Undergoing continuous restoration work. Open Apr–Oct, daily 10am–5pm. Nov–Mar, Wed–Fri noon–4pm, weekends 10am–4pm. Closed 2 weeks at Christmas. £4. ☎01382 200 900. www.frigateunicorn.org.
This 46-gun frigate was commissioned by the Royal Navy in 1824, 19 years after Trafalgar. Today visitors can explore the Captain's Quarters and the main gundeck where the 18 pounder cannon required nine gunners a piece to man them. The gunners ate and slept on the same deck as their cannon. The deck above has the 'Seats of Easement' and gun ports. On the quarter deck were the 32 pounder Carronades, nicknamed "smashers". In the officers' cabins is an exhibition on the Royal Navy.

McManus Galleries & Museum★
Albert Square. Building closed for renovation until Autumn 2008. ☎01382 432 350. www.mcmanus.co.uk.
Sir George Gilbert Scott's fine Victorian Gothic building houses the city's art gallery and museum. On the ground floor, the Trade and Industry gallery gives a good account of the activities that led to Dundee's late-19C and early-20C prosperity and in addition has memorabilia from the Tay Bridge disaster of 1879 (see Tay Railway Bridge, below). Other ground floor sections have reconstructed interiors of a shop and pub and deal with the region's archeology.

Artworks are housed in the first floor galleries, the most sumptuous of which is the **Albert Hall**; here, grouped under the title "Europe and Beyond", is a splendid array of arts and crafts, which the visitor is encouraged to look at from the perspective of the eminent Victorians who assembled the collections. The dark red walls of the Victoria Gallery set off the closely hung 19C portraits, landscapes and genre paintings, while the MacKenzie Gallery contains an excellent survey of 20C Scottish painting. Pride of place is given to works by the long-lived local landscape painter, **James McIntosh Patrick** (b 1907), including his *Autumn, Kinnordy,* a characteristically meticulous study of traditional farming patterns in the Scottish countryside.

Sensation Science Centre Kids
Green Market. ♿⏰*Open year-round daily 10am–5pm. Last admission 4pm.* 🎫*£6.95 (child, £4.95)* ☕.🅿.☎*01382 228 800. www.sensation.org.uk.*
Discover how we use our five senses to explore the world around us at this exciting interactive Science Centre where everything is "hands-on".

St Mary's
This is the oldest surviving building in Dundee. The Old Steeple is all that remains of the original 14C–15C parish kirk. Like many other churches it was subdivided after the Reformation. St Mary's, occupying the east end, has some fine stained glass by Burne-Jones, Morris (east end and north aisle) and a lovely Gethsemane scene (south aisle).

Tay Road Bridge
This bridge, opened in 1966 two years after its Forth counterpart, is one of the longest road bridges in Europe at 1.4mi/2.25km long. It has 42 spans and carries two carriageways each way. The central walkway has observation platforms.

Tay Railway Bridge
The current bridge, completed in 1887, replaced the original which was opened in 1878. The first bridge was built to replace the world's first train ferry (1850) and measured just short of 2mi/3km. On a stormy night in December 1879, disaster struck as the bridge gave way and a train carrying 75 passengers plunged into the river, with no survivors. The

designer Thomas Bouch was greatly afflicted by the tragedy and died shortly afterwards. Some eight years later, the current bridge was opened reusing some of the original ironwork. Memorabilia and relics from the disaster are on display in the McManus Galleries.

Verdant Works★
West Henderson's Wynd. ♿⏰*Open Apr–Oct, Mon–Sat 10am–5pm, Sun 11am–5pm. Nov–Mar, Wed–Sat 10.30am–4.30pm. Sun 11am–4.30pm. Last admission 1hr prior to closing.* ⏰*Closed 25–26 Dec, 1–2 Jan.* 🎫*£5.95 (child, £3.85); combined ticket with Discovery Point £11.20 (child £7).* ☕.🅿. ☎*01382 225 282. www.verdantworks.com.*
At its peak in the mid and late 19C, when there was a huge growth in world demand for baling and packaging material, Dundee's jute industry employed 50,000 local people, many of them living and working in the close-packed Blackness district to the northwest of the city centre. Developed from the late 18C onwards, this was one of Scotland's first industrial areas, but was still countrified enough for David Lindsay's factory of 1833 to be given the name of Verdant Mill. One of the best remaining examples of a Dundee jute mill, it has been converted into a still evolving museum. There are several ingenious exhibits and many audio-visual and hands-on displays which evoke the laborious processes involved in the conversion of the raw jute and the uses to which it was put– the wagons rolling across the Wild West of the United States were covered in material made in Dundee.

Dundee Law
A road leads right up to the War Memorial. This volcanic plug (571ft/174m) affords a circular **panorama** of Dundee and the surrounding countryside. Spread out below is Dundee with the Tay Bridges stretching across to Fife. Visible to the north are Bens Vorlich, Lawers and Macdui.

DUNFERMLINE ★
FIFE
POPULATION 52,105

The "auld grey town", formerly the capital of Scotland, figures largely in Scottish history, mainly in association with its great abbey and royal palace. From earliest times it was a thriving industrial centre with coal mining and later linen weaving; the tradition is maintained today with a variety of new industries.

- **Information:** 1 High Street. ☎01383 720 999.
- ▶ **Orient Yourself:** Dunfermline is 17.5mi/28km northwest of Edinburgh via the A 823, and the A 90 across the Forth Road Bridge.
- **Don't Miss:** the Norman nave of the Abbey Church.
- **Organizing Your Time:** Allow 2hrs to see the city centre. The town centre is small and the main sights can easily be covered on foot.
- **Especially for Kids:** Deep Sea World.
- **Also See:** CULROSS.

A Bit of History

Margaret and Malcolm

In the 11C **Malcolm III** or Canmore (c.1031–93) offered hospitality in his Dunfermline Tower to the English heir to the throne, Edgar Atheling and his family, on their flight from William the Conqueror and the Norman Conquest (1066). Edgar's sister **Princess Margaret** (c.1045–93), a devout Catholic, married the Scottish king in 1070 and was largely responsible for introducing the religious ideas of the Roman Catholic church which were gradually to supplant the Celtic church. Together with her husband, she founded the church in 1072. Three of Queen Margaret's sons ascended the throne: Edgar, Alexander I and David I; it was Alexander who proclaimed the town a royal burgh between 1124 and 1127 and David I (c.1084–1153) who founded the Benedictine abbey. The town prospered as the abbey grew in importance.

Following the untimely deaths of Alexander III and Margaret of Norway, Edward I, during his tour as mediator in the struggle for succession, visited the town and on his departure in 1304, the monastic buildings were a smouldering ruin. **Robert the Bruce** (1274–1329), the great national hero, helped with the reconstruction and is buried in the abbey. His heart is in Melrose Abbey.

Royal Palace

The guesthouse was refurbished for James V's French wife but it was James VI who gave the abbey and palace to his **Queen, Anne of Denmark.** Once more Dunfermline was the home of royalty and three royal children were born here: Elizabeth, known as the Winter Queen, the ill-fated Charles I and Robert who died in infancy. With the Union of the Crowns (1603), the court departed to London. James VI subsequently made two fleeting visits to the town as did Charles I in 1633, and his 20-year-old son, Charles II to sign the Dunfermline Declaration.

Famous citizen

The philanthropist and steel baron, **Andrew Carnegie** (1835–1919), was born in Dunfermline the son of a hand loom weaver. In 1848 the family emigrated to America and young Andrew passed from bobbin boy and telegraphic messenger to working in the railroads before dealing in iron and then the new steel industry. By 1881 he was the foremost steel baron in the USA and in 1901, following the sale of his steel companies, he retired and set about spending his fortune in public benefactions. His many gifts to his home town included the Carnegie Baths, the Library, the Lauder Technical School and Pittencrieff Park.

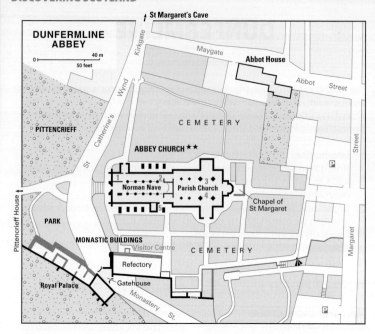

Palace and Abbey★

30min

&♿ ⏱ *Open Apr–Sept daily 9.30am to 6.30pm. Oct–Mar Mon–Wed & Sat 9.30am–4.30pm, Thu 9.30am–1pm, Sun 2–4.30pm.* ⏱*Closed 25–26 Dec, check for New Year. Last admission 30min before closing.* ✆ *£3.50.* ☎ *01383 739026.* *www.historic-scotland.gov.uk.*

The original Celtic church was replaced and dedicated by Malcolm Canmore and Queen Margaret in 1072. Their son David I accorded it abbey status in 1128 and rebuilt the monastic church. The abbey with its extensive lands, property, coal pits, salt pans and ferry dues, accrued enormous wealth and its prestige was enhanced by the fact that it was a royal establishment becoming the "Westminster Abbey of Scotland", where 22 royal persons were buried. The 13C saw the addition of St Margaret's Chapel holding the remains of Malcolm and his consort. The abbey was damaged by fire by Edward I and, although restored by Robert the Bruce, it never attained its former glory. It was during the 14C that a new royal residence was built. At the Reformation the abbey declined and was no longer used as a place of worship; the

east end fell into ruins and only following the collapse of the central tower was the east end rebuilt (1818–21).

Abbey Church★★

Norman nave

The nave of David I's (1128–50) church was restored by William Schaw, Master of Works to Anne of Denmark. The north porch, northwest tower, west front and massive buttresses are all his work.

The interior presents one of Scotland's finest Norman naves with close affinities to both Durham and St Magnus's, Kirkwall, where simple massive forms and round-headed arches predominate. Great cylindrical pillars, four of which have chevron and spiral motifs, separate the seven-bay nave from the aisles and support semicircular arches. Marked on the floor are the outlines (blue on the plan) of the original Celtic church and Queen Margaret's 1072 Church of the Holy Trinity.

The various monuments include **William Schaw's (1)** (1550–1602), near the north porch, erected by Queen Anne to the memory of her Chamberlain and Master of Works who ably restored parts of the building in the 16C and 17C, and the Renaissance one (**2**) to Robert Pit-cairn (1520–84), Commendator from 1560–84, with 16C paintings above on the panels of the vaulting.

East end or parish church

The east end was rebuilt from 1818 to 1821 and now serves as parish church. A memorial brass (**3**) marks the tomb of Robert the Bruce (1274–1329), Scotland's hero. The new royal pew (**4**) commemorates the 900th Anniversary in 1972. Leave the building by the nave and the East Processional Door (**5**), a well-preserved example of Norman work.

Chapel of St Margaret

Foundations only remain of the building which once enclosed St Margaret's Shrine, a popular pilgrimage centre.

Monastic buildings

Of the once great ensemble of abbatial buildings which extended to the south of the abbey church, there remain four walls of the refectory, with chambers below, joined by the gatehouse bestriding the pend to the kitchen and former royal palace.

Royal Palace

In the 14C a new royal palace was built adjacent to the 13C guesthouse. A single wall remains to recall the splendour of this building. Charles I and his sister, the Winter Queen or Elizabeth of Bohemia, were both born here.

Abbot House

Maygate. ♿ ⏱*Open year-round daily 10am–5pm (Nov–Feb Sun 4pm). Last admission 45mins before closing).* ⏱*Closed 25–26 Dec and 1 Jan.* ⊛*£4.* ☕.🅿. ☎*01383 733 266. www.abbot house.co.uk.*
This pink-harled building has a pleasingly irregular outline of turrets, chimney stacks, crow-stepped gables and dormer windows. Now a **heritage centre**, it has colourful displays on such aspects of Dunfermline's history as St Margaret and her shrine, the poet Robert Henryson, and the diarist, Lady Anne Halkett, who resided here between 1670–99. The walled garden evokes Lady Anne's activities as a herbalist, the strik-ing modern ironwork of gates, railings and pergola are tributes to the work of the medieval smiths whose forges lie beneath the garden.

Additional Sights

Andrew Carnegie Birthplace Museum

Moodie Street. ♿ ⏱*Open daily, 11am (Sun 2pm)–5pm, May–Oct.* ⊛ *£2.* ☎*01383 724 302. www.carnegiebirthplace.com.*
On the left is the cottage where Andrew Carnegie (1835–1919) was born, arranged as a typical weaver's home, while the adjoining Memorial Hall houses exhibitions illustrating the great philanthropist's life and work. His many trusts and endowments are too numerous to name but include The Peace Palace in the Hague, the Carnegie Institute of Pittsburgh, and many other much more humble instiutions.

Excursions

Deep Sea World   Kids

At North Queensferry, 5mi/8km south-east. ♿ ⏱ *Open year-round daily, Mon–Fri 10am–5pm; Sat–Sun 10am–6pm. Last admission 1hr before closing time.* ⏱*Closed 25 Dec and 1 Jan.* ⊛ *£11 (child £7.50).* ☕.☎*01383 411 880. www.deepseaworld.com.*
This spectacular and extremely popular aquarium succeeds in its aim of informing and entertaining with lavish features like a piranha display, sand tiger sharks, and an "underwater safari" through a large transparent underwater tunnel.

Loch Leven

12mi/19km north on the M 90. Loch Leven is the largest lowland loch in Scotland (some 5.5sq miles/14km2) and is of international importance for breeding and wintering wildfowl.
The island stronghold of **Loch Leven Castle** (*Ferry service from Kinross*) dates from the 14C to 16C and was the place of imprisonment of Mary, Queen of Scots from June 1567 until her escape on 2 May 1568.

DUNKELD ★
PERTHSHIRE AND KINROSS
POPULATION 273

The particular charm of this modest village on the north bank of the Tay is its ruined cathedral and attractive precinct.

- **Information:** The Cross. ☎01350 727 688. www.perthshire.co.uk.
- ▶ **Orient Yourself:** Dunkeld is 13mi/21km south of Pitlochry on the A 9.
- ◷ **Organizing Your Time:** Allow a day to see Dunkeld and its excursions.
- Kids **Especially for Kids:** Beatrix Potter Exhibition & Garden where little ones can dress up to become Mrs Tiggy-Winkle, Peter Rabbit and Jeremy Fisher, and perhaps listen to story tellers.
- ◔ **Also See:** PITLOCHRY. PERTH.

A Bit of History

Metropolitan See

As early as AD 700 this was the site of a monastic establishment which was to become, for a brief spell, the kingdom's principal ecclesiastic centre under Kenneth MacAlpine in the 9C (AD 843). Confirmed during the reign of Alexander I, the bishopric was held by such historic figures as William Sinclair and the scholar poet, Gavin Douglas (1474–1522). The settlement which developed around the majestic cathedral (14C–16C) never grew to any great size. By 1650 the cathedral itself was a ruin and in 1689 the village was burnt to the ground in the aftermath of Killiecrankie when the Cameronian regiment held out against the remainder of Viscount Dundee's Jacobite Highlander army.

Sights

Dunkeld Cathedral

(HS). ◷Open daily, Apr–Sept 9.30am–6.30pm. Oct–Mar 10am (Sun 2pm)–4.30pm. ☎ 01350 727 601. www.dunkeldcathedral.org.uk.
In an admirable riverside setting surrounded by tree-shaded lawns, the cathedral is divided into two distinct parts, a roofless ruined nave and the choir.

Choir

Begun in 1315 by Robert the Bruce's bishop, William Sinclair, building continued until 1400. In 1600 the choir of the ruined cathedral was renovated to serve as parish church. There have been several restorations since.

Inside, recumbent effigies portray Bishop Sinclair (headless), and Alexander Stewart, the Wolf of Badenoch, in an impressive suit of armour. The 15C chapter-house serves as Atholl mausoleum and houses the small **Chapter House Museum** (◷ open Apr–Sept 9.30am–6.30pm, Oct–Mar 9.30am–4.00pm) covering town and church history. At the choir's west end is a copy of the 1611 Great She Bible.

Nave

☞Restricted access during restoration work.
The nave dating from the 15C was begun by Robert Cardney whose mitred effigy lies in the Chapel of St Ninian (south aisle). Others buried here include Colonel Cleland, leader of the Cameronians, and Count Rohenstart, the last of the Stuart line (d 1854). The windows of the triforium level are unusual. The Late Gothic tower (1469–1501) was the last addition. Inside are two mural paintings, while the platform offers a good view. Behind the cathedral is one of the first larches imported from the Tyrol in 1738 by the Duke of Atholl.

From the grounds can be seen Telford's bridge (1809), the predecessor of which was built by Alexander Mylne, canon at Dunkeld, Abbot of Cambuskenneth, first President of the College of Justice and ancestor of the family of master masons.

The imposing cathedral gates (1730) came from Dunkeld House (*now a hotel*), once the Atholl ducal seat.

Cathedral Street and The Cross★

Cathedral Street and the square known as The Cross were rebuilt to the original street plan after the destruction of 1689. Many of the 17C houses were derelict by the 1950s. An extensive restoration programme, by the National Trust for Scotland and the local authority, has recaptured the 17C–18C aspect of these streets, thus providing an attractive approach to the cathedral.

Cathedral Street is lined with houses where the characteristic door and window trims set off the pale coloured harling, and pends interrupt the succession. **No 19**, Dean's House was where **Gavin Douglas** (1474–1522), the poet and scholar of the Scottish Renaissance, was consecrated Bishop of Dunkeld in 1516. Apart from his politicising for the Douglas faction, Douglas is remembered for his translation of Virgil's *Aeneid* into Scots.

Occupying pride of place on the west side of the Cross is the National Trust for Scotland's **Ell Shop**, named after the ell or weaver's measure fixed to one of its walls. At the heart of the Cross is the restored Atholl Memorial Fountain, erected in 1866 by public subscription in memory of the 6th Duke of Atholl.

Excursions

Birnam

Resting on the opposite bank of the River Tay is the Victorian village of Birnam. In the centre is the smart modern **Birnam Arts & Confernce Centre,** home to the **The Beatrix Potter Exhibition & Garden** (♿ ⏱ open year-round daily. Mid Mar to Nov 10am–5pm. Dec to mid-Mar Mon–Sat 10am–4.30pm, Sun 11am–4.30pm. ⏱ Closed Christmas and New Year.) Beatrix Potter, the English author and illustrator (1866 –1941) developed her interest in wildlife, drawing and painting during her childhood summers spent at Dalguise House near Dunkeld. In 1893 she wrote a letter to a little boy in which she introduced him to Flopsy, Mopsy, Cottontail and Peter, the little rabbits loved by generations of children all over the world. We don't know if Peter Rabbit (published in 1902) was a Scot but other characters from the books were inspired by local personalities, the most famous being Mrs Tiggywinkle, modelled on Potter's Dalguise washerwoman.

Loch of Lowes Wildlife Reserve

2mi/3km northeast by A 923. ♿ ⏱ *Open Apr–Sept 10am–5pm.* ⊙ *£3.* ☎ *01350 727 337. www.swt.org.uk.*

The reserve (242 acres/98ha) covers the freshwater Loch of Lowes and its fringing woodland and has a consequently rich flora and fauna. Visitor access is limited to the south shore, the visitor centre and the observation hide. From the later the tree-top eyrie of a pair of ospreys – one of only two nests accessible to the public in Scotland – can be observed (*binoculars are provided*) between April and late August.

The Hermitage

2mi/3km west, off A 9.

Built in 1758, the **Hermitage,** a woodland walk along the banks of the River Braan has been a famous beauty spot for over two centuries. It overlooks the Falls of Braan, where this Highland torrent rushes through the cleft and under the bridge. Farther on is Ossian's Cave, another folly of the same period as the Hermitage. Britain's tallest tree, a 212 ft/64.5 metre Douglas Fir can also be seen here.

DUNNOTTAR CASTLE★★
ABERDEENSHIRE
⟨LOCAL MAP SEE ABERDEEN: GRAMPIAN CASTLES

The extensive ruins of Dunnottar are impressively set in an almost inaccessible promontory site★★★ with sheer cliffs on three sides. An apt setting for the stirring and also shameful events that have taken place here.

▫ **Information:** ☎01569 762 173. www.dunnottarcastle.co.uk.

▸ **Orient Yourself:** Dunnottar Castle is located just off the A 92, Stonehaven/ Montrose road, just less than 2mi/3km south of Stonehaven.

⟨ **Caution:** The site is unsuitable for elderly or disabled visitors as there are many steep and uneven steps. Some of the Castle chambers are dark so you may wish to take a torch.

⟨ **Also See:** ABERDEEN, MONTROSE, DEESIDE.

A Bit of History

Early religious site

Legend has it that St Ninian founded an early Christian settlement on the crag in the 5C. According to "Blind Harry", a 15C poet, whose epic poem was an inspiration for the 1996 film *Braveheart*, William Wallace set fire to this chapel with a garrison of English soldiers taking refuge inside. (The current chapel was built in the 16C).

By 1276 Bishop Wishart of St Andrews consecrated a stone building which was destroyed 20 years later. In the late 14C Sir William Keith erected the present keep and in so doing was excommunicated for building on consecrated ground. From then on Dunnottar served as the principal seat of the Keiths, Hereditary Earls Marischal of Scotland and Wardens of the Regalia.

The stronghold was the last castle to remain in Royalist hands during the Commonwealth, therefore the natural hiding place for the **Royal Regalia** and royal papers. During the eight-month siege in 1651–52 by Cromwell's troops, the regalia were audaciously smuggled out to be hidden under the floorboards of nearby Kinneff Old Church where it remained secure until the Restoration.

More inglorious was the incarceration of Covenanter prisoners in 1685 following the failure of the Monmouth and Duke of Argyll Rebellions: 122 men and 45 women were kept for two months in Whigs' Vault. Few survived.

In 1715 the estates were forfeited following the 10th Earl's participation in

ES Robertson/ Visit Scotland/ Scottish Viewpoint

Dunnottar Castle

the rising. The castle then gradually fell into disrepair only to be retrieved in the 20C.

Visit

🕐*Open late Jun to late Sept , daily 9am–6pm. Easter–Jun and late Sept to late Oct, Mon–Sat 9am–6pm. Sun 2pm–5pm. Late Oct–Easter Fri–Mon 10.30am–sunset. All opening hours are weather permitting. Last ticket must be purchased 30 minutes before closing. ⊛ £5 ⊟ cash only.*
The main building is the 14C Tower House, battered by Cromwell, but still intact. This is one of 11 buildings which comprise the castle and includes barracks, lodgings, stables and storehouses. At the far end an elegant quadrangle is bounded on three sides by 17C build-

Swimming at Stonehaven

Just along the coast at Stonehaven is Scotland's only Olympic-size outdoor heated saltwater swimming pool. A throwback to the age of Art Deco, it is beautifully preserved in full working order and open from June until late August and the water really is warm! Perversely there's a hardy band of local visitors who insist on using the pool only in bad weather, on the basis that once they are in the water, they're as cosy as can be and can really appreciate the contrast!

ings, including what was once a very large and elegant ballroom extending over 100ft/35m. The fourth side is framed by the castle's 13C Chapel.

DURNESS
HIGHLAND
POPULATION 327

This small hardy village, once a crofting community, is the most northwesterly community in mainland Britain. It now thrives as a stopping-off place for travellers rounding the northwest corner of Scotland.

Information: Durine. ☎0845 225 5121. www.northhighlandsscotland.com. www.durness.org.

Sights

Smoo Cave
An outcrop of limestones accounts for the presence of this, Britain's largest sea cave and the sandy beaches. The waters of the Allt Smoo plunge down a sink-hole to reappear at the mouth of the outer cave. The two inner caves are accessible only to potholers.

Balnakeil Craft Village
1mi/1.5km west by a local road. 🕐*Open Apr–Oct 10am–6pm.* ✗ 🅿 ☎*01971 511 277.*
This former radar station is now occupied by a community of craftspeople. This is a chance to watch craftsmen at work: ceramics, jewellery, weaving, bookbinding and leatherwork.

Excursions

Cape Wrath★★★
By ferry and minibus. The ferry leaves from Keoldale slipway 1.5mi/800m south of Durness. 🕐*Operates Jul–Aug , 9.30am–4.30pm (6 crossings); May–Jun and Sept, 11am, 1pm (3pm if 4 or more passengers). ⊛ £4.50 return. Minibus service after ferries. £7.50 return. ☎01971 511 343 or 287, www.capewrath.org.uk.*
The bus takes 40min for the trip (11.5mi/18km) through bleak moorland country, now MOD territory, to the lighthouse, which marks the most northwesterly point on the British mainland. The lighthouse was built by Robert Stevenson, (the father of Robert Louis Stevenson) in 1828, the name Wrath derives from the Norse word for a turn-

The Lennon Connection

Between the ages of 9 and 14 John Lennon spent long summer holidays at Durness. Lennon and his cousin, Stanley Parkes, used to stay at the family croft at Sango Bay. Parkes recalls "John never forgot those times at Durness. They were among his happiest memories. He loved the wilderness and the openness of the place. John loved going up into the hills to draw or write poetry. John really loved hill walking, shooting and fishing. He used to catch salmon. He would have been quite a laird." Lennon returned in adult life with his wife Yoko Ono and their children. The area had such an impact on the ex-Beatle that it is said it was part of the inspiration for the seminal song, *In My Life*.

The musical connection lives on in **The John Lennon Northern Lights Festival,** voted Britain's best new festival in 2007 and set to light up this part of the world for many years to come (*last weekend Sept. www.northhighlands scotland.com/festival*).

ing point, for here the Norsemen turned their ships to head for home.

Near the lighthouse are the ruins of a coastguard station, built by Lloyds of London, to keep a eye over their insured ships and to ensure that the lighthouse was doing its job properly.

To the east of the lighthouse, above the bay of Kearvaig, is another superlative, the Clo Mor Cliffs, which have a dizzying drop of 281m (nearly 1000ft), making them the highest sea cliffs in mainland Britain.

The totally exposed cape offers a variety of vantage points affording outstanding **views**★★ – especially eastwards and particularly from Clo Mor Cliffs. The churning seas and superb coastal scenery is an unforgettable sight.

THE EAST NEUK★★
FIFE

The East Neuk (meaning corner, as in "nook and cranny") is one of the main attractions of Fife, a stretch of coastline dotted with a series of delightful fishing villages, each clustered around its harbour.

- **Information:** Scottish Fisheries Museum, Anstruther. ☎01333 311 073. Museum & Heritage Centre, Marketgate, Crail. ☎01333 450 869. www.standrews.co.uk.
- ▶ **Orient Yourself:** the East Neuk is the group of fishing villages and their hinterland on the most northerly part of the Firth of Forth.
- **Don't Miss:** Crail Old Centre; Scottish Fisheries Museum, Anstruther.
- **Organizing Your Time:** Allow half a day for Crail, half a day for Anstruther and half a day for the rest (excluding boat trips). A car is best to explore the four villages, even though the distances between them are small.
- **Also See:** ST ANDREWS.

A Bit of History

The golden fringe – As early as the 11C Fife was the hub of the nation, with Dunfermline as the political and St Andrews as the ecclesiastical centres. The villages flourished as active trading ports with the Hanseatic League and the Low Countries. King James VI described Fife as "a beggar's mantle with a fringe of gold". It was the royal burghs along the coast, with their profitable activities of trading, fishing and smuggling, which were the "fringe of gold". With the development of the transatlantic routes, the villages concentrated on fishing.

A jumble of houses at Crail harbour, typical of ancient Neuk of Fife ports

D. Barnes/ Scottish Viewpoint

Crail★★ *Population 1,800*

This busy resort is the most attractive East Neuk burgh. The older heart of the burgh is clustered down by the harbour while the upper town is altogether more spacious.

Upper Crail★

Standing alone in a prominent position overlooking the spacious market place, the **tolbooth** (1598), a tiered tower, is graced by an attractively shaped belfry. The weather vane, a gilded capon (dried haddock), is a reminder that capons were the town's staple export. Behind the tolbooth at nos 62–64 is a **Crail Museum & Heritage Centre** (&ᗢ*Open Easter week, Apr–May Sat–Sun 2–5pm. Jun–Sept Mon–Sat, 10am–1pm, 2pm–5pm; Sun 2pm–5pm. ☜ donations welcome. ☎ 01333 450 869, www.crailmuseum. org.uk*), which gives an insight into the burgh's history, its main buildings and activities. The tree-lined Marketgate is bordered by elegant two- and three-storey dwellings. Of particular note are nos 30 and 44 on the south side and Auld House (16C) and Kirkmay House (early 19C) opposite. The "Blue Stone" just outside the churchyard on the left is said to have been thrown by the devil from the Isle of May in an attempt to destroy the church.
Take Kirk Wynd to pass the 16C circular dovecot, the sole remnant of a priory.

Follow the path round to Castle Walk which skirts the few remains of what was a royal stronghold. Amongst the landmarks visible (*viewfinder*) across the Forth are St Abb's Head, the Bass Rock, Tantallon Castle and the Isle of May.

Old Centre★★

Sloping down to the harbour, **Shoregate** is bordered by an attractive group of cottages (nos 22–28). Crab and lobster boats still use the **inner harbour** with its attractive stonework. On the

Address Book

⚭*For coin ranges, see the Legend on the cover flap.*

WHERE TO STAY

⚬⚬ **The Grange** – *45 Pittenweem Road, Anstruther.* ☎*01333 310 842. www.thegrangeanstruther.com.* This spacious Edwardian house is just outside the village, It features snug lounges, a charming sun room and neat traditional bedrooms.

WHERE TO EAT

⚬⚬⚬ **Cellar** – *24 East Green, Anstruther. Booking Essential.* ☎*01333 310 378.* Close to the picturesque harbour this locally renowned seafood restaurant has a warm ambience with open fires and exposed brick and stone. Bold, original dishes.

waterfront is the three-storey **Customs House** (no 35). Note the boat carving on the pend lintel. The adjoining group of buildings surround a paved courtyard. On the way up, note no 32 Castle Street and the delightful 18C no 1 Rose Wynd with its forestair and attractive door surround.

Anstruther Population 3,640

This linear settlement includes the once independent communities of Cellardyke, Anstruther Easter and Anstruther Wester. There is still some creelfishing (for lobster and crab) and white fish activity from Anstruther, but most of the fishermen now operate from Pittenweem, a mile to the west.

Scottish Fisheries Museum★★

&.⊙*Open Apr–Sept, Mon–Sat 10am–5.30pm. Sun 11am–5pm. Oct–Mar, 10am–4.30pm, Sun noon–4.30pm. Last entries 1hr before closing.* ⊛£5. ⌨. 🅿 ☎01333 310 628, www.scotfishmuseum.org.
Housed in a group of 16C–19C buildings on three sides of a cobbled courtyard, the exhibits, including 18 actual boats, the largest being the 78 ft *Zulu*, recount the history of Scottish fisheries and the harsh life of fisherfolk. Highlights include:

West Room and West Gallery – "The Days of Sail", illustrated by paintings, model boats, tableaux of life-size figures at work, fishing gear, dioramas of fishing methods.

Long Gallery – map of Scotland's fishing communities; ancillary trades tableau showing women gutting and packing herring; coopers making barrels etc.

Whaling – Illustrating a once-important sector of Scotland's industry.

Ship's Loft – "The Days of Steam", devoted to the era of the steam drifter. Paintings, models, original mural, examples of gear and fishing techniques.

Fishing into the Future Gallery – Model boats, fishing equipment, paintings and photos from the advent of motor power in the fishing industry to the present day.

Courtyard and Gallery – Examples of heavier items of machinery, actual small fishing boats, nets, anchors; fully equipped wheelhouse.

Fisherman's Cottage & Loft – This 16C building, once the property of the monks from Balmerino, has been renovated as a fisherman's home c.1900, in a period of relative prosperity. Berthed in the harbour opposite is the Museum's own veteran sea-going 1902 Fifie, *Reaper*, and Bauldie *White Wing*. The *Reaper* houses a small display describing life on board the fishing vessel.

Pittenweem Population 1,537

This burgh is on two levels. **Kellie Lodge** (*private*) in the High Street is the 16C town house of the Earls of Kellie from Kellie Castle (⦿*see KELLIE CASTLE*). Corbelled, pantiled and crow-stepped, it is an excellent example of the vernacular style. **St Fillan's Cave**, and Holy Well, is said to have been the sanctuary of the 7C Christian missionary Fillan.
Take any one of the six wynds down to the harbour which is today Fife's busiest fishing port. Of particular interest on the waterfront are **The Gyles** at the east end and no 18 East Shore, a three-storeyed building with its Dutch-style gable.

St Monance Population 1,450

The village is tightly packed around its small harbour. Wynds and closes lead off into the usual maze of lanes, back alleys and yards; a smuggler's paradise. The **church** was probably begun in the 11C by Queen Margaret. A large part of it is 13C and the choir was rebuilt by King David II in 1346.
Inside, look for the hanging ship, the coats of arms and the painted panel from the laird's loft, and the groined stone roof.

EDINBURGH★★★

CITY OF EDINBURGH

POPULATION 408,822

Edinburgh, the capital of Scotland, is a beautiful city, open and green, attractively set on a series of volcanic hills. The city boasts a rich historic past and two contrasting towns – the Old and New. A wealth of tourist sights, rich museum collections and its prestigious arts festival are all reasons to visit this charming city, its perennial vigour renewed now that it is once again the seat of a Scottish Parliament.

- **Information:** 3 Princes Street. ☎0845 225 5121. Edinburgh International Airport. ☎0870 040 0007. www.edinburgh.org.
- **Parking:** Difficult and expensive; don't drive in central Edinburgh.
- **Don't Miss:** The Royal Mile; an underground tour; the Scottish Parliament Building; the views from the Nelson Monument and Arthur's Seat; Charlotte Square; the Festival Fringe; Royal Museum and Museum of Scotland; Royal Yacht Brittania; Forth Bridges view from Queensferry.
- **Organizing Your Time:** Allow at least three days, preferably longer. It is best to explore on foot, particularly in the Old Town.
- **Especially for Kids:** A ghost tour; Edinburgh Zoo; Our Dynamic Earth; 3D Loch Ness Experience; Museum of Childhood; Brass Rubbing Centre; Royal Museum/ Museum of Scotland.

Viewpoints and Vistas

One of the most attractive features of the central area is the number of spectacular vistas. In addition to the viewpoints afforded by such prominent landmarks as the Scott and Nelson Monuments, the volcanic hills (Calton, Arthur's Seat, Castle Rock, Blackford, Costorphine) provide ideal vantage points.

Edinburgh Festival★★★

Tickets and information from The Hub, Royal Mile. Festival held Aug–Sept. Ticket office open Jul. Mon–Sat 10am– 5pm. ☎0131 473 2000. ww.eif.co.uk.
This prestigious annual festival provides an international quality programme of performances in all art forms. The ever-popular **Military Tattoo** (*first three*

North Bridge, Edinburgh

W. Buss/ MICHELIN

weeks Aug. Tickets from office, 32–34 Market Street. See website for ticket details. Postal bookings deadline mid-Nov. ☎0131 225 1188, www.edinburgh-tattoo.co.uk provides a spectacle rich in colour, tradition, music and excitement under the floodlights of the Castle Esplanade. The capacity audience of 9,000 is entertained by a cast of approximately 600. An integral part of the Festival is **The Fringe** (Tickets and information 180 High Street, see website for booking details First three weeks Aug. ☎0131 226 000. www.edfringe.com) with over 700 productions covering a wide range of entertainment, from the avant-garde to just plain eccentric, The Fringe spills out onto the streets and squares of Edinburgh which become the stage for a variety of entertainers from buskers and jugglers to musicians, dancers, mime artists and showmen of every imaginable kind.

The sister Edinburgh **Folk Festival**, another annual event, dates from 1979. The entertainments include concerts, lectures and workshops. The **Jazz & Blues Festival** (late Jul to early Aug. ☎0131 473 2000, www.edinburghjazzfestival.co.uk) is also a very popular event.

When visiting Edinburgh during the Festival it is absolutely essential to reserve accommodation well in advance. Many museums, galleries and houses extend their opening hours and organise special exhibitions during Festival time.

A Bit of History

The Castle Rock no doubt proved to be a secure refuge for the earliest settlers, although the Romans preferred the attractions of Cramond. The name may in fact be derived from the Northumbrian King Edwin (Edwinesburg – Edwin's fortress) although he actually died before his people captured the site in 638. As a residence, the Castle Rock site was associated with **Malcolm Canmore** and his **Queen Margaret**. Their son

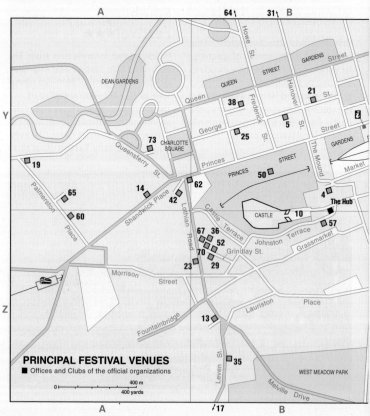

PRINCIPAL FESTIVAL VENUES
■ Offices and Clubs of the official organizations

David I gave great preferment to the settlement by founding the Abbey of Holy Rood and the building of a small chapel to commemorate his mother. During the Wars of Independence, the strategic importance of the castle not only afforded protection to the growing burgh but also made it more susceptible to English attacks.

Medieval Golden Age – The first town wall dated from 1450. With the early Stewarts, Edinburgh slowly assumed the roles of royal residence, seat of government, important religious centre and capital. This Golden Age ended with Flodden when the host of Scots dead included the king and Edinburgh's provost. In haste the town started to build the **Flodden Wall**; although only completed in 1560 this was to define the limits of the Ancient Royalty for over two centuries confining expansion upwards in the characteristic lands (tenements) of as many as 10 and 12 storeys.

Mary, Queen of Scots and the Reformation – Two years after the proclamation of the infant Mary's accession, Henry VIII's army set out on the **"rough wooing"**, creating havoc and destruction in the south and east of the country. Mary was sent to France for safety. Already the Roman Catholic church, wealthier than the Crown, was under attack and the ideas of the Reformation gained ground. The **Reformation** (1560) and the return of the Catholic Mary, Queen of Scots, a year later, made Edinburgh, during her short reign, the stage for warring factions, Protestant and Roman Catholic, pro-French and

Adam Theatre	CZ	2	Calton Community			Castle Esplanade	BZ	10
Assembly Hall	BY	4	Centre	CY	8	Central Hall	BZ	13
Assembly Rooms	BY	5	Calton Studios	CY	9	Cephas Cellar	AY	14

Chaplaincy Centre	CZ	16
Church Hill Theatre	BZ	17
Dance Directions at Belford	AY	19
Festival Club	CZ	
Festival Headquarters	BY	21
Festival Theatre	CZ	22
Filmhouse	BZ	23
Freemason's Hall	BY	25
Fringe Club	CZ	
Fringe Office	CY	
George Square Theatre	CZ	27
Heriott Watt Theatres	BZ	29
Inverleith House	BY	31
Jazz Festival Office	CY	
Jazz Pavillon	CY	33
King's Theatre	BZ	35
Lyceum Studio	BZ	36
Masonic Lodge	BY	38
Military Tattoo Office	CY	
Netherbow Arts Centre	CY	40
Platform One	AY	42
Playhouse Theatre	CY	43
Pleasance Theatre	CZ	45
Queen's Hall	CZ	47
Reid Concert Hall	CZ	49
Ross Bandstand	BY	50
Royal Lyceum	BZ	52
St Cecilia's Hall	CY	55
St Columba's by the Castle	BZ	57
St Giles Cathedral	CY	58
St Mary's Cathedral	AZ	60
The Hub	BYZ	
Theatre West End	AY	62
Theatre Workshop	BY	64
Tic-Toc Theatre	AY	65
Traverse Theatre	BZ	67
Usher Hall	BZ	70
Y.W.C.A.	AY	73

Address Book

For coin ranges, see the Legend on the cover flap.

GETTING AROUND

Bus services are frequent and on time. Tourist passes are valid from 2 to 13 days or a Freedom Ticket valid for one day are available from the tourist office.

VISITOR INFORMATION

3 Princes Street, south of Waverley Station. ☎0845 225 5121. The centre offers an accommodation and theatre booking service. There is also a bureau de change, a tourist information service, a bookshop and a souvenir shop.

WHERE TO STAY

The Beverley – *40 Murrayfield Avenue. ☎0131 337 1128, www. thebeverley.com.* Close to the rugby stadium, a short bus ride from the city centre, this elegant 19C house offers good value rooms with modern facilities and thoughtful extras.

Castle View – *30 Castle Street. ☎0131 226 5784, www.castleviewgh. co.uk.* This is a spacious penthouse apartment on the 3rd and 4th floors of an Edinburgh Georgian townhouse in which Kenneth (*The Wind in the Willows*) Grahame was born. There are views to Edinburgh Castle and the Firth of Forth.

Davenport House – *58 Great King Street. ☎0131 558 8495, www.davenport-house.com.* This traditionally restored 'Grade A' listed Georgian townhouse, set in a cobbled street in the city centre, provides classic luxury accommodation.

Seven Danube Street – *7 Danube Street. ☎0131 332 2755, www. sevendanubestreet.com.* Set in the vibrant and characterful village of Stockbridge, just a short bus ride from the city centre, this luxury guest house has bright traditionally styled rooms with antique furnishings. Breakfasts taken around a single large table add to a feeling of engaging hospitality.

16 Lynedoch Place – *316 Lynedoch Place. ☎0131 225 5507, www.16lynedochplace.co.uk.* This attractive listed Georgian residence close to the West End has been under the same friendly family management for over 20 years and offers beautiful cosy rooms.

Balmoral – *1 Princes Street. ☎0131 556 2414, www.thebalmoral hotel.com.* The haunt of visiting royalty, rock stars and presidents, who enjoy richly furnished rooms in baronial style at this most central of city landmarks.

The George – *19–21 George Street. ☎0131 225 1251. www.edinburgh-georgehotel.co.uk.* Beautifully appointed and recently refurbished, this classic New Town hotel makes the most of Robert Adams' listed 18C design. Carvers **restaurant** sits beneath a magnificent glass dome.

The Glasshouse – *2 Greenside Place. ☎0131 525 8200. www.theetongroup.com.* Possibly the city's most unusual and certainly one of its trendiest places to stay , this boutique hotels mixes ultra-modern styling (glass themes with great views onto Holyrood Park) and all the latest gadgets, set behind the facade of a 19C church.

The Scotsman – *20 North Bridge Street. ☎0131 556 5565, www. thescotsmanhotelgroup.co.uk.* Occupying the grand marble former offices of Edinburgh's principal newspaper, this stunning hotel has top leisure facilities and superbly equipped modern bedrooms. Its beautiful North Bridge **brasserie** is recommended.

Prestonfield – *Priestfield Road. ☎0131 225 7800, www.prestonfield.com.* This superbly restored, opulent 17C country house is on the edge of Holyrood Park just a few minutes walk from the city centre, and offers 22 rooms. Its Rhubarb **restaurant** is recommended.

WHERE TO EAT

Blue – *10 Cambridge Street. ☎0131 221 1222. http://bluescotland.co.uk.* This busy, contemporary city centre restaurant serves Modern Scottish cuisine in an elegant interior of upholstered Danish chairs, modern oak panelling, hand crafted rugs and stunning lighting.

Nargile – *73 Hanover Street. ☎0131 225 5755, www.nargile.com.* An unpretentious welcoming and enthusiastic restaurant serving excellent and authentic Turkish cuisine.

Fenwicks – *15 Salisbury Place.* ☎*0131 667 4265, www.fenwicks-restaurant.co.uk.* This cosy neighbourhood restaurant offers contemporary Scottish cuisine with French flair.

First Coast – *99–101 Dalry Road.* ☎*0131 313 4404. www.first-coast.co.uk.* An informal, smart little bistro near Haymarket Station with a short but interesting menu of trad-modern favourites.

Le Café Saint-Honoré – *34 North West Thistle Street Lane.* ☎*0131 226 2211, www.cafesthonore.com.* Edinburgh's favourite French bistro is furnished in classic fin-de-siecle style and offers good value cuisine.

The Tower – *Museum of Scotland (Fifth Floor), Chambers Street.* ☎*0131 225 3003, www.tower-restaurant.com.* Wonderful rooftop views complement the game, grills and seafood at this popular contemporary brasserie-style restaurant. In good weather ask for a terrace table.

The Vintners Room – *The Vaults, 87 Giles Street, Leith.* ☎*0131 554 6767, www.thevintnersrooms.com.* French cooking in an atmospheric candle-lit 18C spirits warehouse with stone floors and rug-coverd walls, open fireplaces and intricate plasterwork.

Duck's at Le Marche Noir – *2–4 Eyre Place.* ☎*0131 558 1608, www.ducks.co.uk.* This intimate and very personally run bistro serves inventive cuisine with a modern discreetly French character. Outstanding wine list.

Atrium – *Traverse Theatre, 10 Cambridge Street.* ☎*0131 228 8882, www.atriumrestaurant.co.uk.* An ultramodern interior, including twisted copper lamps and tables made of wooden railway sleepers, is the setting for some of the city's most adventurous modern cooking, often voted the best in town.

Forth Floor at Harvey Nichols – *Harvey Nichols Department Store, 30–34 St Andrew Square.* ☎*0131 524 8350.* Stylish restaurant with delightful outside terrace offering views over the city and the Firth of Forth. Modern Scottish cooking with a choice between brasserie-style dining or a more formal setting.

Off the Wall – *105 High Street.* ☎*0131 558 1497, www.off-the-wall.co.uk.* Set discretely on the Royal Mile, this vividly coloured dining room combines French influences with the best of Scottish produce.

Oloroso –*33 Castle Street.* ☎*0131 226 7614, www.oloroso.co.uk.* Very modish restaurant in the heart of the city with a lovely terrace offering fine castle views. The cuisine is stylish and modern with Asian influences. The bar menu opens up Oloroso to diners with thinner wallets.

SIGHTSEEING

Various tours start from Waverley Bridge.

ACCESS FOR DISABLED VISITORS

The *Accessible Scotland* brochure lists almost 1,000 accessible accommodation establishments and visitor attractions across the country. To obtain a copy, call 0845 22 55 121 or order online (*www.visitscotland.com/accommodation/accessiblescotland*).

SHOPPING

Princes Street is the busy main shopping street, but these days has little to offer except popular high-street names – John Lewis (St James Shopping Centre), Marks and Spencer, Boots etc. Only Jenners, the city's famous department store, is a reminder of more elegant times on Princes Street. George Street is now the place to go, lined with trendy shops (Harvey Nichols, Karen Millen). Fashion boutiques and music shops are to be found in Rose Street (parallel to Princes Street). Antique shops are mainly in the area around the Royal Mile, Victoria Street and Grassmarket in the Old Town and in Dundas and Thistle Streets in the New Town.

Quality garments in tweed, tartan, cashmere and wool are sold in Jenners, Burberrys, the Scotch House, Romanes Patterson (Princes Street) and Kinloch Anderson. The Cashmere Store in the Royal Mile and Kinloch Anderson's Retail Shop on the corner of Commercial Street and Dock Street in Leith are also worth a visit.

Edinburgh Crystal in Penicuik – free shuttle bus from Waverley Bridge – has an array of crystal articles on sale in its factory shop.

In the Royal Mile there are gourmet food shops selling smoked salmon, kippers, cheese, haggis, oatcakes, shortbread and Dundee cake as well as malt whisky.

TRACING ANCESTORS

Various organisations specialise in research into ancestry for people of Scottish descent. For addresses see the Practical information chapter at the end of the guide.

ENTERTAINMENT

The List, a fortnightly magazine, lists films, plays and concerts on offer in town. Hotels hold "Scottish Evenings" including traditional fare and entertainment and pubs all over town stage live music of all genres.

PUBLIC HOUSES

The best way to sample the local brews is on a pub crawl, perhaps starting at the **Abbotsford** in Rose Street or the **Café Royal**, the haunt of literary celebrities, in Register Place, with its famous oyster bar. **Deacon Brodie's** in Lawnmarket or **Greyfriars Bobby** in Candlemaker Row are popular with visitors. You'll find noisy pubs with a lively atmosphere popular with students in Grassmarket, and fashionable pubs and wine bars by the riverside in Leith. These establishments all offer simple meals at reasonable prices.

Edinburgh has a wide range of restaurants; those offering Scottish fare are identified by the **Taste of Scotland** logo.

---

pro-English. With the departure of James and his court after the **Union of the Crowns** (1603) Edinburgh lost much of its pageantry and cultural activity.

Religious strife – Relative peace ensued until Charles I, following his 1633 coronation at Holyrood, pushed through Episcopacy (government of the church by bishops) – a policy inherited from his father. **The National Covenant** was drawn up in 1638 and signed in Greyfriars Church. The signatories swore loyalty to the King but fervently opposed his religious policy. A year later, following the General Assembly of Glasgow, episcopacy was abolished. Covenanters took the castle. By 1641 Charles had conceded to the Covenanters (defendants of the Reformed Faith) but the outbreak of the English Civil War brought a pact with the English Parliamentarians, the **Solemn League and Covenant** (1643). The brilliant royalist campaign led by the Marquess of Montrose ended with defeat at Philliphaugh (1645) and the final outcome of the Parliamentary victory at Marston Moor near York was the king's execution (1649).

Cromwell defeated the Scots at Dunbar (1650) and Montrose was executed. His troops entered Edinburgh and the palace and other buildings served as barracks, some like Holyroodhouse suffered through fire. The Commonwealth was a period of uneasy peace in Edinburgh and much was the rejoicing at the Restoration in spite of the fact that it brought the reintroduction of the episcopal system and ruthless persecution of the Covenanters until opposition was finally eradicated.

In the late 17C Edinburgh flourished as a legal and medical centre. The failure of the Darien scheme – its aims were to promote Scottish overseas trade and to control trade between the Atlantic and the Pacific – gave rise to anti-English feelings. In 1707 Edinburgh lost its Parliament when the politicians headed south. The legal profession took over Parliament Hall and began to dominate Edinburgh society.

Of the two Jacobite rebellions, that of 1745 saw the return of a brief period of glory to Holyroodhouse with the installation of the prince's court at the palace.

The Enlightenment – In late-18C Edinburgh a circle of great men flourished, including philosophers David Hume and Dugald Stewart, economist Adam Smith, geologist James Hutton, chemist Joseph Black and architect Robert Adam. Clubs and societies prospered and it was in such a climate of intellectual ferment that plans were put forward for a civic project of great boldness and imagination.

Georgian Edinburgh – Old Edinburgh, on its ridge, was squalid and overcrowded. The earliest moves out were made to George Square in the south before plans for the New Town were drawn up, approved, enacted and accepted socially. The project was encouraged by the early establishment of public buildings in the new area; Theatre Royal (1767–68), Register House (1774–1822), Physicians Hall (1775–77) and the Assembly Rooms (1784–87). Attractive as the elegant streets and squares were, it was to the markets, wynds and closes, taverns and clubs of the Old Town that many still went to earn their livelihood and spend their moments of leisure.

Castle★★ 1hr 30min

Open year-round daily 9.30am–6.00pm (Oct–Mar 5pm). Last entry 45min before closing. During Edinburgh Tattoo and 1–2 Jan call for opening hours. Opening hours for museums vary slightly from castle. Fast track tickets available online. Closed 25, 26 Dec. £11. 0131 225 9846. www.edinburgh castle.gov.uk.

This stately fortress, perched on its strategic **site**★★★ on Castle Rock, is impressive from all sides. The silhouette of the castle figures prominently on the skyline of most views of the city, and the castle's role has been of paramount importance throughout the city's history.

Royal residence to military fortress

As early as the 11C the buildings atop Castle Rock were favoured as a residence by royalty, in particular by Margaret, the queen of Malcolm III, and her sons.
The castle subsequently alternated between Scottish and English forces and in 1313 suffered demolition by the Scots. In the late 14C Bruce's son, David II, built a tower, of which there are no visible remains, on the site of the Half Moon Battery. The infamous **Black Dinner** of 1440 resulted in the execution of the two young Douglas brothers in the presence of their 10-year-old sovereign, James II, in an attempt to quell Douglas power.
In the 16C Regent Morton did much to strengthen the castle's defences which suffered again during Sir William Kirkcaldy of Grange's stout defence (1573) in the name of Mary, Queen of Scots. The end result was prompt execution for Grange and repairs and rebuilding to the castle. In the 1650s Cromwell's troops took over and thus began the castle's new role as a garrison. The 18C

The Edinburgh Military Tattoo

P. Tomkins/VisitScotland/Scottish Viewpoint

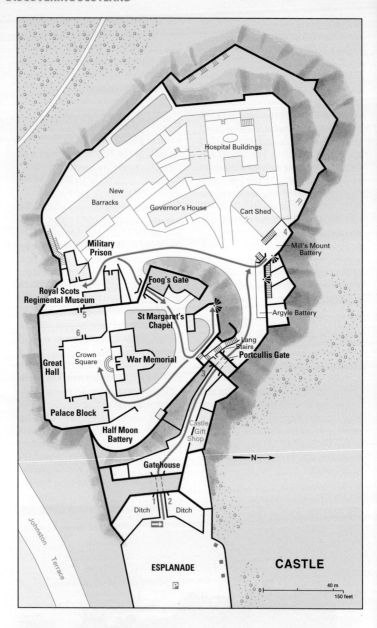

Hospital Buildings

New Barracks

Governor's House

Cart Shed

4

Military Prison

Mill's Mount Battery

Royal Scots Regimental Museum

5

Foog's Gate

Argyle Battery

St Margaret's Chapel

6

Crown Square

War Memorial

Lang Stairs

Portcullis Gate

Great Hall

Palace Block

3

Half Moon Battery

Castle Gift Shop

N →

Gatehouse

1 2

Ditch Ditch

→

Johnston Terrace

ESPLANADE

P

CASTLE

0 ——— 40 m
——— 150 feet

saw two Jacobite attacks, the last by Bonnie Prince Charlie in person from his headquarters at the other end of the Royal Mile. The buildings we see today are basically those which have resulted from the castle's role as a military garrison in recent centuries.

Esplanade

Created as a spacious parade ground in the 18C, the esplanade is the setting for the Festival's most popular event, the **Edinburgh Military Tattoo** (◉ *see Calendar of Events*), when the floodlit castle acts as backdrop. Before entering, note two of the castle's most imposing features from among the tiers of buildings, the appropriately named Half Moon Battery and the Palace Block towering up behind to the left.

Gatehouse

Beyond the ditch, started in the 1650s by Cromwell's troops, is the gatehouse, built as a suitably imposing entrance in the 19C. Two national heroes, Bruce (**1**) and Wallace (**2**) flank the entrance. Once through, the massive walls of the Half Moon Battery loom up ahead. These demarcate the line of the original outer defences. A plaque (**3**) on the left, commemorates Kirkcaldy of Grange's stoic defence of 1573.

Portcullis Gate

The lower part, dating from Regent Morton's 1570s fortifications, has decorative features including Morton's coat of arms, while the upper part is a 19C addition. Farther up, the two batteries, Argyle and Mill's Mount, both afford excellent **views**★★ of Princes Street and the New Town. The **One O'Clock Gun** (**4**) is fired (Mon–Sat) from the upper battery. Following the signs round to the left, on the right is the Governor's House (1742), with adjoining wings for the Master Gunner and Store-Keeper. The imposing building behind is the 1790s New Barracks for the castle garrison.

Royal Scots Regimental Museum

 ♿ 🕐*Open year-round daily 9.30am–5.30pm (Oct–Mar 4pm).* 🕐*Closed 25–26 Dec, 1 Jan.* ☎*0131 310 5014, www. theroyalscots.co.uk.*

The Royal Regiment is the oldest and most senior regiment of the British Army. Raised on 28 March 1633, the unit originally served under King Louis XIII of France where it earned the nickname of "Pontius Pilate's Bodyguard". The regiment was finally recalled to Britain in 1676; two rooms of exhibits trace the regiment's subsequent history: Corunna, Waterloo, Alma, Sebastopol, Marne... There is an impressive display of medals.

Vaults (5)

Two levels of great vaulted chambers, situated under the Crown Square buildings, housed French and American prisoners in the 18C and 19C. In the end chamber stands the 500-year-old siege cannon, **Mons Meg**. Commissioned by the Duke of Burgundy and forged in 1449 at Mons in Hainaut, it was given eight years later to his nephew James II. During an eventful career, Mons Meg is said to have served at Crookston (1489), Dumbarton (1489) and Norham castles (1497) and even to have spent time in the Tower of London. Sir Walter Scott petitioned for its return and in 1829 the huge medieval cannon was returned to Edinburgh.

St Margaret's Chapel

The small rectangular building on the left incorporates remnants of the castle's oldest structure, and perhaps even Edinburgh's. This 12C chapel is dedicated to Malcolm III's Queen Margaret. Once surrounded by other buildings it served various purposes until the mid 19C when its original role was revealed and restoration ensued. Inside, the chancel arch is Norman in inspiration with its cushion capitals and chevron decoration.

The terrace in front offers an extensive **panorama**★★★ of northern Edinburgh, in particular Princes Street and the gardens, and the geometric pattern of the New Town.

Half Moon Battery

The battery was built following the 1573 siege, which saw the destruction of David II's tower house. From here the strategic importance of the original tower with its command of castle approaches and entrance is evident.

The heart of the medieval fortress and one-time royal residence is marked by Crown Square. Of the four buildings overlooking the square today only the southern and eastern ranges are of historic interest.

Scottish National War Memorial

North side. In the 1920s **Robert Lorimer** undertook the task of converting a mid-18C building into Scotland's War Memorial. The exterior, with a strong resemblance to the palace part of Stirling Castle, is in harmony with the earlier buildings.

The interior achieves a suitable atmosphere of dignity and reverence to honour those who served. Wartime scenes are depicted in the stained-glass windows by Douglas Strachan. The low-relief sculptures depict the fighting men and other participants in the struggle. A casket containing the names of the fallen stands in the apse.

National War Museum (6)

West side. East gallery in Palace Block. ⏱ *Open year-round daily, 9.45am–5.45pm (Nov–Mar 4.45pm).* ⏱ *Closed 25 Dec and Bank hols.* ☎ *0131 247 4413. www.nms.ac.uk.*
Displays of uniforms, medals, badges, colours and weapons illustrate the history of the Scottish regiments of the British Army.

Great Hall

South side. The hall built in the late 15C for James IV succeeded a series of earlier buildings. The chief attraction of this spacious apartment intended for great occasions is the **hammerbeam roof**★★ which can be fully appreciated since the 19C restoration. Boards and beams are attractively painted and reward inspection.

Palace Block

East side. This range, which dates from the 15C, contained the royal apartments overlooking the old town. The interior was remodelled in 1617.
Enter by the door nearest the Great Hall range. A room on the right has displays on excavations at Mill's Mount dating back to the Iron Age. Straight ahead, Queen Mary's Room is hung with family portraits of her son James VI, her grandson Charles I, her great-grandsons Charles II and James II, and her first husband Francis II. There is also a plaster cast from Mary's tomb effigy at Westminster Abbey. The adjoining small **chamber**, with its panelling and timber ceiling, is the room where James VI was born in 1566. The decoration dates from the 1617 refurbishing.
Once in the square again, the doorway in the staircase tower leads to the Crown Chamber on the first floor where the Scottish crown jewels, known as the

Honours of Scotland★★★ are displayed. Although of unknown age, the pearl and gem encrusted **crown** is Britain's only pre-Restoration crown to have escaped being melted down by Cromwell. The **sceptre** and **sword** were gifts from two Popes to the Renaissance prince, James IV, the former from the Borgia Pope, Alexander VI (1492–1503), and the latter from his successor, Pope Julius II (1503–13), a great patron of the arts. Pride of place is also given to the **Stone of Destiny**, the ancient symbol of Celtic kingship, which was returned to Scotland in 1996 after 700 years under the Coronation Chair at Westminster Abbey.
The other rooms (*East Gallery*) contain further displays on the Royal Navy, Royal Air Force, Scotland's sole cavalry regiment, the Royal Scots Greys, and the yeomanry regiments. Note the model of the pride of James IV's navy, the magnificent **Great Michael** (1507–11).

Abbey and Palace of Holyroodhouse★★

At the east end of the Royal Mile stands the Palace of Holyroodhouse, the Queen's official residence in Scotland, adjoined by the ruined nave of the abbey. In the background are the green slopes and rocky crags of Holyrood Park rising to Arthur's Seat.

The Holy Rood

Legend has it that **David I**, while out hunting, was thrown from his mount and wounded by a stag. In a defensive gesture he made to grasp the animal's antlers only to find he was holding a crucifix, the animal having made off into the forest. In recognition David founded the Augustinian Abbey of Holy Rood in 1128 and granted to the canons the right to their own burgh, Canongate.
The medieval abbey prospered and benefited from royal patronage in the 15C from the Stewart Kings. James II was born, married and buried here and broke with the Scone tradition to be crowned here. His three successors were all married in the abbey. It was during this period that the guesthouse was used as a royal residence in preference

The Palace of Holyroodhouse from the air with the ruins of Hollywood Abbey to the left

to the castle. James IV, intent on making Edinburgh capital, started transforming the guest house into a palace by building the present northwest tower.

Work continued after his death at Flodden (1513). The abbey buildings suffered damage in 1544, were despoiled at the Reformation and burnt in 1650 when Cromwell's troops were quartered there. A moment of glory in the interval was the coronation of Charles I in 1633. From then on the nave served as parish church for the Canongate until 1688, when the congregation was dislodged by James VII who intended converting it into a Chapel Royal and the headquarters of the Order of the Thistle.

Royal Palace

Although Charles II never set foot in the palace he commissioned **Sir William Bruce** (1630–1710), the Architect Royal, to draw up designs. The architect had been instrumental – acting as an envoy – in Charles II's restoration. Bruce may have been influenced by designs for Whitehall done by Inigo Jones, as the final result is a handsome example of the Palladian style.

Palace *1hr*

🕐 *Palace and Abbey open Easter–Oct 9.30am–6pm. Nov–Easter, 9.30am–4.30pm. Last admission 1hr before closing. 24 Dec, 31 Dec, I Jan, see website for times. Gardens open summer.* 🕐*Closed Good Fri, mid May, first week Jun, last week Jun–first week Jul, 25–26 Dec and during royal visits.* ✆ *£9.80. Joint ticket with Queen's Gallery £13.* ⌨ *.* ☎*0131 556 5100. www.royalcollection.org.uk.*

Exterior

Flanked by columns, the door is surmounted by carved stonework incorporating the Scottish coat of arms, a broken pediment, a cupola and crown. The inner court elevations are an outstanding example of classic Renaissance and one of Scotland's earliest examples.

Interior

The decoration of the State Apartments remains lavish as designed by Sir William Bruce. Highly intricate decorative plasterwork ceilings, lavishly carved woodwork (doors, doorcases, picture frames and swags) and inset canvases were all integral parts of the decor and all of a very high standard of craftsmanship. The seven outstanding **plasterwork ceilings**★★★ in high relief represent 10 years' labour by the "gentlemen modellers" **John Halbert** and **George Dunsterfield.**

The impressive Grand Staircase leads up past Her Majesty's portrait by Her Limner, David Donaldson. Other than the ceilings, the most notable features of the **State Apartments** are: in the Adam-style Dining Room a splendid portrait of

P. Tomkins/ Scottish Viewpoint/ Visit Scotland

George IV in Highland Dress by Sir David Wilkie. In the Throne Room, redecorated in the 1920s, are royal portraits of the brothers Charles II and James VII (the palace's first royal guest) with their respective queens, and Queen Victoria in her coronation robes. Carved door surrounds and 18C Brussels tapestries (market scenes, Asia, Africa) can be seen in the Evening Drawing Room. Finest of all is the Morning Drawing Room sumptuously decorated with a Jacob de Wet medallion above the fireplace and 17C French tapestries (the Story of Diana). The King's Suite was on the east side, overlooking the famous Privy Garden of formal design on the site of the demolished cloister.

In the King's Chamber is a magnificent Red Bed (1672) and ceiling with a De Wet medallion. The Gallery walls are lined with imaginary and real portraits of Scottish Kings from 6C Fergus to James VII. Jacob de Wet completed them in two years.

The **Historic Apartments** in the 16C round tower consist of similar suites on two floors. These were refurbished c.1672 when floor and ceiling levels were adjusted to correspond to the Bruce additions. There are many Mary, Queen of Scots associations. The antechamber has 17C Mortlake tapestries from the workshop founded by her son James VI. Upstairs are two exquisite **16C coffered ceilings**, the first adorned with painted designs. The small chamber adjoining the Bedchamber is closely associated with the murder of Mary's Italian secretary, Rizzio, in 1566. His body was found in the outer chamber (brass plaque marks the spot). Paintings depict Mary's 2nd husband, **Henry Lord Darnley** (1546–67), as a 17-year-old youth with his brother. A second work shows his mourning family, including his son James VI, after Darnley's murder at Kirk o'Field.

A new display within the apartments focuses on **the Order of the Thistle**, the highest honour in Scotland. The Order honours Scottish men and women who have held public office or who have contributed in a particular way to national life.

Shown alongside historic insignia is an example of the mantle worn at the Thistle ceremony at St Giles' Cathedral in Edinburgh, which The Queen attends during her visit to the Palace in July.

Abbey 15min

ⓢ*Same times and charges as Palace.*
The roofless nave is all that remains of this once great abbey. It dates mainly from the late 12C and early 13C and there are some finely sculpted details. Compare the interlaced round-headed blind arcading of the 12C in the north aisle with the pointed 13C work opposite. The south elevation is an attractive fragment of 13C design. Queen Victoria rebuilt the royal burial vault following its destruction on the departure of the Roman Catholic James VII. The remains of David II, James II, James V and Lord Darnley are interred here.

Queen's Gallery 1hr

♿ⓢⓞ*Open same times as palace.* ⓢ*Closed Good Fri, two weeks mid-Apr, late Oct to mid-Nov, 25–26 Dec.* ⊠ *£5. Joint ticket with Queen's Gallery £13.* ⌨ *.* ☎ *0131 556 5100. www.royalcollection.org.uk.*
Built in the shell of the former Holyrood Free Church and Duchess of Gordon's School, the Gallery provides purpose-built, state-of-the-art facilities to enable a programme of changing exhibitions of the most delicate works of art from the priceless Royal Collection to be shown in Scotland for the first time.

Holyrood Park

Holyrood Park, the largest area of open ground within the city, is dominated by Arthur's Seat (823ft/251m) and the Salisbury Crags, both volcanic features. A path from the car park on the Queen's Road, within the park, leads up to **Arthur's Seat** (30min) which affords a tremendous **panorama**★★ of the Edinburgh area.

At the foot of Arthur's Seat, the historic palace buildings are offset by significant structures reflecting the town's dynamic outlook following the devolution of power to Scotland: the futuristic

Holyrood Park, Edinburgh

Dynamic Earth (☾ *see entry, below*); the spectacular Scottish Parliament building; another new building housing the offices of The Scotsman.

Beyond Dunsapie lies the lovely village of **Duddingston** in an attractive setting between park and loch (which acts as bird sanctuary). The 12C church has some good Norman features and its historic inn, **The Sheeps Heid,** is worth the walk in its own right. One of the oldest pubs in Scotland its name dates from 1580 when the landlord was presented with an embellished ram's head ("heid") by King James VI.

Walking Tours

1 **Royal Mile**★★ **Tour**
Castle to Palace, Allow 1 day

The principal thoroughfare of the Old Town runs from the castle, in its strategic site, down the ridge to the abbey and palace. The Royal Mile is in fact a succession of four streets: Castle Hill, the Lawnmarket, the High Street and the Canongate. Daniel Defoe wrote in the early 18C, "This is, perhaps, the largest, longest, and finest street for buildings and number of inhabitants, not in Britain only, but in the world". The few original buildings which remain give some idea of what medieval Edinburgh must have looked like.

The Scotch Whisky Experience
354 Castle Hill ♿ ☾ *Open year-round daily, 10am (9.30am Jun–Aug) to 6pm. Last tour 1hr before closing.* ☾ *Closed 25 Dec.* ✆ *£9.50 (includes Whisky dram or soft drink).* ✕. ☎ *0131 220 0441, www.whisky-heritage.co.uk.*

The ground floor exhibition traces the whisky-making process from peat cutting to bottling and packaging. A 10min film "The Water of Life" explains the different types of whisky and the workings and layout of a typical Speyside distillery. Upstairs, a ride through a series of tableaux gives a pictorial account of whisky making.

Camera Obscura and World of Illusions
Castlehill. ♿ ☾ *Open year-round daily. Jul–Aug, 9.30am–7.30pm. Sept–Oct and Apr–Jun, 9.30am–6pm. Nov–Mar, 10am–5pm.* ✆ *£7.95.* ☎ *0131 226 3709. www.camera-obscura.co.uk.*

From its rooftop position in the Outlook Tower, the **camera obscura** presents a fascinating view of the city on a clear day. Exhibitions deal with illusions, holography, pin-hole photography and space photography.

The Church of Scotland **General Assembly Hall** stands on the site of Mary of Guise's Palace (destroyed 1861). Its blackened towers are a landmark to visitors walking up the hill to the castle.

EDINBURGH

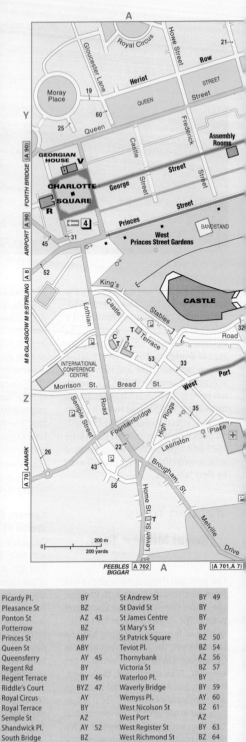

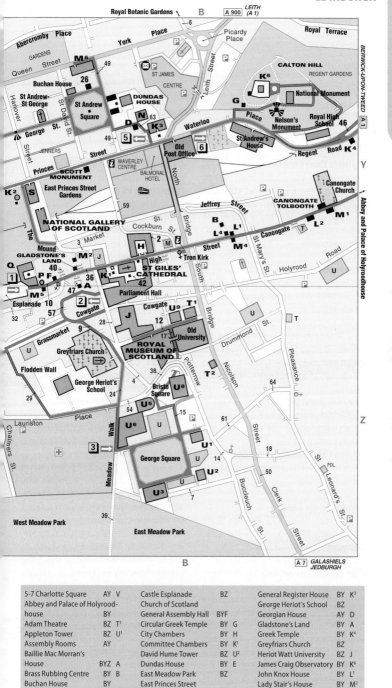

Moray House	BY	L[2]	Outlook Tower and			Scott Monument	BY	F
Mowbray House	BY	L[4]	Camera Obscura	BYP		Scottish National		
Museum of Childhood	BY	M[4]	Parliament Hall	BZ		Portrait Gallery	BY	M[6]
Museum of Edinburgh	BY	M[1]	Ramsay Lodge	BY	Q	St Andrew's House	BY	
National Gallery of			Register House	AY	R	St Andrew-St George	BY	
Scotland	BY	M[4]	Royal Botanic Garden	BY		St Giles Cathedral	BY	
National Monument	BY		Royal High School	BY		Student Centre	BZ	U[8]
Nelson's Monument	BY		Royal Museum of			Tron Kirk	BY	
New Register House	BY	N	Scotland	BZ	M[2]	University Staff Club	BZ	U[9]
Old Post Office	BY		Royal Scottish Academy	BY	S	West Meadow Park	BZ	
Old University	BZ		Scotch Whisky			West Princes		
			Heritage Centre	BZ	M[5]	Street Gardens	AY	

Mylne's Court is a picturesque 1970s reconstruction of what a court looked like once a narrow burgess strip had been built over. The narrow approach passages from the main street are known as closes or wynds with a "pend" at the entrance.

The Hub

⊘*Open year-round daily 10am–6pm.* ✕. ☎ *0131 473 2067, www.thehub-edinburgh.com.*

A tall steeple highlights the former Highland Tolbooth, built in the mid 19C by James Gillespie Graham and Augustus Pugin and imaginatively refurbished as Edinburgh's Festival Centre. The ornate interior boasts contemporary sculpture, tiling and stained glass as well as a splendid sculpture hall. The Hub is a focal point for the city's festivals and a ticket office for the Edinburgh Festival. It's cafe is one of the Royal Mile's favourite daytime meeting eating and drinking places.

Gladstone's Land★

477B Lawnmarket. NTS. ⊘*Open Good Fri–Oct daily 10am–5pm (Jul–Aug 7pm). Last admission 30mins before closing.* ⊘ *£5.* ☎ *0844 4932120. www.nts.org.uk.*

This narrow six-storey "land" (tenement) is typical of 17C Edinburgh when all building was upwards. The property was acquired in 1617 by a merchant burgess, Thomas Gledstanes, who rebuilt and extended it out towards the street. The premises behind the pavement arcade are arranged as a shop with living quarters on the other floors. The first floor is a good example of a 17C town house: original **painted ceilings** and 17C carved Scottish bed and Dutch chests.

Lady Stair's House

Down the close. Built in 1622, this town house takes its name from an occupant of the late 18C, the widow of John Dalrymple, 1st Earl of Stair. It is now home to the **Writers' Museum** (⊘*open year-round daily. Mon–Sat, 10am–5pm, Sun (Aug only) noon–5pm;* ☎ *0131 529 7902, www.cac.org.uk*) which displays manuscripts, relics and other memorabilia of three of Scotland's greatest literary figures: Robert Burns (1759–96), Sir Walter Scott (1771–1832) and R L Stevenson (1850–94).

St Giles' Cathedral★★

⊘*Open year-round daily, May–Sept Mon–Fri 9am–7pm. Sat 9am–5pm, Sun 1–5pm. Oct–Apr Mon–Sat 9am–5pm, Sun 1–5pm.* ⊘*Closed 26 Dec & 1–2 Jan.* ⊘*£3 donation requested. £2 photography permit.* ⊘. ☎ *0131 225 9442, www.stgilescathedral.org.uk.*

The present High Kirk of Edinburgh is probably the third church on this site. The first, dating from the 9C, was probably closer to the castle. It was replaced by a Romanesque structure in 1126 of which remain the four piers supporting the tower. This was burnt down by the English in 1385 following which the present building was raised. Alterations and restorations have radically changed the character of the 15C church. The Reformation brought troubled times to St Giles', when many altars and images, including the precious relic and statue of St Giles, were swept away.

As the capital's principal church it served as meeting place for Parliament and the General Assembly and witnessed many great state occasions such as James VI's farewell to his Scottish subjects and, over 200 years later, George IV's 1822 state visit.

The Jenny Geddes stool-throwing incident (a protest against Episcopacy – statue and plaque on the north side of the Moray aisle), although much disputed historically, preceded the signing of the National Covenant (🔖 *see the Linlithgow copy in the Chepman aisle*) and the ensuing religious strife. Twice during the 17C the church enjoyed a brief spell of cathedral status (1637–38 and 1661–89).

Exterior

Seen from the west, the church is dominated by the square tower raising aloft the delicate imperial or eight-arched **crown spire**★★★ (1495), a most distinctive feature of Edinburgh's skyline. The church's exterior lost much of its original character when it was refaced (19C).

Interior

The original cruciform shape has been lost with the addition of aisle and side chapels. Although the interior was spared the systematic restoration of the exterior, details, and in particular monuments, provide the main points of interest.

▶ *Start in the northwest corner and proceed in a clockwise direction.*

The flowing style and strong glowing colours of the north aisle window (**1**) characterise the work of the Pre-Raphaelites, Burne-Jones and William Morris. In the north aisle stands a statue of **John Knox** (1512–72) (**2**), reformer and minister of St Giles'. The Albany Aisle with its Gothic vaulting was probably built in expiation for the murder of the Duke of Rothesay in 1402. The aisle beyond contains the imposing 19C marble monument (**3**) to the 8th Earl and 1st Marquess of Argyll (1607–61) who was executed only days after the body of his arch rival the Marquess of Montrose had been rehabilitated and interred on the far side of the church. Move back into the south transept to admire Douglas Strachan's great north window (**4**), a glow of blue above the carved stone screen. From here also admire the attractive 15C rib and groin vaulting of the chancel and compare it with that of the nave (19C).

In 1911 Robert Lorimer designed the **Thistle Chapel** in the Flamboyant Gothic style for the most Noble Order of the Thistle founded by James VII in 1687. Under a fan-vaulted ceiling and its multitude of carved bosses, are the richly carved stalls and canopies for the sovereign and 16 knights. It is a lavish display of 20C craftsmanship. Above are helmets, crests and banners with knights' arms on the stall backs.

Beyond the Preston aisle is the side chapel known as the Chepman aisle, the final resting place of the **Marquess of Montrose** (1612–50) (**5**), Covenanter and Royalist whose fame rests on his brilliant 1644–45 campaign. He suffered an ignominious fate at the hands of his enemy, Argyll. The Restoration meant rehabilitation for Montrose and a traitor's execution for Argyll.

The aisle beyond the organ has a 19C marble monument (**6**) to James Stewart,

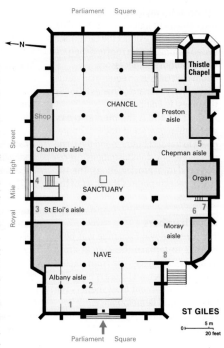

Parliament Square

←—N—

Thistle Chapel

CHANCEL

Shop

High Street

Chambers aisle

Royal Mile

Preston aisle

Chepman aisle

5

Organ

4

SANCTUARY

3 St Eloi's aisle

Moray aisle

6

7

NAVE

8

Albany aisle

2

1

ST GILES

Parliament Square

0 5 m
  20 feet

Earl of Moray (1531–70), with an original 16C brass. Half-brother to Mary, Queen of Scots and Regent for her son, Moray was murdered in Linlithgow (👀 see LIN-LITHGOW) in 1570. A window (**7**) by Noel Paton relates the tale and shows Knox preaching at the funeral service of one of his strongest supporters.

The low relief (**8**) at the end of the Moray Aisle portrays Robert Louis Stevenson (1850–94), offspring of a family of engineers, who achieved fame as an author.

The imposing buildings at the corner of the Lawnmarket and George IV Bridge are the **Committee Chambers**. The Signet Library to the rear of the cathedral dates from 1810–12. Near the Boehm statue of the 5th Duke of Buccleuch in Garter Robes is a heart shape set into the cobbles. This marks the site of the old tolbooth (1466–1817) made famous by Scott in *The Heart of Midlothian*.

Parliament Hall

👀 🕐 *Open Mon–Fri, 9am–4.30pm.* ☎ *0131 225 2595. www.scotcourts.gov.uk.*

Behind the imposing Georgian façade is the 17C Parliament Hall decreed by Charles I and designed by his master mason **John Mylne.** Where the Scottish Parliament met from 1639 to 1707, lawyers now pace under the carved and gilded **hammerbeam roof** and the gaze of their august predecessors.

South of St Giles' is an equestrian statue of the Merry Monarch, Charles II (1685), the oldest in Edinburgh.

At the east end is the **mercat cross**, where merchants and traders congregated to transact business and the scene of celebrations, demonstrations, executions and royal proclamations. The 19C structure incorporates the shaft of the 16C cross.

City Chambers

The former Royal Exchange was built in 1753 to replace the mercat cross as a meeting place. The front, facing Cockburn Street, is 11 storeys high. The screen at pavement level shelters the City's Stone of Remembrance.

The first edition of *Encyclopaedia Britannica* was printed between 1768–71 in

Anchor Close. The original compilers were William Smellie, Colin Macfarquhar and Andrew Bell. They purposely avoided the encyclopaedic dictionary form and their solution became the model for later English language encyclopaedias. The *Encyclopaedia Britannica* still bears a thistle on the covers.

3D Loch Ness Experience [Kids]

1 Parliament Square. 👀 🕐 *Open Apr–Oct 9.30am–6pm, Nov–Mar 10am–5pm. (Jul–Aug late opening until 8pm).* 💷 *£5.95 (child £3.95).* ☎ *0131 225 2290. www.3dlochness.com.*

Written and presented by Loch Ness expert Adrian Shine, designer of the award-winning Loch Ness Exhibition Centre in Drumnadrochit (👀 see *The Great Glen*) this entertaining 3D film explores the myth of Nessie.

Tron Kirk

John Mylne built this church prior to undertaking Parliament Hall. The spire is a 19C replacement. This is the traditional gathering place of Hogmanay revellers.

Museum of Childhood [Kids]

42 High Street. 👀 🕐 *Open Mon–Sat, 10am–5pm. Call for Sun opening times.* 🕐 *Closed 25–26 Dec and 1–2 Jan.* ☎ *0131 529 4142, www.cac.org.uk.*

Anything and everything to do with childhood (not just toys and games) is the theme of this charming collection. Children discover old toys and games while parents reminisce.

Brass Rubbing Centre [Kids]

Chalmers' Close. 🕐 *Open Apr–Sept Mon–Sat, 10am–5pm. Aug, also Sun noon–5pm.* ☎ *0131 556 4364. www.cac.org.uk.*

Try your hand at brass rubbing, choosing from a varied collection of replicas of Pictish stones and brasses, in the only surviving fragment of the Gothic **Trinity College Church,** founded about 1460 by Queen Mary of Gueldres, wife of James II of Scotland.

Farther along the street, 15C **Mowbray House** was the studio of the portraitist **George Jamesone** (1588–1644).

John Knox House

43–45 High Street. ♿🕐*Open year-round Mon–Sat 10am–6pm. Jul–Aug, also Sun noon–6pm.* 🕐*Closed 25–26 Dec and 1–2 Jan.* ☒ *£3.50.* ☎*0131 556 9579 or 2647. www.scottishstorytellingcentre.co.uk.*

This picturesque town house was probably built prior to 1490. The armorial panel on the west wall is that of the goldsmith, James Mossman, whose father was responsible for redesigning the Scottish crown. The **John Knox** connection is now much contested but the house and its exhibits provide an insight into the man, his beliefs and Scotland during the Reformation. The main room on the second floor has a painted ceiling (1600).

The junction with St Mary's and Jeffrey Streets marks the site of the Netherbow Port. The arched gateway with a tower and spire was demolished in 1764.

Beyond was the independent burgh of **Canongate** (gait or way of the canons) where the nobility, ambassadors and other royal officers built residences in close proximity to the royal palace of Holyroodhouse. Only a few of these mansions remain.

The gateway with pyramidal posts and adjoining gable-ended building with first floor balcony are all that remain of **Moray House**, now better known as a College of Education. Tradition has it rightly or wrongly that it was in the summer house of this residence that the Treaty of Union of 1707 was signed.

Canongate Tolbooth (People's Story Museum) ★

🕐*Open year-round Mon–Sat, 10am–5pm; Sun (Aug only) noon–5pm.* ☎*0131 529 4057. www.edinburgh.gov.uk/internet/Leisure.*

The tolbooth for the independent burgh of Canongate, this building with its turreted steeple was built in 1591 and is a good example of 16C architecture.

The museum gives a moving insight into the daily life and work of the citizens from the late 18C to the present day with tableaux, documents, photographs a video and oral and written testimonies.

Canongate Church

This church was built in 1688 for the displaced congregation of Holyrood Abbey when James VII decided to convert the nave into a Chapel Royal for the Most Ancient Order of the Thistle. Above the curvilinear south front is a stag's head bearing a cross, a reminder of the founding legend of Holyrood Abbey. Inside, the royal pew and those of officers of the Royal Household are indicated by coats of arms. Interesting memorials in the churchyard include that of Adam Smith and the young Edinburgh poet Robert Fergusson, whose tombstone was paid for by Burns. Another Burns connection is the plaque to Clarinda (east wall).

Museum of Edinburgh

♿🕐*Open year-round Mon–Sat 10am–5pm, Sun (Aug only) noon–5pm.* ☎*0131 529 4143. www.cac.org.uk.*

Three 16C mansions contain the main city museum of local history. Some of the rooms have 18C Memel panelling. The Edinburgh silver collection contains some particularly fine 18C pieces. The museum has an original parchment of the National Covenant.

Our Dynamic Earth 　　　Kids

Opposite Palace of Holyroodhouse. ♿🕐*Open year-round. Easter Mon–Oct and school hols daily 10am–5pm (Jul–Aug 6pm). Nov–Easter (excl school hols), Wed–Sun 10am–5pm. Last admission 1hr 10mins before closing.* ☒*£9.50.* ▢. ▣. ☎*0131 550 7800. www.dynamicearth. co.uk.*

Against the dramatic backdrop of the Salisbury Crags, rises a striking building with a tented roof designed by Sir Michael Hopkins (1999). An innovative exhibition using state-of-the-art interpretative technology unravels the story of the planet: the Big Bang, the formation of the solar system, volcanoes and earthquakes, glaciers, the evolution of life, the extinction of animal and plant species, the beauty and power of the oceans. Life in the polar regions is dramatically contrasted with the environment of the tundra and rainforest. A stone amphitheatre which seats 1,000 spectators hosts special events.

Scottish Parliament

♿🕐*Visitor Centre open Tue–Thu (Parliament Session "Business Days") 9am–6.30pm. Non-Business Days, normally Mon and Fri and during recess, Apr–Sept 10am–5.30pm. (Oct–Mar 4pm). Sat and public hols, 11am–5.30pm. Last admission 30mins before closing.* 🚻 ☎0131 348 5200, www.scottish.parliament.uk.

The cutting-edge design of this controversial building by Enric Mirales comprises clusters of small buildings shaped like up-turned boats, connected by glass walkways. Public spaces open to visitors include an exhibition about the Scottish Parliament and the public galleries of the Chamber or Committee rooms, in order to see Parliament in action on business days. On non-business days, the Chamber and Committee Room public galleries are open and staff are available to answer questions

2 South of the Royal Mile Tour

Royal Mile to George Heriot's School

Victoria Street★

Descending in a curve to the Grassmarket, this street is lined with an attractive series of boutiques and small traditional shops.

Grassmarket

The railed enclosure marks the site of the gallows where Captain Porteous was hanged (1736) and over 100 Covenanters were martyred. At the southwest corner, **West Port** marks the city's western gate. It was from a close nearby that the body-snatchers Burke and Hare operated.

Cowgate

Although outside the original town wall, this was a fashionable quarter in the 16C. It is now a forlorn underpass.

Curving upwards, Candlemaker Row leads to George IV Bridge, passing the **statue** of a dog, Greyfriars Bobby (🔍*see entry, below*), on the left, at the top.

Greyfriars Church and Churchyard

♿🕐*Open Apr–Oct Mon–Fri 10.30am–4.30pm; Sat 10am–2.30pm. Nov–Mar,* Thu only, 1.30pm–3.30pm. ☎0131 225 1900. www.greyfriarskirk.com.

This early 17C church is famous for being the site where the **National Covenant** (1638) was signed in 1638. There is a copy inside the church together with an exhibition. The churchyard is highly atmospheric. Memorials include the Martyrs Monument (northeast wall) to the Covenanters taken at Bothwell Brig (1679) and imprisoned here for five months, and the grave of John (Jock) Macleod over which Bobby, his faithful Skye terrier, stood watch for 14 years (subsequently the story for a Walt Disney film). Inside the church is the original portrait of "Greyfriars Bobby" painted by MacLeod in 1867.

▸ *Take Forrest Road to Lauriston Place. During the daytime when the gate is open, the churchyard extension offers a short cut to George Heriot's School.*

George Heriot's School

Walk round the outside and into the courtyard.

This great Edinburgh school was endowed by **George Heriot** (1563–1624), goldsmith to James VI who nicknamed him "Jinglin Geordie". On his death, Heriot bequeathed the fortune he had made in London to the city fathers, for the education of "fatherless bairns of Edinburgh freemen". Construction was begun by William Wallace in 1628 but completion was delayed until 1659 when the building was used as a hospital by Cromwell's troops. The symmetrical courtyard building is a good example of an early Renaissance edifice with abundant decorative stone carving and strapwork. The clock tower and statue of Geordie overlooking the courtyard are the work of Robert Mylne (1693).

A fragment of the **Flodden Wall** can be seen to the west of the school, at the head of the Vennel. Opposite is the 1879 Royal Infirmary.

▸ *To reach George Square take Meadow Walk past Rowand Anderson's Medical School.*

③ University Campus Tour

George Square to Chambers Street

George Square

The square, laid out in the 1760s, was the first major residential development outside the Old Town. Distinguished residents included Scott (no 25 west side) and the Duchess of Gordon. The west side is the only complete example of the vernacular Classical style. The remaining sides are occupied by the university: library (1967) by Basil Spence; David Hume Tower (1963) for the Faculty of Social Sciences and the Science Faculty in Appleton Tower (1966).

Old University

The Old College was founded in 1581 and occupied premises within Kirk o'Field Collegiate Church (f 1450) outside the city walls. It was here that Lord Darnley met his death. In 1789 **Robert Adam** provided a grandiose design for a double courtyard building. Only the main front with impressive entrance overlooking South Bridge is his work. Playfair modified the design to one courtyard and completed the surrounding ranges. The **Talbot Rice Gallery** (*Old College Quad, enter from southwest corner, first floor. ♿️☉Open Tue–Sat 10am–5pm. ☎0131 650 2211, www.trg.ed.ac.uk*) occupies Playfair's Georgian gallery, the original home of the Industrial Museum. The permanent Torrie Collection alternates with travelling exhibitions.

Royal Museum and Museum of Scotland ★★★ 🄺🄸🄳🄼

Chambers Street. ♿️☉Open daily 10am–5pm. Free guided tours available. ☉Closed 25 Dec. ✂. ☎0131 225 7534 www.nms.ac.uk.

Capt Fowke RE, of Albert Hall fame, designed the building with an elaborate Venetian Renaissance-style façade. In striking contrast to this masterpiece of Victorian cast iron and plate glass construction, is the landmark building opened in 1998, to house the collections now grouped under the title of the **Museum of Scotland**. Faced in Clasach sandstone from Morayshire, the exterior of this dramatic new structure features a **drum tower** overlooking the junction of Chambers Street with George IV Bridge, and, in contrast to traditional museum buildings, has windows offering passers-by glimpses of the riches within. Inside, an almost bewildering variety of internal spaces ranges from the sublimely light and airy **Hawthornden Court** to mysterious cavities set deep below ground. Spiral staircases seem contained within the thickness of massive walls, while balconies, galleries and windows create stimulating visual relationships both within the building and beyond it to the outside world.

Entered from Chambers Street, the spacious, well-lit **Main Hall** forms the vestibule of the museum, with access both to the older galleries and, via the Hall of Power, to the Hawthornden Court and the displays of the Museum of Scotland.

▶ *Access to the Museum of Scotland is also from the tower at the junction of Chambers Street and George IV Bridge. Free orientation tours are available at various times throughout the day and are recommended. The entries below in italics generally highlight particularly important items of each exhibit.*

Detail of a sculpture of Weituo from Henan Province, China (18C)

National Museums of Scotland

😊 *Some areas of the building will be closed from April 2008 until 2011 for a major redevelopment of the museum. If you want to see a particular exhibit or collection during your visit, call ahead to establish it is still on display. Exhibits may also be moved around galleries during this period so the following should only be treated as a rough guide:*

Level 0 (basement)

Beginnings

- The building blocks of Scotland: *Spectacular rock specimens, including 2,900 million year old Lewisian gneiss*
- History of the Wildlife: *Dioramas of tundra, oakwood and Caledonian pine forest*

Early People

(Scotland's inhabitants from c.8000 BC to AD 1100): *Figures by Sir Eduardo Paolozzi*

- *8C–9C carved stone from Ross and Cromarty with hunting scene*
- *Sculpted stone from Angus of rider drinking from horn*
- *6C–8C BC "Goddess" figure from Ballachulish*
- *Roman funerary sculpture of devouring lioness*
- *Roman carnyx or war horn*
- *Silver treasure from Traprain Law, East Lothian*

Level 1 (Street Level, off Hawthornden Court):

The Kingdom of the Scots

(Scotland from its emergence as a nation to the 1707 Act of Union)

- Scotland Defined: *9C cross from Dupplin, Perthshire*
- *Monymusk reliquary made to hold relic of St Columba*
- *12C Lewis chesspieces*
- *Early 16C carving of St Andrew*
- The Gael: *Highland brooches*
- *Clarsach* (harp)
- Monarchy and Power: *The "Maiden" beheading machine*
- The Renaissance: *Painted ceiling from Rossend Castle*

- Burghs – Life in towns:
- The Medieval Church: *8C St Fillan crozier*
- The Reformed Church:
- New Horizons – Scotland in the 17C: *Portrait of Esther Inglis*

Level 3 Scotland Transformed 1707–1914

- Living on the Land: *Reconstructed cruck-built Dumbartonshire house*
- Power: *Late-18C Newcomen atmospheric engine from Ayrshire coal mine*
- Trade and Industry: *Serf's collar*
- The Jacobite Challenge: *Bonnie Prince Charlie's silver travelling canteen*
- The Spirit of the Age: *Reconstruction of 18C Edinburgh room with painted panels*
- The Church: *Communion vessels*
- Daith Comes In (Level 4): *Late-18C hearse decorated with skulls and hourglasses*

Levels 4/5 Industry and Empire:

- The Workshop of the World (Level 4): *Distilling, ship models, 1861 locomotive Ellesmere*
- Scottish Pottery
- Victorians and Edwardians: *Work by Charles Rennie Mackintosh, Sir Robert Lorimer, Phoebe Traquair and Glasgow women artists*
- The Silver Treasury: *Changing displays of Scottish silver from 16C onwards*
- Innovators: *18C and 19C scientists, explorers, politicians and artists*
- Scotland and the World: *Scots abroad*

Level 6 Twentieth Century

- An extraordinary array of objects chosen by children and adults to represent Scotland in the 20C
- The **Roof Terrace** gives an unusual **panorama** over castle and city

International Galleries

Ground Floor

- Asiatic sculpture, Classical: *Assyrian king and courtier*

- and Middle Eastern art (1,3,4): *Cedarwood totem pole from British Columbia*
- Temporary exhibitions (2)
- Natural Curiosity (6)
- Evolution (7): *350 million year old fish fossils*
- Mammals (8): *78ft/24m long Blue Whale skeleton*
- Carnivores and Reptiles (10)
- World in Our Hands (A/V show) (11)
- British Animals and Birds (12, 13)
- Art and Industry since 1850: *Bauhaus products, bubble car*

First Floor

- European Art 1200–2000 (2): *15C Birth of the Virgin from Lübeck,: Lennoxlove Toilet Service, Beaton Panels c 1540.*
- Ceramics (3): *Charles II slipware dish*
- Glass (4): *Luther glass c 1845*
- Western Decorative Art 1850–2000: *Phoebe Traquair enamel c 1890,*
- (5,6): *German silver nef pre-1874*
- Insects and Molluscs (7, 11,12): *Papier-mâché teaching beetle*
- Enamels and Silver (14)
- Modern Jewellery (17): *Miss Crowford Collection*
- Costume (18)
- Ancient Egypt (20): *Dioramas of Egyptian life*

Second Floor

- Ivy Wu Gallery of Far Eastern Art (2): *Hokusai comic strip, Hiroshige 100 Views of Edo, 1719 model of Dutch East Indiaman "D'Bataviase Eeuw"*
- China (3), Islam and Japan (4): *16C–17C Turkish dish*
- Minerals and Gems (7): *Scottish agates*
- Geology (8), Skeletons (9), Fossils (10)
- Rocks and Minerals (11)
- Within the Middle East (12): *Embroidered hanging from Kerman, Iran*
- Invertebrates (13): *9'6" Giant Japanese Spider-Crab*
- Arms and Armour (14): *14C Pembridge Helm*
- Instruments of Science (18): *Napier's "Bones"*

- Tribal Art (20): *Benin hornblower, New Ireland helmet mask*

New Town★★
1767–1830

When the decision had been taken to extend the Royalty of Edinburgh, a competition was organised and was won by an unknown architect, **James Craig** (c.1740–95). The North Bridge was thrown across the valley and the development of Edinburgh's New Town proceeded apace. The project was to be entirely residential at the outset – business and commerce were to remain in the Old Town centred on the Royal Exchange – and the winning plan had a gridiron layout in which vistas and focal points played an important role.

The plan gave a succession of splendid squares and elegant streets and people were quick to follow the example of Hume and Lord Cockburn in taking up residence.

When exploring Georgian Edinburgh look for the many decorative details which give the New Town so much of its character. The cast-iron work shows great variety of design (Heriot Row and Abercromby Place). Stretches of balcony spanning the frontages (Windsor Street and Atholl Crescent) alternate with window guards; the serried ranks of railings crested with finials are punctuated by lamp standards, brackets and extinguishers or link horns (Charlotte Square, York Place and Melville Street).

4 Charlotte Square to the east end of Princes Street Tour

Charlotte Square★★★

Robert Adam was commissioned in 1791 to design what is now the New Town's most splendid square. Elegant frontages of a unified design frame the garden with a central equestrian statue of **Prince Albert** by Steell. The **north side** is a grand civic achievement where the vertical lines of the advanced central and end blocks are counterbalanced by the rusticated ground floor. The lines of straight-headed windows,

Robert Louis Stevenson (1850–94)

A plaque inscribed with a verse of *The Lamplighter*, a poem for children, marks the site of Stevenson's childhood home at 17 Heriot Row (*private property*) in the New Town. He is famous for adventure stories such as *Treasure Island and Kidnapped* which have enthralled children through the years, and for his more sombre tale *Dr Jekyll and Mr Hyde* which is set in the old town. He took many trips abroad to warmer climes for health reasons including two to France which inspired him to write *An Inland Voyage* (1878) and *Travels with a Donkey in the Cévennes* (1879).

round-headed doorway fanlights and occasional Venetian windows are happily juxtaposed. Note the wrought-iron railings, lamp holders, extinguishers and foot scrapers. The **centrepiece** comprises the headquarters of the National Trust for Scotland (no 5), Bute House (no 6), the official residence of the Secretary of State for Scotland and no 7, **The Georgian House**★ (*open daily; Jul–Aug 10am–6pm, Easter–Jun and Sept–Oct, 10am–5pm; March 11am–4pm, Nov 11am–3pm (last admission 30 mins before closing)*; £5; ☎0844 4932118; www.nts.org.uk). The lower floors have been entirely refurbished by the NTS as a typical Georgian home of the period from 1790 to 1810. Some of the delights include the cheese waggon, rare wine rinsing glasses, lovely Scottish sideboard, moreen hangings, tea table and well equipped kitchen and wine cellar. An introduction to Georgian Edinburgh is provided in one of the basement rooms (*two videos: 33min*).

A mirror image of the north side of the square, the south side has been comprehensively restored in as authentic a manner as possible by the National Trust.

On the west side, St George's Church (1811–14) by Robert Reid provides the focal point for George Street and is now converted into part of the National Archives of Scotland annexe, **West Register House** Famous residents included Lord Cockburn at no 14, Lord Lister (no 9) and Douglas Haig (no 24).

George Street

The principal street of Craig's plan is closed at either end by Charlotte and St Andrew Squares; it is 0.5mi/800m in length and 115ft/35m wide. Many of the houses of this originally residential street are now converted into banks, offices and a whole host of fashionable bars, restaurants and shops. Statues punctuate the street intersections – each of which has good views away to the Forth or down to Princes Street Gardens with the castle and Old Town as backdrop. Note in particular the **view** surveyed by George IV from his pedestal, with the successive landmarks perfectly positioned : Royal Scottish Academy, National Gallery, Assembly Hall and spire of the former Tolbooth Kirk.

Towards the east end are the **Assembly Rooms** (no 54) built in 1784. This fine suite of rooms, with the Music Hall behind, is a magnificent setting for public functions.

St Andrew and St George Church (1785), with its towering spire, was intended to close the George Street vista at the St Andrew Square end, but Dundas beat the planners to it.

Scottish National Portrait Gallery★

1 Queen Street. &Open daily, 10am–5pm (Thu 7pm). Closed 25–26 Dec. Times change during Festival. ☎0131 624 6200., www.nationalgalleries.org.

In the best Victorian tradition a munificent donation by the proprietor of *The Scotsman* provided a building for the illustration of Scottish history. Rowand Anderson designed an Italianate Gothic, statue-decorated building to house the portrait collection founded in 1882. In 1890–91 the Antiquarian Society moved in from its premises in the Mound.

The initial aim of the National Portrait Gallery was to "illustrate Scottish history by likeness of the chief actors in it". Many of the portraits of persons of historic interest are masterpieces of portraiture. Scottish exponents of this tradition include the 16C George Jamesone (*self-portrait*), John Michael Wright, the 18C masters, Ramsay (*David Hume* the companion portrait to the one of J J Rousseau) and Raeburn (*Scott*). In addition there are canvases by Wissing, Lely, Gainsborough, Lawrence... Some of the chief actors portrayed are royalty (*Mary, Queen of Scots, Lord Darnley, James VI, Charles I, Elizabeth of Bohemia and James VII*); statesmen formal and fine (*1st Earl of Dunfermline and Duke of Lauderdale*); 18C to 19C politicians (*Kier Hardie, Ramsay MacDonald* and *W E Gladstone*); literary figures (*Burns, Scott, Byron, Carlyle, Stevenson, Barrie*). There is an excellent cafe, famous for its portrait of Sean Connery.

St Andrew Square

Here **Henry Dundas**, Viscount Melville, better known as King Harry the Ninth for his management of Scottish affairs between 1782 and 1805, still dominates from his fluted column (150ft/46m high). The square, the home of banks and insurance companies, has none of the unified elegance of its counterpart, Charlotte Square, but has individual buildings of charm and splendour. On the north side nos 21 to 26 are examples of the vernacular classical style of the first phase of New Town development. **Dundas House**★ was built (1772–74) for Sir Laurence Dundas on what was originally intended to be a church site. Well set back, this three-storey mansion is adorned with a projecting three-bay pilastered, emblazoned, pedimented central section and a frieze at roof level. Step inside to see the splendours of the original entrance hall where capitals and roof bosses are highlighted in gold leaf. The building was purchased by the Royal Bank of Scotland in 1825 and the domed banking hall was added in 1858.

West Register Street leads past the literary pub **Café Royal** with its oyster bar, to **New Register House** fronted by fine wrought-iron gates and crowned gateposts, indicating the offices of the Court of Lord Lyon with his Heralds and Pursuivants.

The Lord Lyon King of Arms regulates all Scottish armorial matters, adjudicates upon Chiefship of clans, conducts and

Scottish National Portrait Gallery

National Galleries of Scotland

executes Royal Proclamations and state and public ceremonials of all descriptions in Scotland.

The east end of Princes Street is now dominated by Robert Adam's splendid frontage of **General Register House** (1774–1822) headquarters of the National Archives of Scotland. With the projecting pedimented portico and end pavilions crowned by cupolas, it makes a suitably gracious focal point for North Bridge. Changing exhibitions (⏵⏰*Open Mon–Fri 9am–4.45pm.* ⏰*Closed holidays.* ☎*0131 535 1314, www.nas.gov. uk*) are mounted in the front hall. Look through into the splendid domed hall with its characteristic Adam motifs.

The **General Post Office** stands on the site of the Theatre Royal built in 1768, as one of the first buildings in the New Town. During its heyday when Scott was a trustee, famous names such as Sarah Siddons and John Kemble performed here. The theatre closed in 1859 and was burnt down in 1946. Opposite is the Balmoral Hotel with its famous clock tower landmark, and clock always set two minutes fast.

5️⃣ Princes Street and Gardens Tour

Princes Street

Edinburgh's famous shopping street was originally totally residential. Single sided, the street marked the southern extension of the New Town. The 1770s town houses were modest but appreciated for the open view across the valley, which later became a private garden for residents. Following the laying of the railway (1845–46), commercial development slowly took over. Today the street is dominated by modern "bargain" shops and only Jenners is a reminder of past glories.

Princes Street Gardens

The Nor'Loch Valley was infilled during New Town excavation work and later laid out as private gardens for residents. Lord Cockburn was the instigator of the Act of Parliament which safeguarded the south side of Princes Street from further development. With the coming of the railways, shops and hotels replaced houses and in 1876 the gardens were opened to the public. Today the gardens with their greenery, welcome benches and many monuments provide a pleasant respite from the milling crowd in Princes Street.

Scott Monument★

🕐*Open year-round daily. Apr–Sept 9am (10am Sun) to 6pm; Oct–Mar daily 9am (10am Sun) to 3pm.* 🎫*£3.* ♿*the spiral stone staircases are very narrow and can be claustrophobic, especially for larger people.* ☎*0131 529 4068. www.cac.org.uk.*

This pinnacled monument dominating Princes Street is one of Edinburgh's most familiar landmarks. Following Scott's death in 1832, a successful public appeal was launched. Much controversy ensued as to the site and nature of the monument, however the foundation

The Ross Fountain on Princes Street, looking up to Edinburgh Castle

R. Campbell/ELTB

stone was laid in 1840. The neo-Gothic spire (200ft/61m tall) was designed by a joiner and draughtsman, **George Meikle Kemp**, who died before its completion. Steell's Carrara marble statue of Scott and his dog Maida is accompanied by 64 statuettes of characters from his novels (in the niches) and the heads of 16 Scottish poets (on the capitals). The monument became a major attraction. For the agile, four viewing platforms (*287 steps*) give good **views**★ of central Edinburgh.

Dividing Princes Street Gardens into East and West are two imposing Classical buildings on the left: the National Gallery and the Royal Scottish Academy.

National Gallery of Scotland★★

The Mound. ♿🕐*Open daily, 10am–5pm (Thu 7pm). Times change during Festival.* 🕐*Closed 25–26 Dec.* 🅿☎*0131 624 6200. www.nationalgalleries.org.*

The nucleus of the Gallery was formed by the Royal Institution's collection, later expanded by bequests and purchasing. Playfair designed (1850–57) the imposing Classical building to house the works.

▶ *Start with Room 1 on the upper floor by taking the staircase opposite the main entrance.*

The Early Northern and Early Italian holdings include the *Trinity Altarpiece* (c.1470s) by Van der Goes, a unique example of pre-Reformation art commissioned for Edinburgh's now demolished Collegiate Church of the Holy Trinity. Open, the panels represent James III and Margaret of Denmark with patron saints. *The Three Legends of St Nicholas* by Gerard David shows scenes from the life of St Nicholas of Myra, more commonly known as Santa Claus. Early Italian works introduce one of the principal figures of the period, Raphael with his gentle *Bridgewater Madonna* and an excellent example of High Renaissance portraiture by his contemporary, Andrea del Sarto (*Portrait of the Artist's Friend*).

Downstairs, **Galleries I** and **II** introduce the principal figures of early-16C Venetian painting : Jacopo Bassano with the colourful *Adoration of the Kings* and Titian with his religious composition *The*

Three Ages of Man. Two examples of Titian's late style of mythological painting (1550s) display all the painterly qualities of Venetian art : *Diana and Actaeon* and *Diana and Calisto* show a freedom of brushwork and masterly handling of colour and paint. Compare them with the works of other major artists of the second generation of 16C painters: Bassano, Tintoretto's *The Deposition of Christ*, characteristic of his summary style, and Veronese (*Mars and Venus, St Anthony Abbot*) who remained first and foremost a colourist.

Gallery III, arranged as a Kunstkammer, displays a number of miscellaneous 16C and 17C European Cabinet Pictures (Cranach, Holbein, Clouet, Rubens and Avercamp). **Gallery IV** gathers together 17C works by Poussin (*The Mystic Marriage of St Catherine*), Claude Lorrain (*Landscape with Apollo and the Muses*), El Greco (*The Saviour of the World* with its particular colouring, elongation and spiritual power and *Fable* on a rare secular theme), as well as an early work by Velazquez (*An Old Woman Cooking Eggs*).

Poussin's admirable *Seven Sacraments* are enhanced by the gracious setting of **Gallery V**. Note how the marble floor echoes the one in the *Confirmation*. Poussin undertook this second series of formal classical compositions for a Parisian friend, Chantelou.

The diversity of 17C Dutch art is well represented in **Galleries VI, VII** and **IX**. Jan Weenix specialises in large hunting scenes. Cuyp's *View of the Valkhof, Nijmegen* introduces interesting light effects and Koninck's *Onset of a Storm* combines imaginary views with natural scenery. Alongside, the portraits of Frans Hals display a vitality and realism which make them second only to those of Rembrandt represented by his *Self-Portrait Aged 51,* where the use of chiaroscuro focuses attention on the face. In the next gallery (**VII**), landscapes by the specialists Ruisdael and Hobbema hang with Philip Koninck's large-scale *Extensive Landscape* (1666) with a characteristic high viewpoint.

Gallery IX (17C Flemish and Dutch painting) contains canvases by the 17C master Rubens. The swirling movement of his

National Gallery of Scotland

National Galleries of Scotland

Feast of Herod, a large banqueting scene full of colour and realism, contrasts with the staid formalism of Van Dyck's *The Lomellini Family*. Vermeer's early work *Christ in the House of Martha and Mary* shows Mary in an attentive mood.

The principal figures of 18C British art are introduced in **Gallery X**: Gainsborough (*The Hon Mrs Graham, Mrs Hamilton Nisbet*), Reynolds (*Ladies Waldegrave*), Romney, Raeburn and Lawrence. Other 18C schools are represented by three pastoral scenes of joyful frivolity by France's foremost Rococo painter, François Boucher, the last exponent of the Venetian Renaissance tradition; G B Tiepolo's *The Finding of Moses;* and Gavin Hamilton, a pioneer in neo-Classicism (*Achilles mourning the Death of Patroclus*).

19C British and American works (**Gallery XI**) include landscapes by Turner (*Somer Hill, Tunbridge*), Constable (*Vale of Dedham*), Ward (*The Eildon Hills and the Tweed, Melrose Abbey*) and the American, Church (*Niagara Falls*). Next door in **Gallery XII** hang Sir Benjamin West's gigantic work *Alexander III of Scotland rescued from the fury of a stag*, a colourful composition of frenzied action and a collection of full-length Raeburns (*Sir John Sinclair*).

▶ *Take the stairs between Gallery VI and IX to Rooms A2-6 on the upper floor.*

The smaller 18C and 19C paintings in **Rooms A2** and **A3** include Watteau (*Fêtes Vénitiennes*) Greuze, Boucher (*Mme de Pompadour*), Guardi, Chardin, Hogarth, Allan Ramsay (*J J Rousseau*),

Beltane Fire Festival

Since 1988 a festival marking the end of winter is held every year on Calton Hill. Until the beginning of the 20C this celebration, which is derived from an old Celtic tradition, took place on the site of St Anthony's Well on the eve of 1 May.

The main protagonists of this festival are: the May Queen and her retinue, a team of fighters known as the White Women, the Green Man and the Blue Man. Others such as the Red Men holding aloft torches process around a large bonfire to the sound of drums.

Gainsborough, the early-19C landscapist John Crome and Wilkie (*The Confessional*). Precursors to the French Impressionists (**Room A4**) include the romanticism of Corot's landscapes and the realism of Courbet's everyday scenes.

In **Room A5**, note the preoccupation with play of light in the canvases of Monet (*Haystacks* and *Poplars on the Epte*), Sisley and Pissarro. The exoticism of Gauguin is typified by *The Visions after the Sermon* and *Three Tahitians*, Van Gogh's vigorous style and bright colours by the *Olive Trees* and Cézanne's rich tones by *La Montagne*.

▸ *Take the stairs beyond Gallery VII down to the underground wing.*

Galleries B1 to 8

Scottish painting from 1600 to 1900. Portraiture dominates the early works from Jamesone and Aikman to Ramsay's superbly delicate portraits of women. Beyond are numerous examples of Raeburn's works including a *self-portrait* and *The Reverend Robert Walker Skating on Duddingston Loch*. David Wilkie knew great popularity in his time for his realistic Scottish scenes, *Distraining for Rent, The Letter of Introduction* and his first important work *Pitlessie Fair. The Gentle Shepherd* is inspired by Ramsay's poem. Nasmyth's *Edinburgh Castle and the Nor'Loch, The Distant View of Stirling* are soft and atmospheric compositions. William Dyce, precursor of the Pre-Raphaelites, specialised in religious scenes and landscapes (*St Catherine, Christ as the Man of Sorrows*). *Francesca da Rimini* illustrates an episode of Dante's Inferno. *Quarrel and Reconciliation* and *Dawn : Luther* are imaginative works by Paton. *The Porteous Mob* by J Drummond is

based on an historical episode in Scott's *Heart of Midlothian*.

McTaggart excelled in landscapes (*The Storm, The Young Fishers*) where bold brushwork and dramatic light introduced a sense of realism. The follow-up movement was the Glasgow School to which Guthrie and EA Hornel both belonged.

Royal Scottish Academy

🕐 *Open during exhibitions only, Mon–Sat 10am–5pm, Sun noon–5pm.* ⊷ *Admission charges vary.* ☎*0131 225 6671. www. royalscottishacademy.org.*

The Academy was custom built by William Playfair in 1826 to grace the north end of the Mound and counterbalance the Bank of Scotland's imposing building at the south end.

Following a period of relocation due to the major restoration of the RSA building by the National Galleries of Scotland, the RSA returned to its home in spring, 2003 and re-opened as a world-class venue for special temporary exhibitions.

The **Weston Link**, which lies beneath the Royal Scottish Academy and the Scottish National Gallery, connects them together with areas for shopping, learning, eating and drinking.

The Mound

The drained Nor'Loch area was initially crossed by stepping stones laid by an enterprising Lawnmarket clothier as a short cut for his New Town clients. Later, excavated earth from New Town building sites was used to build up the Mound (1781–1805) as it stands today.

Beyond, in West Princes Street Gardens are the **floral clock** composed of 20,000 annuals, the bandstand, a centre for a full programme of open-air entertainment in summer, and statues of the poet Allan Ramsay (east end) and the discoverer of chloroform Sir James Y Simpson.

6 Calton Hill Tour

At the east end of Princes Street rises Calton Hill (328ft/100m) with that familiar skyline of Classical monuments which gave rise to the name, "Edinburgh's acropolis". Another remnant of volcanic activity, Calton Hill (22 acres/9ha) was left undeveloped when the New Town was being built.

The James Craig **Observatory** was the initial building and development continued after 1815 when the ravine to the east of Princes Street had been crossed by Regent Bridge. The flanking porticoes and Classical façades of **Waterloo Place** provide a formal entry, framing Calton Hill in the distance.

On the right, **St Andrew's House**, the former administrative centre of Scotland, stands on the site of two prisons, built to relieve the Old Tolbooth.

Calton Hill

Access by stairs from Waterloo Place (Regent Road) or by a narrow road, suitable for cars, leading off to the left opposite St Andrew's House.

The most striking monument is the 12-columned portico of the **National Monument** to commemorate Scots who died in the Napoleonic Wars. It was intended as a replica of the Parthenon but construction was stopped by lack of funds. The next in a clockwise direction and tallest is the **Nelson Monument★** (*open Apr–Sept, Mon 1pm–6pm, Tue–Sat 10am–6pm; Oct–March, Mon–Sat 10am–3pm; £3; Closed 25–26 Dec, 1–3 Jan; 0131 556 2716, www.cac.org. uk*),a tiered circular tower, 106ft/32m tall. The viewing gallery (*143 steps*) provides a magnificent **panorama★★★** of Edinburgh: up Princes Street, from the castle down the spine of the Royal Mile past the Canongate Church, to Holyroodhouse with Arthur's Seat in the background.

The circular Greek **temple** is Playfair's monument to Dugald Stewart, Professor of Moral Philosophy. The walled enclosure has at its southwest corner

James Craig's 18C Old Observatory which was subsequently replaced by Playfair's building (1818) in the centre, itself superseded by a new Observatory on Blackford Hill. At the southeast corner is another Playfair monument, this time to his uncle, the mathematician and natural philosopher, John Playfair.

Northern and Western Edinburgh

Royal Botanic Garden★★★

1mi/1.5km from city centre by Broughton Street. West Gate, Arboretum Road. Open daily. Apr–Sept 10am–7pm. March and Oct 10am–6pm. Nov–Feb 10am–4pm. Glasshouses close: Mar–Oct 5pm; Nov–Feb 3.30pm. garden free, glasshouses £3.50. 0131 552 7171. www.rbge.org.uk.

The 70 acres of the Royal Botanic Garden are a refreshing haven when you are weary of the city bustle. The terrace café enjoys a beautiful view.

Origins

In the late 17C when Edinburgh was emerging as a centre for medical studies, a physic garden was established (1670) by Dr Robert Sibbald, first Professor of Medicine at Edinburgh University, and Dr Robert Balfour, another eminent physician. The original plot was situated near Holyrood Abbey. In 1676 these gentlemen acquired land near Trinity Hospital – on the present site of Waverley Station – appointing James Sutherland as Intendant. An intermediary move to Leith Walk followed before the final one in c.1820 to a mere 14 acres on the present site.

Garden and buildings

The **rhododendrons** are a major attraction. The modernistic Exhibition Plant Houses (1967) provide unimpeded interiors where winding paths lead through a series of landscaped presentations, a pleasant alternative to serried ranks of pots so normally associated with glasshouses. The Exhibition Hall is devoted to changing displays on various aspects of botany. The Tropical (1834) and Temperate (1858)

Temperate Palm House, Royal Botanic Gardens

Royal Botanic Gardens Edinburgh

Palm Houses have an altogether more traditional and imposing architectural style. High in the centre of the gardens stands 18C **Inverleith House**, formerly the repository for the collection of modern art. From beyond the lawn a view indicator pinpoints Edinburgh's well-known landmarks.

City Outskirts

Leith

Some 2mi/3km north of the city centre Leith has been Edinburgh's port since the 14C. In the second half of the 20C, with the decline of big ships and heavy industry, it slumped into inner city dereliction and acquired a very bad reputation – the tale of low life drug addicts in the 1991 film, *Trainspotting*, originated here. Since the mid 1980s however it has been revitalised in to a trendy dockland development area with the likes of media companies and particularly the new Scottish Office Building, providing well-paid jobs. Loft homes have been created in run-down dockside warehouses, basic pubs have been gentrified and a rash of style bars, gourmet restaurants, a small number of hotels and nightclubs have sprung up.

Ocean Terminal is a large stylish waterside complex devoted to eating drinking and shopping, a muliplex cinema. Moored in front is a very special ship.

Royal Yacht Britannia★

⏱ *Open year-round daily. Jul–Aug 9.30am–4.30pm. Apr–May & Sept–Oct 10am–4.30pm. Nov–March 10am–3.30pm.* ⏱*Closed 25 Dec and 1 Jan* 🚸*To avoid queues pre-book tickets in Aug.* ☎*0131 555 5566.* 🅿. ☎*0131 555 5566. www.royalyachtbritannia.co.uk.*

The Royal Yacht Britannia was launched from a Clydebank shipyard in April 1953. By the time she was decommissioned in December 1997, this symbol of post-Imperial royalty had sailed more than a million miles, carrying Queen Elizabeth II and her family on nearly 1,000 official visits to countries around the world.

The roles Britannia played, from floating palace to venue for the promotion of British exports, are explained in a visitor centre, spacious enough to contain a royal barge afloat in a tank of water. Once aboard, visitors can follow a trail through royal apartments, crew's quarters, bridge and wheelhouse, and engine room. Designed by Sir Hugh Casson in close consultation with the Queen and Prince Philip, the royal apartments have a cool but comfortable style, a subtle combination of country house luxury and shipboard practicality.

The audio tour brings the ship's past alive, explaining the meticulous arrangements for formal dining as well as the rules for the boisterous game of "wombat tennis" played by officers in the wardroom.

Water of Leith Walkway

This recently restored bucolic riverside path links Leith to Dean Village with its two outstanding modern art galleries.

Scottish National Gallery of Modern Art★

Belford Road. ⏰*Open daily 10am–5pm (hours change during festival).* ⏰*Closed 25–26 Dec.* ⛢. 🅿. ☎ *0131 624 6200, www.nationalgalleries.org.*

The Scottish National Gallery of Modern Art (SNGMA)is situated in large wooded grounds, on the western edge of the New Town, which provide a fine setting for sculptures by Bourdelle, Epstein, Hepworth, Moore and Rickey. The Gallery is housed in an imposing neo-Classical building, the former John Watson's School.

The collection has two emphases: international and Scottish art of the 20C. If not fully comprehensive in its international collection, it does nevertheless have fine examples of most of the main artists and movements: the Nabis and Fauvism (Vuillard, Bonnard, Matisse, Derain, Rouault), German Expressionism (Kirchner, Nolde, Jawlensky, Kokoschka, Dix), Cubism and its derivatives (Braque, Picasso, Léger, Delaunay, Lipchitz), Russian Primitivism and Abstract Art (Gontcharova, Larionov, Popova), Abstraction (Moholy-Nagy, Mondrian, Schwitters, Nicholson), School of Paris (De Staël, Balthus, Dubuffet, Soulages, Riopelle, Tápies, Appel, Picasso), Nouveau Réalisme (César, Arman, Tinguely), St Ives School (Nicholson, Hepworth, Lanyon, Hilton), Pop Art (Lichtenstein, Hockney, Hamilton, Paolozzi, Tilson, Kitaj), Minimal Art (Lewitt, Judd, Flavin). The post-war collection also features recent works by artists including Antony Gormley, Gilbert & George, Damien Hirst and Tracey Emin.

The **Scottish Collection** is rich and comprehensive. It has particularly good holdings of the work of the Scottish Colourists (Peploe, Cadell, Hunter, Fergusson) and the Edinburgh School (Gillies, Maxwell, McTaggart and Redpath).

Dean Gallery

75 Belford Road, opposite Gallery of Modern Art. ♿⏰ *same hours, facilites and contact details as SNGMA.*

Built in 1833 as an orphanage, this imposing and idiosyncratic building by the Greek Revival architect Thomas Hamilton makes a surprisingly suitable setting for the National Gallery's specialist collections of contemporary art, with imaginatively redesigned interiors by Terry Farrell.

The **Dada** and **Surrealist** holdings, based on the collections of Sir Roland Penrose and Gabrielle Keiller, include works by Ernst, Dalí, de Chirico, Magritte, Schwitters, Miró, Picasso, Magritte, Delvaux, Tristram Hillier and Henry Moore. Masks, skulls, other *objets trouvés* and the contents of Penrose's cabinet of curiosities help create the bizarre atmosphere favoured by the Surrealists.

The Paolozzi Gift consists of a large number of works by the Edinburgh-born sculptor **Eduardo Paolozzi** (1924–2005), among them the gigantic stainless steel *Vulcan* rising through two floors in the centre of the building. Beyond a room containing a number of the artist's characteristic figures which seem to have survived some unimaginable Armageddon is a reconstruction of Paolozzi's fascinatingly crammed studio.

Temporary exhibitions are held on the upper floor.

National Galleries of Scotland

Scottish National Gallery of Modern Art

P. Tomkins/ Scottish Viewpoint/ Visit Scotland

The ruins of Craigmillar Castle, one of Mary, Queen of Scots favourite residences

City Suburbs

Edinburgh Zoo★★   Kids

*3mi/5km from the city centre, on the A 8.
Open year-round daily 9am–6pm
(Oct & Mar 5pm; Nov–Feb 4.30pm).
£11.50 (child £8.50). 0131 3349171,
www.edinburghzoo.org.uk.*

The 80-acre Scottish National Zoological
Park is attractively set on the south slope
of Corstorphine Hill. Barless and sometimes glassless enclosures for many
of the species allow the visitor better
views of the animals and their antics.
The tables are turned as the orangutans
and chimpanzees, from their pole-top
perch and climbing apparatus, have
grandstand views of the public. The
famous Edinburgh penguin collection
(a colony of 30 Kings and 100 Gentoes)
is the number one attraction with their
daily **Penguin Parade**. A popular new
addition is **Rainbow Landings** where
visitors enter a free-flying aviary and can
buy nectar which attracts Lorikeets to
come to them. In addition to the usual
animals, make a point of looking for
some of the native species : the wild
cat, pine martens, golden eagle.
The **view** from the hilltop (510ft/155m;
view indicator) shows the sprawl of
Edinburgh and from the Pentlands to
the south, round to the mountains of
Loch Lomond.

Craigmillar Castle★

*3mi/5km southeast by St Leonard's Street
and the A 68. (HS). Open Apr–Sept daily
9.30am–6.30pm. Oct–Mar Sat–Wed
9.30am–4.30pm. Last admission 30min
before closing. Closed 1–2 Jan & 25–26
Dec. £4. 0131 661 4445. www.historic-
scotland.gov.uk.*

Dramatically set on an eminence,
even in ruins Craigmillar has an air of
strength and impregnability. The 14C
tower house rises massively above two
successive curtain walls. The outer wall
encloses a courtyard in front and gardens on either side, in all a total area
of over 1 acre. The inner curtain built in
1427 is quartered with round towers,
pierced by gunloops and topped by
attractive oversailing machicolated parapets. Above the inner gate is the Preston family coat of arms. Straight ahead
stands the L-shaped **tower house**, now
flanked by and linked to the later east
(15C) and west ranges (16C–17C). The
Great Hall at first floor level is a grand
apartment with a magnificent hooded
fireplace and three windows with stone
benches lining the embrasures. Climb
to the top to get a view down over the
other buildings and fully appreciate the
strategic excellence of the layout.
It was here that Mary, Queen of Scots
sought refuge after the murder of Rizzio
and that the treacherous plot for the
murder of Darnley was conceived.

EDZELL CASTLE★
ANGUS

The attractive ruin of **Edzell Castle**, seat of the Crawford Lindsays, is unique for its formal walled garden, or pleasance.

- **Information:** ☎01356 648631. www.historic-scotland.gov.uk.
- ▶ **Orient Yourself:** Edzell Castle is 5.5mi/9km north of Brechin on the B 966.
- ⏱ **Also See:** BRECHIN.

Visit

Castle and Grounds
(*HS*). ♿⏱*Open Apr–Sept daily 9.30am–6.30pm. Oct–Mar Sat–Wed 9.30am–4.30pm. Last admission 30min before closing.* ⏱*Closed 1–2 Jan; 25–26 & 28–31 Dec.*

The present entrance leads to the cobbled courtyard of the late-16C mansion. Now in ruins, this extension was never completed. Go through the pend straight ahead to see the original entrance front. To the right is the early-16C tower house. The great hall in the tower house affords a good bird's-eye view of the pleasance.

The Pleasance★★★
The formal walled garden was created in 1604 by **Sir David Lindsay** (c.1550–1610) Influenced by what he had seen abroad, he created a remarkable work displaying elegance and refinement without parallel in Scotland. When the roses of the flower beds and the blue and white lobelia of the wall boxes are in bloom against the rich red of the walls this is a blaze of colour.

The heraldic and symbolic **sculpture** on the walls rewards a closer inspection. Between the wall boxes representing the Lindsay colours and arms are panels portraying the Planetary Deities (*east wall*), Liberal Arts (*south wall*) and Cardinal Virtues (*west wall*). Neatly clipped box hedges spell out the Lindsay motto "Dum spiro spero". The design is completed in the southwest corner by a bath house, a luxury in 17C Scotland, and in the opposite corner, a summer house.

Edzell *Population 751.*
This attractive village was resited here in the 19C. The original settlement was in the vicinity of the castle.

P. Tomkins/ Scottish Viewpoint/ Visit Scotland

Edzell Castle, 16C

ELGIN ★
MORAY
POPULATION 18,702

Set in the rich agricultural area known as the Laich of Moray, the attractive town of Elgin, famous for its cathedral, stands on the banks of the Lossie and is the administrative centre for the Moray district.

🛈 **Information:** 17 High Street. ☎01343 542 666 *or* 543 388.
www.aberdeen-grampian.com

▶ **Orient Yourself:** The medieval plan has been preserved and the High Street links the cathedral to the former site of the castle.

☺ **Don't Miss:** The Cathedral chapter house.

🕓 **Organizing Your Time:** Allow half a day, longer if taking the Glen Moray distillery tour.

Especially for Kids: Older ones may enjoy the Moray Motor Museum.

👣 **Also See:** FORRES.

Elgin Cathedral ★ *30min*

(HS). 🕓*Open Apr–Sept daily 9.30am–6.30pm. Oct–Mar Sat–Wed 9.30am–4.30pm. Last admission 30 min before closing.* 🕓*Closed 1, 2 Jan; 25, 26 Dec.* ⊜£4.50. ☎01343 547171. www.historic-scotland.gov.uk.*

Once one of the most beautiful cathedrals in Scotland, today the biscuit-coloured ruins still stand, majestic, evocative and rich in style, characteristic of the 13C, a period of intensive church building.

The creation of the diocese dated back to 1120 when the Celtic churches of Birnie, Kinneddar and Spynie had served as episcopal seats prior to the final move in 1224 to the Church of the Holy Trinity at Elgin. Both the town and the cathedral suffered ignominious destruction in 1390 at the hands of the **Wolf of Badenoch**, otherwise known as Alexander Stewart, the second son of King Robert II. Although duly repaired, the cathedral suffered gradual deterioration after the Reformation. This was in part due to the fact that it was no longer in

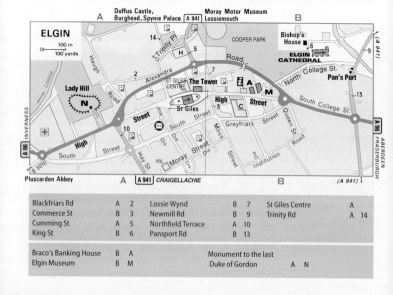

Blackfriars Rd	A	2	Lossie Wynd	B	7	St Giles Centre	A	
Commerce St	B	3	Newmill Rd	B	9	Trinity Rd	A	14
Cumming St	A	5	Northfield Terrace	A	10			
King St	B	6	Pansport Rd	B	13			

Braco's Banking House	B	A			
Elgin Museum	B	M	Monument to the last		
			Duke of Gordon	A	N

use as a place of worship and also due to the protracted struggle over the ownership of church property after the Reformation. In 1711 the collapse of the central tower wreaked much damage and the ruins became a quarry for building materials. Conservation began in the early 19C by the determined efforts of one man.

The Buildings

Between the buttressed twin towers of the west front is a deeply recessed portal with large windows above. Intricate vine and acorn carving frames the doorways. On the internal face is an attractive arcade marking the passageway between the towers at first floor level. This feature is also found at Arbroath (see ARBROATH). The view of the town from the top of the south tower (*134 steps*) is screened by the trees of Cooper Park, although the Duke of Gordon (see *High Street, below*) can be seen on his column on Lady Hill. The transepts are the oldest parts. The two figures in the south aisle originally adorned the outer walls of the central tower. The east end is an impressive arrangement of two rows of five lancets crowned by a rose window. The piers of the choir have unusual spire-like terminations.

The octagonal 13C **chapter-house**★★ was reconstructed in the 15C when it was provided with elaborately rich vaulting and carved bosses. The stone benching is discontinued for the five canopied seats.

Standing within the former cathedral precincts are **Pann's Port**, a former gateway and in the corner of Cooper Park, the ruins of one of the manses, miscalled the **Bishop's House**.

Additional Sights

Elgin Museum

Open Apr–Oct, Mon–Fri 10am–5pm, Sat 11am–4pm. £3. 01343 543 675, www.elginmuseum.org.uk.

This purpose-built Italianate building (1843) houses the local history museum. Items of particular interest

are the local fossil fish and reptiles and incised Pictish stones, especially the **Burghead Bulls.**

High Street

Wynds and pends link the main thoroughfare to the north and south. **Braco's Banking House**, marked by street-level arcades, was the banking house of William Duff of Dipple. His son William Duff of Braco and later Earl of Fife invested the accumulated fortune in the building of Duff House. Farther along on the right as the street widens is a 17C **tower**, now offices. The handsome **Church of St Giles** designed in the Classical style by the Aberdonian, Archibald Simpson, is greatly enhanced by its mid-street site. The steepled tower and fluted columned portico dominate the façades. **Lady Hill** at the far end of the street was the site of the medieval castle. Today it is dominated by the monument to the last Duke of Gordon (d 1836) with his Grace above.

Moray Motor Museum

Bridge Street. Open daily Apr to mid-Oct 11am–5pm. £3.75. 01343 541120.

Admire the classics in this collection of cars and motorcycles: the Ford Model "T"; the 1937 Bentley, a silent sports car; the Bristol 403 (1953), a post Second World War car by the Bristol Aero Company; the 1929 Rolls Royce Phantom I adapted as a shooting vehicle, with a large spotlight for night shooting; and the 1968 E Type Jaguar.

Glen Moray Distillery

Bruceland Road. Open daily. Tours Mon–Fri 9.30am, 11am, 12.30pm, 2pm,3pm. Sat 10.30am, noon, 1.30pm, 3pm. £3 (includes tasting). 5th Chapter tour £15. 01343 550 900. www.glenmoray.com.

Glen Moray has been distilled on the banks of the River Lossie since 1897 at this small friendly distillery. Visitors can take the standard tour or the more in-depth 5th Chapter tour (*advance booking required*) which ends with a tutored tasting of the distilleries premium brands.

EYEMOUTH
SCOTTISH BORDERS
POPULATION 4,000

A busy fishing port and popular holiday resort, Eyemouth stands on the Berwickshire coast at the mouth of the Eye Water.

Information: Auld Kirk. ☎0870 608 0404. www.visitscottishborders.com.

Don't Miss: Eyemouth Museum; The Herring Queen Festival (early July) is the highlight of the summer season; St Abb's Head.

Organizing Your Time: Allow 2hrs for Eyemouth, longer for excursions.

Especially for Kids: Eyemouth beach.

Also See: MANDERSTON.

Sights

Eyemouth Museum★

&.◷Open Apr–Sept, Mon–Sat 10am–4.30pm, Sun 10am–12.30pm (Jul–Aug, 10am–1.30pm). Oct, Mon–Sat 10am–4pm. ◉£2.50. ☎018907 50678.

Displays give glimpses of rural life and attractive presentations touch on all aspects of local fisherfolk's lives : their homes and customs, the fish, the boats, gear and tackle and the ancillary crafts. The **Eyemouth Tapestry**, rich in symbolism, commemorates the Great Fishing Disaster of 1881 and tells the story of the tragedy.

Harbour

The brightly painted boats lining the quayside and the busy **fish market** testify to the importance of fishing to the town. Ever since the 12C fishing has been the main activity in Eyemouth. In 1881, on Black Friday, 14 October, 189 men were lost in the Great East Coast Fishing Disaster; 129 of those men came from Eyemouth. Nineteen boats were lost, almost half the fishing fleet of that time.

Old fishing village

The old fishing area still retains certain of the characteristics described by the Rev Daniel McIver: "Instead of rows of houses, we have clusters of houses, instead of gables facing gables, we have gables facing fronts and fronts facing back courts." Smuggling reached its height in the 18C and Eyemouth was an important centre in the illicit trade in wines, spirits, tea and tobacco.

J. Pringle/ Scottish Viewpoint

Eyemouth Harbour

Driving Tour

Coast North of Eyemouth

Leave Eyemouth, north on the A 1107.

Coldingham

Population 520. This inland village is best-known for its ruined **priory** (◐open Jul–Aug, Wed and Sun 2–4pm; May–Oct, Wed 2pm–4pm; ☎01890 771 820/420, www.stebba-coldinghampriory. org.uk), which was founded in 1098 by King Edgar for Benedictine monks. The present parish church occupies the choir of a 12C–13C building.

▶ *In Coldingham take the B 6438 to the right.*

St Abb's

The church high on the clifftop pinpoints this attractive fishing village clustered round its harbour. Walks in the area include the clifftop path south to the sandy beach of Coldingham Bay and north to St Abb's Head (◐*see below*).

St Abb's Head★★

National Nature Reserve. Access road signposted to the left, off the B6438, just before entering St Abb's. (NTS) ◐ *Visitor Centre open Good Fri–Oct, 10am–5pm.* ☐ Ⓟ(£2). ☎0844 493 2256. www.nts.org.uk.

Two hundred acres in extent, the reserve covers a variety of habitats – coastal grassland, sandy and rocky shores and cliffs – and includes the man-made Mire Loch and the well-known landmark, **St Abb's Head.** The cliffs, some of the finest on the eastern seaboard, rise to over 300ft/91m and provide myriad nesting ledges for seabirds (guillemots, razorbills, puffins, fulmars and gulls). The spectacle of entire cliff faces alive with diving, swooping birds to a background of piercing cries is a fascinating sight. The knoll beside the lighthouse affords **views**★ of the coastline south to Hairy Ness and north to Fast Castle's headland – with, on a clear day, views of the Bass Rock and Fife coast on the horizon. The

reserve is a sanctuary for migrating birds in spring and autumn and a new exhibition and ranger-guided walks interpet the site for visitors who are not specialist bird-watchers.

▶ *Return to A 1107 and continue towards Dunbar.*

Fast Castle

2.3mi/3.5km off the A 1107, signposted. The surfaced road leads to Dowlaw Farm. Leave the car beyond the farm cottages. 15min walk down to castle ruins along a path, steep and stony in places. ⊘*Care is needed on the cliffs.* ☎*www.fast-castle. co.uk.*

Once through the gate, the clifftop site affords a good **view** westwards of the coastline with ever decreasing red sandstone cliffs. The few jagged remains of **Fast Castle** are perched in an audacious **site**★★ teetering on a rocky crag high above the sea, where castle wall and cliff face merge into one another. This once impregnable stronghold dates from the 16C (*excavations are in progress to determine even earlier origins*) and figures as Wolf's Crag in Scott's *The Bride of Lammermoor.* A cave below the castle is reputed to have been used by smugglers.

In June seabirds (guillemots, razorbills, shags and kittiwakes) nesting on the cliffs at the seaward end of the castle, and in November when grey seals pup on the beaches at either side of the castle.

▶ *Return to Eyemouth on A 1107.*

Excursion

Burnmouth

Population 290. 2mi/3km south. ⊘*The road down is steep and narrow and it is advisable to sound the car horn at the corner.* Set on a rocky coastline, the original fishing village – which has the distinction of being the first in Scotland after crossing the border with England – with its harbour below the cliffs make an attractive group.

FALKLAND★
FIFE
POPULATION 960

The Dutch engraver, John Slezer's description of Falkland in the 17C, "a pretty little Town... a stately Palace", sums up the town of today. Tucked away at the foot of the Lomond Hills, safe from the depredations of war and strife so endemic to Scottish history, Falkland has retained the peaceful charm of a royal burgh of yesteryear.

- **Information:** The Merchant's House, 339 High Street, Kirkcaldy. ☎01592 267775, www.standrews.co.uk.
- ▶ **Orient Yourself:** 11mi/18km north of Kirkcaldy.
- 🕓 **Organizing Your Time:** Allow at least 1hr 30 minutes.
- 👣 **Also See:** ST ANDREWS. CUPAR.

A Bit of History

Fife, the centre of the royal kingdom – The original castle belonged to the Macduffs, the Earls of Fife, and its early history was marked by the mysterious death in 1402 of David, Duke of Rothesay, heir to Robert III, while staying with his uncle, Robert, Duke of Albany. David's brother, James I, on his release from imprisonment in England in 1424, set out to restore the power of the monarchy. His revenge was total and in the following year the Albanys were beheaded. Their property, including Falkland, passed to the Crown. James II gifted the castle to Mary of Gueldres in 1451 and followed this in 1458 by raising the town to a royal burgh and the castle to a palace.

Royal residence (15C–16C) – The hunting seat of Falkland became one of the Stewarts' favourite royal palaces. James II built an extension, the north range which originally contained the Great Hall, and it was here that Margaret of Anjou and her son took refuge when Henry VI was imprisoned. The future James III (1451–88) spent his childhood here.

James IV (1473–1513), a typical monarch of the Renaissance, re-established royal authority, and with his Queen, Margaret Tudor, entertained a splendid court. Royal patronage was extended to the poet **William Dunbar** (1465–1530) who dedicated *The Thistle and the Rose* to his

royal patrons. James, who loved to hunt in the Falkland Forest and hawk on the Lomond Hills, built the south range.

James V (1512–42) made extensive alterations in preparation for his marriage, initially to Magdalene, daughter of François I, then after her untimely death, to Mary of Guise in 1538. French workmen prepared the palace for a French

FALKLAND			
Brunton St	2	Horsemarket	6
East Port	3	Parliament Square	8
High St	5		

Birthplace of		Key House	E
Richard Cameron	A	St Andrew's House	F
Bruce Fountain	B	Town Hall	H
Hunting Lodge Hotel	D		

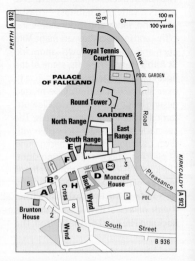

bride. The result was the Renaissance ornament on the courtyard façade of the south range. A radical departure from the Gothic of the time, this stylistic flourish was in fact the earliest of its kind in Britain. James' two sons died as infants and it was to Mary, Queen of Scots that the throne went when her father died heartbroken at the age of 30.

Mary came to hunt occasionally, and her son James VI visited on his 1617 royal progress as did her grandson, Charles I and great-grandson, Charles II. It was the latter who presented the Scots Guards with their Colours here in 1650. Abandoned, the palace fell into a state of disrepair. In the late 19C the Hereditary Keeper carried out restoration work. The palace, although still royal property, is now under the guardianship of the National Trust for Scotland.

Walking Tour

Palace of Falkland ★ 45min

(NTS). &. Palace and Garden: open Mar–Oct, Mon–Sat 10am–5pm, Sun 1pm–5pm. £10 (gardens only, £5). 0844 4932186, www.nts.org.uk.

South Range: street front

This range, built by James IV, consists of two very distinct parts: on the extreme left is the twin-towered gatehouse, which was completed in its present form

Falkland Palace

in 1541 and provided accommodation for the Constable, Captain and Keeper. The corbelled parapet, cable moulding and gargoyles link this with the range to the east where massive buttresses are adorned with canopied niches. The statues are the work of Peter the Flemishman (1538). The street front is a good example of Scottish Gothic.

South Range – From the entrance hall of the **gatehouse**, climb to the Keeper's suite on the 2nd floor. The **bedroom** is dominated by James VI's magnificent canopied bed and the room is hung with copies of full length royal portraits. Adjoining are the dressing room with the Bute Centenary Exhibition and the small panelled bathroom.

The Chapel Royal, Falkland Palace

▶ *Go down one flight to the Drawing Room.*

The **Drawing Room** was restored by the Marquess of Bute in the 1890s. The oak ceiling is emblazoned with the coats of arms of the Stuart Kings and the different Keepers of the palace. The paintings include James VII and Mary, Queen of Scots, Charles II and Catharine of Braganza. The outstanding features of the 16C interior of the **Chapel Royal** are the oak screen between chapel and ante-chapel and the painted ceiling redecorated for Charles I's 1633 visit. The **Tapestry Gallery** is hung with 17C Flemish tapestries and furnished with replicas of 16C and 17C pieces of furniture. The 19C heraldic glass shows sovereigns and consorts closely associated with the palace.

▶ *Take the turnpike up a level.*

The Old Library has memorabilia of the 20C Keepers, the Crichton Stuarts.

▶ *Return to the corridor level before crossing to the East Range.*

East Range

This was built at the same time as the south one, to contain the royal apartments with the king's suite on the first floor and queen's above. This level affords a good view of the delightful courtyard front of the south range, so different from the Gothic street front. The Renaissance influence is most evident in the buttresses embellished with engaged pilasters and pronounced mouldings and the sets of paired medallions. The latter are not unlike Wolsey's terracotta medallions at Hampton Court and the Stirling Heads (see STIRLING).

The **King's Bed Chamber** in the cross house projecting from this range (rebuilt 19C) has been restored. The windows have shutter boards below and leaded glass above and the painted ceiling is resplendent with the monograms of James V and Mary of Guise. The Golden Bed of Brahan is of early 17C Dutch workmanship. James V died here in 1542 several days after learning of the birth of his daughter Mary, Queen of Scots, when he pronounced "It came wi' a lass, and will gang wi' a lass."

Gardens★

The foundations of the North Range and Round Tower of the original Macduff stronghold can be seen in the gardens. Replanted since its use as a potato field in the Second World War effort, the gardens, ablaze with colour, include shrubs, herbaceous borders and a more formal garden. Beyond is the 1539 **Royal Tennis Court**, built for James V.

Village★ 30min

A stroll around Falkland shows off its fine vernacular architecture and gives an insight into the houses and offices of the court officials, royal servants and tradesmen who once resided in the village. Of particular interest are the many **lintel and marriage stones.**

On the south side of the High Street, 17C **Moncreif House** sports a thatch of Tay reeds, a marriage lintel and inscribed panel proclaiming the builder's loyalty to his monarch.

The hotel next door features further panels, and beyond Back Wynd stands the steepled town hall (1801) which is adorned with a sculptured panel of the burgh arms.

On the far side of the street next to the palace is **Key House** with its lintel dated 1713 with, as neighbour, the harled and red pantiled 18C **St Andrew's House**. The Bruce Fountain is 19C.

Cross Wynd is lined by a row of single-storey cottages, interrupted on the left by the cobbled Parliament Square. Glance up Horsemarket to see the building with forestairs.

Dominating Brunton Street is the imposing three-storeyed **Brunton House** (1712), which is the home of the Royal Falconers. Back in the main street, the birthplace of the "Lion of the Covenant", **Richard Cameron** (1648–80), is marked by another inscribed lintel. He headed the extremist Covenanting group, the Cameronians, the nucleus of which was later to form the regiment of the same name.

FLOORS CASTLE
SCOTTISH BORDERS
⬙LOCAL MAP SEE THE TWEED VALLEY

The highly distinctive pinnacled silhouette of **Floors Castle** enjoys a superb terraced site overlooking the Tweed.

▤ **Information:** Town House, The Square, Kelso. ☏0870 6080404. www.scot-borders.co.uk.

◎ **Don't Miss:** The view of the castle from Kelso Bridge.

◷ **Organizing Your Time:** Allow 1 hour for the house.

◔ **Also See:** KELSO, DRYBURGH ABBEY, MELLERSTAIN.

A Bit of History

A Roxburghe seat

Just outside Kelso, Floors Castle occupies a natural terrace overlooking the River Tweed and facing the Cheviot Hills (the heartland of the family's Estate). It lies on the opposite river bank to Roxburgh Castle, once the strongest fortress along the former march with England. Formerly the lands of Kelso Abbey, it was obtained by **Robert Ker of Cessford**, one of King James VI's courtiers, who was created 1st Earl of Roxburghe in 1616. **John, 5th Earl** (d 1740), an active promoter of the Act of Union (1707) was created a duke for his services to the Crown and it was during his lifetime that the house was built (1721) to **William Adam's** designs.

William Playfair was engaged by the 21-year-old **James, 6th Duke** (1816–79), to enlarge and embellish Adam's original building. He took his inspiration from the highly ornamented picturesque style of Heriot's Hospital in Edinburgh. The result is the romantic fairytale castle with its roofscape of turrets, pinnacles and cupolas, that we see today.

Visit

♿◷*Open Easter weekend and Apr– Oct daily 11am–5pm. Last admission 4.30pm.* *£7 (garden and grounds only £3).* ▱. ✕. ☏*01573 223 333. www.floorscastle.com.*

Exterior

On the north front, Adam's original castellated main block quartered by towers rises through three storeys and is flanked by Playfair's additions of wings at right angles, linked at ground level to the main building. The wings, again quartered by taller towers repeat the pattern of the central block. The dramatic roofscape of cupolas, chimneys, battlements and turrets links and unifies the whole.

Interior

Many of the rooms were remodelled by **Duchess May**, the American wife (1876–1937) of the 8th Duke, to accommodate her outstanding collection of tapestries and fine furniture.

From the windows of the **Sitting Room** may be seen a holly tree which marks the spot where James II was killed in 1460 by an exploding cannon while laying siege to Roxburgh Castle.

The **Drawing Room** was altered to accommodate Duchess May's handsome set of six 17C Brussels tapestries.

The **Needle Room** is said to resemble a room in Versailles. The fine post-Impressionist paintings include Matisse's *Corbeille de Fleurs* and a river scene by Bonnard.

The 17C Gobelins tapestries and dark panelling in the **Ballroom** are the background for some fine pieces of French furniture, porcelain and portraits.

The **Bird Room** is a small Gothic room was designed by Playfair to house a collection of stuffed birds.

In the **Gallery** are mementoes and documents including a letter from Mary, Queen of Scots to her warden of the Eastern Marches, the Laird of Cessford.

FORRES
MORAY
POPULATION 8,346

This royal and ancient burgh is situated south of Findhorn Bay. Both the tolbooth and mercat cross are 19C.

- **Information:** 116 High Street. ☎01309 672 938. www.aberdeen-grampian.com.
- **Don't Miss:** Sueno's Stone.
- **Especially for Kids:** Sand dunes and beach at Findhorn.
- **Also See:** BRODIE CASTLE, ELGIN.

Sights

Falconer Museum
Tolbooth Street. ⏱*Open Apr–Oct Mon–Sat 10 am – 5 pm. Nov–Mar Mon–Thu 11am–12.30pm, 1pm–3.30pm.* ⊜*£4.50.* ☎*01309 673 701. www.falconermuseum. co.uk.*
In the throes of a major redevelopment, this lively local museum interprets the town of Forres and Hugh Falconer, a local 19C scientist and discoverer.

Sueno's Stone★★
Outskirts of Forres, close to the Findhorn road, B 9011.
A legacy of the enigmatic Picts, this sandstone cross slab (20ft/6m high, now protected by glass) is superbly carved on all sides and probably dates from the 9C. The purpose of this stone, which has no parallel in Scotland, remains uncertain. Three sides including the one with the wheel cross are decorative. The fourth, the most spectacular, is narrative, depicting horsemen, armed warriors and headless corpses. The theory is that this outstanding piece of craftsmanship represents a commemorative monument for some a battle.

Excursions

Dallas Dhu Distillery
1.25mi/2km south on the A940, then a minor road. (HS). ⏱*Open Apr–Sept daily 9.30am–6.30pm. Oct–Mar, Sat–Wed 9.30am–4.30pm. Last admission 30 mins before closing.* ⏱*Closed 25, 26 Dec and 1, 2 Jan* ⊜*£5.* ☎*01309 676548. www.historic-scotland.gov.uk.*

Built in 1899, this picturesque distillery in stone and slate was closed in the early 1980s, but now provides a fascinating and well-documented experience of the processes involved in producing the "sovereign liquor". After learning about the history of whisky from its monastic beginnings, visitors take a self-guided tour which ends with the customary "wee dram".

Findhorn
4mi/6km north on the B 9011.
The internationally renowned New Age community **Findhorn Foundation,** founded in 1962 is focussed on **Universal Hall**, a strikingly unconventional structure in timber and stone.
The **village** of Findhorn, overlooks the bay of the same name. Its tidal water, sand dunes, fine beach, mud flats and salt-marsh is used for water sports but is also of international significance for wading birds and migrant geese, while seals haul out close to the mouth of the bay. The **Heritage Centre** (⏱*open daily Jun–Aug 2–5pm, May & Sept weekends only 2–5pm;* ☎*01309 690659, www. findhorn-heritage.co.uk*) occupies an old store building and a former ice house West of Findhorn Bay lies an extensive area of dunes, the famous **Culbin Sands,** which were originally held by marram grass. The effects were devastating when the grass was widely removed for thatching in the 17C. Fertile land and the village of Culbin were covered by sand. In 1922 the Forestry Commission started afforestation with Corsican pine, and the **Culbin Forest**, a site of special scientific interest.

FORT WILLIAM★
HIGHLAND
POPULATION 10,805

Fort William lies on the shore of Loch Linnhe in the shadow of Britain's highest mountain, Ben Nevis. As the main town of the Lochaber District, Fort William is ideally situated at the converging point of various routes. The town developed around a succession of strategically sited strongholds and forts at the southern end of the Great Glen. In summer the town is crowded with holidaymakers as Fort William makes an ideal touring centre from which to discover the beauty of the surrounding countryside. Highlights of the tourist calendar are the Ben Nevis Race and the Glen Nevis River Race. The Nevis Range ski resort brings the town to life during the winter months.

- **Information:** Cameron Centre. ☎01397 703 781. www.visithighlands.com.
- **Don't Miss:** Ben Nevis; the Road to the Isles; the Glenfinnan Gathering and Highland Games; the Ardnamurchan Peninsula.
- **Organizing Your Time:** Allow at least 3 days.
- **Especially for Kids:** The Silver Sands of Morar.

Sights

West Highland Museum
Cameron Square. Open Jun–Sept, Mon–Sat 10am–5pm, also Jul–Aug Sun 2pm–5pm. Oct–May, Mon–Sat 10am–4pm. Closed 25–26 Dec and 1–2 Jan. £3. ☎01397 702 169, www.westhighlandmuseum.org.uk.
This local museum covers a wide variety of topics, including the Caledonian Canal, Ben Nevis, the former fort, crofting and Jacobite relics.

Excursions

Ben Nevis★★
4mi/6.4km to the southeast. Start of the footpath: from the road along the north side of the River Nevis or from beside the golf course. Access by footpath: 4/5hr ascent and 3hr descent by a well-marked path.
This snow-capped granite mass is at 4,406ft/1,344m Britain's highest mountain albeit not a particularly shapely one. The Ben is extremely popular with climbers and walkers. Prospective climbers should be suitably clad (boots or strong shoes and waterproofs) and equipped (whistle, map and food etc). At the summit, with its war memorial, once stood a hotel (closed in 1915) and an observatory. Legend has it that if the snow ever leaves the summit, the ownership of Ben Nevis will revert to the Crown.

Nevis Range
Torlundy. 4mi/6.4km north by A 82.
This well-designed resort is the newest of the five Scottish Ski Centres, and boasts the most modern facilities for learning to ski and snowboard. Moreover it offers the highest skiing in Scotland, with an enviable record for good snow-conditions running late into the season.

A **gondola** (cable-car) service (operates daily 10am–5pm, good weather only; closed mid-Nov to mid-Dec for annual maintenance; £8.75 return; ☎01397 705 825, www.nevisrange.co.uk), makes the 2,150ft/655m up the slope of Aonach Mor to the, and the ski resort in just 12 minutes. There are great **views★★** of Skye, Rhum, the Great Glen and the surrounding mountains. The **Mountain Discovery Centre**, located at the top station, interprets the wildlife, mountain habitat and landscape with interactive displays and video footage. In summer the resort also offers many activities such as dry slope skiing, mountain biking, and mountain and forest walks.

Ben Nevis and Loch Lochy

© World Pictures / Photoshot

Driving Tour

Road to the Isles ★★ *46 miles.*

This scenic route, often very busy, passes through country rich in historical associations to the town of Mallaig, one of the ferry ports for Skye and other Inner Hebridean isles.

▶ *Leave Fort William by the Inverness road, A 82, passing on the way the ruins of Inverlochy Castle (closed, unsafe). Turn left to Mallaig taking A 830.*

Neptune's Staircase

Banavie. This flight of eight locks was designed by Telford as part of the **Caledonian Canal** to raise the water level 64ft/19m in 500yds/457m.

From Corpach, with its paper mill (pulping operations ceased in 1980), there are magnificent **views**★★ backwards to Ben Nevis. The road then follows the northern shore of Loch Eil, the continuation of Loch Linnhe.

Glenfinnan Monument Visitor Centre

(NTS) ⏰ *Open daily. Jul–Aug 9.30am–5.30pm, Good Fri–Jun and Sept–Oct 10am–5pm.* ⌨. ☎ *0844 493 2221. www.nts.org.uk.*

In this glorious setting at the head of **Loch Shiel** stands the 1815 monument to commemorate those who died while following Prince Charles Edward Stuart in the 1745 rising. Here, five days after the prince's landing at nearby Loch nan Uamh, the standard was raised before a 1,300-strong army of Highlanders. The "Year of the Prince" ended 14 months later when he left for France from near the same spot.

From the top of the tower (⚠ *61 steps with an awkward trap door exit to viewing area*) there is a splendid **view** of Loch Shiel framed by the mountains, and northwards over the many spanned railway viaduct recently made famous by the flying car sequence in *Harry Potter and the Chamber of Secrets* (2002) .

The **Glenfinnan Gathering and Highland Games** is held annually on the Saturday in August nearest to the anniversary.

▶ *Beyond Glenfinnan, the road and railway part company to go either side of landlocked Loch Eilt. After the Lochailort turn-off, the road passes the head of the sea loch, Loch Ailort, before rising to cross the neck of the Ardnish peninsula.*

The road runs along Loch nan Uamh, providing a seaward **view**★ of the Sound of Arisaig. Down on the foreshore of the north side a **cairn** marks the spot where Prince Charles Edward Stuart came ashore on 19 July 1745 .

Address Book

For coin ranges, see the Legend on the cover flap.

WHERE TO STAY

Lochan Cottage – *Lochyside.*
01397 702 695. www.fortwilliam-guesthouse.co.uk. Minimum booking May–Sept 2 nights. An immaculate little whitewashed cottage 2.5 miles out of town, with homely public areas and a breakfast conservatory overlooking lovely landscaped grounds.

Lawriestone Guest House – *Achintore Road. 01397 700 777. www.lawriestone.co.uk.* This Victorian house just a five-minute walk from the town centre, enjoys views over Loch Linnhe and has spacious airy rooms, some with views.

Ashburn House – *18 Achintore Road. 01397 706 000.* This luxury Victorian house B&B overlooks Loch Linnhe, a 5-min walk from the town centre. Bedrooms are beautifully furnished; very comfortable conservatory lounge.

WHERE TO EAT

Crannog – *The Underwater Centre, An Aird. 01397 705 589, www.crannog.net.* This lakeside seafood restaurant was converted from a baitstore by its former fisherman owner and enjoys wonderful views over Loch Linnhe.

▶ *The road then follows Beasdale Valley, crosses to Borrodale Valley then over the neck of Arisaig Peninsula.*

Arisaig★
Population 177. Facilities. This scattered community looks over the **Sound of Arisaig.** Cruises leave from the pier for Rhum, Eigg and Muck. Beyond Arisaig, the rocky shore is interrupted by a series of sandy bays, the most famous being the **Silver Sands of Morar**★ Kids, known for their white silica sand.

Morar
Population 290. The village lies at the entrance to Loch Morar, the deepest inland loch (over 1,000ft/305m deep) inhabited by a monster Morag, "sister" to Nessie.

Mallaig★
Population 998. The houses spill down the slopes overlooking the bay, sheltered by two headlands. This fishing port is the terminal for the Skye ferry.

Ardnamurchan Peninsula★★
65mi/105km.

▶ *Follow the A 830 to Lochailort (as above), then branch south onto the A 861, skirting the Sound of Arisaig with views of Eigg and Muck. Continue past Loch Moidart and the tip of Loch Shiel to Salen. then on ① the 8007 along Loch Sunart and on to Ardnamurchan Point.*

Ardnamurchan Natural History Centre
Glenmore. Open Apr–Oct, Mon–Sat 10.30am–5.30pm, Sun noon–5.30pm. 01972 500 209, www.ardnamurchannaturalhistorycentre.co.uk.
A fascinating introduction to Ardnamurchan's wild landscape, flora and fauna including the chance to view golden eagles.

Ardnamurchan Point
Crowned by a lighthouse this is Britain's most westerly point and offers dramatic **views**★★ over the Atlantic.

▶ *Return to Salen and bear right onto the A 861 for a scenic run through Glen Tarbert, along the west shore of Loch Linnhe and the south bank of Loch Eil to Kinlocheil. Then take the A 830 back to Fort William. An alternative route is by ferry from Corran to Inchtree and then the A 82 north.*

Glen Nevis★
The road follows the south bank of the River Nevis for 10mi/16km round the foot of the Ben (though there is no view of the summit).

FRASERBURGH
ABERDEENSHIRE
POPULATION 7,789

Though the great days of the herring fishery were in the 19C and early 20C, this austere town on the northeastern tip of Aberdeenshire is still home to a fleet of around 220 fishing boats. The original harbour was the creation of the Fraser family in the 16C and it was they who built the grandiosely named Castle on Kinneard Head, a mansion whose top floor was adapted in 1787 as a base to house Scotland's very first lighthouse.

Information: 3 Saltoun Square. ☎01346 518 315. www.aberdeen-grampian.com.

Also See: BANFF.

Sight

Museum of Scottish Lighthouses

Kinneard Head. ⟐⟐*Open Jul–Aug, Mon–Sat 10am–6pm, Sun 11am–6pm. Apr–Jun and Sept, Mon–Sat 11am–5pm, Sun noon–5pm. Rest of year, Mon–Sat 10am–4pm, Sun noon–4pm.* ⟐£5. ⟐. ☎01346 511 022. www.lighthousemuseum.org.uk.

This museum tells the fascinating story of the "Northern Lights" which have protected shipping from the perils of the country's long coastline with ever-increasing technological sophistication since the first fire tower was lit on the Isle of May in 1636. There are models, maps, drawings and all kinds of objects associated with lighthouse-keeping, but the most compelling exhibits are the great lenses of the lighthouses themselves, gigantic jewels of Art Deco allure. Human interest is not absent. The lives of lighthouse-keepers – a disappearing race due to modern automation – is well evoked with tales such as the mystery of the Flannan Isles lighthouse where three men literally vanished without trace. Also recorded is the extraordinary achievement of five generations of the Stevenson family who between them built around 100 lighthouses.

On Kinnaird Head, on the far side of a fishermen's net drying area, is a cluster of structures including keepers' cottages and the original lighthouse of 1787.

Excursion

Maggie's Hoosie

Inverallochy, 5mi/8km east by ⬚ *9033.* ⟐ *Open Apr–Sept, Mon–Thu 2pm–4pm.* ⟐£2. ☎01346 582 514 761.

The twin fishing villages of Inverallochy and Cairnbulg are extraordinary agglomerations of single-storey granite cottages placed gable-end to the rocky shore. Many have been modernised, but Maggie's Hoosie has been renovated to evoke the simple and harsh life led by local fisherfolk in the late 19C. A tour guide shows visitors around the rooms and talk about the village fishing community in bygone years, Maggie's family and Maggie and her hoosie.

Maggie was born in 1867 and died in 1950. She spent her life preparing and baiting fishing lines, curing, smoking, salting and drying the fish and then selling it, (or bartering it for other produce) around the countryside. She would also barter fish for other goods and produce.

The floor is maintained as it would have been in Maggie's day – beaten down earth covered in fresh sand from the beach. There was no running water in the hoosie, Maggie and her family used the local well and then the pump. Neither was there a toilet; a bucket would be used in the shed.

FYVIE CASTLE ★
ABERDEENSHIRE
&LOCAL MAP SEE ABERDEEN – GRAMPIAN CASTLES

The imposing baronial pile of **Fyvie Castle**, with its centuries of history, is the ideal place to discover the opulence of an Edwardian interior.

Information: 9a The Square, Huntly. ☎01466 792 255. www.aberdeen-grampian.com.

A Bit of History

The original royal stronghold passed in 1390 to the Preston family and then in 1433 to the Meldrums. In 1596 Sir Alexander Seton, later Chancellor of Scotland, purchased Fyvie and remodelled the castle to incorporate the already existing Preston and Meldrum towers. He and created the spectacular **south front** (150ft/45.7m long), a striking example of 17C baronial architecture, and the great wheel staircase. In 1889 the castle was sold to Alexander Forbes-Leith, a man with local origins who had made his fortune in the American steel industry. Lord Leith refurbished Fyvie and, like many other American millionaires assembled a collection of paintings with family or castle connections.

Visit

NTS. & ⊙ Castle open: Jul–Aug daily 11am–5pm. Good Fri–Jun and Sept–Oct, Sat–Wed noon–5pm. Bank Holidays open Fri–Mon. Last admission 4.15. Grounds open: all year, daily dawn–dusk. ☜£8. ⬚. ☎0844 493 2182. www.nts.org.uk.

The spacious 17C **wheel stair** is liberally spangled with the Seton crescent of its builder and rises through five floors. In the Dining Room, with its 19C plasterwork ceiling, are portraits of the first Lord Leith. Other works are by Raeburn, Romney and Opie. Up another floor, the original high hall, now the Morning Room, boasts a 1683 plasterwork ceiling from the Seton period. The Back Morning Room is the unpretentious setting for the Fyvie portraits, masterpieces by **Raeburn**. *Mrs Gregory* is claimed to be his finest female portrait. In the Library the John Burnet painting of the *Trial of Charles I* recalls the royal association. Charles as a four-year-old boy spent time at Fyvie. The Drawing Room in the Gordon Tower has Pompeo Batoni's memorable portrait (1766) of *The Hon William Gordon* as a Grand Tourist. There are other notable works by Lawrence, Hoppner, Romney, Reynolds and Gainsborough.

National Trust for Scotland

Fyvie Castle

GLAMIS★

ANGUS

POPULATION 240

Set in the rich agricultural countryside of Strathmore this attractive village (pronounced "Glarms") stands on the periphery of the Glamis Castle policies (estate).

- **Information:** 21 Castle Street. Dundee. ☎01382 527527. www.angusanddundee.co.uk.
- **Orient Yourself:** Glamis is 12mi/19km north of Dundee and 5mi/8km south west of Forfar.
- **Don't Miss:** Early Christian monuments in Meigle Museum.
- **Also See:** DUNDEE.

Angus Folk Museum★

Kirkwynd Cottages. ♿🕐*Open Mar–Jun and Sept–Oct, Sat–Sun, noon–5pm. Jul–Aug, Mon–Sat 11am–5pm, Sun 1pm–5pm. Bank holiday weekends Fri–Mon noon–5pm.* ☞£5. ☎0844 493 2141. www.nts.org.uk.

An attractive row of 19C cottages houses an outstanding folk collection which depicts rural life of bygone days. In the domestic section (start at the far end) the 19C manse parlour is followed by a dairy, laundry and schoolroom. The next bay recalls the importance in Angus of such cottage industries as spinning and weaving. Beyond the kitchen, room 7 has a box bed and baby shelf.

Across the road the agricultural section has displays of implements large and small, many of local manufacture. Inside, are exhibits of agricultural developments.

Glamis Graveyard & St Fergus Well

According to local legend St Fergus established the local kirk at Glamis, and it was here in the early 8C that he baptised the earliest converts to Christianity in Strathmore in the well which still exists to this day.

Various Pictish stones, together with gravestones describing the trades of long deceased locals, reinforce the importance of Glamis as a holy place. Water from the Well of St. Fergus trickles into the Glamis burn, and baptism and marriage ceremonies still take place in this isolated and atmospheric spot.

Also in the graveyard can be found the headstone of **Margaret Bridie** of Glamis. She made the original bridies (meat-and-potato filled pastries similar to Cornish pasties) in the village and then old them at the Buttermarket in Forfar, hence the origins of the famous Forfar Bridies, still enjoyed all over the region today.

Excursion

Meigle Sculptured Stone Museum★★

7mi/11.5km west by A 94. (HS). ♿🕐*Open Apr–Sept daily 9.30am–5.30pm. Oct Sat–Wed 9.30am–12.30pm, 1.30–4.30pm. Last admission 30 mins before closing. Oct* ☞£3. ☎01828 640612, www.historic-scotland.gov.uk.

The former village school houses an outstanding collection of Old Red Sandstone **Early Christian monuments**★★ (7C–10C AD), all found in the vicinity. Cross-slabs, recumbent gravestones and a variety of fragments vividly illustrate the life and art of the Picts.

Although the exact purpose of the monuments remains obscure the carving everywhere is full of spirit and vitality and shows a high degree of skill. The stones are all numbered. Subject matter includes enigmatic Pictish symbols Celtic-type crosses with associated complex interlace, fretwork, spiral and key patterns; pictorial scenes (including Daniel in the Lion's Den, and fabulous animals and human figures.

GLAMIS CASTLE★★
ANGUS

Set in the rich agricultural Vale of Strathmore, Glamis Castle is the epitome of a Scottish castle with the added interest of many royal connection – it was the childhood home of Her Majesty Queen Elizabeth, the Mother of Queen Elizabeth II – literary associations and a ghost in residence.

- **Information:** 21 Castle Street. Dundee. ☎01382 527527. www.angusanddundee.co.uk.
- **Orient Yourself:** 12mi/19km north of Dundee.
- **Organizing Your Time:** The second weekend of mid July sees the Scottish Transport Extravaganza when around 800 antique vehicles turn the grounds into a carnival of colour.
- **Also See:** Glamis (village). Dundee. Kirriemuir.

A Bit of History

Originally a hunting lodge, Glamis has been the seat of the same family since 1372. In 1376 the Chamberlain of Scotland, Sir John Lyon, married Joanna, the widowed daughter of Robert II. In spite of loyal service to both king and State the family fell out of favour during the reign of James V, in connection with his campaign against the house of Douglas. The 6th Lord Glamis had married a Douglas, sister to the Earl of Angus, who had fled the country. Following her husband's death and after a long period of imprisonment during which the sovereign occupied the castle, James V had Lady Glamis burnt as a witch. Her ladyship's ghost, "The Grey Lady", is said to haunt the castle.

Visit

🕐 Open mid-Mar to Oct, 10am–6pm. Nov–Dec 11am–5pm. Last admission 90 mins before closing. 🕐 Closed 25–26 Dec. ≤£8; park only, £4. ☎01307 840 393, www.glamis-castle.co.uk.

Exterior

When seen from the end of the tree-lined avenue, the castle is grandly impressive. Its central part rises upwards bristling with towers, turrets, conical roofs and chimneys, with windows seemingly placed at random. The 15C L-shaped core has been added to and altered through the centuries, creating the present building.

Interior

Interiors of various periods, family and other portraits and a variety of interesting items highlight the guided tour. The west wing was destroyed by fire in 1800 and in the re-building, the **Dining Room** was given its ornate plaster ceiling. Family portraits include the grandparents and brothers of Queen Elizabeth, the Queen Mother. Jacobean furniture, armour and weapons are displayed in the stone-vaulted **Crypt**, the main hall of the original tower. This opens onto the great circular staircase, a later addition, the central shaft of which served as an early heating system. The Crypt level is the supposed location of the castle's famous "Secret Room" (👜 see Box on the next page).

The splendour of the **Drawing Room** is enhanced by a beautiful vaulted ceiling with **plasterwork decoration** (1621) and a magnificent fireplace (possibly by Inigo Jones) built to commemorate the 1603 Union of the English and Scottish Crowns. Notable among the portraits are the family group showing Patrick, 3rd Earl, strangely attired against the background of the castle and grounds previous to landscaping by Capability Brown, and double-sided wood portraits of the *9th Lord Glamis*, Privy Councillor to James VI, and his secretary, *Boswell* by the school of François Clouet. The Kneller portrait of *Viscount Dundee* is a

Glamis Castle

P. Tomkins/VisitScotland/Scottish Viewpoint

reminder that Claverhouse Castle (*no visible remains*), the principal seat of John Graham of Claverhouse, now lies within Glamis Estate.

The **Chapel's** panelling is decorated with 17C paintings depicting the Twelve Apostles and 15 scenes from the Bible. The paintings are by **Jacob de Wet** (1695–1754), a Dutch artist who also worked at Blair and Kellie castles and Holyroodhouse. The intriguing feature is the painting showing Christ wearing a hat. The chapel is the haunt of the Grey Lady (⌖*see 'A Bit of History' above*). The 20C ceiling of the **Library** makes a good comparison with the 17C one in the drawing room. The finely worked (17C) tapestries were woven at the Mortlake factory founded by James VI and *The Fruit Market* is a combined composition by Rubens and Frans Snyders.

Delicately worked hangings, a plaster ceiling and coat of arms, unusual fireplace and armorial porcelain are the chief points of interest in **King Malcolm's Room.** The most notable features of the **Royal Apartments** arranged for the Duke and Duchess of York are the hangings of the four-poster bed embroidered by Lady Strathmore and the Kinghorne Bed (1606) made for Patrick, Ist Earl. **Duncan's Hall**, the oldest (and eeriest) part, has literary associations with Shakespeare's *Macbeth* written during the reign of James VI, though in historical fact Macbeth did not murder Duncan here. Here also are a pair of portraits of the castle's royal occupants during the 6th Lady Glamis' imprisonment.

Grounds – Statues of James VI and his son Charles I flank the end of the drive. Beyond a fine spreading chestnut tree is the delightful **Italian Garden.**

The Secret Room

It is said that somewhere in the Crypt is a room that harbours a dark secret. One Saturday night Earl Beardie was a guest at Glamis Castle. After a heavy drinking session with Lord Glamis, he demanded a partner to play him at cards. A servant reminded him of the lateness of the hour and that it was almost the Sabbath. 'I care not what day of the week it is,' he roared, and raged that he would play with the Devil himself. At the stroke of midnight there was a knock at the door, and a tall man in dark clothes came into the castle and asked if Earl Beardie still required a partner. The Earl agreed and the two started to play cards. There was a great commotion and when one of the servants peeped through the keyhole to establish the cause of the noise, he saw a bright beam of light, blinding him in one eye. The Earl burst from the room and when he returned, the stranger, who was the Devil, had disappeared along with the Earl's soul, lost in the card game.

GLASGOW★★★
CITY OF GLASGOW
POPULATION 580,700

Scotland's most populous city, with its long-established tradition as an important industrial centre and major port, is nowadays also a flourishing cultural centre. Glasgow was named European City of Culture in 1990. Home to many of the most prestigious national performing arts organisations, Glasgow is internationally acclaimed in the fields of contemporary art, design and music.

- **Information:** Glasgow City Marketing Bureau. 11 George Square. ☎0141 204 4400. www.seeglasgow.com.
- ▶ **Orient Yourself:** Glasgow's main sights are scattered, so it is best to use public transport including the underground railway ("The Clockwork Orange"). Hop-on hop-off tours in open-top buses leave from George Square. ☎0141 204 0444, www.scotguide.com.
- **Parking:** Driving is not advisable due to heavy traffic and the difficulties and cost of parking.
- **Don't Miss:** The Burrell Collection; Glasgow Cathedral; Hunterian Art Gallery, Mackintosh Wing and Whistler Collection; Kelvingrove Museum and Art Gallery; Museum of Transport, Scottish-built cars and Clyde Room of Ship Models; an excursion to the Trossachs.
- **Organizing Your Time:** Allow at least three days in the city centre.
- **Especially for Kids:** Museum of Transport. The Mini Museum (for under 5's), at Kelvingrove Art Gallery & Museum. Glasgow Science Centre.
- **See Also**: THE TROSSACHS.

A Bit of History

"Dear green place" – Although not the capital, Glasgow was part of the British Kingdom of Strathclyde which was bordered to the north by the Picts, to the northwest by the Scots and south by the Angles of Northumbria. St Mungo came to this embattled kingdom in the mid 6C. Proclaimed bishop, he set up a wooden church and the fish and ring in the Glasgow coat of arms refer to a St Mungo legend when he saved an unfaithful wife from the wrath of her royal husband.

The 12C saw the consecration of the see and the new cathedral of Glasgow. Medieval Glasgow developed around its cathedral and its importance increased with the foundation in 1451 of Scotland's second university and the elevation to archbishopric in 1492.

In the religious troubles of the 17C, Glasgow was the scene of the General Assembly responsible for abolishing Episcopacy (see Introduction: History) in Scotland. The town remained a strong supporter of the Covenanting cause, but the restoration of Episcopacy brought renewed repression for the Covenanters.

By the 17C trade with the American colonies via Port Glasgow was a feature of Glasgow's commerce and early fortunes were made in sugar and rum.

Sugar, tobacco and textiles – Glasgow's growing prosperity in the early 18C depended largely on the tobacco trade. The outward cargoes of locally manufactured goods were paid for by the return loads of tobacco, which was then re-exported to the continent. The merchants, known as **Tobacco Lords**, played an important role in Glasgow's economic and social life. With their traditional outfits of scarlet cloaks and black suits they provided a colourful scene on the plainstones, their exclusive trading patch in front of the Tontine Hotel at Glasgow Cross.

Today's street names, Jamaica, Virginia, Glassford, Dunlop, Miller and Buchan are reminders of this flourishing activity and its merchant families. The American War

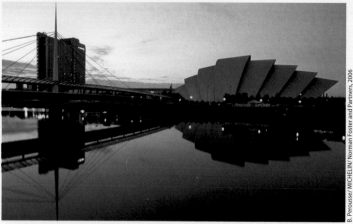

B. Perousse/ MICHELIN/ Norman Foster and Partners, 2006

River Clyde, Scottish Exhibition and Conference Centre

of Independence caused the eventual decline in the tobacco trade but by then many of the merchants had invested their accumulated wealth in other emergent industries (banking, textiles, coal mining and iron manufacturing).

Second City – Cotton manufacturing in particular was responsible for a large increase in the city's population. This trend continued with the impetus of the Industrial Revolution which brought in its wake the centralisation of heavy industries (coal, iron, and steel) in the Glasgow area. Improved communications – building of the Forth-Clyde and Monkland Canals, arrival of the railways and deepening of the Clyde which was made navigable up to Broomielaw – also played an important role in expansion. Once Glasgow had become established as an area of heavy industry, the emphasis moved to shipbuilding with the development of iron ships and screw propulsion. Some of the world's greatest liners were Clyde-built. The prosperity engendered by the Industrial Revolution gave the city its solidly prosperous Victorian face, when it was the workshop of the Empire and came second only to London.

The Glasgow School – Commercial prosperity begat a new generation of business-men interested in art, some making bequests (Mitchell) and others (McLellan, Burrell, Sir William Maxwell

Stirling) collecting. Out of this cultural activity a movement, known as **The Glasgow Boys**, emerged in the last quarter of the 19C partly as a protest against the traditions embodied by the Academicians of Edinburgh and the Victorian artistic conventions.

The leading members were **W Y MacGregor** father of the group, **James Guthrie**, **George Henry**, **E A Hornel** and **John Lavery.** The artists sought to achieve realism as an alternative to the prevalent romanticism, sentimentality and staidness. Masterpieces include *Galloway Landscape* (Henry – Kelvingrove), *Carse of Lecropt* (MacGregor – Hunterian), *The Tennis Party* (Lavery – Aberdeen). This ferment of artistic activity nurtured the development of an Art Nouveau movement in the 1890s. The most brillant exponent was the architect and decorator **Charles Rennie Mackintosh** who, along with H McNair and the Macdonald sisters, was responsible for a rebirth in fine and applied arts.

Cultural centre – Glasgow is home to the **Scottish Opera** , the **Scottish Ballet** and is a rehearsal and recording base for the **Scottish National Orchestra** The city hosts a busy calendar of international class festivals of classical and contemporary music, arts and dance and other kinds of events throughout the year (&*see Calendar of Events*).

The striking new Clyde Auditorium, nick-named the Armadilo, after its exterior

Address Book

For coin ranges, see the Legend on the cover flap.

VISITOR INFORMATION

Tourist Information Centre – The Glasgow City Marketing Bureau (*11 George Square*. ☎*0141 204 4400*. *www. seeglasgow.com*) offers an accommodation and theatre booking service. There is also a bureau de change, a tourist information service, a bookshop and a souvenir shop. There is another office at Glasgow Airport ☎*0141 848 4440*.

GETTING AROUND

The Travel Centre (*St Enoch's Square* ☎*0141 332 7133*) gives information on travel passes for the metro, bus and trains. The SPT **Discovery** ticket valid for one day allows visitors to discover the varied aspects of Glasgow starting from different metro stations.

WHERE TO STAY

The Brunswick – *106 –108 Brunswick Street* ☎*0141 552 0001*. *www. brunswickhotel.co.uk*. In the heart of the Merchant City this fashionable contemporary minimalist hotel with good bar and **restaurant** (pizza, pasta, tapas,) offers excellent value; its smallest double rooms are in the price category.

The Town House – *4 Hughenden Terrace*. ☎*0141 357 086*. *www.thetownhouseglasgow.com*. Elegant, personally run townhouse with nice Victorian touches, spacious rooms and an inviting lounge with a real fire.

Malmaison – *278 West George Street*. ☎*0141 572 1000*. *www. malmaison-glasgow.com*. Visually striking former Masonic chapel with ultra-stylish rooms in bold patterns and colours. The French themed **Brasserie** is recommended.

City Inn – *Finniestone Quay*. ☎*0141 240 1002*, *www.cityinn.com*. This minimalist hotel is part of a stylish chain and enjoys a quayside location with views of the Clyde. Rooms feature CD players, there is a trendy lounge bar and an award-winning **restaurant** .

Sherbrooke Castle – *11 Sherbrooke Avenue, Pollokshields*. ☎*0141 427 4227*. *www.sherbrooke.co.uk*. A celebration of late-19C Baronialist style with rich imposing furnishings, country house refinement and a panelled dining room .

Park Inn– *2 Port Dundas Place*. ☎*0141 333 150*. *www.rezidorparkinn. com*. Super stylish with Japanese or Californian themed loft suites with CD players, computer game systems and a luxurious spa. Oshi **restaurant** (Fusion) is recommended.

Abode – *129 Bath Street*. ☎*0141 221 6789*. *www.abodehotels.co.uk/ glasgow*. Near Mackintosh's School of Art, this early-20C building is decorated with a daring modern palette, making it one of the most distinctive hotels in the city. Michael Caines **Restaurant** is recommended.

Millennium Glasgow – *40 George Square*. ☎*0141 332 6711*, *www. mil-cop.com*. In a very central location and aimed at business travellers, this hotel offers a contemporary interior in a Victorian building. Try its **Brasserie** on George Square .

Carlton George – *44 West George Street*. ☎*0141 353 6373*. *www. carltonhotels.co.uk*. Glasgow's premier boutique hotel affords a quiet oasis from city bustle with attractive tartan bedrooms and a traditional ambience. The recommended Windows **restaurant** offers excellent views.

The Willow Tea Rooms

G. Gonon/ MICHELIN

WHERE TO EAT

Babbity Bowster – *16–18 Blackfriars Street*. ☎*0141 552 5055*. The name comes from an old Scottish courting dance and this fine townhouse pub is attributed to Robert Adam. It serves hearty Scottish dishes and snacks, with daily blackboard specials.

Cafe Gandolfi – *64 Albion Street*. ☎*0141 552 6813. www.cafegandolfi.com*. Established in 1979 and famed for its interior Glasgow School of Art furnishings this relaxed cafe's easy-going professionalism attracts locals and visitors who keep coming back to good honest Scottish cuisine at affordable prices.

Amber Regent – *50 West Regent Street*. ☎*0141 331 1655. www. amberregent.com*. This comfy personally managed restaurant specialises in Cantonese and Szechuan cuisine, combining fresh Scottish produce with traditional Chinese ingredients. Terrific value lunch.

Bouzy Rouge – *111 West Regent Street*. ☎*0141 221 8804, www.bouzy-rouge.co.uk*. A vibrant city centre restaurant with furnishings hand-crafted from Scottish elm and intricate iron work. The menu is eclectic with Modern Scottish and Mediterranean-influenced "casual gourmet" dishes.

Cafe Ostra – *The Italian Centre, 15 John Street*. ☎*0141 552 4433*. Attractive city centre restaurant on two levels with a snappy art deco interior, serving dishes with a seafood emphasis.

The Dhabba – *44 Candleriggs*. ☎*0141 553 1249. www.thedhabba.com*. Large modern North Indian restaurant in the Merchant City with bold colours and huge wall photos, serving authentic and accomplished dishes.

Mao – *84 Brunswick Street*. ☎*0141 564 5161. www.cafemao.com*. This bright buzzy establishment on two floors serves authentic and tasty South East Asian food.

Shish Mahal – *60–68 Park Road*. ☎*0141 339 8256. www.shishmahal.co.uk*. A pan-Indian menu featuring Tandoori specialities, attentive service and an atmospheric interior of etched glass, oak and Moorish tiles have won this long-established favourite many plaudits.

Stravaigin 2 – *8 Ruthven Lane*. ☎*0141 334 7165. www.stravaigin. com*. This lilac-painted cottage with a simple unfussy bistro interior offers a contemporary menu with a diverse range of often original dishes ranging from "the best burgers in Glasgow" to Hanoi Duck.

Two Fat Ladies at The Buttery – *652 Argyle Street*. ☎*0141 221 8188. www.twofatladiesrestaurant.com/ buttery*. This comfortable Glasgow institution, the oldest restaurant in town, has recently been given a new lease of (less formal) life, now specialising in fish and seafood.

Gamba – *225a West George Street*. ☎*0141 572 0899. www.gamba. co.uk*. A compact bright basement with a cosy bar is the place to enjoy an enterprising range of seafood specails with well-priced lunches.

The Ubiquitous Chip – *12 Ashton Lane, off Byres Road* ☎*0141 334 5007. www.ubiquitous chip.co.uk*. The long-established "Chip" mixes traditional Scottish and modern fusion styles and is famous for its glass-roofed courtyard with a more formal but equally lively warehouse dining room.

BARS

The lively atmosphere of Glasgow pubs is famous: **Rab Ha's** in Hutcheson Street, **Times Square** in St Enoch's Square, **Curlers** and **Bonhams** in Byres Road and **Dows** in Dundas Street among many other venues are well worth a visit.

The most famous tea room in town is the delightful **Willow Rooms**, 217 Sauchiehall Street, designed by Charles Rennie Mackintosh. Also serves light meals.

SIGHTSEEING

The **Mackintosh Trail Ticket** (*£12, valid one day*) admits entry to all paying Charles Rennie Mackintosh attractions in the city, the Hill House in Helensburgh, as well as unlimited travel on Subway and FirstBus services.

Boat trips "doon the watter" along the Firth of Clyde past the quays, boatyards and factories which gave Glasgow its industrial might and made it the second city of the British Empire, are also very

popular ☏08451 304 647,
www.waverleyexcursions.co.uk.
Clyde Helicopters, (*City Heliport,
SECC, Glasgow* ☏*0141 226 4261*) offer
spectacular views of the city and of
Loch Lomond.
Loch Lomond Seaplanes (☏*0870 242
1457. www.lochlomondseaplanes.com.
Feb–Nov, weather permitting*) operate
a seaplane service from the Glasgow
Science Centre to Oban Bay (approx 24
mins, flying over areas of outstanding
natural beauty.

SHOPPING

Sauchiehall, Buchanan and Argyle
Streets are pedestrian shopping
precincts. The glass-roofed **Princes
Street** and **Buchanan** shopping
centres in Buchanan Street display the
latest fashions and Scottish items. **The
Italian Centre** on the corner of John
and Ingram Streets has on sale the finest Italian fashion and also offers bars,
brasseries, restaurants and cafés in a
beautiful decor.
The Scottish Craft Centre in Princes
Square displays fine items by Scottish
craftsmen.
The Barras, a large indoor and outdoor
market, is the place to visit not only for
a bargain but also for the spectacle.

ENTERTAINMENT

Glasgow has a dynamic cultural scene
with avant-garde theatre staged by the
Citizens Theatre, the Centre for Contemporary Arts, the Tramway Theatre and
the Tron Theatre. Other venues include
The Mitchell Theatre, the King's Theatre
and the Theatre Royal. Exhibitions are
held at the McLellan Galleries, The Third
Eye Centre, The Lighthouse and the Gait
– recently converted at great expense
from The Old Fruitmarket and City Hall.
The List magazine (published fortnightly; weekly Jul–Aug), is the best guide to
what's on in the Greater Glasgow area.
Tickets for most events are on sale at
the Ticket Centre, City Hall, Candleriggs.

"FITBA CRAZY AND FITBA MAD"

Glasgow offers a choice of first ("premier") and second division matches
by four local football teams: Celtic,
Rangers Partick Thistle, and Queen's
Park. **Celtic** and **Rangers** have long
dominated Scottish football and it is
essential to book in advance for the
"Old Firm" matches between them.
Beware however that strong sectarian
feelings and tempers often run high on
these occasions.

of armour-like plating, is not only the
UK's largest integrated exhibition and
conference centre

The Burrell Collection★★★

*3mi/5km southwest by the M 77. Grounds
of Pollok House.* ♿◷*Open year-round
daily 10am–5pm, Thu and Sun 11am–
5pm.* ◷*Closed 25–26 Dec and 1–2 Jan.*
☕.🅿.☏*0141 287 2550. www.glasgow
museums.com.*

The Collection

The Collection was amassed by one
man, **Sir William Burrell** (1861–1958)
essentially for his own pleasure. Burrell
continued buying for the collection even
after he had handed it over to public
ownership. In about 80 years of collecting, with resources far below those
of the millionaire class such as Frick,
Hearst and Mellon, Burrell showed taste,
insight, discernment and determination
in his pursuit and acquisition of the
more than 8,000 items. He had strong
personal preferences for the medieval
glass and tapestries, Chinese ceramics
and 19C French paintings. In his latter
years he increased the comprehensive-
ness of the collection with a view to its
becoming public.

The Building

In 1983 the Collection found a permanent home and was finally on display to
the public. The elegant modern custom-
built building of warm red sandstone,
light wood and walls of glass in its parkland setting with a woodland backdrop,
successfully enhances the varied items
of the collection.

Visit *1hr 30min*

If you are in a hurry, the major works are located on the plan below; try not to get side-tracked! As only parts of the collection can be shown at any one time, certain sections may change periodically. If you have more time to spare take one of the free guided tours.

Ancient Civilisations

The 2C AD **Warwick Vase (1)**, the centrepiece of the courtyard, is an 18C marble reconstruction incorporating some of the original fragments found at Hadrian's Villa, Tivoli.

The skill of the Greek vase painter is displayed in the 4C BC bell krater from Lucania and the lekythos attributed to the Gela Painter (c. 6C–5C BC).

The noble porphyry **Head of Zeus or Poseidon (2)**, a 4C AD Roman copy of a Greek bronze, shows as much realism as the mosaic cockerel, also Roman, of IC BC. The Mesopotamian terracotta lion head of the Isin-Larsa period (c. 2020–1600 BC) probably belonged to a protective figure in a temple.

Oriental Art – This wide-ranging section has items from the 3rd millennium BC to the 19C. The charming earthenware watchdog and the Boshanlu jar and cover are good examples of the earliest pieces from the Han Dynasty (3C BC–3C AD).

The camel, horse and attendant and tomb figures are 8C Tang Dynasty. These

Self Portrait (1632) by Rembrandt Harmenszoon van Rijn (1606–69), oil on oak panel

earthenware objects all display green, amber and cream lead glazes.

Set against the woodland backdrop is the serenely seated figure of a **lohan (3)** or disciple of Buddha. Almost life-size, this Ming Dynasty (1366–1644) figure dated 1484 is a masterpiece of enamel biscuit ware. The superbly decorated underglaze red-decoration **ewer (4)** is of the late-14C Ming period.

Medieval and Post-Medieval European Art – The tapestry and stained glass sections are the highlights of this department, in particular the 15C Tournai **Peasants Hunting Rabbits with**

The Burrell Collection

© Culture and Sport Glasgow (Museums)

Ferrets (5), alive with detail, and the 16C *Flight of the Heron*.

The stained glass bay rewards close inspection. The 12C fragment from the then Abbey Church of St Denis (near Paris) figures the **Prophet Jeremiah (6)**.

Stained glass is also daringly used in the glass wall south of the building.

The Romanesque bronze, the **Temple Pyx (7)**, shows three sleeping warriors. On the wall above is a delicate alabaster Virgin and Child and opposite stands the Bury Chest. Both are important 14C English works. A Pietà by the workshop of the Rimini Master, a Burgundian altarpiece (**8**) and an alabaster Virgin and Child are fine examples of 15C European sculpture.

Paintings, Drawings and Bronzes

Mezzanine. The early works include Giovanni Bellini's delightful *Virgin and Child* (**9**) with the child dangling a flower by a thread. **Cupid, the Honey Thief (10)** and **The Stag Hunt** are important works by Cranach.

Burrell gathered together a notable holding of 19C French paintings: Géricault's striking *Prancing Grey Horse* (**11**); *The Print Collector* by Daumier; seaside scenes (*The Jetty at Trouville*) by Boudin; Fantin-Latour's *Spring Flowers* and works by the Barbizon School including Corot, Millet and Daubigny. Degas is well represented by examples of his two favourite subjects, dancers and horses. The pastel *Jockeys in the Rain* (**12**) shows a strong

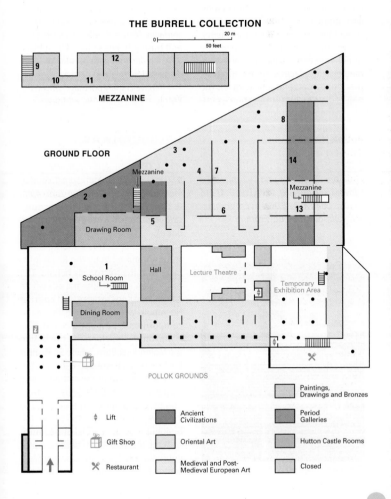

THE BURRELL COLLECTION

MEZZANINE

GROUND FLOOR

Mezzanine

Drawing Room

School Room

Hall

Dining Room

Lecture Theatre

Temporary Exhibition Area

POLLOK GROUNDS

Lift

Gift Shop

Restaurant

Ancient Civilizations

Oriental Art

Medieval and Post-Medieval European Art

Paintings, Drawings and Bronzes

Period Galleries

Hutton Castle Rooms

Closed

sense of movement. *Women Drinking Beer* and *Roses in a Champagne Glass* illustrate Manet's skillful brushwork.

Special displays from the museum's collection include works by the Hague School (the Maris brothers), Joseph Crawhall (Glasgow Boys school), Dürer, Le Nain and Whistler among others.

The 17C–18C period room presents a selection of portraits : **Portrait of a Gentleman** (Frans Hals, **13**) at £14,500 the most expensive item in the original collection; Rembrandt's youthful **Self-Portrait (14),** and Hogarth's *Mrs Ann Lloyd.*

Bronzes (Rodin, Epstein) are displayed in the courtyard and in the southeast gallery on the ground floor.

Hutton Castle Rooms

Burrell stipulated that the Hall, Drawing and Dining rooms from Hutton Castle should be incorporated in the gallery. Arranged around the courtyard they are furnished with fine panelling, tapestries, medieval fireplaces, antique furniture, precious carpets and stained glass. The objets d'art include interesting examples of medieval sculpture.

Pollok House★

3mi/5km southwest by the M 77. NTS. ♿🕐*Open year-round daily 10am–5pm.* 🕐*Closed 25–26 Dec and 1–2 Jan.* 🚫£8 *(Nov–March free).* ✗. 🛍. 🅿. ☎*0141 616 6410 or 0844 4932202. www.nts.org.uk. www.glasgowmuseums.com.*

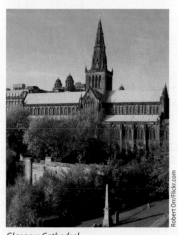

Glasgow Cathedral

The highlight of this 18C mansion, set in spacious parkland a short walk from the Burrell Collection, is a superb collection of paintings acquired by the connoisseur and collector **Sir William Stirling Maxwell** (1818–78, was an authority on the Spanish School of painting.

Paintings★★

The most memorable pictures in the collection are two superb portraits by El Greco (Library). Other important pictures include Tristan's *Adoration of the Kings* and Alonso Cano's *Adam and Eve* in the Drawing Room; the series of etchings *Los Disparates* by Goya in the Dining Room Corridor; Murillo's *Madonna and Child with St John* in the Billiard Room Corridor.

In addition there are canvases by Sanchez Coello, Spanish Court Painter (Billiard Room), Morales, S del Piombo, Jordaens, Mengs, Kneller, Hogarth, Knox and Nasmyth. Works by William Blake (*Chaucer and the Canterbury Pilgrims*) are displayed in the main corridor.

The Maxwell family portraits hang in the Entrance Hall, a late-19C addition.

Cathedral★★★

HS. ♿🕐 *Open Apr–Sept, Mon–Sat 9.30am–6pm, Sun 2pm–5pm. Oct–Mar, Mon–Sat 9.30am–4pm, Sun 2pm–4pm.* ☎ *0141 552 6891. www.glasgow-cathedral.com. www.historic-scotland.gov.uk.*

This imposing Gothic building today stands hemmed in by the Royal Infirmary with the Necropolis behind. The best **view**★ of the cathedral as a whole is from John Knox's stance high up in the Necropolis where the verticality of the composition is best appreciated. This is the fourth church on the site beside the Molendinar Burn, where **St Mungo** built his original wooden church in the 7C. The main part of the cathedral was built in the 13C and 14C with construction progressing from the east end to the nave, and it was the 15C before the building took on its final appearance with the reconstruction of the chapter house and addition of the Blacader Aisle, central tower and stone spire, and the now demolished west front towers. Unusual features of the plan are the non-projecting transepts and two-storeyed east end.

Nave

Stylistically this is later than the choir and the elevation with its richly moulded and pointed arches, ever more numerous at each level, rises to the timber roof. The 15C stone screen or pulpitum, unique in Scotland, marks the change in level from nave to choir. The figures at the top of the screen depict the seven deadly sins; the human figures on the front of the altar platforms may represent 11 disciples.

Choir

The choir and the lower church, both dating from the mid 13C, are of the finest First Pointed style. The triple lancets of the clerestory are echoed in the design of the east window which depicts the Four Evangelists. Four chapels open out of the ambulatory beyond. From the northernmost chapel a door leads through to the upper chapter room, reconstructed in the 15C. It was there that the medieval university held its classes.

Lower Church

Access via stairs to north of the pulpitum.

Here is another Gothic glory where light and shade play effectively amidst a multitude of piers and pointed arches. This lower area was conceived to enshrine the **tomb of St Mungo**, Glasgow's patron saint. A cordoned-off area marks the site. The central panel of the St Kentigern Tapestry (1979) represents the Church and combines the symbols of St Mungo. On the south panel are the ring and salmon of the St Mungo legend. The Chapel of the Blessed Virgin is the area immediately to the east, distinguished by its elaborate net vaulting with intricately carved bosses.

The mid-13C lower chapter room was remodelled at the time of Bishop William Lauder (1408–25). The bishop's arms figure on the canopy. The 15C ribbed vaulting sports heraldic roof bosses including the arms of James I.

Blacader Aisle

Projecting from the south transept, this last addition to the church was designed as a two-storey extension by Glasgow's first Archbishop, Robert Blacader. Only the existing or lower part was finished. The Late Gothic style with its fully developed ribbed vaulting gives an effect of richness. Look for the carved boss (facing the entrance) recalling the legend of the hermit Fergus, who was found near to death by St Mungo. The next day the body was placed on a cart yoked to two bulls with the intention of burying the hermit where they stopped. Some say this chapel marks the site.

Medieval Glasgow

Cathedral Square to Glasgow Green
(see plan)

St Mungo Museum of Religious Life and Art

2 Castle Street. ⏱Open year-round Mon–Thu and Sat 10am–5pm, Fri and Sun 11am–5pm. ⏱Closed 25–26 Dec and 1–2 Jan. ☎0141 553 2557. www.glasgowmuseums.com.

Since its opening in 1993 this museum has sparked controversy with its collections of religious artefacts. They are grouped in three galleries: Religious Art, Religious Life and the Scottish Gallery (its best-known exhibit, Dali's *St John of the Cross*, moved to the Kelvingrove Gallery in 2006). A fourth gallery houses temporary exhibitions and there is an authentic Japanese Zen garden.

Cathedral Square

Prior to the Reformation this was the very heart of the ecclesiastical city. Cathedral, Bishop's Castle and canons' manses overlooked this focal point. The Bishop's Castle (a stone in the Royal Infirmary forecourt marks the site) was destroyed to make way for the Adam brothers' 1792 Royal Infirmary building. The present **Royal Infirmary** is a 20C replacement. It was in a ward of the original that **Sir Joseph Lister** (1827–1912) pioneered the use of carbolic acid as an antiseptic in the treatment of wounds.

The statues in the square include one of the missionary explorer David Livingstone and an equestrian statue of King William of Orange.

Necropolis

Behind the cathedral on the far bank of the Molendinar Burn is the formal burial garden dating from 1833. Pathways bordered by elaborate tombs lead up to the highest point commanded by John Knox atop his column. There is a good **view**★ of the cathedral and Glasgow away to the southwest.

Provand's Lordship

&. ⏲ *Open year-round Mon–Thu and Sat 10am–5pm, Fri and Sun 11am–5pm.* ⏲ *Closed 25–26 Dec and 1–2 Jan.* ☕. ☎ *0141 552 8819, www.glasgow museums.com.*

Provand's Lordship, a former prebendal manse dating from 1471, and the cathedral are the only survivors of the medieval town. The two lower floors are furnished with 16C–20C pieces.

High Street

A plaque on the disused goods yard opposite College Street marks the site of Old College from 1632 to 1870 and the original Hunterian Museum prior to their transfer to Gilmorehill. At 215 High Street, the former British Linen Bank building is still crowned by the figure of Pallas, goddess of wisdom and weaving. The stained glass above the door portrays a flax boat.

Glasgow Cross

Until Victorian times the Cross at the junction of High Street, Saltmarket, Gallowgate and Trongate was the heart of Glasgow. Defoe much admired the Cross set as it was at the centre of a prosperous commercial area known as the "Golden Acre". The **Tolbooth Steeple**★, in the middle of the street, is a striking reminder of this former elegance. The seven-storey tower was originally adjoined by the elegant tolbooth and then the Tontine Hotel. The **mercat cross** nearby is a 1929 replica.

Bridgegate

This now rather dismal street was once a fashionable main thoroughfare to the city's first stone bridge built in 1345. The **steeple**, rising out of derelict warehouses is all that remains of the 1659 Merchants Hall (demolished 1818), the business and social meeting place for Glasgow's merchants. The steeple rising in tiers to a height of 164ft/50m served as a lookout for cargoes coming up the Clyde. The Ship of Trade in full sail symbolises the origins of Glasgow's trade. A new Merchants' House was built in 1877 in George Square.

The Saltmarket took over as the main thoroughfare in the 19C.

Glasgow Green

On the north bank of the Clyde this park is one of Glasgow's most historic sites. Successively or simultaneously it was a place of common grazing, bleaching, public hangings, military reviews and parades, merry-making at Glasgow Fair and above all of public meetings and free speech. Alternating between fashionable and disreputable, it has always been most fiercely defended against encroachment and today lies within the GEAR (Glasgow Eastern Area Renewal Scheme) revitalisation programme. Monuments on the Green include the now sadly abandoned Doulton Fountain – a remarkable piece of pottery figuring Queen Victoria – one to Nelson and the nearby stone commemorating the spot where James Watt, while out on a Sunday walk, worked out his improvement to the steam engine.

People's Palace and Winter Gardens

Enter by Morris Place. &. ⏲ *Open year-round Mon–Thu and Sat 10am–5pm, Fri and Sun 11am–5pm.* ⏲ *Closed 25–26 Dec and 1–2 Jan.* ☕. ☎ *0141 271 2962. www.glasgowmuseums.com.*

The People's Palace museum and Winter Gardens were opened in 1898 as a cultural centre for the east end. It is now a local and social history museum, and the exhibits recount the story of Glasgow from earliest times to the present. There is an exotic plant display in the Winter Gardens.

Templeton Business Centre

This highly unusual, colourful and richly decorated building dating from 1889 was modelled on the Doge's Palace. It originally housed a carpet factory.

The Barras

An assortment of goods at bargain prices, colourful characters and lively street entertainment are the principal ingredients of this famous old weekend market (⊙open Sat–Sun 10am–5pm).

Glasgow University

(ℓ see plan next page)

Bishop William Turnbull founded the university in 1451 and the first classes were held in the cathedral. The early university was greatly dependent on the church and the bishops and archbishops of Glasgow held the office of Chancellor until 1642. The university then acquired properties in the High Street which were used until 1632 when the **Old College**, a handsome building arranged around a double quadrangle, was built. The High Street premises were abandoned and destroyed in 1870 when the university moved to the present site on the estate of Gilmorehill in the west end of the city.

The consequent imposing edifice remains the focal point of a complex of new (Adam Smith, Boyd Orr and Hetherington Buildings, Hunterian Art Gallery and Library) and refurbished buildings throughout the local streets. Today eight faculties (Arts, Divinity, Engineering, Law, Medicine, Science, Social and Veterinary Medicine) welcome over 13,000 students.

Gilmorehill Building

This massive Gothic Revival building, the oldest of the university's present buildings, was designed by George Gilbert Scott. The project was not completed owing to a lack of funds, and it was Scott's son, John Oldrid, who completed the design with Bute Hall (1882) and the tower (1887). The main façade overlooks Kelvingrove Park. In Professors' Square at the west end of the main building is the **Lion and Unicorn**

Staircase from the Old College, as are the staircase and Pearce Lodge facing University Avenue.

The **Visitor Centre** (⊙open Mon–Sat, 9.30am–5pm; ▭; ☎0141 330 5511, www.gla.ac.uk/visitors), has informative displays, interactive computers and a camera obscura showing the panorama from the building's tall tower.

Hunterian Museum

Main building, East Quadrangle, First Floor; enter from University Avenue side. ♿⊙Open Mon–Sat 9.30am–5pm. ⊙Closed public holidays. ☎0141 330 4221. www.hunterian.gla.ac.uk.

William Hunter (1718–83) medical practitioner, anatomist and pioneer obstetrician, was also a great collector, investing in coins, manuscripts, paintings, minerals, and ethnographical, anatomical and zoological specimens. Hunter bequeathed all to the university and in 1807 the Hunterian Museum was opened. His brother John's collection formed the nucleus of a second Hunterian Museum, now in the Royal College of Surgeons, London. Today William's treasured items are divided between the museum and the art gallery.

Museum

The first gallery presents a historical introduction to the university and its many famous sons. The Hunter **coin and medal collection★**, said to be second only to the French Royal Collection is exhibited in a purpose-built gallery. A chronological presentation from a collection of over 30,000 items traces the development of coinage from ancient times to the present. The earliest Scottish coinage appeared in 1136 and by the late 12C–early 13C there were no fewer than 16 mints, the greatest number ever. No coins have been minted in Scotland since the closure of the Edinburgh Mint in the 18C following the Treaty of Union. Note the rare example of Scotland's first gold coin issued c 1357 by David II and one of James V's bonnet pieces using Scottish gold. Exhibits in the main hall, beyond, cover material from Captain Cook's voyages, a pleasant display on the Romans in Scotland, early civilisations and British prehistory. The upper

GLASGOW

Albert Bridge	CZ 2	Great Western Rd	BY
Anderson Quay	BZ	Greendyke St	CZ
Arcadia St	CZ 3	High St	CZ
Argyle St	BCZ	Hillhead St	V
Bain St	CZ 4	Hope St	BY
Baird St	CY	Hospital St	CZ
Ballater St	CZ	Ingram St	CZ
Bath St	BY	Jamaica St	BCZ 28
Bells Bridge	AZ	John Knox St	CZ 29
Berkeley St	BY	Kelvin Way	V
Binnie Pl.	CZ 6	Kilbirnie St	BZ 31
Bridge St	BZ 7	Killermont St	CY 32
Bridgegate	CZ 9	King's Drive	CZ
Broomielaw	BZ	Kingston St	BZ 33
Buccleuch St	BY 10	Kyle St	CY
Buchanan Galleries	CY	Lancefield Quay	BZ
Buchanan St.	CYZ 12	Laurieston Rd	CZ 35
Bunhouse Rd	V	London Rd	CZ
Byres Rd	V	Maryhill Rd	BY
Caledonia Rd	AV 14	Morris Pl.	CZ 36
Cambridge St	BY 15	Morrison St	BZ 38
Castle St	CY 17	Nelson St	BZ
Cathedral Square	CY	Norfolk St	BCZ
Cathedral St	CY	North Canalbank St	CY
Church St	V	North Hanover St	CY
Clyde St	CZ	Old Dumbarton Rd	V
Clydeside Expressway	BY	Oswald St	BZ 39
Commerce St	BZ 18	Oxford St	BCZ 40
Cook St	BZ	Pinkston Rd	CY
Cowcaddens Rd	CY	Pitt St	BY 42
Craighall Rd	CY	Port Dundas St	CY 43
Dobbie's Loan	CY	Queen St	CZ 45
Duke St	CZ	Renfield St	CY 46
Dumbarton Rd	V	Renfrew St	BCY
Eglinton St	BZ	Saltmarket	CZ
Eldon St	BY	Sauchiehall St	BY
Finnieston St	BYZ 21	Scotland St	BZ
Gallowgate	CZ	Scott St	BY 48
Garscube Rd	BY	Seaward St	BZ
George Square	CY	South Portland St	CZ 49
George V Bridge	BZ 22	Springburn	CY
Gibson St	V	St George's Rd	BY
Glasgow Bridge	BZ 25	St. Enoch Shopping Centre	CZ 47
Glassford St.	CZ 26	St. Vincent St.	BCY
Gorbals St	CZ	Stirling Rd	CY 50
Gordon St	BY 27	Stockwell St	CZ 52
Govan Rd	ABZ	Trongate	CZ
Gray St	V	Union St	CYZ
		University Ave	V
		Victoria Bridge	CZ 54

Waterloo St	BYZ
West George St	CYZ
West Graham St	BY 55
West Nile St	CY 56
West Paisley Rd	ABZ
West St	BZ
Woodlands Rd	BY

gallery is devoted to geology and archeology. Don't miss recent finds – the Bearsden Shark and the only evidence of a Scottish dinosaur.

Hunterian Art Gallery★★ (M2)
Hillhead Street. ♿🕐*Open Mon–Sat, 9.30am–5pm.* 🕐*Closed public holidays.* 📷*Art Gallery free; Mackintosh House £3 (free Wed after 2pm).* ☎*0141 330 5431. www.hunterian.gla.ac.uk.*
The 1980 building provides a permanent home for the university's art collection which is particularly noted for the Whistler works, 19C and 20C Scottish art and the Mackintosh wing. Outstanding

among the Old Masters are Rembrandt's *The Entombment* and Rubens' *Head of an Old Man.* Alongside canvases by Raeburn (*Mrs Hay of Spot*), Ramsay (the founder *William Hunter*) Romney and Reynolds, are several by Stubbs and Chardin. The **Whistler Collection**★★★ is an important holding covering most periods of the career of **James McNeill Whistler** (1834–1903). Examples of portraiture include the striking group of full-lengths (*Pink and Silver – The Pretty Scamp; Red and Black – The Fan* and *Pink and Gold – The Tulip*). A master in the art of etching, the French, Thames and Venetian sets demonstrate his stylistic development.

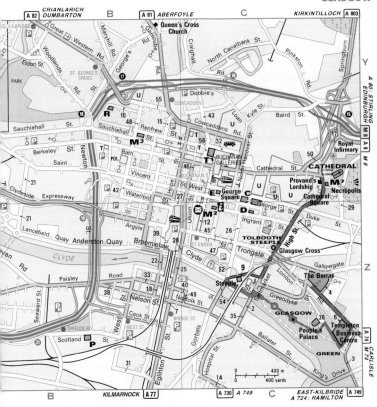

Art Gallery and Museum			Hutchesons' Hall	CZ	D	Scotland Street School	BZ	P
Kelvingrove	V	M¹	Kelvingrove Park	V		St Mungo Museum		
Cathedral	CY		Merchant House	CY	E	of Religious Life and Art	CY	M⁷
City Chambers	CY	C	Museum of Transport	V	M⁶	Steeple	CZ	
Gallery of Modern Art	CZ	M²	Necropolis	CY		Templeton Business		
Glasgow Cross	CZ		People's Palace	CZ		Centre	CZ	
Glasgow Green	CZ		Provand's Lordship	CY		Tenement House	BY	R
Glasgow School of Art	BY	M³	Queen's Cross Church	BY		The Barras	CZ	
Hunterian Art Gallery	V	M⁴	Royal Concert Hall	CY	T¹	The Burrell Collection	AZ	
Hunterian Museum	V	M⁵	Royal Infirmary	CY		Tolbooth Steeple	CZ	

The remaining galleries present 19C and 20C Scottish art together with some French Impressionists. Breaking away from the conventions of Victorian art, William **McTaggart** (1835–1910) developed his own bold style with vigorous brushwork and a sensitive approach to light (*The Sound of Jura, The Fishers' Landing*). He was a precursor of the late-19C group, the **Glasgow Boys**, which originated as a response to the staidness of the Edinburgh art establishment and whose common denominator was realism. Acknowledged father of the group was W McGregor (*Carse of Lecropt*); other members included Hornel (*Gathering*

UNIVERSITY

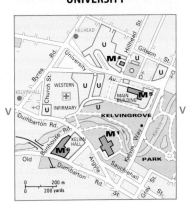

219

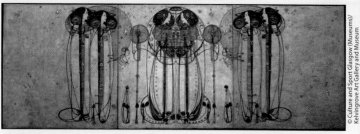

© Culture and Sport Glasgow (Museums)/
Kelvingrove Art Gallery and Museum

The Wassail (1900), one of three gesso panels by Charles Rennie Mackintosh for the Ingram Street Tearooms in Glasgow, Kelvingrove Art Gallery and Museum

Primroses, Japanese figures), Guthrie (*The Gypsy Fires*), Henry, Walton and Lavery. Pringle's townscapes (*Tollcross* 10) in delicate pastel tones herald the **Scottish Colourists**: *Les Eus, Le Voile Persan* by Fergusson, *Iona, Tulips and Cup* by Peploe, *The Red Chair* by Caddell and works by Hunter. The modern section includes an atmospheric canvas by Joan Eardley (*Salmon Nets and the Sea* 1960), Philipson's *Never Mind* (1965) and Davie's *Sea Devil's Watch Tower* (1960).

The gallery also houses the university's print collection and there is a sculpture courtyard.

Mackintosh House★★★

This wing is a reconstruction of the architect designer **Charles Rennie Mackintosh's** (1868–1928) Glasgow home. The domestic interiors with highly distinctive decorative schemes are good examples of Mackintosh's pioneering work in modern architecture and design. Functional, with a restraint and purity of line, painted white woodwork is relieved by decorative motifs. The top floor exhibition gallery displays selections from the many drawings, watercolours and sketches in the Mackintosh collection.

Kelvingrove Art Gallery and Museum ★★

& ♿Open year-round Mon–Thu and Sat 10am–5pm, Fri and Sun 11am–5pm. ♿Closed 25–26 Dec and 1–2 Jan. ✗. ☎ 0141 276 9599. www.glasgow museums.com.

Officially opened in 1902, this imposing red-sandstone building in Kelvingrove Park was partly financed from the profits of the 1888 International Exhibition

on the same site. The nucleus of the permanent collection was formed by the McLellan Bequest (1854) and ever since, prominent citizens and captains of industry such as Graham-Gilbert, James Donald and William McInnes have generously continued to bequeath their art treasures, making this one of the outstanding civic collections.

Ground floor

The centre hall on the ground floor features the Mini Museum for under 5's Kids. Leading from this, the two side courts are the focus for the two wings of the museum, and introduce the themes of Life and Expression. The Art Discovery Centre and the Environment Discovery Centre feature hands-on displays. Galleries on the ground floor include Scottish Art. Featured here is the work of the Glasgow Boys (♿see Introduction: Arts, Painting). The Mackintosh and the Glasgow Style exhibition displays the work of Charles Rennie Mackintosh and his Glasgow contemporaries. Suspended from the roof of the West Court is a World War II Spitfire fighter aircraft.

First floor

The upper galleries are devoted to fine and decorative arts, particularly glass, silver, ceramics and jewellery, and British and European paintings; from Italy, the Netherlands and France (the latter has a strong emphasis on 19C and early 20C works). The highlight is Dalí's stunning *Christ of St John of the Cross*.

Museum of Transport★★   Kids

1 Bunhouse Road. & ♿Open year-round Mon–Thu and Sat 10am–5pm, Fri and Sun

11am–5pm. ⏰ Closed 25–26 Dec and 1–2 Jan. 🍽. ☎0141 287 2720. www.glasgow museums.com.

Trams and trolley buses

A raised catwalk allows visitors to inspect the upper decks of the vintage tramcars which were so much part of Glasgow's street scene from 1872 to 1962.

These vehicles are arranged in chronological order and include: no 543, the horse-drawn one, no 1,089, the 1926 single-deck car and no 1,392 of the type nicknamed the Cunarder because of its comfort, the last tram ever built in the UK (1952). This extremely popular collection was the nucleus around which the museum was established. The trolley-bus is an example from the fleet which operated in Glasgow from 1949 to 1967.

Railway locomotives

Most of the seven items on display are from the former Scottish railway companies. There is also a fascinating model railway, a spell-binder for all ages.

Motor cars

Scottish-built cars★★★ are the thing here, with examples from manufacturers such as Argyll, Albion and Arrol-Johnston, who were all well to the fore in the car industry of the early 20C.

The great traditions of Scottish car manufacturing are represented here by the 1902 Argyll Light Car, the 1906 Arrol-Johnston TT Model 18, fast and powerful for its time and the Argyll Voiturette. The 1963 Hillman Imp, IMP 1 was the first Scottish-built car after a lapse of 30 years.

Horse-drawn vehicles

The varied examples of horse-drawn vehicles on display include the splendid Mail Coach (c 1840) and the two Romany caravans which are brightly painted with traditional decoration.

Kelvin Street

This shop-lined street evokes life as it was on 9 December 1938. The subway station is a cherished reminder of Glasgow's subway prior to modernisation in the 1970s.

Bicycles and motor cycles

Follow the development of the bicycle from the replica of MacMillan's 1839 bicycle (on the wall) through bone-shakers, sociables and tricycles to the gleaming lightweight road racers and fun cycles of today.

The motor cycle section has early examples of British-designed machines from the time when British makers dominated the industry (Zenith, BSA, Triumph, AJS, Beardmore-Precision, Norton, HRD/Vincent and Douglas).

The Clyde Room of Ship Models★★★

This beautifully presented collection displays the products of the Scottish shipyards through the ages and in particular those of the Clyde. Side by side are perfect models of sailing ships (the fully rigged *Cutty Sark*), Clyde River Steamers (*Comet, Columba* and other well-loved excursion steamers), cross-Channel steamers which were often Denny products, ocean-going passenger liners (*The Queens*), warships (HMS *Hood*) and yachts including the Czar Alexander II's circular and unsinkable model.

© Culture and Sport Glasgow (Museums)/Kelvingrove Art Gallery and Museum

Christ of St John of the Cross (1951) by Salvador Dalí

Botanic Gardens

730 Great Western Road &🕐 *Gardens open year-round 7am–sunset. Kibble Palace and Main Range open daily 10am–4.45pm (winter 4.15pm). Visitor Centre open daily 11am–4pm.* ☎0141 334 2422. *www.glasgow.gov.uk.*

The gardens are renowned for their collection of orchids, begonias and tree ferns. The spectacular recently refurbished Kibble Palace, which houses the tree ferns and plants from temperate areas, is a magnificent example of a Victorian iron conservatory. The Main Range contains the tropical and economic plants. A Scottish Garden planted with plants endemic to Scotland is being created.

Central Glasgow

(🕐 see plan)

George Square

The heart of modern Glasgow, this busy square is lined by imposing 19C buildings. Development of the square and adjoining streets began in 1782 and by the beginning of the 19C it had become the city's hotel centre. The initial steps towards a change in character came with the building of the Merchants' House closely followed by the General Post Office and City Chambers.

On the north side is the only hotel to remain (now the Copthorne). The **Merchants' House** (1869) on the west side, and today the home of the Glasgow Chamber of Commerce, is denoted by the Ship of Trade aloft, a replica of the one in Bridgegate. On the south are the post office buildings. Occupying the east side are the **City Chambers**★ (🕐 *visit by guided tour only (45 mins), Mon–Fri 10.30am, 2.30pm;* 🕐*closed public holidays;* ☎0141 287 4018, *www.glasgow.gov. uk*), another of Glasgow's magnificent Victorian buildings, a heritage from the time when Glasgow was the second city of the Empire. Inside, grandeur and opulence reign supreme, particularly in the loggia, council and banqueting halls.

Sir Walter Scott on the central column dominates a series of famous men:

(clockwise) Peel, Gladstone, Lord Clyde, John Moore, Watt...

Hutchesons' Hall

158 Ingram Street. (NTS). 🕐*Open Mon–Tue, Thu–Fri, 10am–5pm.* 🕐*Closed holidays and 2 weeks at the end of Dec.* ☎0844 4932199. *www.nts.org.uk.*

The "hospital" of the original endowment of 1639 for 11 old men and 12 orphan boys was demolished when Hutcheson Street was opened up. The replacement institutional headquarters (1802–05) were designed by David Hamilton to provide the focal point for one of the new thoroughfares of the Merchant City. Statues of the two founding Hutcheson brothers were removed from the original building to occupy niches on the main frontage. Two of Glasgow's best-known public schools originate from the early endowment. The refurbished Hutchesons' Hall is now the Glasgow offices and shop of the National Trust for Scotland.

Gallery of Modern Art★

Queen Street. &🕐*Open year-round Mon–Thu and Sat 10am–5pm, Fri and Sun 11am–5pm.* 🕐*Closed 25–26 Dec and 1–2 Jan.* ▱. ▯. ☎0141 229 1996. *www.glasgowmuseums.com*

Glasgow's collection of modern art (GoMA) is the second most visited contemporary art gallery outside London. It is housed in the city's most splendid late-18C mansion. Built for the tobacco lord William Cunninghame, this great neo-Classical structure boasts a massive Corinthian portico and a magnificent main hall with a barrel-vault ceiling. At the very heart of the commercial city, it served for more than a century as the Royal Exchange, the focal point of Glasgow's business life, then as a library. In the mid 1990s it underwent extensive conversion and now comprises four galleries: Earth (*main hall*), Fire (*basement*), Water (*first floor*) and Air (*roof space*), together with workshops and interactive computer stations.

The range of works selected (sculpture, graphic works, photographs, mobiles and installations as well as paintings) has caused controversy within the art world, not least because of the inclusion of pictures by "popular" painters like Beryl Cook (*Karaoke,* 1992). Contributions from abroad include works by: the Hungarian pioneer of Op Art, Victor Vasarely; Peter Angermann (*Baggersee* 1988); maker of mechanical marvels, Eduard Bersudsky (*The Great Idea, Karl Marx*); Niki de Saint-Phalle (*Autel du Chat Mort* 1962); Australian Aboriginal artist Robert Campbell Jr (*Who Said You Could Fish Here* 1988); Paddy Japaljarri Sims (*The Night Sky Dreaming* 1993).

The Lighthouse
56 Mitchell Lane. ○*Open year-round 10.30am–5pm (Tue 11am, Sun noon).* ⊚*£3.* ☎*0141 221 6362. www.thelighthouse.co.uk.*
The former offices of The Glasgow Herald, designed by C R Mackintosh, have been imaginatively converted into the National Centre for Architecture and Design including the award-winning Mackintosh Centre and Mackintosh Tower with stunning city views and a stylish rooftop café-bar.

Glasgow School of Art★
167 Renfrew Street ☞*Visit by guided tour only (1 hr); booking required. Apr–Oct daily, 9am–5pm each hour on the hour, except 1pm. Oct–March, Mon–Sat 11am, 2pm, 3pm.*○*Closed 21 Dec–2 Jan.* ⊚*£6.50.* ☎*0141 353 4526. www.gsa.ac.uk.*
Charles Rennie Mackintosh designed this major landmark in the history of European architecture when he was only 28. The building was completed in two stages, 1897–99 and 1907–09 and nearly 100 years later it remains highly functional while also housing one of the largest collections of Mackintosh furniture, designs and paintings. Of particular interest is the Library, an architectural *tour de force* with its three-storey high windows and suspended ceiling and Mackintosh's most original and celebrated interior. Visitors can also see his decorative stained glass, metalwork, light fittings etc in the Board Room, Director's Room and the Furniture Gallery, which contains furniture designed for the School, Miss Cranston's Tea Rooms and "Windyhill".

The Tenement House
145 Buccleuch Street. (NTS) ⚕○*Open daily Mar–Oct 1–5pm.* ⊚*£5.* ☎*0844 4932197. www.nts.org.uk.*
The housing demands of Glasgow's ever increasing 19C population were met by building tenements. This tenement flat consists of two rooms, kitchen and bathroom; original fittings include the box-beds, gas lamps and coal-fired ranges with coal bin. Community life centred on the close and back court.

Additional Sights

Queen's Cross Church
870 Garscube Rd. ⚕○*Open Mon–Fri 10am–5pm. Mar–Oct also Sun 2pm–5pm. Last admission 4.30pm.* ○*Closed Christmas through New Year amd various other dates, see website.* ⊚*£2.* 🅿 ☎*0141 946 6600. www.crmsociety.com.*
Mackintosh's innovative design for the galleried, single-aisled church (1898–99) was dictated by its corner site. The spacious interior is enhanced by the Art Nouveau furnishings. The church, which houses the headquarters of the Charles Rennie Mackintosh Society, is now a visitor centre.

Scotland Street School Museum (BZ K)
225 Scotland Street. ⚕○*Open daily, Apr–Sept 10am (Fri and Sun 11am)–5pm.* ○*Closed 25–26, 31 Dec, 1–2 Jan.* ☎*0141 287 0500. www.glasgowmuseums.com.*
This Mackintosh building (1906) features: twin glass stair-towers, fine stonework detailing (south façade), Drill Hall and classrooms. It houses the Museum of Education, with fascinating reconstructions of schoolrooms of various periods.

House for an Art Lover
10 Dumbeck Road, Bellahouston Park. ⚕○*Open Apr– Sept, Mon–Wed 10am–4pm, Thu–Sun 10am–1pm. Oct–Mar, Sat–Sun 10am–1pm. Mon–Fri call for opening times.* ⊚*£3.50.* ☏. ☎*0141 353 4770. www.houseforanartlover.co.uk.*
Completing Glasgow's portfolio of Charles Rennie Mackintosh buildings is this striking villa, based on the archi-

The Clyde Estuary by boat

In the 19C a succession of paddle steamers sailed the Clyde taking Glaswegians "doon the watter" for the day. *The Waverley*, the last of these famous Clyde paddle steamers, still plies her home waters in the high season (○*mid-Jun to Aug; ☎0845 1304 647. www.waverleyexcursions. co.uk*) with departures from Glasgow, Helensburgh, Dunoon, Rothesay, Largs, Millport and Ayr.

tect's entry in a 1901 German design competition. The city council's bold project of implementing the design was completed in 1996 and the building is used by the Glasgow School of Art's postgraduate study centre.

Excursions

The Trossachs★★★ –
⌕*See The TROSSACHS.*

Loch Lomond★★ –
⌕*See LOCH LOMOND.*

The Clyde Estuary ★★

The "Armadillo" , the Glasgow Science Centre and the Tall Ship at Glasgow Harbour are within walking distance of the city centre (around a mile). For other attractions you will need to take public transport.

Clyde Auditorium/Scottish Exhibtion and Conference Centre

Built in 1997 by Foster & Partners the Clyde Auditorium is the futuristic section of the rather more prosaic SECC, which in addition to trade fairs and conventions hosts blockbuster concerts, musicals and other events including the Magners Glasgow International Comedy Festival. Resembling the middle section of an armadillo (after which it is nicknamed) and also called The Poor Man's Sydney Opera House, the inspiration for the designer, was in fact the ship hulls with which the Clyde is historically inextricably linked.

Glasgow Science Centre (GSC) ★ Kids
50 Pacific Quay. ♿○*Open mid-Mar to late Oct daily 10am–5pm (rest of year closed Mon).* ☞*£7.95 Science Mall (£5.95 child). Additional charges: IMAX , Glasgow Tower £2 each.* ☎*0871 540 1000. www.glasgowsciencecentre.org.*

Directly across the water from the SECC (linked by athe Clyde Arc footbridge) and reflecting the same style of architecture (designed 2001 by BDP) this is another bold step in the renovation of Glasgow's docklands. The heart of GSC is the **Science Mall** housed in a gleaming titanium crescent. This is home to three floors with hundreds of interactive exhibits, the Climate Change Theatre and a **planetarium**. Two other important features are Scotland's only **IMAX cinema** and the 127m high **Glasgow Tower**, the tallest tower in the world capable of rotating 360 degrees from the ground up to the top.

The Tall Ship at Glasgow Harbour

Stobcross Road. ○*Open year-round daily 10am–5pm (Nov–Feb 4pm).* ○*Closed 25–26, 31 Dec, 1–2 Jan.*☞*£4.95.* ☎*0141 222 2513. www.thetallship.com.*

The Glenlee first took to the water as a bulk cargo carrier in 1896. She circumnavigated the globe four times and today, restored over a six year period by the Clyde Maritime Trust is one of only five Clydebuilt sailing ships that remain afloat in the world.

Titan Clydebank

6mi/10km north west Glasgow Harbour. Garth Drive, Queens Quays, Clydebank. ♿○*Open May to late Oct 10am–5pm (last admission 4pm). Tours begin at Titan Purser's Office.* ☞ *£4.50.*☎*0141 952 3771. www.titanclydebank.com.*

An "A" listed giant cantilever Titan Crane – the oldest of its kind in the world – has recently been refurbished with a new lift to take visitors up to the jib platform 150ft (46m) off the ground. Here you can see the workings of the Titan wheelhouse and from the jib platform take in the stunning views over the River Clyde and the surrounding countryside.

Hill House, Helensburgh★

Upper Colquhoun Street. (NTS). 🕐 *Open daily Good Fri–Oct 1.30–5.30pm.* 🎫*£8.* ☎. ☎*0844 4932208. www.nts.org.uk.*

On a hillside overlooking the Clyde stands what is considered to be the best example of Mackintosh's domestic architecture. The house was built in 1902–04 as a family home for the Glasgow publisher Walter W Blackie. It was designed as a whole by Mackintosh down to the tiniest detail. Every space corridor, hall, bed or seating alcove was proportioned in itself as well as being part of a harmonious whole. Predominantly white or dark surfaces were highlighted by inset coloured glass, gesso plaster panels, delicate light fittings or stencilled patterns.

Dumbarton Castle

(HS). 🕐*Open daily Apr–Sept 9.30am–6.30pm. Oct–Mar, Sat–Wed 9.30am–4.30pm. Last admission 30 mins before closing.* 🕐*Closed 25, 26 Dec and 1, 2 Jan* 🎫*£4.* ☎ *01389 732167. www.historic-scotland.gov.uk.*

This ruined castle enjoys a fine strategic **site**★ perched on the basaltic plug of Dumbarton Rock (240ft/73m), once the capital of the independent Kingdom of Strathclyde. The remaining fortifications are mainly 18C. Steps (*278 from the Governor's House*) lead up to the viewing-table on White Tower summit and then to the Magazine on the second summit (*an additional 81 steps*). From the former viewpoint there is a vast **panorama** of the Clyde estuary and surrounding area.

GLEN COE★★
HIGHLAND

This splendid glen with its stark and grandiose mountain scenery lies on the principal tourist route from Glasgow to the north. Awe inspiring in sunshine the glen is dramatically more memorable in menacing weather.

- **Information:** Glen Coe Visitor Centre ☎01855 811 729, www.nts.org.uk.
- **Orient Yourself:** For the purposes of the guide, this heading includes the area from the village of Glencoe to the desolation of Rannoch Moor, although the glen proper is a much more limited section, 11mi/18km long.
- **Don't Miss:** Although the glen may be visited in either direction, the most dramatic direction is from the Rannoch Moor end.
- **Walkers:** Be guided by the experts. Do not overestimate your abilities.
- **Also See:** FORT WILLIAM.

A Bit of History

The Massacre of Glen Coe – In the Highlands loyalties ran deep to the Stuart cause and when James VII's short reign (1685–88) ended in flight the clans were reluctant to renounce the cause. After the Convention had offered the Scottish crown to William and Mary (March 1689), John Graham of Claverhouse rallied the Highlanders. Despite victory at Killiecrankie (27 July 1689), all ended a month later in defeat at Dunkeld.

William proposed a pardon to all clans willing to take an oath of allegiance by

1 January 1692. **Maclain, chief of the MacDonalds of Glencoe** arrived in Fort William belatedly but within the deadline, only to be sent to Inveraray where he finally took the oath on the 6 January. At the beginning of February a force of 120 men, under Campbell of Glenlyon, was billeted on the MacDonalds of Glen Coe and for 12 days all cohabited peacefully. Treachery struck on the 13th with the slaughter of their hosts and the burning of their homes. Forty MacDonalds including Maclain were killed and many more subsequently perished of exposure. An official enquiry confirmed that although the king had given orders,

his Scottish Minister, the Master of Stair, undoubtedly exceeded them. Murder was common in these times but even then "Murder under Trust" was a heinous crime.

Sights

Rannoch Moor

see PITLOCHRY. No road disturbs the isolation of this desolate moorland. Glaciers flowed westwards gouging the great U-shaped valleys of Glen Coe and Glen Etive.

Meall à Bhuiridh

3,636ft/1,108m. To the south of the A 82 and Kingshouse rises the Hill of the Roaring Stags, noted for its ski runs on the slopes of the White Corries.

Glen Etive

This glacial valley (10mi/16km long) pushes southwards to the even longer sea loch of the same name, which reaches the open sea north of Oban.

Buachaille Etive Mór

3,345ft/1,022m.
The conically shaped Big Herdsman of Etive guards the entrance to the glen and offers a challenge to the rock climber. Away to the right is the zigzag of the Devil's Staircase, a series of hairpin bends on the old military road leading over to Kinlochleven. To the right, a flat-topped rock, the Study, is said to pinpoint the head of Glen Coe.
From this point there are good views of the Three Sisters on the left.
The road enters the Pass of Glencoe passing the waterfall, and descends slowly towards the valley floor between great rock walls on either side rising to over 3,000ft/900m.

The Three Sisters

These are outliers of the great nine-peaked **Bidean nam Bian** (Peak of the Bens) with a highest point of 3,766ft/1,141m. The Sisters lie from east to west: Beinn Fhada (The Long Mountain), Gearr Aonach (The Short Ridge) and Aonach Dubh (The Black Ridge). Between the first two, although not visible from the glen, is Coire Gabhail (Hidden Valley) where the MacDonalds hid plundered cattle.

Aonach Eagach

On the right is the great unbroken flank of this serrated ridge (The Notched Heights) which continues for 3mi/5km Loch Achtriochtan lies on the flat valley floor.

Glen Coe & Dalness Visitor Centre

(NTS) ♿ ⏰ *Open: Good Fri–Aug 9.30am–5.30pm. Sept–Oct 10am–5pm. Nov to mid-Dec Thu–Sun 10am–4pm. Second week Jan–Feb, Thu–Sun, 10–4. Mar–Good Fri daily 10–4. For times during Christmas and New Year period, see website. Last entry to exhibition 45 mins before closing.* ✆£5. ☎01855 811 729. www.nts.org.uk.
The centre provides a good introduction, historical and geological, to the glen and its environs. Guided walks are available and a ranger will help with advice on hill walking and climbing.

Glencoe

Population 315. On the shores of Loch Leven the village has a small museum, **Glencoe and North Lorn Folk Museum** (⏰*Open Apr–Oct, Mon–Sat 10am–5.30pm.* ✆£2. ☎01855 811 664, www.glencoemuseum.co.uk). Note the glassware engraved with the white rose of the Jacobites, examples of Lochaber axes – some were still in use in 1745 – and the exhibit on the local slate industry.

THE GREAT GLEN★
HIGHLAND

The geological fault of the Great Glen slices across the Highlands. From Loch Lin-
nhe in the south, a series of freshwater lochs linked by stretches of the Caledonian
Canal lead northwards to the Moray Firth. This corridor divides the Central and
Northern Highlands. Loch Ness provides the major tourist attraction.

- **Information:** Cameron Square, FW. ☎0845 2255 121. visithighlands.com.
- **Don't Miss:** Drumnadrochit, Urquhart Castle.
- **Organizing Your Time:** Allow at least a full day.
- **Especially for Kids:** The Official Loch Ness Monster Exhibition.
- **Also See:** FORT WILLIAM, INVERNESS.

A Bit of History

Natural avenue – From earliest times
this route has been used to penetrate
inland. Columba visited the Pictish King
Brude at Inverness. Bruce appreciated
the importance of its strongholds and
In the 18C General Wade exploited this
natural line of communication when
he proposed a military road network
linking the key garrison posts at Fort
William, Fort Augustus and Inverness.
Today the glen is one of the busiest tourist routes to the north.

Caledonian Canal – This feat of civil
engineering was built between 1803
and 1822 to connect the North Sea and
Atlantic Ocean and save vessels the
treacherous waters of the Pentland Firth
and the long haul round Cape Wrath. Initially proposed and surveyed by James
Watt, the work was later supervised by
Thomas Telford (1757–1834). The canal
has a total length of 60mi/96km; lochs
account for 38mi/61km while the remaining 22mi/35km were man-made. Twenty-
nine locks were required to deal with
the varying levels of the lochs. The most
spectacular series, known as **Neptune's
Staircase** (see FORT WILLIAM: Excursions), is at Banavie near Fort William.

Driving Tour

Fort William
to Inverness 65mi/105km.

The main lochside road, the A 82
between Fort William and Inverness,

is very busy and delays at the swing
bridges can cause nose-to-tail driving. A
slower road on the east side of the glen
follows Wade's 18C military road.

▶ *Leave Fort William by the A 82.*

Spean Bridge
Population 235. Small village at the junction of Glen Spean leading to Aviemore
and the Spey Valley.

Commando Memorial
The monument, to the left of the road, is
a memorial to all Commandos who lost
their lives in the Second World War. The site
marks their training ground. On a clear day
Ben Nevis can be seen away to the left.

Loch Lochy
Just under 10mi/16km long, the loch
narrows towards its head. The hill
slopes of the lochsides are blanketed
with forests.

Laggan Locks
Take the chance to go off the road and
watch the many boats negotiate the
locks between Loch Lochy (93ft/28m)
and Loch Oich (106ft/32m).

▶ *The road crosses to the west side.*

Loch Oich
This straight, narrow and relatively shallow loch required considerable dredging
during the construction of the canal.

Boat trips

The Caledonian Canal is used principally by pleasure craft and is operated by the British Waterways Board. Enquire locally about cruiser operators: some offer monster hunting systems as an option. Several companies operate cruises on Loch Ness with departures from Inverness and Fort Augustus.

Fort Augustus

Population 575. This busy little town at the southern end of Loch Ness sits astride the Caledonian Canal and its several locks. It becomes a bottleneck for traffic with the swing bridge.

Loch Ness★★

The lake has a pleasantly pastoral aspect with its forested sides and various settlements. It is 23mi/37km long and has a maximum depth of 754ft/226m. Its dark waters are the home of the elusive Nessie.

It was on Loch Ness that the racing motorist John Cobb (d 1952) lost his life in 1952 in an effort to beat the water speed record. A roadside memorial commemorates his attempt.

There are few glimpses of the loch prior to Drumnadrochit owing to the tree screen.

Urquhart Castle

Fairly steep path and stairs down to the castle. (HS) ⏱*Open daily Apr–Sept, 9.30am to 6.30pm; Oct–Mar, 9.30am to 4.30pm. Last admission 45 mins before closing.* ⏱*Closed 25, 26 Dec.* ✎*£6.50.* ☎*01456 450551, www.historic-scotland. gov.uk.*

The much-photographed castle ruins are strategically set on a rocky promontory jutting into Loch Ness.

Urquhart was one of a chain of strongholds garrisoning the Great Glen, a fact which gave it a turbulent history which is interpreted in the exhibition and audiovisual display in the new visitor centre, alongside medieval artefacts found at the castle. Seen from the roadside, the various parts are easy to distinguish. The gatehouse on the landward side gives access to a double bailey courtyard. To the right the Norman motte is encircled by walls. On the seaward side, beyond the water gate are the basements of a domestic range and on the left the four-storeyed tower house. From the viewing platform (*50 steps*) there are good **views** of the castle's layout and up and down Loch Ness.

There is a good **view** of the northern part of Loch Ness as the road descends to Drumnadrochit.

Drumnadrochit

Population 542. This neat little lochside village is best known for its **Loch Ness Monster Exhibition Centre**★ (🄺 ♿ ⏱*open year-round daily: Jul– Aug 9am–8pm; Jun and Sept 9am–6pm; Oct 9.30am–5.30pm; Nov–Mar 10am– 3.30pm; Apr–May 9.30am–5pm;* ✎*£5.95 (child £4).* ☕; 🅿; ☎*01456 450 573, www. lochnessscotland.com*).

Examine the evidence (or lack of), and judge for yourself. There are, of course, the famous monster's photographs with explanations and scientific judgements. A section covers the various exploration vessels and latest techniques (sonar traces and computer enhancement by NASA) employed in an attempt to solve the mystery. There is also a section on the food chain in the loch.

The final stretch of road provides good **views** of Loch Ness.

Nessie

The initial sighting of a large snake-like, hump-backed monster with a long thin neck in Loch Ness was made in the 8C by a monk. Despite various expeditions, using highly equipped submarines, helicopters and sonar electronic cameras, the loch has failed to reveal its secret. The Loch Ness Monster Exhibition Centre at Drumnadrochit provides an excellent introduction to the Nessie enigma.

HADDINGTON★
EAST LOTHIAN
POPULATION 7,988

Haddington is a handsome market town where the triangular street plan testifies to its medieval origins. The many 18C town houses are witness to the prosperity occasioned by the agricultural improvements of the period. Set on the banks of the Tyne, the town serves the outlying agricultural area.

- ▪ **Information:** 3 Princes Street, Edinburgh. ☎0845 22 55 121. www.visiteastlothian.org.
- ▸ **Orient Yourself:** The compact town centre, including the riverside can easily be covered on foot.
- ◉ **Don't Miss:** High Street architecture; an excursion to the Lammermuir Hills.
- ◕ **Organizing Your Time:** Allow 1 hour for Haddington, half a day for excursions.

A Bit of History

The 12C town grew up around the royal palace in which Alexander II was born in 1198. Royal patronage was extended to the town itself, created a royal burgh by David I, who was responsible for the establishment of two monastic communities. To allow the royal burgh to exercise its foreign trading privileges, Aberlady, 5mi/8km to the north, was designated as the town's port.

By the 16C this was Scotland's fourth largest town. The Reformation saw the destruction of the monastic houses while ensuing strife led to the building of a town wall (c 1604).

The 18C, Haddington's golden age, was the direct result of increasing prosperity created by agricultural improvements.

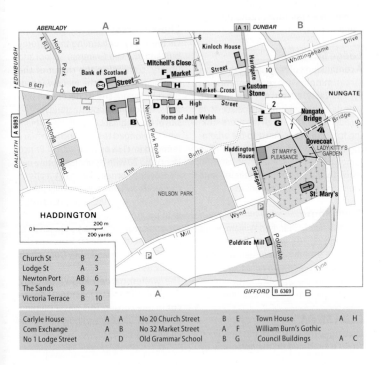

Church St	B	2
Lodge St	A	3
Newton Port	AB	6
The Sands	B	7
Victoria Terrace	B	10

Carlyle House	A	A	No 20 Church Street	B	E	Town House	A	H
Com Exchange	A	B	No 32 Market Street	A	F	William Burn's Gothic		
No 1 Lodge Street	A	D	Old Grammar School	B	G	Council Buildings	A	C

Town Centre

The original market place of this royal burgh was the triangle formed by Market, Hardgate, High and Court streets. The burgesses built gable-ended houses onto this market place with long riggs leading back to the town wall and pends leading off. In the 16C, back to back housing was built in the middle, giving the present layout. The houses themselves were often refronted, and in other cases new fenestration was fitted into a chimney gable end. The streets are lined with some rubblework buildings, some harled and painted, but all with a certain harmony of colour since the 1962 conservation programme. There is a variety of wrought-iron shop signs.

High Street★

The south side has a continuous line of frontages of varying heights, style and colour topped by roofs varyingly pitched, interrupted only by closes. The market cross with the Haddington goat is a 19C replacement. Note in particular no 27 with the decorative chimney, no 31 with the roll skewputts of the dormer window and nos 43 and 45 with the stair turret rising through three storeys.

Lodge Street

A continuation of High Street, this short street mingles markedly contrasting styles. **Carlyle House** – a misnomer, with its highly ornate Italian palace-style façade of the 18C – is all the more striking for its direct contrast to the adjoining vernacular house and its attractive Venetian window. The intervening pend leads to the childhood home of Jane Welsh, wife of Thomas Carlyle.

Town House

This splendidly dignified William Adam building (1748), with pediment and pilasters framing a Venetian window, typified the civic dignity of a town prospering from the agricultural revolution. The steeple was an 1831 addition.

Court Street

Leading to the west port, this tree-lined street is bordered on the north side by splendid town mansions, such as the late-18C Bank of Scotland. Opposite are the 1854 Corn Exchange and William Burn's Gothic Council Buildings on the former site of the royal palace.

Market Street

Late-18C and early-19C three- to four-storey buildings line the north or original side of the triangle. Some gable ends were replaced by new front elevations. Survivals include no 32 with its chimney gable. **Mitchell's Close** on the north side (restored 1967) is more typical of the 17C pattern with rubble masonry, pantiles, inset dormers, crow steps, turnpike stairs – a charming vernacular ensemble.

Hardgate

The most striking building is the white harled **Kinloch House** with its Dutch-style gable, a good example of an 18C laird's town house. The custom stone in front of the George Hotel marks the spot where customs dues were paid in medieval times.

Riverside

Church Street

On the right is a charming three-storey building, the Old Grammar School and library, combining the rigour of the Georgian style and the mellowness of the rubblework and its decorative patterns. The church opposite stands on the site of the original Lamp of the Lothian, which belonged to the Franciscan friary founded in 1138 by Ada, wife of Prince Henry. No 20 with its goat sculpture has a corbelled corner. The street leads to the Sands and down to the riverside.

The sturdily solid 16C **Nungate Bridge** with pointed cutwaters, offers a good view upstream of St Mary's Church in its riverside setting. The far bank was the site of the Cistercian Abbey from which it took its name.

The walled garden known as Lady Kitty's Garden has a cylindrical **dovecot** in one corner. This was a training ground for archery and bowling in the Middle Ages.

St Mary's Parish Church

♿ ⏱ *Open Easter, May–Sept, 11am–4pm, Sun 2pm–4.30pm.* ☎*01620 823 109.*
The cathedral-like dimensions of this church (206ft/163m long and 113ft/34m at the transepts) are enhanced by its unencumbered setting in a spacious churchyard. The first church built in 1134 was rebuilt in the late 14C–early 15C and made a collegiate church in 1540. With successive floods and raids the fabric deteriorated. Extensive alterations were made in the early 19C and the choir was restored in 1971–73.

Restored to some of its original glory, the nave's 19C plaster vaulting replaces the original timber roof; the choir was covered with fibreglass vaulting.

The south window of the south transept is by Burne-Jones (1895). In the Lauderdale Aisle is the 17C marble **Lauderdale Monument** featuring the recumbent alabaster effigies of John Maitland, 1st Lord Thirlestane, his wife Jane Fleming, their son John, 1st Earl of Lauderdale and his countess Isabella Seton. In the floor of the choir is the commemorative slab by Thomas Carlyle to his wife Jane Welsh who was a native of Haddington.

Sidegate

The most notable building is the early 17C **Haddington House**. The street-side entrance was a later addition, the original one being under the turret stair on the garden side. **St Mary's Pleasance** has been re-created as a traditional 17C Scottish garden.

Poldrate Mill

Restored to serve as an arts community centre, this attractive biscuit-coloured stone. 18C corn mill retains its undershot water-wheel, water-mill, storehouses, barns and millers' cottages.

Driving Tour

Lennoxlove★ *1mi/1.5km south by B 6368.* ⏱*See LENNOXLOVE.*

Northern foothills of the Lammermuir Hills★

This rolling countryside conceals a fascinating series of villages each with a spe-

cial charm. Pantiles and the attractive red sandstone are two of the essential contributing factors.

▶ *Take A 6093 out of Haddington.*

Pencaitland

Population 982. Easter and Wester Pencaitland, a double village divided by the River Tyne, has a parish **church** with some unusual features. The octagonal portion of the tower once served as a dovecot. Note the three sundials on the buttress of the south side. The tombstones have some lively depictions of the tools of the trade of the defunct. Watch houses to prevent body snatching stand at each gateway.

▶ *On the outskirts of Pencaitland turn right onto 1 the A 6355.*

East Saltoun

This linear village, with its imposing Gothic church and a line of handsome model cottages, was the work of enterprising landowners, the Fletchers of Saltoun Hall.

▶ *Continue to Gifford.*

Gifford★

Population 665. This late-17C and early-18C estate village was re-sited before the enclosing of the park and rebuilding of Yester House. The main street goes from the church down to the mercat cross then turns at right angles to follow the magnificent avenue of limes leading up to Yester House (*private*), the former home of the Hays of Tweeddale.
The T-shaped **church** dating from 1710 has a laird's loft adorned by the Tweeddale armorial crest.

▶ *Leave by 1 the A 6355 and shortly afterwards branch left onto 1 the A 6370. Take a local road to the right to reach the village of Garvald.*

Garvald

Population 50. Another attractive village with red-sandstone cottages, many of which date from the 1780s when rebuilding followed a disastrous flood. The church, close by the Papana Water, has "jougs" (a kind of pillory) hanging on the west wall.

Stenton★

Population 145. A linear village running between the west green overlooked by the old schoolhouse and adjoining single-storey schoolroom, and the east green punctuated by a now rare feature, the **tron** – for weighing wool. In the churchyard the 16C crow-stepped and saddlebacked tower, with a dovecot in its upper section, marks the site of the former church which was replaced in 1828 by William Burn's Gothic parish church. At the eastern end of the village, by the roadside, is a 16C Rood Well.

▷ *Backtrack to take the local road to East Linton, then turn left onto the A 1. Without going into the village take the local road along the south bank of the Tyne.*

Hailes Castle

This ruined stronghold, which takes full advantage of the rocky outcrop overlooking the River Tyne, was owned at one time by the Hepburns, in particular James, 4th Earl of Bothwell. It is said that Bothwell and Mary, Queen of Scots rested here en route for Dunbar Castle in April 1567.

To the south, the volcanic outcrop of **Traprain Law** (784ft/239m) rises abruptly from surrounding farmland. A good defensive site of early date, it was in all probability the capital of the British tribe, the Votadini. The Law is famous for the **Treasure of Traprain**, a hoard of Roman silver plate, buried in the 5C AD, rediscovered in 1919 and now in the Royal Museum of Scotland in Edinburgh.

▷ *Follow the local road back to Haddington.*

HADDO HOUSE★
ABERDEENSHIRE
⚲ LOCAL MAP SEE ABERDEEN – GRAMPIAN CASTLES

This 18C mansion, stands in Grampian's castle country. Set in lovely wooded grounds it is the ancestral seat of the Gordon Earls of Aberdeen.

🛈 **Information:** 23 Union Street, Aberdeen. ☎ 0124 288 828. www.agtb.org.
▷ **Orient Yourself:** Haddo House is 20 mi/32 km north of Aberdeen on the A 956 and A 90.
🕐 **Organizing Your Time:** Allow 1hr for the house (extra for grounds).
⚲ **Also See:** FYVIE CASTLE, PITMEDDEN GARDEN.

A Bit of History

The history of the house is inextricably that of the Gordon Earls of Aberdeen. The Methlick estate was acquired by a Gordon in 1469. **William, 2nd Earl of Aberdeen** (1679–1745), commissioned William Adam to design a mansion house to replace the earlier family seat destroyed by Covenanters.

The house was an expression of the prosperity engendered by the agricultural improvements. Unfortunately, the next incumbent, George, appropriately named the "wicked earl", dispersed the wealth. A man of great energy, he established three mistresses in residences as far apart as Fraserburgh and Wiscombe Park in Devon, and maintained their offspring, all at the cost of Haddo. **George Hamilton Gordon, 4th Earl** (1784–1860), rose to high office as Prime Minister (1852–55) of a coalition government at the time of the Crimean War. A man of many talents, he nevertheless devoted much time to the improvement of the estate, landscaping the parkland and repairing the house which was by then derelict. Of his three sons, two inherited; the eldest, the

"Sailor Earl", and the youngest. The latter, **John Campbell Gordon, 7th Earl** (1847–1934) embarked on a programme of alterations and refurbishment. Today the house is in the care of the National Trust for Scotland, with the south wing as a private residence for the Gordon family.

Haddo House Choral and Operatic Society

Originally a community centre, the custom-built wooden hall serves as home for various productions (concerts, opera and drama) which attract many visiting artists of international repute. The society was founded by the late 4th Marquess and Lady Aberdeen who, as a professional musician, remains the motivating force.

House

&.🦽🔊*Visit house by guided tours only, Good Fri–Jun & Sept–Oct, Fri–Mon 11am–5pm. Jul–Aug daily 11am–5pm. Last admission to house 4.15. Garden open: year-round daily.*🆗£8. 🚻.☎0844 4932179. www.nts.org.uk.

Interior

The interior of this Palladian country house was entirely transformed when the 1st Marquess refurbished it in the Adam Revival style.

The well lit, elegant reception rooms are a perfect setting for the many family mementoes. From the ground floor entrance hall with its **coffered ceiling**, the staircase leads up to the main apartments. The striking portrait halfway up is Pompeo Batoni's elegant presentation of *Lord Haddo* as the Grand Tourist. His son, the Prime Minister Earl, is commemorated by many souvenirs in the Ante-Room with its 18C panelling and carved overdoors. Alongside Sir Thomas Lawrence's Byronic portrait of the *4th Earl* are portraits of one of his guardians, *Sir William Pitt the Younger*, as well as other political contemporaries such as *Sir Robert Peel* and the *Duke of Wellington* (the 4th Earl was Foreign

Haddo House

National Trust for Scotland

Secretary to both). The bust of Queen Victoria was a personal gift to the former Prime Minister. The Queen's Bedroom was in fact used by the sovereign on her 1857 visit to Haddo.

In the Dining-Room the group of family **portraits** includes the *7th Earl* in his Thistle Robes and the 4th Earl's actor friend *John Philip Kemble*. Part of the 19C alterations included the transformation of a hay loft into the splendid cedar-panelled **library**. The creators of the Library, *We Twa*, are depicted above the fireplaces. The architect GE Street designed the chapel with its Burne-Jones east window.

Grounds

Haddo House Country Park

The **Terrace Garden** features geometric rosebeds and fountain, a lavish herbaceous border and secluded glades and knolls. A magnificent avenue of lime trees leads to adjacent **Haddo Country Park**.

The 180 acres/72ha of parkland with their splendid trees are the result of the 4th Earl's planting programme. The landscaping includes two vistas, Victoria Avenue from the entrance front, and a second on the east side beyond the formal garden, reaching away to the lake, the focal point.

HOPETOUN HOUSE★★
WEST LOTHIAN

Set on the south bank of the Forth, to the west of Edinburgh, this imposing monument stands in landscaped grounds enhanced by manicured lawns and great vistas. Hopetoun House is the place to discover the contrasting exteriors of 17C Sir William Bruce and 18C William Adam and the vastly different interior styles of Bruce and the Adam sons, Robert and James, the whole highlighted by fine furniture and a notable collection of paintings.

- **Information:** High Street, Linlithgow. ☎01506 77 5000. www.edinburgh.org.
- **Don't Miss:** The Hopetoun Summer Fair, if possible, featuring crafts and live entertainment, held the last Sunday in July.
- ▶ **Orient Yourself:** 2mi/3km west of South Queensferry, 12 mi/19km south of Edinburgh. From the south, take the A 90 for the Forth Road Bridge and 'The North'; turn left onto the A 904; right into South Queensferry; then follow the sign to Hopetoun House.
- **Organizing Your Time:** Allow around 1 hour.
- **Also See:** SOUTH QUEENSFERRY (FORTH BRIDGES).

A Bit of History

The Abercorn estate with Midhope Castle was purchased by John Hope in 1678. The original mansion (1699–1703) by **Sir William Bruce** was altered shortly afterwards by John's son, **Charles Hope**, 1st Earl of Hopetoun who commissioned **William Adam**, Bruce's former apprentice, to enlarge his residence. The result was the east front in the Roman baroque manner which we see today. After William Adam's death in 1748 the sons **Robert** and **James** continued the work, in particular the interior decoration of the State Apartments.

Later earls continued to extend their lands with estates in Lanarkshire, West Lothian, East Lothian and Fife, and were widely known as agricultural improvers. The 4th Earl received George IV at Hopetoun during his 1822 state visit to Scotland which was stage-managed by Sir Walter Scott, and occasioned the great revival of all things Scottish and the unspoken acceptance of Highland dress again.

In more recent times, the 1st and 2nd Marquesses of Linlithgow were diplomats and statesmen, serving respectively as Governor-General of Australia and Viceroy of India.

Yellow drawing room, designed by John Adam

Scottish Viewpoint/Visit Scotland

Visit

&. Open Good Fri–Sept, daily 10.30am–5pm (last admission 4pm). £8. Grounds only, £3.70. ☎0131 331 2451. www.hopetounhouse.com.

Exterior

The square form of Bruce's mansion in his mature Classical style, with two main storeys on a rusticated basement, remains the centrepiece of the west front. Seven bays across, the central section is slightly recessed. The straight-headed windows, hood moulds, string courses and quoins contrast with the segmental pediment enclosing an intricate tympanum. In sharp contrast, the more theatrical and certainly very splendid **east front** moves outward from a central unit through curved colonnades to the advanced pavilions and is surely one of William Adam's masterpieces.

Interior

Again the more severe designs of Bruce, who used almost exclusively local materials, can be readily distinguished from the opulence of the Adam interiors of the State Apartments. Move straight through the hall to start with the Bruce rooms.

Library

Two rooms were made into one to create this pine-panelled room now lined with bookshelves. Above the Glen Tilt marble fireplace is David Allan's painting (c 1782) of the two youngest daughters of the 3rd Earl. In the small library with carved and gilded oak wainscotting and a Portsoy marble **fireplace** is a portrait by Sir Nathaniel Dance of *Charles, Lord Hope* (1740–66), one of Adam's companions on the Grand Tour.

Garden Room

Originally the entrance hall, this is an example of Bruce decoration at its best: handsome but sober oak panelling is enhanced by the gilded cornice, door-heads and pilaster capitals and a set of silver armorial candle sconces. Above the fireplace the *4th Earl* is shown in the uniform of Captain of the Royal Company of Archers, the Sovereign's Body-guard in Scotland. The 18C Dutch clock (Jan Henkels) opposite, regularly comes to life with its windmill and musicians.

Bruce Bedchamber

The centrepiece of this sumptuously decorated room is the magnificent **bed** with red damask hangings by Mathias Lock. Painted decoration on a white background alternates with panels of red damask. The original suite included the dressing room and closet with an exhibition on Sir William Bruce, and beyond, the fireproof Charter Room.

Bruce Staircase

Octagonal pine wainscotting admirably carved by Alexander Eizat, echoes the form of the oak handrail and banisters round an octagonal well.

West Wainscot Bedchamber

The room is hung with Antwerp tapestries (c 1700).

▶ *Return to the ground floor.*

Yellow Drawing Room

The proportions of the State Apartments, now reordered, are undoubtedly those of William Adam while the interior decoration has the imprint of Robert Adam.

Above the walls hung with yellow silk damask, the coved **ceiling** is adorned with corner cartouches highlighted in gold and a matching central motif. Details of the frieze, door pediments and cases are also picked out in gold. The paintings include one by Teniers and a contemporary copy of Rembrandt's portrait of *An Old Woman* and the *Adoration of the Shepherds* (school of Rubens). The Cullen pier glasses and console tables between the windows are part of the original 18C dining room furniture. The Cullen commodes on either side of the fireplace came from the State Bedroom. In this room, in 1822 George IV knighted the portrait painter Henry Raeburn.

Red Drawing Room

The ceiling of this room, originally the Saloon, is a Rococo work of gilded **plasterwork** by Clayton and is one of Adam's earliest works. The James Cullen furniture was designed for the room and is arranged in typical parade fashion: mahogany arm and side chairs and the superb gilt console tables, with oval pier glasses above. The white marble fireplace with caryatids is by Michael Rysbrack (1756).

State Dining Room

Refurbished in 1820 this room is typical of the late Regency period with its decorative cornice, leatherised gold cloth on the walls, ornate curtains and pelmets and the ceiling sunburst. The chairs and the marble-topped pier tables with an inlaid H are also by Cullen.

▶ *A staircase leads up to the museum.*

Museum

The subjects covered are the crossing of the Forth from earliest times including the once proposed tunnel to join the Hopetoun estates, costumes, china and the Hope family.

Another staircase leads up to the **rooftop terrace** commanding good **views** of the grounds and the Firth of Forth and the Forth Road Bridges.

Grounds

There are 150 acres of parkland to explore with expansive lawns and a choice walks – the Sea Walk that overlooks the deer park, the Spring Walk with its ever-changing carpet of seasonal flowers and Hope's Walk with its splendid rhododendrons and views of Abercorn Church.

INVERARAY★★
ARGYLL AND BUTE
POPULATION 399

The delightful whitewashed town of Inveraray on the shores of Loch Fyne is a short distance from its castle, the seat of the chief of Clan Campbell.

▫ **Information:** Front Street. ☎08707 200 616. www.visitscottishheartlands.com.
◉ **Don't Miss:** The castle interior and the town itself.
▶ **Orient Yourself:** Inverary lies 37 mi/60km south east of Oban on the A 85 and A 816.
◷ **Organizing Your Time:** Allow one hour for the castle.
▨ **Especially for Kids:** Inverary Jail.
◔ **Also See:** LOCH LOMOND.

A Bit of History

Neil Campbell, one of Robert the Bruce's most faithful supporters, acquired the forfeited MacDougall lands in the 14C and in the 15C the Campbells established their main seat at Inveraray. The medieval settlement arose at the mouth of the River Aray, around the Campbell stronghold. The town achieved royal burgh status in 1648 but it was almost a century later before the 3rd Duke of Argyll envisaged his ambitious scheme to rebuild the castle and settlement, in an area where there were no roads. The military road from Dumbarton arrived in 1745. Building work on the castle took 12 years (1746–58), with Roger Morris as architect and William Adam as clerk of works, although the town took the better part of 100 years to complete.

Castle★★

◷ *Open end Apr–Oct daily 10am (Sun, noon)–5.45pm. Last admission 5pm.* ◷*Closed Aug Bank Holiday Mon for 12 days during Connect Music Festival.* ◉£6.80. ☐. ◻ ☎01499 302 203. www.inveraray-castle.com.

Exterior

Roger Morris' original Gothic Revival edifice was altered externally in the 19C with the addition of a range of dormers at battlement level and conical roofs to the corner towers. On the four fronts, pointed Gothic windows predominate with a tiered central **keep** rising above the general roof line.

Interior★★★

During the 5th Duke's late-18C redecorations the original long gallery was subdivided to give two main rooms on either side of a small entrance hall.

Dining Room

This room is a masterpiece of delicately detailed decoration where roof and walls are perfectly matched. The compartmented **plasterwork ceiling** by a London craftsman is complemented by Clayton's frieze and cornice, and matches admirably the superb painted work of Girard and Guinand (grisaille roundels over doors and in wall panels). The 18C chairs are of Scottish fabrication after a French design and are covered with 18C Beauvais tapestry. Resplendent under the Waterford chandelier (1800) and on the Gillow table are several German silver gilt nefs (c 1900) – elaborate table centrepieces using for holding salt.

Tapestry Drawing Room

The outstanding set of 18C Beauvais **tapestries** and decorative panels and overdoors by Girard rival the compartmented ceiling based on Robert Adam's design. Off this room, the China Turret has an impressive display of porcelain.

Armoury Hall

The hall rises through several storeys to the **armorial ceiling**. The plain pastel-coloured walls provide the ideal background for the impressive display of arms (pole-arms, Lochaber axes and broadswords). From one of these balconies the Duke's personal piper awakes the household with a medley of Campbell tunes.

Saloon

The main family **portraits** hang here where the decoration is confined to an attractive frieze, curtain pelmets and girandoles on the end walls. The principal portraits face each other, namely Pompeo Batoni's *8th Duke of Hamilton* and Gainsborough's portrait of *Conway*, enlarged to match the former. Among the relics in the show cases are some belonging to the Duke who was the Marquess of Montrose's arch enemy.

North West Hall and Staircase

Of the portraits note the builder *3rd Duke* by Allan Ramsay and the *5th Duke* (Gainsborough) and his Duchess Elizabeth Gunning.

Town★★

This tidy township has a showpiece waterfront facing the loch head. The parish church has a prominent site in the axis of the main street.

Bell Tower (All Saints Episcopal Church)

○ *Open Apr–Sept, daily 10am–1pm, 2pm–5pm.* 🅿 ☎*01499 302 203. www.inveraray-castle.com.*
The 10th Duke conceived the idea of building the tower as a memorial to all Campbells who had fallen in war. Each of the 10 bells of the peal is named after a Celtic saint. St Mund, the patron saint of Clan Campbell, is number three. (*Regular bell ringing sessions*). 176 steps lead to the top with a good view of Loch Fyne and the countryside for miles around.

Inveraray Jail
Kids

&○*Open Apr–Oct, daily 9.30am–6pm; Nov–Mar, daily 10am–5pm. Last admission, 1hr before closing.* ○ *Closed 25 Dec and 1 Jan.* ☜*£6.50, child £3.50.* ☎*01499 302 381. www.invererayjail.co.uk.*
This lively attraction re-creates the harsh living conditions of a century or so ago in a real 19C prison. Costumed actors and guides re-enact trials in the courtroom and the punishment meted out to prisoners. Children are both entertained and horrified to learn about the

Loch Fyne Oysters

Loch Fyne is renowned throughout England and Scotland for the quality of its sea-food, particularly its oysters. This reputation is based on the eponymous business which started life as a small oyster bar on the banks of the loch – a venture by Johnny Noble, the owner of the Ardkinglas Estate on the west coast of Scotland, and his colleague Andy Lane – a fish farmer and biologist. They started with one idea – to grow oysters in the clear, fertile waters of Loch Fyne which they first did successfully in 1980. From the humble beginnings of a small, roadside stall on the banks of Loch Fyne, a group of businesses have developed based on the principles of good food, sustainably sourced. The original Loch Fyne Oysters Bar and Shop began life in a small shed at the head of Loch Fyne. In 1985 it moved into the old cow byre at Clachan Farm, Cairndow, 9 mi/14km north of Inverary, (◔open daily 9am–7pm; later opening some weekends, tel to confirm; ☎01499 600236, www.lochfyne.com); it offers excellent value and claims to sell more oysters than anywhere else in the country. Not surprisingly it is often in great demand, so booking ahead is recommended.

The business has subsequently expanded to spawn 38 more Loch Fyne restaurants, though curiously all but one of these are south of the Border – the only other Scottish Loch Fyne is in Edinburgh.

---

draconian punishments doled out to children here: Hector MacNeil, aged 13, was found guilty of stealing a turnip from a field and served 30 days imprisonment; Margaret Cowan, aged 11, stole a pair of shoes and was sentenced to 40 days imprisonment followed by 3 years at reformatory school.

Inverary Maritime Experience

◔Open Apr–Sept daily 10am–6pm. ☜£3.80. ⌣. ☎ 01499 30 2213. www.inverarypier.com.

Moored at the town pier is *The Arctic Penguin*, is a 100ft/30m long triple-masted schooner, built in Dublin in 1911 at a cost of £7,230. It now houses an exhibition on Clyde shipping recounting both the luxuries of the day on board grand Victorian steam ships and the horrors of slavery and awful conditions aboard emigration ships.

Alongide is the Clyde Puffers *Vital Spark*. Puffers were small cargo boats built in the 1940s; specially designed to negotiate the Crinan Canal their maximum length could not exceed 67ft/20m. in summer *Vital Spark* runs short trips across the loch.

Excursions

Oban hinterland★★ –
◔See OBAN: Excursions.

Auchindrain Township Open Air Museum ★

6mi/10km southwest on the A83. &◔Open May–Oct, daily 10am–5pm (*last admission 4pm*). ☜£4.50. 🅿 ☎01499 500 235. www.auchindrain-museum.org.uk.

This open-air folklife museum evokes everyday life as it was for the ordinary people of the West Highlands. Communal tenancy, where a group of tenants hold and work a farm, was the commonest kind of farm in Scotland. This system lasted the longest in the Highlands. Auchindrain is a very ancient settlement, with a history dating back over 1,000 years.

Start the visit with the display centre which gives details on the way of life (field patterns, domestic interiors and occupations), then visit the township where cottages, longhouses, barns and byres have been restored and furnished as museum pieces.

INVEREWE GARDENS★★★
HIGHLAND
POOLEWE – 🌀LOCAL MAP SEE WESTER ROSS

These outstanding gardens in their magnificent west coast setting are at all seasons a source of pleasure and an unrivalled display of beauty.

- 🖹 **Information:** Auchtercairn, Gairloch. ☎01445 712071. www.visithighlands.com.
- ▶ **Orient Yourself:** The Gardens are 6 mi/10km north east of Gairloch.
- 🐾 **Don't Miss:** the rhododendrons and azaleas in April and May, or the herbaceous garden, July through August. The canopy is colourful all year round but excels in the Autumn when the deciduous trees are on the turn.
- 🕐 **Organizing Your Time:** Allow at least two hours.
- 🕯 **Also See:** GAIRLOCH.

A Bit of History

In 1862 the founder, **Osgood Mackenzie** (1843–1922), bought a barren Wester Ross estate including Am Ploc Ard, "the high lump" in Gaelic. The peninsula was exposed to Atlantic gales and salt spray with an acid peaty soil devoid of vegetation. Initial work included rabbit fencing, the creation of a Corsican pine and Scots fir windbreak and the transportation of soil for bedding the plants. A lifetime of patient planning, judicious planting and careful tending, aided by the tempering effects of the Gulf Stream, produced the delightfully informal gardens of today. Osgood's cherished work was continued by his daughter Mrs Sawyer who, in 1952, handed the gardens over to the National Trust for Scotland.

Visit

(NTS) 🛉🕐 *Garden open: year-round daily. Jan to mid-Mar & Nov–Dec 10am–3pm. Mid-Mar to Oct 9.30am–8pm, or sunset if earlier. Last entry 5pm (6pm May–Aug). Visitor Centre open: year-round daily. May–Aug 9.30am–6pm. Oct daily 10am–4pm. Rest of year 9.30am–5pm.* ⊜£8. ✕. ☎0844 4932225, www.nts.org.uk.
Visitors are free to wander at will but a suggested route is indicated by arrows and numbers. Each species is labelled and the guide book contains a list of the more interesting plants. Half of this 64 acre/25ha site is woodland. Here on a latitude similar to that of St Petersburg, flourish some 2,500 species, many of which are exotic but flourish in some sheltered corner. Colour is to be found

Inverewe Gardens, Poolewe

F. Sichet/ MICHELIN

in most seasons: mid-April to mid-May (rhododendrons), May (azaleas), June (rock garden, herbaceous and rose borders), early autumn (heathers) and November (maples).

The twisting paths give unexpected and ever-changing **vistas** of garden, sea and mountain. The high viewpoint affords a **view** back towards Poolewe in its head of the loch setting with the Torridon peaks in the background.

Gairloch

A touring centre for the Northern Highlands, this small low-key holiday resort enjoys attractive sandy beaches and is good walking country.

Housed in a complex of old farm buildings, **Gairloch Heritage Museum** (&Open Mar–Sept daily 10am–5pm, Oct Mon–Sat 10am–1pm; €£3.50; ☎01445 712287, www.ghmr.freeserve.co.uk) is a record of life in the area from pre-history to the present day.

Established in 1989, **Gairloch Marine Life Centre & Cruises** (depart Charleston Harbour Mar–Oct daily; two-hour cruises 10am, 12.30pm, 3pm; one-hour cruise 5.15pm; €£20 for 2 hr cruise, £10 for 1 hr cruise; ☎01445 712636, www.porpoise-gairloch.co.uk) is one of the longest running marine wildlife operators in Europe and has the longest running porpoise survey world-wide. On any cruise you might expect to see Harbour Porpoises, Minke Whale, Common and Grey Seals, Common Dolphins, Bottlenosed Dolphins, Risso's Dolphins and Basking Sharks, all of which swim in the area. More unusual visitors to these water include Killer Whales, White Beaked Dolphins and even Sunfish, all spotted in recent years.

INVERNESS★
HIGHLAND
POPULATION 38,204
&SEE THE TOWN PLAN IN THE MICHELIN GUIDE GREAT BRITAIN AND IRELAND

Inverness stands at the northern end of the Great Glen, astride the outlet of Loch Ness, and has long been known as the capital of the Highlands. At the very hub of the Highland communications system, the town makes an ideal touring centre for much of the Highlands.

- **Information:** Castle Wynd. ☎01463 234 353. www.visithighlands.com.
- **Orient Yourself:** City Sightseeing open-top hop-on hop-off buses tour the city and also Culloden/Cawdor/Fort George (late May–late Sept, www.citysightseeing.co.uk. €£6).
- **Don't Miss:** a cruise on Loch Ness; "monster hunting" trips depart from Inverness and Fort Augustus.
- **Especially for Kids:** Dolphin and Seals of the Moray Firth Visitor Centre.
- **Also See:** THE GREAT GLEN, CROMARTY.

A Bit of History

Hub of the Highlands – The strategic importance of this site has been appreciated from earliest times as testified by the existence in the vicinity of a variety of ancient sites and monuments. St Columba is said to have visited Brude, King of the Picts, at his capital beside the Ness, although the exact site is unsure. By the 11C King Duncan (c. 1010–40), made famous by Shakespeare, had his castle in the town. The town's strategic importance was its downfall in later times when it suffered variously at the hands of the English, Robert the Bruce, turbulent Highland clans, the Lord of the Isles, Mary, Queen of Scots' supporters and Jacobites. The post-1715 Rising law and order policy for the Highlands enacted by General Wade included the creation of a citadel, as one of several

Address Book

♿ *For coin ranges, see the Legend on the cover flap.*

WHERE TO EAT

🍴🍷**Cafe 1** – *Castle Street.* ☎01463 226 200. www.cafe1.net. Local ingredients feature in the Modern Scottish menu of this attractive contemporary restaurant. (Cafe Express menu 🍴 is superb value)

🍴🍷**Chez Christophe** –*16 Ardross Street.* ☎01463 717 126. Top quality Scottish and French ingredients combine well at this small two-room restaurant (dinner only).

WHERE TO STAY

🛏️**Craigside Lodge** – *4 Gordon Terrace.* ☎01463 231 576. www.craigsideguesthouse.co.uk. Delightfully located by the banks of the river Ness, views of the river, castle and mountains can be enjoyed from many rooms.

🛏️**Old Rectory** – *9 Southside Road.* ☎01463 220 969. Victorian residence with a secluded garden, set in a quiet residential area, a 6-minute walk to the town centre.

strategic strongholds in the Highland fringes. Culloden and its tragic aftermath was the ultimate action of the 1745 Rising.

Such a troubled history means that there are few historic buildings. The architecture of the town today is largely that of the 19C, one of expansion due in large to Telford's construction of the Caledonian Canal (1803–22) and the arrival of the railway.

Northern Meeting Piping Competitions (♿*see Calendar of Events*) are held annually in Eden Court Theatre and are the oldest of all piping contests, dating back to 1781.

Sights

Inverness Castle

Several earlier castles have preceded the present 19C building which serves as court house and administrative offices. The esplanade with the **statue** of Flora MacDonald affords a good **view** of the Ness and the town.

Inverness Museum and Art Gallery★

Castle Wynd. ♿🕐*Open Mon–Sat 10am–5pm.* 🕐*Closed 25–26 Dec, 1 and 2 Jan.* ☕. ☎01463 237 114. http://inverness.highland.museum.

The imaginative and well presented exhibition "Inverness, Hub of the Highlands" interprets the rich heritage of the Highlands. Topics of special local

significance range from the Great Glen; the vitrified Fort Craig Phadrig (visible from the window); the Picts and their surviving works; the engineering feats of more recent times, such as the military roads of General Wade, Telford's Caledonian Canal and the Kessock Bridge. Exhibits on the Highland way of life include the former silver-producing centres of Inverness, Tain and Wick and there are a presentation pair of **Doune pistols** (♿*see DOUNE*) by John Murdoch. These guns of exquisite craftsmanship are dated c. 1790.

The Museum is also home to the Highland Photographic Archive.

Town House

At the foot of Castle Wynd. This Victorian replacement was the scene in 1921 of the first ever Cabinet Meeting outside London. The base of the mercat cross incorporates the Clach-na-Cuddain or "stone of the tubs" used as a resting place by washerwomen on their way to and from the Ness. As long as the stone remains Inverness will continue to flourish.

Abertarff House

Church Street. This renovated 16C house is the oldest in inverness.

Inverness Cathedral

Ardross Street. 🕐*Open Apr–Sept daily 9.30am–6.30pm. Oct–Mar Mon–Sat 9.30am–4.30pm, Sun 2–4.30pm.* ☎01463 233 535. www.invernesscathedral.co.uk.

This imposing richly decorated neo-Gothic edifice was built 1866–9 for the diocese of Moray, Ross and Caithness. The nave piers are columns of polished Peterhead granite. The choir screen and rood cross are by Robert Lorimer.

Excursions

Kessock Bridge

1.25 mi/2km north on the A9. Opened in 1982 this suspension bridge spanning the Beauly Firth carries the A 9 north to the Black Isle. With a total length of 3,451ft/1,052m the bridge's main span has a clearance of 95ft/29m above high water. There is a good **view**★ of Inverness from the bridge, while the **Dolphin and Seals of the Moray Firth Visitor Centre** (&⟨⟩*open Jun–Sept, daily 9.30am–12.30pm, 1.30–4.30pm;* � ; ☎*01463 731 866*) in the car park of the Tourist Information Centre on the A 9 gives information on the marine life of the Moray and Beauly Firths. Bottlenose dolphins, harbour porpoises and upwards of 1,000 seals inhabit these waters; the seals' mating roars and the mysterious sounds emitted by the dolphins can sometimes be heard with the aid of the Centre's sophisticated listening equipment.

Culloden

6mi/10km east by the A 9 and the B 9006. (NTS). &⟨⟩*Open daily: Apr–Oct, 9am–6pm, Nov–Mar 10am–4pm.* ⟨⟩*Closed 24–26 Dec, 1 and 2 Jan.* ⟨⟩. ⟨⟩*£10 (inc £2 for audio tour).* ☎*0844 493 2159. www.culloden.org.uk.*

On 16 April 1746 this bleak moor saw the end of the Jacobite Rising of 1745 when Prince Charles Edward Stuart's army was defeated by a government army under the Duke of Cumberland, the younger son of King George II. After months in hiding as a fugitive the prince escaped to France and lifelong exile.

The dynamic new **visitor centre** features interactive characters that witnessed or were involved in the battle the Immersion Theatre where you can experience first hand what it was like to be in the middle of the action at Cul-

loden, and weapons and artefacts found on the battlefield.

The **Old Leanach Cottage** which survived the battle has been restored as it was at the time of the battle. Stones and monuments mark the graves of the clans. A hand held audio device is available to take onto the battlefield to help you further understand the armies' manoeuvres and tactics.

Clava Cairns★

Head east on the A 9 and the B 9006. Turn right at the Cumberland Stone then continue for 1mi/1.5km.

This impressive site includes three cairns, girdled by stone circles, and a small ring of boulders. The middle cairn was a ring-cairn with its centre always open to the sky. The two others, now unroofed, had entrance passages leading to a burial chamber. Some of the stones of the cairns bear cup marks. The complex dates c. 4400–2000 BC, and each cairn and stone ring formed a single design.

Beauly

12mi/18km west on the A 862. In a sheltered position at the head of the Beauly Firth this delightful village takes its name *Beau Lieu* from the 13C Burgundian monks who founded a priory here.

Fortrose

This busy little town is the chief community of the Black Isle. Away from the bustle of the main street, the remnant of the **cathedral church** makes an attractive picture in its peaceful **setting**★ of green lawns enclosed by the charming red sandstone houses of the former close.

The remaining south aisle has attractive vaulting and the damaged tomb of its builder, Euphemia, Countess of Ross, widow of the Wolf of Badenoch. The detached two-storey building may have been a sacristy and chapter-house.

Rosemarkie – ⟨⟩*See CROMARTY EXCURSIONS.*

Cromarty★ – ⟨⟩*See CROMARTY.*

Strathpeffer
19mi/30km northwest on the A 9, the A 862 and the A 834.

Framed by monkey puzzle trees and other exotic conifers, the ornate villas and hotels of this delightful Victorian spa town adorn the slopes at the head of a lush valley. Like many of the European spas which it resembles, Strathpeffer had its heyday in the years before the First World War; the branch line up the valley from the market town of Dingwall was opened in 1885, enabling well-heeled visitors to arrive by direct sleeping car express from London. A small pump room and the spa pavilion survive, and the "singular variety of Mineral Water dispensed by Nature" may be tried in one of a jolly trio of modern pavilions in The Square.

Highland Museum of Childhood
&. ⊙Open Apr–Oct, Mon–Sat 10am–5pm, Sun 2pm–5pm (Jul–Aug Mon–Fri 10am–7pm. ⊗£2. P. ☎01997 421 031. www.highlandmuseumofchildhood.org.uk. Strathpeffer's charming station building, complete with glazed canopy on ornate cast-iron columns, survived the closing of the railway in 1951 and part of it now houses this equally charming little museum with a particularly good collection of doll's houses.

Cruises on Loch Ness –
&. *See The GREAT GLEN.*

ISLE OF IONA★
ARGYLL AND BUTE
POPULATION 128

This remote and lonely windswept Inner Hebridean isle is one of the most venerated places in Scotland. Over 1,400 years ago St Columba and his companions landed on its southern shore to establish a monastic settlement. Today the island is an important place of pilgrimage although there are few tangible remains.

- ▪ **Information:** The Pier, Tobermory, Mull. ☎08452 255 121. www.visitscottishheartlands.com, www.isle-of-iona.com.
- ▶ **Orient Yourself:** CalMac ferries make the short trip from Fionnphort on the southwest tip of the Isle of Mull (www.calmac.co.uk). The island is about 3 mi/5km long and 1 mi/1.6km wide. The main sights are easily reached on foot from the pier at Baile Mór. A taxi or rented bikes (from Fionnphort) will take you farther afield.
- ☻ **Don't Miss:** St Oran's Chapel, Maclean's Cross, St Martin's Cross, the Cross of St John.
- ☻ No private cars are allowed on Iona.
- ⊙ **Organizing Your Time:** Allow the best part of a day if you want to explore the whole island.
- ☪ **Also See:** ISLE OF MULL.

A Bit of History

The Columban Settlement – In AD 563, 166 years after St Ninian's mission (☪see WHITHORN) **St Columba** (521–597) and a group of followers set off from Ireland. Their chosen site, this bare and somewhat inhospitable island, suited the tenets of their monastic traditions. The community flourished and was successful in converting the native people of the mainland. It was from Iona that St Aidan set out to establish Irish Christianity in Northumbria in 636. Even after the death of Columba in 597, and the decisions of the Synod of Whitby (664), the community went from strength to strength and was to become the mother house for the Columban monasteries. Although nothing remains of St Columba's monastery, the period was one of great artistic achievement. There were beautiful intricately carved crosses and grave slabs, and it has been suggested that the sacred work of art, the *Book of Kells*, was undertaken in whole or in part, by the scribes and illuminators of the Iona community. This period was brought to an end by the Norse raids of the 8C and 9C.

Some of the monks accepted refuge at Dunkeld, which became the new centre of the Columban Church. Following a particularly savage raid in AD 803 when 68 monks lost their lives, the remaining members, with the relics of St Columba and perhaps the *Book of Kells*, returned to Kells in Ireland.

Medieval foundation – At the beginning of the 13C Reginald, son of Somerled, King of the Isles, founded a Benedictine monastery and a nunnery to be headed by his sister. Iona became part of the mainstream of medieval monasticism but its importance was purely local. With the forfeiture of the Lordship of the Isles at the end of the 15C, the principal source of patronage, the monastery lost its independence. For a short period in the 16C the church was elevated to cathedral status but by the Reformation, disrepair had already set in.

Rebirth – Following the foundation in 1938 of the Iona Community, originally a Church of Scotland brotherhood and now an ecumenical community of women and men, a programme of restoration of the monastic buildings was undertaken, and completed in 1966. The Abbey is now open all year round as a place of hospitality, reflection and worship. Although the sacred precincts belong to the Church of Scotland Trust, the rest of the island is in keeping for the nation under the auspices of the National Trust for Scotland.

Walking Tour

▶ *Take the road straight up from the pier continuing past the post office.*

Nunnery

The nunnery was founded at the same time as the monastery and the ruins here are a good example of a typical, small medieval nunnery. The cloister-garth is bordered by the early 13C church and the ranges of the conventual buildings, parts of which date from the late medieval period.

Fragments of the cloister arcade are on display in the Infirmary Museum.

Beyond the main group is a simple rectangular building, St Ronan's Church, with narrow triangular-headed windows.

Across the road, in the old Manse, is the **Iona Heritage Centre** (🕐 *open Easter–Oct, Mon–Sat 10.30am–4.30pm.* ✆£2. ☎01681 700 439) with exhibits on the social history of the isle.

▶ *Continue along the road.*

Maclean's Cross★

The cross, which dates from the 15C, is a product of the local school of carvers. On the west face is a Crucifixion while on the reverse the intricately carved patterns maintain the Celtic traditions.

Map of Baile Mór, Iona, showing: Infirmary Museum, Michael Chapel, Tor Abb, ABBEY, High Crosses, St Columba's Shrine, St Oran's Chapel, Street of the Dead, Reilig Odhrian, St Columba Hotel, Maclean's Cross, Baile Mór, St Ronan's Church, NUNNERY, Pier, FIONNPHORT, Sound of. Scale: 100 m / 500 feet.

▶ *Follow the road round past St Columba Hotel.*

Reilig Odhrian

This early Christian burial ground is reputed to be the burial place of Scotland's kings from Kenneth MacAlpine to Malcolm III, the Lords of the Isles and other chieftains. The most notable medieval effigies and grave slabs are now in the Infirmary Museum.

St Oran's Chapel★

The chapel, the island's oldest surviving building, dates from the 12C (restored 20C). The simple rectangular structure has a worn but rather fine Norman west door with three arches of beak-head and chevron decoration.

▶ *Pass through to the abbey precincts.*

Street of the Dead

Part of the paved processional way, which led from the landing place to the abbey, is uncovered at this point.

Tor Abb

This hillock is said to mark the site of St Columba's cell.

High Crosses

Of the three standing crosses **St Martin's**★ (8C), complete and original, displays figure scenes on the west face. Only the truncated shaft of St Matthew's (9C–10C) remains. The third one is a replica of St John's Cross (8C). On the latter the decorative work is divided into panels.

Abbey

(*HS*). &. ⏱*Open year-round daily 9.30am to 5.30pm (Oct–Mar 4.30pm). Last admission 30 mins before closing.* ⏱*Closed 25–26 Dec, 1–2 Jan.* ◉£4.50. ☎01681 700 512, www.historic-scotland.gov.uk.*

The present church no doubt stands on the site of its Columban predecessor. The original 13C church was altered towards the end of the century and enlarged in the 15C. Conversion work included the adding of a tower at the crossing and a south aisle to the choir. Fragments of the 13C Benedictine church include

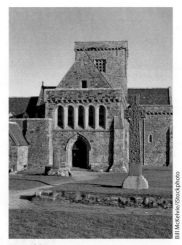

Iona Abbey

Bill McKelvie/iStockphoto

the north transept and an arcade of the choir's north wall. The elaborate trefoil-headed doorway below was inserted when the north aisle was converted into a sacristy in the 15C. Note the carved capitals of the arcade and the piers of the crossing. The pale creamy green communion table is of Iona marble. A door in the north wall of the nave leads into the cloisters with the unusual twin-columned arcade. There are two originals in the west side.

▶ *Return to the west front of the church.*

To the north of the west front is St Columba's Shrine, said to be the original burial place of the saint. The exact whereabouts of the saint's relics remain a mystery.

▶ *Go right round the far side of the buildings to the back.*

Infirmary Museum★

⏱*Times and charges same as Abbey; admission included on same ticket.*

The museum houses an outstanding collection of early Christian and medieval stones. The 8C Celtic **Cross of St John**★ has pride of place. The early Christian works (nos 1–49) dating from AD 563 to the second half of the 12C include incised crosses (nos 3–33) and ring crosses

The End of the World

Will Iona be the only place to survive the effects of global warming?

An ancient island prohecy runs thus:

*Seachd bliadhna 'n blr'ath
Thig muir air Eirinn re aon tr'ath
'S thar lle ghuirm ghlais
Ach sn'amhaidh I Choluim Chl'eirich*

In seven years before the day of judgement the ocean will sweep over both Ireland and Islay. Yet the Isle of St Columba will swim above the waves.

(nos 23–33 and 38–48). The medieval section (nos 50–110) has examples of the Iona School of carving (14C–15C). Their work included grave slabs, effigies and free-standing crosses (&see *Maclean's Cross*). The group (nos 71–83) of grave slabs includes human figures and the distinctive West Highland galleys. Nos 98–101 show the armour of the period.

Michael Chapel

This small chapel is used for public worship in the winter months.

JEDBURGH★

SCOTTISH BORDERS

POPULATION 4,053
&LOCAL MAP SEE THE TWEED VALLEY

The historic royal burgh of Jedburgh, lying astride the Jed Water, is on one of the main routes into Scotland, as taken by the Roman Dere Street and the present A 68. At one time the site of a castle and abbey, the town was granted royal burgh status in 1165 by William the Lion. However, it remained vulnerable in this troubled border region and its history reflects that of the area. It is now a peaceful market town, with some attractive vernacular buildings.

- **Information:** Murray's Green, Jedburgh. ☎0870 6080 404. www.scot-borders.co.uk, www.jedburgh.org.uk.
- ▶ **Orient Yourself:** Jedburgh is just 10 mi/16km north of the Border with England on a main route north, the A 68.
- **Don't Miss:** Jedburgh Abbey; the view from the Waterloo monument.
- **Organizing Your Time:** Allow 3 hours for the town centre, including 30mins for the Abbey.
- **Kids Especially for Kids:** Jedforest Deer and Farm Park.
- **Also See:** ABBOTSFORD, DRYBURGH ABBEY.

Jedburgh Abbey★★

(*HS*). ⏱*Open year-round daily 9.30am–5.30pm (Oct–Mar 4.30pm). Last admission 30min before closing.* ⏱*Closed 25–26 Dec, 1–2 Jan.* ✏£5. ☎01835 863 925. *www.historic-scotland.gov.uk.*
One of the most famous Border abbeys, Jedburgh was founded by **David I** in 1138 as a priory for Augustinian canons from Beauvais in France and elevated to abbey status 14 years later (1152). Work started at the church's east end in 1140 and continued for 75 years before the

cloister buildings were commenced. A majestic building, it witnessed in its early days such royal events as the coronation of the founder's grandson, Malcolm IV (1153–65) and the marriage of Alexander III (1249–86) to his second wife, Yolande de Dreux. Constant attack and plundering were the fate of many of the great buildings in the region. The destruction of the 1545 raid ended abbey life although the church continued to be used as a place of worship until 1875.

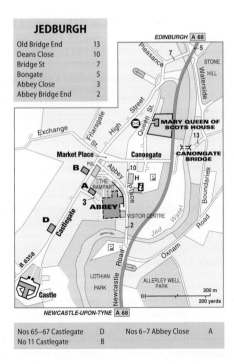

JEDBURGH	
Old Bridge End	13
Deans Close	10
Bridge St	7
Bongate	5
Abbey Close	3
Abbey Bridge End	2

Nos 65–67 Castlegate	D	Nos 6–7 Abbey Close	A
No 11 Castlegate	B		

Abbey Church

The visitor centre gives a good introduction to the abbey. The mellow-toned stone building is roofless but otherwise comparatively complete. Seen from Abbey Close, the late-12C transitional **west front** is a powerful and most original feature. The main section with a deeply recessed, round-headed doorway crowned by three pedimented gables, has above a tall, fairly narrow window rising through the upper two sections to a rose-adorned gable, the whole being flanked by solid buttresses. Strength, originality and soaring height are its chief characteristics. The rhythm and regularity of the **nave** display the assurance of an art well mastered. The increasing number of elements per bay pulls the eye upwards from the pointed arches on solid clustered columns, through the triforium section of round-headed arches, subdivided by two smaller lancets, to the clerestory and the serried ranks of lancets.

The tower above the crossing is trimmed with a delicate balustrade.

Beyond, the mid-12C east end, the earliest part of the church, is highly unorthodox. Massive round pillars rise upwards to the clerestory, buttressing the truncated arches of the main arcade. Distinctive Norman style includes the rounded arches and chevron decoration.

Cloister buildings

On a sloping site and now reduced to the foundations, these follow the usual pattern around the cloister, with, in the east range, the parlour, chapter-house and treasury below, and dormitory above. The refectory, cellars and kitchens border the south side and offer a good view of the south elevation. Compare the Norman doorway giving access from

Jedburgh traditions

The Common Riding or **Jethart Callant's Festival** comprises a series of rides out to historic places. Another long-established local event is the mid-February Ba' Games when those born above the mercat cross, the Uppies, oppose the Downies, with the respective goals ("hails") being the Castle Jail grounds and Townfoot.

the south aisle to the cloister, weathered but with a variety of sculptural motifs still discernible, to the replica on the left, resplendent with the full wealth of detail.

Additional Sights

Mary Queen of Scots Visitor Centre★

🕐 *Open early Mar– Nov, Mon–Sat 10am–4.30pm, Sun 11am–4.30pm.* 👝*£3.* ☎*01835 863 331.*

This is an attractive 16C L-shaped tower house in the vernacular style, standing in its own well-tended garden. Originally the property of the Kerrs of nearby Ferniehirst, it took its present name following Mary, Queen of Scots' visit in 1566 when she lodged here. Her stay was prolonged by ill health (to the point of fearing for her life) after her famous ride to visit the injured Earl of Bothwell, her future husband, at Hermitage Castle some 20mi/32km distant.

The ground floor kitchen is cobbled and barrel-vaulted. The window embrasures indicate the thickness of the walls.

As in all Kerr houses, the spiral staircase is left-handed to allow this Kerry-fisted family to use their sword hands. Engraved glass panels, paintings, documents and relics tell the story of the hapless Queen's life. Portraits include her death mask and the Antwerp Portrait and contentious Breadalbane Portrait by George Jamesone. The second room at first floor level is decorated with a series of inset paintings of people closely associated with Mary, Queen of Scots.

Jedburgh Castle Jail and Museum

♿🕐*Open late Mar–Oct Mon–Sat 10am– 4.30pm, Sun 1–4pm.* 👝*£2.* ☎ *01835 863 254.*

This Georgian prison, built in the 1820s, was the site of the original Jedburgh Castle, a favourite residence of royalty in the 12C and well placed for hunting parties in the ancient Jed Forest. In the 15C the castle was pulled down by the townsfolk to prevent it falling into English hands.

In 1823 the present building, a Howard Reform Prison, was considered one of the most modern of its time in Scotland.

Buildings

Three prison blocks arranged around the central governor's block were linked to the latter by first floor gangways. The top floor terrace of the central block served as point of surveillance and was expediently provided with a bell to sound the alarm in times of escape.

The three cell blocks had a similar disposition with cells leading off a central passage. Inmates' cells included two windows, a wooden bed and central heating – the grate at floor level covered the hot air ducts which were supplied by a stove in the windowless cell on the ground floor.

Two blocks of this fascinating building are open to the public. Some of the cells have displays evoking the life that went on in this "comfortable place of confinement", and there are exhibits on many aspects of local history.

Castlegate

Leading downhill to Market Place, the way to the castle is bordered by some attractive houses (restored). On the left, nos **65** and **67** have incorporated into their walls two sculptures, one of which may well represent the Turnbull bull. Abbey Close, leading off down to the right to the abbey, is where in 1803 the Wordsworths received Scott who read them part of his *Lay of the Last Minstrel* (plaques **6** and **7**).

Continuing down Castlegate, no **11** on the left is where Bonnie Prince Charlie lodged in 1745 when leading his Jacobite army into England.

Market Place

A plaque in the road marks the original site of the mercat cross around which clustered the stalls. The plaque on the County Buildings (H) commemorates Sir Walter Scott's first appearance as an advocate in 1793.

The Canongate continues down to A 68 which borders the Jed Water, bridged at this point by the **Canongate Bridge**★, a mid-12C triple-arched bridge. Stout

Thorsten Schmitz /iStockphoto

Jedburgh Abbey

piers with pointed cutwaters support the narrow bridge provided with pedestrian recesses.

Excursions

Waterloo Monument

3mi/5km north on the A 68 and then the B 6400. A path leads from the Harestanes Countryside Visitor Centre.   ♿ ⏰ *Open Good Fri–Oct, daily 10am–5pm.* ☕. ☎ *01835 830 306), to the base of the monument.*

Standing on the summit of Peniel Heugh (744ft/227m), the Waterloo Monument (⊶ *no access to viewing platform*), one of the Border's most prominent landmarks, was built to commemorate Wellington's victory of 1815. Formerly the site of pre-Roman camps, with Dere Street on its western flank, the craggy eminence offers a splendid **panorama**★★ of the surrounding countryside: the fertile Teviot Valley to the Cheviots in the south and east; great stretches of arable land and Smailholm Tower due north; the Eildon Hills to the northwest.

Ferniehirst Castle

1.5mi/2.5km south on the A 68.   ♿ 🚌 *visit by guided tours only, Jul Tue–Sun 11am–4pm.* ☞ *£3.50.* ☎ *01835 862 201. www.ferniehirst.com.*

The original castle was built in 1450 and has been in the hands of the Kerr family ever since. Strategically important, it guarded the road to Otterburn and made an ideal base for the Wardens of the Middle March. The present building with its attractive rubble stonework dates from 1598 and has recently been restored following use as a youth hostel. The visit includes the Border Clan Centre in the former chapel, the Kerr Chamber in the basement, the entrance and great halls hung with portraits as well as the delightful turret room which is beautifully panelled.

Jedforest Deer and Farm Park   [Kids]

5mi/8km south on the A 68. Mervinslaw Estate ⏰ *Open Easter–Aug 10am–5.30pm; Sept–Oct 11am–4.30pm.* ☞*£4.50, (child £2.50).* ☕. ☎ *01835 840 364. www.jedforestdeerpark.co.uk.*

This Borders farm (820 acres/332ha) welcomes visitors with an array of rare breeds of sheep, cattle, pigs, goats and poultry. Beyond the belts of trees sheltering the farmstead paddocks from the wind are more extensive enclosures, the domain of muntjac, fallow and sika deer. Birds of Prey displays are given each lunchtime starring falcons, hawks, owls and eagles.

An extensive adventure playground keeps little ones happy.

KELLIE CASTLE ★
FIFE

One of the chief charms of this laird's house is the chance to appreciate an example of unspoilt 16C and 17C Scottish traditional Lowland architecture.

- **Information:** ☎ 01333 720 271. www.nts.org.uk.
- ▶ **Orient Yourself:** 2 mi/3km inland, northwest, from the East Neuk villages of Pittenweem and St Monan's and 10mi/16km south of St Andrews.
- 🅿 **Parking:** £3 pay and display.
- **Also See:** ST ANDREW'S, THE EAST NEUK.

A Bit of History

Originally the seat of the Oliphants, once home to the youngest daughter of Robert the Bruce, in 1613 Kellie Castle passed to the Erskines or Earls of Mar and Kellie. It is said that the first Earl saved the life of King James I, and the 5th Earl, who fought on the side of the Jacobites at the Battle of Culloden, spent the entire summer of 1746 hidden in an old beech tree in the gardens at Kellie where his butler secretly brought him food every day.

The castle and lands were dissociated in the late 18C and a period of neglect followed from 1830 until a lease was granted in 1876 to Professor James Lorimer, an Edinburgh jurist. His rescue of the castle is commemorated by a Latin inscription "This mansion snatched from rooks and owls is dedicated to honest ease amongst labours, 1878". The castle stayed in the Lorimer family , and was the childhood summer home to the internationally renowned architect Sir Robert Lorimer, and his brother the accomplished artist John Henry Lorimer. Sir Robert's son, Hew Lorimer, an acclaimed sculptor, took over the lease in 1937, refurbished it and finally bought the castle in 1957. It has since gradually been restored to its former glory by the NTS.

Castle

(NTS) ⚐ 🕐 *Castle open: Good Fri–Oct daily 1–5pm. Gardens and Park open: year-round daily 9.30am–5.30pm.* 🎫 *£8 (gardens only, £3).* ☕.

Built of rubble sandstone to a T-shaped plan, each wing of the T forms a tower. Around 1573 a second, quite separate tower was added to the east. Finally between 1573 and 1605 an L-shaped addition completed the T-plan. The southwest **tower**, containing the entrance door, is a splendid work – corbelled turrets with conical roofs, pedimented dormers, crow-stepped gables, chimney stacks, varyingly pitched roofs and string courses.

Interior

The late-17C **plasterwork ceilings** are notable, in particular the **Vine Room** ceiling with its delicate trailing vine branches on the coving and painted central panel, *Mount Olympus* by Jacob de Wet. Typical of the period is the Memel pine panelling in the **Withdrawing-Room** painted with over 60 romantic landscapes. The Scottish furniture is designed by Sir Robert Lorimer and there is an exhibition on the life and work of his son, Hew.

Grounds

The Arts & Crafts garden is filled with scent of old roses and the beautiful herbaceous borders. The walled garden includes formal gardens and orchards. and a summerhouse (designed by Sir Robert) exhibits a display on the history of the walled garden.

There are woodland and meadow walks, with extensive views of the Firth of Forth and the Bass Rock.

KELSO ★
SCOTTISH BORDERS
POPULATION 6,150
🎇LOCAL MAP SEE THE TWEED VALLEY

Kelso stands at the confluence of the Tweed and its main tributary, the Teviot. A handsome market town, it is remarkable for its Georgian architecture and serves a rich agricultural hinterland. Although arable farming predominates in the rich Merse, the outlying hill regions maintain the tradition of hill sheep farming; however, the area is also known as horse country.

- 🅸 **Information:** Town House. ☏0870 608 0404. www.scot-borders.co.uk.
- ▶ **Orient Yourself:** Kelso is 23mi/37km southwest of Berwick-upon-Tweed via the A 698 and B 6350, and 10mi/16km from the Border with England.
- 👀 **Don't Miss:** The Square; the views from Kelso Bridge, and (out of town) from the Maxwellheugh Road and Smallholm Tower.
- 🕐 **Organizing Your Time:** Allow half a day for the town.
- 👓 **Also See:** FLOORS, MELLERSTAIN, DRYBURGH ABBEY.

A Bit of History

The original settlement grew up at a fording point, the first west of Berwick, and then developed round the abbey here in 1128. Kelso flourished when the nearby prosperous royal burgh of Roxburgh was destroyed in 1460 and her prosperity increased with the abbey's although she also suffered the fate of the abbey in 1545 when English troops led by the Earl of Hertford attacked. The town was raised to a burgh of barony in 1614 in favour of Robert Ker, 1st Earl of Roxburghe.

Sights

Kelso Bridge
The attractive five-arched bridge, built (1800–03) by John Rennie served as a model for his Waterloo Bridge. The lamp standards at the south end came from its London version when it was replaced in the 19C. The bridge offers a splendid **view**★ upstream over the lazy flowing Tweed, of Kelso on the right with Floors in its fine setting and the mound of Roxburgh Castle on the left.
An elegant toll-house still stands on the north bank.

Abbey Court
The previous bridge opened onto this close which is dominated by a church on the left and the white-harled 17C **Turret House**.

Abbey
The abbey was founded in 1128, the monks having moved from two previous sites at Selkirk and Roxburgh before finally settling here. With royal patronage the abbey grew and acquired extensive lands to become the richest in the land and the abbot claimed seniority among the Scottish clergy. The building itself, a vast edifice, took 84 years to complete. Following the death of James II while besieging Roxburgh Castle, the infant **James III** was crowned in the abbey. Time and again the abbey suffered from invading forces, the most destructive being that of Hertford's "Rough Wooing" in 1545 despite a desperate fight by the monks. By 1587 the abbey was officially defunct and in 1592 James VI granted it and the lands to Robert Ker of Cessford, 1st Earl of Roxburghe. From 1649 to 1771 the roofed-over transept served as parish church, then the ruins were pillaged for dressed stone. In 1919 the abbey was presented to the nation by the Duke of Roxburghe.
The **ruins** date from the last quarter of the 12C. This once mighty abbey with its grandiose double transept plan was

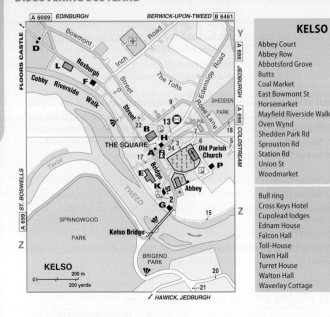

KELSO		
Abbey Court	Z	2
Abbey Row	Z	3
Abbotsford Grove	Z	5
Butts	Z	6
Coal Market	Y	7
East Bowmont St	Y	9
Horsemarket	Y	13
Mayfield Riverside Walk	Z	15
Oven Wynd	Z	17
Shedden Park Rd	Y	18
Sprouston Rd	Z	20
Station Rd	Z	21
Union St	Y	22
Woodmarket	Z	24

Bull ring	Z	A
Cross Keys Hotel	Y	B
Cupolead lodges	Y	D
Ednam House	Z	E
Falcon Hall	Y	F
Toll-House	Z	G
Town Hall	YZ	H
Turret House	Z	K
Walton Hall	Y	L
Waverley Cottage	Z	P

undoubtedly the largest and the most unusual of the Border group.

From the entrance only part of the south recessed doorway is visible, with a variety of sculpture on the arches, while rising above is the west transept tower, again massive in construction. Pass through to the abbey churchyard and turn around to admire the elevation. Three sections with round-headed openings rise above very attractively carved intersecting arcading.

The modern partial cloister (1933) by Reginald Fairlie is the Roxburghe family vault. The sculpture is interesting for the use of Celtic designs.

The **west front** and **tower** are best seen from the churchyard outside the abbey grounds. This is by far the most imposing part with its unique ordinance. In the transitional style, the recessed round-headed doorway with its pediment is surmounted by successive horizontal sections, each adorned with varying architectural elements. The whole is flanked by stout buttresses crowned with round turrets. The overall impression of this unique composition is one of soaring strength.

Pass through the churchyard to the car park. In the far corner is **Waverley Cottage**, the house, adorned with a statue of a dog, where Walter Scott spent some of his time while attending Kelso Grammar School.

Old Parish Church

&. ⏱ Open May–Sept, Mon–Fri noon–2pm. 🅿. ☎01572 226 254.

The highly unusual and controversial octagonal-shaped church was built in 1773 by a local man, James Nisbet. The ground floor straight-headed windows and the round-headed ones above are all equipped with hood moulds, a common architectural feature of the region. The eight-sided roof is topped by a lantern.

Return to cobbled Bridge Street. Set back on the left is **Ednam House**, now a hotel. This fine Georgian mansion dates from 1761.

The Square★★

Spacious and elegant, this vast square is dominated by the 19C **Town Hall** which was built by public subscription and surrounded by a selection of 18C and 19C town buildings: three-storeyed, parapeted hipped roofs with dormers, straight-headed windows – some with straight hoods on scroll brackets, some in colourful harling, others of dressed stone, all a delight in summer with colourful hanging baskets and window box displays. On the west side

Rams, Races and Rides

Kelso is famous for its Ram Sales (*September*), the Horse and Pony Sales (*April and September*), and an agricultural show, the Border Union Show (*July*).

Kelso races take place at Berrymoss and point-to-point races are held across the river at Friarshaugh (*February and March*).

Kelso Civic Week has a varied programme including the Kelso Laddie leading his supporters on the Whipman's Ride. Also popular is the Tweed Raft Race from Kelso to Carham.

the **Cross Keys Hotel** was one of the staging points on the Edinburgh–London coaching route. The names of the adjoining streets – Horsemarket, Woodmarket – are reminders of the original role of the square as the market place, as is the bull ring embedded in a star formation in the cobbles.

The dilapidated Tudor building with oriel windows in Woodmarket (now furniture storage premises) was built in 1885 as the corn exchange.

Roxburgh Street

Leading off down towards the river is an alley that gives access to the **Cobby Riverside Walk**, affording pleasant views of the river, the weir, the eminence and former site of Roxburgh Castle, Floors Castle in its splendid setting, and the backs of a series of town houses. Climb back up to Roxburgh Street where on the left is the majestic entrance to Floors built in 1929 by Reginald Fairlie. Two lodges with cupolas are linked by grandly gilded gates.

Return to the town centre by Roxburgh Street passing **Walton Hall** behind massive wooden gates, the former home of James Ballantyne, a schoolfellow of Scott's and later business partner in his printing business. **Falcon Hall** is also noteworthy.

Driving Tour

Floors Castle★
See FLOORS CASTLE.

▶ *Take B 6397 to the left, crossing rich arable farmland then turn left onto B 6404. Take the road signposted Sandyknowe Farm up to the right*

then branch left towards the steading (stables and farm outbuildings). Continue through the steading and over the cattle grid up to the car park at the foot of the tower.

Smailholm Tower★
Open Apr–Sept daily 9.30am–5.30pm. Oct Sat–Wed 9.30am–4.30pm. Nov–Mar Sat–Sun 9.30am–4.30pm. Last admission 30mins before closing. Closed 25, 26 Dec & 1, 2 Jan. £3.50 01573 460365. www.historic-scotland.gov.uk.

Standing like a sentinel, this lone tower house (57ft/17m tall) captures the history of the Borders, when these marches were controlled by a day and night watch. This attractive 16C example is built of rubble masonry and contrasting red-standstone trims. Restored in the 1980s, the interior houses an exhibition of beautifully detailed dolls, representing characters from the Border ballads. The adjacent village of Sandyknowe was where the young Walter Scott spent his childhood years with his grandparents listening to the rousing tales of the Border ballads.

The rocky outcrop at the base of the tower commands a **panoramic view**★★ of the Border countryside over a patchwork of rich arable farmland with in the distance other local landmarks: the Waterloo Monument (*see JEDBURGH: Excursions*) on Peniel Heugh due south and two of the Eildon Hills to the west.

▶ *Make for Smailholm village and then on to Mellerstain by the B 6397.*

Mellerstain★★ *see MELLERSTAIN.*

Greenknowe Tower

▶ *Make for the A 6089, turning left towards Gordon and at the road junction take the A 6105 left, and continue for about 1mi/1.5km.*

Greenknowe Tower

On an elevated site, surrounded by marshland, this 16C L-shaped tower house, now a roofless ruin, still stands sentinel. Over the entrance the lintel comprises the owner's coat of arms, dated 1581.

Internally the layout is typical of such a building with cellar and kitchen on the ground floor, the laird's hall on the first and bedchambers above.

▶ *Return to Gordon and continue out to the east by the A 6105 in the direction of Greenlaw. Turn sharp right onto the B 6364.*

The imposing edifice high on the right is **Hume Castle**. The present structure dates from the 18C. From its foot there are splendid views of the Merse.

▶ *Continue on the A 6089 to Kelso.*

KINTYRE
ARGYLL AND BUTE

Kintyre is the southern part of the long West Coast peninsula. The western shores are pounded by the great Atlantic rollers while the east coast looks over the sheltered Kilbrannan Sound to Arran.

🛈 **Information:** Mackinnon House, The Pier, Campbeltown. ☎08452 255 121. www.visitscottishheartlands.com.

▶ **Orient Yourself:** The varying scenery and seascapes afford a pleasant drive. The western (A 83) road is wider and faster with good views of Ireland, while the eastern route is single track with passing places. The points of interest are described below in alphabetical order, allowing you to decide your own route.

⊙ **Don't Miss:** Carradale; Gigha gardens in spring time.

🕐 **Organizing Your Time:** Allow 1–2 hours.

Kids **Especially for Kids:** Sandy beaches on the west coast.

Sights

Carradale★

Population 262. Facilities. This small village has a pleasant site, fringing the tiny harbour, a haven for a busy fishing fleet.

Campbeltown

Population 6,077. The main market and shopping town of the peninsula, Campbeltown is also a holiday centre.

In the 19C the town boasted a large fleet based on the Loch Fyne herring fishery and over 30 distilleries producing a variety of malt whiskies. Both sectors have declined drastically, although the industries are still represented. The cross near the pier is 15C.

Clachan

At nearby Ronachan Point grey seals may be seen basking offshore.

Claonaig

Pier for the ferry to Lochranza on Arran (*summer only*).

Kennacraig

The ferry port for Islay and Jura.

Machrihanish

Population 540. This west coast town is known for its huge sandy beach 🄺🄸🄳🅂 (6mi/10km long) and 18-hole golf course. A nearby farm was the home of the artist **William McTaggart** (1835–1910) who was inspired by local landscapes.

Mull of Kintyre

The Campbeltown Pipe Band and, of course, Paul McCartney, brought worldwide publicity to this headland (only 13mi/21km from Ireland) with the eponymous song in 1977.

Saddell

Overgrown ruins are all that remain of this once important West Highland abbey founded c. 1207. The founder Reginald, who was the ruler of Kintyre and Islay, is said to be buried here. In the churchyard a **collection**★ of 14C–16C grave slabs displays the unusual panoply of West Highland subjects: warriors, weapons and galleys. The black galley with its sails furled symbolises the end of a voyage.

Skipness Castle

Leave the car at the entrance to the grounds. (HS) Exterior view only.

This vast courtyard fortress incorporates an early-13C hall house and 16C tower house. An Old Red Sandstone door and window trims add a decorative touch to this imposing stronghold which marked the southern limit of Campbell territory. There are good views across the Kilbrannan Sound to Arran.

Tayinloan

This is the ferry port for the small island of **Gigha**, lying 3mi/5km off the Kintyre coast. The island is known for its remarkable woodland **gardens** at Achamore (🕐*Open daily, sunrise to sunset*. 💷£3.50. 🖂. ☎01583 505 390. www.gigha.org.uk). The rhododendrons, azaleas and camellias burst into colour in late spring.

Tarbert

Population 1,429.

At the head of East Loch Tarbert, this small town marks the isthmus dividing Kintyre from Knapdale to the north. The houses fringe the harbour and bay, lively with fishing boats and yachts in summer. There are scant overgrown remnants of Bruce's castle. In imitation of the 11C Magnus Barefoot, (King of Norway), Bruce dragged his boats across the isthmus on his way to attack Castle Sween in 1315.

Tarbert

P. Tomkins/ Scottish Viewpoint/ Visit Scotland

KIRKCUDBRIGHT★
DUMFRIES AND GALLOWAY
POPULATION 3,352

Kirkcudbright (pronounced Cur-coo-bree), set on the east bank of the Dee, derives its livelihood from farming, fishing and tourism. The open waterfront was once a bustling port and the town itself a royal burgh and county town.

- ⓘ **Information:** Harbour Square. ☎ 01557 330 494. www.kirkcudbright.co.uk, www.visitdumfriesandgalloway.co.uk.
- ▶ **Orient Yourself:** 28mi/45km southwest of Dumfries on the A 75.
- ⓒ **Organizing Your Time:** Allow 2–3 hours for Kirkcudbright, a full day for excursions. 3 hours for the coastal drive.
- **Kids Especially for Kids:** Fish ladder at Tongland Power Station, Galloway Wildlife Conservation Park.
- ⓒ **Also See:** THREAVE GARDEN.

Sights

Broughton House

(NTS) ⓒ⅁ *House and garden open: Good Fri–Jun & Sept–Oct, Thu–Mon noon–5pm. Jul–Aug daily noon–5pm. Garden also open: Feb–Good Fri, Mon–Fri 11am–4pm. ☎£8. ☎0844 4932246. www.nts.org.uk.*
At the beginning of the century this 17C house became the home of the artist, **Edward Atkinson Hornel** (1864–1933), known for his Galloway scenes and the originality of his bold and colourful style. It now contains the **Hornel Art Gallery** and the works on display include some of his Japanese paintings, the result of an extended visit to Japan. His fine **Japanese garden** is another by-product of his fascination for the country.

MacLellan's Castle

(HS). ⓒ *Open Apr–Sept daily 9.30am–5.30pm. Oct Sat–Wed 9.30am–4.30pm Last admission 30 mins before closing. ☎£3. 50. ☎01557 331 856, www.historic-scotland.gov.uk.*
In 1582 the former provost of the town, **Sir Thomas MacLellan**, quarried the adjoining ruined monastery to build his town residence, which is impressive for its sheer size. A spacious staircase, with straight flights, leads from the ground floor cellars and kitchen to the great hall where the massive fireplace is equipped with a **laird's lug** or spy hole. By 1752 the mansion was roofless.

Greyfriars Kirk

Formerly part of a 15C monastery, the kirk shelters the memorial of MacLellan, the castle builder, who is portrayed as a knight in full armour.

High Street

The west and south sides of this L-shaped street provide a mixture of styles, some with a vernacular flavour and others with a Georgian sophistication, interrupted by cobbled closes or pends. No 14 was the home of the artist, Charles Oppenheimer, while the mosaic on no 44 commemorates the husband and wife artists team of E A Taylor and Jessie M King. At the far end are the 1610 mercat cross and the 16C–17C tolbooth, complete with jougs.

Tolbooth Art Centre

⅁ⓒ *Open Jul–Aug, Mon–Sat 10am–5pm, Sun 2pm–5pm; May–Jun and Sept–Oct Mon–Sat 11am–5pm (4pm Oct), Sun 2pm–5pm. Nov–Apr Mon–Sat 11am–4pm. P ☎01557 331 556. www.dumgal.gov.uk.*
In the late 19C–early 20C Kirkcudbright had an active artists' colony, attracted here by the charm of the townscape, the unspoiled nature of the surrounding countryside, and the quality of the light. Their work and their contribution to the life of the town is celebrated in the handsome steepled 17C Tolbooth, where there is an audio-visual show, artists' studios and pictures.

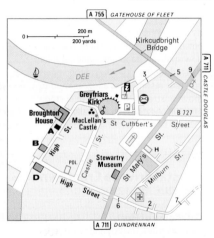

KIRKCUDBRIGHT	
Rues	
Victoria Park	9
Silver Craigs Rd	7
St Mary's Pl.	6
Bridge St	5
Beaconsfield Pl.	3
Barrhill Rd	2
Tolbooth Art Centre	D
Home of E.A. Taylor and	
Jessie M. King	B
Home of Charles Oppenheimer	A

The Tollbooth's past includes service as a prison, its most famous occupant being the American John Paul Jones.

Stewartry Museum

♿ 🕐 *Open Mon–Sat 10am–5pm, Sun 2–5pm.* 🅿️ . ☎ *01557 331 643. www.dumgal.gov.uk.*
This small local museum, bursting with items, has particularly interesting exhibits on curling and quoiting, an old game played with iron rings resembling horseshoes, which used to be popular in every parish, and on local personalities such as Thomas Telford and John Paul Jones.

Excursions

Galloway Wildlife Conservation Park Kids

1mi/1.5km east on the B 727. ♿ 🕐 *Open Feb–Nov daily 10am–dusk (last admission 6pm).* ≈£5, child £3. 🍴. ☎01557 331 645, www.gallowaywildlife.co.uk.
Set in woodland, the park has some 150 animals from around the world, though the highlight is perhaps the opportunity to see the rare Scottish wildcat.

Dundrennan Abbey★

5mi/8km southeast by the A 711. (HS) ♿ 🕐 *Open Apr–Sept daily 9.30am–5.30pm. Oct Sat–Wed 9.30am–4.30pm. Nov–Mar, Sat–Sun only 9.30am–4.30pm. Last admission 30mins befpre closing.* 🕐 *Closed 25–26 Dec, 1–2 Jan.* ≈£3. ☎ 01557 500262, www.historic-scotland.gov.uk.

This Cistercian abbey was founded in 1142 by King David. The monastery prospered but by the time it passed into secular hands at the Reformation it was in a precarious state. In 1568 Mary, Queen of Scots halted here on her flight into England.
The ruins have a grandeur and austere simplicity true to the Cistercian tradition. The parts still standing include a section of the west wall, the transepts, chapter-house and some outbuildings. As an early example of the Gothic style the 12C transepts combine the use of the pointed arch (main arcade and triforium level) with the round arch of the clerestory. The remains of the chapter-house, rebuilt in the 13C show a more decorative Gothic style, in particular the charming group of entrance doorways.

▶ *Continue on the A 711 for a farther 9mi/14.5km. At the junction with the B 736 to Castle Douglas, take the single track road to the right.*

Tongland Power Station (Galloway Hydros Visitor Centre) Kids

2mi/3km north by A 711. 🔭 *Visit by guided tour only, May–Sept Mon–Fri 9.30am–5pm.* ≈ *call for charges.* 🍴. ☎01557 330 114. www.scottishpower.com/GallowayHydrosVisitorCentre.asp.
Following the creation of a national grid system in 1926, Tongland was built between 1931–36 as headquarters for the Galloway Hydroelectric Scheme. The tour includes the turbine hall with origi-

nal turbo generators, the arch and grav-ity dam (984ft/300m along its crest and 66ft/20m above the river bed), the over-flow spillway, flood gates and popular **fish ladder.** Twenty-nine stepped pools and four resting ones allow salmon to move upstream to spawn. An average of 4,000 pass through annually.

Driving Tour

Coastal drive to Creetown
20mi/32km. Take A 755 west

Gatehouse of Fleet
Population 894. This tidy and picturesque town is an example of late late-18C town planning.

▶ *Take A 75 the Newton Stewart road which follows the coast.*

Cardoness Castle
This mid-15C tower house is prominently set on a rocky outcrop overlooking the tidal Fleet. A turnpike, linking the differ-ent floors, leads to the parapet (79 steps)

which affords a view across the Fleet and the estuary with Wigtown peninsula on the horizon.

▶ *6mi/9.5km further on, turn right off the main road to the Cairn Holy site.*

Cairn Holy
0.5mi/800m from the main road. Bear left twice up a farm road. Park at the first monument.
These two chambered cairns are in a commanding site with a good outlook over the Solway.

▶ *Proceed for 1mi/1.6km*

Carsluith Castle
The well-preserved ruin of a 16C tower house. The 18C ranges of outhouses are still in use by a farmer

Creetown
Population 760. This delightful village, famous in the past for its granite quar-ries, has a gem and rock museum with a dazzling collection of Scottish and worldwide specimens.

KIRRIEMUIR
ANGUS
POPULATION 5,308

The small town of Kirriemuir, with its narrow winding streets lined by red-sandstone houses, has a certain charm. Set on the slopes of the Highland rim overlooking the great sweep of Strathmore, Kirriemuir is at the heart of the raspberry growing country. This was the birthplace of the playwright JM Barrie and the Thrums of his books.

🛈 **Information:** Brechin Castle Centre, Haughmuir, Brechin. ☎01356 623050. www.angusanddundee.co.uk.
▶ **Orient Yourself:** Kirriemuir is 19mi/30km north of Dundee via the A 929 and A 90.
Kids **Especially for Kids:** Fans of Peter Pan may enjoy the chance to visit JM Barrie's Birthplace.
🕒 **Also See:** BRECHIN, DUNDEE.

Sights

JM Barrie's Birthplace   **Kids**
No 9 Brechin Road. (NTS) ♿⏰*Open Good Fri–Jun & Sept–Oct, Sat–Wed (also Fri bank hol weekends) noon–5pm, Sun 1pm–5pm. Jul–Aug daily 11am–5pm,*

(Sun 1pm–5pm). Bank Holiday weekends from Fri– Mon. Last admission 4.30. 💷£5 *(inc free admission to Camera Obscura), child £4.* 🖵*.* ☎*0844 493 2142. www.nts. org.uk.*
The four-roomed cottage was where **James Matthew Barrie** (1860–1937),

the playwright and author of *Peter Pan*, was born in 1860. The ground floor room with albums and other memorabilia was no doubt where Barrie's father originally had his linen-weaving hand-loom.

Upstairs on the left is the Barrie kitchen and opposite, the bedroom with a box-bed and the portrait of the St Bernard, Porthos, the model for Nana. Of particular interest are the two historic Peter Pan costumes: one with the shadow and the second with the detachable "kiss". The small wash-house outside served as a makeshift theatre and no doubt provided the inspiration for the Wendy House built by the Lost Boys in Never Never Land.

There is summer holiday entertainment in the Pirates Workshop for 5–8 year olds (booking required).

Cemetery
Turn left off Brechin Road to take Cemetery Road right to the top.
Barrie's grave is signposted. The short walk has good views of the agricultural patchwork of Strathmore below.

Camera Obscura
Barrie Pavilion, Kirriemuir Hill. (NTS) 🕐 *Good Fri–Sept Mon–Sat noon–5pm, Sun 1pm–5pm.* 🌂 *Poor weather may prevent operation. Last viewing 4.40pm.* 🎫 *£3 (combined admission with JM Barrie's Birthplace, £5).* ☎ *0844 493 2143. www.nts.org.uk.*
Gifted by JM Barrie, this is one of only three public Camera Obscuras in Scotland. Weather permitting it offers excellent views of the Highlands north and south over Strathmore to Dundee.

KYLE OF LOCHALSH
HIGHLAND
POPULATION 803
📍LOCAL MAP SEE WESTER ROSS

Formerly famous as the ferry port for Skye – before the bridge was built to the island in 1995 – this small town is still a very busy place in summer.

- 🛈 **Information:** Car Park. ☎08452 255 121. www.visithighlands.com.
- ▶ **Orient Yourself:** 78mi/126km west of Inverness via the A 82 and A 887. Kyle of Lochalsh also makes a good excursion point for discovering Torridon and Applecross to the north or Kintail to the east. The areas to the south remain remote and secluded.
- 👜 **Don't Miss:** Eilean Donan Castle.
- 👟 **Also See:** ISLE OF SKYE.

Driving Tour

Northwards to Ullapool
via Gairloch★★★ –
👟*See WESTER ROSS.*

Eilean Donan Castle★
9mi/14.5km east by A 87. 🕐 *Open mid-Mar to mid-Nov daily 10am(Jul–Aug 9am)–6pm.* 🎫*£4.95.* 🍽. ☎*01599 555 202/291, www.eileandonancastle.com.*
One of the most iconic images of Scotland, Eilean Donnan has an idyllic island site★★ (today linked by a bridge) with a picture-postcard mountain and loch

setting. it has starred many times on the big screen, recently in the James Bond film *The World is Not Enough* (1999). Following the abortive Jacobite rising of 1719 the ruins were abandoned for 200 years until the 20C when a complete reconstruction was undertaken. The Banqueting Hall, bedrooms and kitchen (as it would have looked in 1932) as well as courtyard are open to visitors. The outer ramparts offers excellent **views** of the three lochs.

- ▶ *Continue to the head of Loch Duich (8mi/13km southeast on the A 87).*

Eilean Donan Castle

Glen Shiel★

This grandiose V-shaped valley passes from the head of Loch Duich through to Loch Cluanie. Stretching 6mi/9.5km down the left side of the Glen are the **Five Sisters of Kintail.** Rising up from the lochside some of the peaks top 3,000ft/900m. The valley was the site of the Battle of Glen Shiel which ended the Jacobite rising of 1719.

LANARK

SOUTH LANARKSHIRE

POPULATION 9,673

This busy market town has one of the biggest livestock markets in Scotland. Historically it boasts William Wallace associations and in sport possibly the oldest horse-racing trophy in the world, the Silver Bell. Its biggest visitor attraction however, is the new model village of New Lanark.

- **Information:** Horse Market. ☎01555 661 661. www.seeglasgow.com.
- **Orient Yourself:** Lanark is 31mi/50km southeast of Glasgow via the M 74. New Lanark is 1.2mi/2km south of Lanark.
- **Don't Miss:** New Lanark: the Lanimer Festival (6–12 June) with the traditional riding of the marches and the unusual "Whuppity Scourie" ceremony (1 March) (*see Calendar of Events*).
- **Organizing Your Time:** Allow at least half a day.
- **Also See:** BIGGAR.

New Lanark★★ *2hr*

Down on the floor of the deep gorge of the River Clyde, New Lanark is a fine-example of an 18C planned industrial village. When the Glasgow tobacco trade collapsed owing to the American War of Independence (1776–83) cotton manufacturing was quick to take its place, exploiting a workforce skilled in linen making.

In 1783, a Glasgow manufacturer and banker, **David Dale** (1736–1806), brought Richard Arkwright, inventor of the spinning power frame, to the area to prospect suitable sites for a new factory. The present site was chosen and the smallest of the Falls of Clyde harnessed to provide water power for the mills. Building started in 1785 and by 1799 the four mills and associated housing comprised Scotland's largest cotton mill supporting a village population of over 2,000.

In 1800 Dale sold the mills to his future son-in-law, **Robert Owen** (1771–1858) a social reformer, who took over as managing partner and was to remain so for 25 years. The mills were a commercial success enabling Owen to put a series of social experiments into practice. He created the Nursery Buildings, the Institute for the Formation of Character, the village store and school. In an age of increasing industrialisation **Owenism** was widely acclaimed but was eventually eclipsed by government and employer resistance.

Cotton continued to be manufactured here until 1968. A major restoration programme followed; in 1986 the village was nominated a World Heritage Site and today New Lanark is one of the country's most popular visitor attractions.

Village

The best approach is on foot from the car park. Stop on the way down at viewpoint with the orientation table. ○*Open Jun –Aug, daily 10.30am–5pm; Sept–May, daily 11am–5pm.* ⊗*£5.95.* ☎*01555 661 345, www.newlanark.org.*

The centrepiece, **New Buildings** (1798), pinpointed by the bell tower is prolonged to the right by the **Nursery Buildings** (1809) to house the pauper apprentices who worked and usually lived in the mills, and then the cooperative **store** (1810) – now refurbished with an exhibition about Owen's original store and a period-style shop. The bow-ended **counting house** terminates a line of restored tenements which took its name, **Caithness Row,** from the storm-bound Highlanders on their way to America who were accommodated and subsequently settled here.

At the other end of the village, beyond Dale and Owen's houses, is more tenement housing, while between the river and the lade stands the massive **mill**, divided in to units.

The **Visitor Centre**, is home to working textile machines and the entertaining **New Millennium Experience** ride where visitors travel in time. There is also an interactive Gallery of light, sound and colour. The building which was Robert Owen's School for Children now houses **Annie McLeod's Story**, where the ghost of a mill-girl appears on stage. A **Millworker's House** shows living conditions of the 1820s and 1930s.

Mill no 3 is the most handsome building and the only one to have been rebuilt by Owen, in 1826. **Mill 1** was fully reconstructed in 1995 and has been converted recently into a hotel. The engine house gives access to a glass bridge – to the pattern of the original rope-race – which leads to mill 3.

Mill 2 is home to the Edinburgh Woollen Mill and on the very top of the building is a **Roof Garden** where a viewing platform giving a fantastic birds-eye view of the village, woodland, and Falls of Clyde

▶ *The riverside path leads upstream to the gorge section of the Clyde*

Falls of Clyde

The Old Mill Dyeworks, by the river, now serve as the **Falls of Clyde Visitor Centre** with an audio-visual show and displays on the wildlife. ♿○*Visitor centre open Jan–Feb, daily noon–4pm, Mar–Dec 11am–5pm.* ○ *Closed 25–26 Dec and 1–2 Jan. Reserve open summer 8am–8pm. Winter during daylight hours.* ⊗*£2.* ☎*01555 665 262. www.swt. org.uk.*

This stretch of river with four spectacular falls – now used for hydro-electricity – was once one of Scotland's most visited beauty spots, portrayed by Turner and described by Wordsworth, Coleridge and Scott.

A viewpoint beyond Bonnington Power Station provides an excellent **view** of the highest falls, **Corra Linn** where the drop is 60ft/18m. These are spectacular on days when the water is turned on and thunders over the rocky lips down to a boiling mass below with a pall of vapour hanging above.

LENNOXLOVE ★
EAST LOTHIAN

Historic associations and rich royal collections plus objects from the near-legendary Hamilton Palace make Lennoxlove a fascinating outing. You can even stay the night in a bed fit for a queen.

- **Information:** ☎01620 828 604. www.lennoxlove.com.
- ▶ **Orient Yourself:** Orient Yourself: Lennoxlove is 1 mi/1.6km south of Haddington on the B 6369 Gifford/Duns Road and 22mi/36km east of Edinburgh.
- ⏱ **Organizing Your Time:** Allow 45 minutes.
- **Also See:** HADDINGTON.

A Bit of History

Originally known as Lethington Tower, the oldest parts were built by the Gifford family c.1250. The tower was then acquired by the Maitlands. The best-known family member was **William Maitland** (1525–73), Secretary to Mary, Queen of Scots, described by Queen Elizabeth of England as "The Flower of the Wits of Scotland". His brother John became Lord High Chancellor to James VI, was created 1st Earl of Lauderdale and began the enlargement of the old tower.

On the death of the Duke of Lauderdale, Lethington passed to his stepson, Lord Huntingtower, and was purchased by the Trustees of Frances Teresa Stewart, Duchess of Lennox, known as "La Belle Stewart" (1647–1702), a favourite at the court of Charles II and subsequently immortalised as Britannia on British coins. On her death Lethington then formed a bequest to Walter Stewart, Master of Blantyre, the son of the Duchess of Lennox's cousin, later 5th Lord Blantyre. The house was renamed Lennoxlove as a condition of the bequest, and to signify the love of the Duchess for the Duke of Lennox.

It was purchased in 1946 by the 14th Duke of Hamilton. In 1933 he had won international fame as chief pilot of the first expedition to fly over Mount Everest and in 1941 he was to gain even more, albeit less welcome, publicity when, to his astonishment, Rudolph Hess, Adolf Hitler's deputy, parachuted into Renfrewshire demanding to see him (they had mutual friends) in an attempt to negotiate peace with the United Kingdom.

Visit

♿ 🚻 *Visit by guided tours only, every 30 mins, Apr–Oct, Wed, Thu & Sun, 1.30–4pm (last tour time).* ⏱*Closed certain days in Jul & Sept, see website for dates.* 💷*£4.50.*

Interior

The portraits bring to life the story of this historic home and its many famous owners. Of special interest in the **Front Hall** are the portraits attributed to Mytens of *James, 2nd Marquess of Hamilton*, who accompanied James VI to England in 1603. Portrayed by Ponsford is the *Marquess of Huntly*, uncle of Susan Beckford who married the 10th Duke of Hamilton. On the first floor landing are portraits by Kneller of *William Douglas*, Earl of Selkirk, who became the 3rd Duke of Hamilton, and of his wife *Anne*. There are also portraits of *Sir William Hamilton*, the celebrated art collector and diplomat, and of his wife *Emma*, mistress of Lord Nelson, who figures in a triple portrait by Angelica Kauffmann.

The wall cabinets of the **China Hall** display 18C–20C armorial porcelain. By the entrance to the **Blue Room**, William Beckford, collector, eccentric and author, is pictured as a boy. He was the father of the 10th Duchess. There is also a portrait by David Wilkie of the *10th Duke of Hamilton* (1767–1852), known as "El Magnifico" who enlarged Hamilton Palace, added to the collections of furniture and paintings and built his own mausoleum at Hamil-

Lennoxlove House, Blue Room

P. Tomkins/ Scottish Viewpoint/ Visit Scotland

ton. The Palace, built 1695, was said to be the largest house in the Western world aside from royal houses, but was demolished in 1921. There are also portraits by Henry Raeburn of the *8th* and *11th Dukes,* the latter as a child. The former is portrayed riding from Edinburgh to Hamilton in under three hours in fulfilment of a wager. Several French items include furniture by Courtois, a piano by Pleyel, Napoleon's bedside table, and a portrait of the *Marquis of Marigny,* brother of Madame de Pompadour.

In the **Petit Point Room** is an ebony and pewter Boulle cabinet. The damask wall hangings are appliqued with older petit point embroideries. In the **Yellow Room** a double portrait of the *2nd Duke of Hamilton* and the *Duke of Lauderdale* establishes the link between the original and present owners of Lennoxlove. There are also portraits by Lely of the *Duke and Duchess of Lennox.* The **Stuart Room** is dominated by the inlaid tortoiseshell writing cabinet, a gift from Charles II to La Belle Stewart. The **Great Hall**, which represented the whole living portion of the original tower, was remodelled in 1911–12 by Robert Lorimer. The **Tower Room** contains one of the four original death masks of Mary, Queen of Scots, and also her silver casket, a betrothal gift from her first husband, François II of France. There is also a portrait believed to be of *John Knox.*

A section devoted to the 20C features memorabilia from Rudolph Hess's flight to Scotland and the 14th Duke of Hamilton's historic first flight over Mount Everest .

Bed and Breakfast

In 2006 Lennoxlove closed for a year of major refurbishment and reopened in 2007 with 11 newly created luxury suites allowing visitors for the first time to be able to sleep in the house.

A 16th century four-poster bed, reputedly slept in by Mary Queen of Scots, was also unveiled for the first time. Made of solid black oak and beautifully refurbished, the bed is thought to have been used by the much persecuted Mary when under guard at Arden Hall in North Yorkshire. It is intricately carved and has been restored to the magnificent comfort and style that befitted a monarch at the time. It is draped in long, deep red velvet curtains which have been embroidered in the exact style of the Tudor times, replicating many of the embroideries known to have been stitched by Mary herself. In the 16C higher nobility literally travelled with their beds. As a result, they were made exceptionally well and the framework of this bed is still more or less as it was four hundred years ago.

Most remarkably, set in The Lady's Bower, a room within Lennoxlove's original 14C tower, it is available for guests to sleep in and not just admire.

LINLITHGOW★★
WEST LOTHIAN
POPULATION 9,524

The now quiet residential town of Linlithgow gives little hint of its dramatic past which centred on the royal palace. Today the town remains little altered in plan, on the south bank of a loch, away from the busy M 9 motorway.

- 🏛 **Information:** Burgh Halls, The Cross. ☎01506 844 600. www.edinburgh.org.
- 👁 **Don't Miss:** The Palace fountain and hooded fireplace.
- ▶ **Orient Yourself:** Linlithgow is 22mi/35km east of Edinburgh via the M 9.
- 🕐 **Organizing Your Time:** Allow 2–3 hours.
- 🧒 **Especially for Kids:** A trip on the Bo'ness and Kinneil Railway.
- 🔆 **Also See:** SOUTH QUEENSFERRY.

A Bit of History

Royal burgh – The history of the town is essentially that of its palace. The royal burgh grew up around the manor house and as early as Edward I's time its strategic role controlling the east-west route was appreciated. The burgh with its port at Blackness flourished and in 1368 its importance was such that it was included in the Court of the Four Burghs. With the rebuilding of both the palace and St Michael's, the 15C and 16C was a time of great prosperity which ended with the Union of the Crowns.

Despite the introduction of the leather industry during the Commonwealth, the smaller landward burghs like Linlithgow declined in the face of competition from the great industrial centres of the west coast flourishing on Atlantic trade. In 1822 the **Union Canal** was opened and prospered for 20 years. The barges were eclipsed with the coming of the railway in 1842, reviving the town's fortunes.

Linlithgow Palace★★
45min

(HS) ♿🕐*Open year-round daily 9.30am– 5.30pm (Oct–Mar 4.30pm). Last admission 45mins before closing. 🕐Closed 25–26 Dec, 1–2 Jan. ✇£5. ☎01506 842 896. www.historic-scotland.gov.uk.*

The formidably bare and vast form of the former royal residence dominates the town and loch of Linlithgow from its promontory site. The layout of this now roofless 15C–17C building with its

Linlithgow Palace

W. Buss/ MICHELIN

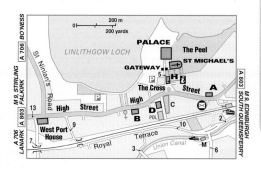

many staircases and corridors is typical of a search for comfort and a more logical disposition.

Manor house

Originally on an island site it was appreciated for its strategic location and for the good hunting in the surrounding countryside. The original manor house, accompanied by a conveniently near place of worship, was encircled by a wooden palisade by Edward I on his 1301–02 winter campaign. David II rebuilt the manor and it was his edifice that was gutted by a fire which ravaged the town, church and manor in 1424. On the return of the third Stewart king, James I, from 18 years' captivity in England, he undertook the first phase of construction from 1425 to 1435.

Favourite royal residence

It was during the reigns of James IV and V that Linlithgow became a favoured royal residence. **James IV** was responsible for another period of building and alterations (1490–1530) probably partly in preparation for his new bride Margaret Tudor, whom he married in 1503 and who spent most of her married life here. This was Scotland's Golden Age and their court was a glittering one with Linlithgow Palace fully participating in the round of merry pursuits. On 10 April 1512 the future James V was born here. Following this, the dowager queen left with her children for Stirling.

James V had his father's same love for Linlithgow Palace and often resided here. It was his second wife, Mary of Guise, who declared "she had never seen such a princely palace". Having lost two sons, Mary of Guise gave birth

to the future Mary, Queen of Scots on 8 December 1542 only days before the king died. As Regent, Mary of Guise continued to visit the great palace as did Mary, Queen of Scots on several occasions but its heyday was past and decline set in with the removal of the court to London following the Union of the Crowns (1603).

The north wing was rebuilt, after the roof collapsed, from 1618 to 1620; later occupants included Cromwell and troops (1650–59). There was a fleeting visit by Bonnie Prince Charlie in 1745 and subsequently by the Duke of Cumberland's troops after whose stay fire gutted the palace leaving it the roofless ruin now standing.

Gateway★

The single-storey gateway, built by James V c.1535 at the head of the Kirkgate, gives access to the Royal Park wherein stand the palace and St Michael's Church. The town side of the gateway is adorned with four gaily painted orders, 19C representations of the originals, showing The Garter, The Thistle, The Golden Fleece and St Michael.

Courtyard

The centrepiece of the inner close is the magnificently intricate stone **fountain**★★ built by James V in the 1530s. Octagonal in shape, the three basins decreasing in size are adorned by figures, buttresses, roundels, arms and various bearers.

The courtyard elevations present a variety of styles and decorative devices.

Of the four ranges three are 15C–16C while the north one is 17C. On the east side above the round-headed arch of the former entrance, three canopied niches with angels above are surmounted by an elaborate moulding. The more strictly symmetrical north elevation (1618–20) with its regular string courses has window pediments sporting some of the national emblems.

Take the northeast spiral staircase to reach the main apartments on the first floor.

Interior at first floor level

To the left of the Screens Passage is the kitchen with its vast fireplace. The **Great Hall**, of impressive dimensions, runs the full length of the east range. At the dais end is a superb **hooded fireplace**★★ with delicately carved ornamentation. Beyond the corner solar, the **chapel** retains four elaborately carved, but statueless, canopied niches between the windows. The remaining part of this wing is occupied by a hall followed by a corner chamber. Both of these ranges have the innovative feature of a corridor running along the courtyard side.

The apartments of the west range include the King's Hall, the Presence Chamber with an unusual window and, at the end, the King's Bed Chamber.

The adjoining **King's** and **Queen's Oratories** have beautifully carved bosses figuring the unicorn. A wooden gangway leads through the shell of the range, remodelled by William Wallace in the early 17C. The new style is clearly visible in the decoration of the remaining fireplaces.

Look in the various ground floor cellars and guard-rooms and take one of the turnpikes (*northwest*) for an overall view of the palace and its setting.

Exterior

The striking feature of the entrance façade is the group of five closely-set **lancet windows** indicating the chapel. As one moves round to the east façade, the original entrance is flanked by elongated canopied niches with, above, the royal coat of arms. The Great Hall is identifiable by the great window and six fairly large windows slightly higher up. The openings of the 17C north front are more numerous and regular while on the plainer west face the corner towers are more easily distinguished.

St Michael's

🕐 *Open May–Sept Mon–Sat 10am–4pm, Sun 12.30pm. Oct–Apr Mon–Fri 10.30am–1.30pm.* ☎ *01506 842 188. www.stmichaelsparish.org.uk.*

The present building is essentially the 15C reconstruction of an earlier one destroyed by fire. This burgh church is one of the largest pre-Reformation ecclesiastic buildings and took over a century to complete. Construction started with the nave progressing to the choir (1497), the tower and finally the apse (c.1531).

Exterior

The most striking external feature of this aisled cruciform building with transeptal chapels and a polygonal apse is the west end tower with its **spire**, which however controversial, maintains the medieval tradition that any addition to a church should be in the style of the period to emphasise that it is both ancient and modern. The Geoffrey Clarke laminated timber and aluminium spire was erected in 1964 to replace an earlier crown spire. Also original is the **south porch** with an unusual oriel window above, flanked by a turret staircase. Farther round on the southwest buttress the only statue to survive the "cleansing" by the Lords of the Congregation in 1559 is a weathered, bewinged and armoured St Michael.

Interior

Pleasingly plain with little sculptural ornament, the pointed arcades and clustered piers of the five-bay **nave** continue for three bays into the chancel, separated only by the great chancel arch, and terminate with the tall windows of the three-sided apse. The elevation in both parts is similar excepting the blind triforium in the chancel. The nave, chancel and apse are roofed with a 19C plaster ceiling (replacing an 1812 oak roof) while the original rib vaulting still covers the aisles and transept chapels. Particularly worthy of attention are the **tracery** and **stained glass**. Perpendicular tracery fills the three tall apse windows while the stained glass of the central one (eight lights) portrays Psalm 104 (The Creation). The window overlooking the war memorial in the chancel's south aisle traces the history of the church and depicts three sovereigns: James IV, David I and Queen Victoria. Note, above, the stonemasons at work. Just before the transept chapel is a lovely Burne-Jones design (1899) in muted colours. The jewel of the church is the Flamboyant **window** in the south transept chapel with highly decorative and unusual tracery above the six lights. It was in this chapel that James IV was said to have seen the ghost forewarning him of impending doom at Flodden.

Town★

The town has conserved its medieval layout, with a long main street backed by its burgess plots, widening at the market place and closed by its ports. The arrival of the railway destroyed the town wall to the north.

The Cross
This, the former market place, has in the centre the **cross well**, a 19C replica of its predecessor. On the north side is the grandly imposing **Town Hall** which dates from the 17C. Cromwell destroyed the original. The present divided staircase is a 20C replacement for a wrought-iron loggia.
Inside is the Tourist Information Centre with an exhibition on the town and its surroundings "The Burgh and Beyond".

High Street
In East High Street **nos 40–48** are known as Hamilton Lands (⚷ *not open to the public*). These rubblework, crow-stepped and gable-ended dwellings are typical of the late 16C–early 17C when Linlithgow was still at the height of its mercantile prosperity. The narrow frontages corresponded to the width of the burghal lot (rig) and the round-arched pend was a typical feature of such layouts. There are more in West High Street.

A plaque on the wall of the Sheriff Court marks the approximate site of Archbishop Hamilton's house, from which the Regent Moray was shot in 1570. The latter died and the archbishop was later hanged for suspected complicity in this incident and the Darnley murder.
Annet House has displays which tell **The Linlithgow Story** (ⓘ *open Good Fri–Oct Mon–Sat 11am–5pm, Sun 1pm–4pm;* ⌨ *£2;* 🅿; ☎01506 670 677, www.linlithgowstory.org.uk), with emphasis on the town's royal connections and the development of crafts and trades. **West Port House**, as the name suggests, marked the site of the west gate. The three-storey, L-plan house dating from 1600 retains a turret staircase.
In a charming setting just above the town, at the Manse Street Basin, is the **Linlithgow Canal Centre** (♿ⓘ *open Jul–Aug daily 2pm–5pm; Easter Sat–Jun and Sept–first weekend Oct, Sat–Sun 2pm–5pm;* ⌨; 🅿; ☎01506 671 215, www.lucs.org.uk). There is a small museum here and boat trips can be made along the Union Canal to the 12-arch aqueduct over the River Avon, 2.5mi/4km to the west.

Excursions

Bo'ness and Kinneil Railway 🧒
4mi/6.5km north on the A 706. ♿ⓘ*Trains run Jul–Aug daily; mid-Mar to mid-Oct, Sat–Sun. Exhibition open: Apr–Oct during train operating times. Phone or see website for details.* ⌨. 🅿. ☎01506 822 298. www.srps.org.uk.
A station and a track (3.5mi/6km) have been rebuilt by the Scottish Railway Preservation Society to display its large collection of items from the country's railway heritage. The station complex, with booking office, footbridge, canopy and signalbox evokes the era of the North British, one of the major Scottish railway companies. A large shed by the disused whaling dock is home to the **Scottish Railway Exhibition** which displays locomotives, rolling stock and general railway paraphernalia.
Steam trips run along the foreshore, inland to Birkhill station, and to the underground **Birkhill Fireclay Mine**

(☎ visits by guided tour only Jul–Aug daily; Apr–Jun and early Sept–mid-Oct, Sat–Sun; ♿ Be sure to wear suitable clothes; ₤3.50; ☎01506 822 298, www.srps.org.uk).

Blackness Castle

4mi/6.5km northeast on the A 803 and B 903. (HS). ◷Open Apr–Sept daily 9.30am–5.30pm. Oct–Mar Sat–Wed 9.30am–4.30pm. Last admission 30mins before closing. ◷Closed 25–26 December, 1–2 January. ₤4. ☎01506 834807, www.historic-scotland.gov.uk.

The now peaceful village of Blackness was once the flourishing seaport for Linlithgow. Likewise its castle, standing on a rocky promontory, jutting out into the Firth of Forth, was formerly one of the most important in the kingdom.

Following the Union of 1707, it was one of four Scottish strongholds (the others were Edinburgh, Stirling and Dumbarton) to be garrisoned. It has also served as a royal castle, a prison for Covenanters, an ordnance depot and latterly a youth hostel.

The stronghold was built in the shape of a ship. The south or "stern" tower is 16C with curtain walls of the same period enclosing a 15C central tower and meeting at the north or "bow" tower, reduced to serve as a gun platform. The latter affords a fine **view** across the Firth of Forth and its famous bridges.

The Binns

4mi/6.5km northeast by a 803, then after crossing the M 9 take the A 904 to the right. ♿See The BINNS.

LOCH LOMOND ★★
ARGYLL, BUTE AND STIRLING

The legendary beauty of the "Queen of Scottish Lochs", so often celebrated in song and verse, is one of blue waters flanked by shapely mountains or fringed by pastoral wooded shores. The loch is 23mi/37km long and 5mi/8km at its widest and has a maximum depth of 653ft/200m. The water discharges into the Firth of Clyde by the River Leven.

- ▮ **Information:** Balloch Road, Balloch. ☎08707 200 607. www.visitscottishheartlands.com, www.lochlomond-trossachs.org.
- ▶ **Orient Yourself:** Balloch, at the southernmost point of Loch Lomond, is 20mi/32km northwest of Glasgow via the A 82.
- ⓟ **Parking:** Difficult in high season.
- ◉ **Don't Miss:** Luss, Ben Lomond.
- ◉ **Drivers:** It is advisable to avoid summer weekends, as traffic on the busy west shore road is often very dense.
- ◷ **Organizing Your Time:** Allow a full day.
- ▦ **Especially for Kids:** Loch Lomond Shores (Loch Lomond Aquarium and The Ceramic Experience).
- ◔ **Also See:** STIRLING.

Loch

This area of outstanding natural beauty has been designated as the **Loch Lomond & the Trossachs National Park** – Scotland's first national park. The ruggedly mountainous scenery of the narrow northern end changes in the south to a more pastoral setting of wooded islands and shores. For walkers, part of the West Highland Way from Glasgow to Fort William follows the east shore.

Loch Lomond Shores ▦

Ben Lomond Way, Balloch. ♿◷Open year-round daily 10am–5pm, extended hours in summer. ☎ 0845 4580 885. www.lochlomondshores.com.

This spectacular visitor centre on the water's edge is the perfect introduc-

Loch Lomond

tion to the Loch and National Park. It hosts a range of activities and attractions including the **Loch Lomond Aquarium** (£8.46, child £5.91; ☎01389 721500, www.sealifeeurope.com); **The Ceramic Experience** (☎01389 750760; www.theceramicexperience.com; create your own ceramic ware from £2); canoe, kayak, pedal boat and mountain bike hire and boat trips (Apr–Oct. The complex is also, somewhat confusingly, home to the **Loch Lomond & the Trossachs National Park Gateway Centre** (☎0845 345 4978, www.lochlomond

-trossachs.org) explores the nature, geology and social history of the National Park, and includes a pond and wetland area, direct access to Loch Lomond and woodland walks incorporating specially commissioned environmental artworks.

Sites and Towns

Inchmurrin
The largest of the 30 or so islands speckling the wider southern part of the loch.

Address Book

⚓For coin ranges, see the Legend on the cover flap.

WHERE TO STAY
Lomond View – Tarbet. ☎0130 170 2477. www.lomondview.co.uk. Three spacious light airy bedrooms are tastefully decorated in tartan with Norwegian pine furniture; a terrace offers panoramic loch views.

Lodge on Loch Lomond – Luss. ☎01436 860 201. www.lochlomond.co.uk. This hotel merges the traditional and the contemporary to provide luxury accommodation and has attracted two United States Presidents. Colquhouns **restaurant** () is recommended).

De Vere Cameron House Hotel, Balloch – ☎01389 755 565, www.cameronhouse.co.uk. Extensive Victorian House in a picturebook setting on the loch among wooded parkland. Luxurious rooms and superb leisure facilities include spa and golf.

WHERE TO EAT
Lomonds – De Vere Cameron House Hotel, Balloch. ☎01389 755 565. www.cameronhouse.co.uk. A refined and elegant meal, using notably fine local ingredients, served in superb lochside surroundings.

Boat trips

By far the best way to discover the charms of Loch Lomond is to take to the water. Boat trips depart in summer from Balloch with the Loch Lomond Steamship Company, aboard the last paddle steamer built in Britain (*www.maidoftheloch.co.uk*, ☎01389 711865); and with Sweeney Cruises (☎01389 752 376, *www.sweeneyscruises.com*). Cruise Loch Lomond operate from Tarbet (☎£5.50. ☎01301 702 356, *www.cruiselochlomondltd.com*). Stopping points are Balloch Luss, Rowardennan, Tarbet and Inversnaid.

At the southern tip are the ruins of what was once a Lennox stronghold.

Inchcailloch

Nature Reserve. Balmaha marks the passage of the Highland Boundary Fault where mountains suddenly rise out of lowlands.

Luss★

Population 256. A very attractive village with mellow coloured-stone cottages. Beyond Luss the loch narrows and the mountains close in.

Rowardennan Hotel

The loch's eastern road ends at this landmark. A path leads from the pier to the summit of Ben Lomond.

Ben Lomond★★

The shapely form of this 3,192ft/974m peak rises on the east shore behind Rowardennan. This is the most southerly of the Highland Munros.

On a level with Tarbet, the dramatic pile of Ben Arthur (2,891ft/881m), better known as the Cobbler, rises in the distance.

Tarbet

Population 257. Tarbet lies at the head of a short valley which leads southwestwards to Arrochar. The Vikings are said to have hauled their galleys over this neck of land to claim sovereignty over the peninsula.

Inversnaid – See The TROSSACHS.

From here there is a splendid **view**, across the loch, of the mountains on the far shore: left to right the craggy shaped **Cobbler**, then a group of four, A'Chrois, Beinn Ime (3,318ft/1,011m) and Chorranach farther back with Ben Vane rising from the lochside.

MANDERSTON★
SCOTTISH BORDERS

Manderston is a splendid Edwardian country house, in immaculate grounds, where the hallmark of extravagant splendour applies throughout.

- **Information:** ☎01361 882 010. www.manderston.co.uk.
- **Orient Yourself:** 2 mi/3km east of Duns and 16mi/25km west of Berwick-upon-Tweed via the A 6105.
- **Don't Miss:** The stables, where traditional Edwardian cream teas are served.
- **Also See:** ST ABB'S HEAD, MELLERSTAIN, EYEMOUTH, BERWICK-UPON-TWEED.

Visit

House open mid-May through Sept, Thu & Sun 1.30pm–5pm. Last admission 4.15pm Gardens open 11.30am–sunset. ☎£8 (gardens only, £4.50).

Exterior

The long, low, two-storeyed building beneath a balustraded roof is interrupted on the south or garden front by two gracefully curved projections and a front porticoed entrance.

Manderston, an Edwardian country house

Interior

The supreme craftsmanship of **plaster-work ceilings**, doors, fireplaces and furnishings are matched by the quality of the materials – marble, rosewood, mahogany, alabaster, brass, silver... and the refinement of the objets d'art. John Kinross' interior designs are in the manner of Robert Adam.

Ground floor

The impressively spacious **Hall** heightened by the dome, fringed by delicate plasterwork, opens into the Anteroom with alabaster panels, leading to the Dining Room. Completed in 1905 with an elaborate compartmented ceiling, it holds a unique Blue John collection.

The Library, doubling as a billiard room, is hung with crimson silk damask Double door lead to the richly decorated **Ballroom** with embossed silk and velvet wall hangings, and century-old curtains woven with gold or silver threads. In the Tea Room a Lutyens painting shows the Miller children grouped round a dog by Landseer. Sir James, responsible for the house as it stands today, is on the left.

First Floor

The same luxury and attention to detail applies to bedrooms and bathrooms.

Basement

One of the more fascinating aspects of the visit is the vast domain of kitchen, scullery, five larders, housekeeper's room, linen store and servants' hall, a highly organised realm, where the housekeeper and the butler reigned supreme over an impressive army of domestic staff.

Grounds, gardens and outbuildings

The south front overlooks terraced gardens and grassy slopes down to the lake with, on the far side, the Woodland Garden (rhododendrons and azaleas) and on a clear day the Cheviots as backdrop.

On the entrance front, manicured lawns and majestic trees precede gates to formal gardens. Beyond, the Marble Dairy, in the form of a chapter-house, has an oak-panelled tea room above. Nearby is the head gardener's house with its walled garden.

The refinement of the **stables**★, arranged around two courtyards, is all the more striking for being unexpected. Teak and brass predominate while in the mahogany panelled harness room both the floor and the central table are of marble.

Manderston is now the home of Lord and Lady Palmer, of Huntley & Palmers biscuit fame. A **Biscuit Tin Museum** celebrates the history of this colourful container.

MELLERSTAIN★★
SCOTTISH BORDERS
⚙LOCAL MAP SEE THE TWEED VALLEY

Mellerstain is famous for the amazing detail and delicacy of Robert Adam interiors, gracing a house of homely proportions.

- **Information:** ☎01573 410 225, www.mellerstain.com.
- ▶ **Orient Yourself:** Mellerstain is 7 mi/11km northwest of Kelso, just off the A 6089.
- ⊙ **Don't Miss:** The ceilings, the Library.
- ⊙ **Organizing Your Time:** Allow 1hr.
- ⚙ **Also See:** FLOORS CASTLE, KELSO, DRYBURGH ABBEY, MANDERSTON.

A Bit of History

The Mellerstain estate was purchased in 1642 by a Lanarkshire man and passed in 1646 to his son Robert Baillie, a staunch Covenanter. Imprisoned in Edinburgh's Tolbooth he was visited by his friend's daughter, Grisell Hume, who on that occasion met for the first time her future husband, the young **George Baillie** (1664–1738). Several years were to pass, including exile and hardship in Holland for both families, before a return in 1688 to their native Borders and the marriage of Grisell to George Baillie in 1692. **Lady Grisell Baillie** (1665–1746), a remarkable woman of many parts, was Mellerstain's heroine and mistress, ruling her household with efficiency, unbounded energy and gentleness. She lived to see the completion of the William Adam wings but on her death the estate passed to her grandson George Baillie who engaged **Robert Adam** (1728–92) to bridge the gap between the two wings.

House

⊙*House open: Easter weekend, May–Jun & Sept Wed, Sun and Mon Bank Hols 12.30pm–5pm. Jul–Aug Wed–Thu & Sun–Mon 12.30pm–5pm. Oct Sun only 12.30pm–5pm. Last admission 4.15pm. Gardens open: same dates, 11.30am–5.30pm. Snowdrop Days: mid and late Feb and early Mar (see website for dates) 11.30am–4pm, ✎guided walk at 2pm. ⊙£6 (gardens only, £3.50). ⊙.*

Exterior
Rarely did Robert Adam plan a house from beginning to end, as he did here; Mellerstain is even more rare in that Adam's father designed the wings for this home.
Imposingly plain, the exterior comprises the yellow stone castellated centre by Robert Adam flanked at right angles by the two earlier wings by his father William. Although only 45 years separate the constructions, the contrast in architectural styles is striking and best seen from the courtyard front. The wings of 1725 have a certain vernacular charm compared with the severity and plainness of the castellated Gothic centre.

Interior
Less grandiose than elsewhere (Culzean, Osterley, Syon) but nonetheless so typically Adam, it boasts a series of remarkable **ceilings★★★**, often with matching fireplaces, woodwork and furniture.

Stone Hall
Part of the William Adam wing, this room has a Delft tile-adorned fireplace. On display in the east corridor is an original copy of the National Covenant subscribed by the 2nd Earl of Haddington. In the eastern section of the main corridor are several portraits including *Lady Grisell Baillie* by Aikman (1717) and *Lady Murray*, her daughter, by Richardson.

Sitting Room
Adam designed a Gothic ceiling and a fireplace with Dutch tiles for this room. The furniture is principally from the

Queen Anne period. The ornate mirror over the fireplace is in the style of Adam. There are many sporting paintings.

Library★★★

An initial impression of colour – pale green, ivory white, pink, blue-grey – and of an overall grand design with the delicately detailed ceiling as centrepiece, slowly gives way to a perception of constituent components: the Zucci roundels – *Minerva, Learning* and *Teaching* – vases, medallions, trophies and figure panels and recesses, with the unifying pattern echoed in the bookcases, frieze, fireplace, superbly carved doors and mirror cupboards of the window wall. The Roubiliac busts of Lady Grisell Baillie and her daughter face each other above the end wall doors.

Music Room

It was designed as the Dining Room; the plain claret-coloured walls provide a sharp contrast to the highly decorative ceiling with plaster reliefs of urns, eagles, sphinxes, medallions, rinceaux and fan ornaments surrounding the central medallion. The end wall pier glasses are to Adam's designs; above the fireplace is *Patrick Hume* by William Aikman with, to the left and right, his granddaughters by Maria Varelst, *Grisell, Lady Murray* and *Rachel, Lady Binning* respectively.

Drawing Room

The room is rich and ornate, with heavily patterned silk brocade wall hangings and Aubusson carpet, ormolu mounted furniture, and the overall effect is again in sharp contrast to the two preceding rooms. The ceiling colour scheme is subdued and includes a griffin and vase pattern which is repeated in the frieze. The Adam design on the satinwood side table is echoed in the marble fireplace. Of the portraits, several are by Allan Ramsay, or Old Mumpy as Adam called him, including *Lady Murray, Lord Binning* and *Dr Torriano* (1738), one of the first paintings executed by the artist while in Italy.

Small Drawing Room

Originally a bedchamber, the Adam imprint is everywhere, in the octagon designed ceiling, frieze, fireplace and massive mirror. The Italian commode and small cupboards are late 18C.

Small Library

This small room, originally two dressing-rooms, has the distinction of having two different Adam ceilings.

Main Corridor

The ceiling design again differs from that of the eastern section and is decidedly Gothic in inspiration. The paintings include family portraits.

Main Staircase

A majestic double staircase climbs and unites to rise as a single flight to the first floor, where an early-16C Flemish hunting tapestry is displayed. Several bedrooms are open; note in particular in the Manchineel Bedroom, the 19C carpet, handwoven in Alloa.

Great Gallery

The final surprise, on the second floor, is a noble apartment with screens of Ionic columns at either end, alas unfinished. Adam's proposed design is on display, as is his father's project for the central block. *Lady Grisell Baillie* and *George Baillie* are portrayed by Medina. The enigma remains – what was the function of this gallery and why was it never completed?

Return to the Inner Hall; the mirror and table are Adam works. Among the canvases there is a beautiful conversation piece by Nasmyth.

Grounds and gardens

In the vaulted halls of the old servants' quarters, the **Mellerstain Art Gallery** offers temporary exhibitions of modern Scottish paintings.

The Italian-styled terraced garden was laid out in 1909 by Sir Reginald Blomfield and commands a glorious view overlooking the lake to the Cheviot Hills in the distance.

MELROSE ★
SCOTTISH BORDERS
POPULATION 2,143
🔎 LOCAL MAP SEE THE TWEED VALLEY

Grouped round its beautiful abbey ruins, in the middle reaches of the Tweed, Melrose is overshadowed by the triple peaks of the Eildons. This attractive town bustles with visitors in the summer and makes an ideal touring centre for exploring the surrounding countryside. The town's Summer Festival and the day of the Melrose Sevens (7-a-side rugby football tournament) are lively occasions.

- **Information:** Abbey House. ☎08706 080404. www.scot-borders.co.uk.
- ▶ **Orient Yourself:** Melrose is in the heart of the Scottish Borders 43 mi/69km south of Edinburgh via the A 68.
- **Don't Miss:** Melrose Abbey decorative sculptures; the panoramas from Eildon Hill North and Scott's View; Dryburgh Abbey.
- **Organizing Your Time:** One hour for the Abbey, an hour for the town.
- **Also See:** ABBOTSFORD, TWEED VALLEY.

Melrose Abbey ★★

(HS) ⏱*Open year-round daily 9.30am–5.30pm (Oct–Mar 4.30pm). Last admission 30min before closing.* ⏱*Closed 25–26 December, 1–2 January.* £5. ☎01896 822562. www.historic-scotland.gov.uk.
The fertile Tweed haughlands were traditionally the site of early settlers and the Cistercian monks who settled **David I's** 1136 foundation proved no exception when choosing the site of their new abbey. The monks from Rievaulx built an original 12C church which was damaged by 14C raids, in particular by Edward II's retreating army of 1322. Robert the Bruce ensured the rebuilding of the abbey and it was here that his heart was buried. The community grew and prospered becoming probably the richest abbey in Scotland, a fact which was not to save it from the fate of most Scottish abbeys: passing into secular hands, decline of the community and subsequent decay of the building. The ruins date from the late 14C–early 16C and are in a pure Gothic style. It was Sir Walter Scott who initiated repairs between 1822 and 1826 securing for posterity some of the loveliest ruins and establishing them as a must for travellers in the mid 19C.

Abbey Church
The harmony of the stone, with tints varying from ochre to red, the profusion of decorative sculptural work, so uncharacteristic of the Cistercian order, and the purity of the Gothic style make for an extremely impressive and attractive group of ruins.

Exterior
To appreciate fully the **decorative sculpture** ★★★ walk round the outside. The chapels of the south side are lit by a series of large pointed windows with elegant tracery, separated by pinnacled buttresses. The south transept gable is a profusion of detailed sculptural work. The pointed-arched, moulded doorway is surmounted by the great south window. The east gable with the great oriel and its fragile tracery is crowned at the apex with the *Coronation of the Virgin*.

Interior
A pulpitum divides the lay brothers' choir from the monks' choir. On the nave's south side the clustered piers support moulded pointed arches which open onto eight chapels. The **choir** beyond the pulpitum has later buttressing work and barrel-vaulting, as this once served as parish church. The north transept still has statues of St Peter and St Paul

above the west clerestory windows. The south transept frames the impressive **window**.

Cloister

Conforming to usual practice, buildings border the garth and walks on all sides. The east range housed the chapter-house in the centre and dormitory above, the north the kitchens and refectory, the west the early frater with the lay brothers' cloister beyond. The arcading on the east wall and north processional doorway with a highly ornamental accolade to the right are the main features.

Commendator's House

Across the road and over the Great Drain.

A museum in this restored building contains sculptural fragments, explanations on construction methods, in addition to exhibits on Trimontium and Sir Walter Scott's associations with Melrose.

Additional Sights

Trimontium

The Ormiston, The Square. ⏱*Open Apr–Oct daily 10.30am–4.30pm.* ✆*£3 (tea/coffee included).* ☎*01896 822 651/463.*
Trimontium was the largest Roman fort in Scotland, built by Agricola in the 1C AD, at nearby Newstead. Finds made here in the early 20C (now at Edinburgh) gave an unparalleled insight into the life of the Roman soldier on this far frontier of the Empire. This small museum features more recent excavations.

Priorwood Garden

Entrance Abbey Street. (NTS) ♿⏱*Open Good Fri–24 Dec Mon–Sat noon–4pm, Sun 1pm–5pm.* ✆*£3.* ☎*0844 4932 257. www.nts.org.uk.*
Next to the abbey precincts this small garden specialises in flowers for drying; their shop (*open all year*) sells the results of their labours. The roadside wall has attractive ironwork by Lutyens.

High Street

The street is bordered by some fine 18C buildings in the vicinity of the Market Square, with its 17C mercat cross.

Address Book

♿*For coin ranges, see the Legend on the cover flap.*

WHERE TO STAY

◖◗ **Fauhope House** – *off Monkswood Road, Gattonside.* ☎*01896 823 184. www.fauhopehouse. com.* Melrose Abbey is just visible from this stylish and charming 19C Arts and Crafts-type house with antiques and fine furniture.

◖◗◗ **Burt's Hotel** – *Market Square.* ☎*01896 822 285. www.burtshotel. co.uk.* This one-time coaching inn on the main square is now a friendly family-run hotel with unpretentious rooms and an excellent **restaurant** ◖◗. This cosy clubby place with hunting scenes and rich tartans, serves modern Scottish cuisine featuring well-sourced local produce.

Eildon Hills

Leave Melrose by the Lilliesleaf B 6359 road, turning left at the signpost Eildon Walk. Cross the bridge then follow the path leading up to the saddle between the two summits. 1hr 30min there and back. Wear sturdy shoes for the grassy slopes if it is wet.

The Eildons are of volcanic origin, but legend has it that this triple-peaked hill was the work of the 13C wizard **Michael Scott**, who is buried in Melrose Abbey. Scott was in fact a mathematician, philosopher, doctor of theology and friend of the Emperor Frederick II. He figures in Dante's *Inferno* as Michele Scotto. The peaks are a conspicuous landmark in the region and the Eildon Hill North (1,325ft/404m), which was successively an Iron Age hill fortress and Roman signal station, now provides a magnificent **panorama**★★★: Melrose and its abbey, the Leaderfoot viaduct, Smailholm Tower, east and south to the Cheviots, Peniel Heugh with its monument round to the Tweed again and the Gala Water Valley with Galashiels.

Driving Tour

Scott's View★★

Leave Melrose by the B 6361. Continue down towards the river passing the viaduct, turn left onto the A 68, then right once over the river to climb down towards the river at Leaderfoot taking the local road up the flank of Bemersyde Hill. Turn right onto the B 6356.

Scott's View★★

Viewfinder 593ft/181m. This panoramic view of typical Border scenery encompasses the Tweed Valley with Melrose and Galashiels, the Eildons sloping down to Newtown St Boswells, then round to Minto, Rubers and Black Laws. In the near foreground is Bemersyde House, presented in 1921 by a grateful nation to Earl Haig who is buried in Dryburgh Abbey. Down on the Tweed meander is Old Melrose, the original site of the Cistercian settlement.

▶ *Continue by the local road to Dryburgh Abbey in its fine setting.*

Dryburgh Abbey★★ –
See DRYBURGH ABBEY.

▶ *Return to Leaderfoot and take B 6360 under A 68 overpass and viaduct to follow the north bank of the Tweed.*

This stretch of road has most attractive views over the valley and Melrose, before reaching Gattonside, once the site of the abbey orchards.

▶ *Turn left over the Tweed and left again back into Melrose.*

Newstead

Population 195. East of Melrose this attractive hamlet was the home of the stonemasons who built Melrose Abbey and is reputedly the oldest inhabited place in Scotland. A memorial by the roadside just out of Newstead marks the site of Trimontium.

MOFFAT
DUMFRIES AND GALLOWAY
POPULATION 1,990
LOCAL MAP SEE THE TWEED VALLEY

A small town at the head of Annandale, Moffat is set in the heart of beautiful countryside. Once a flourishing spa in the 18C, the town is now principally a market centre for the surrounding hill sheep farming area and a tourist centre handily placed for the ample excursions into the hills around.

- **Information:** Churchgate. ☎01683 220 620. www.visitdumfriesandgalloway.co.uk
- ▶ **Orient Yourself:** Moffat is just off the M 74, 21 mi/34km north of Dumfries on the A 701.
- **Don't Miss:** the Grey Mare's Tail waterfall.
- **Also See:** BOWHILL, DUMFRIES.

Moffat House Hotel

High Street. John Adam built this 18C mansion as a residence for the 2nd Earl of Hopetoun. The severity of the design is relieved by the contrasting colours and textures of the building materials. It was during his stay as a tutor that James Macpherson (1738–96) "translated" the Ossian Fragments.

Colvin Fountain

High Street. The bronze ram on the fountain testifies to the importance of sheep farming in the area.

Moffat Museum

The Neuk. Open Easter and Whitsun–Sept, Thu–Sat and Mon–Tue 10.30am–5pm, Sun 2.30–5pm. ☎01683 220 868.

A snow topped Hart Fell in the Moffat Hills

A. Devlin/ Scottish Viewpoint

The story of Moffat through the centuries with such topics as clan warfare, Covenanting and its heyday as a spa.

Excursion

Tweedsmuir Hills
The route climbs out of the Annan Valley over into the wilder scenery of the Moffat Water Valley, a classic U-shaped glacially deepened valley.

Grey Mare's Tail★★
The Tail Burn forms this spectacular waterfall as it plunges 200ft/61m from the hanging valley to join the Moffat Water. A sheep pen near the roadside car park provides explanatory notes on the geological history of the site. Two paths lead to the waterfall. The one on the left, the easier, leads to the bottom of the waterfall, while the one on the right, much steeper and stonier (🅿 Stout footwear needed) climbs up to the valley and Loch Skeen.
The road moves up the narrow V-shaped valley to cross the pass and descend into another glacially valley of the Little Yarrow Water. Between the Loch of Lowes and St Mary's Loch, originally one, stands Tibbie Sheil's Inn, the meeting place of **James Hogg** (1770–1835), "the Ettrick Shepherd" and his friends, made famous by Christopher North's accounts. On the slope beyond the souvenir shop and café is a statue of him.

St Mary's Loch
The handsome hill setting is reflected in the waters of the loch which provides good sailing and trout fishing.

Take the road left, signposted Tweedsmuir (11 mi/18km) following Megget Water.

Megget Dam and Reservoir
With its curved grass-covered embankment the dam, which part supplies the Lothian Region, blends well into the landscape. There are good viewing points on the road running along the north shore of the reservoir.

The road down suddenly affords a splendid view of the Talla Reservoir – source of Edinburgh's water supply – in its hill setting. Turn left onto A 701. Pass on the left the source of the Tweed on the northern side of the Tweedsmuir Hills.

Devil's Beef Tub
This steep-sided depression between the Tweedsmuir and Lowther Hills was so named after its use as a shelter for stolen cattle in reiving days.

Continue down Annandale where the valley is wider and the scene is one of a gentle arable landscape with Moffat nestling on the valley floor in the far distance.

MONTROSE
ANGUS
POPULATION 12,127

The East Coast town of Montrose sits on a peninsula between a tidal basin and the sea. The steeple of the parish church pinpoints the town from afar. Ever popular with summer visitors the town has a vast stretch of golden sand, several golf courses and scenic countryside nearby to explore. Montrose has always been a busy shopping centre and market town for the rich agricultural hinterland and a thriving port. Increased prosperity has accrued from North Sea Oil with the establishment of an oil base on the Ferryden side of the River South Esk.

- **Information:** Bridge Street. ☎01674 672000 www.angusanddundee.co.uk.
- ▶ **Orient Yourself:** Montrose is 29mi/47km northeast of Dundee on the A 92.
- **Organizing Your Time:** Allow two hours.
- **Especially for Kids:** The town's golden beach and sand dunes.
- **Also See:** ARBROATH.

A Bit of History

In the difficult times leading up to the Reformation, Montrose had more than its fair share of martyrs, most notably David Straton (d 1534) and **George Wishart** whose execution at St Andrews (*see ST ANDREWS*) in February 1546 sparked off reprisals which resulted in the stabbing of Cardinal Beaton. Protestant connections continued with John Knox who was a regular visitor to John Erskine at the nearby House of Dun. Erskine was the town's provost and one of the first Moderators. The tradition continued with Knox's follower, the scholar and linguist **Andrew Melville** (1554–1622), and his nephew James, who led a determined fight against James VI's policy to introduce Episcopacy. The former is remembered for his admonition to James VI that he was but "God's silly vassal".

Sights

High Street
The elongated triangular layout is medieval and many of the original wynds and closes between the burgess plots still remain. Interspersed between the substantial 17C and 18C buildings are a number of gable-ended houses from which the Montrosians acquired their nickname "gable endies". This feature is a relic of trading days with the Low Countries.

Old Town House
This 18C building, with a 19C addition, has an elegant arcade on the High Street side. It faces the statue of local worthy, Joseph Hume (1777–1855), a radical politician and reformer.

Old Church and Steeple
The Gothic steeple (220ft/68m), a notable landmark, was added to this 18C church by Gillespie Graham in the 19C. The famous Panniter Panels in the Museum of Scotland in Edinburgh came from the earlier church on this site.

Castlestead
At the south end of the High Street this castellated building is now used as offices. It was the site of a 13C castle which later became the town house of the Graham family and it may have been here that the town's most colourful historical character, James Graham, 5th Earl and 1st Marquis of Montrose was born in 1612. Accomplished in many fields, elegant, fastidious and vain, he was a natural military commander and fought as a Covenanter before switching his allegiance to the Royalist cause. He was defeated and betrayed however and executed in Edinburgh in 1650.

Montrose Museum

Panmure Place. ⟨♿⟩⟨🕐⟩*Open year-round Mon–Sat 10am–5pm.* ⟨🕐⟩*Closed 25–26 Dec and 1–2 Jan.* 🅿️. ☎ *01374 673 232. www.angus.gov.uk/history/museums/ montrose.*

The collection includes sections on the town's activities in the past (salmon fishing, 18C tobacco trade and whaling), natural history dioramas and biographical sections on famous citizens from James Graham, Marquis of Montrose, leader of the Royalist party, to the politician and reformer Joseph Hume, and William Lamb, the 20C sculptor. Note in particular the bust of his contemporary Hugh McDiarmid; one of Scotland's finest 20C poets, he was editor of the local paper in the 1920s.

William Lamb Sculpture Studio

Market Street. ⟨♿⟩⟨🕐⟩*Open Jul–mid-Sept, daily 2pm–5pm. Rest of year by appointment.* ☎ *01674 673 232. www.angus.gov. uk/history/museums/montrose.*

In this small studio is a display of sculptures, paintings and sketches by the relatively unknown but highly talented artist, **William Lamb** (1893–1951) – "one of the few original minds in Scottish art of this century". The bronzes have a verve and sureness of touch which is all the more remarkable given Lamb's history. Following a war wound to his favoured right hand, he taught himself to work anew with the left. The furniture of the panelled sitting room upstairs is reminiscent of Mackintosh's work. One of his life-size works, *The Seafarer*, cast posthumously, stands down by the harbour.

Excursion

Glen Esk★

29mi/47km via Brechin and Edzell. Leave Montrose by the A 935 west. ⟨♿⟩*See BRECHIN.*

House of Dun & Montrose Basin Nature Reserve

3mi/5km west on the A 935 Brechin Road.

⟨♿⟩⟨🕐⟩*Open Good Fri– Jun and Sept–Oct Wed–Sun (closed Mon and Tue, except Bank Hols when open Fri–Mon), 12.30– 5.30pm; Jul–Aug, daily 11.30am–5.30pm. (☞Visit by guided tours only, Wed– Sat). Last admission 45 mins before closing.* ⟨£⟩*£8.* ⟨☕⟩. *Garden and grounds open: year-round daily 9am–sunset.* ☎ *01674 810 264. www.nts.org.uk.*

William Adam built this fine Palladianstyle mansion in the early 18C for the Erskine lairds of Dun to replace an earlier castle. The house was remodelled in the 19C. The recent restoration combines features from both periods. The **reception rooms** show decorative features typical of "stone and lime": the garlands, swags, regalia, armorial trophies and allegorical scenes in the **Saloon** are by Joseph Enzer (1742–43).

On the first floor the decoration of the private rooms and the bedrooms re-creates the 19C setting. The Red Bedroom and the Tapestry Room contain 17C Flemish tapestries. The domestic rooms give an insight into life below stairs. The gardens are also being re-created. The parkland offers stunning views of the adjacent **Montrose Basin Nature Reserve** with access to Widgeon and Shellduck bird hides.

Montrose Basin Wildlife Centre

1mi/1.5km southwest by A 92. ⟨♿⟩⟨🕐⟩ *Visitor centre open: mid Mar to mid Nov daily. Rest of year Fri–Sun 10.30am–4pm. Reserve open: summer 8am–8pm, winter dawn–dusk.* ⟨🕐⟩*Closed 25–26 Dec & 1–2 Jan.* ⟨£⟩*£3.* 🅿️.☎ *01674 676 336. www.swt.org.uk.*

A striking modern visitor centre built by the Scottish Wildlife Trust perches on the southern rim of the splendid tidal tract of sheltered tidal water known as the Montrose Basin. The wetlands of the relatively unpolluted and undamaged basin are of great conservation interest and of first importance for migrating birds. Displays explain the ecology of tidal basins while the wildlife can be observed through high-powered binoculars (provided) and television cameras.

ISLE OF MULL★
ARGYLL AND BUTE
POPULATION 2,605

The Inner Hebridean island of Mull with its varied scenery and peacefulness is an ideal holiday centre and the stepping-stone for Iona.

🅸 **Information:** Pier Head. ☎08452 255 121. www.visitscottishheartlands.com.

▶ **Orient Yourself:** Caledona MacBrayne ferries connect Mull with Oban (40 mins), Kilchoan and Lochaline on the mainland. If travelling in summer book ahead (☎0800 066 5000, www.calmac.co.uk). The island roads are twisting and narrow – with the exception of two stretches from Craignure to Fionnphort and Craignure to Salen – but perfectly suited to a leisurely discovery of Mull's charms. The sights are listed alphabetically.

☺ **Don't Miss:** Calgary Bay; Torosay Castle gardens; in summer the Mull Music Festival.

☺ **Don't Forget:** Petrol stations are widely scattered. Keep the tank topped up.

🕒 **Organizing Your Time:** If you want to experience the island atmosphere allow at least a day and a night on Mull.

🄺🄸🄳🅂 **Especially for Kids:** Calgary Bay beach: Isle of Mull railway; Young fans of *Balamory* will easily recognise Tobermory.

Scenery

The sheltered Sound of Mull separates the island (24mi/38km long and 26mi/42km wide) from the mainland. The deeply indented coastline (300mi/483km) varies from the rocky cliffs of the Ross of Mull with offshore skerries, to the small creeks and sheltered sandy beaches like Calgary Bay. Inland the scenery can be desolate and dramatic like the moorlands which rise to the island's highest peak, **Ben More** (3,169ft/966m), or peaceful and pastoral, dotted with crofting townships. As with all the Hebridean Islands, the seaward vistas are superb.

Sights

Calgary Bay★★ 🄺🄸🄳🅂
This unspoilt west coast bay with its strand of white shell sand is an ideal spot for bathing.

Craignure
This is one of the two terminal points for the Oban ferry. The island's two castles are nearby. A coach runs from here to Duart Castle at 10.45am and 12.50pm on days when the castle is open.

Isle of Mull Railway 🄺🄸🄳🅂
🕒*Trains run Easter–late Oct.* 🚄*Return fare £4.50, child £3.* ☎*01680 812494. www.mullrail.co.uk.*
"Scotland's original island passenger railway" operates steam and diesel trains on a narrow-gauge track 1.25mi/2 km) from Craignure to Torosay.
The train chugs slowly alongside the Sound of Mull with views of Ben Nevis, the Glencoe hills, the island of Lismore and the mass of Ben Cruachan, In Spring the wild flowers along the way can be spectacular, with primroses, wild garlic and bluebells.

Torosay Castle
1.5mi/2.5km from Craignure. 🕒*Open daily Apr–Oct 10.30am–5pm. Gardens 9am–7pm (winter, sunrise–sunset).* 🚄*£5.50 (gardens only, £4.75).* 🍽. 🅿.
☎*01680 812 421. www.torosay.com.*
Torosay Castle, built 1856, is an example of **David Bryce**'s fluency in the Scottish baronial style. Inside are mementos of the Guthrie family, owners since the early 19C. Murray Guthrie (see the Sargent sketch in the library) commissioned Robert Lorimer to lay out the delightful **gardens**★. These include the fountain and lion terraces, the water and Japanese gardens and the statue walk. The

Address Book

For coin ranges, see the Legend on the cover flap.

WHERE TO STAY

Birchgrove – *Lochdon, Craignure.* 01688 812 364, www.birchgrovebandb.co.uk. Modern guesthouse close to ferry pier, in a peaceful setting with landscaped gardens and good views.

Brockville – *Breadalbane Street, Tobermory.* 01688 302 741, www.brockville-tobermory.co.uk. Modern house a 5-minute walk from the harbour; its breakfast room has sea views and the pretty, cottagey bedrooms include videos and CDs.

WHERE TO EAT

Highland Cottage – *Raeric Road (by Back Brae), Tobermory.* 01688 302 030, www.highlandcottage.co.uk. This modern small luxury hotel by the harbour features a pretty dining room and an excellent locally sourced menu. It also has individually styled rooms ( ) with good views.

Italian terraced gardens have superb-far-reaching **views**★, with Duart Castle (*2mi/3.5km footpath to Duart Castle*) in the foreground and the mountains of the mainland on the horizon. Ben Nevis may even be seen on a clear day.

Duart Castle

3mi/5km from Craignure. Open Apr Sun–Thu 11am–4pm. May–mid-Oct daily 10.30am–5.30pm. £5. . 01680 812 309. www.duartcastle.com.
Duart, home of the chief of **Clan Maclean**, is on a strategic site perched on a rocky crag, guarding the Sound of Mull. The earliest keep, built c 1250, was extended, only to be stormed in the 17C, garrisoned by Redcoats in the 18C then abandoned to fall into a ruinous condition. The 26th clan chief restored the stronghold to its present-day appearance. Clan and family mementoes are on show. On the upper floor a Scouting Exhibition recalls Lord Maclean (1916–90), 27th clan chief, and his lifetime devotion to the movement and his role as Chief Scout. The ramparts have good views across to the mainland.

Isle of Iona★ – *See Isle of IONA. Access from Fionnphort on the Ross of Mull.*

Loch na Keal

A west coast sea loch.

Staffa

Boats from Dervaig, Ulva Ferry, Fionnphort and Iona.
This basaltic island, lying on the western seaboard of Mull, owes its fame to Mendelssohn's overture *Fingal's Cave* composed following his 1829 visit.

Tobermory

Population 843. The main town and ferry port of Mull, Tobermory is famous for the cheerful colours of its waterfront buildings and the yachts bobbing in the natural harbour and was the setting for the BBC children's television show *Balamory*.
While being a popular yachting centre Tobermory Bay is also known as the last resting place of a galleon which had sailed with the Spanish Armada and there are tales of treasure deep in the Bay.

Island Festivals

The **Mull Music Festival** (*see Calendar of Events*) features concerts for accordions, fiddles, pipes and Gaelic choirs. Ceilidhs give summer visitors a chance to participate. The **Tobermory Highland Games** are known for the piping and clan march. The **Mull Little Theatre** (*open May–Sept,* 01688 302 828, www.mulltheatre.com) has a summer season with plays adapted for a two-person cast. There are only 37 seats so book ahead.

NAIRN
HIGHLAND
POPULATION 7,366

This favourite seaside resort, on the southern shore of the Moray Firth, is popular thanks to a combination of sun (it is one of the driest and sunniest places in Scotland), sea, sand and golf (two good courses). It is an ideal touring centre.

- **Information:** 62 King Street. ☎0845 225 5121. www.visithighlands.com.
- **Orient Yourself:** Nairn is 17mi/27km northeast of Inverness via the A 96.
- **Also See:** INVERNESS.

Excursions

Cawdor Castle★
See CAWDOR CASTLE.

Fort George★
10mi/16km west. (HS) ⏱Open year-round daily 9.30am–5.30pm (Oct–Mar 4.30pm). Last admission 45min before closing. ⏱Closed 25–26 Dec. ⮝£6.50. ☎01667 460232. www.historic-scotland.gov.uk.

Set on a peninsula jutting into the Moray Firth, this outstanding artillery fortress was built 1748–69 to serve as a stronghold for the troops of George II. It is impressive for its size and the elaboration of its defences. Although Fort George is a working army barracks, the public may visit several of its buildings, where displays and audio-visual presentations give a glimpse into the living and working conditions in an 18C fort. Beyond the emblazoned main gate and entrance tunnel are **guard-rooms** for the officers and regular soldiers. The **historic barrack rooms** show the evolution in living conditions with two rank and file rooms from 1780 and 1868. The 1813 Officer's Room is surprisingly spartan. The **grand magazine** was the store for 2,500 powder barrels. A plain galleried **chapel** stands on its own.

The Lieutenant-Governor's and fort major's houses are now occupied by the **Queen's Own Highlanders Regimental Museum**. The history of the regiment is evoked through displays of uniforms, colours, weapons, campaigns and medals, and militia silver.

NORTH BERWICK
EAST LOTHIAN
POPULATION 4,861

This ancient royal burgh is a popular holiday and golfing resort and provides a complete range of amenities—vast sandy beaches, golf courses and putting greens, sailing and sea angling facilities. It faces onto the Bass Rock, world famous for its bird population. The town is also favoured by commuters with the railway giving rapid access to Edinburgh.

- **Information:** Quality Street. ☎01620 892 197. www.edinburgh.org.
- **Orient Yourself:** North Berwick is on the southern shore of the Firth of Forth 29mi/46km northeast of Edinburgh via the A 1.
- **Don't Miss:** The view from North Berwick Law.
- **Organizing Your Time:** Allow half a day for North Berwick itself; more if you are interested in birds.
- **Especially for Kids:** Sandy beaches; Myreton Motor Museum; the Museum of Flight.
- **Also See:** DIRLETON. TANTALLON CASTLE.

Sights

Auld Kirk

On the harbour promontory, dividing the two sandy beaches, are the scant remains of the town's first parish church (12C), notoriously associated with a gathering of witches in 1590 to plot the death of James VI. The burial place for the Lauder and Douglas families, it was abandoned in the 1680s on account of the expense of the upkeep of the connecting bridge, to what was then an island promontory.

Old Parish Church

Kirk Port. Now a ruin, this was the 17C replacement for the Auld Kirk. In the churchyard is a headstone commemorating **John Blackadder**, the Covenanting preacher who died in prison on the Bass Rock (*see Bass Rock, below*).

The Lodge

This 18C white harled building was the town house of the Dalrymple family. It has now been divided into flats and the grounds form a public park.

Town House

At the corner of Quality Street and High Street stands an attractive 18C building with outside stairs and a clock tower. The upper chamber still serves as a meeting place for committees and community councils.

North Berwick Law

612ft/187m. 1mi/1.5km south of the town centre by Law Road. Signposted path with occasional seats.
One of East Lothian's many volcanic hills and distinguishing landmarks, the Law, with the town spread out at its feet, has a commanding **panorama**★★★. At the very top is a a pair of ancient weathered whale's jawbones and a view indicator. On a clear day you can use it to pick out: St Abb's Head, inland to the Lammermuir Hills, the Traprain and the Garleton Hills backed by the Moorfoots and Pentlands, perhaps even as far as Ben Lomond on a really clear day; the Forth, the Ochils and the Grampians with the East Neuk of Fife on the northern shore of the Firth.

The Law is the scene of an annual hill race in August.

Scottish Seabird Centre

Open Apr–Sept 10am–6pm. Feb–Mar & Oct 10am–5pm (Sat–Sun 5.30pm). Nov–Jan 10am–4pm (Sat–Sun 5.30pm). Last admission 45 mins before closing. Closed 25 Dec. £7.15. 01620 890 202. www.seabird.org.

This new birdwatching centre enjoys a stunning location overlooking the sea and islands of the Forth, most notably the famous **Bass Rock** (*see Bass Rock, below*)**.** The latest technology in remote viewing, with cameras on the islands, beam back live panoramas and close-ups onto giant screens with such clarity that visitors can even read the rings on individual birds' feet. In spring you can expect to see Bass Rock gannets, puffins, guillemots huddled together like penguins on the sea cliffs and the fluffy white newborn seals on the Isle of May. There are wading birds along the shore in winter and the occasional rare and often spectacular sightings of dolphins, porpoises and whales in summer.

Bass Rock

Boat trips May–end Sept. Please phone for details. 01620 892 838.
At the entrance to the Firth of Forth, 3mi/5km from North Berwick, the rounded form of this volcanic hill rises to 350ft/107m above sea level. It is

---

The Gannet

The gannet comes to land during the breeding season only (Feb–May). The single egg is protected, in turn, by the parents who cover it with first one then the other webbed foot. They leave in August and the deserted fledgling is driven by hunger down to the sea where it usually floats, protected by excess fat, for about 3 weeks before learning to fly. The birds are excellent divers capable of descending at least 50ft/15m for their prey.

now equipped with a lighthouse and foghorn for Forth shipping. Its role has varied throughout history: a retreat for St Baldred; a fortress; a Covenanters' prison; the last stronghold of the Stuart monarchy's cause to surrender (1691–94); and a present-day sanctuary of a myriad of seabirds.

A boat trip makes it possible to observe the wildlife at fairly close quarters, depending on the weather. Every conceivable crevice and ledge of the vertical cliffs is the domain of some seabird be it guillemot, razorbill, cormorant, puffin, tern, eider duck, gull or the famous **Gannet**, also known as Solan Goose, which takes its latin name *Sula Bassana* from this island (see Box on previous page).

Driving Tour

Coastal road★ North Berwick to Port Seton

Leave North Berwick to the west by the A 198.

Dirleton – See DIRLETON.

Gullane
Population 2,124. With five golf courses, this is a golfer's paradise, best known for the famous Muirfield Course, home of the Honourable Company of Edinburgh Golfers (founded 1744) and one of the regular venues for the British Open Golf Championship. With its fine sandy beach the village has always been popular for day outings from the capital and recently it has been growing in popularity as a commuter haven too.

▶ *Once over the Peffer Burn take the local road to the left.*

Myreton Motor Museum [Kids]
 Open Apr–Oct daily 11am–4pm. Nov–Mar Sat–Sun only, 11am–3pm. £6. ☎01875 870 288. www.aberlady. org/Myreton.
This privately owned, rather cramped collection presents a panorama of roadworthy vehicles, motorcycles and bicycles; it is a far cry from the spit and polish image of more traditional motor muse-

ums. The cars, each with their individual case histories, tell a story of misfortune and neglect or loving care and attention. They include the Galloway with its thistle-adorned footplates, an exhibit at the 1926 Scottish Motor Show, a 14-seat charabanc from Ford (1920), *Eve* (1892) by A Benz, the oldest car in Scotland, the Standard Beaverette looking like something out of science fiction and the Bollee Motor Tricycle c 1896, which once belonged to the Hon C S Rolls of Rolls-Royce fame.

Circular tour from North Berwick

21mi/34km. Leave North Berwick to the east by A 198.

Tantallon Castle★ –
 See TANTALLON CASTLE.

Whitekirk
Population 70. The parish church of St Mary's, a 15C mellow red-sandstone building, originally belonged to Holyrood Abbey. The presence of a Holy Well made this a great pilgrimage centre, visited in 1435 by the Papal Legate, Aeneas Sylvius Piccolomini, later Pope Pius II. Burnt by suffragettes in 1914, the church was restored by Robert Lorimer.
In the field behind, the 16C three-storey building was probably the tithe barn.

Tyninghame★
Population 186. Most of the houses in this pretty estate village are single-storey pink sandstone with pantiled roofs. The original village situated in the grounds of Tyninghame House was removed in 1761.

▶ *Take the B 1407 through the village.*

Preston Mill & Phantassie Doocot ★
(NTS). Open Jun–Sept Thu–Mon noon–5pm. £5. P £2. ☎0844 4932128. www.nts.org.uk.
Picturesque 16C Preston Mill, with its red-pantiled roofs and rubble masonry, is one of Scotland's rare working watermills, believed to be of Dutch design. In the cone-shaped kiln, damp oats were dried on perforated metal plates before being transferred by chute to the mill.

In a field beyond (*5min walk*) is the oddly truncated, beehive-shaped **Phantassie Doocot** (*Fantasy Dovecote* – *See Introduction: Arts and Culture*). It is circular with two string courses – to prevent rats climbing up – and the south-facing side has a sloping roof and two sets of flight holes. Inside, the 500 nests are reached by a revolving ladder.

▶ *Take the A 1 west in the direction of Haddington. Turn right onto the B 1347.*

National Museum of Flight★   Kids
East Fortune Airfield. Open daily, Apr–Oct 10am–5pm. Nov–Mar Sat–Sun only 10am–4pm. £5.50, child free. Concorde, adult extra £3, child £2. Booking ahead at busy times advisable. 0870 421 4299. ☐. ☎01620 897 240. www.nms.ac.uk.
In a vast hangar, this outstation of the National Museums of Scotland displays its superb collection of aircraft ranging from a wooden DH Dragon biplane to Concorde. The latter has its own special exhibition area.

The model airship on show is "Tiny", otherwise known as **HM Airship R 34**. It was from this historic airfield that she set out on the historic first ever double Atlantic crossing in 1919.

A larger hangar displays another 18 aircraft with a Comet airliner and a Vulcan bomber parked outside.

Hangar 4 is home to the pride of the museum, Concorde G-BOAA. Visitors can see her being reconstructed after her final voyage by land and sea from Heathrow. G-BOAA became the first of the British Airways fleet to fly commercially when she flew from London to Bahrain in January 1976.

▶ *B 1377, then B 1347 lead back to North Berwick.*

OBAN
ARGYLL AND BUTE
POPULATION 8,500

Scotland's most popular west-coast holiday town is built round Oban Bay and is backed by a ring of low hills. Much of the town's activity is concentrated in and around the harbour, where fishing vessels, ferries, excursion steamers and a variety of pleasure craft find refuge, protected by the island of Kerrera.

- **Information:** Argyll Square. ☎08707 200 630. www.visitscottishheartlands.com.
- ▶ **Orient Yourself:** Looking across to the Isle of Mull, 44 mi/71km south of Fort William, Oban makes an ideal West Coast touring centre, by land and sea.
- **Don't Miss:** Loch Awe; Loch Fyne. If you are here during late August visit the Argyllshire Highland Gathering: visit www.obangames.com for details.
- **Driving:** The town is very busy in summer with long traffic queues.
- **Organizing Your Time:** Allow two hours to see the town, at least a full day for excursions.
- Kids **Especially for Kids:** The Scottish Sea Life Sanctuary.
- **Also See:** ISLE OF MULL. INVERARY.

A Bit of History

Oban has long been a service centre as livestock market and fishing port for the outlying area and islands, but today its economy is geared to tourism. Hotels and boarding houses line the seafront, a far cry from the situation in 1773 when Dr Johnson had to content himself with "a tolerable inn".

The town became a fishing port in the 18C and really developed a century later with the arrival of the steamboats and then the railway, giving Oban its present very Victorian aspect.

Address Book

🍷For coin ranges, see the Legend on the cover flap.

WHERE TO STAY

🍽**The Old Manse** – Dalriach Road. ☎01631 564 886. www.obanguesthouse. co.uk. Set just outside the town this former manse is perched on the hillside with views out to sea. Rooms are spacious and well equipped and the gardens feature wood decking.

🍽**Alltavona** – Corran Esplanade. ☎01631 565 067. www.alltavona.co.uk. This elegant 19C villa is set on a smart esplanade with fine views of Oban Bay across to the Isle of Mull. The attractive interiors and fittings are contemporary to the house and bedrooms are individually styled.

🍽🍽**The Barriemore** – Corran Esplanade. ☎01631 566 356. www. barriemore-hotel.co.uk.
A gabled 1890s house with fine views over the town (a 10min walk away) and islands, this is a comfortable mix of modern and period styling.

WHERE TO EAT

🍽🍽🍽 **Ee-Usk at the North Pier** – The North Pier. ☎01631 565 666. www. eeusk.com. This smart modern award-winning fish restaurant (ee-usk is the phonetic for fish in Gaelic) enjoys excellent views over the bay and harbour.

🍽🍽**The Waterfront** – No. 1 The Pier. ☎01631 563 110. www.waterfrontoban. co.uk. Set on the pier with great views over the bay and harbour, this converted quayside mission has its own fishing boats and therefore guarantees the best and freshest fish and seafood.

🍽🍽 **Coast** – 104 George Street. ☎01631 569 900. www.coastoban.com. The appealing reasonably priced modern menus at this former bank building in the centre of town include plenty of fish and shellfish. Attractive minimalist contemporary interiors of stripped wooden floors and khaki coloured walls.

Driving Tour

Hinterland★★

▶ Leave Oban by the A 85. Turn left at Dunbeg and continue for 1mi/1.6km.

Dunstaffnage
HS. 🕐Open Apr–Sept daily 9.30am–5.30pm.Oct–Mar Sat–Wed 9.30am–4.30pm. Last admission 30 mins before closing. 🕐Closed 25–26 Dec, 1,2 Jan.

🎫£3.50. ☎01631 562465. www.historic-scotland.gov.uk.
This impressive 13C castle, one of the principal seats of the MacDougalls, rises out of a rocky outcrop on a promontory commanding the entrance to Loch Etive.
The thick curtain walls are punctuated by three towers and a 17C tower house. It was captured by Robert the Bruce in 1309 and remained in royal possession for some years. In fact it is claimed that Dunstaffnage was the home of the

McCaig's Tower

Dominating the Oban skyline, high on the hill above, is a replica of the **Colosseum**, known as McCaig's Tower, or McCaig's Folly. The project was initiated in 1897 by the philanthropic Oban banker John Stuart McCaig in order to relieve unemployment and act as a family memorial. It cost around £5,000, an enormous sum at the time. He planned it to include a museum, art gallery and central tower, but the building has remained incomplete since McCaig died in 1902.

It's a short if steep walk to its viewing platform and well worth the effort. Go at sunset to enjoy the Mountains of Morvern providing a spectacular backcloth for the isles of Kerrera and Lismore, the Maiden Isle and Mull.

Scots court prior to Kenneth MacAlpine's unification of the country and removal of the seat of power to Scone (☞see SCONE PALACE).

Flora MacDonald (☞see ISLE OF SKYE) was held prisoner here on her way to The Tower of London in 1746.

▷ *Continue by the A 85 to Taynuilt and bear left onto the B 845.*

Bonawe Historic Iron Furnace★

HS. ◷*Open Apr–Sept daily 9.30am– 5.30pm. Last admission 30 mins before closing.* ◷*Closed 25–26 Dec, 1,2 Jan.* ☜*£4.* ☏*01866 822432. www.historic-scotland.gov.uk.*

The most complete charcoal-fuelled ironworks in Britain, Bonawe was founded in 1753 and in production until the 1870s. Displays bring to life the industrial heritage of the area and illustrate how pig iron was made.

▷ *Return to the A 85 and proceed east.*

Cruachan Power Station★

Dalmally. ◷ ☞*Visit underground by guided tours only, every 30 mins, Easter– Nov daily 9.30am–5pm. Winter hours available on request.* ☜*£5.* ☖*.* ☏*01866 822 618.*

Lying deep within the mountain of Ben Cruachan, on the shores of Loch Awe, is one of the country's most amazing engineering achievement, a power station buried over half a mile/1 km below the ground. At its centre lies a massive cavern, high enough to house the Tower of London, where enormous turbines convert the power of water into electricity.

Part of the Awe scheme, the Cruachan power station, opened in 1965, has an annual output of 450 million units of electricity. The pump turbines are reversible and are used to pump water from Loch Awe to the high level reservoir in the corrie on Ben Cruachan, which in turn feeds, by means of two shafts, an underground power station in the heart of the mountain. A road tunnel (1mi/1.5km long) leads to the Generating Hall.

A visitor centre on the surface provides an introdction to this ambitious scheme. Once inside the mountain visitors walk past sub-tropical plants that grow well in the warm humid conditions, and then onto the viewing gallery looking into the mighty main hall.

▷ *The road follows Loch Awe, skirting the lower slopes of Ben Cruachan.*

Loch Awe★★

This is Scotland's longest loch, stretching over 25mi/40km. It drains via the River Awe and the Pass of Brander where the former is harnessed for hydroelectric power. This is the heart of Campbell country with the family seat formerly situated on Innischonnail Island, then at Kilchurn, at the head of Loch Awe.

D. Ha/ Scottish Viewpoint

Kilchurn Castle, Loch Awe

▶ *Turn right onto the A 819.*

From this road there are very pictur-esque views of the ruins of **Kilchurn Castle**, the 15C stronghold built by Sir Colin Campbell, on a spit of land jutting out into the headwaters of Loch Awe. .

Inveraray★★ – *See INVERARAY.*

Loch Fyne★★ – *See INVERARAY.*

Auchindrain★ – *See INVERARAY: Excursions.*

Crarae Garden
Visitor Center open: Good Fri–Sept daily 10am–5pm. SIte open: daily 9.30am–sun-set. £5. ☎0844 4932210. www.nts. org.uk.
This delightful Himalayan-style wood-land garden (100 acres/40ha) occupies a steep sloping site overlooking Loch Fyne. The beautiful natural setting in a small glen with its rushing burn and waterfalls is complemented by judicious planting and includes the national col-lection of Southern Beech trees.
The garden is at its best in spring, par-ticularly for its rhododendrons, or in autumn when the leaf colours are a blaze of russet shades. The winding climbing paths afford splendid viewpoints and glimpses of the loch and mountains.

Crinan★
This delightful hamlet stands at the west-ern end of the Crinan Canal (9mi/14.5km long) which links the Sound of Jura and Loch Fyne. The canal, with its 15 locks, was opened in 1801 to save fishing boats the long sail round the Mull of Kintyre. Today yachts and pleasure craft make a colourful spectacle as they manoeuvre and jostle for position in the holding pool and locks.

▶ *Return to the A 816 and continue north.*

Dunadd Fort
Access by the farm road to the left.
The rocky eminence rising abruptly out of the flat lands of the Great Moss was a Dark Ages fortification.

▶ *The road enters Kilmartin Glen, leading through a pass to reach the southern end of Loch Awe.*

Kilmartin
There are over 350 ancient monuments within a 6mi/10km radius of the village of Kilmartin, of which 150 are prehistoric. This extraordinary concentration and diversity of monuments distinguishes **Kilmartin Glen** as an area of outstand-ing archaeological importance. **Kilmar-tin House Museum** (*open Mar–Oct daily 10am–5.30pm, Nov–23 Dec reduced hours; £4.60; ; ; ☎01546 510 278, www.kilmartin.org*), is an award-winning world-class centre for archaeology and landscape interpretation and includes 'The Valley of Ghosts' audio-visual with atmospheric imagery and music.
In Kilmartin churchyard is a fine collec-tion of **sculptured stones** dating from the 14C to 16C. Inside the church, **Cross no 3** (16C) is outstanding.

▶ *Follow the A 816 2mi/3km north*

Carnasserie Castle
On a strategic site commanding the route northwards to Loch Awe, the remains of this 16C castle are remarkable for their carved detail and mouldings.

▶ *Follow the A 816 back to Oban.*

Scottish Sea Life Sanctuary★ Kids
11mi/18km north of Oban, just off the A 828. Open Mar–Oct 10am–5pm (last admission 4pm). Call for prices and times during winter. ☎0870 608 2608. www.sealsanctuary.co.uk .
Discover the living creatures of the marine world in this spectacular aquarium and seal rescue centre. Walk around, over and under the tanks, to view the occupants. The touch tank with its sea urchins, starfish and crabs is always a firm favourite. Other popu-lar areas are a fish farming exhibit, a seal pool with feeding times and an otter sanctuary.

ORKNEY ISLANDS★★
ORKNEY ISLANDS
POPULATION 19,040

The archipelago of the Orkney Islands, located off the northern tip of Scotland where the North Sea and the Atlantic Ocean meet, is made up of 67 islands, about half of which are uninhabited.

- **Information:** 6 Broad Street. ☎01856 872 586. www.visitorkney.com.
- ▶ **Orient Yourself:** The principal island, Mainland, is divided into Eastern Mainland and Western Mainland with the capital, Kirkwall, at the dividing point. Causeways link a small number of the islands, Orkney Ferries (☎01856 872044) and Loganair (☎01856 872494) service the other principal inhabited islands. Several British airports fly to Orkney, mainland ferries run from Aberdeen (6hrs), Scrabster (90mins), Gills Bay (1hr) and John O'Groats (40mins), which is 10mi/16km south of the islands. In summer, bus tours take in all the major sites. Bicycle hire is also popular.
- **Don't Miss:** St Magnus Cathedral, Kirkwall; Maes Howe: Skara Brae; The Old Man of Hoy.
- **Organizing Your Time:** Allow at least three days.
- **Also See:** SHETLAND ISLANDS, WICK.

A Bit of History

Prehistory – The first settlers were established on the islands by the 4th millennium BC and the island has a great wealth of impressive prehistoric remains. Among the most remarkable are the Neolithic settlement at Skara Brae, the outstanding tomb of Maes Howe, the Bronze Age stone circle of Brodgar, the Iron Age brochs (see SHETLAND ISLANDS) of Birsay and Gurness, and the Pictish earth houses.

The Golden Age – With the arrival of the Norsemen in the 8C and 9C this Pictish land became Scandinavian. The Norse settlement was a peaceful and gradual process and in due course Orkney, as part of a Norse earldom, became the pivot of Viking Britain. The history of the earls of Orkney, who ruled as sovereigns, is traced in The Orkneyinga Saga. They include such notable figures as Thorfinn the Mighty, St Magnus the martyr and the crusader Rognvald.

It is this Norse heritage which differentiates the Orkney and Shetland Islands from the rest of Scotland. Even today the imprint is clear in place names, in the form of a magnificent cathedral, and in literature much influenced by the sagas, as well as in artistic designs and in time-honoured traditions. As late as the 19C, Norn – a form of Norse – was the language spoken rather than Gaelic.

Surety for a dowry – The late medieval period brought Scottish rule when the islands were given in security (1468) for the dowry of Margaret of Denmark, future bride of James III. The period is often associated with misrule and the despoiling of Orkney lands by Scottish overlords, and more particularly with tyranny, in particular that of the Stewart Earls of Orkney.

The 18C was an era of prosperity with the making of **kelp**. Seaweed was burned to obtain an ash residue rich in potash and soda which was in demand for the glass and soap manufacturing industries. The kelp industry (c. 1780–1830) brought great prosperity to the local nobility who were nicknamed the "Kelp Lairds". Many of the fine mansions on the islands belong to this period.

Today – In these low-lying and fertile islands agriculture is the main economy with the cattle rearing and dairying the main activities. Distilling and tourism follow in order of importance. The traditional crafts, such as knitwear and straw-backed Orkney chairs, continue to flourish. A new element in the economy

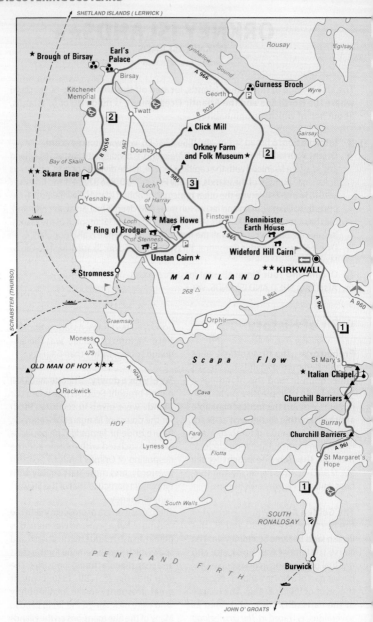

is oil with the creation of an oil handling terminal at Flotta on Scapa Flow.

Brough of Birsay★
(Island)

This tidal island lying just offshore from the northwestern point of Mainland,

features important remains of Pictish and Norse settlements.

Access
The island can be reached on foot at low tide across a causeway. For times of low tide ask at the local tourist offices in Stromness or Kirkwall. ☞ *Admission fee mid-Jun–Sept, £2.*

Pictish metalworkers

The earliest remains are houses and metalworking debris of the Pictish period. Recent excavations have thrown doubt on the original interpretation of the remains as a monastery. There is a replica of a fine Pictish symbol stone.

Norse occupation

In the 10C and 11C Norsemen lived on the Brough and a group of farmsteads marks this period. The Norse Earls (Jarls) of Orkney, made Birsay one of their principal seats in Orkney.

Visit

Because excavations have uncovered evidence of the above periods piecemeal; the result can be confusing. Take your bearings from the most prominent feature, the church.

Norse Church

The church on the Brough dates from the 12C. It is set within an enclosure representing the **Norse graveyard**. Both Pictish and Norse graves have been uncovered. An important example of the former is the **Birsay Stone** (replica) portraying three armed warriors. On the far side (to the north) of the church are the domestic buildings of the priests, in three ranges enclosing a courtyard.

Norse long houses

To the southwest and higher up the slope are typical Norse houses with the living quarters at the upper end and byre lower down. The walls had cores of turf. Between the church and the cliff (to the east) are the complex remains of Norse buildings of various periods, some of which have been thought to represent Earl Thorfinn's palace.

Kirkwall★★ (Mainland)

Population 8,500. Kirkwall stands on the northern end of the Kirkwall-Scapa isthmus which divides Mainland into eastern and western parts. The town is dominated by its splendid 800-year-old cathedral and spreads up the hillside from the harbour. Kirkwall has been the island fulcrum since it was a Norse trading centre and today it combines its role of capital with that of shopping and business centre. Its central location The central situation of Kirkwall makes it an ideal touring centre.

The town is famous for its Christmas and New Year's Day **Ba' Games** (ball games)

St Magnus Cathedral, interior

when the Uppies play the Downies in an anything-goes (within reason!) football-cum rugby match. Historically it symbolises the rivalry between the bishop and the town's secular authorities.

St Magnus Cathedral★★

 🕐*Open Apr–Sept daily 9am (Sun 1pm)–6pm. Oct–Mar Mon–Sat 9am–1pm, 2pm–5pm. 📷Tours of upper floor Tue and Thu 11am and 2pm, book with the custodian. ☏01856 874 894.*

The founder, Earl Rognvald, started to build his new cathedral in 1137 with the intention of dedicating it to his murdered kinsman, **Earl Magnus**. Building operations supervised by the earl's father Kol were completed rapidly in 1152. Two years later the Orkney See became part of the Norwegian diocese centred on Trondheim, an arrangement that was to continue until 1472. The cathedral is Norman in character and contemporary with two other masterpieces of this style, Durham and the nave of Dunfermline Abbey (*see DUNFERMLINE*). The exterior, severe and quite plain, is dominated by the tower and steeple. The three west front doorways added later, are very beautiful, although much weathered, and show originality in the alternate use of red and yellow sandstone.

Interior

The initial impression is one of vastness although the dimensions of this cruciform church are relatively small. The admirable proportions, strong sense of unity, and warm tones of the red stone make for a pleasing result. The **view** is best from the west end. The design of the nave elevation moves eastwards in seven bays as slowly as it moves upwards through the triforium and clerestory, where there is no quickening of the rhythm. Ornamental detail is confined to decorative mouldings on the recessed arches of the main nave arcade, the interlaced wall arcading of the nave aisles and transepts and the grotesque heads of the choir consoles. The square pillars on either side of the organ screen enshrine the relics of St Magnus (right) slain in 1115, and his nephew Earl Rognvald, the builder.

Sights

The other main sights stand within what must have been the cathedral precinct.

Earl's Palace★

🕐*Open Apr–Sept 9.30am–5.30pm. October check site for times.*

Although in ruins, this early-17C palace still displays much architectural sophistication and beauty. The refinement is all the more surprising in that the builder was the villainous despot, **Patrick Stewart**, Earl of Orkney (d 1615). Like his father he was executed, but only after the final hour had been postponed to allow the condemned man time to learn the Lord's Prayer.

The palace, built 1600–1607, is an early example of Renaissance style. Details of interest on the exterior include the corbelling—ornate and varied—of the windows, chimney breast and corbel course, the sculptured panel above the main entrance and the oriel windows. Inside, a splendidly spacious staircase with straight flights rises to the Great Hall and the other principal apartments. The vaulted chambers on the ground floor have exhibits on Orkney's other notable historic monuments and prehistoric sites.

Bishop's Palace

Open Apr–Sept 9.30am–5.30pm. October check site for times.

A new episcopal palace was built in the 12C alongside the new cathedral, the original seat having been at Birsay (*see Brough of Birsay, above*). It was in the original palace that the Norwegian King Haakon died in December 1263 after the Battle of Largs. His death and the palace are described in one of the Sagas. Two

rebuildings followed in the 16C and 17C, the latter by Earl Patrick as part of his scheme to create a vast lordly residence incorporating his new palace across the road. The round tower on the corner is part of Bishop Reid's 16C remodelling. The yellow-sandstone figure of a bishop in a red niche is 13C.

Orkney Museum

Tankerness House. Open May–Sept, Mon–Sat 10.30am–12.30pm & 1.30pm– 5pm. 01856 873 191. www.orkney.org/ museums.

This fine 16C town mansion houses a well-presented museum portraying life in Orkney from its prehistoric beginnings to the present day. The island's many outstanding prehistoric sites are described chronologically and accompanied by artefacts. This makes an ideal introduction prior to exploring the islands. Do not miss the St Magnus Reliquary, a simple wooden casket. Upstairs the exhibits portraying domestic life include an example of the straw-backed Orkney chairs, excellent draught excluders.

Address Book

For coin ranges, see the Legend on the cover flap.

WHERE TO STAY

Polrudden – *Peerie Sea Loan, Kirkwall.* 01856 874 761. www.polrudden.com. Large modern house just outside the town centre with picture windows looking out over quiet fields. Well kept rooms and friendly owners.

Sands – *Burray.* 01856 731 298. www.thesandshotel.co.uk. This former fishing store has been totally modernised with six stylish seaview rooms, a popular bar and spacious dining room ( ) also with views of the bay.

Shoreside – *St Margaret's Hope, South Ronaldsay.* 01856 831 560. A superbly positioned guesthouse with fine views of West Sound and stylishly decorated bedrooms. It is famous for its seafood dinners, taken communally.

Merkister – *Loch Harray, Eastern Mainland.* 01856 771366. www.a1tourism.com/uk/merkister. Sited on the edge of the loch this peaceful family-run small hotel offers trim bedrooms, a lively public bar and a restaurant ( ) offering an extensive Scottish menu.

WHERE TO EAT

Foveran – *St Ola, Kirkwall.* 01856 872389. Enjoy a beautiful view of Scapa Flow with an aperitif served in a lounge with an open fire. Meals are exclusively fresh local produce specialising in seafood and the signature Orkney fudge cheesecake.

Creel – *Front Road, St Margaret's Hope, South Ronaldsay.* 01856 831 311. www.thecreel.co.uk. This smart contemporay restaurant with stylish rooms ( ) serves flavourful dishes using local produce; try their seafood specials and home-made ice creams.

Main Street

Stroll along the town's main thoroughfare, a narrow stone-flagged way that incorporates **Broad Street, Albert Street** and **Bridge Street,** and ends at the harbour. Former town houses of country lairds, now occupied by shops some still emblazoned with coats of arms, provide the main points of interest, along with pends leading to attractive paved courtyards.

Driving Tours

1 Eastern Mainland
23mi/37km to Burwick.

This excursion offers the opportunity to visit more of the Orkney Islands (Lamb Holm, Glims Holm, Burray and South Ronaldsay) without taking a boat or plane. The road passes through some of Orkney's finest agricultural land.

▶ *Take the airport road out of Kirkwall then fork right onto the A 961, South Ronaldsay road.*

The early stretch has a good view of **Scapa Flow**, the famous naval base where on 21 June 1919 the entrapped German Grand Fleet was scuttled. Activity has most recently returned with the Island of Flotta being used as a pipeline landfall and tanker terminal for gas and oil from the Piper and Claymore Fields. Lyness on Hoy serves as a supply base. and is also home to the **Scapa Flow Visitor Centre & Museum** (⏱*open Mon–Fri 9am–4.30pm.*☎*01856 791 300)* which includes extensive photographic displays, many artefacts and an impressive audio-visual display sited inside a huge oil tank

▶ *After St Mary's, follow signposts to St Margaret's Hope.*

Beyond is the first of the **Churchill Barriers** linking Mainland to three outlying islands. These concrete causeways were built during the Second World War after the torpedoing of the battleship *HMS Royal Oak*, to protect the eastern entrances to Scapa Flow. The work was undertaken by Italian prisoners who completed the four sections totalling 1.5mi/2.4km in length.

▶ *Turn left immediately after crossing the first causeway.*

Italian Chapel★
Lamb Holm. ⏱*Open daily sunrise-sunset.* ☎*01856 873 191. www.orkneyheritage. com.*

Two Nissen huts were converted into a chapel with the materials to hand, by the prisoners working on the construction of the causeways between 1943 and 1945. With its rood screen and fresco paintings, it stands as a testimony to faith in times of adversity.

On either side of the following two causeways there are rusting hulks which are valuable as scallop breeding grounds.

On the island of South Ronaldsay a roadside viewpoint with indicator offers **views**★ across the Pentland Firth of Dunnet Head and John O'Groats on the Scottish mainland.

Burwick
In summer a passenger ferry operates between Burwick and John O'Groats (♿*see WICK: Excursions).*

2 Western Mainland★★
53mi/85km. Allow a full day.

This tour combines important prehistoric sites with the tranquil agricultural landscape of the interior and dramatic coastal scenery. The tour may be taken in either direction and started from either Kirkwall or Stromness.

▶ *Leave Kirkwall by the A 965 Stromness road .*

Rennibister Earth House
Leave the car on the road up to the farm. The site is behind the farmhouse. Access by a trap door and ladder down into the chamber.

This earth house, or souterrain, consists of an oval chamber with five wall recesses and an entrance passage. Human bones were found in the chamber, but its original purpose is uncertain. Souterrains are Iron Age in date; some belong to the period of the brochs (☞*see SHELTAND ISLES*), but both earlier and later examples are known. They are usually found under or by round houses of stone or timber.

▶ *Turn left twice following the HS signposts to Wideford Hill Cairn.*

Wideford Hill Cairn
1mi/1.5km on foot from the road. The site is on the flank of the hill, follow the path. Access by a trap door and ladder.
This chambered tomb, within its cairn, dates from between 3500 and 2500 BC and has a main chamber with side cells. From the hillside there is a lovely **view** northwards over the Bay of Firth.

▶ *Return to the main road, the A 965 and at Finstown turn right onto the A 966 in the direction of Georth (Evie). Gurness Broch is signposted to the right.*

Gurness Broch
A sandy track suitable for cars continues beyond the first car park round the shore to the Sands of Evie beach. ⓢ*Open Mar–Sept.* ☎*01856 751414.*
At the point of Aikerness promontory are the remains of a broch altered by subsequent phases of occupation. The result is a cluttered complex of later settlements inside and beyond the broch. The road offers fine **views** across the Sound of Rousay and to the island of Eynhallow.

▶ *Continue around the north coast to the village of Birsay, then turn right.*

There are good **views**★ of Marwick Head.

Brough of Birsay★ –
ⓖ*See Brough of Birsay.*

▶ *Return to the village.*

Earl's Palace
In the village of Birsay are the ruins of a residence built around three sides of a courtyard, by the late-16C earls of Orkney. This once sumptuous building is another example of the outstanding architectural heritage from the builder earls.

▶ *Take the A 967 then turn right onto the B 9056 to the Bay of Skaill.*

The prominent headland pinpointed by the Kitchener Memorial is Marwick Head, known for its sea bird colony.

Skara Brae★★ –
ⓖ*See SKARA BRAE over page.*

▶ *Continue via the B 9056 then turn right onto the A 967 and right again towards Stromness.*

Stromness★ –
ⓖ*See STROMNESS over page.*

▶ *Leave by the A 965 and once over the outlet of the Loch of Stenness take the farm road to the left.*

Unstan Cairn★
Park in front of the house. �*The key hangs in a box at the back door.*
The cairn on the edge of the Loch of Stenness contains an excellent example of a communal chambered tomb typical of Neolithic times. The main chamber is divided by upright slabs into compartments. The pottery found here gave rise to the name Unstan Ware which dates from the middle of the fourth millennium BC.

▶ *Turn left onto the B 9055.*

Pass the Stones of Stenness, with their few remaining stones, on the right.

Ring of Brodgar★
This Bronze Age stone circle stands in an impressive site on a neck of land between the lochs of Stenness and Harray. Of the original 60 stones 27 remain upright. Two entrance causeways interrupt the encircling ditch.

▶ *Once back onto the main road continue for a short distance. Park beside Tormiston Mill.*

Maes Howe★★ –
♿See MAES HOWE below.

▶ *Return to Kirkwall.*

3 Kirbuster Farm Museum

14mi/22.5km from Kirkwall via the A 965 and A 986. 🕐*Open Mar–Oct Mon–Sat 10.30am–1pm & 2–5pm, Sun 2–5pm.* ☎ *01856 771 268. www.orkney.org/ museums.*

This group of 18C buildings has been restored to its mid-19C appearance to form a delightful museum of farming and rural life. The original "firehouse" has been subdivided by a gable fireplace into "in-by" and "oot-by". The out-by (**1a**) had pig stalls and recessed goose nests. The in-by (**1b**) was the family room with sleeping area beyond. The present exhibition area (**3**) was the byre, which was later replaced by a separate building (**4**) with its ingenious flagstone stalls, drain and angle nooks for hens' nests. The following building contains the stable for the working Clydesdales (**6**) with a small lean-to for the ponies (**7**) and a barn with threshing floor (note position of doors for winnowing), kiln (**9**) and peat store (**10**).

▶ *Continue along the A 986 to Dounby, turn right onto the B 9057 to reach Click Mill after 2mi/3.2km.*

Click Mill
This is the last working example in Orkney of a horizontal watermill.

Maes Howe★★ (Mainland)

The Neolithic chambered cairn of Maes Howe is an outstanding piece of skill and craftsmanship in an age when the only tools were of flint or stone. It was built prior to 2,700 BC (around the time when Stonehenge began), the ingenuity of construction and quality of workmanship are such that it has been suggested this was the tomb of a chieftain or ruling family. The whole is covered by a mound (Maes Howe means great mound) 26ft/8m high and 115ft/35m in diameter, and was encircled by a ditch.

Interior
A passage (39ft/12m long) leads to the inner chamber, off which open three burial cells. The tomb was pillaged in the 12C by Norsemen, and according to the rich collection of runic inscriptions to be found within, there was so much treasure to remove, it took them three nights to accomplish the robbery.

Skara Brae★★ (Mainland)

On the west coast of Mainland, overlooking the Bay of Skaill, clusters a group of Stone Age dwellings. Long protected by sand, the site of the prehistoric village is well preserved and provides a vivid picture of life in Neolithic times.

Period of occupation
This is the best preserved of all northwest European Neolithic villages. Radiocarbon dating shows the two main periods of settlement belong between about 3,100 BC and 2,500 BC.

The inhabitants and their activities
The first inhabitants grew grain and kept cattle, sheep and pigs. They fished in the sea which at that time was much farther than now from the village. To supplement their diet they hunted deer. Their tools were of wood, stone, bone and horn. They dressed in skin clothing, and had shell and bone necklaces and ornaments. Their pottery, heavily decorated, ranges from small fine cups to large coarse storage vessels. They belonged to a culture which buried its dead in tombs like Maes Howe.

The settlement
0.5mi/800m walk from the car park.
Today several dwellings (nos 1–10) remain, linked by once-covered passageways (A, B and F). Seven are well preserved, remains of several others are less prominent. Only driftwood and scrubby trees were available for timber and even the furniture was built of stone.

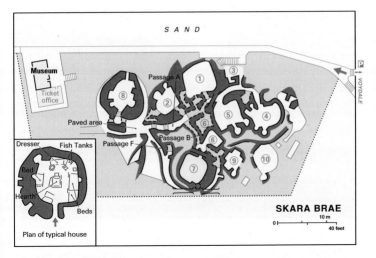

Plan of typical house

SKARA BRAE

Rectangular in shape with rounded corners, the huts had regularly coursed flagstone walls. Each dwelling had a short entrance passage guarded by a door at the inner end. The hearth for the fire was in the middle and smoke was allowed to escape by a hole in the roof. Stone slabs were used to fashion the beds against the walls, the shelved dressers and wall cupboards. Privies were connected to an underground sewer system. The boxes lined with clay, which are let into the floor, may have served as tanks for bait. The best preserved house (no 7) has been roofed over.

Some artefacts found on site are displayed in the small museum (custodian's office); others are in the Royal Museum of Scotland, Edinburgh.

Stromness★ (Mainland)

Population 2,100. The second Mainland centre and principal fishing port, Stromness is often the visitor's first view of the islands as it is the terminal for the boat service from the Scottish mainland. Although used as a haven by the Norsemen, the settlement only really developed in the 18C as a trading centre and the last port of call for the Hudson Bay Company's ships. Whaling and herring fishing then took over as the principal activities. The dominance of the sea in the past is reflected in the physical layout. A long, winding and paved main street is overlooked on the seaward side by gable-ended dwellings, each with their own jetties.

Sights

The Pier Arts Centre

♿🕐*Open year-round Mon–Sat 10.30am–5pm.* ☎*01856 850 209. www.pierarts centre.com.*
Recently reopened following a major renovation, this "glowing postmodern shed of dark metal and glass" was voted best building of the year in 2007 by the Royal Incorporation of Architects in Scotland.

It features a permanent collection of **abstract art**★ highlighted by some of the greatest works of the 1929–63 period. Ben Nicholson and Barbara Hepworth are represented by some of their early works, together with canvases of other St Ives painters including Peter Lanyon, Patrick Heron, and Naum Gabo.

Stromness Museum

🕐*Open Apr–Sept daily 10am–5pm, Oct–Mar Mon–Sat 11am–3.30pm.* 🕐*Closed mid-Feb–1st wk Mar.* ✉*Call for details.* ☎*01856 850 025. www.scbf. co.uk/museum.*
Orkney's natural history and maritime museum includes displays on whaling, fishing, the Hudson Bay Company and

W. Richard/ Britainonview.com

Old Man of Hoy

the scuttled German Fleet in Scapa Flow (ⓒ*see KIRKWALL: EASTERN MAINLAND*).

Excursions

Pentland Firth Crossing

The 2hr car ferry between Stromness and Scrabster is an ideal way of seeing the outstanding cliff scenery of Hoy (the name means high island). The sheer cliffs of **St John's Head** (1,140ft/347m) marks where the mountains meet the sea. Even more spectacular is the sight of the 450ft/137m sea stack, **The Old Man of Hoy**★★★, rising sheer out of turbulent waters. This red-sandstone stack was climbed for the first time in 1966 but it is more usually the domain of a myriad screeching and hovering seabirds.

PAISLEY
RENFREWSHIRE
POPULATION 84,330

The industrial town of Paisley is the largest "town" (as opposed to a city) in Scotland. It may not be well known for its visitor attractions but it has long been famed for its Paisley shawls and thread production.

- 🗊 **Information:** 9A Gilmour Street. ☎0141 889 0711. www.seeglasgow.com. www.paisley.org.uk
- ▶ **Orient Yourself:** Paisley is 9.5mi/15km west of Glasgow via the M 8.
- ⓒ **Also See:** GLASGOW.

Sights

Paisley Abbey

ⓒ*Open Mon–Sat 10.30am–3.30pm.* 🚻. ☎*0141 889 7654. www.paisleyabbey. org.uk.*

Rght In the heart of Paisley, the church is an impressive sight as it stands unencumbered by encroaching buildings. Walter Fitzalan founded a priory in 1163 bringing monks from the Cluniac estab-lishment at Wenlock. Elevated to abbey status in 1245, the monastery became one of the richest and most powerful in Scotland.

Although the priory was a 12C foundation, the present-day church is mostly 15C and the result of many rebuildings and extensive restorations. The deeply recessed west front **doorway** is 13C Early Pointed Gothic. Inside, the corbelled galleries at the clerestory level of the nave are unusual in that they go round the outside of the pillars. The St Mirin Chapel, in the south transept, commemorates St Columba's friend and contemporary. The long choir, a 19C and 20C restoration, has Robert Lorimer furnishings. Here also is the **tomb of Marjory Bruce** the daughter of King Robert the Bruce. Tradition has it that she fell from her horse near Paisley Abbey. She was pregnant at the time and, although the baby was saved, Marjory died. The baby became Robert II of Scotland, the first of the Stewart monarchs and an ancestor of the present queen.

The **Place (Palace) of Paisley** is all that remains of the monastic buildings which, after the Reformation, were appropriated as the commendator's residence.

Paisley Museum and Art Gallery

High Street. ◷*Open Tue–Sat 10am–5pm, Sun 2–5pm.* ☎*0141 889 3151. www.paisley .org.uk.*

This 19C building, one of the Coats bequests, houses a series of well displayed collections. The comprehensive **Paisley Shawl Section**★ outlines the development of this specialised local activity and includes examples of its varied products (☙*see Box below*). The art gallery has a number of works by the Scottish School (including Gillies, Walton and George Henry). Other sections include a good pottery collection, and local and natural history exhibits.

Coats Observatory

Oakshaw Street. ◷*Open Tue–Sat 10am– 5pm, Sun 2–5pm. Public telescope view-ing: Oct–Mar Thu 7.30–9.30pm.* ☎*0141 889 2013. www.paisley.org.uk.*

When built in 1882–3 this was one of the best equipped small observatories in the country. Its array of telescopes, including a 10inch model, is open to the public, and there are displays on astronomy, meteorology and space flight.

Sma' Shot Cottages

11/17 George Place. ◷*Open Apr–Sept Wed & Sat noon–4pm.* ☐. ☎*0141 889 1708. www.smashot.co.uk.*

The fully restored and furnished 18C weavers cottages evoke bygone Paisley with photographs and artifacts, such as bone cutlery and old looms. The adjacent row of mill workers houses from the 1840s. One of them has been turned into a cosy tearoom.

Excursion

Kilbarchan Weaver's Cottage

5mi/8km west off the A 737. ◷*Open Good Fri–Sept Fri–Tue 1–5pm.* ⊛*£5.* ☎*0844 4932205. www.nts.org.uk.*

This 18C weaver's cottage, with its typical interior of the period, is a reminder of the local cottage industry which still reigned supreme at the turn of the last century. Displayed throughout the cottage are examples of locally woven work including tartan which was produced more recently. The handlooms in the basement are used for demonstration purposes.

An attractive cottage garden has an interesting collection of herbs and local historical artefacts.

Paisley shawls

It was in 1805 that an Edinburgh manufacturer introduced the art of imitation Kashmir shawls to Paisley, where it prospered, initially as a cottage industry. Such was the success that all patterned shawls with the traditional "pine" or tear-drop motifs came to be known as **Paisley shawls**. With the introduction of the Jacquard loom in the 1820s the industry became more factory based, and intricate overall patterns with as many as 10 colours were popular. Printed shawls were introduced in the 1840s and were followed in the 1860s by the reversible shawl which never gained any real popularity.

The local museum has an excellent collection, demonstrating all the beauty and intricacy of these multicoloured, fine garments which were appreciated equally for their warmth, lightness and softness.

PERTH★
PERTHSHIRE AND KINROSS
POPULATION 43,450

Perth, "the Fair City on the Tay", is pleasantly situated beside the river between two vast parklands, and although this former royal burgh has few historic buildings, it has succeeded better than most in retaining the atmosphere of a Scottish county town. Within driving distance of many major Scottish cities and attractions, Perth is an ideal touring centre.

- **Information:** Lower City Mills. ☎01738 450 600, www.perthshire.co.uk.
- ▶ **Orient Yourself:** The town centre is compact and can be covered on foot with bus tours to outlying sites.
- **Don't Miss:** The city's Georgian terraces; Perth Museum and Art Gallery; an excursion to Scone Palace; the view from Glenshee.
- **Organizing Your Time:** Allow two hours for the town centre.
- **Also See:** DUNKELD.

A Bit of History

The town achieved royal burgh status in the 12C and both William the Lion and Robert the Bruce gave confirming charters.

During the reign of James I, Perth became the meeting place on several occasions for Parliament. The town would no doubt have become the centre of government or national capital had the king not been murdered in Blackfriars Monastery. By the 16C the walled town was a prosperous burgh, and the various trades and crafts are remembered today by street names: Cow Street, Meal Street, Flesher's Street, Cutlog Street, Baxter's (Bakers) Street, Mercer Terrace, Glover Street and Skinnergate.

Inland port – From earliest times the Tay was important in bringing trade to the town and river traffic included both foreign and coastal vessels. Between 1814 and the 1930s a steamboat service plied the river between Dundee and Perth. Today, Perth's port, situated downstream, imports and handles fertilisers, with grain, timber, malt and potatoes as the main exports.

With its reputation as a salmon river, the Tay also boasts pearl fishing. The gems obtained from freshwater mussels range in colour from grey to gold and lilac.

Walking Tour

Black Watch Regimental Museum★

🕐 *Open May–Sept Mon–Sat 10am–4.30pm. Oct–Apr Mon–Fri 10am–3.30pm.* 🕐*Closed last Sat in Jun, 23 Dec–6 Jan.* ▱. ☎*0131 310 8530. www.theblackwatch. co.uk.*

Balhousie Castle, the former home of the Earls of Kinnoull, is now the setting for the the Black Watch Regimental Museum. The origins of the regiment date back to the early 18C when General Wade was given the task of bringing

Tay Street and Smeaton Bridge, Perth

VisitScotland Perthshire

peace, law and order to the Highlands. During his subsequent programme of road and bridge building, Wade enlisted and armed groups of Highlanders to keep the peace. These companies were known as **The Black Watch** (&*see ABER-FELDY*) for the watch they kept on the Highlands and for their dark tartan, a direct contrast to the red of the Government troops. The Regiment was formed in 1739. This well-presented museum is organised chronologically to unfold the regimental history through its battles and campaigns with paintings, silver, Colours and uniforms, plus medals won in battle as recently as 2005.

North Inch

The 100 acres of this park, extending northwards along the west bank of the Tay are mainly given over to sports facilities. Its outstanding feature is the domed form of Bell's Sports Centre built in 1978. It was on the North Inch that the great **Clan Combat** took place in 1396 between 30 champions from clans Chattan and Kay. There were few survivors in this event which Scott describes in his novel, *The Fair Maid of Perth*. Robert III and his Queen spectated from the Blackfriars Monastery, which once stood at the south end of the park.

Georgian terraces★

On the completion of Perth Bridge in 1772 the town began to spread beyond the medieval limits. Entire streets were built in the new Georgian style, such as **Barossa Place** with its substantial villas, and **Rose Terrace** dominated by its centrepiece, the Old Perth Academy (1807). The art critic John Ruskin (1819–1900) spent much of his childhood at no 10. Continue round to the delightful curve of **Atholl Crescent**, the first extension in the new town development. A plaque on the southwest corner of Blackfriars Street marks the site of Blackfriars Monastery. Founded in 1231, this was the scene of James I's assassination in 1437. In 1559 it was destroyed along with all of Perth's other monastic establishments.

North Port leads to **The Fair Maid's House**, the home of Scott's heroine, Catherine Glover; it is now used mainly as an art centre. Charlotte Street, leading round to Tay Street, is backed by a short Georgian row, the last house of which has an attractive fire plaque. Smeaton's elegant nine-arched **Perth Bridge** bestrides the Tay.

▶ *Take George Street, overlooked on the right by Perth Museum and Art Gallery.*

Perth Museum and Art Gallery★

&⊙*Open year-round Mon–Sat 10am–5pm.* ⊙*Closed 25 Dec, 1 Jan.* ☎*01738 632 488. www.pkc.gov.uk.*

The building is distinguished by an imposing portico and dome. In addition to displays on natural history and furniture there are particularly interesting sections on the local glass (Monart and Vasart ware), silver and clock-making industries.

The art gallery includes works by **John Millais**, Cadell, Henry and David Wilkie. At the woodland display you can see and listen to red squirrel and capercaillie, and marvel at the 64lb (29kg) salmon, a British record, caught by a Miss Ballantine on the Tay in 1922.

▶ *George Street leads to High Street. Then take St John Street.*

St John's Kirk

&⊙ *Open Easter–Oct 10am–noon, 2–4pm.* ☎*01738 638 482. www.st-johns-kirk.co.uk.* The church, with its steepled tower, is an example of the great burgh kirks. Founded in the 12C, this mainly 15C church was restored in 1925–26 to house a war memorial. It was probably from this church that Perth took its early name of "St John's toun", perpetuated today by the name of the local football team (St Johnstone).

At the junction with South Street, a plaque on the building on the left, marks the former site of the Bishops of Dunkeld's house. The Salutation Hotel (1699) with its Venetian-style window was used by Bonnie Prince Charlie.

▶ *Continue down South Street towards the Tay and turn right onto Tay Street. From here there is a good* **view** *of Perth Bridge.*

PERTH

York Pl.	Z	North Port	Y	27	George St	YZ	17
Watergate	Z	North Methven St	Y	25	Edinburgh Rd	Z	15
Victoria St	Z	New Row	Z		Dunkeld Rd	Y	
Tay St	Z	Mill St	Z		Dundee Rd	Z	
Strathmore St	Y	36	Melville St	Y		County Pl.	Z	14
South St	Z	Marshall Pl.	Z		Charterhouse Line	Z	13
South Methven St	Z	34	Main St	Y		Charlotte St	Y	
Skinner Gate	Z	35	Lochie Brae	Y		Charlotte Pl.	Y	10
Shore Rd	Z	32	Leonard St	Z		Carpenter St	Y	9
Scott St	Z		Kirk Gate	Z	24	Canal St	Z	
Saint Leonard's Bank	Z	31	Kinnoull St	YZ		Caledonian Rd	YZ	
Saint John's St	Z	29	King St	Z		Bowerswell Rd	Y	7
Saint John's Pl.	Z	28	King ,s Pl.	Z	22	Blackfriars St	Y	6
Saint John's Centre			King Edward St	Z	21	Barrack St	Y	5
Rose Terrace	Y		Keir St	Y		Barossa Pl.	Y	
Queen's Bridge	Z		Isla Rd	Y		Balhousie St	Y	
Princes St	Z		Hospital St	Z	20	Balhousie Ave	Y	3
Perth Bridge	Y		High St	Z		Atholl St	Y	
		Hay St	Y		Atholl Crescent	Y	2
		Gowrie St	Y				

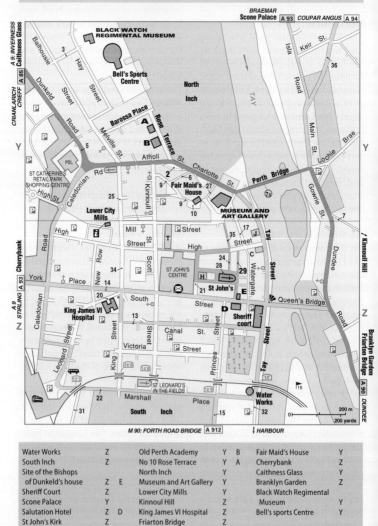

The Gowrie Conspiracy

Who knows what really happened on 5 August 1600 at Gowrie House? The basic facts are that King **James I** and a small retinue visited John Ruthven, 3rd Earl of Gowrie, and his brother Alexander. There ensued a fight, during which John and Alexander were both killed. On the royalist side it was claimed that the king was lured here falsely, then threatened with kidnap, and the deaths of the Ruthvens were as a result of self defence. But it is also clear that the Ruthvens were known to be disloyal to James and, moreover, owed him a large sum of money, so James had at least one motive to get rid of them. Whether it was the king or the Ruthvens who engineered the situation is lost in the mists of time.

Tay Street

The colonnaded frontage of the **Sheriff Court** (1820) is typical of Robert Smirke's Greek-inspired work. A plaque to the left commemorates and represents the once magnificent Gowrie House (1520). It was the scene of the mystery-shrouded **Gowrie Conspiracy** (5 August 1600) when the descendants of the Ist Earl of Gowrie were murdered. Theories abound on whether this was an attempted regicide, kidnapping, or a plot on the part of James VI (☉ see Box above).

The Water Works (Fergusson Gallery)

This handsome circular building is girdled by a balustrade, crowned by an elegant dome and guarded by an urn-topped tower. Formerly the city's water works the building now houses the **Fergusson Gallery** (☉ open Mon–Sat 10am–5pm, also Sun early May–late Aug 1–4.30pm; ☉ closed 25 Dec, 1 Jan; ☎01738 441 944, www.pkc.gov.uk), which exhibits in rotation the works of J D Fergusson (1874–1961), a leading member of the **Scottish Colourists**. The muted tones of his early landscapes and portraits (*Princes Street Gardens, The White Dress*) contrast with the vibrant colours and luminous quality of later scenes which reflect the influence of Fauvism (*People and Sails at Royan, Cassis from the West*). There is also a striking group of female nudes in vivid colours and with dark outlines (*Bathers: The Parasol, Bathers in Green, Danu Mother of the Gods*). His Scottish paintings include Highland landscapes and Glasgow scenes.

Address Book

☉ For coin ranges, see the Legend on the cover flap.

WHERE TO STAY

🛏🛏**Kinnaird** – 5 Marshall Place. ☎01738 628 021. www.kinnaird-guesthouse.co.uk. This neat Georgian terrace house offers sensitively appointed period style and lovely park and garden views.

🛏🛏**Beechgrove** – Dundee Road. ☎01738 636 147. Set in 1.25 acres this sturdy Georgian manse (vicarage) is a short walk from the town centre; bedrooms with mahogany furniture.

🛏🛏**Taythorpe** – Isla Road. ☎01738 447994. An immaculately kept modern guesthouse, a short walk from the city centre and close to Scone Palace, with cosy bedrooms, an inviting lounge and friendly communal breakfasts.

WHERE TO EAT

🍴🍴**Deans @ Let's Eat** – 77–79 Kinnoull Street. ☎01738 643 377. www.letseatperth.co.uk. Vibrant, modern Scottish cuisine is served in a relaxed neighbourhood setting.

🍴🍴**63 Tay Street** – 63 Tay Street. ☎01738 441 451. www.63taystreet.co.uk. Light airy and modern, this contemporary restaurant close to the riverside serves well-priced modern cuisine with an emphasis on the finest seasonal ingredients.

Perth on show

Perth is famous for its Aberdeen Angus Shows and sales (*February and October*), the Perthshire Agricultural Show (*August*) and is the home of both the Aberdeen Angus and Highland Cattle Societies.

Notable events in the year's calendar include five race meetings (*April, May, August, September and October*) as well as Perth Horse Show, a Carriage Driving Championship (*May*) at Scone racecourse, the Perth Highland Games (*August*) and Curling Championships.

King James VI Hospital
In 1429 James I founded the only **Carthusian Monastery** in Scotland on this site. The murdered founder, his Queen Joan Beaufort and Margaret Tudor, James IV's Queen, were all buried within its walls. The monastery was destroyed in 1559. The present four-storeyed, H-plan building, now divided into flats, was founded by James VI in 1587 originally as a hospital.

City Mills
West Mill Street.
A fine group of early industrial buildings straddles Perth's Town Lade, the channel bringing water from a tributary of the Tay. The Upper City Mills have been converted into a hotel and the Lower City Mills is now home to the tourist office.

Outskirts

Branklyn Garden★
Signposted off the A 85. (NTS). &⊙*Open Good Fri–Oct daily 10am–5pm.* ⊕*£5.* ⊞*£2 pay and display.* ☎*0844 4932193. www.nts.org.uk, www.branklyngarden. org.uk.*
"Small is beautiful" aptly applies to Branklyn which began life in 1922 as a private garden on the east bank of the Tay, overlooking Perth. It is only two acres but it has a wide variety of plants. Branklyn is famed for its rhododendrons, which start to come into colour as early as February, frosts permitting, and many

species are still in bloom in July in the most vibrant of colours. Another speciality is the lovely blue Himalayan poppy

Kinnoull Hill
Take Bowerswell Road; 20min walk from Braes Road car park to the view indicator. The summit (792ft/241m) commands an extensive **view**★, away from the Highland rim, over Perth, to the New Friarton Bridge, then follows the Tay round into the Carse of Gowrie with the Ochils and Lomonds in the distance. The craggy cliffs of Kinnoull, towering 700ft/213m above the Tay, are dominated by the follies of Kinnoull Watchtower and its counterpart a mile to the east on Binn Hill, both imitations of Rhineland castles.

Excursions

Scone Palace★★ – *2mi/3.2km NE via the A 93.* ☁*SCONE PALACE.*

Huntingtower Castle★
3mi/5km northwest on the A 9 and then the A 85. (HS). ⊙*Open Apr–Sept daily 9.30am–5.30pm. Oct–Mar, Sat–Wed 9.30am–4.30pm. Last admission 30 mins before closing.* ⊙*Closed 25–26 Dec, 1–2 Jan.* ⊕*£4.* ☎*01738 627 231. www.historic-scotland.gov.uk.*
Originally known as the Castle of Ruthven, this was the hunting seat of the family of the same name and scene of the **Raid of Ruthven** in 1582. William, 4th Lord Ruthven, created Earl of Gowrie the previous year, invited the 16-year-old James VI to the castle, where he was held captive for 10 months by a group of nobles resentful of the influence the Earl of Arran and Duke of Lennox exercised over the young monarch. Although officially pardoned, the Earl of Gowrie was beheaded in 1584 at Stirling, on charges connected with an attack on Stirling Castle. Revenge was to follow with the counterplot, the Gowrie Conspiracy (☁*see Gowrie Conspiracy Box above*) in 1600. The castle was confiscated, its name changed to Huntingtower and the family name of Ruthven proscribed. In 1643 the castle passed into the hands of William Dysart, "whipping-boy" for Charles I and

father of Elizabeth Dysart, Duchess of Lauderdale.

This typical 15C–16C tower house consists of two towers, which were joined in the 17C to provide more commodious accommodation. Both towers have three storeys plus a garret served by turnpikes. Note in particular the roofline with corbelled wall walk, corner turrets, punctuated by chimneys and crow-stepped gable ends. The **painted timber ceiling** on the first floor of the eastern tower is one of the earliest of its kind (c. 1540). An unusual feature is the dovecot in the garret of the western tower.

Elcho Castle★

Leave Perth by the A 912 and before the motorway turn left onto a local road in the direction of Rhynd. HS signposting leads down to the castle by a farm road and through the steading. (HS). ◷*Open Apr–Sept daily 9.30am–5.30pm. Oct, Sat–Wed 9.30am–4.30pm. Last admission 30 mins before closing.* ◎£3. ☎01738 639 998. www.historic-scotland.gov.uk.

Overlooking the Tay, the Earls of Wemyss' family seat is reputedly on or near the site of an earlier stronghold and former retreat of William Wallace. Built in the second half of the 16C, Elcho Castle is a handsome and remarkably complete 16C fortified mansion with three projecting towers. Above the plain walls, pierced by windows with wrought-iron grills and gun ports, the wallhead is an intriguing composition of decorative elements: pediments, roll-moulded window surrounds, corbelled turrets, crow-stepped gables and chimney stacks. The north and west fronts are good examples of the imaginative Scottish masons at their best.

The southwest tower has an unusually elegant and spacious **staircase**.

Abernethy

8mi/13km southeast by A 912 and A 913. Population 881. Happily the main road by-passes the old centre of this peaceful village on the lower slopes of the Ochils. As the village stood at the heart of the Pictish kingdom, some claimed this was the early capital. Later it was the site of a Celtic settlement and the only relic of its ancient past is an **11C Round Tower**★. This Irish-type tower served the dual purpose of place of refuge and belfry. Standing alone at the kirkyard gate this tower (74ft/22.5m tall) tapers slightly. Two periods of construction are clearly visible. Note the elevated position of the door, a defensive feature, the jougs attached to the wall and the Pictish symbol stone at its foot.

Glenshee – *40mi/64km. Leave Perth to the north by the A 93.*

Scone Palace★★

↻*See SCONE PALACE.*

Glenshee, winter landscape

L. McGowran/ Scottish Viewpoint

Meikleour Beech Hedge
This hedge (100ft/30.5m high) was planted in 1746.

Blairgowrie
Population 7,028. Set in the heart of an area famous for soft fruit-growing, in winter Blairgowrie becomes the main ski centre for the resort of Glenshee (see *Glenshee entry below*).

The road follows the Black Water up Glenshee, a typical Angus Glen, as far as the Spittal of Glenshee. The final ascent to the Cairnwell Pass (2,199ft/665m) was famous for the zigzag bend, appropriately called the **Devil's Elbow**, now bypassed by a new stretch of the A 93.

In the romantically wooded valley of the River Ericht just upstream from Blairgowrie stands **Keathbank Mill**. Once a flax and jute mill with the largest wheel in Scotland, the imposing structure is now private housing.

Glenshee
The Glenshee ski area lies to either side of the A 93.

This is the busiest **ski resort** in Scotland. The season generally commences around late December and runs until Easter, but can be longer or shorter depending on snow cover. The lifts run December through April, with 22 ski tows and two chair-lifts operating on three peaks, giving access to 36 ski runs ranging from easy to expert (*for more information contact the Ski Centre.* ☎013397 41320, *www.ski-glenshee. co.uk*). Facilities include an artificial slope. At the summit (3,059ft/933m) there is a restaurant and **panorama**★★ which encompasses Ben Macdui, Beinn à Bhuird, Lochnagar and Glas Maol on the far side of the valley, plus several Munros. In summer Glenshee is a centre for hang-gliding.

PITLOCHRY★
PERTHSHIRE AND KINROSS
POPULATION 2,194

Set in the lovely Tummel Valley, this holiday resort makes an ideal touring centre for the magnificent scenery of the surrounding countryside. The busy main street is a succession of hotels, guest houses, restaurants, cafés, and tweed and Highland craft shops.

- **Information:** 22 Atholl Road. ☎01796 47221. www.perthshire.co.uk.
- ▶ **Orient Yourself:** Pitlochry is 27mi/43 km north of Perth on the A 9.
- **Don't Miss:** The Queen's View panorama.
- **Organizing Your Time:** Allow at least a day and a night here.
- **Especially for Kids:** The Salmon Ladder at The Hydro Electric Story.
- **Also See:** DUNKELD, BLAIR CASTLE.

A Bit of History

One of the main drove roads from the north followed the alignment of the Tummel valley and in the 1720s and 1730s **General Wade** (1673–1748) built one of his first military roads from Dunkeld to Inverness through Pitlochry. Prior to this the main settlement was Moulin, and as late as the 1880s Pitlochry numbered barely 300 people. The town's growth was due in large part to its popularity as a health resort in Victorian times, and more recently as a tourist centre situated astride the Great North Road.

Sights

The Hydo Electric Story (Pitlochry Power Station) Kids
♿ ⏰ *Open Apr–Oct Mon–Fri 10am– 5.30pm.* ⏰ *Closed Bank Hols.* ✦£3. *Viewing Salmon Ladder only, free.* ☎01796 473 152. www.scottish-southern.co.uk.

Address Book

🪙 *For coin ranges, see legend cover flap.*

WHERE TO STAY

🛏️ **Dunmurray Lodge** – *72 Bonnethill Road.* ☎01796 473 624, *www.dunmurray. co.uk.* This charming immaculately kept 19C cottage has a homely sitting room and smallish but cosy bedrooms, all in soothing shades of cream. Good value.

🛏️ **Torrdarach** – *Golf Course Road.* ☎01796 472 136. *www.a1tourism. com/uk/torrdarach.html.* This substantial Edwardian country house lies in secluded wooded gardens with views over the Tummel Valley; reasonably-priced bedrooms in bright colours.

🛏️ **Beinn Bhracaigh** – *Higher Oakfield.* ☎01796 470 355. *www. beinnbhracaigh.com.* This restored Victorian Country House has been extended and decorated with a blend of antique and contemporary style.

WHERE TO EAT

🍽️ **Old Armoury** – *Armoury Road.* ☎01796 474 281. *www. theoldarmouryrestaurant.com.* This former armoury, now a tearoom and restaurant, has a lovely al fresco dining area. Inside is a bright lounge; traditional menus with a distinct Scottish accent.

Part of the North of Scotland Hydroelectric Board's Tummel Valley Scheme, the dam (54ft/16.5m high and 457ft/139m long) retains Loch Faskally to even out the flow of water. There is an interactive exhibition which includes videos on the Tummel Scheme and the life cycle of the salmon. The main attraction is the **Salmon Ladder**, which permits salmon to move upstream to their spawning grounds between April and October: 34 pools, three of which are "resting pools", rise up in steps to the level of the loch. The salmon can be observed at close quarters through windows in the observation room. The artificial Loch Faskally (3mi/5km long) is stocked with salmon and trout. It provides good angling and boating facilities and a pleasant walk (*1hr*) around the shores.

Excursions

Rannoch Moor – *38mi/60km to Rannoch Station from Pitlochry*

The B 8019 follows the northern shore of Lochs Tummel and Rannoch with mountains and loch scenery as fine as any in the Central Highlands. By contrast the excursion ends with the desolation of Rannoch Moor.

Queen's View★★

Access from the Forestry Commission car park and information centre.

This famous viewpoint, named after Queen Victoria's 1866 visit, has a truly royal vista up Loch Tummel, which is dominated by the conical shape of Schiehallion (3,547ft/1,083m).

Loch Tummel

Hydroelectric works in the vicinity have been responsible for increasing the size of the original loch from about 3mi/4.5km to 7mi/11km in length and its depth by 17ft/5m. The power station at the Tummel Bridge end is powered by water from the Loch Errochty reservoir, high in the mountains to the north, which arrives by a 6mi/10km tunnel.

Loch Rannoch

The larger of the two lochs is almost 10mi/16km long and an average of 0.75mi/1km wide.

The road runs close to the loch side. On the south shore are the remains of the native pine forest, the Black Wood of Rannoch.

Beyond the head of Loch Rannoch the B 846 continues a further 6mi/10km to Rannoch Station, on the West Highland Railway (Glasgow–Fort William). The terrain is hummocky with glacial debris and erratics all around. The Gaur is a typical Highland river with a boulder-strewn course.

Once over the watershed, Rannoch Moor stretches away to the horizon.

Rannoch Moor
The vastness of this desolate wilderness is legendary. At an average height of 1,000ft/305m the granite floor is mainly covered with blanket bog and occasional lochans with the peat in places reaching a depth of 20ft/6m. The moor was a centre of ice dispersal during the Ice Age, with glaciers radiating outwards and gouging, among others, the troughs of the Rannoch-Tummel Valley and Glen Coe in the west.

Killiecrankie
Leave Pitlochry north to join the A 9. Beyond Garry Bridge, leading to lochs Tummel and Rannoch, the river, road and railway all run parallel to negotiate the narrow Pass of Killiecrankie.

Killiecrankie Visitor Centre
(NTS). &. ⓒ *Open Good Fri–first weekend Nov 10am–5.30pm. Site open all year.* ☕. 🅿 (£2). ☎0844 4932194. www.nts.org.uk.

The centre interprets the rich natural history of the Pass (it is famous for its spectacular Autumn colours) and the story of the **Battle of Killiecrankie** (27 July 1689). This was the major event in the first of the Jacobite uprisings, fought on high ground to the north of the Pass. The Jacobite followers were rallied by **John Graham of Claverhouse, Viscount Dundee** (c. 1649–89), who, having seized Blair Castle, moved south to meet the government troops under Mackay. The encounter was brief, and a decisive victory for Dundee even though he was mortally wounded in the fray. A month later however the leaderless Highlanders were beaten at Dunkeld (ⓒ see DUNKELD). The final Jacobite saga ended in 1746 with Culloden (ⓒ see INVERNESS: Excursions).

From the Visitor Centre a path (signposted) leads to the **Soldier's Leap** where a fleeing government soldier is said to have jumped an impossibly wide gap to escape from his Jacobite pursuers. A second path leads down through the wooded Pass of Killiecrankie to the car park beside Garry Bridge.

PITMEDDEN GARDEN★★
ABERDEENSHIRE

The formal Great Garden at **Pitmedden** is a rare jewel in the northeast area and a magnificent sight in summer when the extravagant scale of its planting is revealed in a riot of colour.

- 🛈 **Information:** ☎0844 4932177. www.nts.org.uk.
- ▶ **Orient Yourself:** The Gardens, at Ellon, are 16.5mi/26.5km north of Aberdeen on the A 90.
- 👁 **Don't Miss:** a visit in July or August when over 40,000 flowers are in bloom and the gardens are at their very best.
- ⓒ **Organizing Your Time:** Allow at least two hours.
- & **Also See:** HADDO HOUSE, ABERDEEN.

A Bit of History

The creator – In the early 17C the Pitmedden Estate was acquired by the Setons. When John, the 3rd laird, was killed at the Battle of Brig O'Dee (1639) his two young sons were entrusted to a relative, George Seton, 3rd Earl of Winton. An improving laird and man of advanced tastes, he had established gardens at Winton and Pinkie. It was **Sir Alexander Seton** (c. 1639–1719), the younger brother, who In 1675 began to transform this treeless and stony area into an extraordinary formal garden.

Re-creation – By 1951, when the donation of the garden was made to the

The National Trust for Scotland

Pitmedden Garden

National Trust for Scotland, time had all but effaced the formal designs and the lower area was a vegetable garden. The original plans had been lost when Pitmedden Castle was burnt in 1818. New designs were established based on Charles II's garden at Holyroodhouse.

Visit

(NTS). ♿🕐*Walled Garden and Museum of Farming Life open: May–Sept 10am–5.30pm (last admission 5pm). Grounds open: all year daily. ⬤£5 (grounds only, free).* ☕. 🅿.

The gardens today – Pitmedden features over 5mi/8km of box hedging arranged in intricate patterns to form six parterres, made from trim boxwood hedges. Each parterre is filled with some 40,000 plants bursting with colour in the summer months. The initial impression is of immaculately tended gardens where neatly clipped yews, neat hedges and shaven lawns edge masses of colour and contrast with the more natural exuberance of the extensive herbaceous borders and a spectacular lupin border The **walled garden** is planned on two levels. An upper western half, mostly lawns and hedges with a herb garden, overlooks the lower formal garden area. Honeysuckle, jasmine and roses create a succession of fragrances, while fountains, topiary, sundials, and a fascinating herb garden add to the sense of discovery around the walled garden. A belvedere provides a good **viewing point**. The colour is provided by annuals, coloured gravels and green turf paths. Three of the designs are geometric while a fourth represents the armorial display of Sir Alexander Seton. Also part of the original plan are two gazebos with their ogee-shaped roofs, the central fountain (rebuilt) and the entrance staircase linking the two levels.

Over 80 varieties of apple trees adorn the high granite walls, offering a spectacular show of blossom and scent in spring. On the last Sunday in September harvest celebrations feature dancing and music, and fruits harvested from the gardens are on sale.

Grounds – In the surrounding policies, a woodland walk and nature trail shows off rare breeds of livestock and endangered species. It also takes in ponds, rhododendrons, a lime kiln and a nature hut with information about the wider estate. The outbuildings house a **Museum of Farming Life** with implements, artefacts and domestic utensils from a bygone era. The farmhouse, bothy (unmarried farm servant's home) and the stables, with a display on the era of the horse, are of particular interest.

ROSSLYN CHAPEL★★
MIDLOTHIAN
7MI/11KM SOUTH OF EDINBURGH, NEAR ROSLIN

Set on the edge of the Esk Valley, the 15C **Rosslyn Chapel** famous for its stone carvings and legends, is a masterpiece of astonishing craftsmanship.

- **Information:** ☎0131 440 2159. www.rosslynchapel.org.uk.
- ▶ **Orient Yourself:** Roslin Village is 8mi/13km south of Edinburgh, via the A 701 towards Penicuik/Peebles. Bus 15 comes here direct.
- **Guided tours:** Rosslyn Chapel is one of Scotland's most talked about and interpreted sites. If you would like a guide to help you decipher its myriad symbols and mysterious history, try Celtic Trails ☎0131 448 2869. www.celtictrails.co.uk.
- **Organizing Your Time:** Allow half an hour.
- No interior photography or video is allowed.
- **Also See:** EDINBURGH.

A Bit of History

The founder, **Sir William St Clair**, third and last Prince of Orkney (1396–1484) and lord of nearby Rosslyn Castle, assembled workmen from various European countries with the very intention of creating a unique work. This began in 1446 and came to a halt in 1486 two years after Sir William's death. Of the planned cruciform collegiate church only the choir was completed. Damaged in 1592, used as a stable for the horses of General Monck's troops in 1650, it was restored in 1861 and today serves as an Episcopalian place of worship.

Visit

Open year-round Mon–Sat 9.30am–6pm (Oct–Mar 5pm), Sun noon–4.45pm. Last admission 30 min before closing. Closed Dec 24–25 & 31, Jan 1. ₤7.50.

Exterior
A foretaste of the richness to come, the pinnacled flying buttresses, window hood moulds, heraldic roof cornice, corbels and canopies of niches are covered with elaborate **decorative sculpture**.

Interior
A five-bay **choir** with clerestory above is bordered by north, south and east aisles, the latter being prolonged by a Lady Chapel stretching the full width

of the building and raised by one step. The five compartments of the vaulted choir, spangled with stars, roses and other decorative paterae are separated by sculptured ribs. In the side aisles, architraves between the pillars and outer walls separate pointed vaulting, with the apex running in a north-south direction, while the Lady Chapel has groined vaulting with pendants.

Amid this wealth of detail the outstanding feature is the **Apprentice Pillar**★★★ (see illustration, Introduction: Arts and Culture). Legend has it that while the master mason was on a tour abroad prior to executing this work, the apprentice produced the pillar we see today. On his return the enraged master mason, in a fit of jealousy, killed the apprentice (see **30**, **29** and **27**). From the base with eight intertwined dragons, foliage winds up the column to the carved capital. The Stafford Knot is visible on the south side. Some of the scenes from this Bible of Stone are listed below and pinpointed on the accompanying plan.

North Aisle
(**1**) wall pillar to the right of the door: Crucifixion; (**2**) wall pillar: plaited crown of thorns; (**3**) pillar: imp; (**4**) pillar: lion's head; (**5**) wall pillar: shield; (**6**) wall pillar: shield displaying the arms of the founder and his wife; (**7**) architrave, east side: Our Blessed Lord seated in Glory; (**8**) windows: two of the Twelve Apostles;

Rosslyn Chapel (carved ceiling, detail)

P. Tomkins/ Scottish Viewpoint/ Visit Scotland

(**9**) arch: Samson pulling down the pillars of the House of Dagon.

Lady Chapel

(**10**) and (**11**) roof ribs: the Dance of Death is portrayed by a series of 16 figures; (**12**) pendant: Star of Bethlehem with eight figures evoking the Birth of Christ; (**13**) pillars: angels; (**14**) **Apprentice Pillar★★★**; carvings above include Isaac on the altar and a ram caught in a thicket; (**15**) and (**16**) roof ribs: series of eight figures.

South Aisle

(**17**) architrave: inscription in Lombardic letters: "Wine is strong, the King is stronger, Women are stronger but above all truth conquers"; (**18**) window: two of the Twelve Apostles; (**19**) architrave; east side: The Virtues; west side: The Vices; (**20**) window arch: Nine Orders of the Angelic Hierarchy.

Choir

(**21**) niche: modern Virgin and Child replacing the statue destroyed at the Reformation; (22) floor: founder's burial slab; (**23**) pillar: human figures and animals; (**24**) pillar: Anna the Prophetess; (**25**) arch: Twelve Apostles and Four Martyrs each with the instruments of their martyrdom; (**26**) pillar: Jesus as the Carpenter of Nazareth, two men wrestling and Samson or David with a lion; (**27**) under niche: the widowed mother;

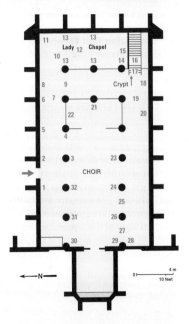

(**28**) pillar: crowned figure; (**29**) cornice level: the master mason; (**30**) cornice level: the apprentice with the scar on his left temple; (**31**) pillar: Prodigal son feeding the swine; (**32**) pillar: three figures looking north to (**1**).

In the Movies

In 2006 millions of people saw Rosslyn Chapel on screen in the blockbuster movie *The Da Vinci Code*.

ST ANDREWS★★
FIFE
POPULATION 10,525

St Andrews, on the Fife coast, is famous as both a seat of learning and the home of golf. As the former metropolitan *see* of Scotland, the city was in the mainstream of Scottish history and its rich heritage includes a 12C cathedral, 13C castle and 15C university. Today it has a quieter charm, detached from national matters, although it is a buzzing holiday resort in summer, and reverts to the role of a university town in term time with a very busy social and cultural scene.

- **Information:** 70 Market Street. ☎01334 472 021. www.visitfife.com. www.standrews.co.uk. www.visit-standrews.co.uk.
- ▶ **Orient Yourself:** St Andrews is 54mi/86km northeast of Edinburgh, across the Firth of Forth, The town centre is compact and can be covered on foot with open-top bus tours (mid-Jun through Sept) to outlying sites.
- **Parking:** Vouchers, available from the tourist office and some local shops, are required.
- **Don't Miss:** the view from the cathedral tower; the West Port; an excursion to the East Neuk villages.
- **Organizing Your Time:** Allow at least half a day plus a day for excursions.
- **Especially for Kids:** The Scottish Deer Centre; St Andrews Aquarium; Craigtoun Country Park.

A Bit of History

The Celtic settlement of St Mary on the Rock, associated with the relics of St Andrew, grew in importance with the founding of the St Regulus Church, a priory in the 12C and finally a grandiose cathedral. The monastic establishment renowned as a seat of learning was the precursor of the university. With a growing university attracting scholars and students of a high calibre, 15C St Andrews was an active and prosperous burgh well meriting the attribution of a national role as ecclesiastical capital of Scotland in 1472.

Prosperity and the population declined in the 17C, owing in part to the loss of the archbishopric (in the 1689 Revolution), the changing trading patterns (now with the American colonies), as well as the political changes after the 1707 Act of Union. The 18C was one of general decline for St Andrews

The Old Course, St. Andrews

P. Tomkins/VisitScotland/Scottish Viewpoint

Golf, a Royal and Ancient Game

Since the 15C St Andrew's has been a place for playing golf or at least the early ball and stick version of the sport. So popular was the game that by 1457 an Act of Scottish Parliament was passed requiring that "futeball and the golfe be utterly cry it down" in favour of church attendance and archery practice. Mary, Queen of Scots played occasionally and her son, **James VI**, popularised golf in England.

Founded in 1754, the Society of St Andrews Golfers had the title **Royal and Ancient** conferred on it by **William IV** in 1834 and is now recognised as the sport's ruling body. To meet the increasing popularity of the game, new courses (New 1895, Jubilee 1897, Eden 1912) were laid out, supplementing the Old Course, which was established several centuries before.

By the beginning of the 20C St Andrews was firmly established as Scotland's golfing mecca, and the town now regularly hosts the British Open, the British Amateur Championships, Walker Cup Matches and other big money tournaments which draw the stars of the professional circuit, bringing huge crowds despite television coverage. Two of the greatest names in golfing history are immortalised by hole names on the Old Course: Tom Morris (18th) and Bobby Jones (10th).

The 19C saw the beginning of the growth of golf as a sport and by the turn of the century the town had achieved renown as a mecca of golf. Its popularity as a holiday and golfing resort has gone from strength to strength.

St Andrews University – Founded in 1410 by **Henry Wardlaw,** Bishop of St Andrews, this was the first university in Scotland and third in Great Britain after Oxford and Cambridge. The present student population is over 4,250.

Cathedral★

(HS). ♿🕐*Open year-round daily 9.30am–5.30pm (Oct–Mar 4.30pm). Last admission 30min before closing; last entry to St Rules Tower, Dec–Jan 3pm.* 🕐*Closed 25–26 Dec, 1–2 Jan.* 🎫*£4, includes entry to Museum and St Rule's Tower. Joint ticket with St Andrews Castle £7.* ☎*01334 472 563. www.historic-scotland.gov.uk.*

Bishop Robert founded the **priory** c 1159 and his successor Bishop Arnold began work on the new cathedral, which was consecrated in 1318 by Bishop Lamberton in the presence of Robert the Bruce. Only the 12C east end, the late-13C west gables and the south wall of the nave remain of this once immense building with its 10-bay nave. Following

the depredations of the Reformation, subsequent neglect and 17C quarrying for stone, the cathedral was reduced to its present ruined state.

To the south were the buildings of what must have been one of the most powerful monastic establishments in Scotland. The 16C precinct wall encloses the cathedral ruins and the church of St Regulus (St Rule). The imposing **St Regulus Church** with its lofty western tower may well have been the shrine built to shelter St Andrew's relics. Queen Margaret's son, Alexander I, nominated Robert, Prior of Scone as Bishop of St Andrews, and it was he who built the church between 1127 and 1144. **St Rule's Tower** *(151 steps)* offers a magnificent **panorama**★★ of St Andrews and its main monuments.

The **museum (M¹)** has a good collection of early and later medieval sculpture and other relics found on the site.

Castle

(HS) ♿🕐 *Open year-round daily 9.30am–5.30pm (Oct–Mar 4.30pm). Last admission 30 mins before closing.* 🕐*Closed 25–26 Dec, 1–2 Jan.* 🎫*£5. Joint ticket with St Andrews Cathedral £7.* ☎*01334 477 196. www.historic-scotland.gov.uk.*

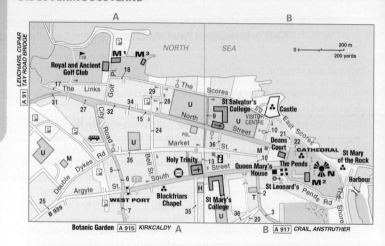

A powerful See

Overlooking the foreshore, the castle ruins once formed part of the palace and stronghold of the bishops and archbishops of St Andrews. Founded c. 1200, it suffered greatly during the Wars of Independence. Bishop Henry Wardlaw, founder of the university, was tutor to James I and it is possible that his young charge spent time here prior to his captivity in England. Bishop Kennedy taught James II how to break the power of his nobles by comparing them to a bundle of arrows, with the suggestion he snap each one individually.

Many reformers suffered imprisonment here, including George Wishart whom Cardinal Beaton had burnt at the stake in front of his palace, and Patrick Hamilton another martyr. Following the martyrdom of Wishart, a group of Protestants seeking revenge gained admission to the castle disguised as stonemasons and stabbed Cardinal Beaton to death (see MONTROSE). They were besieged in the castle for a year and were joined at intervals by others such as John Knox; the siege was only lifted when the garrison capitulated to the French fleet. The defenders were taken to France and Knox was sent to the galleys.

The late-16C entrance range with the central Fore Tower, originally flanked by two round towers, was the work of Archbishop Hamilton and it was supposedly from this façade (the exact spot is contested) that the body of Cardinal Beaton was displayed to the crowd. The buildings were arranged around a courtyard. In what remains of the northwest or Sea Tower is the grim **Bottle Dungeon** of late-14C construction; it is 24ft/7.3m deep and was hewn out of the solid rock. The body of Beaton was dropped into here. The other interesting features are a **mine** and **counter mine** (*enter from the ditch in front of the entrance building*) excavated during the 1546–47 siege.

In the pavement in front of the castle are carved the initials "G W", for George Wishart, marking the spot where he was burnt at the stake in 1546.

Address Book

For coin ranges, see the Legend on the cover flap.

WHERE TO STAY

Deveron House – *64 North Street.* ☎*01334 473 513. www.deveron-house. co.uk.* Centrally located Victorian guest house with a cosy lounge, sunny breakfast room and flowery, pine bedrooms.

18 Queens Terrace – *18 Queens Terrace.* ☎*01334 478849. www.18queensterrace.com.* Very attractive characterful Victorian guesthouse in smart street next to one of the colleges. Lovely light and airy bedrooms and lounge, all furnished and decorated in modern-traditional style.

Aslar House – *120 North Street.* ☎*01334 473 460. www.aslar.com.* This Victorian guesthouse features good value homely bright modern-traditional bedrooms with DVD player; most overlook a quiet rear garden.

Albany – *56–58 North Street.* ☎*01334 47737. www.thealbanystandrews.co.uk.* An elegant well run Georgian townhouse with unfussy bedrooms. The homely firelit lounge is stocked with books and a bar.

WHERE TO EAT

The Seafood Restaurant – *The Scores* ☎*01334 479475. www.theseafoodrestaurant.com.* Floor to ceiling glass on all four sides of this award-winning restaurant ensure everyone gets a sea view. Excellent service accompanies the changing seafood menus.

University

Tours usually only open to prospective students and guests. Call the University for details. The exteriors of the following buildings are open for viewing at any reasonable hours. ☎*01334 462 245.*

St Salvator's College

St Salvator's was founded in 1450 by Bishop James Kennedy. The chapel and tower, above the entrance archway, form the North Street frontage and are a good example of 15C Gothic ecclesiastical style. The two ranges around the quadrangle are 19C reconstructions. **St Salvator's Chapel** was, according to Dr Johnson, "the neatest place of worship he had seen". The collegiate church was restored in the 19C and 20C. Inside is the **founder's tomb**, an amazingly intricate 15C work of art in the Gothic style. The pulpit opposite, with the preacher's hourglass, is supposedly the one used by John Knox.

The initials "P H" laid in the pavement before the entrance, mark the spot where **Patrick Hamilton** (1504–28), an early reformer, was burned on 29 February 1528.

St Leonard's Chapel

The chapel belonged to the college of the same name. The original buildings were a hospital for pilgrims to St Andrew's shrine, then a nunnery, before being acquired to form the nucleus of the new college of St Leonard's. When St Leonard's and St Salvator's were united in 1747, the chapel was neglected while the buildings and grounds were eventually taken over by St Leonard's girls' school. The 1950s restoration re-created the medieval layout with a screen and organ loft.

St Mary's College

Archbishop James Beaton founded St Mary's College in 1537. The buildings on the west side of the quadrangle are 16C. On the ground floor, College Hall has portraits of past principals including Cardinal Beaton. Up two flights of stairs is one of the original student chambers with box beds. On the north side is the old **University Library**, on the site of the original Pedagogy, which is now refurbished as the Psychology Department. On the street front there are a series of arms of University Chancellors. The first floor Senate Room is part of a 19C extension. The two Joseph Knibb longcase clocks flanking

St Andrews Alumni

When William Wales, better known as Prince William, graduated from St Andrews with a 2:1 geography degree in June 2005, he became not only the most famous man at St Andrews for quite some while, but also the first member of the royal family to ever receive a masters degree. The only other royal to have attended St Andrews was James II, back in the early 15C. Other famous ex-students include John Knox, Edward Jenner, and, more recently, Alex Salmond, currently the First Minister of Scotland and leader of the Scottish National Party.

the fireplace were part of Gregory's equipment. The Upper Hall (1612–43) is a galleried room panelled with pale Baltic pine. This was where **Gregory**, the Astronomer (1638–75) and inventor of the reflecting telescope, worked. The ground floor Parliament Hall completed in 1643 is where the Scottish Parliament sat in 1645–46 following the Battle of Philiphaugh.

Additional Sights

The town has retained its original layout with three main streets – South Street, Market Street and North Street – converging on the cathedral.

West Port★
The main entrance to the old town was built in 1589 and opens onto South Street.

Blackfriars Chapel
This is all that remains of a mid-15C foundation for Dominican Friars. The chapel dates from the 16C. The imposing building behind is part of Madras College.

Holy Trinity Church
⏱Open year-round daily 10am–noon, 2–4pm. ☎01334 478 317.
This burgh church, rebuilt in 1410, was modified in the late 18C and restored in the 20C. The corbelled tower with the stone steeple is 15C. Inside, Archbishop Sharp's monument graphically records his death in 1679 on Magus Muir.

Queen Mary's House
A 16C house in attractive rubble stonework with a pantile roof.

Deans Court
This 16C building is now a post-graduate students' residence.

The Pends
A 14C vaulted gatehouse which was the main entrance to the priory. The road follows the precinct wall down to the harbour.

Harbour
This was rebuilt in the 17C with stone from the castle and cathedral.

Church of St Mary of the Rock
This was the site of the 12C Celtic settlement which was gradually superseded by St Regulus and the new cathedral and priory.

Royal and Ancient Golf Club
Club members only. The imposing 1854 clubhouse overlooks the 1st and 18th holes of the Old Course and is the headquarters of the Royal and Ancient Golf Club (see Box above).

British Golf Museum
⏱*Open Mar–Oct Mon–Sat 9.30am–5.30pm, Sun 10am–5pm. Nov–Mar, daily 10am–4pm. Last admission 45 mins before closing.* £5.50. ☎01334 460 046. www.britishgolfmuseum.co.uk.
A must for golfing enthusiasts. 500 years of golf history both in Britain and abroad, come alive by means of audiovisual displays and interactive screen presentations including the origins of the game, the development of the equipment and famous golfing events and personalities.

St Andrews Aquarium Kids
The Scores. ⏱*Open year-round daily 10am–5pm (Nov–Easter Mon–Fri 4pm). Last admission 1hr before closing.* ⏱*Closed 25–26 Dec, 1 Jan.* £6.50,

child £4.60. ✕. ☏ *01334 474 786. www. standrewsaquarium.co.uk.*

Nestled by the cliffs with great views of the famous West Sands, the aquarium has one of the best locations in town. Stingrays, sharks, conger eels, piranha, catfish, mudskippers and many other exotic fish and marine creatures come under the microscope in this lively place. There is also an outdoor seal pool.

Botanic Garden

The Canongate. ⏱ *Open daily: May–Sept, 10am–7pm; Oct–Apr 10am–4pm.* ☏ *£2.* 🅿. ☏ *01334 476 452. www.st-andrews-botanic.org.*

Attractions here include the rhododendrons of the Peat Garden, the colourful Heath Garden, the alpine varieties of the Rock Garden, the Water Garden with exotic species and moor plants, and the glasshouses.

Excursions

Scotland's Secret Bunker

10mi/16km southeast on the B 9131 and the B 940. ⏱ *Open daily mid-Mar through Oct 10am–5pm.* ☏ *£8.60.* ✕. 🅿. ☏ *01333 310 301. www.secretbunker.co.uk.*

Deep below the surface of Fife's farmlands, the sinister chambers and corridors of this once top-secret installation evoke all the menace of the Cold War era.

The bunker was built as one of a chain of early warning radar stations along Britain's eastern coastlines. Redundant in this role, it was then modified to become a nuclear command centre, one of several regional seats of government which would have administered what was left of the country following an atomic holocaust. Following the disappearance of the Soviet threat, it was opened to the public in 1994.

Set in an excavation (130ft/40m deep), protected by 10ft/3m of reinforced concrete and approached down a corridor (500ft/153m long), the bunker is entered via the guardhouse, cunningly designed to resemble a traditional farm building. All stages of its 40-year operational existence are brought hauntingly to life. Contemporary films and videos recall the Orwellian atmosphere of

possible nuclear attack, while figures with dishevelled hair plot the extent of fall-out and members of the emergency services communicate with the contaminated surface. The Secretary of State's office with its bedstead overlooks the Operations Room. In the chapel, a plaque commemorates "those who gave their lives keeping the peace throughout the Cold War".

The East Neuk★★ –
👆*See The EAST NEUK.*

Driving Tour

Inland Fife★

34mi/54km.

This tour through the agricultural hinterland of St Andrews offers a varied selection of places of interest to visit.

▸ *Leave St Andrews to the northwest by the Cupar Road (A 91). Once over the Eden turn right onto the A 919 in the direction of Guardbridge.*

Guardbridge

This small village with an important paper mill and narrow 15C bridge was built by Bishop Wardlaw.

Leuchars

Population 2,203. The fame of the village of Leuchars derives in part from its RAF station and Leuchars Junction, the railway station for St Andrews. However, pride of place is taken by the **parish church**★ (⏱*open Apr–Oct daily 9am–6pm;* ☏*01334 870 038*), which dominates the village from its elevated position. The 12C chancel and semicircular east end are exceptional examples of **Norman work**. On the external walls, under the cornice of grotesque heads, are two fine bands of arcades. The tower and lantern are 17C. Inside, the perspective towards the apse is framed by the richly moulded chancel and apse arches.

Cupar

Population 6,662. Formerly the county town of Fife. Cupars boasts some interesting buildings including two 17C survivors, Preston Lodge and Chancellor's House – the birthplace of John Campbell who became Lord Chancellor in 1859.

The Scottish Deer Centre   Kids
2mi/3.2km west of Cupar on the A 91. Rankeilour Park. ♿🕐*Open year-round daily 10am–4.30pm.* 🕐*Closed 25–26 Dec, 1 Jan.* ⊜*£6.95, child £4.95.* 🅿. ☎*01337 810 391. www.tsdc.co.uk.*

Deer are normally associated with the Highlands, but were once common in Lowland Scotland too, before woodland clearance and farming drove them away. This Georgian farmstead and its surrounding parkland are now used to introduce the public, particularly children, to these fascinating creatures. In the 50 acres/22ha of paddocks there are not only red deer but eight other species totalling around 140 deer in all. These are supplemented by rare breeds, such as a black Highland Cow and Soay sheep. There are native red foxes and in the wolf wood (segregated from the deer) you can watch the wolves feeding time (*Sat–Thu 3pm*). There are also daily bird-of- prey demonstrations in the outdoor theatre.

Rangers give regular guided tourswhile treetop walkway with viewing platforms allow visitors to look down on the animals.

> ▸ *Return to Cupar and take the A 914 southeast, then fork second left onto the A 916.*

Hill of Tarvit
(*NTS*). 🕐*Open Jun–Aug daily 1–5pm, May & Sept–Oct Thu–Mon 1–5pm.* ⊜*£8.* 🍴. ☎*0844 4932185. www.nts.org.uk.*

This elegant Edwardian country house. was commissioned by Frederick Bower Sharp (d 1932), a jute manufacturer and financier from Dundee. In 1904 Sharp purchased the estate that included the original house, Wemysshall (1696) – attributed to Sir William Bruce – and the 16C Scotstarvit Tower. Sharp was an art collector of note and his remodelled family residence was designed as a suitable setting for his important **private collection** of fine French and Chippendale-style furniture, Old

Masters, tapestries, Chinese porcelain and bronzes.

Visitors can sample the "Upstairs, Downstairs" nature of the Edwardian period, the grandeur and charm of the main rooms the fascination of the kitchen with its old utensils, and the laundry in the garden.

A nature trail leads through the wild garden to the hilltop (692ft/211m) with viewpoint indicator and a **panorama** of Fife and beyond.

The house wil loan you a picnic hamper, sell you the provisions to go inside and give you a map to find your very own picnic spot!

Scotstarvit Tower
Keys available from Hill of Tarvit House. Park the car on the side of the A 916.

This L-shaped tower house dates from c. 1579 and rises through five storeys. The vertical accommodation, consisting of six chambers with a well-lit main hall on the first floor, is reached by a turnpike stair. The cap-house is of an unusual variety.

> ▸ *Once through Craigrothie turn sharp left onto the B 939 towards St Andrews.*

Ceres★
Population 850. This picturesque village with its arched bridge and village green is the home of the **Fife Folk Museum** (🕐*open mid-April through Sept daily 1.30–4.30pm.* ⊜*£2.50;* ☎*01334 828 180, www.fifefolkmuseum.org*), with comprehensive displays of everyday items, a cottar's living-room and a tool and agricultural section.

> ▸ *Continue along the B 939 past Pitscottie. At the Strathkinness junction turn right. Once up the hill a signpost to the right indicates the footpath to follow (5min).*

Magus Muir
When level with the railed enclosure in the field, veer right towards the pyramid-shaped monument. This marks the spot where Archbishop Sharp of St Andrews was ambushed and murdered on 3 May 1679.

Craigtoun Country Park Kids
⏱*Open Apr–Sept daily 10.30am–6.30pm.
Last admission 5.30pm.* 🚫*Call for admission charge.* ☎*01334 473 666.*
Originally laid out as parkland attached to adjacent Mount Melville House, this has been a country park since 1947. Much of the formal design, including the avenue of Lawson Cypress, the Italian Garden and the much loved Dutch Village are part of the original design. Little ones will enjoy the adventure playground, miniature railway, trampoline, bouncy castle, boating, putting, crazy

Running on the beach

The famous stirring opening sequence to the movie *Chariots of Fire* (1981), with the athletes running in slow-motion to the music of Vangelis, was filmed on the West Beach beside the Aquarium.

golf, pets' corner and aviaries while parents and grandparents will also appreciate the formal gardens, glasshouses and bowling green.

SCONE PALACE★★
PERTHSHIRE AND KINROSS

On the east bank of the Tay, Scone Palace (pronounced "skoon") includes one of Scotland's most hallowed historic sites. The Palace itself is a treasure house with superb collections of French furniture, ivories and porcelain.

- **Information:** ☎01738 552 300, www.scone-palace.net.
- **Orient Yourself:** Scone Palace is 2 mi/3 km north of Perth via the A 93. Buses run here from the city centre.
- **Organizing Your Time:** Allow 1hr 30min.
- **Also See:** PERTH.

A Bit of History

Heartland of a Scoto-Pictish Kingdom – Although the exact role of the site in Pictish times is unsure, its considerable importance is in no doubt. The

tradition was perpetuated by Kenneth MacAlpine in the mid-9C when he made Scone the centre of his new Scoto-Pictish Kingdom. From this time on Scottish Kings were ceremonially enthroned on the **Stone of Scone** also known as the

Scone Palace library

Stone of Destiny (⊘ see Box on following page).

Robert the Bruce was the first of many Scottish kings to be crowned here, right up to James VI, the last being Charles II in 1651. Such was the stone's importance that in 1296, Edward I, following his defeat of the Scots and imprisonment of King John Balliol, had the Stone and other regalia carried off to Westminster Abbey where it has been part of the Coronation Chair ever since, except for a notable interlude in 1950–51. In 1996 the Stone was transferred to Edinburgh Castle in acknowledgement of its symbolic importance. It will be returned to Westminster Abbey for future coronations.

Religious Centre – The original Celtic community was superseded when Alexander I founded an Augustinian priory c. 1120, the first of that Order in Scotland. The abbey and abbot's palace, as was the custom, served as a royal residence.

The abbey was sacked in the 1559 wave of destruction following John Knox's inflammatory sermon in Perth, and it became the property of the Earls of Gowrie who built a 16C house, Gowrie Palace, using the old palace stones. Following the Gowrie Conspiracy (⊘ see PERTH) and the forfeiture of their property in 1600, James VI bestowed the estate on the Murray family, later the Earls of Mansfield. The 3rd Earl commissioned William Atkinson to build a neo-Gothic palatial mansion (1802–08).

Visit

&. ⊙Open Good Fri–Oct daily 9.30am–5.30pm. Last entry 5pm. Grounds close 6pm. Nov–Mar by appointment. ⊗£8; grounds only, £4.50.

Interior

Throughout the suite of richly furnished apartments in neo-Gothic style are superb pieces of French furniture and a series of unusual and interesting timepieces. Outstanding in the **Dining Room** is the collection of 17C–19C **European ivories**, a wonder of delicate carv-

ing. Arranged around the table, set with an armorial damask cloth and service, are locally made chairs in the Chippendale style. His Grace the **Hon. William Murray** (1701–79), the eminent lawyer, politician and embellisher of Kenwood House (Hampstead Heath, London), is portrayed here, as is the Ist Earl. In the adjoining **Anteroom** Sir David Murray, the Cup Bearer to James VI, was the lucky recipient of the forfeited Gowrie lands and palace.

In the **Drawing Room**, against the 18C Lyons silk-hung walls, are a series of **portraits,** including Allan Ramsay's pair of royal portraits (1765) of King George III and Queen Charlotte, and Reynolds' portrait of the Ist Earl of Mansfield, William Murray as Lord Chief Justice of England (1776). One of the greatest lawyers of his day, he was known as "Silver-tongued Murray" and was the lifelong opponent of William Pitt the Elder.

The Pierre Bara set of French fauteuils with fine needlework are dated 1756, and flanking the fireplace are two Boulle commodes. However the finest piece is Marie Antoinette's exquisite Riesener (1734–1806) **writing table**. The magnificent array of fine **porcelain** in the **Library** was collected by the Ist and 2nd Earls. The Ist Earl's portrait shows his prized possession, Bernini's bust of Homer which Alexander Pope had given him, and flanking this is Rysbrack's bust of the Lord Chief Justice.

The **Ambassador's Room** is named after the 2nd Earl, politician, statesman and ambassador, who served in Dresden, Vienna and subsequently Paris, where he became the confidant of Louis XVI and Marie-Antoinette and acquired much of the fine French furniture now in the house. The bed was a royal piece commissioned for His Grace the Ambassador, who is portrayed here by Pompeo Batoni. Zoffany's portrait of the Ambassador's daughter, Lady Elizabeth Murray, shows her in the grounds of Kenwood, the Earl's English country house and permanent home after rioting crowds destroyed his Bloomsbury residence.

Stretching 168ft/51m, the appropriately named **Long Gallery** retains its original oak and bog-oak flooring but sadly has

Romancing the Stone

The Stone of Scone, also known as The **Stone of Destiny** is an oblong block of red sandstone, which measures around 26 inches (660 mm) by 16 inches (410 mm) by 10.5 inches (270 mm) and weighs approximately 336 pounds (152 kg). At each end of the stone is an iron ring, presumably for carrying, or perhaps securing it.

Legends abound as to its provenance. It is said to have been Jacob's Pillow when he saw the angels of Bethel, another story suggests it was brought to Scotland by Scotia, daughter of an Egyptian pharaoh, and yet another theory is that it was a portable altar used by St Columba in his missionary work in Caledonia. The most likely explanation is that it was a royal stone used by the early Irish kings, brought from Antrim to Argyll and then to Scone in 838 from Dunstaffnage (☞ see OBAN: Excursions) by Kenneth MacAlpine.

Its recent history is hardly less colourful. On Christmas Day 1950, a group of four Scottish students managed to steal the Stone from Westminster Abbey – no mean feat given its size and weight. However In the process of removing it they broke it into two pieces. The Stone was passed to a pro-Nationalist senior Glasgow politician who arranged for it to be professionally repaired by a Glasgow stonemason. Meanwhile a nationwide hunt continued for the Stone.

On 11 April 1951, over 15 months after its disappearance, the Stone was found on the altar of Arbroath Abbey, the site of the signing of the Declaration of Arbroath and a hallowed site for Scottish Nationalists. A relieved and red-faced government hastily returned it to Westminster. Meanwhile rumours circulated among Scottish Nationalists that a copy had been made of the Stone while it was in hiding, and that the block of sandstone now sitting in Westminster was not the real thing. A film of this escapade, *Stone of Destiny,* starring Christopher Lee and Robert Carlyle, is due for release in 2008–2009.

---

lost its painted ceiling. Outstanding among the paintings and fine furniture is a unique collection of **Vernis Martin** *objets d'art*, all made of papier mâché. David Wilkie's *The Village Politicians* hangs here.

Grounds

Facing the palace is **Moot Hill**, now occupied by a 19C chapel. Explanations for the name Moot are various. The Gaelic derivation (*Tom-a-mhoid*) would have it as a place where justice was administered, while another version, **Boot Hill**, though more unlikely on first hearing, is perhaps the more credible. It was said that when the earls, chieftains and other men of consequence came to swear fealty to the Lord High Ardh, they carried earth in their boots from their own lands – since fealty could only be sworn for their land while standing on it! Having taken the oath they then emptied the contents on the spot.

The avenue opposite the main entrance leads down to the **Old Gateway**, emblazoned with the arms of James VI and the Ist Viscount. Beyond was the original site of the village of Scone, before it was moved during 19C alterations to the palace.

The **pinetum** (50 acres/20ha) has some of the oldest firs including the Douglas species. The first such tree was sent by its namesake the celebrated botanist, David Douglas (1798–1834) who was born and worked on the estate.

SHETLAND ISLANDS ★
SHETLAND ISLANDS
POPULATION 22,000

The most northerly of Scotland's islands, some 60mi/100km to the north of Orkney, this archipelago comprises 100 isles, of which less than 20 are inhabited.

- **Information:** The Market Cross, Lerwick. ☎08701 999 440. www.visitshetland.com.
- ▶ **Orient Yourself:** The capital Lerwick, which is the islands' hub, is on the east coast of the largest island, known as Mainland, 70mi/112km long, and 20mi/32km at its widest point. Most places are 3mi/5km from the sea. There are daily sailings from Aberdeen to Lerwick and flights from Aberdeen, Edinburgh, Glasgow, Inverness and London to Sumburgh.
- 👁 **Don't Miss:** Jarlshof, Mousa Broch.
- 👁 **Weather warning** : Be prepared for poor weather at any time of year.
- 🕐 **Organizing Your Time:** Allow three days minimum.

A Bit of History

By contrast with Orkney, Shetland has few tracts of flat land. It is deeply penetrated by the sea and until recently had an economy dominated by fishing and crofting. The oil boom of the 1970s led to the disruption of this traditional and well balanced economy. Today, with one of the largest oil ports in Europe sited at Sullom Voe, the oil industry comes second after fishing. It is planned to use oil revenues to bolster the traditional industries (crofting, fishing, fish processing and knitwear).

Thankfully for visitors oil-related industrialisation is limited to Sullom Voe. Elsewhere the islands retain their attractions of wild beauty, solitude and empty spaces. In Mainland with all its coastal indentations, the sea is ever present. The long coastline is varied and of outstanding beauty, be it rocky and rugged or sandy and smooth. The wildlife is varied and plentiful.

The archeological treasures of the Shetland Islands, often preserved by the shifting sand dunes, reveal fascinating information on the early human settlements. Recent excavations have uncovered an Iron Age village at Sumburgh.

Jarlshof ★★ (Mainland)

25mi/40km from Lerwick

Set on the seashore not far from one of the more recent constructions, Sumburgh airport, is the prehistoric site of **Jarlshof** (*HS,* ♿🕐 *open Apr–Sept daily 9.30am–5.30pm, Oct Sat–Wed 9.30am–4.30pm; last admission 30 mins before closing;* 🕐*closed 25–26 Dec, 1–2 Jan;* 💷*£4.50;* ☎*01950 460 112, www. historic-scotland.gov.uk*). The sequence of occupation is clearly distinguished, covering a span of over 3,000 years from the mid-2nd millennium BC to the 17C.

▶ *Visit the site in chronological sequence. The numbers below are those used on the official plan.*

Stone Age

Only fragments remain of the earliest settlers' village, contemporary with Skara Brae (👁*see ORKNEY ISLANDS*), on the landward side of the site.

Bronze Age

Six oval-shaped houses with cubicles built into the walls; Dwelling III is the best preserved. Later settlement of the early Iron Age period brought about the alteration of the original plan including the addition of earth houses.

Shetlands Wildlife

Shetland offers probably the best wildlife-watching in Scotland. This includes over a million breeding seabirds, the highest density of otters in Europe, regular sightings of Killer Whales and superb displays of rare sub-arctic flora.

The cliffs around **Sumburgh Head**, a protected RSPB reserve, attract thousands of summer breeding seabirds, including puffins, guillemots, shags and fulmars.

On Mousa Island Arctic skuas and Arctic terns defend their nesting grounds by dive-bombing all intruders, people included, so if visiting there do try to walk round the breeding colonies, for their sakes as well as yours.

For more details on all Shetlands wildlife including specialist holidays and tours visit www.shetlandwildlife.co.uk.

Late Iron Age
This settlement is clustered around the ruins of a broch, partly eroded by the sea. The broch itself is equipped with a well. The plan is confused by post-broch dwellings (wheelhouses 1–4) both inside and outside the main structure. No 2 is the best completely preserved example of a wheelhouse (a circular hut divided radially).

Viking era
The remains include numerous long houses (1–8), the layout of which is complex reflecting various centuries of occupation.

Medieval farmstead
Only parts of the original house and barn, from the 13C to 16C, are preserved.

Jarlshof
The 16C New Hall was built for Earl Robert Stewart. It was converted into kitchens when a new Laird's House was added in the early 17C.

Museum
This displays finds from excavations and a plan of the entire Jarlshof site.

Lerwick (Mainland)

Population 8,000. The port capital of Lerwick is set on a promontory overlooking the natural harbour, sheltered by the Island of Bressay. The town has always been important as a fishing port, and the oil boom has brought new activities.

A port through the centuries
As a haven, Lerwick provided shelter for King Haakon's and other Viking fleets. in the early 17C, It became an illegal marketplace servicing the Dutch herring fleets before being demolished by order of the Scalloway court. The Dutch burnt the fort in 1673 and the French set fire to Lerwick in 1702. Both the German and British navies sheltered here in the 20C and now there is an assorted flotilla of oil vessels.

Most of the sandstone buildings on the waterfront date from the 18C although a few, such as No 10 Commercial Street, are older. The narrow main street still follows the old shoreline but modern harbour works have been built out in front of shops and warehouses that once stood in the sea. Perched on a hillside overlooking the harbour – now home to pleasure boats – the town's lanes retain their charm and their shelter from the prevailing south-westerly gales.

Commercial Street
Known affectionately as The Street, this paved and twisting thoroughfare winds its way along the shore. Steep lanes lead off uphill.

Fort Charlotte
From the walls of this 17C fort, rebuilt in the 18C, there is a good view of Bressay Sound and island of the same name.

Town Hall
Stained-glass windows depict Viking history.

Shetland Museum
&⏱ *Open year-round Mon–Sat 10am–5pm (Thu 7pm), Sun noon–4pm.* ✕. ☎01595 695 057. www.shetland-museum.org.uk.
Set in a stunning new modern-traditional harbourside building, the Museum displays over 3,000 artefacts on two floors, a wealth of easily accessible archive material, a temporary exhibition area, a boat hall and sheds, an art gallery, auditorium, shop and an excellent café-restaurant.

Böd of Gremista
Gremista, 1.25 mi/2km north of Lerwick. ⏱ *Open May to mid-Sept Wed–Sun 10am–1pm & 2–5pm.* ☎01595 695 057. www.shetland-museum.org.uk.
This typical 18C booth (böd) provided family accommodation as well as a working store for the nearby fish drying beach. Remarkably this was the birthplace of Arthur Anderson (1792–1868), co-founder of what is now P & O Ferries, and is furnished in a basic Shetland style. It also features displays on the life and times of Arthur Anderson.

Clickhimin Broch★
1mi/1.6km south west of Lerwick
This particular broch (fortified farm, 🡒 *see below*: MOUSA BROCH) is the outstanding structural feature of this islet, and gives evidence of successive occupations. Although only 17ft/5m high, the characteristic layout of this defensive structure with its mural chambers and staircase can still be seen. At its peak around 60 people would have lived at the Clickhimin settlement

Driving Tour

Lerwick to Jarlshof★
20mi/32km.

This run takes in various aspects of Shetland. Discover its desolate moorland scenery (at times interrupted by peat cutting), the varied and attractive shoreline with crofting townships down by the sea, and the numerous vestiges of man's occupation in the past.

▶ *Leave Lerwick by the A 970.*

The main road, before the turnoff for Scalloway, provides a good **view**★ of the inlet of Gulber Wick. Such deeply penetrating arms of the sea (known as *voes*) are typical of Shetland.

▶ *Take the B 9076 to the right to join the A 970.*

On the right is the valley which is the setting for Tingwall Loch. The head of the loch is reputed to be the site of the Law Ting Holm or meeting place of the old Norse Parliament.

Scalloway
Population 1,018. Attractively set round its bay, Scalloway was the former islands capital and is still dominated by the ruin of **Scalloway Castle,** built in 1600 (*HS,* ⏱ *open Mon–Sat 9.30am–5pm; Sun, key available from the Royal Hotel;* ☎01856 841 815, www.historic-scotland.gov.uk). Scalloway was the principal island seat of **Patrick**, **Earl of Orkney** (🡒 *see ORKNEY ISLANDS: Kirkwall*), renowned for his cruelty, and the castle was constructed by forced labour. This grand example of a Scottish fortified house is just as splendid as his other residences and attractive details include the corbelling of the corner turrets, sculptured panel above the entrance doorway and sandstone window, door and angle trims. It was occupied for less than a century and is now roofless. Beneath the grand banqueting hall are large kitchens and a dungeon where 17C 'witches', condemned to die on nearby Gallows Hill, awaited their fate.

▶ *Return to the A 970.*

The road provides a succession of fine views of the east coast all the way down. Mousa Broch can be espied on its island site.

▶ *Turn right to take the B 9122, and right again in Bigton.*

St Ninian's Isle
An attractive beach links this idyllic island to the mainland. It was in the

ruins of an early Christian church that **St Ninian's Treasure**, one of the most important troves of silverware ever found in Britain, was discovered. The originals are now in the Museum of Scotland in Edinburgh while the Shetland Museum has replicas.

The B 9122 offers views of a succession of small bays sheltered by headlands.

▶ *Return to the A 970.*

Shetland Croft House Museum★
Lower Hillhead. 🕐 *Open mid-Apr through Sept daily 10 am–1pm & 2pm–5pm.* ☎*01595 695 057. www.shetland-museum. org.uk/crofthouse.*
Set in the typical crofting township of Boddam, this farmhouse grouping reproduces an accurate picture of rural life in the mid-19C. The croft steading itself comprises kitchen, sleeping accommodation and byre with the barn behind and a small horizontal watermill down by the stream. Note the roofing of cured turf with straw on top.

▶ *Return to the main road, heading south again towards the site of Sumburgh Airport on its isthmus separating the waters of the Atlantic and North Sea.*

Jarlshof★★ – 🕐*See Jarlshof.*

Mousabroch (Mousa Island)

12mi/19km south of Lerwick. Accessible by ferry from Sandwick Apr–Sept ☎*01950 431367. www.mousaboattrips.co.uk.*

Mousa Island is uninhabited and you may well glimpse seals basking on the shore and wild Shetland ponies.
Mousa Broch itself is an outstanding example of a **broch**, a structure unique to Scotland and the north in particular.

Broch period
Brochs are the culmination of a tradition of small stone fortified farms, sometimes referred to as towers, stretching back to 500 BC. Mousa, which probably dates back to the first two centuries of our era, is the finest surviving exam-

ple and may have been more strongly built than the other 500 known brochs in Scotland most of which are found in the Highlands and Islands. Around 120 were built throughout Shetland alone, as times became more troubled. Most are now mere rubble.

The Broch
Impressive from the outside, it is awesome and fascinating inside. Ingeniously constructed, the tower (43ft 6in/13m high and 50ft/15m in diameter at the base) swells out at the base like a bottle kiln. Enter by a passage (16ft/5m long) which had a door midway along. The courtyard, with a central hearth, was surrounded by lean-to timber structures supported by the scarcements (ledges) still visible on the inner faces of the walls. Three doorways lead to mural chambers, a fourth opens into a staircase, again with a mural, which leads to the wallhead. Above the uppermost scarcement, the hollow wall is divided by stone slabs into galleries which open onto the courtyard by means of three sets of ladder-like openings.

Mousa Broch was mentioned in the ancient Sagas as an eloping lovers' hideout, and today is home to Storm petrels nesting within its stone chambers

Sullom Voe (Mainland)

35mi/56km north of Lerwick

From the main A 970 the only indication of this major oil terminal is the flame on the flare stack. The decisive factors in siting an oil terminal and accompanying port facilities at Sullom Voe were the presence of a deep sheltered inlet and its proximity to the oilfields in the East Shetland Basin. The port with its four specialised jetties can berth ships of up to 300,000t, and at its peak it once handled a staggering 1.4 million barrels of oil a day. The oil arrives via two pipelines from over a dozen offshore oilfields some 100mi/160km to the northeast. The gases (propane and butane) are separated from the oil and then stored prior to shipment. The terminal has no refining facilities. Calback Ness peninsula is the site for 16 huge storage tanks.

ISLE OF SKYE★★
HIGHLAND
POPULATION 9,000
ACCESS: SEE THE MICHELIN GUIDE GREAT BRITAIN AND IRELAND

Skye evokes the mystery and enchantment of a Hebridean isle famous for its spectacular scenery and wealth of legends. An aura of mysticism remains, which had its origins in Norse and Gaelic times when the isle was known variously as the Cloud Island, Misty Isle or Winged Isle. The enchantment derives in part from the isle's rapidly changing moods. It is hard not to be spellbound when a heavy mist is pierced by fingers of sunshine prior to rolling away, or when persistent rain clears to reveal a landscape of purest colours and streaming sunshine.

- **Information:** The Car Park, Broadford; 2 Lochside, Dunvegan; Bayfield House, Bayfield Road, Portree. All: ☎01845 22 55 121. www.visithighlands.com. www.skye.co.uk.
- ▶ **Orient Yourself:** At 48mi/77km long and up to 25mi/40km in breadth, Skye is the largest of the Inner Hebrides group. Portree is the capital. Skye is joined to the mainland by the Skye Bridge at Kyle of Lochalsh and it also has two mainland ferry connections from Mallaig (150mi/242km northwest of Glasgow) and Glenelg, the latter summer only. From Mallaig to Armadale is the most picturesque entrance route and takes 30mins by ferry (www.calmac.co.uk).
- **Don't Miss:** The Cuillins; the Trotternish Peninsula.
- **Language:** Gaelic is spoken by 58% of the island's population.
- **Especially for Kids:** Glendale Toy Museum.
- ○ **Organizing Your Time:** At least two days; more if you enjoy hill walking.

Access

A **toll-bridge** (opened in 1995), links the romantic island to the mainland. The structure between Kyleakin and Kyle of Lochalsh, the longest cantilever bridge (780ft/238m main span) in Europe, has aroused controversy on aesthetic and conservation grounds, as well as for putting ferry operators out of business.

The Cuillins★★★

These dramatic, often harsh mountains figure large in most views of Skye. The

The Black Cuillin Ridge and Loch Brittle

C. Weston/BRITAIN ON VIEW

Address Book

For coin ranges, see the Legend on the cover flap.

WHERE TO STAY

Almondbank – *Viewfield Road, Portree. 01470 532 326. www.skye. uk.com/almondbank.* High standards are kept at this self-catering apartment in a modern house away from the town centre. (4 nights minimum stay).

Rosedale – *Beaumont Crescent, Portree. 01478 613 131. www.rosedalehotelskye.co.uk. Restaurant.* This converted quayside terrace of former fisherman's houses enjoys views over the harbour. There is a pub bar and compact, but immaculately kept floral bedrooms.

Bosville – *Bosville Terrace, Portree. 01478 612 846. www. bosvillehotel.co.uk.* Skye's first boutique-style hotel overlooks the town harbour and hills; rooms are modern and stylish

and the award-winning Chandlery dining room offers excellent Scottish cuisine with a French twist.

WHERE TO EAT

Three Chimneys & The House Over-By – *Colbost, Dunvegan. 01470 511258. www.threechimneys.co.uk.* This renowned restaurant, with 6 spacious rooms, is set in an atmospheric crofter's cottage on the shore of Loch Dunvegan. It serves accomplished Skye gourmet seafood dishes and Highland sourced meat. Bedroom suites are characterful, sumptuous and enjoy spectacular views of the sea.

Loch Bay Seafood – *1 Macleod Terrace, Stein, Waternish. 01470 592 235. www.lochbay-seafood-restaurant.co.uk.* Housed in a white cottage overlooking the sea, this tiny atmospheric dining room features a menu filled with locally caught fish.

Black Cuillins are a horseshoe-shaped range encircling the glacial trough of Loch Coruisk. Gabbro rocks form over 20 sharp peaks, all over 3,000ft/900m with the highest point being Sgurr Alasdair (309ft/993m). This ridge, intersected by ravines and vertical gulleys, provides a real challenge for climbers.

Facing these across Glen Sligachan are the conical summits of the **Red Cuillins**. The pink granite here has weathered to more rounded forms. The Cuillins are a favourite haunt for climbers, geologists and holidaymakers; however treacherous weather, scree slopes and steep ascents and descents require skill and experience.

Dunvegan Castle

Open mid-March–Oct daily 10am–5pm, rest of year daily 11am–4pm. Closed 25–26 Dec, 1–2 Jan. £7.50 (gardens only, £5) Seal boat trip £6.50. .01470 521 206. www.dunvegan castle.com.

Famous as the seat of the MacLeods, this Hebridean fortress is set on a rocky

platform commanding Loch Dunvegan. The visit reveals a fascinating story, a mixture of personalities, clan legends and mementoes.

The castle enshrines several priceless heirlooms, notably the **Fairy Flag**. According to one legend this was the parting gift to Iain, the 4th Chief from his fairy wife with whom he had lived for 20 years. The fabric, thought once to have been dyed yellow, is silk from the Middle East (Syria or Rhodes); experts have dated it between the 4th and 7th centuries A.D. Perhaps it was the robe of an early christian saint, or maybe the war banner of Harold Hardrada, King of Norway, killed in 1066. It is said that the Flag has the power of warding off disaster to the clan and has twice been successfully invoked.

Among other prized possessions is the Dunvegan Cup and Horn of Sir Rory Mor the 15th Chief. Tradition requires that the heir, on coming of age, quaffs the horn filled with claret without falling down drunk! Family portraits include canvases by Zoffany, Raeburn and Ramsay.

During summer a boat trip runs across Loch Dunvegan to small islets colonised

B.PEROUSSE/MICHELIN

Trotternish Peninsula, Isle of Skye

by **seals**, where these playful sea mammals can be observed at close quarters. Herons also nest on these islands and Arctic Terns and many other species of bird can frequently be seen.

Driving Tours

Duirinish Peninsula★

This westernmost wing of Skye spreads out into the Little Minch, the channel that separates the Western Isles from the Isle of Skye.

Dunvegan

Population 301. This is the main settlement on the west coast, though aside from the castle (see *Dunvegan Castle, above*) there is little to detain visitors.

▶ *From beyond Dunvegan the B 884 crosses the peninsula to Glendale.*

Looming large on the horizon are **MacLeod's Tables**, two flat-topped mountains where a Macleod chief is said to have entertained James V to a torch-lit banquet.

Colbost Folk Museum

⏱ *Open Apr–Oct, daily 10am–6pm.* £1.50. 🅿 01470 521 296.
The Black House shows a typical abode of the 19C, with the family quarters and byre under one roof. Behind is an interesting

example of an illicit whisky still. Documents on display recall how an uprising of local crofters highlighted the problems of 19C crofting. The resultant Croft Act accorded among other things the much sought after security of tenure. Today the area around here is popular with "white settlers" from England.

▶ *A road forks to the right at Totaig, in the direction of Dunvegan Head.*

Pipers' Monument

A cairn monument overlooking Loch Dunvegan marks the site of a piping school of the MacCrimmons, the hereditary pipers to the MacLeods. A piping centre was re-established nearby in 1976.

▶ *Return to the main road.*

Glendale

This typically scattered crofting community is home to the very untypical **Glendale Toy Museum** (Kids ⏱ *open year-round Mon–Sat 10am–6pm;* £3 adult, £1 child; 01470 511240, www.toy-museum.co.uk) Set in the sturdy Victorian built Holmisdale House, it is unusual in that many of its exhibits – trains and boats and dolls and teddys and games from Victorian Times to Star Wars – are hands-on.
There is a mill down in the bay. Over 200 years ago, crofters came with their grain and a supply of peat, some even from the Outer Hebrides, to mill their

grain here. The kiln was used to reduce the moisture content prior to grinding.

Trotternish Peninsula★★

▶ *Follow the A 855 and A 87.*

This peninsula (20mi/32km long) to the north of Portree is known for its unusual rock formations. A coastal road circles it with lovely seascapes over the Sound of Raasay and Loch Snizort.

Portree
Population 1,533. Set around a bay sheltered by two headlands, the isle's capital is a popular yachting centre.

The Storr
A ridge (10mi/16km long) rising to 3,000ft/914m, the Storr is a succession of jagged rock shapes. Rising to 160ft/49m on the northeastern flank is the rock pinnacle **The Old Man of Storr**.

Kilt Rock
Leave the car at the picnic area and walk along the clifftop.
There are interesting cliff formations of basaltic columns.

Quiraing
From Staffin Bay, this great ridge with its numerous rocky bastions is clearly visible. At the northern end towers the Needle (100ft/30m).

Duntulm
The jagged tooth of a ruined ancient MacDonald stronghold stands on its cliff-top site commanding the sea route to the Outer Hebrides.

Kilmuir
In the churchyard is a Celtic cross monument to **Flora MacDonald** (1722–90) commemorating her bravery when she organised **Prince Charles Edward Stuart**'s escape from the Outer Hebrides dressed as her maid. The Prince was soon to arrive in France and lifelong exile, having spent months wandering the Highlands, a hunted fugitive with £30,000 on his head. A quarter of a century later Dr Johnson and Boswell visited Flora at her nearby home.

Skye Museum of Island Life
Open Easter–Oct Mon–Sat 9.30am–5pm. £2.50. 01470 522 206. www.skyemuseum.co.uk.
The museum groups a late-19C crofter house, a weaver's house, a smithy and a ceilidh house. The latter has an interesting display of photographs and documents including newspaper cuttings, which give a flavour of crofting life in the late 19C.

Uig
Population 103. The ferry port for Lewis and Uist.

Sleat Peninsula
The moorland of the north gives way to a much greener and more fertile area, especially on the west coast, known as the Garden of Skye.

Armadale Castle Gardens and Museum of the Isles
Museum open: mid-Mar through Oct daily 9.30am–5.30pm. Gardens open year-round. £5.60. 01471 844 305. www.clandonald.com.
The restored stable block serves as an entertaining and instructive visitor arrival point. One end of Armadale Castle houses a museum-cum-exhibition featuring the 'Sea Kingdom', the story of the Lords of the Isles and the Gaelic culture. There are also special exhibitions that change each year plus children's trails and interactive exhibits. The former grounds offer 40 acres of exotic trees, shrubs and flowers a selection of woodland walks, nature trails and scenic viewpoints overlooking the Sound of Sleat.

Minginish Peninsula

The attraction here is the **Talisker Distillery** (*visit by guided tour only, mid-Mar–Oct Mon–Sat 9.30am–5pm; Jul–Aug also Sun 12.30–5pm; Jan through mid-Mar 1.30pm, 3.30pm; £5, includes discount voucher and free dram; 01478 614308 www.discovering-distilleries.com*) set on the shores of Loch Harport with dramatic views of the Cuillins.

SOUTH QUEENSFERRY
CITY OF EDINBURGH
POPULATION 7,485

Former royal burgh and once a traffic-congested ferry port, this now quiet, small town nestles on the south shore of the Firth of Forth, overshadowed by the two Forth bridges.

- **Information:** 3 Princes Street, Edinburgh. ☎845 22 55 121 www.edinburgh.org/lothians.
- ▶ **Orient Yourself:** 10mi/16km west of Edinburgh on the A 90.
- **Kids Especially for Kids:** Deep Sea World.
- ☀ **Also See:** HOPETOUN HOUSE; DUNFERMLINE.

A Bit of History

Forth Crossing – The narrowest point of the Forth, this has been the natural crossing point from earliest times. The first ferry, instituted by **Queen Margaret**—hence the town's name—for pilgrims travelling north to Dunfermline, was operated by the Dunfermline monks, then local seamen. By the 17C it was one of Scotland's busiest ferry crossings and was linked to the capital by one of the first turnpike (toll) roads.

In the 18C, a tunnel was proposed to link the Hopetoun Estates on either side of the Forth and also a chain bridge. Steam ferry ships were introduced in 1821 and in 1850–51, in the wake of the railway age, both the Forth and the Tay saw the inauguration of the first railway ferries in the world, albeit for goods traffic only. This service continued to operate until the building of the Tay Bridge in 1878 and the Forth Bridge in 1890. Throughout this time the Queen's ferry continued to ply between North and South Queensferry right up until 1964 when HM Queen Elizabeth II made the last crossing, in the electric paddle ferry *Queen Margaret*, after opening the New Road Bridge.

Forth Bridges★★

The esplanade is an excellent **viewing point** for the Bridges, in particular for the Rail Bridge, while the service area at the south end of the Road Bridge has a viewing terrace. On the north bank (*signposted off the Road Bridge approach and part of the Queensferry Lodge Hotel*) there is a small **Visitor Centre** which tells the story of both bridges.

Forth Rail Bridge

Widely acclaimed as a great engineering achievement in its day, the familiar outline of this cantilever bridge is well known. Built between 1883 and 1890 at a total coast of £3,177,206 it was an intrepid endeavour so soon after the great Tay Bridge Disaster of 1879 and was achieved not without injury and loss of life. The 135 acres/54ha of steel surface representing 50,000t of girders, take at least three years and 7,000 gallons of a special paint to respray from end to end.

Forth Road Bridge

Upstream stands the slim elegant form of the suspension bridge with its amazing "curve". With two carriageways (24ft/7.3m wide), cycle tracks and pathways, the bridge took six years (1958–64) to complete using 39,000t of steel and 150,000cu yd/114,750m^2 of concrete at a total cost of £20,000,000.

Additional Sights

Hawes Inn

At the east end of the esplanade, part of this building dates from the 17C. The Inn probably stands on the site of one of Queen Margaret's pilgrims' hospices and it figures in novels by Scott and R L Stevenson.

Main Street

The winding street has been attractively repaved, setting off to advantage the many fine houses, some of which, built by the once-flourishing merchant community, give on to raised terraces reached by steps and ramps. Note in particular the elevated **terraces**, West, Mid and East, which are lined on the south side by houses which belonged to the flourishing merchant community. Note in particular **Black Castle** with its pedimented dormer windows, one of which bears the date 1626, a heart, love-knot and initials. The 17C tolbooth tower has several public clocks.

The little **Queensferry Museum** (◷ open Thu–Sat and Mon 10am–1pm, 2.15pm–5pm; Sun noon–5pm; ☎0131 331 5545, www.cac.org.uk), offers fine views over the Forth complete with telescopes and binoculars for studying details. As well as relating the history of the road and rail bridges, it has a full-size figure of the Burry Man.

Excursions

Deep Sea World   Kids

See DUNFERMLINE: Excursions.

Inchcolm Island

Haws Pier. ◷ *Call for sailing times.* ⌖£10, *£14.70 to include HS landing and Abbey admission fees.* ☎*0131 331 5000. www. maidoftheforth.co.uk.*

Known as the "Iona of the East", Inchcolm Island lies 1.5mi/2.5km due south of Aberdour and is famous for its abbey ruins, the best-preserved group of monastic buildings in Scotland. The outward journey on the *Maid of the Forth* gives a good view of the south shore and Hound Point. Beyond, on the foreshore, is the 12C Barnbougle Castle (*private*). Cormorants and seals can be seen on the skerries and on Inchcolm Island itself.

Inchcolm Abbey

◷*Open Apr–Sept daily 9.30am–5.30pm. Oct Sat–Wed 9.30am–4.30pm.* ⌖*£4.50.* ☎*01383 823332. www.historic-scotland. gov.uk.*

In 1123 **Alexander I** was stormbound on the island and in gratitude for the hospitality he received from a hermit, he founded a monastery for Augustinian canons. The priory was later raised to abbatial status. Despite many English raids the abbey flourished up to the Reformation when it passed to the Stewarts as commendators and finally the Earls of Moray. The conventual buildings are very well preserved and include a 13C octagonal **chapter-house**, one of the few in Scotland, and 14C cloisters.

STIRLING

POPULATION 36,640

Strategically important from time immemorial as focal point for all Scotland, the long and eventful history of the town has been essentially that of its famous stronghold and former royal residence.

- **Information:** Dumbarton Road. ☎08452 255 121. www.visitscottishheartlands.com. www.visitstirling.org.
- ▸ **Orient Yourself:** Stirling is 43mi/70km north west of Edinburgh via the M 9. All the sights are clustered tightly together in the Old Town, adjacent to the castle. The hop-on hop-off City Sightseeing Tour (www.citysightseeing.co.uk) bus is useful for seeing outlying sights including the Wallace Monument.
- **Don't Miss:** Stirling Heads in the Castle; view from National Wallace Monument.
- ◷ **Organizing Your Time:** Allow a day to see the town and Wallace Monument.
- Kids **Especially for Kids:** Old Town Jail and Stirling Ghost Tour; Blair Drummond Safari and Adventure Park.
- **Also See:** DUNBLANE, THE TROSSACHS.

Address Book

WHERE TO STAY

Number 10 – *Gladstone Place.*
☎*01786 472 681. www.cameron-10.co.uk.*
Set in a pleasant suburb within walking distance of the old town this 19C terrace house is deceptively spacious and offers smart newly decorated modern-traditional bedrooms.

Premier Travel Inn – *Whins of Milton, Glasgow Road.* ☎*08701 977 241. www.premiertravelinn.com.* This chain-owned lodge, 3 mi/5km from the town centre offers excellent motorway connections, comfortable modern bedrooms with ample space and informal dining.

West Plean House – *Denny Road.*
☎*01786 812208. www.westpleanhouse. com.* This homely traditional early 19C house, surrounded by extensive lawns and with a duck pond, is set 3.5 miles south of town. Friendly owners, slmple en-suite accopmmodation, neat gardens, communal breakfast. Good value.

A Bit of History

Strategic location – The site of Stirling has always been of paramount strategic importance, controlling a crossing of the Forth at its tidal limit, a passage northwards between the Ochils and Gargunnock Hills, and being fortuitously endowed with a superb and nigh impregnable strongpoint, the crag. It comes as no surprise then that so many important battles have been fought in the vicinity: Stirling Bridge 1297, Falkirk 1298, 1766; Bannockburn 1314; Sauchieburn 1488; Kilsyth 1645, and Sheriffmuir 1715.

Early royal connections – Royal associations began in 1124 with the death of Alexander I. In 1126 his brother, David I, granted the settlement royal status and the ensuing privileges ensured the town's subsequent prosperity and growth, becoming, in the 12C, one of the "Court of the Four Burghs" along with Berwick, Edinburgh and Roxburgh. It was from here that David I no doubt supervised the building of his abbey at Cambuskenneth (founded 1147) down on the carselands of the Forth.

Wars of Independence (1296–1305) – Owing to its vital strategic importance the castle was attacked and counterattacked by both the English and Scots during this turbulent period, which figures largely in the castle's own history and features two of Scotland's most famous heroes, **William Wallace** and **Robert the Bruce**. The castle was recaptured from Edward I's garrison following **William Wallace**'s victory at the **Battle of Stirling Bridge** (1297), which was no doubt fought upstream from the present bridge. In 1304 the castle was the last Scottish stronghold in Wallace's hands and after capitulation there followed 10 years of English occupation. The castle again became the centre of a struggle in 1313, and the **Battle of Bannockburn** (*see Excursions below*) the following year was fought in the short term for possession of Stirling Castle with, as long term aim, the achieving of independence from the English.

Royal abode of the House of Stewart – With the accession of the Stewarts, Stirling Castle became a permanent royal residence. James III (1451 –88) strengthened the defences and built the gatehouse to the castle of his birth, as well as building the Great Hall as a meeting place for Parliament and other State occasions.
Stirling's Golden Age corresponded with the reigns of James IV and V (1488 –1542). **James IV**, a true Renaissance prince initiated the building of the Palace Block.
A notable escapade in the merry round of festivities, which was an important feature of his court, was that of a courtier named Damian, who thought he would attempt to emulate Icarus. Winged only with cocks' feathers he launched himself

from the battlements and surprisingly he survived his maiden flight!

On James' death at Flodden his queen, Margaret, brought her son to Stirling where he was crowned in the chapel (21 September 1513). as James V. Thirty years later his daughter, **Mary, Queen of Scots** (1542 –87), was crowned in the old Chapel Royal on 9 September 1543. Her infant son James was baptised in 1566, with the absent Elizabeth I as royal godmother, although the queen was already estranged from her husband, Darnley. The following year, prior to his mother's abdication, the 13-month-old prince was crowned in the parish church and it was here that he lived under the stern tutorship of George Buchanan. James rebuilt the Chapel Royal (1594) for the baptism of his own son, Prince Henry, in the same year. With the departure of James VI to Whitehall, Stirling's role as a royal residence ceased.

A prosperous royal burgh – This royal burgh, with its exclusive trading privileges and the stimulus of the court, greatly prospered in the 15C and 16C, with the town itself spreading downhill from its august neighbour.

Stirling was once again to play its military role of garrison town during the Covenanting troubles and the Commonwealth. Associations with the Jacobite rebellion included the Battle of Sheriffmuir which, although indecisive, ended the 1715 campaign, while the 1745 links are even more numerous since Bonnie Prince Charlie wintered in the area prior to his final defeat at Culloden (👆 see INVERNESS: Excursions).

The 19C saw the growth of textile, coal mining and agricultural engineering industries. In 1967 Stirling was chosen as the site for a new university and the electronics industry is now so firmly established in the Central Belt that it has acquired the nickname, Silicon Glen. The town is also a leading agricultural service centre with a modern cattle market.

Stirling Castle

(HS). 🕐 Castle open: year-round daily 9.30am–6pm (Nov–Mar 5pm). Tapestry Studio open daily 11–5pm (Nov–Mar 4pm). Last admission 45 mins before closing. 🕐 Closed 25–26 Dec and 1, 2 Jan. ⊚£8.50 (includes admission to Argyll's Lodging). ✕. 🅿️ £2 (4 hours). ☎01786 450 000. www. historic-scotland.gov.uk.

With a magnificent **site**★★★, high on a crag dominating the Forth carselands, Stirling Castle was one of Scotland's strongest and most impregnable fortresses. The castle is approached, up the tail formation of the crag, through the old town. Standing sentinel on the esplanade (car park) is Bruce's statue.

Pass the Town Visitor Centre and after crossing the ditch and first gateway continue upwards passing through the Inner Gateway. On the left are the

Stirling Castle, perched up high on a volcanic rock

BRITAIN ON VIEW/V K Guy Ltd

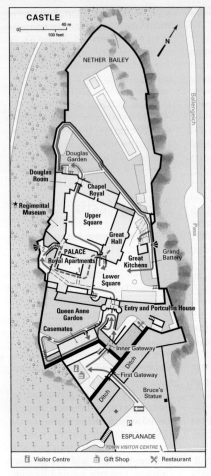

CASTLE

0 ___ 40 m
0 ___ 100 feet

N

NETHER BAILEY

Ballengeich

Douglas Garden

Douglas Room

Regimental Museum

Chapel Royal

Upper Square

Great Hall

PALACE
Royal Apartments

Great Kitchens

Grand Battery

Pass

Lower Square

Queen Anne Garden

Casemates

Entry and Portcullis House

Inner Gateway

Ditch

First Gateway

Ditch

Bruce's Statue

ESPLANADE
TOWN VISITOR CENTRE

Visitor Centre   Gift Shop   Restaurant

Queen Anne Garden, once a bowling green, the ramp up to the terrace, and the **Casemates**, where there is an entertaining exhibition area.
The 15C **Entry and Portcullis House**, the work of James IV, opens onto the Lower Square.

Lower Square

This is overlooked on the left by the ornate façade of the palace, with the Great Hall straight ahead and the Grand Battery to the right.

Palace

Begun in 1496 by **James IV**, it was completed by 1540 in the reign of his son and is a masterpiece of Renaissance ornamentation. Stirling and the other royal residences of Falkland and Linlithgow

remain isolated examples of the then current European Renaissance ideas and were to have little direct effect on Scottish architecture in general.

External elevations★★★

The outstanding architectural feature of the palace, which is simple in plan with four buildings round a courtyard, is the elaborate design of the external elevations (♿ *for further details see Upper Square, below*).
Turn left into the covered passageway, passing the entrance to the Lion's Den (**1**).

Lady's Hole (2)

This terrace has good **views** to the west and in particular of the **King's Knot** below. Now all grass, the outlines of this garden can still be distinguished as laid out in 1627 by William Watt within the confines of the royal park. Away to the left the flagstaff of the rotunda at Bannockburn (♿ *see Bannockburn Heritage Centre, below*) pinpoints another historic site.

Royal Lodgings (Apartments)

This area has recently undergone major refurbishment to present the Royal Lodgings based on the latest historical research and archaeological evidence using materials and craftsmanship of appropriately high quality.
The Palace Block has cellars below with the royal apartments on the main floor and accommodation for the courtiers above. The Queen's Outer and Own Halls are two nobly proportioned chambers where examples of the famous 16C **Stirling Heads**★★ are on display. This series of oak medallions is an extremely fine and rare example of Scottish Renaissance wood carving. The medallions were originally set into a compartmented ceiling in the King's Presence Chamber (Own Hall). Of the original 56, roughly a quarter are missing, three are in the Royal Museum of Scotland in Edinburgh and the rest are at Stirling awaiting reinstatement. Set in circular frames the medallions portray

kings and queens, courtiers, and mythical and Biblical figures. (As part of the ongoing refurbishment of the Castle, a Renaissance Gallery on the upper floors of the Palace will eventually house the original Stirling Heads).

Great Hall

This free-standing building was sadly much altered when used as a barracks in the 18C. However an important programme of restoration has re-created the former splendour of this chamber to the period when it was used by the Stewart court. A fine example of late-Gothic domestic architecture it was described by Defoe as "the noblest I ever saw in Europe". The original arrangement of the Gothic chamber included a dais at the south end flanked by magnificent oriel windows, with the screens and minstrel gallery at the opposite end. The hall with its oak **hammerbeam roof** was lit by paired windows.

Upper Square

This courtyard provides a good vantage point for comparing the façades of the Great Hall (1460–88), the Palace (1496–1540) and Chapel (1594) showing clearly how styles changed in under 150 years.

The original front of the Great Hall had four pairs of deeply embrasured windows with, below, a lean-to roof protecting outside stairs leading up to the main chamber. Above the cornice was a crenellated parapet with wall-walk. The **palace façade** by contrast has a variety of unusual sculptured decoration: between the windows, recessed and cusped arches are the setting for carved figures (*left to right*: James V; young man holding cup; Stirling Venus; bearded man; woman in flowing drapery) which are on the baluster wall shafts.

Chapel Royal

The present church was hurriedly erected on the site of an earlier chapel by James VI for the baptism of Prince Henry. In the early classic Renaissance style, the courtyard front is most pleasing with three pairs of round-headed windows on either side of the elaborate **doorway**. The interior has elaborate wall decoration. The chapel now serves as memorial hall for the regiment.

Argyll and Sutherland Highlanders Regimental Museum

🕐 *Open Easter–Sept daily 9.30am–5pm. Oct–Easter daily 10am–4.15pm.* 📧*Donation requested.* ☎*01786 475 165. www.argylls.co.uk/museum.htm.*

Battle Honours, Colours, medals, peace and wartime uniforms, documents and pictures, all tell the story of nearly 200 years of regimental history and its heroic moments: The Thin Red Line at Balaclava 1854 and the Relief of Lucknow. The regiment is the proud possessor of an outstanding **collection of silver**.

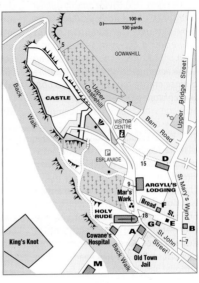

Pass through to the Douglas Garden. It was in the building (Douglas Room) on the left that Black Douglas was treacherously murdered in 1452 by **James II**.

Battlements

The wall-walk round the battlements on the east side has good **views** of the Forth carselands. From the **viewpoint** at the Grand Battery, pick out below the medieval Stirling Bridge bestriding the Forth with, in the middle distance, the tower of Cambuskenneth Abbey, the Wallace Monument and the Ochils.

The Great Kitchens

Steps from the Lower Square lead down into the Great Kitchens, where, lit by fires and flickering torchlight, there is a vivid recreation of the chaos and confusion involved in the preparation of a right royal medieval feast.

Old Town

Explore the old town on foot starting from the esplanade. The medieval town with its steep streets and narrow wynds spills downhill from the castle to the new centre of present-day Stirling. A 1960s restoration programme has brought the area's past to life.

Argyll's Lodging★

Castle Wynd. (HS) ⏱Visit only by guided tour, year-round daily 9.30am–6pm (Nov–Mar 5pm). Last admission 30 mins before closing. ⏱Closed 25–26 Dec and 1, 2 Jan. ✆£4.50 (free admission with Stirling Castle ticket). ☎01786 431 319. To ensure a place on the tour ☎ 01786 450 000. www.historic-scotland.gov.uk.
Scotland's most splendid and complete example of a 17C townhouse was built in 1632 by Sir William Alexander, founder of Nova Scotia. On his death the property passed to the Argyll family when alterations and extensions were made. The street side of this courtyard mansion is enclosed by a screen wall pierced by a fine rusticated Renaissance gateway. The courtyard façades are rich with Scottish **Renaissance decoration**★: strapwork on dormer and window heads, and an armorial panel above the entrance.

Mar's Wark

Top of Broad Street.
Ruined but nonetheless impressive, the **façade** is all that remains of this still-born palace, with ornamental sculpture and heraldic panels adorning the street front. It was started in 1570, for John Erskine (1510–72), Regent and Ist Earl of Mar, but never completed. As Hereditary Keeper of the castle and guardian of Prince James, it was thought only appropriate that his Grace should have a private residence close at hand. It is said that Cambuskenneth Abbey (⏱*see Driving Tours, below*) was quarried for the stone which went towards Mar's Wark. The unusual name comes from the fact that in the 1730s the town council made plans to convert it into a workhouse.

Church of the Holy Rude★

♿⏱*Open Easter–Sept daily 11am–4pm. ✉Donations welcome. ☎01786 475 275.*
This burgh church was built in stages on the site of an earlier church destroyed by fire. The oldest parts, the nave and lower part of the tower, date from the first half of the 15C. Of interest in the nave, with its round piers supporting pointed arches, is the original 15C oak **timberwork roof**. Almost a century older, the choir and pentagonal apse (1507–46) were partitioned off from the rest between 1656 and the 1936–40 restoration. The **east end** is most impressive when seen from St John's Street, looming up massively with sloped intake buttresses between the great windows, characteristic of the Scottish Gothic style. It was here that the infant James VI was crowned in 1567 and John Knox preached the sermon.

Stirling Cowane's Hospital

St John Street ⏱Open daily 9am–4pm. ⏱Closed 25–26 Dec, 1 Jan. ☎ 01786 472 247.
Until recently used as the Guildhall, and now for concerts, meetings and ceilidhs, the building was founded by **John Cowane** (c. 1570–1633) as an almshouse to accommodate 12 "decayed" brethren. Built between 1633 and 1639 the premises included a refectory with sleeping accommodation above. The donor, a member of the Council of Royal

Burghs and Scots Parliament, a man of some substance, stands jauntily above the doorway. The figure is said to come to life at Hogmanay!

At no 39 St John Street is **Bothwell House** a three-storey rubble stonework house with a projecting tower. Nearby stands the **Old Town Jail** (Kids 👤⏰*open daily; Apr–May 9.30am–5.30pm; Jun–Sept 9am–6pm; Oct 9.30am–5pm. Nov–Mar 10am–4pm; last admission 1 hour before closing. ⏰Closed 25–26 Dec and 1 Jan; 💷£5 (without actor guide),£5.95 (with guide, Apr–Oct and Christmas period only);* 🅿️*;* ☎*01786 450 050, www. oldtownjail.com),* where visitors can get an idea of the harsh treatment meted out as punishment to prisoners. **The Stirling Ghost Tour** walk departs from the Jail (⏰*year-round Fri 7.45pm.*💷£6 , *child £4.* ☎*01592 872788, www.stirling. org).*There are fine **views** of Stirling from the roof top of the Jail.

Broad Street

Once the centre of burgh life, Broad Street with its **mercat cross**, marks the site of the market and place of execution. **Sir William Bruce** designed the elegant **tolbooth** (1701 –04), shortly after his release from Stirling Castle where he had been held for Jacobite sympathies. The design is unusual in that the stairs climb internally over the cells and up to the panelled rooms. The crowning feature of the six-storey tower is an unusual pavilion with delicate crestings. Across the street at no 16 the narrow gable-ended house has inscribed window pediments.

At the bottom of Broad Street is **Darnley's House** a four-storeyed town house where Lord Darnley is supposed to have stayed while Mary Queen of Scots attended to affairs of state at the castle. Farther down in St Mary's Wynd is the now roofless **John Cowane's House**.

Additional Sight

Stirling Smith Art Gallery and Museum

Dumbarton Road. 👤⏰*Open Tue– Sat,10.30–5pm, Sun 2pm–5pm.* ☕*.*

☎*01786 449 523. www.smithartgallery. demon.co.uk*

Founded by Thomas Stuart Smith (1814 –1869), a local collector and painter of portraits, landscapes, oils and watercol- ours, this enjoyable small gallery and museum contains much 19C artwork, and oddities such as the world's oldest football, made from a pig's bladder, and dating from the 1540s. **The Story of Stirling** is its principal collection, relat- ing the history of the royal burgh.

Driving Tours

8mi/13km. Leave Stirling to the north by the A 9 and at the Causewayhead rounda- bout take the B 998.

National Wallace Monument★★

Shuttle bus or 10min walk from the car park. ⏰*Open daily: Jun 10am–6pm. Jul–Aug 9am–6pm. Sept 9.30am– 5.30pm. Oct and March–May 10am–5pm. Nov–Feb 10.30am–4pm.* 💷£6.50. 🅿️. ☎*01786 472 140, www.nationalwallace monument.com.*

A famous landmark, the 19C Wallace monument stands sentinel on Abbey Craig (362ft/110m) to commemorate

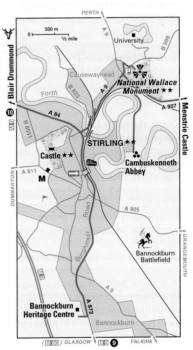

the patriot, **Sir William Wallace** (1270–1305), responsible for rallying Scottish forces against English rule in the period from 1297 to 1305. Hero of the hour at the Battle of Stirling Bridge (1297), he became Guardian, prior to the introduction of a collective system of rule. Following the Scots submission in 1304, Wallace was hunted and captured and died a traitor's death in London the year after. The 19C cult of Wallace was unexpectedly revived towards the end of the 20C, with the popular success of Mel Gibson's film *Braveheart*, a highly romantic account of the hero.

An upper chamber within the monument contains Wallace's War Tent, with a gripping audio-visual presentation of his conflict with the English. Another chamber, the Hall of Heroes, is lined with the busts of such figures as Sir Walter Scott, Robert the Bruce, and Robert Burns. The viewing platform (*246 steps*) has a tremendous **panorama**★★ of Stirling in the flat carselands of the Forth.

Also visible is the **University of Stirling** in its lake and parkland setting, with the Ochils as backdrop. Airthrey Castle, another of Adam's castle houses in the baronial style, serves as administrative centre while the MacRobert Centre is the focus of cultural activity for both town and gown.

▶ *Return to the Causewayhead roundabout and take the Alloa Road (A 907). The abbey is signposted to the right shortly afterwards.*

Cambuskenneth Abbey

The remains of this once great abbey lie within a loop on the flat and fertile carselands of the Forth. Around 1147 King David founded an Augustinian monastery which grew to become one of the most prosperous and influential houses, and its abbots were often statesmen of note. Proximity to Stirling meant royal patronage and the abbey was used for meetings of the Scottish Parliament. The remains include an attractive, free-standing 13C **belfry** which rises through three storeys to a height of 79ft/24m. Within the church there is a 19C monument marking the graves of **James III** (1451–88), victim of the rebel lords after

the Battle of Sauchieburn (1488), and his Queen, Margaret of Denmark.

▶ *Return to the A 907 and turn right. At the roundabout turn left onto the A 91.*

Menstrie Castle

Signposted off the main street. ⏱*Open Easter & May–Sept Wed & Sun 2–5pm.* ☎*01259 211 701. www.menstriecastle.co.uk.*

Built in the 16C, Menstrie Castle has been partially converted into holiday apartments while part of the ground floor is a museum and a National Trust for Scotland shop. Exhibits on the former Scottish colony of Nova Scotia relate to the fact that Menstrie was the birthplace of the founder of the colony, **Sir William Alexander**, 1st Earl of Stirling (1567–1640). The title was created to further the development of the colony and replenish impoverished royal coffers, as, in return for a payment, each Earl was granted land in Eastern Canada. The project ceased when Nova Scotia was returned to the French in 1631 – even though charters continued to be granted until 1637!

Bannockburn Heritage Centre

2mi/3km south on the A 9. (NTS) ⏱*Open Mar–Oct, daily 10am–5.30pm.* ✉*£5.* 🅿*.*☎*0844 4932139. www.nts.org.uk.*

The equestrian statue (1964) of King **Robert the Bruce** (1274–1329) marks Bruce's command post on the eve of the historic **Battle of Bannockburn**, 24 June 1314. Although numerically superior, the English forces, led by Edward II in person, were routed and Bannockburn was a turning point in the **Wars of Independence** (see HISTORY). Since his coronation at Scone in 1306 and Edward I's death in 1307, the Bruce had been steadily regaining his kingdom and by 1314 Stirling Castle was the most important stronghold still in English hands.

The **visitor centre** has an audio-visual presentation on the battle and exhibitions on the Kingdom of the Scots, Robert the Bruce and the Struggle for Independence.

STRANRAER
DUMFRIES AND GALLOWAY
POPULATION 10,766

At the head of Loch Ryan, the agricultural market town of Stranraer depends heavily on the ferry service to Larne (Northern Ireland). Although there's little of interest in the town itself, Stranraer is a good base from which to visit the Rhinns of Galloway peninsula.

- **Information:** 28 Harbour Street. ☎01776 702 595. www.visitdumfriesandgalloway.co.uk.
- ▶ **Orient Yourself:** 72mi/116km south west of Dumfries via the A 75.
- **Don't Miss:** Logan Botanic Garden.
- **Organizing Your Time:** Allow one or two days for an excursion.
- **Especially for Kids:** Logan Fish Pond; Mull of Galloway beaches.

Excursions

Castle Kennedy Gardens

3mi/5km east by A 75. &⏱*Open Easter weekend or Apr 1 (whichever is earlier) through Sept daily 10am–5pm.* ⚬*£4.* ✉.☎*01776 702 024. www.castlekennedygardens.co.uk.*

The natural beauty of the **site**, on a peninsula between two lochs, is an essential part of these gardens where vistas, sweeping lawns and tree-lined avenues are a delight, often the more so for their unexpectedness. The **ruins** are those of Castle Kennedy, former seat of the powerful Ayrshire family of the same name. The stronghold had passed in the 17C into the hands of the infamous Ist Earl of Stair, Sir John Dalrymple, who had ordered the Glencoe Massacre. It was the **2nd Earl** who created the gardens following the castle's destruction by fire (1716).

He commissioned **William Adam** to create an informal garden to harmonise with the setting. In the words of Samuel Boyse, another contemporary exponent of the natural, the gardens are "Too form'd for Nature – yet too wild for Art".

In 1842 following a period of neglect, Loudon restored the gardens to their original aspect, which we see today. Using the Castle Kennedy ruins, the 19C baronial Lochinch Castle (the present seat of the Earls of Stair) and several water features (the Round Pond, canal and lochs) to form focal points, vistas and avenues. The garden is at its best during the rhododendron and azalea season (usually April–May).

Glenluce Abbey

10mi/16km from Stranraer on the A 75 towards Dumfries. After 9mi/14.5km turn sharp left beside a railway viaduct up a farm road.

Castle of Park

This tower house, rising tall in a commanding site overlooking Luce Bay and glen, was built in 1590 by Thomas Hay, son of the last abbot of Glenluce. The door has an inscribed **lintel**.

- ▶ *Return to the main road and turn left after crossing the river. Continue for 1mi/1.6km up the valley.*

Glenluce Abbey

(HS) ⏱*Open Apr–Sept daily 9.30am–5.30pm. Oct Sat–Wed 9.30am– 4.30pm. Last admission 30 mins before closing.* ⏱*Closed 25–26 Dec and 1, 2 Jan.* ⚬*£3.* ☎*01581 300541. www.historic-scotland.gov.uk.*

The abbey was founded in the late 12C by Roland, Lord of Galloway, on a beautiful **site** in the Water of Luce Valley, befitting a Cistercian establishment. The outstanding features of the ruins are the 15C **chapter-house** with some fine sculptural work and the drainage system with some of the original earthenware pipes still in place. There is an exhibition of objects excavated on the site.

Driving Tour

Mull of Galloway

48mi/77km round tour. Leave Stranraer to the south by the A 77.

This drive along quiet back roads explores the southern arm of the Rhinns of Galloway right down to the extremity, the Mull of Galloway. The coutryside is more rugged where small fields are enclosed by stone dykes and where gorse and whin abound. This is dairy country where Friesian cows reign.

Along the splendid **coastline** sandy beaches alternate with stretches of rugged cliffs and occasional bays harbour peaceful villages and ports. Thanks to the Gulf Stream, the region enjoys Scotland's mildest climate.

Sandhead   Kids

Population 250. A typical seaside village with great stretches of sandy beach overlooking Luce Bay.

▶ *Beyond Sandhead take the local road inland to Kirkmadrine Church.*

Kirkmadrine Church

The porch has been glazed in to shelter some of Scotland's earliest existing **Christian monuments**. Three of the tombstones bear Latin inscriptions and the Chi-Rho monogram. They date from the 5C and 6C. These stones are reminders of the early Christian mission established at Whithorn (*see WHITHORN*) and are typical examples of work by the Whithorn School.

Ardwell House Garden

  Open Mar–Sept daily 10am–5pm. £3. P 01776 860 227.

There are three types of garden to vist, Woodland, Heath and Kitchen. The best time to come is around April–May when the daffodils are out, or the rhododendrons and azaleas are in bloom.

▶ *Continue to the small village of Drummore from where B 7041 leads to the southernmost tip. The last part of the road is single track with passing places.*

Mull of Galloway

Short walk from car park.

This rugged headland is fringed with cliffs some 200–250ft/61–76m high. The waters offshore are notorious for strong tides. Good **views** of Cumberland and Ireland can be had on a clear day.

▶ *Continue on the B 7041*

Logan Fish Pond   Kids

  Open Feb–Sept, daily noon–5pm. Oct–early Nov 10am–4pm. £3.50, child £1.25. 01776 860 300. www.loganfish-pond.co.uk.

Set on the far side of the bay the rock pool (30ft/9m deep) here was onceused as a Victorian fish larder for Logan House. It is now stocked with trout, eels, plaice, rays and turbot and the coley can be fed by hand. There are also touch pools, a cave aquarium and a bathing pool.

Logan Botanic Garden★

  Open Apr–Sep daily 10am–6pm. Mar and Oct daily 10am–5pm. Feb Sun only 10am–4pm. £4. 01776 860 231. www.rbge.org.uk.

This annexe of the Royal Botanic Garden (*see EDINBURGH*) has a large variety of well labelled **exotic plants** which flourish in the warmth of the Gulf Stream. Impeccably kept with something to delight everyone, the garden has two main parts, walled and woodland. Outstanding among the many plants from warm temperate regions of the world are the cabbage palms (actually members of the lily family), and the tree ferns.

▶ *At Ardwell take the B road to Portpatrick.*

Portpatrick   Kids

Population 595. On the west coast, this popular seaside village is the peninsula's most important community. The houses climbing the slopes at the back of the bay overlook the small harbour which in pre-steam days was the terminal for the Irish crossing.

The **Southern Upland Way** links Portpatrick to Cockburnspath on the east coast.

▶ *The A 77 returns to Stranraer.*

TANTALLON CASTLE★★
EAST LOTHIAN
3MI/5KM EAST OF NORTH BERWICK

In its splendid **clifftop site**★★★ facing the Bass Rock, the formidable ruin of **Tantallon Castle** defies the pounding waves and howling easterly gales.

- **Information:** ☎01620 892727. www.historic-scotland.gov.uk.
- **Orient Yourself:** Tantallon Castle lies 3mi/5km east of North Berwick on the A 198.

Visit

(HS) ⏱*Open Apr–Sept daily 9.30am–5.30pm. Oct–Mar Sat–Wed 9.30am–4.30pm. Last admission 30 mins before closing.* ⏱ *Closed 25–26 Dec and 1, 2 Jan.* ☕. 🍴*£4.50* ☎ *01620 892 727. www.historic-scotland.gov.uk.*

The Visitor Centre is the best introduction to exploring the castle. Two ditches and earthen ramparts defend the landward side and access to the bailey is by the now ruined Outer Gate. The lectern type dovecot is 17C. The inner ditch stretches right across the headland at the foot of the curtain walls.

Dating from the late 14C, with 16C alterations, Tantallon is one of the great castles of enclosure. The massive curtain wall (50ft/15m tall) links the gatehouse and flanking circular towers and cuts off the impregnable promontory site. The attractively weathered red sandstone enhances the foreboding, stark ruin.

Mid Tower

In the late 14C a barbican, distinguished here by green stone with red string courses, was added to the gatehouse and followed by an outwork in the 16C. The Earl of Angus' coat of arms is high up on the forework. Pass through the passage to the original doorway. To the right is a guard-room and to the left a passage leading to a turnpike which gives access to the four floors above, each consisting of a single apartment with garderobe and small adjacent chambers.

The **well** in the close goes down to a depth of 106ft/32m.

East Tower

The five storeys are reached by a turnpike. At each level there are apartments with fireplaces, stone benches and mural garderobes.

Douglas Tower

Above the pit prison with a bedrock floor, are six storeys of apartments similar to those in the East Tower.

Tantallon Castle

W. Buss / MICHELIN

A vivid impression

The dramatic scenery is aptly described by **Sir Walter Scott** in his narrative poem Marmion.

"...Tantallon vast
Broad, massive, high and
stretching far,
And held impregnable in war
On a projecting rock it rose,
And round three sides the ocean flows,
The fourth did battled walls enclose..."

Curtain Walls

Over 12ft/3.5m thick and 50ft/15m high, they connect the towers by a wall-walk and originally had their own independent stairways with mural chambers. The wall-walk was once roofed over and edged by a parapet wall.

Northern Courtyard Range

The western part included the Laigh and Long halls and was contemporary with the towers and curtain walls. It was altered in the 16C when the eastern part was added.

LOCH TAY★★
PERTHSIRE AND KINROSS

Loch Tay is an attractive freshwater loch in a mountain setting with Ben Lawers rising to majestic heights on the north shore. It measures over 14mi/22.5km long from Killin to Kenmore, but is never more than 1mi/1.5km wide. The loch is fed by the Dochart and Lochay, and at the east end the River Tay.

- **Information:** Breadalbane Folklore Centre, Falls of Dochart, Killin. ☎08707 200 627. www.visitscottishheartlands.com.
- ▶ **Orient Yourself:** Killin, head of Loch Tay is 44mi/71km west of Perth on A 85.
- 🕐 **Organizing Your Time:** Allow half a day for the north shore tour, plus a full day if you intend ascending Ben Lawers.
- 👍 **Also See:** ABERFELDY.

Driving Tour
North Shore:
Killin to Kenmore

17mi/27.5km – 30min

Killin

Population 545. Killin is busy with passing trade in summer. To the west (best seen from the bridge) the River Dochart tumbles into the **Falls of Dochart**, towards the loch. The old watermill has been converted into the **Breadalbane Folklore Centre** (🕐 *open Apr–Oct 10am–5pm (Jul–Aug 5.30pm);* ✆£2.75; ☎01567 820 254, www.breadalbanefolklorecentre.com), where visitors are introduced to the area's history and clans like the MacDonalds and MacGregors. The Tourist Information Centre is also here. On a rocky outcrop overlooking the loch stand the tree-sheltered and overgrown ruins of **Finlarig Castle**, seat of Black

Duncan of the Cowl, the ruthless chief of **Clan Campbell**. Finlarig was notorious for its beheading pit.

Ben Lawers★★

2.5mi/4km by single track road. (NTS). 🕐 *Visitor Centre open Good Fri–Sept daily 10am–5pm (closed half hour for lunch 1–2pm.* ✆£2. ☎0844 4932136. *www.nts.org.uk.*

The **Visitor Centre** provides an excellent audio-visual programme on the mountain, its formation and the rare alpine flora. The summit (3,984ft/1,214m) and southern slopes of the mountain are a National Nature Reserve, and access is controlled in order to protect the fragile ecology of the area. A **nature trail** (*1hr 30min*) introduces visitors to some of the fascinating plants and makes clear the need for careful conservation of their vulnerable habitat.

VISITSCOTLAND/SCOTTISH PERTHSHIRE

Scottish Crannog Centre, Kenmore, Loch Tay

On the way down the road provides good **views** of Loch Tay.

Isle of Loch Tay

○━*No access.* When Alexander I's Queen Sybilla died in 1122, the king granted her burial place, the isle, to the monks of Scone. A nunnery succeeded the monastery until the late 15C.

Kenmore★

Population 211. The sites of 18 crannogs have been discovered in Loch Tay. A crannog is an artificial or modified natural island, found throughout Scotland and Ireland, the oldest dating back some 5,000 years. Many crannogs were built as defensive homesteads and represented symbols of power and wealth. The multi-award-winning **Scottish Crannog Centre** (⚿⏰*open mid Mar–Oct daily 10am–5.30pm, Nov Sat–Sun only 10am–4pm; ☞£5.75; ☎01887 830 583, www.crannog.co.uk*), features a unique reconstruction of an early Iron Age loch-dwelling, based on the excavation evidence from a 2,600 year old site.

THURSO
HIGHLAND
POPULATION 8,828

Most visitors use this small town as a gateway to the Orkneys, from Thurso's car ferry port, Scrabster, to Stromness. Busy in summer, it also makes a good centre for visiting the very scenic north coast, from Durness to Duncansby Head.

🛈 **Information:** Riverside. ☎08452 255 121. www.visithighlands.com.

▶ **Orient Yourself:** Thurso is 20mi/32km west of John O'Groats on the A 836.

👁 **Don't Miss:** The views from Strathy Point; the views of the Kyle of Tongue from Torrisdale Bay; view of Loch Eriboll.

🄺🄸🄳🅂 **Especially for Kids:** The beach at nearby Dunnet Bay.

⚓ **Also See:** WICK, DUNCANSBY HEAD, ORKNEY ISLANDS.

A Bit of History

The origins of this north-facing **Caithness**town go back to Norse times, but the oldest (and most interesting) part of the present town is medieval, and overlooks the harbour at the mouth of the River Thurso. There are many

Dounreay

Scotland became a **nuclear** country in August 1957 when the first reaction occurred in a test cell at Dounreay – its fast reactor was the first of its kind to produce electricity for public consumption. For over four decades, the coastal landscape around Sandside Bay has been dominated by the futuristic dome of this nuclear power station, but it is now in the process of demolition and decommissioning, which is planned to finish by 2036. The public are no longer allowed near the plant but its story is told in the exhibition in Thurso.

Exhibits from the plant will also be on display at the new visitor attraction which promises artefacts from the Stone Age to the Atomic Age.

dignified late Georgian/early Victorian houses, many of them built with thick walls of blue Caithness flintstone. In the 1950s and 60s the town expanded three-fold in response to the construction of the nearby Dounreay nuclear power station (see Box, above).

Driving Tour

North coast
Thurso to Durness
74mi/119km by the A 836 and the A 838. Bleak moorland scenery gives way to the glories of coastal scenery beyond, with an ever-changing pattern of sandy bays, lochs and headlands.

Scrabster
This is the terminal port for the car ferry to Stromness in the Orkneys.

Melvich Bay
From the War Memorial behind the hotel in the crofting community of Melvich, there is a splendid **view** over Melvich Bay with the sand bar. The island of Hoy is visible in the distance.

▶ *The road beyond Melvich is single track with passing places. Cross the River Strathy which opens into another sandy estuary, Strathy Bay. Then turn right to the point.*

Strathy Point★
15min walk from the car park to the point.
There are excellent **views**★★★ along the coast to the east of Strathy Bay in the

foreground, with Dounreay and Hoy in the distance.
The landscape then becomes scoured and hummocky with the stately outline of the granite peaks of **Ben Loyal**★★ (2,504ft/764m) ahead, rising above the plateau.

Bettyhill
Population 177. This is one of the crofting communities which originated at the time of the Highlands Clearances when crofters were evicted, in this case from Strathnaver, to make way for sheep. The story of the Highlands Clearances is one of several subjects in the **Strathnaver Museum** (open Apr–Oct Mon–Sat 10am–1pm, 2pm–5pm; £1.90; 01641 521 418, www.strathnavermuseum.org.uk) housed in Farr Church.
The road then follows the sandy estuary of **Torrisdale Bay**★, crosses the river, then climbs out of Strathnaver to ascend to the scoured plateau surface dotted with reed-choked lochs. Go round Cnoc an Fhreiceadain and just before reaching Coldbackie there are excellent **views**★★ of the great sea loch, the Kyle of Tongue, with Rabbit Islands in the middle.

Tongue
Population 129. This small village lies on the shores of the sea loch.
The Kyle of Tongue is bridged by a causeway which offers a new **view** inland towards Ben Loyal and, ahead, a ruined Mackay stronghold perched on an eminence.

▶ *The road becomes double track beyond Tongue.*

The outline of Ben Hope appears on the horizon. Peat banks are visible from time to time. On the descent there are glimpses of Loch Hope stretching away to the left. From the west side of Loch Hope, there are fine views of the loch stretching away to **Ben Hope**★ (3,040ft/927m) in the background. A little farther on, a magnificent **view**★★★ unfolds of Loch Eriboll, another deeply penetrating sea loch.

▸ *The road becomes single track on the east side. Do not impede the flow of traffic by parking in passing points. Go round the loch. Sangobeg has a lovely sandy beach.*

Durness – &See DURNESS.

Smoo Cave
&See DURNESS: Excursions.

Dunnet Head
26mi/42km there and back.

Castletown
5.5 miles east on the A 836. London's famous Strand was paved with Caithness flagstones, exported from the little harbour at Castletown. Other reminders of the more prosperous times of the 19C and early 20C are the stump of a windmill, a dam, and the quarry workers' cottage. The industry was killed off by the introduction of concrete paving slabs.

Mary-Ann's Cottage
On the northern edge of the village of Dunnet, 8.5mi/13km east by A 836. Westside Dunnet. &☉*Open June –Sept, Tue–Sun 2pm–4.30pm.* ☞*£2.* 🅿☎ *01593 721 325.*
The home of Mary-Ann Calder, born here in 1897, this typical crofting cottage, together with its outbuildings, is being actively conserved as an important social document. Far from being a static exhibit, it shows the evolution of this type of habitat, with modern developments like the 1950s kitchen as well as a wealth of indicators of the traditional, pre-Improvement, rural way of life.

Dunnet Head
13mi/21km northeast by A 836 and B 855. Reached by a single-track road across a wild landscape with lochans, Dunnet Head is the most northerly point on the British mainland, almost 2.5 mi/4 km further north than John O'Groats, which is traditionally known as the northernmost point.
The lighthouse, which stands on the 300ft (90m) cliff top of Easter Head is 345ft (105m) tall and it was built in 1831 by Robert Stevenson, the grandfather of Robert Louis Stevenson.
The buildings nearby (bunker, radar and montoring stations etc) date from World War II and were part of the protection of the naval base at Scapa Flow.
The cliffs are rich in sea birds.

TRAQUAIR HOUSE★★
SCOTTISH BORDERS
LOCAL MAP SEE THE TWEED VALLEY

The white walls of **Traquair** peep out from the tree cover on the south bank of the Tweed. The long and peaceful history of house and family, visited or lived in by no less than 27 Scottish kings and queens, is vividly illustrated by a wealth of relics, treasures, traditions and legends.

▣ **Information:** ☎01896 830 323. www.traquair.co.uk.
▸ **Orient Yourself:** Traquair House is 1.5mi/2.4km south of innerleithen (29 mi/47km south of Edinburgh on the A 702/A 703) on the B 709
☉ **Organizing Your Time:** Allow around two hours.
& **Also See:** ABBOTSFORD, BIGGAR, TWEED VALLEY.

P. Tomkins/VISITSCOTLAND/SCOTTISH VIEWPOINT

Traquair House

A Bit of History

Royal hunting lodge – As early as 1107, Alexander I stayed at Traquair and it remained a royal residence up to the 13C, used initially as a hunting seat for the surrounding forests. The favourite residence of William the Lion, it was transformed during the Wars of Independence into a Border peel or fortified tower. In the late 13C the tower was in English hands and both Edward I and II stayed here, but it was returned to the Scottish Crown in the early 14C. James III gave Traquair to his Master of Music, William Rogers, and he sold the property to James, Earl of Buchan, uncle to the King.

Tower house to mansion – The Earl's son, **James Stuart**, inherited Traquair in 1491 and the present owners are direct descendants. James' plans to extend the property were cut short by his untimely death at Flodden in 1513 and it was not until the 16C–17C that the original peel was transformed into a mansion house. James' grandson, **Sir John Stuart**, 4th Laird of Traquair, was Captain of Mary, Queen of Scots' Bodyguard and played host to the Queen and Lord Darnley in 1566, which is why the house has so many personal belongings of Mary and associations with this period.

Another notable figure was **John Stuart, Ist Earl of Traquair** (1600–59), who rose to the high office of Lord High Treasure. However misfortune befell him and loss of office obliged the earl to return to his estate and preoccupy himself with home affairs. He changed the course of the Tweed and added a storey to the house. It was during his son John's lifetime that the Catholic faith was adopted by the family, a tradition that has been maintained and which was to make Traquair an active centre for the Jacobite cause in the 18C.

Charles, 4th Earl (1659–1741), a staunch Jacobite sympathiser, married Lady Mary Maxwell uniting the Maxwell and Stuart estates. One of the Maxwell seats was the now demolished Terregles House in Dumfriesshire and many of its treasures are at Traquair. Charles commissioned James Smith to make certain alterations (1695–99). The side wings were remodelled, a wrought-iron screen erected in the forecourt, a formal garden was created and given two attractive pavilions with ogee-shaped roofs. Ever since then the exterior of Traquair has remained unaltered.

Visit

& ⓒOpen Jun–Aug daily 10.30am–5pm. May & Sept noon–5pm. Easter weekend, Apr Sat–Sun only noon–5pm. Oct daily 11am–3pm. Nov Sat–Sun only 11am–3pm. Last admission 1 hour before closing). ⌖£6.50. Grounds only £3.50. ✗.

Ground floor

The oak armorial in the hall displaying Scotland's royal arms dates from Mary, Queen of Scots' 1566 visit. The corner cupboards in the panelled still room contain Chinese and English porcelain. The elm chairs are part of a Scottish-made set dating from around 1750. The main staircase leads off the hall. Note at the bottom the vigorously carved oak door from Terregles House.

First floor

The width of the drawing room gives some indication of the narrowness of the building. Other noteworthy features include the fragments of 16C painted beams, the 1651 Andreas Ruckers harpsichord, and portraits of the *4th Earl*, *Dryden* and another by George James-one (c. 1620). Pass through the dressing room to reach the **King's Room**, dominated by the splendidly ornate yellow State Bed, again from Terregles and said to be the one used by Mary, Queen of Scots. The bedspread was the work of Mary and her companions, the four Marys, and the cradle was used by her son, King James VI. Beside the powder closet is the door giving access to the unevenly stepped, steep narrow stairs of the original 12C tower and the secret stairs.

Second floor

This may be reached by the secret or main stairs. The **Museum Room** display includes a variety of historical documents, mementoes and other interesting items such as the 1530 fragment of wall painting and a collection of Amen glasses.

▶ *Return to the main stairs and go up another flight.*

Third floor

The **Library** remains almost intact, as formed in 1700–40, with books still bearing the mark of their shelf number and place. Adjoining is a second library with 19C works. At the end of the corridor the **Priest's Room** originally served as the chapel and it was in these cramped quarters that the chaplain lived his furtive existence, as testified by the hidden stairs, with the false cupboard entrance.

▶ *Return to the ground floor.*

Take the passage to the left to see the **vaulted chamber** of the original construction. This is where the cattle used to be herded in times of raids.

South wing

In the Dining Room there is another group of family **portraits**, with Medina's one of the *4th Earl and Countess of Traquair* who had 17 children, and another of the Jacobite *Charles 5th Earl*. Above the fireplace is the *1st Earl* with the rod of office as Lord High Treasurer.

North wing

Following the Catholic Emancipation Act of 1829, the chapel replaced the priest's room as the place of worship. The set of 12 16C carved **wood panels** depicts episodes from the Life of Christ.

Outbuildings

Next to the chapel is the reception centre and shop while above is a fully equipped wash-house. Take a tour around the **brew-house**; one of the oldest working breweries in Britain, dating back to the 18C, its highly regarded Traquair House Ales are available to sample and purchase. Several independent craft shops also occupy old buidings and lunch is served in the old walled garden at the 1745 Cottage Restaurant.

The site of the Well Pool marks the former bed of the Tweed and the grounds include a choice of woodland walks which boasts some of the oldest yew trees in Scotland .

The Steekit Yetts (Bear Gates)

This famous entrance, built 1737–38, lies at the end of a grassy tree-lined avenue. Tradition has it that the gates were closed by the 5th Earl on the departure of **Bonnie Prince Charlie** with a vow to reopen them only on the Restoration of a Stuart monarch.

THE TROSSACHS ★★★
STIRLING

One of Scotland's most famous beauty spots, the Trossachs conjures up an idyllic landscape of great scenic beauty where rugged, but not so lofty mountains, and their wooded slopes, are reflected in the sparkling waters of the lochs.

- **Information:** Trossachs Discovery Centre, Main Street, Aberfoyle. ☎08707 200 604. Rob Roy & Trossachs Visitor Centre, Ancaster Square, Callander. ☎08707 200 628. Breadalbane Folklore Centre, Falls of Dochart, Killin. ☎08707 200 627. Main Street, Tyndrum. ☎08707 200 626. www.visitscottishheartlands.com.
- **Orient Yourself:** The Trossachs are delimited by the head of Loch Achray in the east, the foot of Loch Katrine to the west, Ben An (1,750ft/533m) to the north and Ben Venue (2,393ft/727m) to the south. The term is more generally taken to cover a wider area from Loch Venachar in the east to the shores of Loch Lomond.
- **Don't Miss:** The Hilltop viewpoint panorama; a boat trip on Loch Katrine.
- **Organizing Your Time:** Allow a day for the round tour including visits and boat trip. To appreciate to the full the solitude and scenic splendours, it is advisable to visit early in the morning when the coaches are not yet about and driving on the narrow roads is still a pleasure.
- **Especially for Kids:** Go Ape at the Queen Elizabeth Forest Park.
- **Also See:** LOCH LOMOND, DOUNE, DUNBLANE.

*"So wondrous and wild, the
whole might seem
The scenery of a fairy dream."*

Sir Walter Scott put the Trossachs on the map in the early 19C with his novels *Lady of the Lake*, and *Rob Roy* and its untamed peaks, glens and deep forests have attracted visitors from England and Scotland (thanks in no small part to its proximity to the great urban populations of Edinburgh, Glasgow and the Central Valley, ever since.

National Park

🕐*The Old Station, Balloch Road, Balloch.*
☎ *0845 345 4978 . www.lochlomond-trossachs.org.*
The Trossachs is part of the **Loch Lomond & The Trossachs National Park.** It embraces the deep waters of Loch Lomond, the wild glens of the Trossachs, Breadalbane's high mountains and the sheltered sea lochs of the Argyll Forest. The Visitor Centre contains a state-of-the-art interpretation centre exploring the nature, geology and social history of the National Park and a peaceful outdoor

area with accessible walks down to Loch Lomond. Various events are held here.

The area described here under the heading Trossachs has been intentionally extended towards Loch Lomond in the west and in the south to the Lake of Menteith for the convenience of the round tour described below, which has Callander as its starting point. An alternative day tour combining boat and bus trips covers the western part of the area, starting from Balloch.

Driving Tour from Callander

59 miles

Callander★ – 🕯*See CALLANDER.*

- *Leave Callander by the A 84 in the direction of Crianlarich (Lochearnhead). After 1mi/1.5km branch left to take The Trossachs A 821 road.*

This road climbs up with the great shoulder of **Ben Ledi** (2,882ft/879m) on the right. On looking backwards Callander

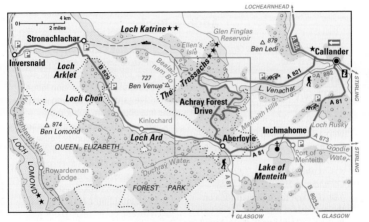

🏕	Picnic site
🚶	Forest walk

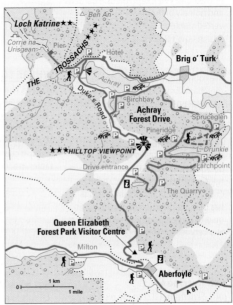

can be seen nestling in the valley floor. As the road moves round the lower slopes of Ben Ledi, it approaches **Loch Venachar** (4mi/6.5km long; *parking and picnic places*).

Brig o'Turk

This widely scattered village at the mouth of Glen Finglas is closely associated with the Ruskins and Millais who spent an extended holiday in the area in 1853. Brig o'Turk was also one of the early summer haunts of the Glasgow Boys art movement.

Once across the Finglas Water, the road enters the **Achray Forest**, part of the Queen Elizabeth Forest Park (⚭ *see main entry, below*). After Loch Achray, the second tallest peak of the area, **Ben Venue** (2,393ft/727m), stands out in the distance with the white form of Loch Achray Hotel at its feet. Pass on the right the castellated 20C reconstruction of the Trossachs Hotel. At the end of the Loch, the road continues on to Loch Katrine (dead end).

Address Book

For coin ranges, see the Legend on the cover flap.

WHERE TO STAY

⊜⊜ **Priory** – *Bracklinn Road, Callander.* ☎*01877 330 001. www.thepriory. co.uk* This spacious Victorian house with a walled garden features homely bedrooms and an elegant sitting room with antiques.

⊜⊜ **Lubnaig House** – *Leny Feus, Callander.* ☎*01877 330 376. www. lubnaighouse.co.uk.* Built in 1864 on the outskirts of town, this characterful house boasts well kept, mature gardens and homely bedrooms—two in converted stables.

⊜⊜ **Brook Linn** – *Leny Feus, Callander.* ☎*01877 330 103. www.brooklinn-scotland.co.uk.* Built 150 years ago as the country house of a wealthy wool merchant, Brook Linn has an elevated, peaceful position on the edge of Callander. Homely lounge and traditional bedrooms.

⊜⊜ **Dunmor House** – *Leny Road, Callander.* ☎*01877 330 756. www. dunmorhouse.co.uk.* This large Victorian house nestles underneath Callander Crags on the fringes of the village. It has been refurbished to provide high quality contemporary accommodation at a very reasonable price.

⊜⊜⊜ **Roman Camp Country House** – *Main Street, Callander.* ☎*01877 330 003. www.romancamphotel.co.uk.* A very peaceful part-17C hunting lodge in extensive gardens replete with antiques and fine objets d'art. Public rooms include a secret chapel. Bedrooms are decorated in comfy country-house style.

⊜⊜⊜⊜ **Forest Hills** – *Kinlochard, Aberfoyle.* ☎*0870 194 2105. www. macdonaldhotels.co.uk/foresthills.* This luxury country-house hotel enjoys a lovely location overlooking Loch Ard, with extensive leisure facilities and individually styled rooms. The Garden Restaurant (⊜⊜⊜) enjoys glorious views and offers Modern Scottish cuisine.

WHERE TO EAT

⊜⊜⊜ **The Restaurant** – *Roman Camp Country House, Main Street, Callander.* ☎*01877 330 003, www. romancamphotel.co.uk.* Attentive staff serve skilfully prepared modern Scottish cuisine on crisp linen-covered tables in a vibrant modern dining room.

Loch Katrine★★

1mi/1.5km from A 821 to the pier and car park. No access round loch for vehicles.
Other than hill walking, the only (very rewarding) way to discover this famous loch is to take a **boat trip** (*operates daily late Mar–late Oct, see website for times and prices;* ☎ *01877 376 315/6, www. lochkatrine.com*).
The loch (10mi/16km long and 2mi/3.2km at its widest) has been Glasgow's water supply since 1859, when Queen Victoria officiated at the inauguration. On the northeastern slopes of the twin-peaked Ben Venue are Corrie na Urisgean (Goblin's Cave), the traditional meeting place of Scotland's goblins, and Bealach nam Bo (Pass of the Cattle), a route much favoured by the drover Rob Roy when returning home with cattle. Ellen's Isle (Eilean Molach) figures in Scott's *The Lady of the Lake*.

The boat turns about at Stronachlachar from where a road leads westwards to Inversnaid on the shores of Loch Lomond. Glen Gyle, at the head of Loch Katrine, was the birthplace of Rob Roy and on the north shore is a MacGregor burial place. Factor's Isle, another Rob Roy haunt, is where the outlaw held the Duke of Montrose's factor, Baillie Nicol Jarvie, in reprisal for having evicted Rob Roy's family.

▶ *Return to the junction with the A 821 and take Duke's Road, in the Aberfoyle direction, to pass round the head of Loch Achray.*

From the **car park** there is a good view up the loch. Once round to the south side, the road climbs with good views over Loch Achray.

Hilltop viewpoint★★★
Park at the roadside; 5min climb to viewing table.
There is an excellent **panorama**★★★ of the Trossachs, encompassing Ben Venue, Loch Katrine with its mountain ring, Ben An, Finglas Reservoir, Ben Ledi with Brig o'Turk at its feet, Loch Venachar and due east round to the Menteith Hills. In the immediate foreground is Loch Drunkie in the heart of Achray Forest.

Achray Forest Drive
This forest road (7mi/11km long) makes an excellent outing for those wanting an afternoon away from it all (*ample parking and picnic places with a choice of walks*) but since it is through forested countryside it has few views of the surrounding countryside.
Away on the right can be seen scars of now disused slate quarries.

Queen Elizabeth Forest Park Visitor Centre
David Marshall Lodge Visitor Centre. ♿🕐Open Mar–Dec. Picnic area. ✗ P (fee). ☎01877 382 258.
The audio-visual presentation is an excellent introduction to the forest park. The centre is also the base for **Go Ape** (Kids 🕐 *open school hols,daily mid Mar–Oct; Sat–Sun Nov, see website for Dec; 9am–5pm, during busy periods 8.30am–6pm); ⬛£25, child £20. Height/ weight and adult supervision restrictions apply; ☎0845 643 9215, www.go.ape. co.uk).* This is an exciting tree top trail for

The Fairy Folk
Local folklore includes such mythical creatures as the Water Bull of Loch Katrine and the Water Horse of Loch Venachar, the latter recently made into a movie, *The Water Horse* (2008). An Aberfoyle minister, the Reverend Robert Kirk, published *The Secret Commonwealth of Elfs, Fawns and Fairies* (1691) and another supernatural tale is that of the first commercial steamboat to ply the waters of Loch Katrine, *The Water Witch*.

children and adults, traversing a series of rope ladders, bridges, Tarzan swings, trapezes, stirrup crossings and zip wires, including the longest zip wire in Great Britain, measuring 1,400ft/426 m.
A variety of **trails** are open to the public including the Fairy Trail on Doon Hill, the site from where the Rev Robert Kirk was spirited away (🔲*see Box above*).
The road then descends into Aberfoyle leaving behind the mountainous rim of the Central Highlands.

Aberfoyle
Population 546. Aberfoyle was made famous as the meeting place of Rob Roy and Nicol Jarvie. Today it is busy with tourists in summer, many of whom throng the sales floor of **The Scottish Wool Centre** (♿🕐*open daily 9.30am– 5pm; ✗ P ; ☎01877 382 850, www. scottishwoolcentre.co.uk*). The story of 2,000 years of Scottish wool is told by means of an entertaining live show where most of the models and actors have four legs; there is also a small farm for children.

A land of romance and adventure
Much of the Trossachs was MacGregor country and is closely associated with the daring exploits of **Rob Roy MacGregor** (1671–1734), an outlaw and the leader of the MacGregor Clan, which Sir Walter Scott recounted in *Rob Roy* (1818).

Scott also popularised the Trossachs with his romantic poem, *The Lady of the Lake*. Such was the public desire to follow in the footsteps of Scott's characters that the Duke of Montrose built **Duke's Road** in 1820, a connecting road north from Aberfoyle. Famous visitors who came this way included the Wordsworths and Coleridge in 1830, following which Wordsworth wrote *To a Highland Girl*.

▶ *Leave Aberfoyle to the west by the B 829, a single track road.*

This **scenic road**, ending beside Inversnaid Hotel on Loch Lomond, makes a pleasant drive through the southwest of the Queen Elizabeth Forest Park.

Loch Ard

The road along the north shore runs close to the water's edge of Loch Ard described by **Queen Victoria** in 1869 as "a fine long loch with trees of all kinds overhanging the road, heather making all pink, bracken, rocks, high hills of such fine shape and trees growing up them as in Switzerland. Altogether the whole view was lovely". The **scenery** has lost none of its attraction with the southern shore clothed with the trees of Loch Ard Forest. The prominent outline of Ben Lomond looms large on the horizon. There is a fine **view** of Loch Chon, backed by the 'Arrochar Alps' in the distance.

Loch Chon

This is the smaller of the two lochs.

▶ *At the road junction the branch to the right leads to Stronachlachar.*

Stronachlachar

On the south shore of Loch Katrine. The *SS Sir Walter Scott* makes a stop at this point (🌀*see Loch Katrine above*)

▶ *Return to the junction and carry straight on.*

Loch Arklet

This artificial loch (reservoir) lies in a glacially created hanging valley.
The ruins to the right are those of Inversnaid barracks built in the early 18C to curb the MacGregors.

Inversnaid

On Loch Lomondside, the Inversnaid Hotel overlooks the pier and is one of the stopping places for steamer cruises. The far side of Loch Lomond (🌀*see LOCH*

LOMOND) is dominated by the peaks of the Cobbler, Bens Vorlich, Vane and Ime. The **West Highland Way** follows this shore of Loch Lomond, on its way north to Fort William.

▶ *Return towards Aberfoyle, leaving to the east. At the junction with the A 81 turn left. The road skirts the great rounded spine of the Menteith Hills.*

Lake of Menteith

On the northern edge of Flanders Moss, the lake is the venue for The Bonspiel, or Grand Match, an outdoor curling tournament between teams from the north and south, which historically has drawns thousands of participants. However it is only played when the ice is sufficiently thick enough (around 10 inches) to make it safe to do so – the last time was in 1979!

▶ *Pass the lake and then turn right in the direction of Arnprior. The car park is 0.5mi/800m down the road.*

Inchmahome Priory

This is an island monastery. To attract the ferryman's attention when he is on the island, turn the white board on the jetty. (HS) 🕐*Open Apr–Sept daily 9.30am–6pm; Oct Mon–Fri 9.30am– 4.30pm. Last ferry out 1hr 15min before closing.* ▫️*£4.50 (inc ferry)* ☎ *01877 385294. www.historic-scotland.gov.uk.*
The mid-13C ruins include the church of the Augustinian priory with its deeply recessed west doorway strongly resembling the one at Dunblane and the chapter-house which shelters an unusual **double effigy**★ tomb monument.
In 1547 Mary, Queen of Scots was brought here for her own safety – she was only four years old at the time – after the battle of Pinkie Cleugh and stayed for three weeks prior to embarking for France.

▶ *Return to Callander by the A 81.*

THE TWEED VALLEY★★
SCOTTISH BORDERS

The Tweed is one of Scotland's longest and most beautiful waterways, with long vistas and graceful curves. A series of famous landmarks and quiet, pleasant, well-to-do market towns adorn its banks.

- **Information:** Shepherd's Mill, Whinfield Road, Selkirk; Murray's Green, Jedburgh; Town House, The Square, Kelso; High Street, Peebles; Abbey House, Abbey Street, Melrose. ☎0870 608 0404 (all offices). www.visitscottishborders.com.
- ▶ **Orient Yourself:** The River Tweed rises in the Tweedsmuir Hills to the west of the Borders and flows eastwards, acting as the frontier with England for the latter part of its journey, ending at Berwick-upon-Tweed, some 97mi/155km later. This section of the guide relates to the Middle Tweed Valley. For the description of sights along the upper reaches of the Tweed see MOFFAT and BIGGAR. For sights downriver see KELSO and COLDSTREAM.
- **Don't Miss:** DRYBURGH ABBEY, SCOTT'S VIEW, ABBOTSFORD, TRAQUAIR HOUSE. The **Glorious Tweed Festival** (see Calendar of Events) is a varied programme of events celebrating the Borders heritage.
- **Organizing Your Time:** Allow a full day to explore the Middle Tweed; though you could easily spend longer here.

A Bit of History and Geography

River and landscapes – The Tweed, is the third longest Scottish river after the Tay and Clyde, and drains the Border region. The Tweed basin is ringed by hills, with the Cheviots to the south, the Southern Uplands to the west and the Lammermuir Hills to the north. Tributaries include the Yarrow, Ettrick, Gala, Leader and Teviot.

In its upper reaches the Tweed cuts discordantly across the major structures and its valley is constricted and irregular. In its middle reaches, between the uplands and the Merse, it is broad with majestic curves, overlooked by ruined abbeys and prosperous Border towns.

A rich heritage – From earliest times the region has been favoured as an area of settlement. Iron Age remains, Roman forts and great monastic houses all chose its fertile haughlands as ideal sites. The area is best-known for the troubled times (13C–16C) of Border raids and reiving as recounted in the ballads. The Border Laws accepted by both kingdoms were enforced by Wardens of the March, three for each country. It was the responsibility of these officers, often hereditary, to repel invasion and keep the peace. The Tweed Valley has a rich heritage from this period with the traditional Border peels or fortified tower houses. Outstanding examples are Neidpath, Smailholm and Greenknowe. The memory of these times is also kept alive by the **Common Ridings** when groups of citizens ride the burgh boundaries.

The Tweed today – The valley is noted primarily for its agriculture with hill sheep farming on the uplands and mixed arable farms on the flatter and richer till soils of the Merse. The traditional woollen and knitwear industries are of paramount importance to the Tweed towns. The Tweed, Queen of the Salmon rivers, and its tributaries provide several hundred miles of freshwater fishing with a possible catch of 16 different species of fish, and stillwater or loch fishing for trout, pike and perch.

Driving Tour

Middle Tweed from Kelso to Neidpath Castle 40mi/64km.

Kelso★ – ⓘSee KELSO.

▶ *Leave Kelso by A 699 which follows the south bank.*

Floors Castle (ⓘ*see FLOORS CASTLE*) enjoys an attractive terraced setting on the north bank. A visit to Mellerstain (ⓘ*see MELLERSTAIN*) is also very worthwhile. Pass on the left the site of Roxburgh Castle (ⓘ*see KELSO*).

St Boswells

Population 1,086. The village was once the site of an important livestock fair.

▶ *Take the local B 6404 northeast to cross the Tweed.*

Dryburgh Abbey★★ – ⓘSee DRYBURGH ABBEY.

▶ *Continue by the local B 6356 which skirts Bemersyde Hill.*

Scott's View★★
ⓘ*See MELROSE: Excursions.*

▶ *Turn left onto the local road and once under the main road cross the river to take the B 6361.*

Pass the 19-span Leaderfoot Viaduct. Farther on, a monument to the left of the road marks the site of the Roman settlement of **Trimontium** ⓘ*See MELROSE: Additional Sights..*

Melrose★ – ⓘSee MELROSE.

▶ *Leave to the west by the A 7 and at the second roundabout follow the signs to Abbotsford.*

Abbotsford★★
ⓘ*See ABBOTSFORD.*

▶ *Once back on the A 7 cross the Tweed.*

Galashiels

Population 12,294. On the narrow floor of the Gala Water this busy tweed and knitwear manufacturing and shopping centre is one of the largest Border towns. The **Braw Lad's Gathering** (*last weekend Jun*) is a famous Common Ridings. Local history can be traced at **Old Gala House** (ⓘ *open Jul–Aug, Mon–Sat 10am–4pm, Sun 2–4pm; Apr–Sept & Oct, Tue–Sat 10am (Oct 1pm)–4pm;* ☕; P; ☎01750 20096, www.galashiels.border-net.co.uk /oldgalahouse), a late-16C stone house with a 17C painted ceiling.

Lochcarron Cashmere Wool Centre (♿ⓘ*open year-round Mon–Sat 9am–5pm, Sun 11am–4pm;* •ⷮGuided tours (40min), Mon–Thu 10.30am, 11.30am, 1.30pm, 2.30pm. ⓘ closed public and local hols); P; ☎01896 751 100, www.lochcarron.com) is a working mill, museum and visitor centre with displays on the evolution of the town and its industries, and tours showing the process of tartan manufacture.

▶ *Continue by the A 72 to rise out of the constricted valley of the Gala Water to go round Meigle Hill.*

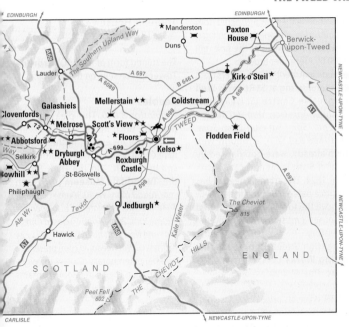

Clovenfords

Population 270. The hotel, once a coaching inn, was patronised by Sir Walter Scott who came to fish the Tweed. This hamlet was the site of the Tweed Vineries, where the Duke of Buccleuch's gardeners produced the famous Clovenford Tweed grapes.

▶ *The A 72 then follows the north bank quite closely as the forested valley sides move in.*

Innerleithen

Population 2,397. In a lovely setting at the meeting of Leithen Water with the River Tweed, wide and meandering at this point, the small woollen-textile

Address Book

For coin ranges, see the Legend on the cover flap.

WHERE TO STAY

Bellevue House – *Bowmont Street, Kelso.* ☎01573 224 588. This Victorian House five minutes from the town centre offers good hospitality with individually decorated bedrooms and a choice of breakfast dishes.

Ednam House – *Bridge Street, Kelso.* ☎01573 224 168. www.ednamhouse.com. Set on the banks of the Tweed, this Georgian mansion retains impressive period features and offers a bar, traditional bedrooms and a spacious dining room that overlooks the river and grounds.

Edenwater House – *off Stichill Road, Ednam.* ☎01573 224 070, www.edenwaterhouse.co.uk. This charming house enjoys an idyllic rural location next to a 17C kirk, 2 miles north of Kelso. Bedrooms and lounges boast antique furniture. Excellent Modern Scottish cuisine is served in the elegant dining room.
See also MELROSE .

WHERE TO EAT

The Hoebridge Inn – *Gattonside, Melrose.* ☎01896 823 082. www.thehoebridgeinn.com. This charming rustic converted 19C bobbin mill serves top class traditional Scottish fayre with a modern twist.
See also MELROSE.

town of Innerleithen has prospered from its beginngs as a modest rural village, following the opening of the first mill in 1790 by Alexander Brodie.

The medicinal merits of the waters from the mineral spring at **St Ronan's Well Interpretive Centre** (*St Wells Brae.* ♿ ⏰*Open Apr–Oct, Mon–Fri 10am–1pm, 2pm–5pm; Sat–Sun 2pm–5pm.* 🅿 ☎ *01896 833 583*), although well known already, were popularised by Sir Walter Scott in his novel *St Ronan's Well* of 1824. The spring's heyday has long since passed, but the little pavilion above the town has been restored and houses a museum recounting the spa's history.

On the High Street, **Robert Smail's Printing Works** (*NTS,* ⏰*open Good Fri–Oct, Thu–Mon noon–5pm. Sun 1–5pm, last admission 4.15;* ☜*£5.* 🅿☎*0844 4932259, www.nts.org.uk*), is a fascinating time-capsule of a Victorian Letterpress Printing Works. The caseroom, and machine room illustrate printing methods at the turn of the century and stillproducing commercial work today.

▶ *Take the B 709 to the left.*

Traquair House★★
♿*See TRAQUAIR HOUSE.*

The ruined form of the 16C **Cardrona Tower** can be seen on the far side.

Peebles
Population 8,000. This pleasant and peaceful town makes a good excursion centre for exploring the Tweeddale countryside. It was a flourishing spa in the 19C. On the High Street the **Tweeddale Museum** (♿⏰*open year-round Mon–Fri 10.30am–12.30pm, 1–4pm; Easter Sat–late Oct also open Sat 10am–1pm, 2pm–4pm;* ⏰*closed Christmas and New Year holidays;* ☎*01721 724 820, www.visittweeddale.com*) presents a number of temporary displays throughout the year. The Secret Room contains interesting historical plaster **friezes**.

▶ *Take the A 72 0.5 mi/0.8km west*

Neidpath Castle
This 14C tower house (☎*01875 87020, call for admission details*) is dramatically situated on a rocky outcrop overlooking the Tweed. It is of the traditional Scottish L-plan and an interesting example of the adaptation of a medieval tower house to 17C requirements.

ULLAPOOL★
HIGHLAND
POPULATION 1,006
♿LOCAL MAP SEE WESTER ROSS

Set on the shore of Loch Broom, the white houses of the fishing port and resort of Ullapool make an attractive picture. In summer the waterfront is a lively throng of yachtsmen and holidaymakers. Ullapool makes an ideal touring centre for the Wester Ross coast and is an unrivalled centre for sea angling.

- 🛈 **Information:** 20 Argyle Street. ☎ 08452 255 12. www.visithighlands.com.
- ▶ **Orient Yourself:** Ullapool is 57mi/91.5km NE of Inverness via the A 835.
- 👁 **Don't Miss:** the Falls of Measach; Loch Broom; the view of Ullapool from the A835 near Morefield; Loch Assynt.
- 🕐 **Organizing Your Time:** Allow half a day for the excursion around Loch Broom and additional time for a day trip to Lewis on the Western Isles and a boat trip to the Summer Isles.
- ♿ **Also See:** WESTER ROSS, INVEREWE.

A Bit of History

The village was laid out in the late 18C by the British Fisheries Society and flourished as a fishing port during the herring boom. Fishing is still an important activity, based on the Minch fishery, and in season the trawlers anchor in the loch while a fleet of factory ships can usually be seen in attendance at the mouth of Loch Broom. The port is also the terminal for the car ferry to Stornoway (the capital of the Isle of Lewis in the Outer Hebrides) and a haven for many small pleasure craft in summer.

Ullapool and Loch Broom with the ferry departing for Stornaway, Isle of Lewis

Visit

Ullapool Museum

8 West Argyle Street . ○*Open Good Fri (or 1 Apr if earlier)–Oct Mon–Sat 10am–5pm.*☞*£3.* ☎*01854 612 987. www.ullapoolmuseum.co.uk.*

Housed within a restored Thomas Telford church, built in 1829, this award-winning museum tells the story of Ullapool and Lochbroom through a mix of traditional and multimedia displays. It includes natural history and the story of Ullapool as a gateway for emigrants from Scotland to Nova Scotia.

Excursions

Summer Isles

○*Operates Apr–Sept. Summer Islands Cruise: Mon–Sat 10am (4 hrs, inc landing on Tanera Mhor), Sun 11am (3 hrs, no landing). Nature cruises (2 hrs no landing) daily 2.15pm*☎*01854 612 472, www.summerqueen.co.uk.*

The *Summer Queen* sails to this group of offshore islands where dolphins, seals and seabirds are the principal attractions. Tanera Mhor, the last inhabited Summer Isle is also the last place in Britain to print its own stamps. These are on sale at the post office.

Falls of Measach★★

11mi/18km south by the A 835.
The road follows the northern shore of **Loch Broom**★★ (21mi/39km long) in a beautiful mountain setting. The loch

sides are dotted with houses and traces of former field patterns are visible on the south side. From a point near the head of the loch there are particularly fine **views**.

Falls of Measach★★

In the wooded cleft of the mile-long **Corrieshalloch Gorge**★, the waters of the River Droma make a spectacular sight as they drop over 150ft/46m. The bridge over the chasm and a viewing platform (☞*£1 honesty box*) provide excellent vantage points.

Northwards to Lochinver★★

37mi/60km. Although the run follows the main road, it passes through splendid scenery punctuated by some of the most impressive peaks.

▸ *Take the A 835 north.*

Just before Morefield there is an excellent **view**★★ of Ullapool below in its lochside setting with the blue waters of Loch Broom stretching away to its mountain fringe. From the lay-by on the top of the rise, a path (*7min*) leads out to the point of a craggy promontory from where there is another **view**★ of Loch Broom and the distant Summer Isles.

Ardmair

A hamlet on the shore of Loch Kanaird. Before entering the small valley look

Address Book

For coin ranges, see the Legend on the cover flap.

WHERE TO STAY: ULLAPOOL

Dromnan – *Garve Road.* ☎01854 612 333. www.dromnan.com. 2 night min stay Jul–Aug. This modern guest house on the village outskirts overlooks Loch Broom; pretty rooms vary in decor from light pastels to dark tartan.

Point Cottage – *West Shore Street.* ☎01854 612 494. www.pointcottage.co.uk. A converted fisherman's cottage dating from the 18C with bright modern bedrooms and lovely views across Loch Broom.

The Sheiling – *Garve Road.* ☎01854 612 947. www.thesheiling ullapool.co.uk. Set in an acre of grounds, including a sauna, this modern guest-house enjoys spectacular views of Loch Broom and the mountains. Breakfast may include smoked fish platters.

back to the view over Isle Martin in Loch Kanaird, and farther out to sea. The road crosses Strath Kanaird, and Ben More Coigach (2,438ft/743m) rises to the left as sheer as a cliff wall.

Knockan Crag Visitor Area

Unmanned visitor centre, open all hours throughout the year. ☎ 01854 613 418, www.knockan-crag.co.uk.

The centre is on the edge of the Inverpolly National Nature Reserve covering an area of 26,827 acres/11,000ha. This glacially scoured countryside with its many lochs and lochans, the largest of which is Loch Stonascaig, has three important landmarks, the peaks of **Cul Mor** (2,786ft/849m), **Cul Beag** (2,523ft/769m) and **Stac Pollaidh** (2,010ft/613m) – the latter pronounced, stack polly. These upstanding masses of Torridonian Sandstone lie on a base of Lewisian gneiss. The geological sequence exposed at Knockan Cliff is explained on the nature-cum-geological **trail** from the centre. From the centre there is a **view** across the main road of the main peaks, with, from left to right, Cul Beag, Stac Pollaidh and Cul Mor with its whitish quartzite summit.

Before reaching Ledmore junction there is a **view** to the left over the waters of Cam Loch to the sheer slopes of **Suilven** (2,399ft/731m), a twin-peaked mountain when seen from the north or south.

▶ *Turn left at Ledmore junction to take the A 837.*

The road passes Loch Awe and its outlet, the River Loanan with, to left and right, the majestic forms of **Canisp** (2,779ft/846m) and the rounded outliers of **Ben More Assynt** (3,273ft/998m). The Inchnadamph area at the head of Loch Assynt is a Cambrian limestone outcrop noted for its underground features. At the **Inchnadamph Nature Reserve** a track leads to the **Allt nan Uamh caves**, where human remains at least 4500 years, along with the bones of animals now extinct in Scotland, have been found.

Just before the fork in the lochside road there is a splendid **view** of the ruins of Ardvreck Castle, a 16C MacLeod stronghold.

Loch Assynt★★

The road along this loch (6mi/10km long) is particularly scenic. The waters are flanked to the left by Beinn Gharbh, with Canisp peeping from behind, and to the right lofty **Quinag** (2,654ft/808m). The road follows the loch's change of direction and then the winding River Inver.

Lochinver★

Population 283. Set round the head of a sea loch, this attractive village with its mountainous backdrop is best seen from the sea. It is a busy holiday centre, renowned for the outstandingly beautiful scenery of the **Stoer Peninsula**, with its many charming crofting communities and sandy coves. The port is a haven for a busy fishing fleet and pleasure boats.

WESTERN ISLES
WESTERN ISLES
POPULATION 23,224

The chain of islands known as the Western Isles extends some 130mi/209km from Barra Head in the south to the Butt of Lewis in the north. The islands – Lewis, Harris, North Uist, South Uist and Barra – are buffeted by the Atlantic waves, treeless and windswept, but boast moorlands, glistening lochans, superb sandy beaches and crystal clear water. Their isolation has helped to preserve their cultural identity. Gaelic is widely spoken and many islanders are bilingual.

- **Information:** 26 Cromwell Street, Stornoway, Lewis ☎01851 703088; Pier Road, Tarbert, Harris ☎01859 502011; Pier Road, Lochmaddy, North Uist ☎01876 500321; Pier Road, Lochboisdale, South Uist ☎01878 700 286; Main Street, Castlebay, Barra ☎01871 810336. www.visithebrides.com.
- **Orient Yourself:** Lewis and Harris in fact form one island. A ferry makes the short journey from Lewis and Harris to the southern chain of islands (North Uist, Benbecula, South Uist, Eriskay and Barr), which are linked by bridges and causeways. Boat services to the mainland are Stornoway–Ullapool and Lochboisdale/Castle Bay–Oban. There is also a service between Uig and Skye.
- **Don't Miss:** Callanish Standing Stones.
- **Sunday rest, midges, outings:** Very little happens on Sundays. Midges (small, biting insects) are a constant nuisance, so wear protection. It is advisable to take a picnic lunch and keep the tank full, as places to buy refreshments and petrol are scarce.
- **Organizing Your Time:** Allow 2–3 days.
- **Especially for Kids:** To the northeast of Stornoway the Eye Peninsula has some fine sandy beaches; Barra is also renowned for its sand.
- **Also See:** ISLE OF SKYE.

Sights

Lewis and Harris
Sights listed in alphabetical order.

An Lanntair 'The Lantern'
Open Mon–Sat 10am–late.
On the Stornoway Waterfront, near the ferry terminal, this arts centre is a good introduction to the island' arts and culture with all-day food, exhibitions, live music and events, and shopping.

Arnol Black House
Signposted off the main A 858. (HS)
Open Apr–Sept Mon–Sat 9.30am–5.30pm. Oct Mon–Sat 9.30am–4.30pm. Last admission 30 mins before closing. £5. ☎01851 710 395. www.historic-scotland.gov.uk.
This traditional, fully furnished, straw-thatched house shelters under one roof a sleeping area with box beds, a living area, a byre and stable-cum-barn. This type of dwelling, known as a Black House – due to its open hearth – was common up until 50 to 70 years ago. Beside the Black House, a furnished 1920s crofthouse can also be seen.

Callanish Standing Stones★★
Signposted off the A 858.
This famous group of stones (the locals say you never count the same number twice!) forms a circle with alignments radiating outwards at the compass points. The site is one of a series in the vicinity and it is generally assumed they were used for astronomical observations. It dates from the late Stone Age and early Bronze Age (3000–1500 BC), making it over 4,000 years old and roughly contemporary with Stonehenge. Composed of Lewisian gneiss the stones were once partially buried under peat. The central cairn or burial chamber was a later addition by the Neolithic people (2500–2000 BC).

Colin Weston / BRITAIN ON VIEW

Callanish standing stones, excavated in 1857

Carloway Broch★

Signposted off the A 858. Although it is not a complete example of a broch (◖*see SHETLAND ISLANDS*), enough remains of this structure to intrigue. The galleried walls and entrance guard chamber are still visible.

Leverburgh

The township of Obbe was renamed by the English soap magnate, Lord Leverhulme in 1923. He acquired Harris in 1919, and Lewis later the same year, and dreamed of developing the islands. However his grand schemes, including a project to make Leverburgh an important fishing port, failed. The **An Clochan** café and shop (☎*01859 520370*). It currently displays **The Harris Tapestry**, a locally famous collage (1998–2000) which illustrates the past and present. (Call before visiting to make sure it is still here)

St Clement's Church

In the township of Rodel near the southern tip of Harris is a church with the outstanding **tomb**★ of the 16C builder, Alexander MacLeod (d. 1546). Splendid carvings decorate the arch and the back of the recess above the effigy of the 8th Chief of MacLeod.

Shawbost Museum

◷*Open Apr–Oct Mon–Sat 10am–5pm.* ☎*01851 710 212.*
This small folk museum gives an insight into the life and customs of the past.

Stornoway

Population 8,660. The capital and only town of any size lies on a narrow neck of the Eye Peninsula. The main shopping area fronts the landlocked harbour which is also overlooked by the 19C castle (now a technical college) and its wooded

Harris Tweed

The **orb** trademark guarantees that this fine quality cloth is hand woven by the islanders in their homes. Weaving tweed originated in Harris and in the mid 19C it was commercialised in Lewis where today all processes after weaving are done in the mills of Stornoway and Shawbost. In the mid to late 20C the industry went into decline, due in no small part to its antiquated looms which are costly to maintain and produce cloth of a width not suitable for modern cutting equipment. The recent invention of a new loom, which is easier to operate, and weaves cloth twice as wide as previously, as well as producing more intricate designs, has helped to stem the decline, thus reducing a threat to the way of life of whole communities.

The Lewis Chessmen

The **Lewis Chessmen**, a unique hoard of 80 pieces carved from walrus ivory, are of Norse origin and date from the mid 12C. Most of the pawns are missing but the superbly crafted main pieces include the kings, queens, knights and bishops with their distinctive attributes: crowns, shields, swords and croziers. The demonic expressions of the gaming pieces, uncovered by a storm, terrified the finder who suspected witchcraft. According to tradition a curse is attached to the chessmen and previous owners have met horrible deaths. The pieces changed hands several times until they were acquired by the British Museum. Some are also displayed at the Museum of Scotland in Edinburgh.

grounds. A good view of the town can be had from the foot of the War Memorial on the hill behind the hospital. Stornoway makes a good base. (⬤see *An Lanntair 'The Lantern' above*).

Tarbert
Population 504. The main community of Harris, Tarbert sits on the isthmus between West and East Lochs. It is the ferry terminal for Skye and North Uist.

Uig
This township is famed on two counts, as the home of the Brahan Seer, a legendary 17C clairvoyant, and as the place where the Lewis Chessmen (⬤*see Box, above*) were found in 1831.

Uist and Benbecula
Bridges and causeways link the islands which offer spectacular land and seascapes: rolling hills and moorland, white sand dunes and beaches, sparkling sea lochs and pounding waves. The chambered cairns and stone circles, castles and chapels attest to the islands' rich history. There is a rich birdlife and in summer a profusion of wild flowers, good walking and fishing.

Barra   Kids
The romantic small island, which takes great pride in its Norse heritage, is famous for its fine beaches.

WESTER ROSS ★★★
HIGHLAND

The Atlantic seaboard of Wester Ross includes such notable areas of Highland scenery as the shores of Loch Maree, the Torridon area and the fastness of the Applecross peninsula. Discover the rugged beauty of a wild and rocky landscape, the splendour of majestic mountains (Beinn Eighe, Liathach, Slioch and An Teallach), the beauty of lochs Maree, Torridon, Broom and Ewe and the charm of small isolated communities like Plockton, Poolewe, Kinlochewe and Applecross.

- **Information:** 20 Argyle Street. ☎08452 255 12. www.visithighlands.com.
- ▶ **Orient Yourself:** Explore the area from any one of the main touring centres, Kyle of Lochalsh, Gairloch or Ullapool.
- **Don't Miss:** the views from Bealach-na-Bo; Loch Maree; the view of Loch Maree from the A832.
- **Drivers:** Keep the petrol tank well topped up.
- **Organizing Your Time:** Allow at least two days for sightseeing, but to enjoy this glorious area to the full, take extra to walk ,climb, sail or fish.
- **Also See:** INVEREWE GARDENS, ULLAPOOL.

Driving Tours

1 Kyle of Lochalsh to Gairloch

102mi/164km – allow at least 1 day. ⓒsee local map on following pages.

The itinerary described covers 102mi/164km although there are alternatives which reduce the distance to 74mi/119km. This is a landscape where mountains, lochs and seashore, woods and moorland all come together in nearly perfect proportions. Parts of the route are busy in the tourist season but other stretches still permit the luxury of enjoying it all in solitude.

Kyle of Lochalsh – ⓒ*See KYLE OF LOCHALSH.*

▶ *Leave Kyle to the north by the coast road which has good views seawards to Skye with the Cuillins prominent on the skyline.*

Plockton★

Population 425. This lovely village, with its palm tree-lined main street, has an ideal **site** facing east overlooking a sheltered bay. Originally a refugee settlement at the time of the clearances, it is now a holiday centre popular for yachting and windsurfing.

▶ *At Achmore take the A 890 left.*

Down on the shore, pass Stromeferry, a former railhead and ferry point. The lochside road on the southern shore has fine **views** of the loch.

Loch Carron

This sea loch has two branches, Loch Kishorn and Upper Loch Carron, backed by the glen of the same name.

▶ *At the junction take the A 896 left.*

Lochcarron

Population 900. A small linear settlement down on the loch shore.

▶ *Follow the A 896 as it branches to the right beyond Lochcarron and rises to cross moorland, and then take a narrow valley down to the shore of Loch Kishorn.*

On the far side are the Applecross mountains, from left to right, are Meal Gorm (2,328ft/710m), Sgurr a' Chaorachain (3,355ft/1,053m), forming the sides of the valley to be ascended, and Beinn Bhàn (2,938ft/896m).

▶ *The A 896 is a possible short cut to Shieldaig. The itinerary follows the narrow road to the left to cross the Applecross Peninsula via Bealach-na Bo (Pass of the Cattle).*

This route has hairpin bends and 1:4 gradients and is not recommended for learner drivers, caravans or heavy vehi-

Loch Torridon

B. Perousse/MICHELIN

cles. The pass is closed to traffic in wintry conditions. However the splendid views make it all worthwhile.

Bealach-na Bo

2,053ft/626m. The road winds upwards then rises gradually following the east flank. Striated rock and scree slopes are overlooked by rocky overhangs. Hairpin bends allow the final ascent of the back wall of the corrie. The **vista**★★ framed by the hanging valley is spectacular with Loch Kishorn, Loch Carron, Loch Alsh and the Isle of Skye below in the distance.

The rocky moorland surface is dotted with lochans. From the car park there are superb **views**★★★ westwards of Skye, the Cuillins, and the fringing islands.

The descent to Applecross and the coast is more gradual.

Applecross

Population 235. This picturesque village is situated on a bay with a popular red sandy beach. This was the site in the 7C of St Maelrubha's monastery.

The coastal road has good **views** across the Inner Sound to Raasay and Rona with Skye beyond.

▶ *Continue round the south shore of Loch Torridon, Loch Shieldaig and Upper Loch Torridon.*

Torridon

The village lies at the foot of Liathach at the head of Upper Loch Torridon.

Torridon Countryside Centre

NTS. ♿🕐*Countryside Centre open Good Fri–Sept daily 10am–5pm. Estate, Deer Enclosure and Deer Museum (unstaffed), open all year, daily.* ✆£3. ☎0844 4932 229. www.nts.org.uk.

The centre offers an audio-visual introduction to the Torridon area. Nearby is a small deer museum. In addition, information is available on climbing and walking routes. Remember, these mountains can be dangerous and are only for experienced, fit and properly equipped explorers. Changeable weather makes them treacherous. Always leave behind a detail of routes and objectives with an estimated time of return.

▶ *The A 896 is single track with passing places.*

Glen Torridon

The glen leads through a flat-bottomed glacial valley. The lower part of the glen is overlooked to the north by **Liathach**, "Grey One" (3,456ft/1,054m); with its seven peaks it is an impressive sight. The valley to the south, containing Loch Clair, leads through to Glen Carron (*no through road for cars*). The imposing range of **Beinn Eighe** (3,309ft/1,010m) to the north is a long ridge also of seven peaks; the most easterly ones have a whitish quartzite capping.

Kinlochewe

Population 85. The village has retained the loch's original name and is known as a good centre for climbing, hill walking and fishing.

▶ *Take the A 832 to the left.*

Aultroy Visitor Centre

Analcaun. ♿🕐*Open Easter–Oct, daily 10am–5pm.* 🅿 ☎01445 760 254.

The centre is the gateway to the **Beinn Eighe National Nature Reserve**, a 12,350acres/5,000ha mountain area of Caledon pinewoods (one of the few remaining fragments of the native Scots Pine Forest), barren moors and lochans with breathtaking views over Loch Maree and Torridon. Among the wildlife can be found pine marten, red deer and the more elusive wildcat.

From the centre are a number of short trails suitable for all, including a wheelchair friendly route. All routes have descriptive panels giving an insight into the surrounds.

A roadside picnic area makes an ideal vantage point for viewing the loch and Slioch (the Spear) on the far side. This is also the starting point of a nature and mountain **trail** (4mi/6.5km) on the lower slopes of Beinn Eighe. This is a 4–5hr hike, and it is advisable to wear boots.

Loch Maree★★★

This magnificent loch epitomises the rugged scenic grandeur of the west coast. Measuring 12mi/20km long and 3mi/5km wide, it is ensconced

P. Tomkins/VISITSCOTLAND/SCOTTISH VIEWPOINT

Fishing in Loch Maree with view of Ben Slioch

between the towering form of **Ben Slioch** (3,217ft/980m) to the north and a shoulder of Beinn Eighe. At its widest part the loch is studded with isles and it was on the Isle Maree that St Maelrubha set up his cell in the 7C. The isle became a popular place of pilgrimage and Loch Ewe was rechristened Maree, a corruption of Maelrubha. In the 17C the lochside slopes were the site of iron smelting.

Victoria Falls★
Car park off the main road.
A viewing platform and riverside path afford good views of these falls as they drop in two stages over great slabs of rock. The falls are named after Queen Victoria who visited the area in 1877.
A roadside viewing-point overlooks the dammed Loch Bad an Sgalaig. The surrounding country is hummocky and dotted with small lochs.

▶ *Pass the bay of Charlestown.*

Gairloch
Population 125. As a holiday centre, Gairloch lies at close proximity to the majestic mountain scenery of the Torridon area and the splendid sandy beaches of the immediate coastline. At the head of Loch Gairloch the pier still has the lively bustle of a fishing port.

The **Gairloch Heritage Museum** (*Achtercain.* 👍🕐 *open Easter–Sept, Mon–Sat 10am–5pm, Oct Mon–Fri 1.30pm.* 💷£3. 🅿☎*01445 712 287, www.gairlochheritagemuseum.org.uk*), has won national awards and illustrates all aspects of life in the past in a typical West Highland parish. Displays include a croft interior of 100 years ago, a schoolroom, dairy and shop. Other topics of interest include the Loch Maree ironworks of the 17C, illicit whisky distilling and Queen Victoria's 1877 visit to the area.

2 Gairloch to Ullapool
56mi/90km – about 4hr

The run reveals the scenic coastline to the north where bays, beaches and headlands succeed one another backed, inland, by breathtaking mountain scenery. The A 832 leads northeastwards across the rock and moorland neck of the Rubha Reidh peninsula.

▶ *Stop before descending to the Ewe.*

The roadside viewpoint has a superb **view★★★** of Loch Maree with its forested islands and majestic mountain flanks. **Loch Ewe** stretches ahead enclosed by the peninsulas of Rubha Reidh and Rubha Mor.

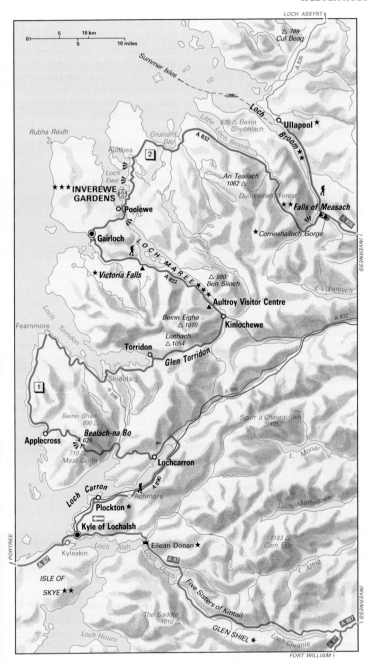

Poolewe
Small village at the head of Loch Ewe.

Inverewe Gardens★★★ –
See INVEREWE GARDENS.

View indicator
This vantage point has a lovely **view**★ of Loch Thurnaig in the foreground, the Inverewe Garden promontory behind, then Loch Ewe backed by Rubha Reidh, and the Isle of Ewe to the right.

Second viewpoint

The Isle of Ewe is straight ahead while Aultbea shelters in a bay to the right.

▶ *The road rises up and over Rubha Mor Peninsula.*

The descent offers a wide **view** over Gruinard Bay and Island of the same name, once the scene of an anthrax experiment (◦▬*the public is strictly forbidden to land*).

As the road follows the southern shore, straight ahead is **An Teallach** (3,484ft/1,062m) with, away to the left, the twin peaks of Beinn Ghobhlach, the Forked Mountain.

At the head of the loch the road follows the wooded Strath Beag up to the moors of Dundonnell Forest. This stretch of the road, known as Destitution Road, was made during the potato famine of 1851 to give work to starving men.

There is an excellent roadside vantage point with a **view**★ over the farmland and woodland of Strath More at the head of Loch Broom.

▶ *Turn left at Braemore Junction.*

Falls of Measach★★

☙*See ULLAPOOL: Excursions.*

Loch Broom★★

☙*See ULLAPOOL: Excursions.*

Ullapool★ – ☙*See ULLAPOOL.*

WHITHORN
DUMFRIES AND GALLOWAY
POPULATION 990

Whithorn is the cradle of Scottish Christianity and predates the more famous shrine of Iona, by over 150 years. Today's unassuming town, with its wide main street, serves the surrounding dairy farming community of the Machars.

🛈 **Information:** Burns House, 28 Harbour Street, Stranraer. www.visitdumfriesandgalloway.co.uk www.whithorn.info.

▶ **Orient Yourself:** Whithorn is in the south westernmost corner of Scotland, 64mi/103km south west of Dumfries via the A 75.

☺ **Don't Miss:** the early Christian crosses in the museum.

🕐 **Organizing Your Time:** Allow 1 hour to 1 hour 30 mins.

☙ **Also See:** STRANRAER, LOGAN BOTANIC GARDEN.

A Bit of History

Candida Casa – In the year 397 when the Roman legions were still in Britain, St Ninian, Scotland's first saint, established the first Christian mission beyond Hadrian's Wall. Reputed to be a local man, **St Ninian** (c. 360–c. 432) was educated and consecrated bishop in Rome. On his return to Scotland he built a small stone building – the first Christian church in Scotland – daubed with light-coloured plaster, and known as **Candida Casa**, the White House (in Anglo-Saxon *huit aern*, hence today's name). The bishop's influence was widespread albeit overshadowed by the later Celtic Columban mission. None the less St Ninian's tomb became a place of pilgrimage which was to remain popular until the beginning of the 16C. The bishopric lapsed during a period of Viking rule which ended after 1100. In 1128 Fergus, Lord of Galloway, built a priory cathedral over the ruins of the *Candida Casa* which was served by Premonstratensians, reviving the original See, which remained under the sway of York. Severance from York came in 1472 when the See of St Andrews was raised to a Bishopric. Twenty years after this Galloway was put under the jurisdiction of Glasgow which had recently acquired episcopal status.

Sights

From the main street a pend leads through the former priory gatehouse, built in the 15C by Bishop George Vaus, and emblazoned with the pre-Union Scottish coat of arms supported by two unicorns. In one of the cottages on the right is the museum.

Whithorn Priory and Museum

Access through The Whithorn Story, 45–47 George Street. &⃝Open Easter/Apr (whichever is earlier)–Oct daily 10.30am–5pm. ☞£3.50, includes Museum, The Whithorn Story, Priory and Dig. ☏01988 500508. www.historic-scotland.gov.uk, www.whithorn.com.

The museum gives a short history of the priory and houses a notable collection of **early Christian crosses**★★. These standing crosses or headstones denoted individual graves and date from the Christian period in Whithorn. The earliest Christian memorial in Scotland is the **Latinus Stone** (no 1) dated AD 450 and inscribed with the name of the relative who erected it. Typical of the more decorative Whithorn School is no 7. Later stones (nos 3 and 5) show a Northumberland influence (eg Ruthwell). St Peter's Stone (no 2) is 7C or early 8C.

Priory

The ruins (nave, south and Lady Chapels), set on a knoll, are scanty and belong mainly to the medieval cathedral. The building to the left, originally the nave, served as a parish church until 1822. Note the reset Norman doorway in the south wall. The rest of the structure is mainly 13C, much altered. To the right, the paved area and low walls mark the east end with crypts underneath. The probable site of *Candida Casa* is beyond.

The Whithorn Dig

The audio-visual show and exhibition in the visitor centre (are a good introduction to the excavation programme which has revealed evidence of more than 1,500 years of human occupation

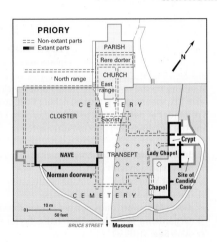

in the area. On a site to the south of the priory have been found traces of an early Christian community (5C), an 8C Northumbrian settlement – the ground plan of a church, burial chapel, hall and other buildings can be viewed – a graveyard (16C) and finally a market garden. The site of a Viking trading post to the west of the priory is also being investigated.

Excursion

Isle of Whithorn

14mi/22km. Leave Whithorn by A 746 south and bear left onto B 7004. Population 222.

The village, a popular yachting centre, is known for the ruined St Ninian's Chapel which stands on the rocky foreshore (*5min walk from pier*). At one time thought to be the site of *Candida Casa*, this 13C chapel with its enclosure wall may well mark the site where St Ninian himself landed, or else was for the convenience of pilgrims coming by sea.

▸ *Take the Port William road B 7004 then A 747.*

St Ninian's Cave

This cave, with some crosses carved in the rock, is said to be St Ninian's place of retreat.

▸ *Return to Whithorn by A 747.*

WICK
HIGHLAND
POPULATION 7,770

Standing on the river of the same name, Wick takes its name from the Norse term Vik, meaning bay. A small fishing fleet operates out of the harbour and is a reminder of past glories; in its heyday over 1,000 boats operated out of Wick and the neighbouring port of Pulteneytown.

- **Information:** The Norseman Hotel. ☎01955 602 596. www.visithighlands.com.
- **Orient Yourself:** Wick is in the northeastern corner of the Highlands, just 16mi/26km south of John O'Groats.
- **Don't Miss:** The Long Cairn of Camster; the view to the Stacks of Duncansby.
- **Organizing Your Time:** Allow half a day for excursions.
- **Also See:** THURSO.

A Bit of History

Wick was one of the first towns to develop the herring fishery on a large scale and by the early 19C was the largest herring fishing port in the country. The British Fisheries Society commissioned Thomas Telford to draw up the plans for this new fishing settlement, attempting to bring some order to the jumble of undecked boats and mass of masts all over the harbour. The quays and all available dockside space spilt over with the paraphernalia of the curing industry. Curing, which had to be done within 24hrs of landing the catch, entailed gutting the fish, salting and packing them in barrels and was carried out by large teams of itinerant workers, mostly women.

Sights

Wick Heritage Centre
♿ 🕐 *Open Easter–Oct, Mon–Sat 10am–3.45pm.* ♿£2.75. 🅿 ☎01955 605 393. *www.wickheritage.org.*
A number of fully furnished rooms take visitors back in time to typical local houses between 1900 and 1925.
Other displays and exhibits traces the town's history and heritage, most notably: a model of the herring port; the complete optical and mechanical working of Noss Head Lighthouse; a fine display of Caithness glassware which was

produced in Wick between 1960 and 2005, when the business moved away from the area.

Excursions

Prehistoric Caithness
30mi/48km south on the A 9.
This run takes the visitor through flat, moorland countryside to two prehistoric sites.

The Hill o'Many Stanes★
To the right off the main road.
With its 22 rows of small stones this is a Bronze Age monument (c. 1850 BC). The purpose of the fan-shaped arrangement may have been astronomical.

Grey Cairns of Camster★
5mi/8km off the main road by a narrow road with passing places.
This is typical Highland crofting country – a bleak expanse of moorland dotted with small cultivated areas and crofts. The first of the two cairns is the **Round Cairn** with its entrance passage (20ft/6m long, *to be negotiated on hands and knees*) and chamber. The much larger second one, the **Long Cairn**★★ is 195ft/60m long by 33ft/10m wide. This long-horned structure incorporates two earlier beehive cairns. The main chamber is tripartite, subdivided by large slabs. The chambered cairns of

the area date from the Neolithic period (4000–1800 BC).

Duncansby Head★

21mi/34km including detours to the north following the A 99.

This excursion takes in the northeastern tip of the Scottish mainland and is notable for its magnificent coastal scenery. Sheltered coves and sandy bays alternate with giddily steep cliffs, rock stacks, natural arches and bridges, and narrow inlets, known locally as goes. Rock ledges are the home of guillemots, shags, fulmars, kittiwakes, a variety of gulls and other species.

▸ *Leave Wick to the north by the road signposted Noss Head. Leave the car in the car park then take the path through the fields; 15min walk.*

Girnigoe Castle and Sinclair Castle

The jagged ruins of two adjacent castles are dramatically set on a peninsula, overlooking the great sandy sweep of Sinclair's Bay on one side and a typical goe on the other. Nearest to the point of the peninsula is the late-15C Castle Girnigoe with its evil-looking dungeon. The part known as Castle Sinclair, an early-17C addition, stands to the left beyond a ditch. Both were the seat of the Sinclair Earls of Caithness, a clan with a dark and often violent history in these parts. The castles are currently being restored.

▸ *Return to the outskirts of Wick to take the John O'Groats A 99 road.*

Pass on the way the tall remains of Old Keiss Castle, occupying a dramatic locations at the top of sheer cliffs overlooking the sea. (⚠ *Beware the castle is in a dangerous state. There have been recent collapses and under no circumstances should the structure be entered*). Standing nearby is the white form of its successor, New Keiss Castle, remodelled in 1860 (*private*).

Northlands Viking Centre

Auckengill. 🕐 *Open June–Sept, daily 10am–4pm.* ☎ *01955 607 771.*

The artifacts on display here were found by John Nicolson during a lifetime of excavating many of Caithness's 100-plus Iron Age brochs (👆 *see SHETLAND ISLANDS*).

The road climbs and once over the rise, South Ronaldsay, the southernmost isle of the Orkneys, can be seen in the distance.

John o'Groats

Traditionally this is the northernmost extremity of the mainland United Kingdom. In actual fact that particular honour goes to Dunnet Head (also known as Easter Head) some 11mi/18 northwest of here, though John o'Groats is certainly the most northernmost settlement. It lies 876mi/1,410km from its southern counterpart, Land's End in Cornwall and is the starting or finishing point for various feats of endurance, usually undertaken for charity, with the challenge of going from one end of the country to the other in a certain time, or even non-stop.

The scattered community takes its name from a Dutchman, Jan de Groot, who started a regular ferry service to the Orkney Islands in the 16C. The octagonal tower of the hotel recalls the story of the ferryman, who, to settle problems of precedence among his seven descendants, built an eight-sided house with eight doors and an octagonal table.

A passenger boat service operates from the harbour to Burwick on South Ronaldsay from May to September (☎01955 611 353, www.jogferry.co.uk).

▸ *Take the road to the east to Duncansby Head 2mi/3.2km away.*

Duncansby Head★

From around the lighthouse, which commands this northeastern headland of mainland Scotland, there is a good view across the Pentland Firth, a channel (7mi/11km wide) notorious for its treacherous tides. A path leads to another clifftop viewpoint overlooking the Stacks of **Duncansby**★★. Standing offshore these pointed sea-stacks rise to a spectacular height of 210ft/64 m.

A

INDEX

INDEX

INDEX

INDEX

WHERE TO STAY

INDEX

WHERE TO EAT

MAPS AND PLANS

LIST OF MAPS

COMPANION PUBLICATIONS

A map reference to the appropriate Michelin map is given for each chapter in the Sights section of this guide.

REGIONAL MAP

The Michelin map 501 (Scale 1 : 400 000 – 1cm = 4km – 1in : 6.30miles), on one sheet, covers Scotland, the network of motorways and major roads and some secondary roads. It provides information on shipping routes, distances in miles and kilometres, town plans of Edinburgh and Glasgow, services, sporting and tourist attractions, a list of Unitary Authorities of Scotland and an index of places; the key and text are printed in four languages.

COUNTRY MAPS

The Michelin Tourist and Motoring Atlas – Great Britain & Ireland (Scale 1 : 300 000 – 1cm = 3km – 1in : 4.75 miles - based on 1 : 400 000) covers the whole of the United Kingdom and the Republic of Ireland, the national networks of motorways and major roads. It provides

information on route planning, shipping routes, distances in miles and kilometres, over 60 town plans, services, sporting and tourist attractions and an index of places; the key and text are printed in six languages.

The Michelin map 713 – Great Britain & Ireland (Scale 1 : 1 000 000 – 1cm = 10km – 1inch : 15.8 miles), on one sheet, covers the whole of the United Kingdom and the Republic of Ireland, the national networks of motorways and major roads. It provides information on shipping routes, distances in miles and kilometres, a list of Unitary Authorities for Wales and Scotland; the key and text are printed in six languages.

INTERNET

Users can access personalised route plans, Michelin mapping on line, addresses of hotels and restaurants featured in the Michelin Guides and practical and tourist information through the internet: **www.ViaMichelin.com**

LEGEND

★★★ **Highly recommended**

★★ **Recommended**

★ **Interesting**

Tourism

Sightseeing route with departure point indicated

Ecclesiastical building

Synagogue – Mosque

Building (with main entrance)

Statue, small building

Wayside cross

Fountain

Fortified walls – Tower – Gate

AZ B — Map co-ordinates locating sights

Tourist information

Historic house, castle – Ruins

Dam – Factory or power station

Fort – Cave

Prehistoric site

Viewing table – View

Miscellaneous sight

Recreation

Racecourse

Skating rink

Outdoor, indoor swimming pool

Marina, moorings

Mountain refuge hut

Overhead cable-car

Tourist or steam railway

Waymarked footpath

Outdoor leisure park/centre

Theme/Amusement park

Wildlife/Safari park, zoo

Gardens, park, arboretum

Aviary, bird sanctuary

Additional symbols

Motorway (unclassified)

Junction: complete, limited

Pedestrian street

Unsuitable for traffic, street subject to restrictions

Steps – Footpath

Railway – Coach station

Funicular – Rack-railway

Tram – Metro, underground

Bert (R.)... Main shopping street

Post office – Telephone centre

Covered market

Barracks

Swing bridge

Quarry – Mine

Ferry (river and lake crossings)

Ferry services: Passengers and cars

Foot passengers only

Access route number common to MICHELIN maps and town plans

Abbreviations and special symbols

C — County council offices

H — Town hall

J — Law courts

M — Museum

POL. — Police

T — Theatre

U — University

Park and Ride

Motorway

Primary route

Hotel

Battlefield

381

Michelin Apa Publications Ltd

A joint venture between Michelin and Langenscheidt

Suite 6, Tulip House, 70 Borough High Street, London SE1 1XF, United Kingdom

No part of this publication may be reproduced in any form
without the prior permission of the publisher.

© 2009 Michelin Apa Publications Ltd
ISBN 978-1-906261-45-0
Printed: July 2008
Printed and bound: Himmer, Germany

Although the information in this guide was believed by the authors and publisher to be accurate
and current at the time of publication, they cannot accept responsibility for any inconvenience,
loss, or injury sustained by any person relying on information or advice contained in this guide.
Things change over time and travellers should take steps to verify and confirm information,
especially time-sensitive information related to prices, hours of operation, and availability.

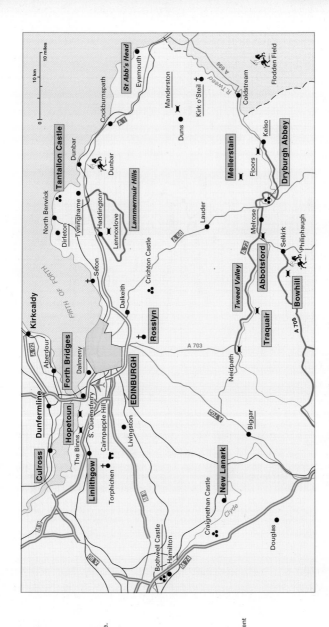

GLASGOW ★★★ Highly recommended

Stirling ★★ Recommended

Jedburgh ★ Interesting

Stranraer   Other sight described in this guide.

The names of towns or sights described
in the guide appear in black on the maps.
See the index for the page number

Glossary

Ben : mountain

Broch, Brough : prehistoric round tower

Cairn : pile of stones marking a funerary monument

Firth : tidal part of an estuary

Glen : narrow steep-sided valley

Kyle : sound, strait

Loch : lake

Mull : promontory

Strath : broad river valley

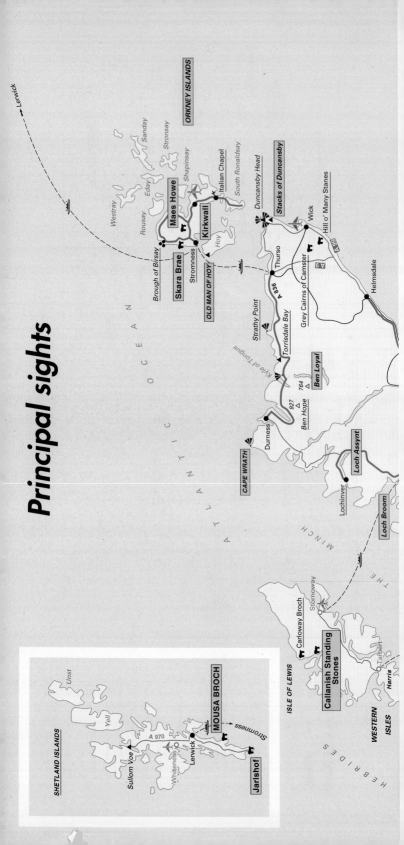

Principal sights